Chrysler LH-series Automotive Repair Manual

by Eric Godfrey
and John H Haynes
Member of the Guild of Motoring Writers

Models covered:
Chrysler LHS, Concorde, 300M and Dodge Intrepid
1998 through 2003

(12K8 - 25026)

A

Haynes Publishing Group
Sparkford Nr Yeovil
Somerset BA22 7JJ England

Haynes North America, Inc
861 Lawrence Drive
Newbury Park
California 91320 USA

Acknowledgements

We are grateful to the Chrysler Corporation for assistance with technical information, wiring diagrams and certain illustrations. Technical writers who contributed to this project include Richard Thomas Smith, Jay Storer, Jeff Kibler and Bob Henderson.

A book in the Haynes Automotive Repair Manual Series

Printed in the U.S.A.

ISBN 1 56392 493 5

Library of Congress Control Number 2002117270

02-320

Contents

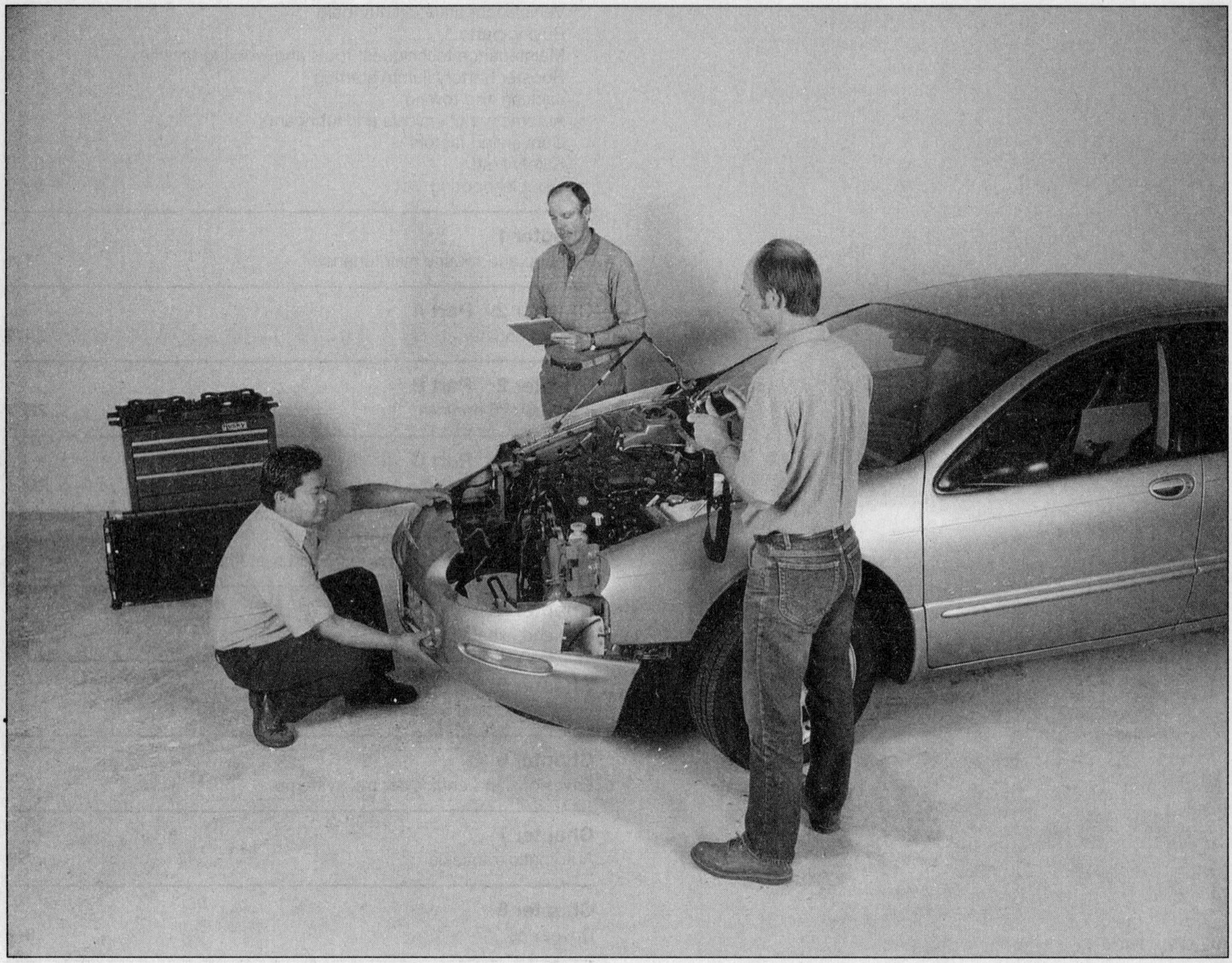

Haynes photographer, mechanic and author with 1999 Chrysler Concorde

About this manual

Its purpose

The purpose of this manual is to help you get the best value from your vehicle. It can do so in several ways. It can help you decide what work must be done, even if you choose to have it done by a dealer service department or a repair shop; it provides information and procedures for routine maintenance and servicing; and it offers diagnostic and repair procedures to follow when trouble occurs.

We hope you use the manual to tackle the work yourself. For many simpler jobs, doing it yourself may be quicker than arranging an appointment to get the vehicle into a shop and making the trips to leave it and pick it up. More importantly, a lot of money can be saved by avoiding the expense the shop must pass on to you to cover its labor and overhead costs. An added benefit is the sense of satisfaction and accomplishment that you feel after doing the job yourself.

Using the manual

The manual is divided into Chapters. Each Chapter is divided into numbered Sections, which are headed in bold type between horizontal lines. Each Section consists of consecutively numbered paragraphs.

At the beginning of each numbered Section you will be referred to any illustrations which apply to the procedures in that Section. The reference numbers used in illustration captions pinpoint the pertinent Section and the Step within that Section. That is, illustration 3.2 means the illustration refers to Section 3 and Step (or paragraph) 2 within that Section.

Procedures, once described in the text, are not normally repeated. When it's necessary to refer to another Chapter, the reference will be given as Chapter and Section number. Cross references given without use of the word "Chapter" apply to Sections and/or paragraphs in the same Chapter. For example, "see Section 8" means in the same Chapter.

References to the left or right side of the vehicle assume you are sitting in the driver's seat, facing forward.

Even though we have prepared this manual with extreme care, neither the publisher nor the author can accept responsibility for any errors in, or omissions from, the information given.

NOTE

A **Note** provides information necessary to properly complete a procedure or information which will make the procedure easier to understand.

CAUTION

A **Caution** provides a special procedure or special steps which must be taken while completing the procedure where the Caution is found. Not heeding a Caution can result in damage to the assembly being worked on.

WARNING

A **Warning** provides a special procedure or special steps which must be taken while completing the procedure where the Warning is found. Not heeding a Warning can result in personal injury.

Introduction to the Chrysler LHS, Concorde, 300M and Dodge Intrepid

The second generation Chrysler LH is available in Chrysler LHS, Concorde and 300M as well as Dodge Intrepid models only in the four-door sedan body style. They feature longitudinally mounted V6 engines, equipped with electronic multi-port fuel injection. The engine drives the front wheels through a four-speed automatic transaxle via independent driveaxles.

The fully independent front suspension consists of coil spring/strut units, lower control arms with tension struts and a stabilizer bar. The independent rear suspension uses coil spring/strut units and spindle/hub units located by trailing arms and lateral links.

The power-assisted rack-and-pinion steering unit is mounted behind the engine.

Front and rear brakes are disc-type. Power assist is standard.

Vehicle identification numbers

Vehicle identification numbers

Modifications are a continuing and unpublicized process in vehicle manufacturing. Since spare parts manuals and lists are compiled on a numerical basis, the individual vehicle numbers are essential to correctly identify the component required.

Vehicle Identification Number (VIN)

The Vehicle Identification Number (VIN), which appears on the Vehicle Certificate of Title and Registration, is also embossed on a gray plate located on the upper left (driver's side) corner of the dashboard, near the windshield **(see illustration)**. The VIN tells you when and where a vehicle was manufactured, its country of origin, make, type, passenger safety system, line, series, body style, engine and assembly plant.

VIN engine and model year codes

Two particularly important pieces of information in the VIN are the engine code and the model year code. Counting from the left, the engine code letter designation is the 8th digit and the model year code is the 10th digit.

On models covered by this manual the engine codes are:

1998 and 1999

G .... 3.5L 24-valve SOHC
J .... 3.2L 24-valve SOHC
R .... 2.7L 24-valve DOHC

2000 and 2001

G .... 3.5L 24-valve SOHC
J .... 3.2L 24-valve SOHC
R .... 2.7L 24-valve DOHC
U .... 2.7L 24-valve DOHC
V..................... 2.7L 24-valve DOHC

The model year codes (10th digit of the VIN) are:

W 1998
X..................... 1999
Y 2000
1...................... 2001
2...................... 2002
3...................... 2003

Body Code Plate

The body code plate, which is riveted to the front of the battery tray, provides more specific information about the vehicle - type of engine, transaxle, paint, etc. - to which it's attached **(see illustration)**. The information codes are useful when ordering parts or matching paint and trim. On certain models, the right headlight housing must be removed to see the plate (refer to Chapter 12 for headlight housing removal).

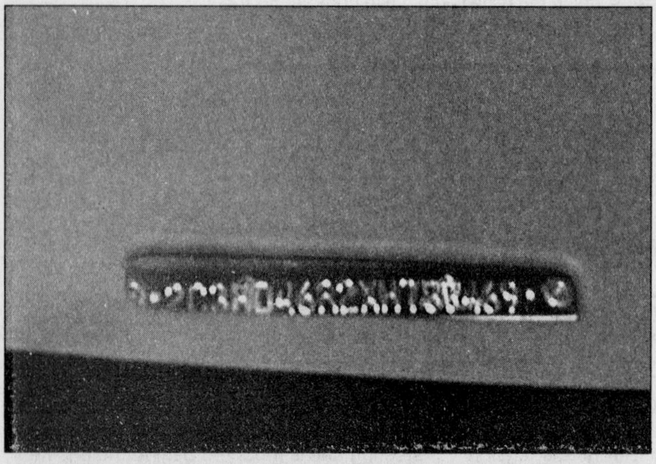

The Vehicle Identification Number (VIN) is stamped into a metal plate fastened to the dashboard on the driver's side - it's visible through the windshield

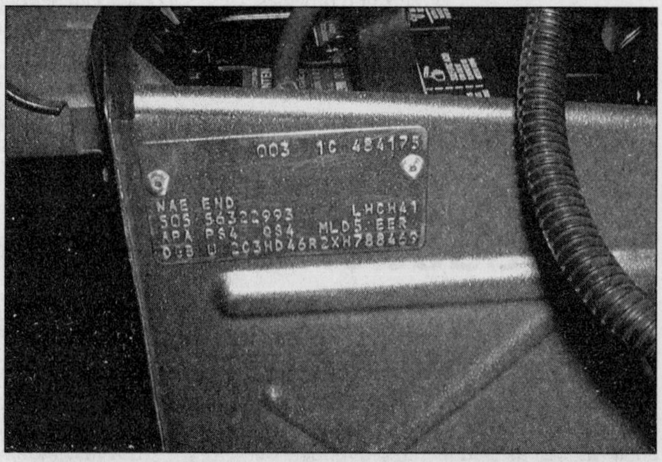

The Body Code Plate is located on the front of the battery tray, and the right headlight housing must be removed to see it (see Chapter 12) - the plate provides information about the type of engine, transaxle, paint, etc.

Typical Safety Certification label

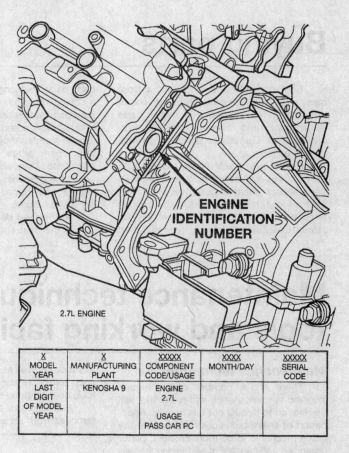

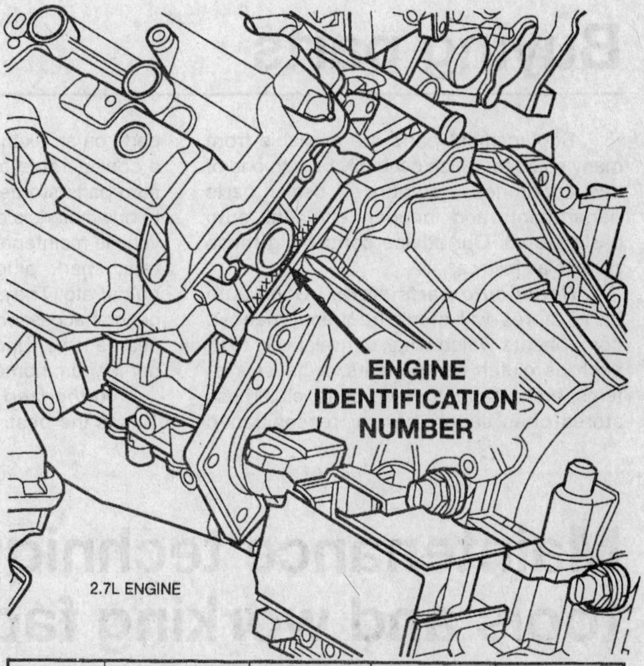

X MODEL YEAR	X MANUFACTURING PLANT	XXXXX COMPONENT CODE/USAGE	XXXX MONTH/DAY	XXXXX SERIAL CODE
LAST DIGIT OF MODEL YEAR	KENOSHA 9	ENGINE 2.7L USAGE PASS CAR PC		

The Engine Identification Number is located on the engine block, just below the cylinder head (2.7L shown, 3.2L/3.5L similar)

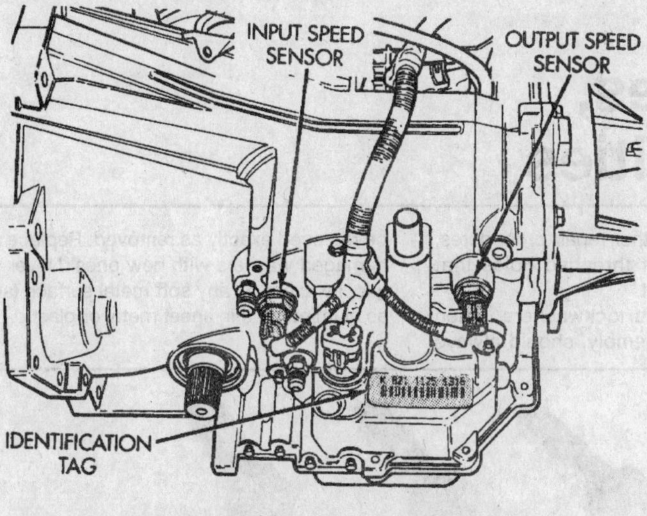

The automatic transaxle identification number is located on a sticker at the left (driver's) end of the transaxle

Vehicle Safety Certification label

The Safety Certification label is affixed to the left front door pillar or the pillar-side of the door **(see illustration)**. The plate contains the name of the manufacturer, the month and year of production, the Gross Vehicle Weight Rating (GVWR) and the safety certification statement. This label also contains the original tire sizes and recommended pressures, and the paint code. It is especially useful for matching the color and type of paint during repair work.

Engine Identification Number (EIN)

The Engine Identification Number (EIN) is stamped into the rear of the engine block just below the cylinder head **(see illustration)**.

Transaxle Identification Number (TIN)

The Transaxle Identification Number (TIN) is located on a sticker on top of the left end of transaxle housing **(see illustration)**.

Buying parts

Replacement parts are available from many sources, which generally fall into one of two categories - authorized dealer parts departments and independent retail auto parts stores. Our advice concerning these parts is as follows:

Retail auto parts stores: Good auto parts stores will stock frequently needed components which wear out relatively fast, such as clutch components, exhaust systems, brake parts, tune-up parts, etc. These stores often supply new or reconditioned parts on an exchange basis, which can save a considerable amount of money. Discount auto parts stores are often very good places to buy materials and parts needed for general vehicle maintenance such as oil, grease, filters, spark plugs, belts, touch-up paint, bulbs, etc. They also usually sell tools and general accessories, have convenient hours, charge lower prices and can often be found not far from home.

Authorized dealer parts department: This is the best source for parts which are unique to the vehicle and not generally available elsewhere (such as major engine parts, transmission parts, trim pieces, etc.).

Warranty information: If the vehicle is still covered under warranty, be sure that any replacement parts purchased - regardless of the source - do not invalidate the warranty!

To be sure of obtaining the correct parts, have engine and chassis numbers available and, if possible, take the old parts along for positive identification.

Maintenance techniques, tools and working facilities

Maintenance techniques

There are a number of techniques involved in maintenance and repair that will be referred to throughout this manual. Application of these techniques will enable the home mechanic to be more efficient, better organized and capable of performing the various tasks properly, which will ensure that the repair job is thorough and complete.

Fasteners

Fasteners are nuts, bolts, studs and screws used to hold two or more parts together. There are a few things to keep in mind when working with fasteners. Almost all of them use a locking device of some type, either a lockwasher, locknut, locking tab or thread adhesive. All threaded fasteners should be clean and straight, with undamaged threads and undamaged corners on the hex head where the wrench fits. Develop the habit of replacing all damaged nuts and bolts with new ones. Special locknuts with nylon or fiber inserts can only be used once. If they are removed, they lose their locking ability and must be replaced with new ones.

Rusted nuts and bolts should be treated with a penetrating fluid to ease removal and prevent breakage. Some mechanics use turpentine in a spout-type oil can, which works quite well. After applying the rust penetrant, let it work for a few minutes before trying to loosen the nut or bolt. Badly rusted fasteners may have to be chiseled or sawed off or removed with a special nut breaker, available at tool stores.

If a bolt or stud breaks off in an assembly, it can be drilled and removed with a special tool commonly available for this purpose. Most automotive machine shops can perform this task, as well as other repair procedures, such as the repair of threaded holes that have been stripped out.

Flat washers and lockwashers, when removed from an assembly, should always be replaced exactly as removed. Replace any damaged washers with new ones. Never use a lockwasher on any soft metal surface (such as aluminum), thin sheet metal or plastic.

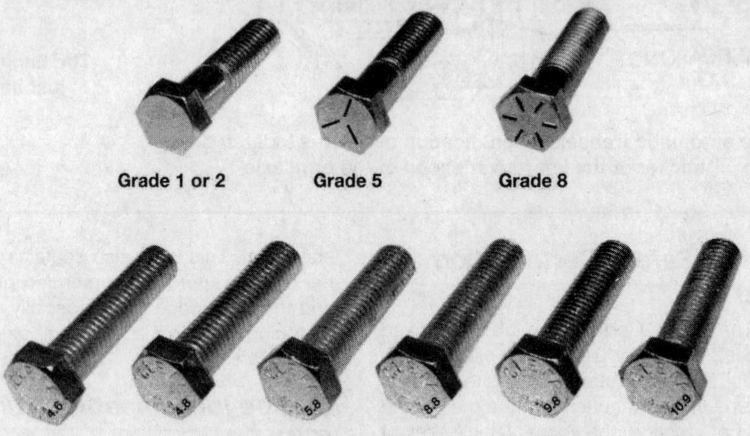

Bolt strength marking (standard/SAE/USS; bottom - metric)

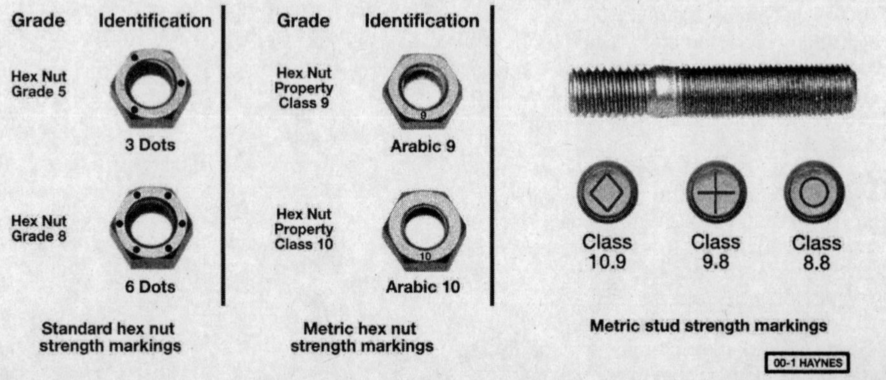

Standard hex nut strength markings

Metric hex nut strength markings

Metric stud strength markings

Fastener sizes

Modern vehicles use almost exclusively metric fasteners. However, it is still important to be able to tell the difference between standard (sometimes called U.S. or SAE) and metric hardware, since they cannot be interchanged.

All bolts, whether standard or metric, are sized according to diameter, thread pitch and length. For example, a standard 1/2 - 13 x 1 bolt is 1/2 inch in diameter, has 13 threads per inch and is 1 inch long. An M12 - 1.75 x 25 metric bolt is 12 mm in diameter, has a thread pitch of 1.75 mm (the distance between threads) and is 25 mm long. The two bolts are nearly identical, and easily confused, but they are not interchangeable.

In addition to the differences in diameter, thread pitch and length, metric and standard bolts can also be distinguished by examining the bolt heads. To begin with, the distance across the flats on a standard bolt head is measured in inches, while the same dimension on a metric bolt is sized in millimeters (the same is true for nuts). As a result, a standard wrench should not be used on a metric bolt and a metric wrench should not be used on a standard bolt. Also, most standard bolts have slashes radiating out from the center of the head to denote the grade or strength of the bolt, which is an indication of the amount of torque that can be applied to it. The greater the number of slashes, the greater the strength of the bolt. Grades 0 through 5 are commonly used on automobiles. Metric bolts have a property class (grade) number, rather than a slash, molded into their heads to indicate bolt strength. In this case, the higher the number, the stronger the bolt. Property class numbers 8.8, 9.8 and 10.9 are commonly used on automobiles.

Strength markings can also be used to distinguish standard hex nuts from metric hex nuts. Many standard nuts have dots stamped into one side, while metric nuts are marked with a number. The greater the number of dots, or the higher the number, the greater the strength of the nut.

Metric studs are also marked on their ends according to property class (grade). Larger studs are numbered (the same as metric bolts), while smaller studs carry a geometric code to denote grade.

It should be noted that many fasteners, especially Grades 0 through 2, have no distinguishing marks on them. When such is the case, the only way to determine whether it is standard or metric is to measure the thread pitch or compare it to a known fastener of the same size.

Standard fasteners are often referred to as SAE, as opposed to metric. However, it should be noted that SAE technically refers to a non-metric fine thread fastener only. Coarse thread non-metric fasteners are referred to as USS sizes.

Since fasteners of the same size (both standard and metric) may have different strength ratings, be sure to reinstall any bolts, studs or nuts removed from your vehicle in their original locations. Also, when replacing a fastener with a new one, make sure that the new one has a strength rating equal to or greater than the original.

Metric thread sizes	Ft-lbs	Nm
M-6	6 to 9	9 to 12
M-8	14 to 21	19 to 28
M-10	28 to 40	38 to 54
M-12	50 to 71	68 to 96
M-14	80 to 140	109 to 154

Pipe thread sizes	Ft-lbs	Nm
1/8	5 to 8	7 to 10
1/4	12 to 18	17 to 24
3/8	22 to 33	30 to 44
1/2	25 to 35	34 to 47

U.S. thread sizes	Ft-lbs	Nm
1/4 - 20	6 to 9	9 to 12
5/16 - 18	12 to 18	17 to 24
5/16 - 24	14 to 20	19 to 27
3/8 - 16	22 to 32	30 to 43
3/8 - 24	27 to 38	37 to 51
7/16 - 14	40 to 55	55 to 74
7/16 - 20	40 to 60	55 to 81
1/2 - 13	55 to 80	75 to 108

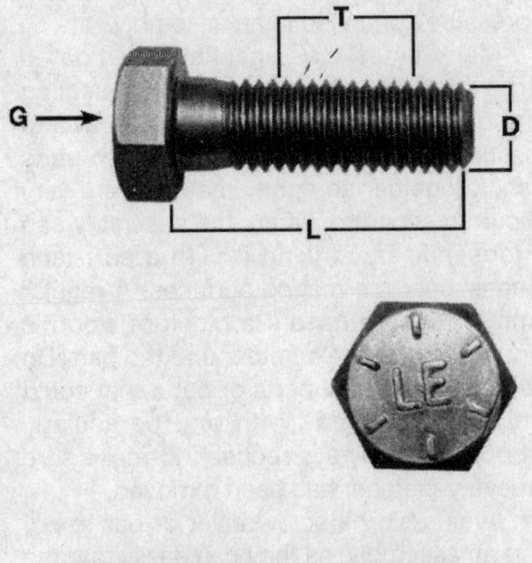

Standard (SAE and USS) bolt dimensions/grade marks

G *Grade marks (bolt strength)*
L *Length (in inches)*
T *Thread pitch (number of threads per inch)*
D *Nominal diameter (in inches)*

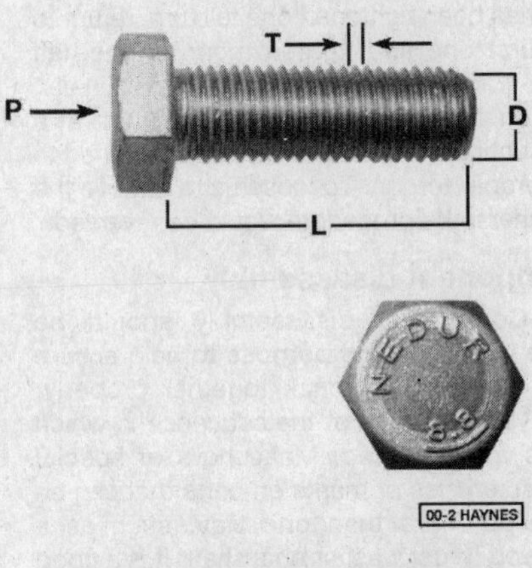

Metric bolt dimensions/grade marks

P *Property class (bolt strength)*
L *Length (in millimeters)*
T *Thread pitch (distance between threads in millimeters)*
D *Diameter*

Tightening sequences and procedures

Most threaded fasteners should be tightened to a specific torque value (torque is the twisting force applied to a threaded component such as a nut or bolt). Overtightening the fastener can weaken it and cause it to break, while undertightening can cause it to eventually come loose. Bolts, screws and studs, depending on the material they are made of and their thread diameters, have specific torque values, many of which are noted in the Specifications at the beginning of each Chapter. Be sure to follow the torque recommendations closely. For fasteners not assigned a specific torque, a general torque value chart is presented here as a guide. These torque values are for dry (unlubricated) fasteners threaded into steel or cast iron (not aluminum). As was previously mentioned, the size and grade of a fastener determine the amount of torque that can safely be applied to it. The figures listed here are approximate for Grade 2 and Grade 3 fasteners. Higher grades can tolerate higher torque values.

Fasteners laid out in a pattern, such as cylinder head bolts, oil pan bolts, differential cover bolts, etc., must be loosened or tightened in sequence to avoid warping the component. This sequence will normally be

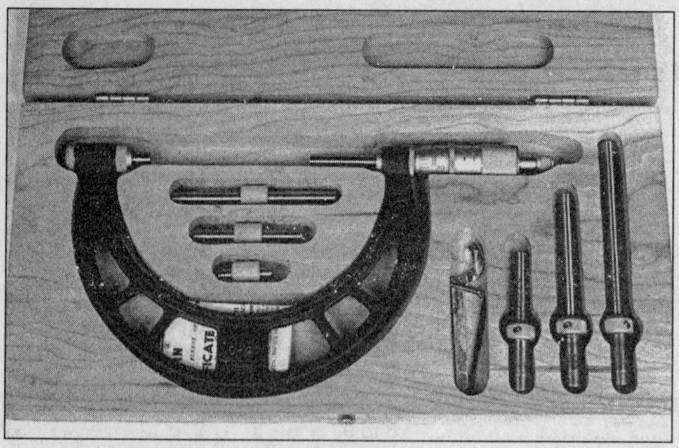

Micrometer set

Dial indicator set

shown in the appropriate Chapter. If a specific pattern is not given, the following procedures can be used to prevent warping.

Initially, the bolts or nuts should be assembled finger-tight only. Next, they should be tightened one full turn each, in a criss-cross or diagonal pattern. After each one has been tightened one full turn, return to the first one and tighten them all one-half turn, following the same pattern. Finally, tighten each of them one-quarter turn at a time until each fastener has been tightened to the proper torque. To loosen and remove the fasteners, the procedure would be reversed.

Component disassembly

Component disassembly should be done with care and purpose to help ensure that the parts go back together properly. Always keep track of the sequence in which parts are removed. Make note of special characteristics or marks on parts that can be installed more than one way, such as a grooved thrust washer on a shaft. It is a good idea to lay the disassembled parts out on a clean surface in the order that they were removed. It may also be helpful to make sketches or take instant photos of components before removal.

When removing fasteners from a component, keep track of their locations. Sometimes threading a bolt back in a part, or putting the washers and nut back on a stud, can prevent mix-ups later. If nuts and bolts cannot be returned to their original locations, they should be kept in a compartmented box or a series of small boxes. A cupcake or muffin tin is ideal for this purpose, since each cavity can hold the bolts and nuts from a particular area (i.e. oil pan bolts, valve cover bolts, engine mount bolts, etc.). A pan of this type is especially helpful when working on assemblies with very small parts, such as the carburetor, alternator, valve train or interior dash and trim pieces. The cavities can be marked with paint or tape to identify the contents.

Whenever wiring looms, harnesses or connectors are separated, it is a good idea to identify the two halves with numbered pieces of masking tape so they can be easily reconnected.

Gasket sealing surfaces

Throughout any vehicle, gaskets are used to seal the mating surfaces between two parts and keep lubricants, fluids, vacuum or pressure contained in an assembly.

Many times these gaskets are coated with a liquid or paste-type gasket sealing compound before assembly. Age, heat and pressure can sometimes cause the two parts to stick together so tightly that they are very difficult to separate. Often, the assembly can be loosened by striking it with a soft-face hammer near the mating surfaces. A regular hammer can be used if a block of wood is placed between the hammer and the part. Do not hammer on cast parts or parts that could be easily damaged. With any particularly stubborn part, always recheck to make sure that every fastener has been removed.

Avoid using a screwdriver or bar to pry apart an assembly, as they can easily mar the gasket sealing surfaces of the parts, which must remain smooth. If prying is absolutely necessary, use an old broom handle, but keep in mind that extra clean up will be necessary if the wood splinters.

After the parts are separated, the old gasket must be carefully scraped off and the gasket surfaces cleaned. Stubborn gasket material can be soaked with rust penetrant or treated with a special chemical to soften it so it can be easily scraped off. A scraper can be fashioned from a piece of copper tubing by flattening and sharpening one end. Copper is recommended because it is usually softer than the surfaces to be scraped, which reduces the chance of gouging the part. Some gaskets can be removed with a wire brush, but regardless of the method used, the mating surfaces must be left clean and smooth. If for some reason the gasket surface is gouged, then a gasket sealer thick enough to fill scratches will have to be used during reassembly of the components. For most applications, a non-drying (or semi-drying) gasket sealer should be used.

Hose removal tips

Warning: If the vehicle is equipped with air conditioning, do not disconnect any of the A/C hoses without first having the system depressurized by a dealer service department or a service station.

Hose removal precautions closely parallel gasket removal precautions. Avoid scratching or gouging the surface that the hose mates against or the connection may leak. This is especially true for radiator hoses. Because of various chemical reactions, the rubber in hoses can bond itself to the metal spigot that the hose fits over. To remove a hose, first loosen the hose clamps that secure it to the spigot. Then, with slip-joint pliers, grab the hose at the clamp and rotate it around the spigot. Work it back and forth until it is completely free, then pull it off. Silicone or other lubricants will ease removal if they can be applied between the hose and the outside of the spigot. Apply the same lubricant to the inside of the hose and the outside of the spigot to simplify installation.

As a last resort (and if the hose is to be replaced with a new one anyway), the rubber can be slit with a knife and the hose peeled from the spigot. If this must be done, be careful that the metal connection is not damaged.

If a hose clamp is broken or damaged, do not reuse it. Wire-type clamps usually weaken with age, so it is a good idea to replace them with screw-type clamps whenever a hose is removed.

Tools

A selection of good tools is a basic requirement for anyone who plans to maintain and repair his or her own vehicle. For the owner who has few tools, the initial investment might seem high, but when compared to the spiraling costs of professional auto maintenance and repair, it is a wise one.

To help the owner decide which tools are needed to perform the tasks detailed in this manual, the following tool lists are offered: *Maintenance and minor repair*, *Repair/overhaul* and *Special*.

The newcomer to practical mechanics

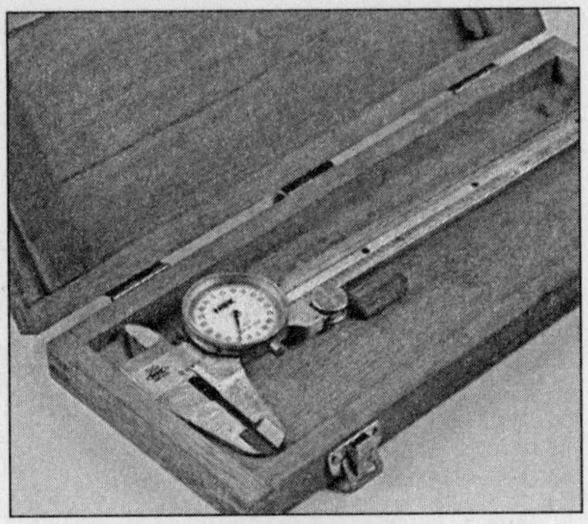

Dial caliper

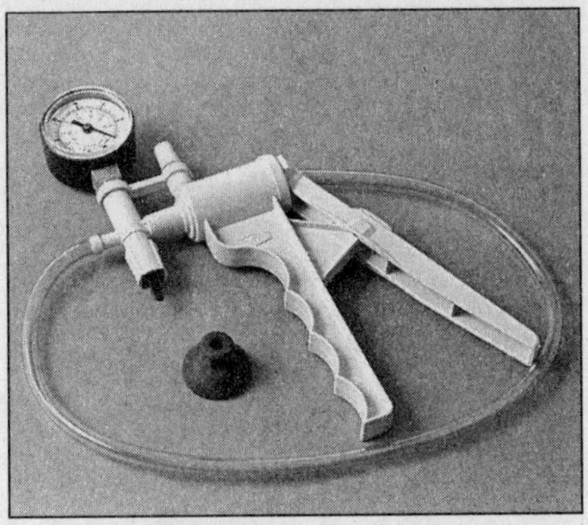

Hand-operated vacuum pump

Timing light

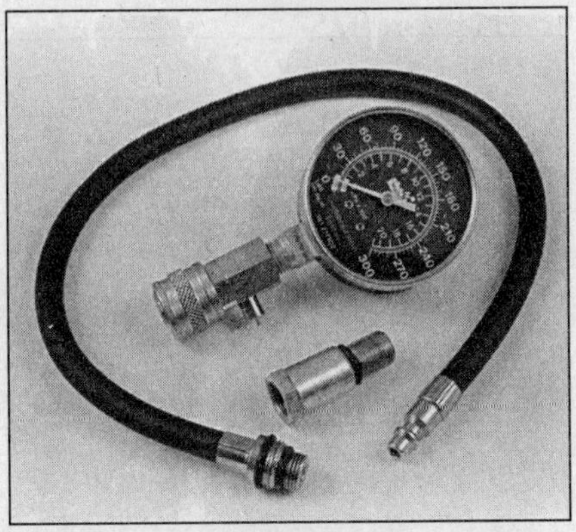

Compression gauge with spark plug hole adapter

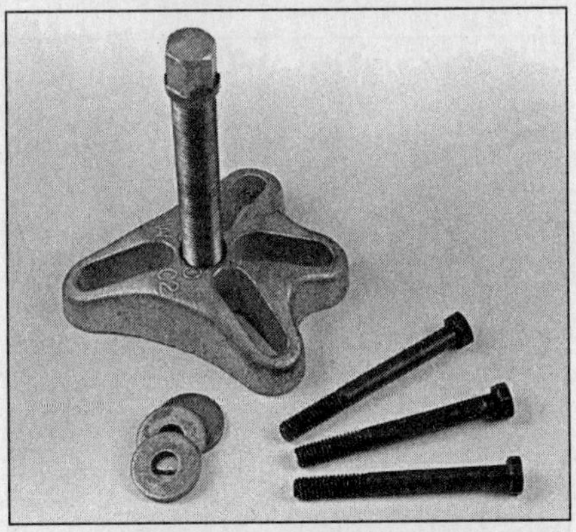

Damper/steering wheel puller

General purpose puller

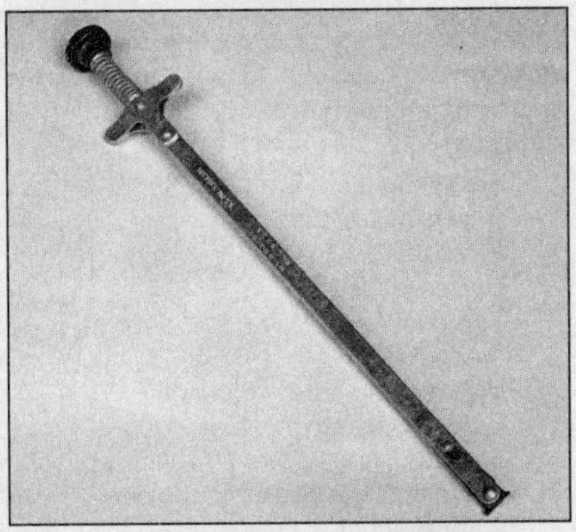

Hydraulic lifter removal tool

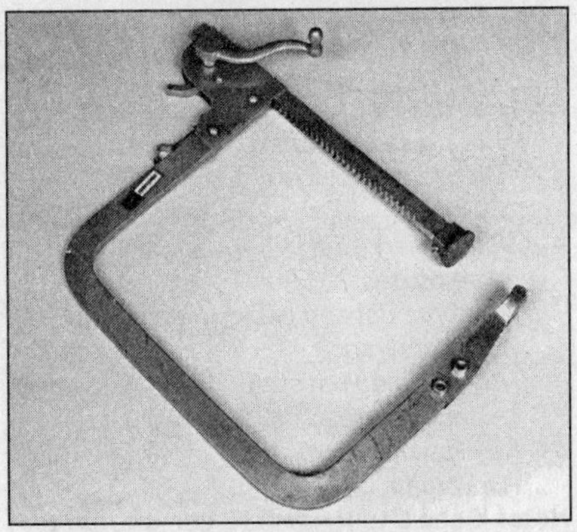

Valve spring compressor

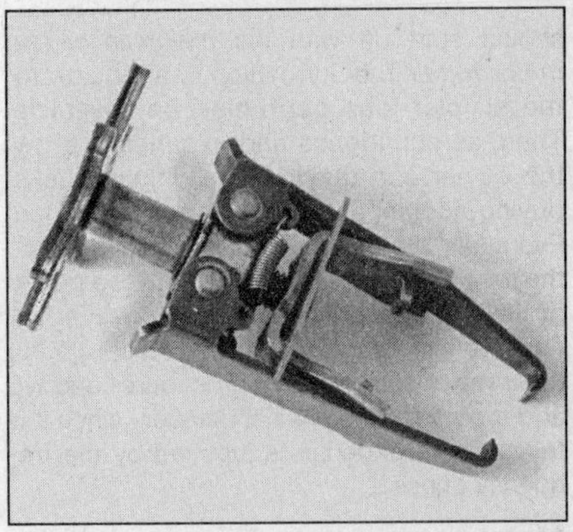

Valve spring compressor

Ridge reamer

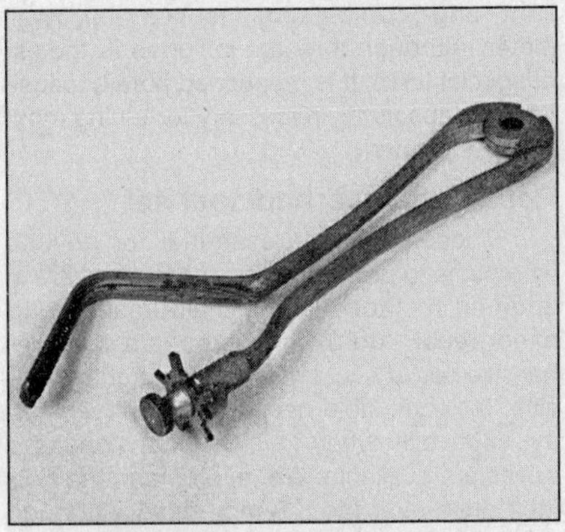

Piston ring groove cleaning tool

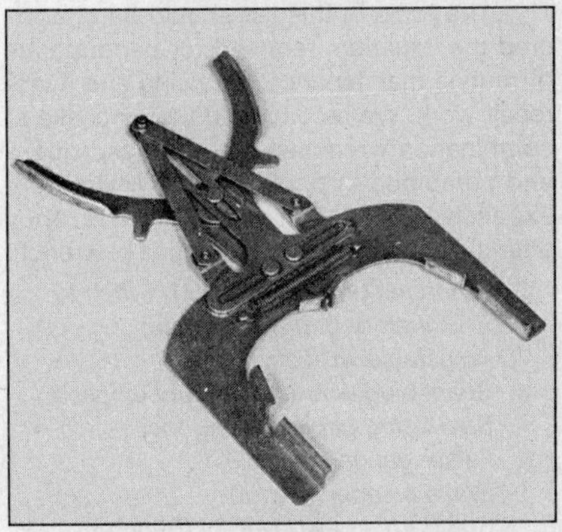

Ring removal/installation tool

Ring compressor

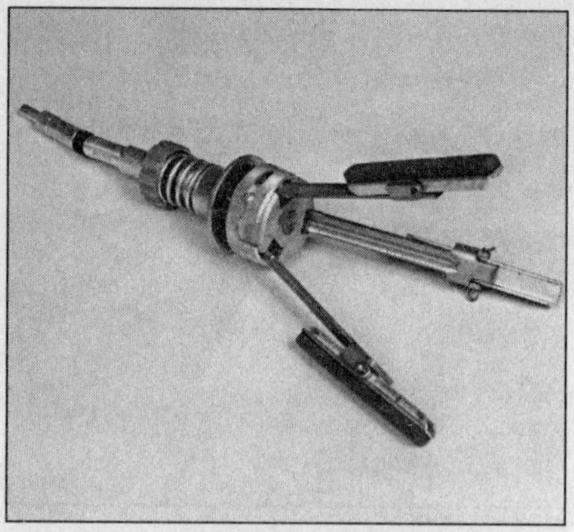

Cylinder hone

Brake hold-down spring tool

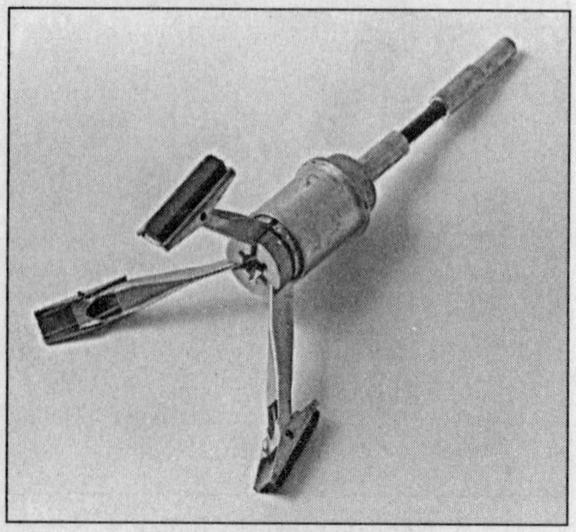

Brake cylinder hone

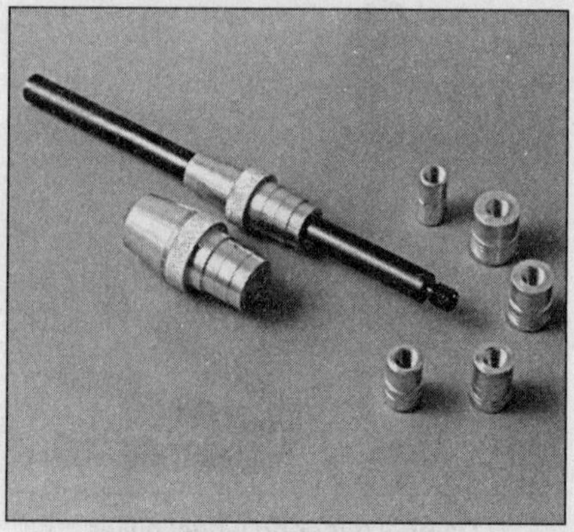

Clutch plate alignment tool

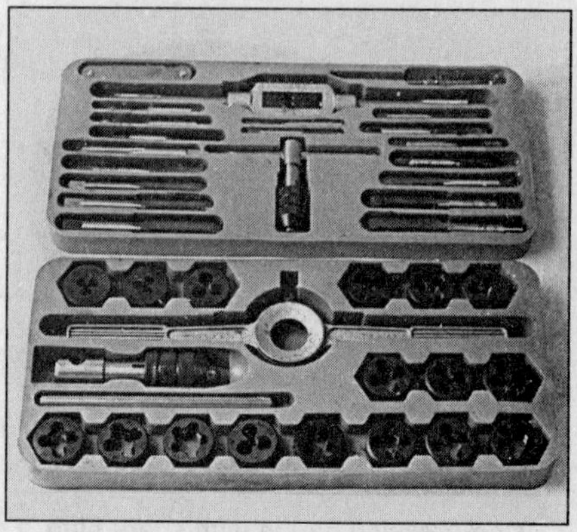

Tap and die set

should start off with the *maintenance and minor repair* tool kit, which is adequate for the simpler jobs performed on a vehicle. Then, as confidence and experience grow, the owner can tackle more difficult tasks, buying additional tools as they are needed. Eventually the basic kit will be expanded into the *repair and overhaul* tool set. Over a period of time, the experienced do-it-yourselfer will assemble a tool set complete enough for most repair and overhaul procedures and will add tools from the special category when it is felt that the expense is justified by the frequency of use.

Maintenance and minor repair tool kit

The tools in this list should be considered the minimum required for performance of routine maintenance, servicing and minor repair work. We recommend the purchase of combination wrenches (box-end and open-end combined in one wrench). While more expensive than open end wrenches, they offer the advantages of both types of wrench.

Combination wrench set (1/4-inch to 1 inch or 6 mm to 19 mm)
Adjustable wrench, 8 inch
Spark plug wrench with rubber insert
Spark plug gap adjusting tool
Feeler gauge set
Brake bleeder wrench
Standard screwdriver (5/16-inch x 6 inch)
Phillips screwdriver (No. 2 x 6 inch)
Combination pliers - 6 inch
Hacksaw and assortment of blades
Tire pressure gauge
Grease gun
Oil can
Fine emery cloth
Wire brush
Battery post and cable cleaning tool
Oil filter wrench
Funnel (medium size)
Safety goggles
Jackstands (2)
Drain pan

Note: If basic tune-ups are going to be part of routine maintenance, it will be necessary to purchase a good quality stroboscopic timing light and combination tachometer/dwell meter. Although they are included in the list of special tools, it is mentioned here because they are absolutely necessary for tuning most vehicles properly.

Repair and overhaul tool set

These tools are essential for anyone who plans to perform major repairs and are in addition to those in the maintenance and minor repair tool kit. Included is a comprehensive set of sockets which, though expensive, are invaluable because of their versatility, especially when various extensions and drives are available. We recommend the 1/2-inch drive over the 3/8-inch drive. Although the larger drive is bulky and more expensive, it has the capacity of accepting a very wide range of large sockets. Ideally, however, the mechanic should have a 3/8-inch drive set and a 1/2-inch drive set.

Socket set(s)
Reversible ratchet
Extension - 10 inch
Universal joint
Torque wrench (same size drive as sockets)
Ball peen hammer - 8 ounce
Soft-face hammer (plastic/rubber)
Standard screwdriver (1/4-inch x 6 inch)
Standard screwdriver (stubby - 5/16-inch)
Phillips screwdriver (No. 3 x 8 inch)
Phillips screwdriver (stubby - No. 2)
Pliers - vise grip
Pliers - lineman's
Pliers - needle nose
Pliers - snap-ring (internal and external)
Cold chisel - 1/2-inch
Scribe
Scraper (made from flattened copper tubing)
Centerpunch
Pin punches (1/16, 1/8, 3/16-inch)
Steel rule/straightedge - 12 inch
Allen wrench set (1/8 to 3/8-inch or 4 mm to 10 mm)
A selection of files
Wire brush (large)
Jackstands (second set)
Jack (scissor or hydraulic type)

Note: *Another tool which is often useful is an electric drill with a chuck capacity of 3/8-inch and a set of good quality drill bits.*

Special tools

The tools in this list include those which are not used regularly, are expensive to buy, or which need to be used in accordance with their manufacturer's instructions. Unless these tools will be used frequently, it is not very economical to purchase many of them. A consideration would be to split the cost and use between yourself and a friend or friends. In addition, most of these tools can be obtained from a tool rental shop on a temporary basis.

This list primarily contains only those tools and instruments widely available to the public, and not those special tools produced by the vehicle manufacturer for distribution to dealer service departments. Occasionally, references to the manufacturer's special tools are included in the text of this manual. Generally, an alternative method of doing the job without the special tool is offered. However, sometimes there is no alternative to their use. Where this is the case, and the tool cannot be purchased or borrowed, the work should be turned over to the dealer service department or an automotive repair shop.

Valve spring compressor
Piston ring groove cleaning tool
Piston ring compressor
Piston ring installation tool
Cylinder compression gauge
Cylinder ridge reamer
Cylinder surfacing hone
Cylinder bore gauge
Micrometers and/or dial calipers
Hydraulic lifter removal tool
Balljoint separator
Universal-type puller
Impact screwdriver
Dial indicator set
Stroboscopic timing light (inductive pick-up)
Hand operated vacuum/pressure pump
Tachometer/dwell meter
Universal electrical multimeter
Cable hoist
Brake spring removal and installation tools
Floor jack

Buying tools

For the do-it-yourselfer who is just starting to get involved in vehicle maintenance and repair, there are a number of options available when purchasing tools. If maintenance and minor repair is the extent of the work to be done, the purchase of individual tools is satisfactory. If, on the other hand, extensive work is planned, it would be a good idea to purchase a modest tool set from one of the large retail chain stores. A set can usually be bought at a substantial savings over the individual tool prices, and they often come with a tool box. As additional tools are needed, add-on sets, individual tools and a larger tool box can be purchased to expand the tool selection. Building a tool set gradually allows the cost of the tools to be spread over a longer period of time and gives the mechanic the freedom to choose only those tools that will actually be used.

Tool stores will often be the only source of some of the special tools that are needed, but regardless of where tools are bought, try to avoid cheap ones, especially when buying screwdrivers and sockets, because they won't last very long. The expense involved in replacing cheap tools will eventually be greater than the initial cost of quality tools.

Care and maintenance of tools

Good tools are expensive, so it makes sense to treat them with respect. Keep them clean and in usable condition and store them properly when not in use. Always wipe off any dirt, grease or metal chips before putting them away. Never leave tools lying around in the work area. Upon completion of a job, always check closely under the hood for tools that may have been left there so they won't get lost during a test drive.

Some tools, such as screwdrivers, pliers, wrenches and sockets, can be hung on a panel mounted on the garage or workshop wall, while others should be kept in a tool box or tray. Measuring instruments, gauges, meters, etc. must be carefully stored where they cannot be damaged by weather or impact from other tools.

When tools are used with care and stored properly, they will last a very long time. Even with the best of care, though, tools will wear out if used frequently. When a tool is damaged or worn out, replace it. Subsequent jobs will be safer and more enjoyable if you do.

How to repair damaged threads

Sometimes, the internal threads of a nut or bolt hole can become stripped, usually from overtightening. Stripping threads is an all-too-common occurrence, especially when working with aluminum parts, because aluminum is so soft that it easily strips out.

Usually, external or internal threads are only partially stripped. After they've been cleaned up with a tap or die, they'll still work. Sometimes, however, threads are badly damaged. When this happens, you've got three choices:

1) *Drill and tap the hole to the next suitable oversize and install a larger diameter bolt, screw or stud.*
2) *Drill and tap the hole to accept a threaded plug, then drill and tap the plug to the original screw size. You can also buy a plug already threaded to the original size. Then you simply drill a hole to the specified size, then run the threaded plug into the hole with a bolt and jam nut. Once the plug is fully seated, remove the jam nut and bolt.*
3) *The third method uses a patented thread repair kit like Heli-Coil or Slimsert. These easy-to-use kits are designed to repair damaged threads in straight-through holes and blind holes. Both are available as kits which can handle a variety of sizes and thread patterns. Drill the hole, then tap it with the special included tap. Install the Heli-Coil and the hole is back to its original diameter and thread pitch.*

Regardless of which method you use, be sure to proceed calmly and carefully. A little impatience or carelessness during one of these relatively simple procedures can ruin your whole day's work and cost you a bundle if you wreck an expensive part.

Working facilities

Not to be overlooked when discussing tools is the workshop. If anything more than routine maintenance is to be carried out, some sort of suitable work area is essential.

It is understood, and appreciated, that many home mechanics do not have a good workshop or garage available, and end up removing an engine or doing major repairs outside. It is recommended, however, that the overhaul or repair be completed under the cover of a roof.

A clean, flat workbench or table of comfortable working height is an absolute necessity. The workbench should be equipped with a vise that has a jaw opening of at least four inches.

As mentioned previously, some clean, dry storage space is also required for tools, as well as the lubricants, fluids, cleaning solvents, etc. which soon become necessary.

Sometimes waste oil and fluids, drained from the engine or cooling system during normal maintenance or repairs, present a disposal problem. To avoid pouring them on the ground or into a sewage system, pour the used fluids into large containers, seal them with caps and take them to an authorized disposal site or recycling center. Plastic jugs, such as old antifreeze containers, are ideal for this purpose.

Always keep a supply of old newspapers and clean rags available. Old towels are excellent for mopping up spills. Many mechanics use rolls of paper towels for most work because they are readily available and disposable. To help keep the area under the vehicle clean, a large cardboard box can be cut open and flattened to protect the garage or shop floor.

Whenever working over a painted surface, such as when leaning over a fender to service something under the hood, always cover it with an old blanket or bedspread to protect the finish. Vinyl covered pads, made especially for this purpose, are available at auto parts stores.

Booster battery (jump) starting

Observe these precautions when using a booster battery to start a vehicle:

a) *Before connecting the booster battery, make sure the ignition switch is in the Off position.*
b) *Turn off the lights, heater and other electrical loads.*
c) *Your eyes should be shielded. Safety goggles are a good idea.*
d) *Make sure the booster battery is the same voltage as the dead one in the vehicle.*
e) *The two vehicles MUST NOT TOUCH each other!*
f) *Make sure the transaxle is in Neutral (manual) or Park (automatic).*
g) *If the booster battery is not a maintenance-free type, remove the vent caps and lay a cloth over the vent holes.*

The battery on these vehicles is located inside the wheelwell of the right front fender. Due to the lack of accessibility, remote battery connections are provided inside the engine compartment for jumping and easy battery disconnection **(see illustration)**.

Connect the red-colored jumper cable to the positive (+) terminal of the booster battery and the other end to the positive (+) remote terminal in the engine compartment. Then connect one end of the black jumper cable to the negative (-) terminal of the booster battery, and the other end of the cable to the negative (-) remote terminal.

Start the engine using the booster battery, then, with the engine running at idle speed, disconnect the jumper cables in the reverse order of connection.

The remote battery terminals are located in the engine compartment and well marked - when connecting the jumper cables connect the cable to the positive terminal (A) first, then the negative cable (B)

Jacking and towing

Jacking

The jack supplied with the vehicle should be used only for raising the vehicle when changing a tire or placing jackstands under the frame. **Warning:** *Never work under the vehicle or start the engine when this jack is being used as the only means of support.*

The vehicle should be on level ground with the wheels blocked and the transaxle in Park (automatic). If a tire is being changed, loosen the lug nuts one-half turn and leave them in place until the wheel is raised off the ground. Make sure no one is in the vehicle as it's being raised off the ground.

Place the jack under the side of the vehicle at the jacking point nearest the wheel to be changed **(see illustration)**. If you're using a floor jack, place it beneath the crossmember at the front or rear. Operate the jack with a slow, smooth motion until the wheel is raised off the ground. If you're using jackstands, position them beneath the support points along the front or rear side sills. Remove the lug nuts, pull off the wheel, install the spare and thread the lug nuts back on with the beveled sides facing in. Tighten them snugly, but wait until the vehicle is lowered to tighten them completely.

Lower the vehicle, remove the jack and tighten the lug nuts (if loosened or removed) in a criss-cross pattern. If possible, tighten them with a torque wrench (see Chapter 1 for the torque figures). If you don't have access to a torque wrench, have the nuts checked by a service station or repair shop as soon as possible. Retighten the lug nuts after 500 miles.

Use only the indicated lifting points (arrows) when jacking up the vehicle with the factory jack

If the vehicle is equipped with a temporary spare tire, remember that it is intended only for temporary use until the regular tire can be repaired. Do not exceed the maximum speed that the tire is rated for.

Towing

The vehicle must be either towed with the front (drive) wheels off the ground or carried on a flatbed truck to prevent damage to the transaxle. A wheel lift is recommended.

While towing, the parking brake must be released and the transaxle must be in Neutral. The steering must be unlocked (ignition switch in the OFF position). Don't exceed 30 mph.

Safety is a major consideration while towing and all applicable state and local laws must be obeyed. A safety chain system must be used at all times. Remember that power steering and power brakes will not work with the engine off.

Automotive chemicals and lubricants

A number of automotive chemicals and lubricants are available for use during vehicle maintenance and repair. They include a wide variety of products ranging from cleaning solvents and degreasers to lubricants and protective sprays for rubber, plastic and vinyl.

Cleaners

Carburetor cleaner and choke cleaner is a strong solvent for gum, varnish and carbon. Most carburetor cleaners leave a dry-type lubricant film which will not harden or gum up. Because of this film it is not recommended for use on electrical components.

Brake system cleaner is used to remove grease and brake fluid from the brake system, where clean surfaces are absolutely necessary. It leaves no residue and often eliminates brake squeal caused by contaminants.

Electrical cleaner removes oxidation, corrosion and carbon deposits from electrical contacts, restoring full current flow. It can also be used to clean spark plugs, carburetor jets, voltage regulators and other parts where an oil-free surface is desired.

Demoisturants remove water and moisture from electrical components such as alternators, voltage regulators, electrical connectors and fuse blocks. They are non-conductive, non-corrosive and non-flammable.

Degreasers are heavy-duty solvents used to remove grease from the outside of the engine and from chassis components. They can be sprayed or brushed on and, depending on the type, are rinsed off either with water or solvent.

Lubricants

Motor oil is the lubricant formulated for use in engines. It normally contains a wide variety of additives to prevent corrosion and reduce foaming and wear. Motor oil comes in various weights (viscosity ratings) from 0 to 50. The recommended weight of the oil depends on the season, temperature and the demands on the engine. Light oil is used in cold climates and under light load conditions. Heavy oil is used in hot climates and where high loads are encountered. Multi-viscosity oils are designed to have characteristics of both light and heavy oils and are available in a number of weights from 5W-20 to 20W-50.

Gear oil is designed to be used in differentials, manual transmissions and other areas where high-temperature lubrication is required.

Chassis and wheel bearing grease is a heavy grease used where increased loads and friction are encountered, such as for wheel bearings, balljoints, tie-rod ends and universal joints.

High-temperature wheel bearing grease is designed to withstand the extreme temperatures encountered by wheel bearings in disc brake equipped vehicles. It usually contains molybdenum disulfide (moly), which is a dry-type lubricant.

White grease is a heavy grease for metal-to-metal applications where water is a problem. White grease stays soft under both low and high temperatures (usually from -100 to +190-degrees F), and will not wash off or dilute in the presence of water.

Assembly lube is a special extreme pressure lubricant, usually containing moly, used to lubricate high-load parts (such as main and rod bearings and cam lobes) for initial start-up of a new engine. The assembly lube lubricates the parts without being squeezed out or washed away until the engine oiling system begins to function.

Silicone lubricants are used to protect rubber, plastic, vinyl and nylon parts.

Graphite lubricants are used where oils cannot be used due to contamination problems, such as in locks. The dry graphite will lubricate metal parts while remaining uncontaminated by dirt, water, oil or acids. It is electrically conductive and will not foul electrical contacts in locks such as the ignition switch.

Moly penetrants loosen and lubricate frozen, rusted and corroded fasteners and prevent future rusting or freezing.

Heat-sink grease is a special electrically non-conductive grease that is used for mounting electronic ignition modules where it is essential that heat is transferred away from the module.

Sealants

RTV sealant is one of the most widely used gasket compounds. Made from silicone, RTV is air curing, it seals, bonds, waterproofs, fills surface irregularities, remains flexible, doesn't shrink, is relatively easy to remove, and is used as a supplementary sealer with almost all low and medium temperature gaskets.

Anaerobic sealant is much like RTV in that it can be used either to seal gaskets or to form gaskets by itself. It remains flexible, is solvent resistant and fills surface imperfections. The difference between an anaerobic sealant and an RTV-type sealant is in the curing. RTV cures when exposed to air, while an anaerobic sealant cures only in the absence of air. This means that an anaerobic sealant cures only after the assembly of parts, sealing them together.

Thread and pipe sealant is used for sealing hydraulic and pneumatic fittings and vacuum lines. It is usually made from a Teflon compound, and comes in a spray, a paint-on liquid and as a wrap-around tape.

Chemicals

Anti-seize compound prevents seizing, galling, cold welding, rust and corrosion in fasteners. High-temperature anti-seize, usually made with copper and graphite lubricants, is used for exhaust system and exhaust manifold bolts.

Anaerobic locking compounds are used to keep fasteners from vibrating or working loose and cure only after installation, in the absence of air. Medium strength locking compound is used for small nuts, bolts and screws that may be removed later. High-strength locking compound is for large nuts, bolts and studs which aren't removed on a regular basis.

Oil additives range from viscosity index improvers to chemical treatments that claim to reduce internal engine friction. It should be noted that most oil manufacturers caution against using additives with their oils.

Gas additives perform several functions, depending on their chemical makeup. They usually contain solvents that help dissolve gum and varnish that build up on carburetor, fuel injection and intake parts. They also serve to break down carbon deposits that form on the inside surfaces of the combustion chambers. Some additives contain upper cylinder lubricants for valves and piston rings, and others contain chemicals to remove condensation from the gas tank.

Miscellaneous

Brake fluid is specially formulated hydraulic fluid that can withstand the heat and pressure encountered in brake systems. Care must be taken so this fluid does not come in contact with painted surfaces or plastics. An opened container should always be resealed to prevent contamination by water or dirt.

Weatherstrip adhesive is used to bond weatherstripping around doors, windows and trunk lids. It is sometimes used to attach trim pieces.

Undercoating is a petroleum-based, tar-like substance that is designed to protect metal surfaces on the underside of the vehicle from corrosion. It also acts as a sound-deadening agent by insulating the bottom of the vehicle.

Waxes and polishes are used to help protect painted and plated surfaces from the weather. Different types of paint may require the use of different types of wax and polish. Some polishes utilize a chemical or abrasive cleaner to help remove the top layer of oxidized (dull) paint on older vehicles. In recent years many non-wax polishes that contain a wide variety of chemicals such as polymers and silicones have been introduced. These non-wax polishes are usually easier to apply and last longer than conventional waxes and polishes.

Conversion factors

Length (distance)

Inches (in)	X	25.4	= Millimetres (mm)	X	0.0394	= Inches (in)
Feet (ft)	X	0.305	= Metres (m)	X	3.281	= Feet (ft)
Miles	X	1.609	= Kilometres (km)	X	0.621	= Miles

Volume (capacity)

Cubic inches (cu in; in^3)	X	16.387	= Cubic centimetres (cc; cm^3)	X	0.061	= Cubic inches (cu in; in^3)
Imperial pints (Imp pt)	X	0.568	= Litres (l)	X	1.76	= Imperial pints (Imp pt)
Imperial quarts (Imp qt)	X	1.137	= Litres (l)	X	0.88	= Imperial quarts (Imp qt)
Imperial quarts (Imp qt)	X	1.201	= US quarts (US qt)	X	0.833	= Imperial quarts (Imp qt)
US quarts (US qt)	X	0.946	= Litres (l)	X	1.057	= US quarts (US qt)
Imperial gallons (Imp gal)	X	4.546	= Litres (l)	X	0.22	= Imperial gallons (Imp gal)
Imperial gallons (Imp gal)	X	1.201	= US gallons (US gal)	X	0.833	= Imperial gallons (Imp gal)
US gallons (US gal)	X	3.785	= Litres (l)	X	0.264	= US gallons (US gal)

Mass (weight)

Ounces (oz)	X	28.35	= Grams (g)	X	0.035	= Ounces (oz)
Pounds (lb)	X	0.454	= Kilograms (kg)	X	2.205	= Pounds (lb)

Force

Ounces-force (ozf; oz)	X	0.278	= Newtons (N)	X	3.6	= Ounces-force (ozf; oz)
Pounds-force (lbf; lb)	X	4.448	= Newtons (N)	X	0.225	= Pounds-force (lbf; lb)
Newtons (N)	X	0.1	= Kilograms-force (kgf; kg)	X	9.81	= Newtons (N)

Pressure

Pounds-force per square inch (psi; lbf/in^2; lb/in^2)	X	0.070	= Kilograms-force per square centimetre (kgf/cm^2; kg/cm^2)	X	14.223	= Pounds-force per square inch (psi; lbf/in^2; lb/in^2)
Pounds-force per square inch (psi; lbf/in^2; lb/in^2)	X	0.068	= Atmospheres (atm)	X	14.696	= Pounds-force per square inch (psi; lbf/in^2; lb/in^2)
Pounds-force per square inch (psi; lbf/in^2; lb/in^2)	X	0.069	= Bars	X	14.5	= Pounds-force per square inch (psi; lbf/in^2; lb/in^2)
Pounds-force per square inch (psi; lbf/in^2; lb/in^2)	X	6.895	= Kilopascals (kPa)	X	0.145	= Pounds-force per square inch (psi; lbf/in^2; lb/in^2)
Kilopascals (kPa)	X	0.01	= Kilograms-force per square centimetre (kgf/cm^2; kg/cm^2)	X	98.1	= Kilopascals (kPa)

Torque (moment of force)

Pounds-force inches (lbf in; lb in)	X	1.152	= Kilograms-force centimetre (kgf cm; kg cm)	X	0.868	= Pounds-force inches (lbf in; lb in)
Pounds-force inches (lbf in; lb in)	X	0.113	= Newton metres (Nm)	X	8.85	= Pounds-force inches (lbf in; lb in)
Pounds-force inches (lbf in; lb in)	X	0.083	= Pounds-force feet (lbf ft; lb ft)	X	12	= Pounds-force inches (lbf in; lb in)
Pounds-force feet (lbf ft; lb ft)	X	0.138	= Kilograms-force metres (kgf m; kg m)	X	7.233	= Pounds-force feet (lbf ft; lb ft)
Pounds-force feet (lbf ft; lb ft)	X	1.356	= Newton metres (Nm)	X	0.738	= Pounds-force feet (lbf ft; lb ft)
Newton metres (Nm)	X	0.102	= Kilograms-force metres (kgf m; kg m)	X	9.804	= Newton metres (Nm)

Vacuum

Inches mercury (in. Hg)	X	3.377	= Kilopascals (kPa)	X	0.2961	= Inches mercury
Inches mercury (in. Hg)	X	25.4	= Millimeters mercury (mm Hg)	X	0.0394	= Inches mercury

Power

Horsepower (hp)	X	745.7	= Watts (W)	X	0.0013	= Horsepower (hp)

Velocity (speed)

Miles per hour (miles/hr; mph)	X	1.609	= Kilometres per hour (km/hr; kph)	X	0.621	= Miles per hour (miles/hr; mph)

*Fuel consumption**

Miles per gallon, Imperial (mpg)	X	0.354	= Kilometres per litre (km/l)	X	2.825	= Miles per gallon, Imperial (mpg)
Miles per gallon, US (mpg)	X	0.425	= Kilometres per litre (km/l)	X	2.352	= Miles per gallon, US (mpg)

Temperature

Degrees Fahrenheit = (°C x 1.8) + 32

Degrees Celsius (Degrees Centigrade; °C) = (°F - 32) x 0.56

**It is common practice to convert from miles per gallon (mpg) to litres/100 kilometres (l/100km), where mpg (Imperial) x l/100 km = 282 and mpg (US) x l/100 km = 235*

Safety first!

Regardless of how enthusiastic you may be about getting on with the job at hand, take the time to ensure that your safety is not jeopardized. A moment's lack of attention can result in an accident, as can failure to observe certain simple safety precautions. The possibility of an accident will always exist, and the following points should not be considered a comprehensive list of all dangers. Rather, they are intended to make you aware of the risks and to encourage a safety conscious approach to all work you carry out on your vehicle.

Essential DOs and DON'Ts

DON'T rely on a jack when working under the vehicle. Always use approved jackstands to support the weight of the vehicle and place them under the recommended lift or support points.

DON'T attempt to loosen extremely tight fasteners (i.e. wheel lug nuts) while the vehicle is on a jack - it may fall.

DON'T start the engine without first making sure that the transmission is in Neutral (or Park where applicable) and the parking brake is set.

DON'T remove the radiator cap from a hot cooling system - let it cool or cover it with a cloth and release the pressure gradually.

DON'T attempt to drain the engine oil until you are sure it has cooled to the point that it will not burn you.

DON'T touch any part of the engine or exhaust system until it has cooled sufficiently to avoid burns.

DON'T siphon toxic liquids such as gasoline, antifreeze and brake fluid by mouth, or allow them to remain on your skin.

DON'T inhale brake lining dust - it is potentially hazardous (see *Asbestos* below).

DON'T allow spilled oil or grease to remain on the floor - wipe it up before someone slips on it.

DON'T use loose fitting wrenches or other tools which may slip and cause injury.

DON'T push on wrenches when loosening or tightening nuts or bolts. Always try to pull the wrench toward you. If the situation calls for pushing the wrench away, push with an open hand to avoid scraped knuckles if the wrench should slip.

DON'T attempt to lift a heavy component alone - get someone to help you.

DON'T rush or take unsafe shortcuts to finish a job.

DON'T allow children or animals in or around the vehicle while you are working on it.

DO wear eye protection when using power tools such as a drill, sander, bench grinder, etc. and when working under a vehicle.

DO keep loose clothing and long hair well out of the way of moving parts.

DO make sure that any hoist used has a safe working load rating adequate for the job.

DO get someone to check on you periodically when working alone on a vehicle.

DO carry out work in a logical sequence and make sure that everything is correctly assembled and tightened.

DO keep chemicals and fluids tightly capped and out of the reach of children and pets.

DO remember that your vehicle's safety affects that of yourself and others. If in doubt on any point, get professional advice.

Asbestos

Certain friction, insulating, sealing, and other products - such as brake linings, brake bands, clutch linings, torque converters, gaskets, etc. - may contain asbestos. Extreme care must be taken to avoid inhalation of dust from such products, since it is hazardous to health. If in doubt, assume that they do contain asbestos.

Fire

Remember at all times that gasoline is highly flammable. Never smoke or have any kind of open flame around when working on a vehicle. But the risk does not end there. A spark caused by an electrical short circuit, by two metal surfaces contacting each other, or even by static electricity built up in your body under certain conditions, can ignite gasoline vapors, which in a confined space are highly explosive. Do not, under any circumstances, use gasoline for cleaning parts. Use an approved safety solvent.

Always disconnect the battery ground (-) cable at the battery before working on any part of the fuel system or electrical system. Never risk spilling fuel on a hot engine or exhaust component. It is strongly recommended that a fire extinguisher suitable for use on fuel and electrical fires be kept handy in the garage or workshop at all times. Never try to extinguish a fuel or electrical fire with water.

Fumes

Certain fumes are highly toxic and can quickly cause unconsciousness and even death if inhaled to any extent. Gasoline vapor falls into this category, as do the vapors from some cleaning solvents. Any draining or pouring of such volatile fluids should be done in a well ventilated area.

When using cleaning fluids and solvents, read the instructions on the container carefully. Never use materials from unmarked containers.

Never run the engine in an enclosed space, such as a garage. Exhaust fumes contain carbon monoxide, which is extremely poisonous. If you need to run the engine, always do so in the open air, or at least have the rear of the vehicle outside the work area.

If you are fortunate enough to have the use of an inspection pit, never drain or pour gasoline and never run the engine while the vehicle is over the pit. The fumes, being heavier than air, will concentrate in the pit with possibly lethal results.

The battery

Never create a spark or allow a bare light bulb near a battery. They normally give off a certain amount of hydrogen gas, which is highly explosive.

Always disconnect the battery ground (-) cable at the battery before working on the fuel or electrical systems.

If possible, loosen the filler caps or cover when charging the battery from an external source (this does not apply to sealed or maintenance-free batteries). Do not charge at an excessive rate or the battery may burst.

Take care when adding water to a non maintenance-free battery and when carrying a battery. The electrolyte, even when diluted, is very corrosive and should not be allowed to contact clothing or skin.

Always wear eye protection when cleaning the battery to prevent the caustic deposits from entering your eyes.

Household current

When using an electric power tool, inspection light, etc., which operates on household current, always make sure that the tool is correctly connected to its plug and that, where necessary, it is properly grounded. Do not use such items in damp conditions and, again, do not create a spark or apply excessive heat in the vicinity of fuel or fuel vapor.

Secondary ignition system voltage

A severe electric shock can result from touching certain parts of the ignition system (such as the spark plug wires) when the engine is running or being cranked, particularly if components are damp or the insulation is defective. In the case of an electronic ignition system, the secondary system voltage is much higher and could prove fatal.

Troubleshooting

Contents

This section provides an easy reference guide to the more common problems, which may occur during the operation of your vehicle. These problems and their possible causes are grouped under headings denoting various components or systems, such as Engine, Cooling system, etc. They also refer you to the chapter and/or section, which deals with the problem.

Remember that successful troubleshooting is not a mysterious black art practiced only by professional mechanics. It is simply the result of the right knowledge combined with an intelligent, systematic approach to the problem. Always work by a process of elimination, starting with the simplest solution and working through to the most complex - and never overlook the obvious. Anyone can run the gas tank dry or leave the lights on overnight, so don't assume that you are exempt from such oversights.

Finally, always establish a clear idea of why a problem has occurred and take steps to ensure that it doesn't happen again. If the electrical system fails because of a poor connection, check the other connections in the system to make sure that they don't fail as well. If a particular fuse continues to blow, find out why - don't just replace one fuse after another. Remember that failure of a small component can often be indicative of potential failure or incorrect functioning of a more important component or system.

Engine

1 Engine will not rotate when attempting to start

1 Battery terminal connections loose or corroded (Chapter 1).
2 Battery discharged or faulty (Chapter 1).
3 Automatic transaxle not completely engaged in Park (Chapter 7).
4 Broken, loose or disconnected wiring in the starting circuit (Chapters 5 and 12).
5 Starter motor pinion jammed in flywheel ring gear (Chapter 5).
6 Starter solenoid faulty (Chapter 5).
7 Starter motor faulty (Chapter 5).
8 Ignition switch faulty (Chapter 12).
9 Starter pinion or flywheel teeth worn or broken (Chapter 5).
10 Engine seized.

2 Engine rotates but will not start

1 Fuel tank empty.
2 Battery discharged (engine rotates slowly) (Chapter 5).
3 Battery terminal connections loose or corroded (Chapter 1).
4 Leaking fuel injector(s), fuel pump, pressure regulator, etc. (Chapter 4).
5 Fuel not reaching fuel injection system (Chapter 4).
6 Ignition components damp or damaged (Chapter 5).
7 Worn, faulty or incorrectly gapped spark plugs (Chapter 1).
8 Broken, loose or disconnected wiring in the starting circuit (Chapter 5).
9 Broken, loose or disconnected wires at the ignition coils or faulty coils (Chapter 5).

3 Engine hard to start when cold

1 Battery discharged or low (Chapter 1).
2 Malfunctioning fuel system (Chapter 4).
3 Fuel injector(s) leaking (Chapter 4).

4 Engine hard to start when hot

1 Air filter clogged (Chapter 1).
2 Fuel not reaching the fuel injection system (Chapter 4).
3 Corroded battery connections, especially ground (Chapter 1).

5 Starter motor noisy or excessively rough in engagement

1 Pinion or flywheel gear teeth worn or broken (Chapter 5).
2 Starter motor mounting bolts loose or missing (Chapter 5).

6 Engine starts but stops immediately

1 Loose or faulty electrical connections at coils or alternator (Chapter 5).
2 Insufficient fuel reaching the fuel injector(s) (Chapters 1 and 4).
3 Vacuum leak at the gasket between the intake plenum/fuel injection throttle body (Chapters 1 and 4).

7 Oil puddle under engine

1 Oil pan gasket and/or oil pan drain bolt washer leaking (Chapter 2).
2 Oil pressure sending unit leaking (Chapter 2).
3 Valve covers leaking (Chapter 2).
4 Engine oil seals leaking (Chapter 2).
5 Oil pump housing leaking (Chapter 2).

8 Engine lopes while idling or idles erratically

1 Vacuum leakage (Chapters 2 and 4).
2 Leaking EGR valve (Chapter 6).
3 Air filter clogged (Chapter 1).
4 Fuel pump not delivering sufficient fuel to the fuel injection system (Chapter 4).
5 Leaking head gasket (Chapter 2).
6 Timing belt and/or pulleys worn (Chapter 2).
7 Camshaft lobes worn (Chapter 2).

9 Engine misses at idle speed

1 Spark plugs worn or not gapped properly (Chapter 1).
2 Vacuum leaks (Chapter 1).
3 Uneven or low compression (Chapter 2).

10 Engine misses throughout driving speed range

1 Impurities in the fuel system (Chapter 1).
2 Low fuel output at the injector(s) (Chapter 4).
3 Faulty or incorrectly gapped spark plugs (Chapter 1).
4 Incorrect ignition timing (Chapter 5).
5 Faulty emission system components (Chapter 6).
6 Low or uneven cylinder compression pressures (Chapter 2).
7 Weak or faulty ignition system (Chapter 5).
8 Vacuum leak at the fuel injection throttle body, intake manifold, or vacuum hoses (Chapter 4).

11 Engine stumbles on acceleration

1 Spark plugs fouled (Chapter 1).
2 Check injector driver circuit (Chapter 4) and injector resistance.
3 Throttle Position Sensor (TPS) binding or sticking (Chapter 6).
4 EVAP system leaking or malfunctioning (Chapter 6).
5 Alternator output low or excessive (Chapter 5).

12 Engine surges while holding accelerator steady

1 Intake air leak (Chapter 4).
2 Fuel pump faulty (Chapter 4).
3 Loose fuel injector wire harness connectors (Chapter 4).
4 Contaminated or defective oxygen sensors (Chapter 6).
5 Fuel system rich or lean (Chapters 4 and 6).

13 Engine stalls

1 Accelerator cable linkage binding or sticking (Chapter 4).
2 Idle air control system malfunctioning (Chapter 4).
3 Water and impurities in the fuel system (Chapters 1 and 4).
4 MAP sensor or circuit defective (Chapter 6).
5 EGR valve stuck open (Chapter 6).
6 Check cylinder compression (Chapter 2C).

14 Engine lacks power

1 Incorrect ignition timing.
2 Faulty or incorrectly gapped spark plugs (Chapter 1).
3 Faulty coils (Chapter 5).
4 Rear brakes binding (Chapter 9).
5 Automatic transmission fluid level incorrect (Chapter 1 and 7).
6 Fuel filter clogged and/or impurities in the fuel system (Chapters 1 and 4).

15 Engine backfires

1 Emission control system not functioning properly (Chapter 6).
2 Faulty secondary ignition system; cracked spark plug insulator, or faulty coils, (Chapters 1 and 5).
3 Fuel injection system malfunction (Chapter 4).
4 Vacuum leak at fuel injectors, intake manifold or vacuum hoses (Chapter 4).
5 EGR stuck open all the time (Chapter 6).

16 Pinging or knocking engine sounds during acceleration or uphill

1 Incorrect grade (octane) of fuel.
2 Fuel injection system faulty (Chapter 4).
3 Improper or damaged spark plugs or wires (Chapter 1).
4 Faulty or incorrect thermostat (Chapter 3).
5 Low coolant levels (Chapter 1).
6 Knock sensor system faulty (Chapter 6).
7 Vacuum leak (Chapter 2C and 4).
8 EGR system not functioning properly (Chapter 6).

17 Engine runs with oil pressure light on

1 Low oil level (Chapter 1).
2 Short in wiring circuit (Chapter 12).
3 Faulty oil pressure sender (Chapter 2).
4 Worn engine bearings and/or oil pump (Chapter 2).

18 Engine diesels (continues to run) after switching off

Excessive engine operating temperature (Chapter 3).

Engine electrical system

19 Battery will not hold a charge

1 Alternator drivebelt defective or not adjusted properly (Chapter 1).
2 Battery electrolyte level low (Chapter 1).
3 Battery terminals loose or corroded (Chapter 1).
4 Alternator not charging properly (Chapter 5).
5 Loose, broken or faulty wiring in the charging circuit (Chapter 5).
6 Short in vehicle wiring (Chapter 12).
7 Internally defective battery (Chapters 1 and 5).

20 Alternator light fails to go out

1 Faulty alternator or charging circuit (Chapter 5).
2 Alternator drivebelt defective or out of adjustment (Chapter 1).
3 Alternator voltage regulator inoperative (Chapter 5).

21 Alternator light fails to come on when key is turned on

1 Warning light bulb defective (Chapter 12).
2 Fault in the printed circuit, dash wiring or bulb holder (Chapter 12).

Fuel system

22 Excessive fuel consumption

1 Dirty or clogged air filter element (Chapter 1).
2 Incorrectly set ignition timing (Chapter 1).
3 Emissions system not functioning properly (Chapter 6).
4 Fuel injection system malfunction (Chapter 4).
5 Low tire pressure or incorrect tire size (Chapter 1).

23 Fuel leakage and/or fuel odor

1 Leaking fuel feed or return line (Chapters 1 and 4).
2 Tank overfilled.
3 Evaporative canister filter clogged (Chapters 1 and 6).
4 Fuel injection system malfunction (Chapter 4).

Cooling system

24 Overheating

1 Insufficient coolant in system (Chapter 1).
2 Water pump defective. (Chapter 3).
3 Radiator core blocked or grille restricted (Chapter 3).
4 Thermostat faulty (Chapter 3).
5 Electric coolant fan blades broken or cracked, or problem in fan circuit (Chapter 3).
6 Radiator cap not maintaining proper pressure (Chapter 3).

25 Overcooling

1 Faulty thermostat (Chapter 3).
2 Inaccurate temperature gauge sending unit (Chapter 3).

26 External coolant leakage

1 Deteriorated/damaged hoses; loose clamps (Chapters 1 and 3).
2 Water pump seal defective (Chapter 3).
3 Leakage from radiator core or coolant reservoir (Chapter 3).
4 Engine drain or water jacket core plugs leaking (Chapter 2).

27 Internal coolant leakage

1 Leaking cylinder head gasket (Chapter 2).
2 Cracked cylinder bore or cylinder head (Chapter 2).

28 Coolant loss

1 Too much coolant in system (Chapter 1).
2 Coolant boiling away because of overheating (Chapter 3).
3 Internal or external leakage (Chapter 3).
4 Faulty radiator cap (Chapter 3).

29 Poor coolant circulation

1 Inoperative water pump (Chapter 3).
2 Restriction in cooling system (Chapters 1 and 3).
3 Thermostat sticking (Chapter 3).

Automatic transaxle

Note: *Due to the complexity of the automatic transaxle, it is difficult for the home mechanic to properly diagnose and service this component. For problems other than the following, the vehicle should be taken to a dealer or transmission shop.*

30 Fluid leakage

1 Automatic transmission fluid is a deep red color. Fluid leaks should not be confused with engine oil, which can easily be blown onto the transaxle by air flow.
2 To pinpoint a leak first remove all built-up dirt and grime from the transaxle housing with degreasing agents and/or steam cleaning. Then drive the vehicle at low speeds so air flow will not blow the leak far from its source. Raise the vehicle and determine where the leak is coming from. Common areas of leakage are:

a) Pan (Chapters 1 and 7)
b) Dipstick tube (Chapters 1 and 7)
c) Transaxle oil lines (Chapters 3 and 7)
d) Speed sensor (Chapter 7)

31 Transaxle fluid brown or has a burned smell

Transaxle fluid burned (Chapter 1).

32 General shift mechanism problems

1 Chapter 7 deals with checking and adjusting the shift linkage on automatic

transaxles. Common problems, which may be attributed to poorly adjusted linkage, are:

a) *Engine starting in gears other than Park or Neutral.*
b) *Indicator on shifter pointing to a gear other than the one actually being used.*
c) *Vehicle moves when in Park.*

2 Refer to Chapter 7B for the shift linkage adjustment procedure.

33 Transaxle will not downshift with accelerator pedal pressed to the floor

Fault in the transaxle electronic controls.

34 Engine will start in gears other than Park or Neutral

Shift linkage out of adjustment (Chapter 7B).

35 Transaxle slips, shifts roughly, is noisy or has no drive in forward or reverse gears

There are many probable causes for the above problems, but the home mechanic should be concerned with only one possibility - fluid level. Before taking the vehicle to a repair shop, check the level and condition of the fluid as described in Chapter 1. Correct the fluid level as necessary or change the fluid and filter if needed. If the problem persists, have a professional diagnose the cause.

Driveaxles

36 Clicking noise in turns

Worn or damaged outboard CV joint (Chapter 8).

37 Shudder or vibration during acceleration

1 Excessive toe-in (Chapter 10).
2 Worn or damaged inboard or outboard CV joints (Chapter 8).
3 Sticking or worn inboard CV joint assembly (Chapter 8).

38 Vibration at highway speeds

1 Out-of-balance front wheels and/or tires (Chapters 1 and 10).
2 Out-of-round front tires (Chapters 1 and 10).
3 Worn CV joint(s) (Chapter 8).

Brakes

Note: *Before assuming that a brake problem exists, make sure that:*

a) *The tires are in good condition and properly inflated (Chapter 1).*
b) *The front end alignment is correct (Chapter 10).*
c) *The vehicle is not loaded with weight in an unequal manner.*

39 Vehicle pulls to one side during braking

1 Incorrect tire pressures (Chapter 1).
2 Front end out of line (have the front end aligned).
3 Front or rear tires not matched to one another.
4 Restricted brake lines or hoses (Chapter 9).
5 Malfunctioning caliper (Chapter 9).
6 Loose suspension parts (Chapter 10).
7 Loose calipers (Chapter 9).
8 Excessive wear of brake shoe or pad material or disc on one side (Chapter 9).

40 Noise (high-pitched squeal when the brakes are applied)

1 Front disc brake pads worn out. The noise comes from the wear sensor rubbing against the disc (does not apply to all vehicles). Replace pads with new ones immediately (Chapter 9).
2 Incorrectly installed new pads (many require an anti-squeal compound on the backing plates).

41 Brake roughness or chatter (pedal pulsates)

1 Excessive lateral runout of brake disc (Chapter 9).
2 Uneven pad wear (Chapter 9).
3 Defective disc (Chapter 9).

42 Excessive brake pedal effort required to stop vehicle

1 Malfunctioning power brake booster (Chapter 9).
2 Partial system failure (Chapter 9).
3 Excessively worn pads (Chapter 9).
4 Piston in caliper stuck or sluggish (Chapter 9).
5 Brake pads contaminated with oil or grease (Chapter 9).
6 New pads installed and not yet seated. It will take a while for the new material to seat against the disc.

43 Excessive brake pedal travel

1 Partial brake system failure (Chapter 9).
2 Insufficient fluid in master cylinder (Chapters 1 and 9).
3 Air trapped in system (Chapters 1 and 9).

44 Dragging brakes

1 Incorrect adjustment of brake light switch (Chapter 9).
2 Master cylinder pistons not returning correctly (Chapter 9).
3 Restricted brake lines or hoses (Chapters 1 and 9).
4 Incorrect parking brake adjustment (Chapter 9).
5 Caliper piston sticking (Chapter 9).

45 Grabbing or uneven braking action

1 Malfunction of proportioning valve (Chapter 9).
2 Malfunction of power brake booster unit (Chapter 9).
3 Binding brake pedal mechanism (Chapter 9).
4 Brake fluid, grease or oil on brake pads (Chapter 9).

46 Brake pedal feels spongy when depressed

1 Air in hydraulic lines (Chapter 9).
2 Master cylinder mounting bolts loose (Chapter 9).
3 Master cylinder defective (Chapter 9).

47 Brake pedal travels to the floor with little resistance

1 Little or no fluid in the master cylinder reservoir caused by leaking caliper piston(s) (Chapter 9).
2 Loose, damaged or disconnected brake lines (Chapter 9).

48 Parking brake does not hold

Parking brake linkage improperly adjusted (Chapters 1 and 9).

Suspension and steering systems

Note: *Before attempting to diagnose the suspension and steering systems, perform the following preliminary checks:*

a) Tires for wrong pressure and uneven wear.
b) Steering universal joints from the column to the steering gear for loose connectors or wear.
c) Front and rear suspension and the steering gear assembly for loose or damaged parts.
d) Out-of-round or out-of-balance tires, bent rims and loose and/or rough wheel bearings.

49 Vehicle pulls to one side

1 Mismatched or uneven tires (Chapter 10).
2 Broken or sagging springs (Chapter 10).
3 Wheels in need of alignment (Chapter 10).
4 Front brake dragging (Chapter 9).

50 Abnormal or excessive tire wear

1 Wheel alignment (Chapter 10).
2 Sagging or broken springs (Chapter 10).
3 Tire out of balance (Chapter 10).
4 Worn strut damper (Chapter 10).
5 Overloaded vehicle.
6 Tires not rotated regularly.
7 Incorrect tire pressure (Chapter 1).

51 Wheel makes a thumping noise

1 Blister or bump on tire (Chapter 10).
2 Improper strut damper action (Chapter 10).

52 Shimmy, shake or vibration

1 Tire or wheel out-of-balance or out-of-round (Chapter 10).
2 Loose or worn wheel bearings (Chapters 1, 8 and 10).
3 Worn tie-rod ends (Chapter 10).
4 Worn lower balljoints (Chapters 1 and 10).
5 Excessive wheel runout (Chapter 10).
6 Blister or bump on tire (Chapter 10).
7 Steering gear mounting bolts loose (Chapter 10).

53 Hard steering

1 Lack of lubrication at balljoints, tie-rod ends and steering gear assembly (Chapter 10).
2 Front wheel alignment (Chapter 10).
3 Low tire pressure(s) (Chapters 1 and 10).
4 Power steering fluid low (Chapter 1).
5 Defective power steering pump or steering gear (Chapter 10).

54 Poor returnability of steering to center

1 Lack of lubrication at balljoints and tie-rod ends (Chapter 10).
2 Binding in balljoints (Chapter 10).
3 Binding in steering column (Chapter 10).
4 Lack of lubricant in steering gear assembly (Chapter 10).
5 Front wheels in need of alignment or bent front suspension components (Chapter 10).

55 Abnormal noise at the front end

1 Lack of lubrication at balljoints and tie-rod ends (Chapters 1 and 10).
2 Damaged strut mounting (Chapter 10).
3 Worn control arm bushings or tie-rod ends (Chapter 10).
4 Stabilizer bar loose (Chapter 10).
5 Wheel nuts loose (Chapters 1 and 10).
6 Suspension bolts loose (Chapter 10).

56 Wander or poor steering stability

1 Mismatched or uneven tires (Chapter 10).
2 Lack of lubrication at balljoints and tie-rod ends (Chapters 1 and 10).
3 Worn strut assemblies (Chapter 10).
4 Stabilizer bar loose (Chapter 10).
5 Springs broken or sagging (Chapter 10).
6 Wheels out of alignment (Chapter 10).

57 Erratic steering when braking

1 Worn wheel bearings (Chapter 10).
2 Broken or sagging springs (Chapter 10).
3 Leaking caliper (Chapter 9).
4 Brake discs warped (Chapter 9).

58 Excessive pitching and/or rolling around corners or during braking

1 Stabilizer bar loose (Chapter 10).
2 Worn strut dampers or mountings (Chapter 10).
3 Broken or sagging springs (Chapter 10).
4 Overloaded vehicle.

59 Suspension bottoms

1 Overloaded vehicle.
2 Worn strut dampers (Chapter 10).
3 Incorrect, broken or sagging springs (Chapter 10).

60 Cupped tires

1 Front wheel or rear wheel alignment (Chapter 10).
2 Worn strut dampers (Chapter 10).
3 Wheel bearings worn (Chapter 10).
4 Tire or wheel runout excessive (Chapter 10).
5 Worn balljoints (Chapter 10).

61 Excessive tire wear on outside edge

1 Inflation pressures incorrect (Chapter 1).
2 Excessive speed in turns.
3 Front end alignment incorrect (excessive toe-in). Have professionally aligned.
4 Suspension arm bent or twisted (Chapter 10).

62 Excessive tire wear on inside edge

1 Inflation pressures incorrect (Chapter 1).
2 Front end alignment incorrect (toe-out). Have professionally aligned.
3 Loose or damaged steering components (Chapter 10).

63 Tire tread worn in one place

1 Tires out of balance.
2 Damaged or buckled wheel. Inspect and replace if necessary.
3 Defective tire (Chapter 1).

64 Excessive play or looseness in steering system

1 Worn wheel bearing(s) (Chapter 10).
2 Tie-rod end loose (Chapter 10).
3 Steering gear loose (Chapter 10).
4 Worn or loose steering intermediate shaft (Chapter 10).

65 Rattling or clicking noise in steering gear

1 Insufficient or improper lubricant in steering gear assembly (Chapter 10).
2 Steering gear attachment loose (Chapter 10).

Notes

Chapter 1
Tune-up and routine maintenance

Contents

Specifications

Recommended lubricants and fluids

Note: *Listed here are manufacturer recommendations at the time this manual was written. Manufacturers occasionally upgrade their fluid and lubricant specifications, so check with your local auto parts store for current recommendations.*

Engine oil	API grade "certified for gasoline engines"
Viscosity	See accompanying chart
Fuel	Unleaded gasoline, 87 octane minimum
Automatic transaxle fluid	Mopar ATF +4 Type 9602 automatic transmission fluid
Differential lubricant	SAE 75W90 gear oil
Power steering fluid	Chrysler power steering fluid (not automatic transmission fluid) or equivalent
Brake fluid	DOT 3 brake fluid
Engine coolant	50/50 mixture of Mopar orange-colored 5 year/100,000-mile antifreeze/coolant and distilled water
Parking brake mechanism grease	White lithium-based grease NLGI no. 2

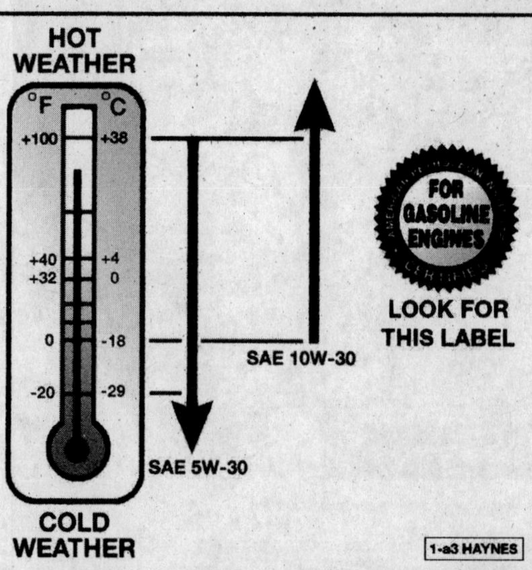

Engine oil viscosity chart - For best fuel economy and cold starting, select the lowest SAE viscosity grade for the expected temperature range

Recommended lubricants and fluids (continued)

Chassis lubrication grease	NLGI GC chassis grease
Hood, door and trunk hinge lubricant	Engine oil
Door hinge and check spring grease	NLGI no. 2 multi-purpose grease
Key lock cylinder lubricant	Graphite spray
Hood latch lubricant	NLGI no. 2 multi-purpose grease
Door latch lubricant	NLGI no. 2 multi-purpose grease

Capacities*

Engine oil (including filter)	5.0 qts
Automatic transaxle	
From dry (including torque converter)	
Through 2000	9.9 qts
2001 and later	9.3 qts
Fluid and filter change	4.5 qts
Cooling system	9.4 qts

All capacities approximate. Add as necessary to bring to appropriate level.

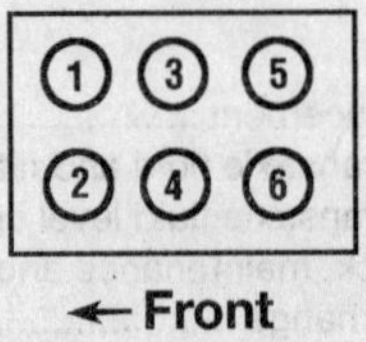

Engine cylinder identification

Brakes

Disc brake pad lining thickness (minimum)	3/32 inch
Parking brake shoe lining thickness (minimum)	1/16 inch

Ignition system

Spark plug type	
3.2/3.5L engine	Champion RC12PEC5, or equivalent
2.7L engine	Champion RE10PMC5, or equivalent
Spark plug gap	
3.2/3.5L engine	0.048 to 0.053 inch
2.7L engine	0.048 to 0.058 inch
Firing order, all engines	1-2-3-4-5-6

Torque specifications

Torque specifications	Ft-lbs (unless otherwise indicated)
Spark plugs	
3.2/3.5L engine	20
2.7L engine	156 in-lbs
Drivebelt tensioner pulley locknut	40
Wheel lug nuts	100
Automatic transaxle	
Pan bolts	19
Filter-to-valve body screws	40 in-lbs
Differential	
Fill plug	35
Drain plug	60 in-lbs

Typical engine compartment layout (2.7L shown)

1. *Automatic transaxle dipstick*
2. *Brake master cylinder reservoir*
3. *Windshield washer fluid reservoir*
4. *Battery (below air filter housing)*
5. *Power steering fluid reservoir*
6. *Engine oil dipstick*
7. *Fuse and relay center*
8. *Individual spark plug coil*
9. *Engine oil filler cap*
10. *Air filter housing*
11. *Engine coolant reservoir*
12. *Positive battery booster cable post*
13. *Negative battery booster cable post*

Typical engine compartment underside components

1 Engine oil filter
2 Front brake caliper
3 Strut/coil spring assembly
4 Inner CV joint boot
5 Exhaust system
6 Engine oil drain plug
7 Automatic transaxle fluid pan
8 Differential oil drain plug
9 Outer CV joint boot

Typical rear underside components

1 *Rear resonator/tailpipe*
2 *Fuel tank*
3 *Fuel filler hose*
4 *Strut/coil spring assembly*
5 *Rear wheel toe adjuster*
6 *Muffler*
7 *Parking brake cable*
8 *Rear stabilizer bar*
9 *Rear disc brake caliper*
10 *Rear lateral links*

1 Chrysler LH model maintenance schedule

The following maintenance intervals are based on the assumption that the vehicle owner will be doing the maintenance or service work, as opposed to having a dealer service department do the work. Although the time/mileage intervals are loosely based on factory recommendations, most have been shortened to ensure, for example, that such items as lubricants and fluids are checked/changed at intervals that promote maximum engine/driveline service life. Also, subject to the preference of the individual owner interested in keeping his or her vehicle in peak condition at all times, and with the vehicle's ultimate resale in mind, many of the maintenance procedures may be performed more often than recommended in the following schedule. We encourage such owner initiative.

When your vehicle is new, follow the maintenance schedule to the letter, record the maintenance performed in your owners manual and keep all receipts to protect the new vehicle warranty. In many cases, the initial maintenance check is done at no cost to the owner.

Every 250 miles or weekly, whichever comes first

Check the engine oil level; add oil as necessary (see Section 4)
Check the engine coolant level; add coolant as necessary (see Section 4)
Check the windshield washer fluid level (see Section 4)
Check the battery electrolyte level (see Section 4)
Check the brake fluid level (see Section 4)
Check the tires and tire pressures (see Section 5)
Check the automatic transaxle fluid level (see Section 6)
Check the power steering fluid level (see Section 7)
Check the operation of all lights
Check the horn operation

Every 3,000 miles or 3 months, whichever comes first

Change the engine oil and filter (see Section 8)*

Every 7,500 miles or 6 months, whichever comes first

Check the seat belts (see Section 9)
Check the wiper blade condition (see Section 10)
Check and clean the battery (see Section 11)
Check the drivebelt tension (see Section 12)
Inspect the underhood hoses (see Section 13)
Check the cooling system (see Section 14)
Rotate the tires (see Section 15)

Every 15,000 miles or 12 months, whichever comes first

Check the fuel system hoses and connections for leaks and damage (see Section 16)
Check the exhaust system (see Section 17)
Check the brakes (see Section 18)*
Check the suspension, steering and driveaxle boots (see Section 19)*
Check the differential lubricant level (see Section 20)

Every 30,000 miles or 24 months, whichever comes first

Check and replace if necessary, the PCV valve (see Section 21)
Drain and replace the engine coolant (see Section 22)
Brake fluid change (see Section 23)
Change the automatic transaxle fluid and filter (see Section 24)**
Replace the air filter element (see Section 25)*

Every 60,000 miles or 48 months, whichever comes first

Replace the spark plugs (see Section 26)
Replace the differential lubricant (see Section 27)

Every 90,000 miles or 72 months, whichever comes first

Replace the timing belt (see Chapter 2)**

** This item is affected by "severe" operating conditions as described below. If your vehicle is operated under "severe" conditions, perform all maintenance indicated with an asterisk (*) at 3000 mile/3 month intervals. Severe conditions are indicated if you mainly operate your vehicle under one or more of the following conditions:*

Operating in dusty areas
Towing a trailer
Idling for extended periods and/or low speed operation
Operating when outside temperatures remain below freezing and when most trips are less than 4 miles

*** If operated under one or more of the conditions noted above or below, change the timing belt every 60,000 miles:*

In heavy city traffic where the outside temperature regularly reaches 90-degrees F (32-degrees C) or higher
In hilly or mountainous terrain
Frequent trailer pulling

2 Introduction

This Chapter is designed to help the home mechanic maintain the Chrysler LH models with the goals of maximum performance, economy, safety and reliability in mind.

Included is a master maintenance schedule, followed by procedures dealing specifically with each item on the schedule. Visual checks, adjustments, component replacement and other helpful items are included. Refer to the accompanying illustrations of the engine compartment and the underside of the vehicle for the locations of various components.

Adhering to the mileage/time maintenance schedule and following the step-by-step procedures, which is simply a preventive maintenance program, will result in maximum reliability and vehicle service life. Keep in mind that it's a comprehensive program - maintaining some items but not others at the specified intervals will not produce the same results.

As you service the vehicle, you'll discover that many of the procedures can - and should - be grouped together because of the nature of the particular procedure you're performing or because of the close proximity of two otherwise unrelated components to one another.

For example, if the vehicle is raised, you should inspect the exhaust, suspension, steering and fuel systems while you're under the vehicle. When you're rotating the tires, it makes good sense to check the brakes, since the wheels are already removed. Finally, let's suppose you have to borrow or rent a torque wrench. Even if you only need it to tighten the spark plugs, you might as well check the torque of as many critical fasteners as time allows.

The first step in this maintenance program is to prepare before the actual work begins. Read through all the procedures you're planning to do, then gather up all the parts and tools needed. If it looks like you might run into problems during a particular job, seek advice from a mechanic or an experienced do-it-yourselfer.

3 Tune-up general information

The term "tune-up" is used in this manual to represent a combination of individual operations rather than one specific procedure.

If, from the time the vehicle is new, the routine maintenance schedule is followed closely and frequent checks are made of fluid levels and high wear items, as suggested throughout this manual, the engine will be kept in relatively good running condition and the need for additional work will be minimized.

More likely than not, however, there will

4.4a The engine oil dipstick is located at the left front of the engine

be times when the engine is running poorly due to lack of regular maintenance. This is even more likely if a used vehicle, which hasn't received regular and frequent maintenance checks, is purchased. In such cases, an engine tune-up will be needed outside of the regular routine maintenance intervals.

The first step in any tune-up or diagnostic procedure to help correct a poor running engine is a cylinder compression check. A compression check (see Chapter 2, Part C) will help determine the condition of internal engine components and should be used as a guide for tune-up and repair procedures. For instance, if a compression check indicates serious internal engine wear, a conventional tune-up will not improve the performance of the engine and would be a waste of time and money. Because of its importance, the compression check should be done by someone with the right equipment and the knowledge to use it properly.

The following procedures are those most often needed to bring a generally poor running engine back into a proper state of tune:

Minor tune-up

Check all engine related fluids (see Section 4)
Clean, inspect and test the battery (see Section 11)
Replace the spark plugs (see Section 26)
Check and adjust the drivebelts (see Section 12)
Check all underhood hoses (see Section 13)
Check the PCV valve (see Section 21)
Service the cooling system (see Section 22)
Check the air filter (see Section 25)

Major tune-up

All items listed under Minor tune-up plus . . .
Check the fuel system (see Section 16)
Replace the air filter (see Section 25)
Check the charging system (see Chapter 5)

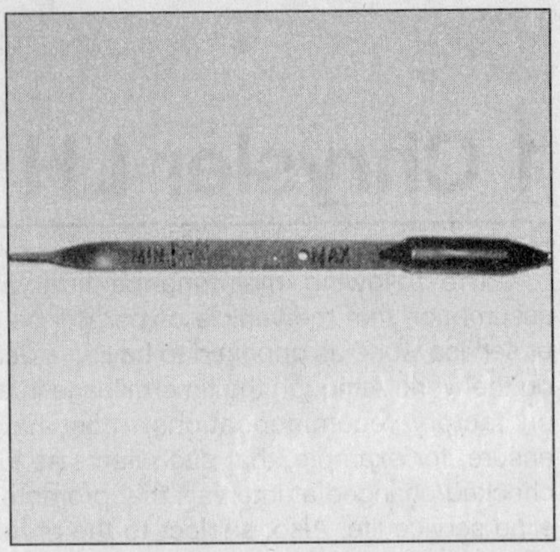

4.4b The oil level should be between the MIN and MAX marks on the dipstick - if it isn't, add enough oil to bring the level up to or near the MAX mark (it takes one quart to raise the level from the MIN mark to the MAX mark)

4 Fluid level checks (every 250 miles or weekly)

Note: *The following are fluid level checks to be done on a 250 mile or weekly basis. Additional fluid level checks can be found in specific maintenance procedures that follow. Regardless of the intervals, develop the habit of checking under the vehicle periodically for evidence of fluid leaks.*

1 Fluids are an essential part of the lubrication, cooling, brake and window washer systems. Because the fluids gradually become depleted and/or contaminated during normal operation of the vehicle, they must be replenished periodically. See *Recommended lubricants and fluids* at the beginning of this Chapter before adding fluid to any of the following components. **Note:** *The vehicle must be on level ground when fluid levels are checked.*

Engine oil

Refer to illustrations 4.4a, 4.4b and 4.5

2 The engine oil level is checked with a dipstick, which is located at the front, left (driver's) side of the engine. The dipstick extends through a tube and into the oil pan at the bottom of the engine.

3 The oil level should be checked before the vehicle has been driven, or about 5 minutes after the engine has been shut off. If the oil is checked immediately after driving the vehicle, some of the oil will remain in the upper engine components, resulting in an inaccurate reading on the dipstick.

4 Pull the dipstick out of the tube **(see illustration)** and wipe all the oil off the end with a clean rag or paper towel. Insert the clean dipstick all the way back into the tube, then pull it out again. Note the oil level at the end of the dipstick. Add oil as necessary to keep the level at the Max mark **(see illustration)**.

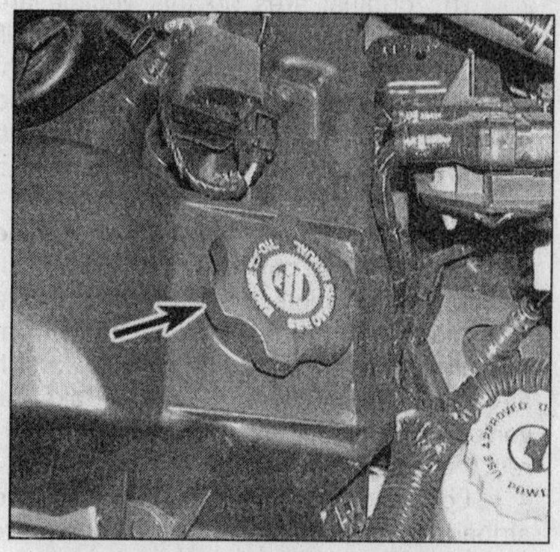

4.5 **Turn the oil filler cap (arrow) counterclockwise to remove it**

5 Oil is added to the engine after removing a cap located on the valve cover **(see illustration)**. The cap will be marked "Engine oil" or something similar. A funnel may help reduce spills as the oil is poured in.

6 Don't allow the level to drop below the Min mark or engine damage may occur. On the other hand, don't overfill the engine by adding too much oil - it may result in oil fouled spark plugs, oil leaks or seal failures.

7 Checking the oil level is an important preventive maintenance step. A consistently low oil level indicates oil leakage through damaged seals, defective gaskets or past worn rings or valve guides. If the oil looks milky in color or has water droplets in it, the block may be cracked. The engine should be checked immediately. The condition of the oil should also be checked. Each time you check the oil level, slide your thumb and index finger up the dipstick before wiping off the oil. If you see small dirt or metal particles clinging to the dipstick, the oil should be changed (see Section 8).

Engine coolant

Refer to illustration 4.8

Warning: *Do not allow antifreeze to come in contact with your skin or painted surfaces of the vehicle. Rinse off spills immediately with plenty of water. Antifreeze is highly toxic if ingested. Never leave antifreeze lying around in an open container or in puddles on the floor; children and pets are attracted by its sweet smell and may drink it. Check with local authorities about disposing of used antifreeze. Many communities have collection centers that will see that antifreeze is disposed of safely.*

Note: *Non-toxic antifreeze is now manufactured and available at local auto parts stores, but even this type should be disposed of properly.*

8 All vehicles covered by this manual are equipped with a pressurized coolant recovery system, which makes coolant level checks very easy. A coolant reservoir attached to the inner fender panel or the radiator itself is connected by a hose to the radiator filler neck **(see illustration)**. As the engine warms up,

4.8 **Make sure the coolant level in the reservoir is at or near the MAX mark - if it's below the MIN mark, add more coolant mixture or water**

some coolant escapes through a valve in the radiator cap and travels through the hose into the reservoir. As the engine cools, the coolant is automatically drawn back into the cooling system to maintain the correct level.

9 The coolant level should be checked when the engine is at normal operating temperature. Simply note the fluid level in the reservoir - it should be above the Cold Fill mark when the engine is at normal operating temperature.

10 If only a small amount of coolant is required to bring the system up to the proper level, regular water can be used. However, to maintain the proper antifreeze/water mixture in the system, both should be mixed together to replenish a low level. High-quality antifreeze/coolant should be mixed with water in the proportion specified on the antifreeze container.

11 Coolant should be added to the reservoir after removing the cap **(see illustration 4.8)**. **Warning:** *Don't remove the cap when the engine is warm!* Wait until the engine has cooled, then wrap a thick cloth around the cap and turn it to the first stop. If any steam escapes from the cap, allow the engine to cool further, then remove the cap.

12 As the coolant level is checked, note the condition of the coolant as well. It should be relatively clear. If it's brown or rust colored, the system should be drained, flushed and refilled (see Section 22).

13 If the coolant level drops consistently, there may be a leak in the system. Check the radiator, hoses, filler cap, drain plugs and water pump (see Section 14). If no leaks are noted, have the filler cap pressure tested by a service station.

Windshield washer fluid

Refer to illustration 4.14

14 The fluid for the windshield washer system is stored in a plastic reservoir. The level inside each reservoir should be maintained about one inch below the filler cap. The reservoir is accessible after opening the hood **(see illustration)**.

4.14 **Flip up the cap (arrow) to add more fluid to the windshield washer reservoir**

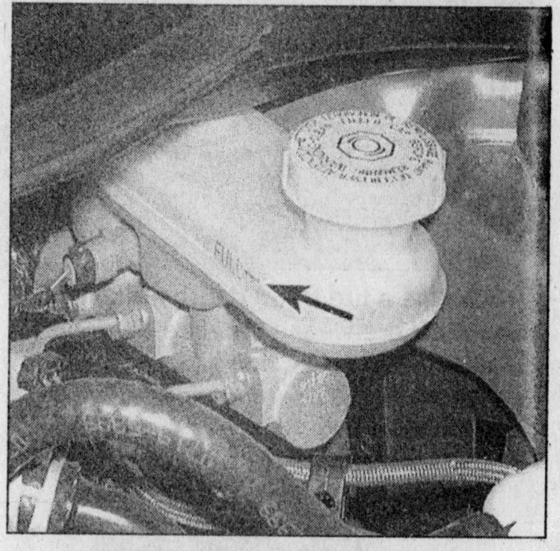

4.17 **The brake fluid level on the translucent white plastic brake fluid reservoir should be kept at the Full mark (arrow)**

15 In milder climates, plain water can be used in the reservoir, but it should be kept no more than two-thirds full to allow for expansion if the water freezes. In colder climates, use windshield washer system antifreeze, available at any auto parts store, to lower the freezing point of the fluid. Mix the antifreeze with water in accordance with the manufacturer's directions on the container. **Caution:** *Don't use cooling system antifreeze - it'll damage the vehicle's paint. To help prevent icing in cold weather, warm the windshield with the defroster before using the washer.*

Brake fluid

Refer to illustration 4.17

16 The brake master cylinder is located on the driver's side of the engine compartment firewall.

17 The level should be maintained at the Full mark on the reservoir **(see illustration)**.

18 If additional fluid is necessary to bring the level up, use a rag to clean all dirt off the top of the reservoir. If any foreign matter enters the master cylinder when the cap is removed, blockage in the brake system lines can occur. Also, make sure all painted surfaces around the master cylinder are covered, since brake fluid will ruin paint. Carefully pour

new, clean brake fluid into the master cylinder. Be careful not to spill the fluid on painted surfaces. Be sure the specified fluid is used; mixing different types of brake fluid can cause damage to the system. See *Recommended lubricants and fluids* at the beginning of this Chapter or your owner's manual.

19 At this time the fluid and the master cylinder can be inspected for contamination. Normally the brake hydraulic system needs only the recommended periodic draining and refilling, but if rust deposits, dirt particles or water droplets are seen in the fluid, the system should be dismantled, cleaned and refilled with fresh fluid (see Section 23).

20 Reinstall the master cylinder cap.

21 The brake fluid in the master cylinder will drop slightly as the brake shoes or pads at each wheel wear down during normal operation. If the master cylinder requires repeated replenishing to keep the level up, it's an indication of leaks in the brake system, which should be corrected immediately. Check all brake lines and connections, along with the wheel cylinders and booster (see Chapter 9 for more information).

22 If you discover that the reservoir is empty or nearly empty, the brake system should be bled (see Chapter 9).

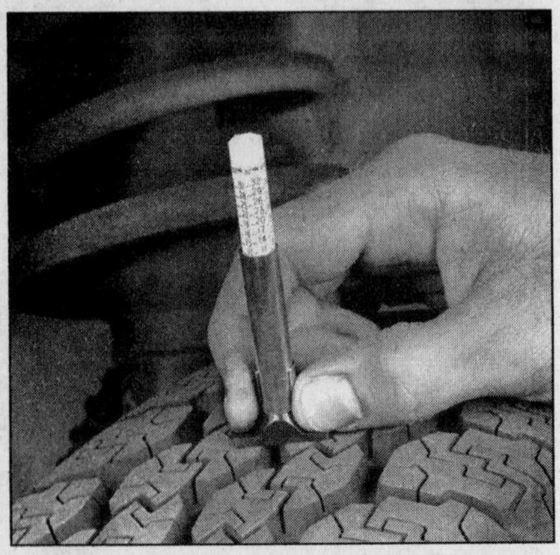

5.2 Use a tire tread depth indicator to monitor tire wear - they are available at auto parts stores and service stations and cost very little

5 Tire and tire pressure checks (every 250 miles or weekly)

Refer to illustrations 5.2, 5.3, 5.4a, 5.4b and 5.8

1 Periodic inspection of the tires may spare you the inconvenience of being stranded with a flat tire. It can also provide you with vital information regarding possible problems in the steering and suspension systems before major damage occurs.

2 The original tires on this vehicle are equipped with 1/2-inch wide bands that will appear when tread depth reaches 1/16-inch, at which point the tires can be considered worn out. Tread wear can be monitored with a simple, inexpensive device known as a tread depth indicator **(see illustration)**.

3 Note any abnormal tread wear **(see illustration)**. Tread pattern irregularities such as cupping, flat spots and more wear on one side than the other are indications of front end alignment and/or balance problems. If any of these conditions are noted, take the vehicle to a tire shop or service station to correct the problem.

4 Look closely for cuts, punctures and embedded nails or tacks. Sometimes a tire will hold air pressure for a short time or leak down very slowly after a nail has embedded itself in the tread. If a slow leak persists, check the valve stem core to make sure it's tight **(see illustration)**. Examine the tread for an object that may have embedded itself in the tire or for a "plug" that may have begun to leak (radial tire punctures are repaired with a plug that's installed in a puncture). If a puncture is suspected, it can be easily verified by spraying a solution of soapy water onto the puncture area **(see illustration)**. The soapy solution will bubble if there's a leak. Unless the puncture is unusually large, a tire shop or service station can usually repair the tire.

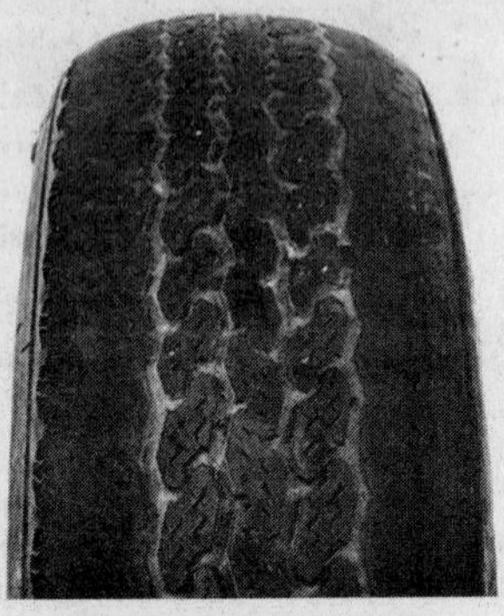

UNDERINFLATION

CUPPING

Cupping may be caused by:

- **Underinflation and/or mechanical irregularities such as out-of-balance condition of wheel and/or tire, and bent or damaged wheel.**
- **Loose or worn steering tie-rod or steering idler arm.**
- **Loose, damaged or worn front suspension parts.**

OVERINFLATION

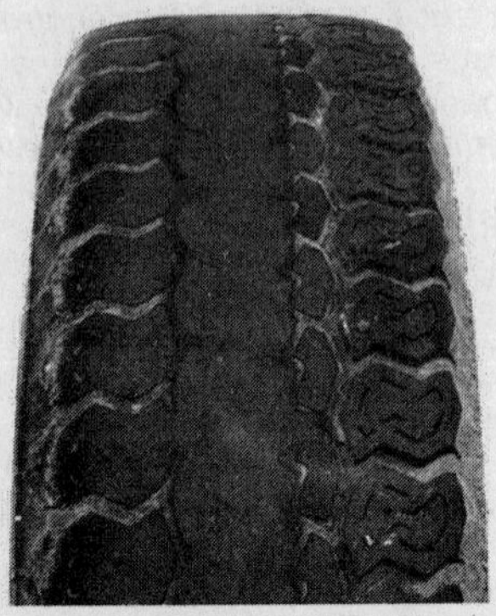

INCORRECT TOE-IN OR EXTREME CAMBER

FEATHERING DUE TO MISALIGNMENT

5.3 This chart will help you determine the condition of the tires, the probable cause(s) of abnormal wear and the corrective action necessary

5.4a If a tire loses air on a steady basis, check the valve core first to make sure it's snug (special inexpensive wrenches are commonly available at auto parts stores)

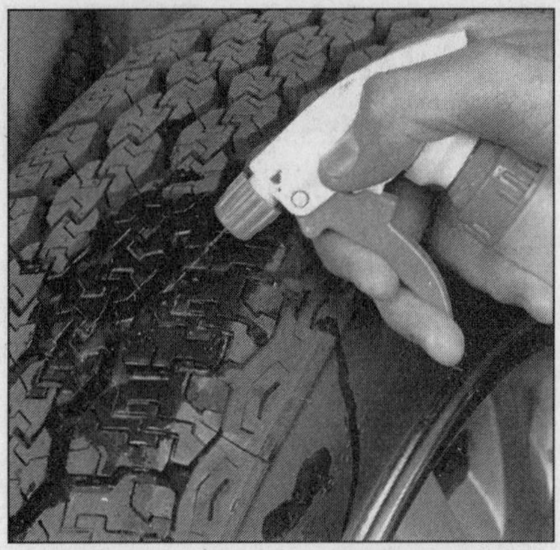

5.4b If the valve core is tight, raise the corner of the vehicle with the low tire and spray a soapy water solution onto the tread as the tire is turned slowly - leaks will cause small bubbles to appear

5.8 To extend the life of the tires, check the air pressure at least once a week with an accurate gauge (don't forget the spare!)

5 Carefully inspect the inner sidewall of each tire for evidence of brake fluid leakage. If you see any, inspect the brakes immediately.

6 Correct air pressure adds miles to the lifespan of the tires, improves mileage and enhances overall ride quality. Tire pressure cannot be accurately estimated by looking at a tire, especially if it's a radial. A tire pressure gauge is essential. Keep an accurate gauge in the vehicle. The pressure gauges attached to the nozzles of air hoses at gas stations are often inaccurate.

7 Always check tire pressure when the tires are cold. Cold, in this case, means the vehicle has not been driven over a mile in the three hours preceding a tire pressure check. A pressure rise of four to eight pounds is not uncommon once the tires are warm.

8 Unscrew the valve cap protruding from the wheel or hubcap and push the gauge firmly onto the valve stem **(see illustration)**. Note the reading on the gauge and compare the figure to the recommended tire pressure shown on the placard on the driver's side door pillar. Be sure to reinstall the valve cap to keep dirt and moisture out of the valve stem mechanism. Check all four tires and, if necessary, add enough air to bring them up to the recommended pressure.

9 Don't forget to keep the spare tire inflated to the specified pressure (refer to your owner's manual or the tire sidewall). Note that the pressure recommended for the compact spare is higher than for the tires on the vehicle.

6 Automatic transaxle fluid level check (every 250 miles or weekly)

Refer to illustrations 6.3 and 6.4

1 The level of the automatic transaxle fluid should be carefully maintained. Low fluid level can lead to slipping or loss of drive, while overfilling can cause foaming, loss of fluid and transaxle damage. The fluid inside the transaxle should be at normal operating temperature to get an accurate reading on the dipstick. This is done by driving the vehicle for several miles, making frequent starts and stops to allow the transaxle to shift through all gears.

2 Park the vehicle on a level surface, place the gear selector lever in Park and leave the engine running.

3 Remove the transaxle dipstick **(see illustration)** and wipe all the fluid from the end with a clean rag.

4 Push the dipstick back into the transaxle until the cap seats completely. Remove the dipstick again and note the fluid on the end. The level should be in the area marked Hot (between the two upper holes in the dipstick) **(see illustration)**. If the fluid isn't hot (temperature about 100-degrees F), the level should be in the area marked Warm (between the two lower holes).

5 If the fluid level is at or below the Add mark on the dipstick, add enough fluid to raise the level to within the marks indicated for the appropriate temperature. Fluid should be added directly into the dipstick hole, using a funnel to prevent spills.

6 Do not overfill the transaxle. Never allow the fluid level to go above the upper hole on the dipstick - it could cause internal transaxle

6.3 The automatic transaxle fluid dipstick is located on the left side of the engine compartment - don't confuse it with the engine oil dipstick

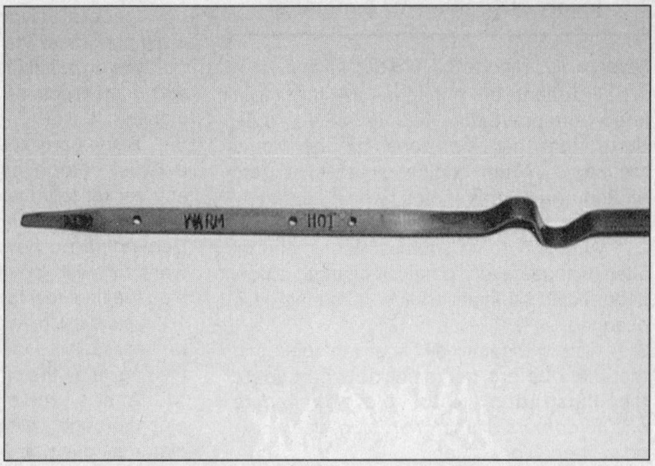

6.4 Check the fluid with the transaxle at normal operating temperature - the level should be kept in the HOT range (between the two upper holes or marks)

damage. The best way to prevent overfilling is to add fluid a little at a time, driving the vehicle and checking the level between additions.

7 Use only the transaxle fluid specified by the manufacturer. This information can be found in the *Recommended lubricants and fluids* section at the beginning of this Chapter.

8 The condition of the fluid should also be checked along with the level. If it's a dark reddish-brown color, or if it smells burned, it should be changed. If you're in doubt about the condition of the fluid, purchase some new fluid and compare the two for color and smell.

7 Power steering fluid level check (every 250 miles or weekly)

Refer to illustration 7.2

1 Unlike manual steering, the power steering system relies on fluid which may, over a period of time, require replenishing.

2 The reservoir for the power steering pump is located at the front of the engine on the left (driver's) side of the engine compartment **(see illustration)**.

3 The power steering fluid level can be checked with the engine either hot or cold.

4 With the engine off, use a rag to clean the reservoir. Looking at the fluid level view area on the side of the reservoir, check that the fluid is at the Max Cold mark or Max Hot, according to the engine temperature **(see illustration 7.2)**.

5 If additional fluid is required, remove the cap and pour the specified type directly into the reservoir using a funnel to prevent spills.

6 If the reservoir requires frequent fluid additions, all power steering hoses, hose connections, the power steering pump and the steering box should be carefully checked for leaks.

7.2 The power steering reservoir is located at the front of the engine on the left side - check the fluid level at the indicator (arrow)

8 Engine oil and filter change (every 3000 miles or 3 months)

Refer to illustrations 8.3, 8.9, 8.14 and 8.19

1 Frequent oil changes are the most important preventive maintenance procedures that can be done by the home mechanic. When engine oil ages, it gets diluted and contaminated, which ultimately leads to premature engine wear.

2 Although some sources recommend oil filter changes every other oil change, a new filter should be installed every time the oil is changed.

3 Gather together all necessary tools and materials before beginning this procedure **(see illustration)**. **Note:** *To avoid rounding off the corners of the drain plug, use a six-point wrench or socket.*

4 In addition, you should have plenty of clean rags and newspapers handy to mop up any spills. Access to the underside of the vehicle is greatly improved if it can be lifted on a hoist, driven onto ramps or supported by jackstands. **Warning:** *Don't work under a vehicle that is supported only by a jack!*

5 If this is your first oil change on the vehicle, crawl underneath it and familiarize yourself with the locations of the oil drain plug and the oil filter. Since the engine and exhaust components will be warm during the actual work, it's a good idea to figure out any potential problems beforehand.

6 Allow the engine to warm up to normal operating temperature. If oil or tools are needed, use the warm-up time to gather everything necessary for the job. The correct type of oil to buy for your application can be found in the *Recommended lubricants and fluids* section at the beginning of this Chapter.

7 With the engine oil warm (warm oil will drain better and more built-up sludge will be removed with it), raise the vehicle and support it securely on jackstands. They should be placed under the portions of the body designated as hoisting and jacking points (see *Jacking and towing* at the front of this manual).

8 Move all necessary tools, rags and newspapers under the vehicle. Place the drain pan under the drain plug. Keep in mind that the oil will initially flow from the engine with some force, so position the pan accordingly.

9 Being careful not to touch any of the hot exhaust components, use the breaker bar and socket to remove the drain plug near the bottom of the oil pan **(see illustration)**. Depending on how hot the oil is, you may want to wear gloves while unscrewing the plug the final few turns.

10 Allow the oil to drain into the pan. It may be necessary to move the pan further under the engine as the oil flow reduces to a trickle.

11 After all the oil has drained, clean the plug thoroughly with a rag. Small metal particles may cling to it and would immediately contaminate the new oil.

12 Clean the area around the oil pan opening and reinstall the plug. Tighten it securely.

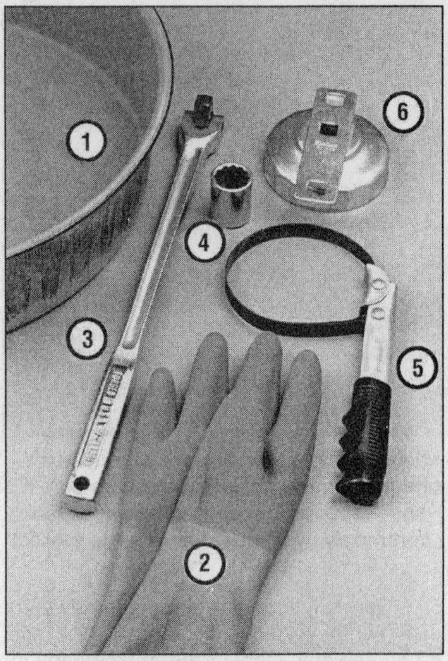

8.3 These tools are required when changing the engine oil and filter

1 ***Drain pan*** - *It should be fairly shallow in depth, but wide to prevent spills*
2 ***Rubber gloves*** - *When removing the drain plug and filter, you will get oil on your hands (the gloves will prevent burns)*
3 ***Breaker bar*** - *Sometimes the oil drain plug is tight, and a long breaker bar is needed to loosen it*
4 ***Socket*** - *To be used with the breaker bar or a ratchet (must be the correct size to fit the drain plug - six-point preferred)*
5 ***Filter wrench*** - *This is a metal band-type wrench, which requires clearance around the filter to be effective*
6 ***Filter wrench*** - *This type fits on the bottom of the filter and can be turned with a ratchet or breaker bar (different-size wrenches are available for different types of filters)*

8.9 To avoid rounding off the corners, use the correct size box-end wrench or a socket to remove the engine oil drain plug

8.14 The oil filter is usually on very tight and normally will require a special wrench for removal - DO NOT use the wrench to tighten the filter!

8.19 Lubricate the oil filter gasket with clean engine oil before installing the filter on the engine

13 Move the drain pan into position under the oil filter.

14 Now use the filter wrench to loosen the oil filter **(see illustration)**.

15 Sometimes the oil filter is on so tight it cannot be loosened, or it's positioned in an area inaccessible with a conventional filter wrench. Other type of tools, which fit over the end of the filter and turned with a ratchet/breaker bar, are available and may be better suited for removing the filter. If the filter is extremely tight, position the filter wrench near the threaded end of the filter, close to the engine.

16 Completely unscrew the old filter. Be careful, it's full of oil. Empty the old oil inside the filter into the drain pan.

17 Compare the old filter with the new one to make sure they're identical.

18 Use a clean rag to remove all oil, dirt and sludge from the area where the oil filter mounts on the engine. Check the old filter to make sure the rubber gasket isn't stuck to the engine mounting surface.

19 Apply a light coat of oil to the rubber gasket on the new oil filter **(see illustration)**.

20 Attach the new filter to the engine following the tightening directions printed on the filter canister or packing box. Most filter manufacturers recommend against using a filter wrench due to the possibility of over-tightening and damaging the canister.

21 Remove all tools and materials from under the vehicle, being careful not to spill the oil in the drain pan. Lower the vehicle off the jackstands.

22 Move to the engine compartment and locate the oil filler cap on the engine.

23 If the filler opening is obstructed, use a funnel when adding oil.

24 Pour the specified amount of new oil into the engine. Wait a few minutes to allow the oil to drain to the pan, then check the level on the dipstick (see Section 4 if necessary). If the oil level is at or above the Add mark, start the engine and allow the new oil to circulate.

25 Run the engine for only about a minute, then shut it off. Immediately look under the vehicle and check for leaks at the oil pan drain plug and around the oil filter. If either one is leaking, tighten with a bit more force.

26 With the new oil circulated and the filter now completely full, recheck the level on the dipstick. If necessary, add enough oil to bring the level to the Full mark on the dipstick.

27 During the first few trips after an oil change, make it a point to check for leaks and keep a close watch on the oil level.

28 The old oil drained from the engine cannot be reused in its present state and should be disposed of. Check with your local auto parts store, disposal facility or environmental agency to see if they will accept the oil for recycling. After the oil has cooled, it should be drained into containers (plastic bottles with screw-on tops are preferred) for transport to one of these disposal sites. Don't dispose of the oil by pouring it on the ground or down a drain!

9 Seat belt check (every 7,500 miles or 6 months)

1 Check the seat belts, buckles, latch plates and guide loops for obvious damage and signs of wear.

2 See if the seat belt reminder light comes on when the key is turned to the Run or Start positions. A chime should also sound.

3 The seat belts are designed to lock up during a sudden stop or impact, yet allow free movement during normal driving. Make sure the retractors return the belt against your chest while driving and rewind the belt fully when the buckle is unlatched.

4 If any of the above checks reveal problems with the seat belt system, replace parts as necessary.

10 Wiper blade inspection and replacement (every 7,500 miles or 6 months)

Refer to illustrations 10.3 and 10.4

1 The windshield wiper blade elements should be checked periodically for cracks and deterioration.

2 Lift the wiper blade assembly away from the glass.

3 Press the release lever and slide the blade assembly out of the hook in the end of the wiper arm **(see illustration)**.

4 Use needle-nose pliers to compress the two metal clips, then slide the element out of the frame **(see illustration)**.

5 Slide the new element into the frame until the metal prongs are engaged fully into the slots in the frame.

6 Installation is the reverse of removal.

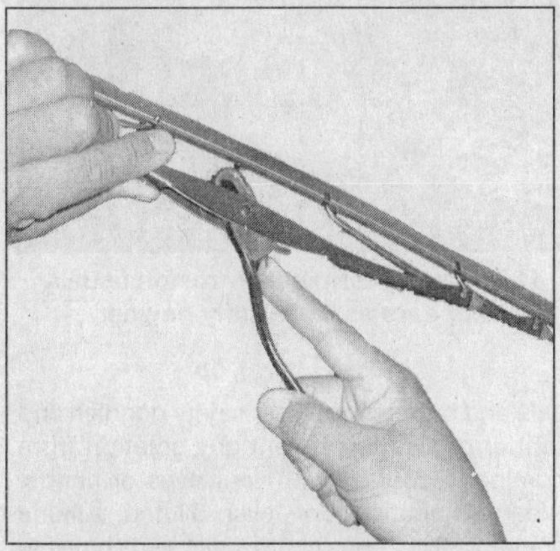

10.3 Depress the release lever (finger is on it here) and slide the wiper assembly down the wiper arm and out of the hook in the end of the arm

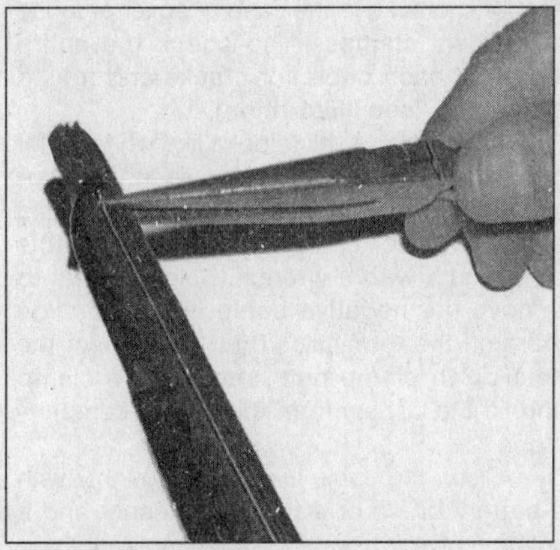

10.4 Squeeze the two silver metal prongs on the blade element to allow it to slide out of the assembly

11 Battery check, maintenance and charging (every 7,500 miles or 6 months)

Refer to illustrations 11.1, 11.6a, 11.6b, 11.7, 11.8a and 11.8b

1 A routine preventive maintenance program for the battery in your vehicle is the only

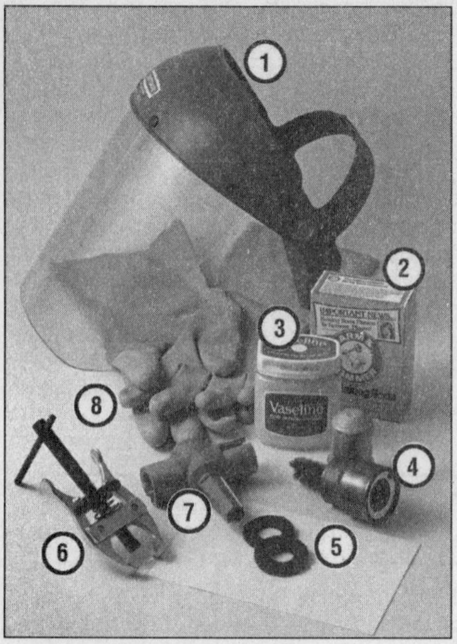

11.1 Tools and materials required for battery maintenance

1 ***Face shield/safety goggles*** *- When removing corrosion with a brush, the acidic particles can easily fly up into your eyes*
2 ***Baking soda*** *- A solution of baking soda and water can be used to neutralize corrosion*
3 ***Petroleum jelly*** *- A layer of this on the battery posts will help prevent corrosion*
4 ***Battery post/cable cleaner*** *- This wire brush cleaning tool will remove all traces of corrosion from the battery posts and cable clamps*
5 ***Treated felt washers*** *- Placing one of these on each post, directly under the cable clamps, will help prevent corrosion*
6 ***Puller*** *- Sometimes the cable clamps are very difficult to pull off the posts, even after the nut/bolt has been completely loosened. This tool pulls the clamp straight up and off the post without damage*
7 ***Battery post/cable cleaner*** *- Here is another cleaning tool that is a slightly different version of Number 4 above, but it does the same thing*
8 ***Rubber gloves*** *- Another safety item to consider when servicing the battery; remember that's acid inside the battery!*

way to ensure quick and reliable starts. But before performing any battery maintenance, make sure that you have the proper equipment necessary to work safely around the battery **(see illustration)**.

2 There are also several precautions that should be taken whenever battery maintenance is performed. Before servicing the battery, always turn the engine and all accessories off and disconnect the cable from the negative terminal of the battery.

11.6a The original equipment battery has a state-of-charge indicator (arrow) - green indicates 75% or better charge, black indicates it needs charging, and clear indicates the battery needs to be replaced

3 The battery produces hydrogen gas, which is both flammable and explosive. Never create a spark, smoke or light a match around the battery. Always charge the battery in a ventilated area.

4 Electrolyte contains poisonous and corrosive sulfuric acid. Do not allow it to get in your eyes, on your skin on your clothes. Never ingest it. Wear protective safety glasses when working near the battery. Keep children away from the battery.

5 The battery on the LH series vehicles is located in the right fenderwell. Because accessibility is limited, you must make a point to do regular inspections, since the battery isn't visible every time you open the hood. Refer to Chapter 5 for the procedure to access the battery.

6 Note the external condition of the battery. Check the state-of-charge indicator at the top of the battery **(see illustration)**. If the positive terminal and cable clamp on your vehicle's battery is equipped with a rubber protector, make sure that it's not torn or damaged. It should completely cover the terminal. Look for any corroded or loose connections, cracks in the case or cover or loose hold-down clamps. Also check the entire length of each cable for cracks and frayed conductors **(see illustration)**.

7 If corrosion, which looks like white, fluffy deposits **(see illustration)** is evident, particularly around the terminals, the battery should be removed for cleaning. Loosen the cable clamp nuts with a wrench, being careful to remove the negative cable first, and slide them off the terminals. Then disconnect the hold-down clamp nuts, remove the clamp and lift the battery from the engine compartment.

8 Clean the cable clamps thoroughly with a battery brush or a terminal cleaner and a solution of warm water and baking soda **(see illustration)**. Wash the terminals and the top of the battery case with the same solution but make sure that the solution doesn't get into the battery. When cleaning the cables, terminals and battery top, wear safety goggles and rubber gloves to prevent any solution from coming in contact with your eyes or hands. Wear old clothes too - even diluted, sulfuric acid splashed onto clothes will burn holes in them. If the terminals have been extensively corroded, clean them up with a terminal cleaner **(see illustration)**. Thoroughly wash all cleaned areas with plain water.

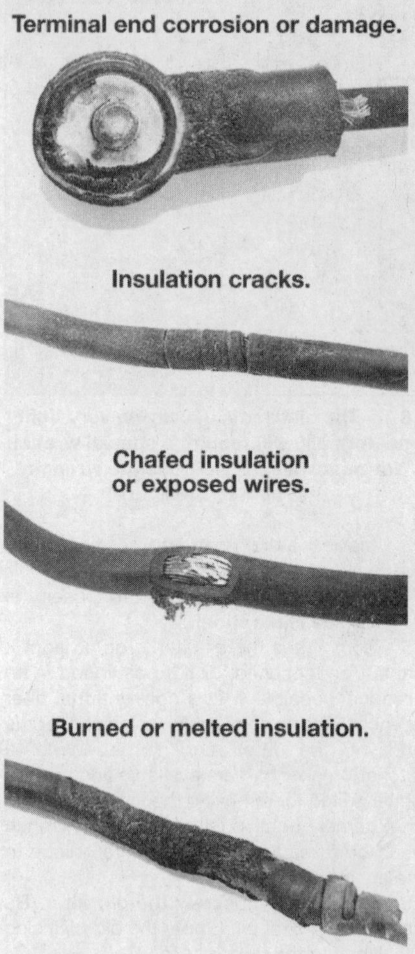

11.6b Typical battery cable problems

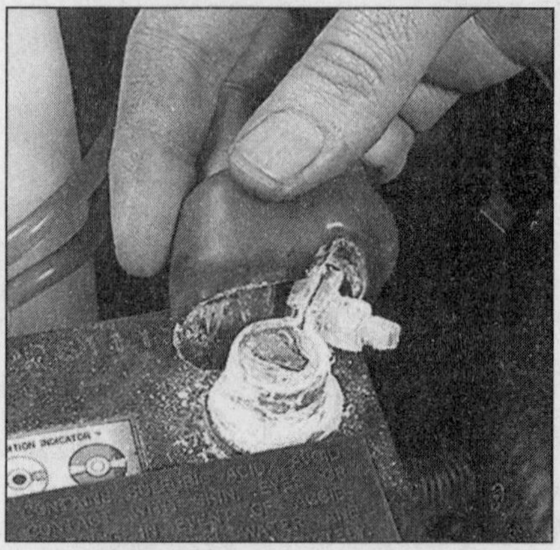

11.7 Battery terminal corrosion usually appears as light, fluffy powder

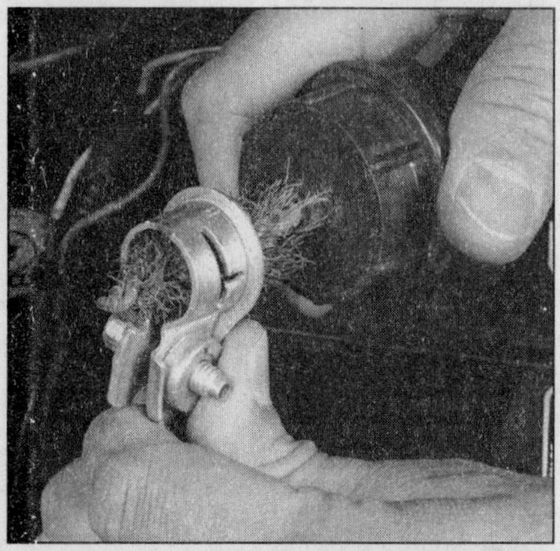

11.8a When cleaning the cable clamps, all corrosion must be removed (the inside of the clamp is tapered to match the taper on the post, so don't remove too much material)

9 Before reinstalling the battery in the engine compartment, inspect the plastic battery carrier. If it's dirty or covered with corrosion, remove it and clean it in the same solution of warm water and baking soda. Inspect the metal brackets that support the carrier to make sure that they are not covered with corrosion. If they are, wash them off. If corrosion is extensive, sand the brackets down to bare metal and spray them with a zinc-based primer (available in spray cans at auto paint and body supply stores).

10 Reinstall the battery carrier and the battery back into the compartment. Make sure that no parts or wires are laying on the carrier during installation of the battery.

11 Install a pair of specially-treated felt washers around the terminals (available at auto parts stores), then coat the terminals and the cable clamps with petroleum jelly or grease to prevent further corrosion. Install the cable clamps and tighten the nuts, being

11.8b Regardless of the type of tool used on the battery posts, a clean, shiny surface should be the result

careful to install the negative cable last.

12 Install the hold-down clamp and nuts. Tighten the nut only enough to hold the battery firmly in place. Overtightening this nut can crack the battery case.

Charging

13 Refer to Chapter 5 and remove the battery, hook the battery charger leads to the battery posts (positive to positive, negative to negative), then plug in the charger. Make sure it is set at 12 volts if it has a selector switch.

14 If you're using a charger with a rate higher than two amps, check the battery regularly during charging to make sure it doesn't overheat. If you're using a trickle charger, you can safely let the battery charge overnight after you've checked it regularly for the first couple of hours.

15 Factory batteries with sealed tops have built-in hydrometers on the top that indicate the state of charge by the color displayed in the hydrometer window. Green indicates 75% or better charge, black indicates the battery needs charging, and clear indicates the battery needs to be replaced.

16 If the battery has a sealed top and no built-in hydrometer, you can hook up a digital voltmeter across the battery terminals to check the charge. A fully charged battery should read 12.6 volts or higher.

17 Further information on the battery and jump starting can be found in Chapter 5 and at the front of this manual.

12 Drivebelt check, adjustment and replacement (every 7,500 miles or 6 months)

Refer to illustrations 12.2a, 12.2b, 12.3a, 12.3b, 12.4, 12.5 and 12.6

Warning: *The electric cooling fan on these models can activate at any time the ignition switch is in the On position. Make sure the ignition is Off when working in the vicinity of the fan.*

Check

1 The drivebelts at the front of the engine play an important role in the overall operation of the vehicle and its components. Due to their function and material makeup, the belts are prone to failure after a period of time and should be inspected and adjusted periodically to prevent major damage.

2 On all models, two drivebelts are used; one to turn the air conditioning compressor and another for the alternator and power steering pump **(see illustrations).** On 2.7L engines, both belts are multi-rib, while on the 3.2L/3.5L engines the air conditioning belt is a V-belt and the alternator/power steering belt is multi-rib.

3 With the engine off, open the hood and locate the drivebelts at the front of the engine. With a flashlight, check each belt: On V-belts, check for cracks and separation of

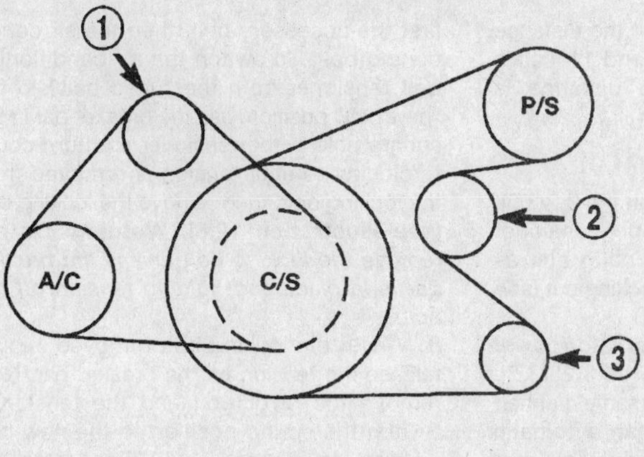

12.2a 2.7L engine serpentine drivebelt layout

1 *Idler*
2 *Idler*
3 *Alternator*

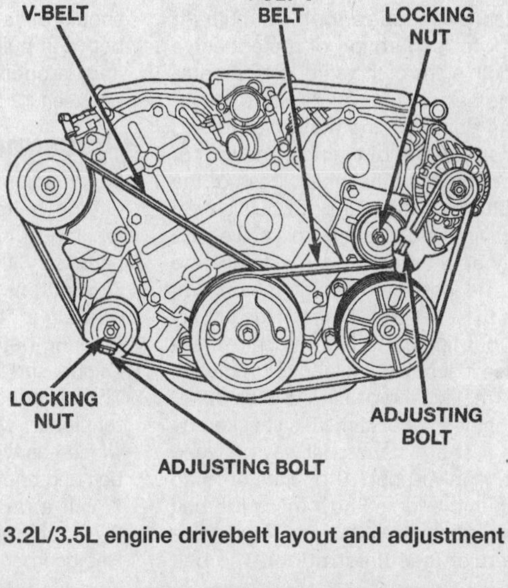

12.2b 3.2L/3.5L engine drivebelt layout and adjustment details

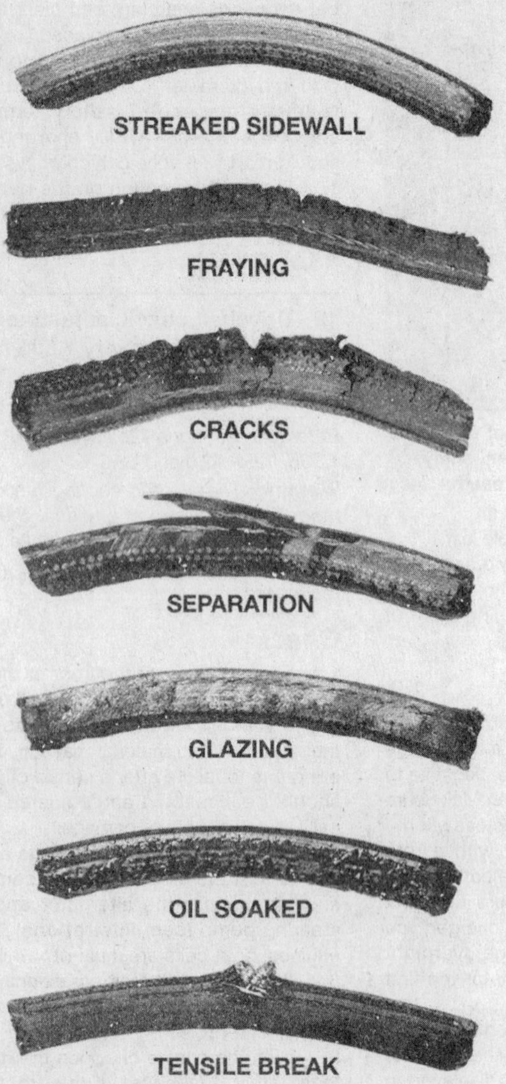

12.3a Here are some of the more common problems associated with V-belts (check the belts very carefully to prevent an untimely breakdown)

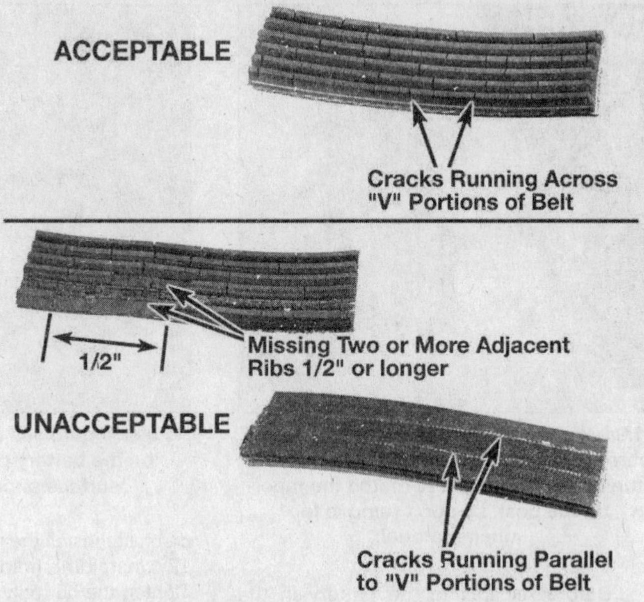

12.3b Check V-ribbed belts for signs of wear like these - if the belt looks worn, replace it

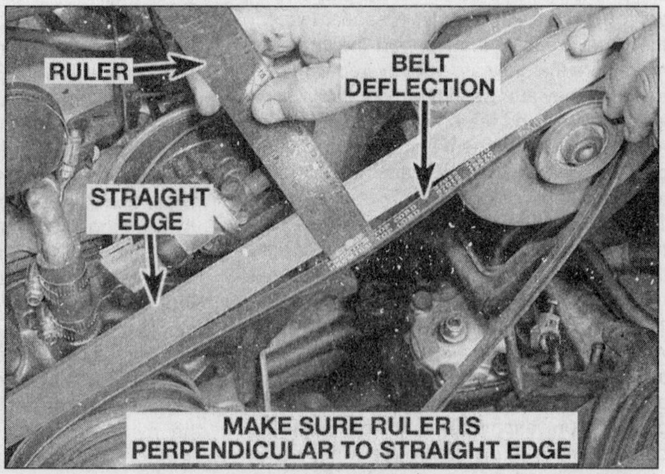

12.4 Measuring drivebelt deflection with a straightedge and ruler

the belt plies **(see illustration)**. On multi-rib belts, check for separation of the adhesive rubber on both sides of the core, core separation from the belt side, a severed core, separation of the ribs from the adhesive rubber, cracking or separation of the ribs, and torn or worn ribs or cracks in the inner ridges of the ribs **(see illustration)**. On both belt types, check for fraying and glazing, which gives the belt a shiny appearance. Both sides of the belt should be inspected, which means you will have to twist the belt to check the underside. Use your fingers to feel the belt where you can't see it. If any of the above conditions are evident, replace the belt (go to Step 9).

4 The tightness of each belt is checked by pushing on it at a distance halfway between the pulleys. Apply about 10 pounds of force with your thumb and see how much the belt moves down (deflects). Measure the deflection with a ruler **(see illustration)**. The belt should deflect about 1/4-inch if the distance between pulleys is between 7 and 11 inches and around 1/2-inch if the distance is between 12 and 16 inches.

Adjustment

5 If adjustment is required on the 3.2/3.5L engine belts, loosen the proper tensioner locking nut and turn the adjusting bolt as necessary, then retighten the locking nut **(see illustration)**.

6 On 2.7L engines, the alternator/power steering belt has an idler like the 3.2L/3.5L engine, and it is adjusted in the same manner. The air conditioning belt has an automatic tensioner, which is not fully adjustable, but which has two spring positions: one for a new belt and one for a used belt **(see illustration)**.

7 If a new belt is to be installed on the 2.7L air conditioning side, follow the Replacement procedure below for removing first the accessory belt, then the air conditioning belt. To switch the air conditioning belt tensioner from the "used belt" to the "new belt" position, use the breaker bar in the square hole in the tensioner and turn counterclockwise until tension is removed from the locking bolt, then remove the locking bolt **(see illustration 12.6)**. **Warning:** *Do not remove the locking bolt unless the breaker bar is in place and holding tension off the bolt.*

8 With the locking bolt removed, slowly release the tension on the breaker bar. Now remove the pivot bolt and the tensioner. Switch the spring position to the new belt position **(see illustration 12.6)** and install the tensioner with the pivot bolt. Insert the breaker bar and turn the tensioner until the locking bolt can be install and tightened almost all the way. Tighten the locking bolt only after the new belt is installed.

12.5 On all 3.2L/3.5L belts, and 2.7L alternator belt, the idler is adjustable - loosen the locknut (A), then turn the adjuster bolt (B) until proper tension is achieved, then retighten the locknut

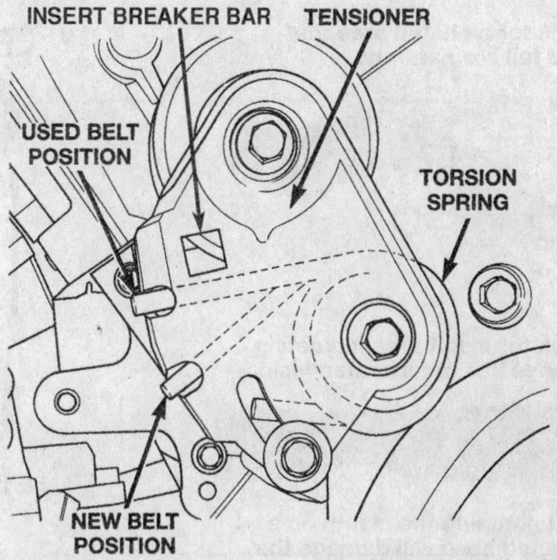

12.6 The spring behind the 2.7L air conditioning belt tensioner can be installed in two positions, once installed, tension is automatically maintained - use a breaker bar in the square hole

Replacement

9 To replace a belt on the 3.2L/3.5L engines, follow the above procedures for drivebelt adjustment but loosen the adjuster bolt until the belt can be slipped off the crankshaft pulley and removed. If you are replacing the air conditioner compressor belt on any of the V6 engines, you have to remove alternator belt first because of the way they are arranged on the crankshaft pulley. To remove the air-conditioning belt on the 2.7L engine, use a 1/2-inch drive breaker bar in the square hole of the tensioner and turn it counterclockwise until the belt can be slipped off. If a new belt is installed, follow the *Adjustment* procedure to change the tensioner spring position.

10 Because belts tend to wear out more or less together, it is a good idea to replace both belts at the same time. Mark each belt and its appropriate pulley groove so the replacement belts can be installed in their proper positions.

11 Take the old belt(s) to the parts store in order to make a direct comparison for length, width and design.

12 After replacing a multi-ribbed drivebelt, make sure it fits properly in the ribbed grooves in the pulleys. It is essential that the belt be properly centered.

13 Adjust the belt(s) in accordance with the procedure outlined above.

13 Underhood hose check and replacement (every 7,500 miles or 6 months)

Warning: *Replacement of air conditioning hoses must be left to a dealer service department or air conditioning shop equipped to depressurize the system safely. Never remove air conditioning components or hoses until the system has been depressurized and the refrigerant recovered.*

General

1 High temperatures under the hood can cause the deterioration of the rubber and plastic hoses used for engine, accessory and emission systems operation. Periodic inspection should be made for cracks, loose clamps, material hardening and leaks.

2 Information specific to the cooling system hoses can be found in Section 14.

3 Some hoses use clamps to secure the hoses to fittings. Where clamps are used, check to be sure they haven't lost their tension, allowing the hose to leak. Where clamps are not used, make sure the hose hasn't expanded and/or hardened where it slips over the fitting, allowing it to leak.

Vacuum hoses

4 It's quite common for vacuum hoses, especially those in the emissions system, to be color coded or identified by colored stripes molded into the hose. Various systems require hoses with different wall thickness, collapse resistance and temperature resistance. When replacing hoses, make sure the new ones are made of the same material.

5 Often the only effective way to check a hose is to remove it completely from the vehicle. Where more than one hose is removed, be sure to label the hoses and their attaching points to insure proper reattachment.

6 When checking vacuum hoses, be sure to include any plastic T-fittings in the check. Check the fittings for cracks and the hose where it fits over the fitting for enlargement, which could cause leakage.

7 A small piece of vacuum hose (1/4-inch inside diameter) can be used as a stethoscope to detect vacuum leaks. Hold one end of the hose to your ear and probe around vacuum hoses and fittings, listening for the "hissing" sound characteristic of a vacuum leak. **Warning:** *When probing with the vacuum hose stethoscope, be careful not to allow your body or the hose to come into contact with moving engine components such as the drivebelts, cooling fans, etc.*

Fuel hose

Warning: *There are certain precautions that must be taken when inspecting or servicing fuel system components. Work in a well-ventilated area and do not allow open flames (cigarettes, appliance pilot lights, etc.) or bare light bulbs near the work area. Mop up any spills immediately and do not store fuel soaked rags where they could ignite. The fuel system is under high pressure, so if any fuel lines are to be disconnected, the pressure in the system must be relieved first* (see Chapter 4 for more information).

8 Check all rubber fuel hoses for damage and deterioration. Check especially for cracks in areas where the hose bends and just before clamping points, such as where a hose attaches to the fuel injection unit.

9 High quality fuel line, made specifically for high-pressure fuel-injection systems, must be used for fuel line replacement. Never, under any circumstances, use unreinforced vacuum line, clear plastic tubing or water hose for fuel lines.

10 Spring-type clamps are commonly used on fuel lines. These clamps often lose their tension over a period of time, and can be "sprung" during removal. Replace all spring-type clamps with screw clamps whenever a hose is replaced.

Metal lines

11 Sections of metal line are routed along the frame, between the fuel tank and the engine. Check carefully to be sure the line has not been bent or crimped and that cracks have not started in the line.

12 If a section of metal fuel line must be replaced, only seamless steel tubing should be used, since copper and aluminum tubing don't have the strength necessary to withstand normal engine vibration.

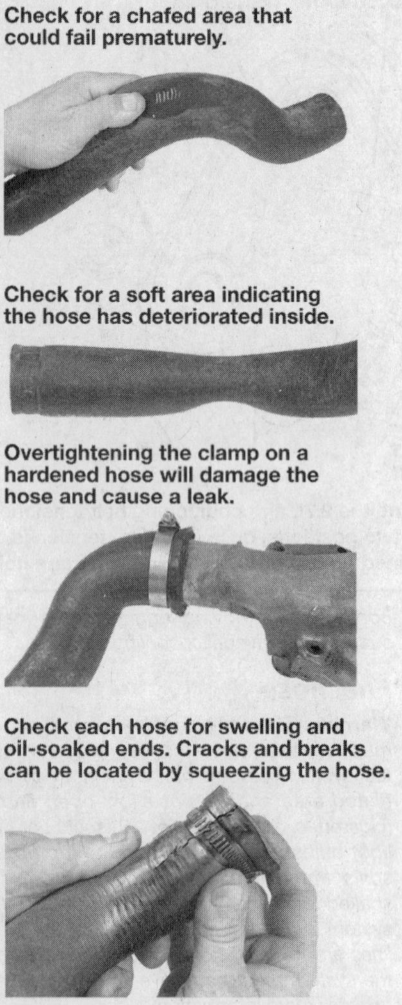

Check for a chafed area that could fail prematurely.
Check for a soft area indicating the hose has deteriorated inside.
Overtightening the clamp on a hardened hose will damage the hose and cause a leak.
Check each hose for swelling and oil-soaked ends. Cracks and breaks can be located by squeezing the hose.

14.4 Hoses, like drivebelts, have a habit of failing at the worst possible time - to prevent the inconvenience of a blown radiator or heater hose, inspect them carefully as shown here

13 Check the metal brake lines where they enter the master cylinder and ABS unit (if equipped) for cracks in the lines or loose fittings. Any sign of brake fluid leakage calls for an immediate and thorough inspection of the brake system.

14 Cooling system check (every 7,500 miles or 6 months)

Refer to illustration 14.4

Warning 1: *Wait until the engine is completely cool before beginning this procedure.*

Warning 2: *The electric cooling fan on these models can activate at any time the ignition switch is in the On position. Make sure the ignition is Off when working in the vicinity of the fan.*

1 Many major engine failures can be attributed to a faulty cooling system. If the vehicle is equipped with an automatic transaxle, the cooling system is also used to cool the transaxle fluid.

2 The cooling system should be checked with the engine cold. Do this before the vehicle is driven for the day or after it has been shut off for three or four hours.

3 Thoroughly clean the cap on top of the coolant recovery tank, inside and out, with clean water. Also clean the filler neck on the tank. All traces of corrosion should be removed. The coolant inside the tank should be relatively transparent. If it is rust-colored, the system should be drained, flushed and refilled (see Section 22). If the coolant level is not up to the top, add additional antifreeze/coolant mixture (see Section 4).

4 Carefully check the large upper and lower radiator hoses along with the smaller diameter heater hoses that run from the engine to the firewall. Inspect each hose along its entire length, replacing any hose that is cracked, swollen or shows signs of deterioration. Cracks may become more apparent if the hose is squeezed **(see illustration)**. Regardless of condition, it's a good idea to replace hoses with new ones every two years.

5 Make sure all hose connections are tight. A leak in the cooling system will usually show up as white or rust-colored deposits on the areas adjoining the leak. If wire-type clamps are used at the ends of the hoses, it may be a good idea to replace them with more secure screw-type clamps.

6 Use compressed air or a soft brush to remove bugs, leaves, etc. from the front of the radiator or air conditioning condenser. Be careful not to damage the delicate cooling fins or cut yourself on them.

7 Every other inspection, or at the first indication of cooling system problems, have the cap and system pressure tested. If you don't have a pressure tester, most repair shops will do this for a minimal charge.

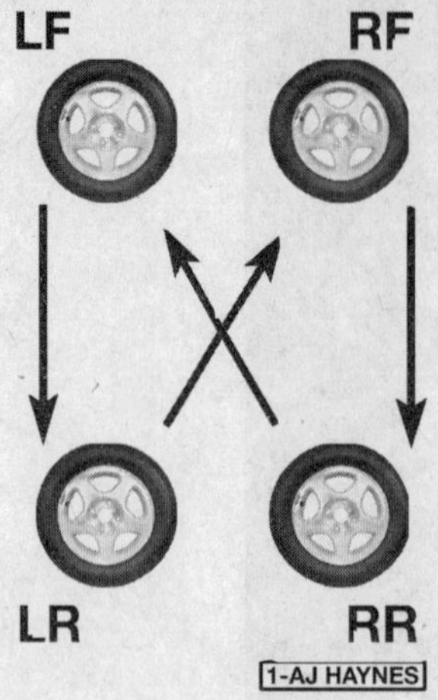

15.2a The recommended four-tire rotation pattern for non-directional radial tires

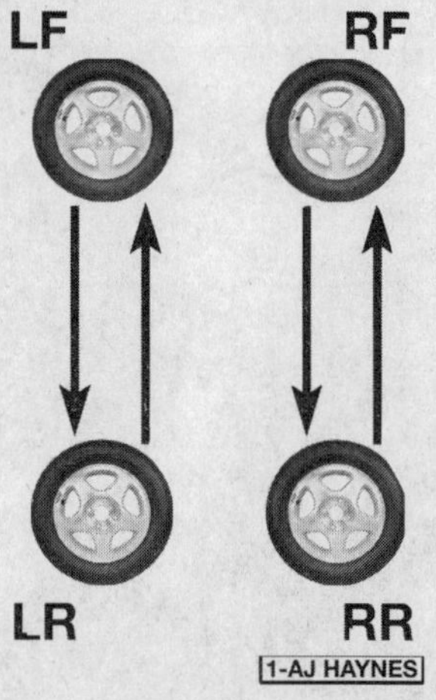

15.2b The recommended four-tire rotation pattern for directional radial tires

15 Tire rotation (every 7,500 miles or 6 months)

Refer to illustrations 15.2a and 15.2b

1 The tires should be rotated at the specified intervals and whenever uneven wear is noticed. Since the vehicle will be raised and the tires removed anyway, this is a good time to check the brakes (see Section 18).

2 Radial tires must be rotated in a specific pattern **(see illustrations)**. **Note:** *Most vehicles are sold with non-directional radial tires, but some replacement performance tires are available that are directional, and have a different rotation pattern. Directional tires have an arrow on the sidewall indicating the direction they must turn when mounted on the vehicle.*

3 See the information in *Jacking and towing* at the front of this manual for the proper procedures to follow when raising the vehicle and changing a tire; however, if the brakes are to be checked, don't apply the parking brake as stated. Make sure the tires are blocked to prevent the vehicle from rolling.

4 Preferably, the entire vehicle should be raised at the same time. This can be done on a hoist or by jacking up each corner of the vehicle and lowering it onto jackstands. Always use four jackstands and make sure the vehicle is safely supported.

5 After the tire rotation, check and adjust the tire pressures as necessary and be sure to check wheel lug nut tightness.

16 Fuel system check (every 15,000 miles or 12 months)

Refer to illustration 16.5

Warning: *Gasoline is extremely flammable, so take extra precautions when you work on any part of the fuel system. Don't smoke or* *allow open flames or bare light bulbs near the work area, and don't work in a garage where a natural gas-type appliance (such as a water heater or clothes dryer) with a pilot light is present. Since gasoline is carcinogenic, wear latex gloves when there's a possibility of being exposed to fuel, and, if you spill any fuel on your skin, rinse it off immediately with soap and water. Mop up any spills immediately and do not store fuel-soaked rags where they could ignite. The fuel system is under constant pressure, so, if any fuel lines are to be disconnected, the fuel pressure in the system must be relieved first* (see Chapter 4 for more information). *When you perform any kind of work on the fuel system, wear safety glasses and have a Class B type fire extinguisher on hand.*

1 If you smell gasoline while driving or after the vehicle has been sitting in the sun, inspect the fuel system immediately.

2 Remove the gas filler cap and inspect if for damage and corrosion. The gasket should have an unbroken sealing imprint. If the gasket is damaged or corroded, remove it and install a new one.

3 Inspect the fuel feed and return lines for cracks. Make sure the connections between the fuel lines and the fuel injection system are tight.

4 Since some components of the fuel system - the fuel tank and part of the fuel feed and return lines, for example - are underneath the vehicle, they can be inspected more easily with the vehicle raised on a hoist. If that's not possible, raise the vehicle and support it securely on jackstands.

5 With the vehicle raised and safely supported, inspect the gas tank and filler neck for punctures, cracks and other damage. The connection between the filler neck and the tank is particularly critical. Sometimes a rubber filler neck will leak because of loose clamps or deteriorated rubber **(see illustration)**. These are problems a home mechanic can usually rectify. **Warning:** *Do not, under any circumstances, try to repair a fuel tank (except rubber components). A welding torch or any open flame can easily cause fuel vapors inside the tank to explode.*

6 Carefully check all rubber hoses and metal lines leading away from the fuel tank. Check for loose connections, deteriorated hoses, crimped lines and other damage. Carefully inspect the lines from the tank to the fuel injection system. Repair or replace damaged sections as necessary (see Chapter 4).

17 Exhaust system check (every 15,000 or 12 months)

Refer to illustrations 17.2a and 17.2b

1 With the engine cold (at least three hours after the vehicle has been driven), check the complete exhaust system from its starting point at the engine to the end of the tailpipe. This should be done on a hoist where unrestricted access is available.

2 Check the pipes and connections for signs of leakage and/or corrosion indicating a potential failure. Make sure that all brackets and hangers are in good condition and tight **(see illustrations)**.

3 At the same time, inspect the underside of the body for holes, corrosion and open seams which may allow exhaust gases to enter the passenger compartment. Seal all body openings with silicone sealant or body putty.

4 Rattles and other noises can often be traced to the exhaust system, especially the mounts and hangers. Try to move the pipes, muffler and catalytic converter. If the components can come into contact with the body, secure the exhaust system with new mounts.

5 This is also an ideal time to check the running condition of the engine by inspecting the very end of the tailpipe. The exhaust deposits here are an indication of engine state-of-tune. If the pipe is black and sooty or coated with white deposits, the engine may be in need of a tune-up (including a thorough fuel injection system inspection).

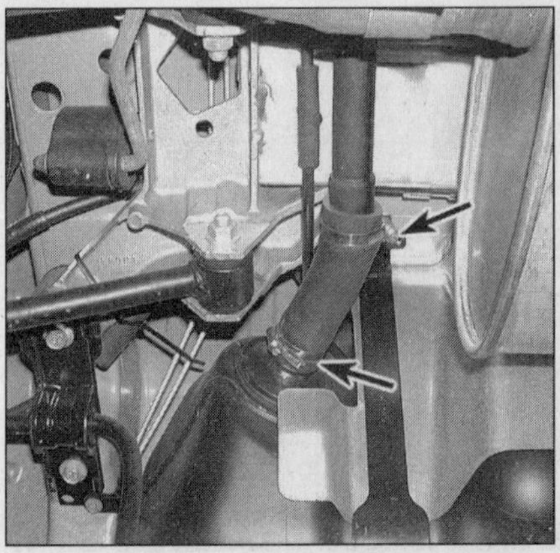

16.5 Inspect fuel filler hoses for cracks and make sure the clamps (arrows) are tight on all hoses in the system

18 Brake system check (every 15,000 miles or 12 months)

Warning: *The dust created by the brake system may contain asbestos, which is harmful to your health. Never blow it out with compressed air and don't inhale any of it. An approved filtering mask should be worn when working on the brakes. Do not, under any circumstances, use petroleum-based solvents to clean brake parts. Use brake system cleaner only! Try to use non-asbestos replacement parts whenever possible.*

Note: *For detailed photographs of the brake system, refer to Chapter 9.*

1 In addition to the specified intervals, the brakes should be inspected every time the wheels are removed or whenever a defect is suspected.

17.2a Starting at the front of the exhaust system, check the clamps (arrow) securing the catalytic converter to the exhaust manifolds

17.2b Check the exhaust system components

A Clamp
B Hanger
C Mufflers

18.7a With the wheel off, check the thickness of the inner pad (arrow) through the inspection hole (front caliper shown, rear calipers are inspected similarly)

18.7b The outer pad (arrow) is more easily checked at the edge of the caliper

2 Any of the following symptoms could indicate a potential brake system defect: The vehicle pulls to one side when the brake pedal is depressed; the brakes make squealing or dragging noises when applied; brake pedal travel is excessive; the pedal pulsates; or brake fluid leaks, usually onto the inside of the tire or wheel.

3 Loosen the wheel lug nuts.

4 Raise the vehicle and place it securely on jackstands.

5 Remove the wheels (see *Jacking and towing* at the front of this book, or your owner's manual, if necessary).

Disc brakes

Refer to illustrations 18.7a, 18.7b, 18.9 and 18.11

6 There are two pads (an outer and an inner) in each caliper. The pads are visible with the wheels removed. Both front and rear brakes are disc-type.

7 Check the pad thickness by looking at each end of the caliper and through the inspection window in the caliper body **(see illustrations)**. If the lining material is less than the thickness listed in this Chapter's Specifications, replace the pads. **Note:** *Keep in mind that the lining material is riveted or bonded to a metal backing plate and the metal portion is not included in this measurement.*

8 If it is difficult to determine the exact thickness of the remaining pad material by the above method, or if you are at all concerned about the condition of the pads, remove the caliper(s), then remove the pads from the calipers for further inspection (refer to Chapter 9).

9 Once the pads are removed from the calipers, clean them with brake cleaner and re-measure them with a ruler or a vernier caliper **(see illustration)**.

10 Measure the disc thickness with a micrometer to make sure that it still has service life remaining. If any disc is thinner than the specified minimum thickness, replace it (refer to Chapter 9). Even if the disc has service life remaining, check its condition. Look for scoring, gouging and burned spots. If these conditions exist, remove the disc and have it resurfaced (see Chapter 9).

11 Before installing the wheels, check all brake lines and hoses for damage, wear, deformation, cracks, corrosion, leakage, bends and twists, particularly in the vicinity of the rubber hoses at the calipers **(see illustration)**. Check the clamps for tightness and the connections for leakage. Make sure that all hoses and lines are clear of sharp edges, moving parts and the exhaust system. If any of the above conditions are noted, repair, reroute or replace the lines and/or fittings as necessary (see Chapter 9).

Brake booster check

12 Sit in the driver's seat and perform the following sequence of tests.

13 With the brake fully depressed, start the engine - the pedal should move down a little when the engine starts.

14 With the engine running, depress the brake pedal several times - the travel distance should not change.

15 Depress the brake, stop the engine and hold the pedal in for about 30 seconds - the pedal should neither sink nor rise.

16 Restart the engine, run it for about a minute and turn it off. Then firmly depress the brake several times - the pedal travel should decrease with each application.

17 If your brakes do not operate as described, the brake booster has failed. Refer to Chapter 9 for the replacement procedure.

Parking brake

18 One method of checking the parking brake is to park the vehicle on a steep hill with the parking brake set and the transmission in Neutral. If the parking brake cannot prevent the vehicle from rolling, it's in need of adjustment (see Chapter 9).

19 Suspension, steering and driveaxle boot check (every 15,000 miles or 12 months)

Note: *The steering linkage and suspension components should be checked periodically. Worn or damaged suspension and steering linkage components can result in excessive and abnormal tire wear, poor ride quality and vehicle handling, and reduced fuel economy.*

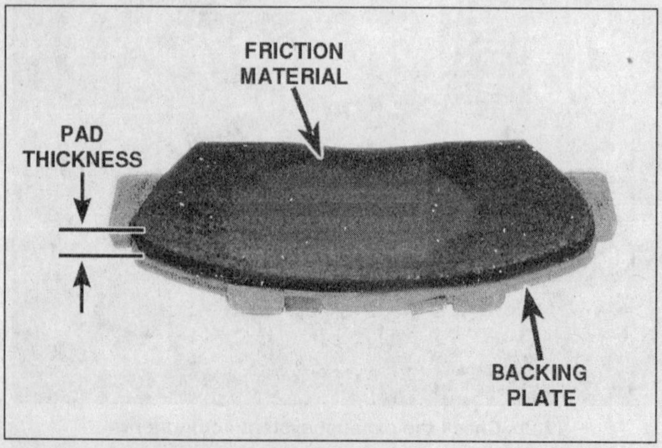

18.9 If a more precise measurement of pad thickness is necessary, remove the pads and measure the remaining friction material

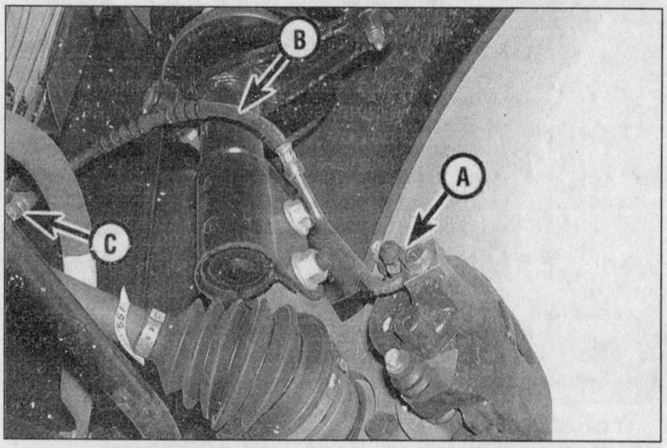

18.11 Check the fitting at the caliper (A), look along the brake hose (B) for signs of cracking or fluid leakage, and check the fitting (C) where the flexible brake hose meets the steel line on the chassis

19.6 Pull up the boot on front and rear struts to check for signs of fluid leakage at the point (arrow) where the shaft enters the strut (front strut shown, rear similar)

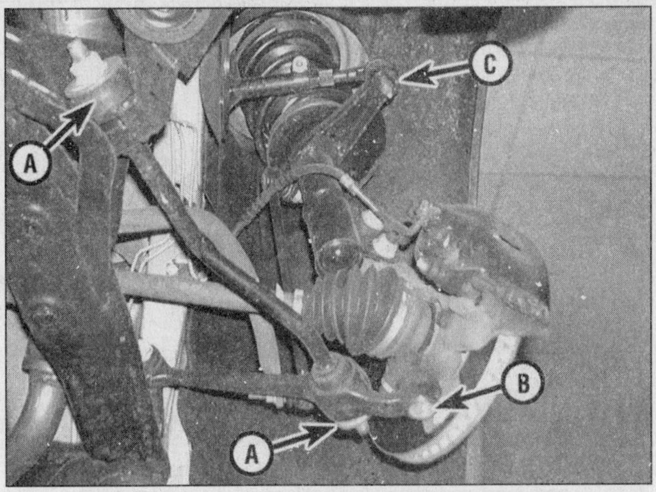

19.9a Examine the front suspension components

A Tension strut
B Lower balljoint
C Tie-rod end

For detailed illustrations of the steering and suspension components, refer to Chapter 10.

Strut (shock absorber) check

Refer to illustration 19.6

1 Park the vehicle on level ground, turn the engine off and set the parking brake. Check the tire pressures.

2 Push down at one corner of the vehicle, then release it while noting the movement of the body. It should stop moving and come to rest in a level position within one or two bounces.

3 If the vehicle continues to move up-and-down or if it fails to return to its original position, a worn or weak strut is probably the reason.

4 Repeat the above check at each of the three remaining corners of the vehicle.

5 Raise the vehicle and support it securely on jackstands.

6 Check the struts for evidence of fluid leakage **(see illustration)**. A light film of fluid is no cause for concern. Make sure that any fluid noted is from the struts and not from some other source. If leakage is noted, replace the struts as a set.

7 Check the struts to be sure that they are securely mounted and undamaged. Check the upper mounts for damage and wear. If damage or wear is noted, replace the struts as a set (front or rear).

8 If the struts must be replaced, refer to Chapter 10 for the procedure.

19.9b Examine the rear suspension components

A Rear crossmember isolator bushings (one shown, there are four)
B Lateral link bushings (there are four links)
C Stabilizer bar link bushings
D Trailing arm bushings

Steering and suspension check

Refer to illustrations 19.9a, 19.9b, 19.10 and 19.12

9 Visually inspect the steering and suspension components (front and rear) for damage and distortion. Look for damaged seals, boots and bushings and leaks of any kind. Examine the bushings where the lower control arm meets the chassis, and where the strut rod is bushed, either at the lower control arm or the chassis end **(see illustrations)**.

10 In the engine compartment, look behind the engine and inspect the rack-and-pinion steering gear boots for signs of cracking or lubricant leakage **(see illustration)**. If the boots need replacing, refer to Chapter 10.

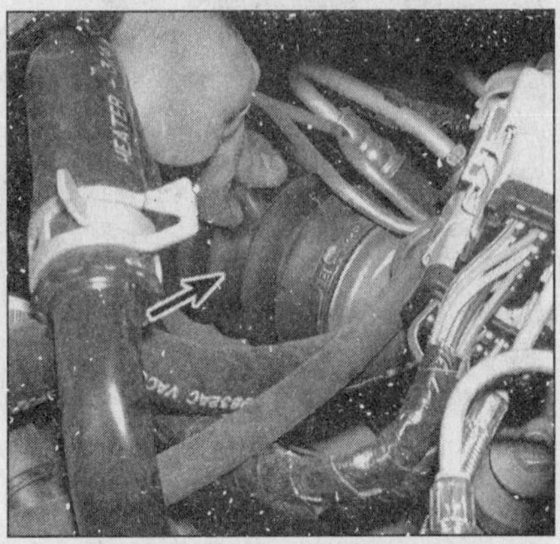

19.10 Flex the steering gear boots (arrow) to check for cracks or signs of leakage

19.12 Check for tie-rod end play by moving the wheel/tire front and rear, and check for balljoint play by moving the top and bottom of the tire

19.15 Inspect the inner and outer driveaxle boots for loose clamps, cracks of signs of leaking lubricant (outer boot shown)

11 Clean the lower end of the steering knuckle. Have an assistant grasp the lower edge of the tire and move the wheel in-and-out while you look for movement at the steering knuckle-to-control arm balljoint. If there is any movement the suspension balljoint(s) must be replaced.

12 Grasp each front tire at the front and rear edges, push in at the front, pull out at the rear, then reverse the motions and feel for play in the steering system components. If any freeplay is noted, check the tie-rod ends for looseness **(see illustration)**.

13 Additional steering and suspension system information and illustrations can be found in Chapter 10.

Driveaxle boot check

Refer to illustration 19.15

14 The driveaxle boots are very important because they prevent dirt, water and foreign material from entering and damaging the constant velocity (CV) joints. Oil and grease can cause the boot material to deteriorate prematurely, so it's a good idea to wash the boots with soap and water. Because it constantly pivots back and forth following the steering action of the front hub, the outer CV boot wears out sooner and should be inspected regularly.

15 Inspect the boots for tears and cracks as well as loose clamps **(see illustration)**. If there is any evidence of cracks or leaking lubricant, they must be replaced as described in Chapter 8.

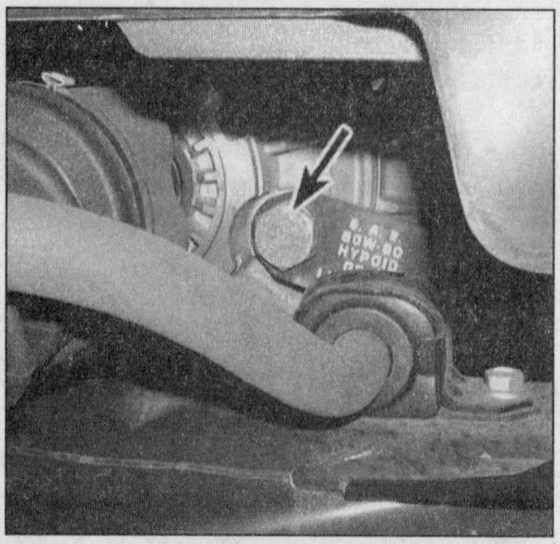

20.1 Unscrew the fill plug (arrow) from the side of the differential housing to check the lubricant level - note the plastic tag that contains information on lubricant type

20 Differential lubricant level check (every 15,000 miles or 12 months)

Refer to illustration 20.1

1 On these models the differential lubricant supply is separate from the transaxle. The differential has a fill plug that must be removed to check the lubricant level **(see illustration)**. **Warning:** *If the vehicle is raised to gain access to the plug, be sure to support it safely on jackstands - DO NOT crawl under a vehicle that is supported only by a jack!*

2 Remove the plug from the differential and use your little finger to reach inside the housing to feel the lubricant level. The level should be at or near the bottom of the plug hole.

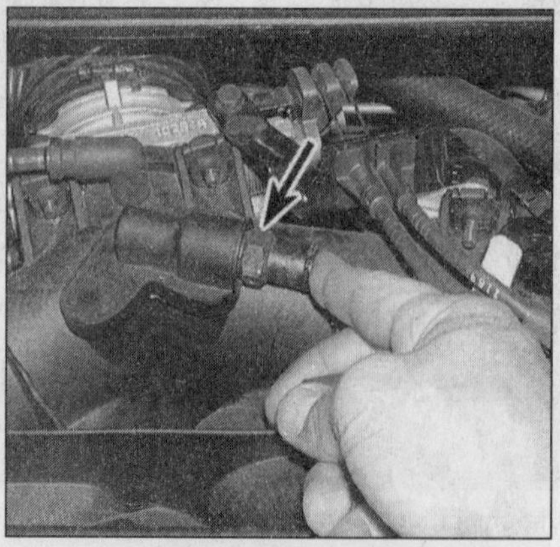

21.3 Feel for vacuum at the PCV valve (arrow) with the engine running and the hose off (2.7L shown)

3 If it isn't, add the recommended lubricant through the plug hole with a syringe or squeeze bottle.

4 Install and tighten the plug and check for leaks after the first few miles of driving.

21 Positive Crankcase Ventilation (PCV) valve check and replacement (every 30,000 miles or 24 months)

Refer to illustration 21.3

1 The PCV valve is located on the intake plenum. On 2.7L engines it is on top, and on 3.2L/3.5L engines it's at the rear of the plenum, to the left of the throttle body.

2 With the engine idling at normal operating temperature, remove the clamp and detach the hose from the valve fitting.

3 A hissing sound should be heard. Place your finger over the valve opening **(see illustration)**. If there's no vacuum at the valve, check for a plugged hose, plenum port or valve. Replace any plugged or deteriorated hoses.

4 To replace the valve, use a wrench to unscrew it from the plenum.

5 When purchasing a replacement PCV valve, make sure it's for your particular vehicle and engine size. Compare the old valve with the new one to make sure they're the same.

6 Screw the valve into the plenum until it's seated and push the hose securely into position, then install the clamp.

22 Cooling system servicing (draining, flushing and refilling) (every 100,000 miles or 5 years)

Warning: *Do not allow antifreeze to come in contact with your skin or painted surfaces of the vehicle. Rinse off spills immediately with*

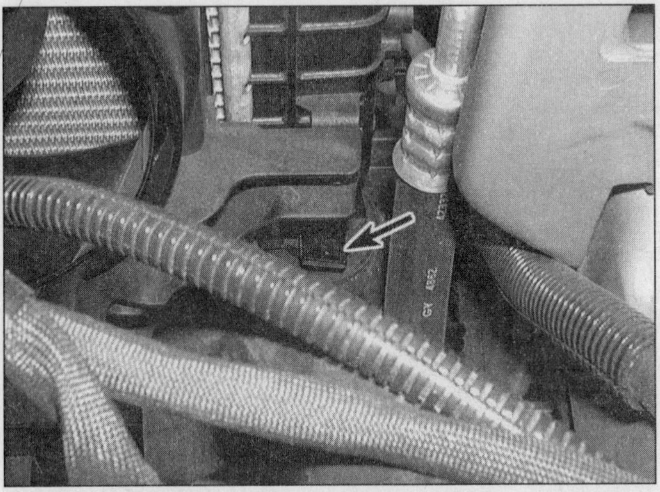

22.3 From below on the right side of the radiator, turn the plastic drain valve (arrow) - the coolant will come out the drain hole below

22.4 Use a socket and long extension to reach the block drain plugs (arrow indicates right-side plug, left side similar)

plenty of water. Antifreeze is highly toxic if ingested. Never leave antifreeze lying around in an open container or in puddles on the floor; children and pets are attracted by its sweet smell and may drink it. Check with local authorities about disposing of used antifreeze. Many communities have collection centers that will see that antifreeze is disposed of safely.

Note: *Non-toxic antifreeze is now manufactured and available at local auto parts stores, but even this type should be disposed of properly.*

Draining

Refer to illustrations 22.3 and 22.4

1 Periodically, the cooling system should be drained, flushed and refilled to replenish the antifreeze mixture and prevent formation of rust and corrosion, which can impair the performance of the cooling system and cause engine damage. When the cooling system is serviced, all hoses and the radiator cap should be checked and replaced if necessary.

2 Apply the parking brake and block the wheels. **Warning:** *If the vehicle has just been driven, wait several hours to allow the engine to cool down before beginning this procedure.*

3 Move a large container under the radiator drain to catch the coolant. The drain plug is located on the lower right side of the radiator **(see illustration)**. Attach a hose to the drain fitting (if possible) to direct the coolant into the container, then open the drain fitting (a pair of pliers may be required to turn it). Remove the coolant reservoir cap.

4 After coolant stops flowing out of the radiator, move the container under the engine block drain plugs - there's one on each side of the block **(see illustration)**. Remove the plugs and allow the coolant in the block to drain.

5 While the coolant is draining, check the condition of the radiator hoses, heater hoses and clamps (refer to Section 14 if necessary).

6 Replace any damaged clamps or hoses.

Flushing

Refer to illustration 22.9

7 Once the system is completely drained, remove the thermostat from the engine (see Chapter 3). Then reinstall the thermostat housing without the thermostat. This will allow the system to be thoroughly flushed.

8 Reinstall the lower radiator hose and twist the radiator drain valve shut. Turn your heating system controls to Hot, so that the heater core will be flushed at the same time as the rest of the cooling system.

9 Disconnect the upper radiator hose, then place a garden hose in the upper radiator inlet and flush the system until the water runs clear at the upper radiator hose **(see illustration)**.

10 In severe cases of contamination or clogging of the radiator, remove the radiator (see Chapter 3) and have a radiator repair facility clean and repair it if necessary.

11 Many deposits can be removed by the chemical action of a cleaner available at auto parts stores. Follow the procedure outlined in the manufacturer's instructions. **Note:** *When the coolant is regularly drained and the system refilled with the correct antifreeze/water mixture, there should be no need to use chemical cleaners or descalers.*

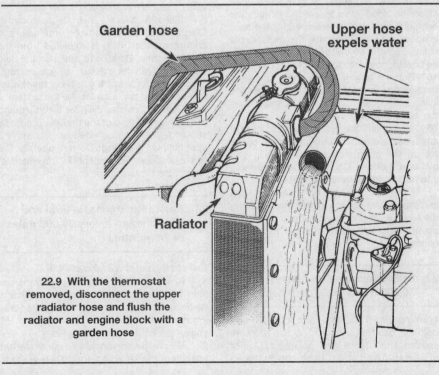

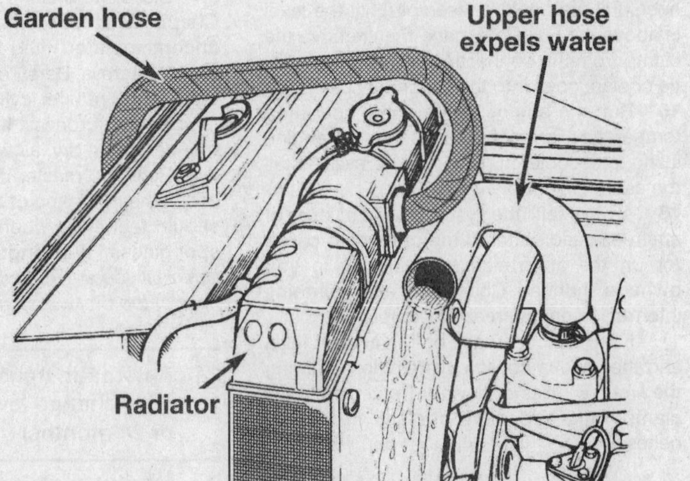

22.9 With the thermostat removed, disconnect the upper radiator hose and flush the radiator and engine block with a garden hose

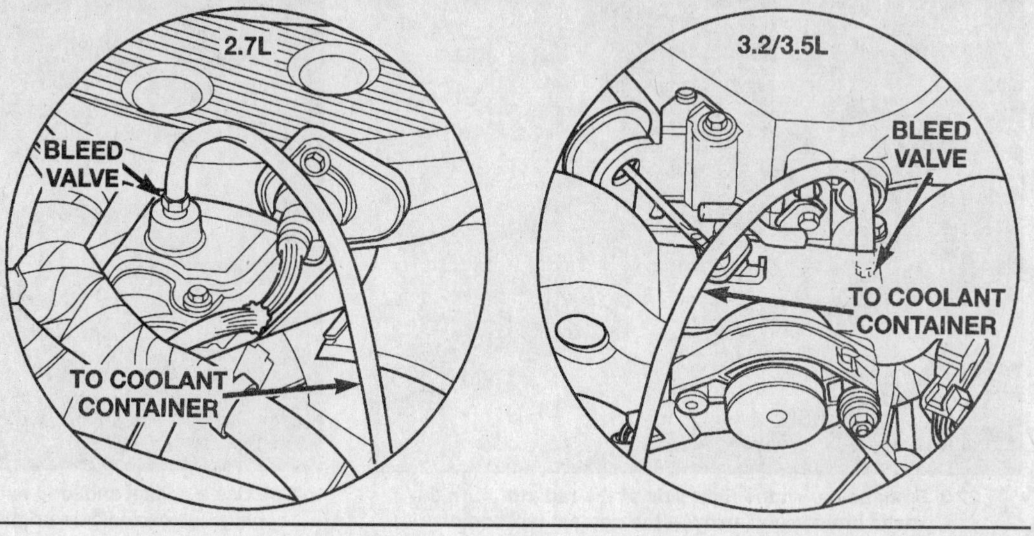

22.13 Connect a clear hose to the bleeder screw and run the hose into an empty container, then open the bleeder and begin filling the system at the coolant reservoir

Refilling

Refer to illustration 22.13

12 Install the coolant reservoir, reconnect the hoses, close the drain fitting hand tight and install the block drain plugs. Use a clamp to pinch off the hose connecting the two chambers of the coolant reservoir (the chamber with the cap is pressurized, the secondary chamber is only for overflow).

13 Connect one end of a four foot long piece of 1/4-inch diameter clear plastic tubing to the bleed screw and run the other end into an empty coolant container **(see illustration)**. **Caution:** *Keep the bleeder hose away from hot or moving components on the engine.*

14 Open the bleed valve screw and slowly add coolant to the reservoir until the coolant stream running from the hose is bubble-free. Squeeze the upper radiator hose gently to make sure all remaining air is expelled, then close the bleed valve screw and remove the hose. Fill the coolant reservoir until the level is above the Full Cold mark, then remove the clamp from the connecting hose so that a little coolant goes into the secondary chamber.

15 Run the engine until normal operating temperature is reached and, with the engine idling, add coolant up the correct level. Install the cap on the coolant tank.

16 Always refill the system with a mixture of antifreeze and water in the proportion called for on the antifreeze container or in you owner's manual. Chapter 3 also contains information on antifreeze mixtures.

17 Keep a close watch on the coolant level and the various cooling system hoses during the first few miles of driving. Tighten the hose clamps and add more coolant mixture as necessary.

23 Brake fluid change (every 30,000 miles or 24 months)

Warning: *Brake fluid can harm your eyes and damage painted surfaces, so use extreme caution when handling or pouring it. Do not use brake fluid that has been standing open or is more than one year old. Brake fluid absorbs moisture from the air. Excess moisture can cause a dangerous loss of braking effectiveness.*

1 At the specified intervals, the brake fluid should be drained and replaced. Since the brake fluid may drip or splash when pouring it, place plenty of rags around the master cylinder to protect any surrounding painted surfaces.

2 Before beginning work, purchase the specified brake fluid (see *Recommended lubricants and fluids* at the beginning of this Chapter).

3 Remove the cap from the master cylinder reservoir.

4 Using a hand suction pump or similar device, withdraw the fluid from the master cylinder reservoir.

5 Add new fluid to the master cylinder until it rises to the base of the filler neck.

6 Bleed the brake system as described in Chapter 9 at all four brakes until new and uncontaminated fluid is expelled from the bleeder screw. Be sure to maintain the fluid level in the master cylinder as you perform the bleeding process. If you allow the master cylinder to run dry, air will enter the system.

7 Refill the master cylinder with fluid and check the operation of the brakes. The pedal should feel solid when depressed, with no sponginess. **Warning:** *Do not operate the vehicle if you are in doubt about the effectiveness of the brake system.*

24 Automatic transaxle fluid and filter change (every 30,000 miles or 24 months)

Refer to illustrations 24.6 and 24.9

1 At the specified intervals, the transmission fluid should be drained and replaced. Since the fluid will remain hot long after driving, perform this procedure only after the engine has cooled down completely.

2 Before beginning work, purchase the specified transmission fluid (see *Recommended lubricants and fluids* at the front of this Chapter) and a new filter.

3 Other tools necessary for this job include a floor jack, jackstands to support the vehicle in a raised position, a drain pan capable of holding at least four quarts, newspapers, clean rags and RTV sealant.

4 Raise the vehicle and support it securely on jackstands.

5 Place the drain pan underneath the transmission pan. Remove the rear and side pan mounting bolts, but only loosen the front pan bolts approximately four turns.

6 Carefully pry the transmission pan loose with a screwdriver, allowing the fluid to drain **(see illustration)**.

7 Remove the remaining bolts and the pan. Carefully clean the gasket surface of the transmission to remove all traces of the old gasket and sealant.

8 Drain the fluid from the transmission pan, clean the pan with solvent and dry it with compressed air, if available. **Note:** *All models are equipped with a magnet in the transmission pan to catch metal debris. Clean the magnet thoroughly. A small amount of metal material is normal at the magnet. If there is considerable debris, consult a dealer or transmission specialist.*

9 Remove the filter from the valve body

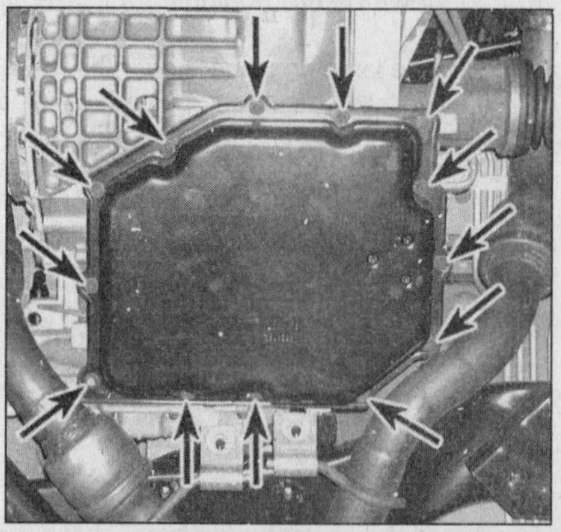

24.6 Remove the transmission oil pan bolts (arrows)

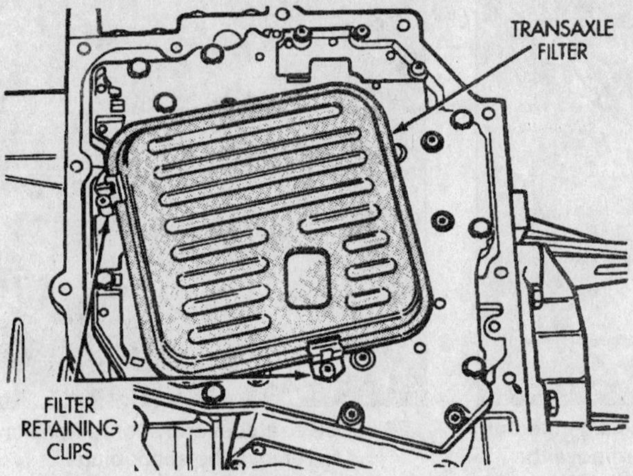

24.9 Detach the clips and lower the filter - be careful, it still contains residual fluid

25.3 Press open the clips at the front of the air filter housing, lift the lid and remove the filter

inside the transmission **(see illustration)**. Use a gasket scraper to remove any traces of old gasket material or sealant that remain on the valve body. **Note:** *Be very careful not to gouge the delicate aluminum gasket surface on the valve body.*

10 Install a new gasket and filter. On many replacement filters, the gasket or O-ring is attached to the filter to simplify installation.

11 Make sure the gasket surface on the transmission pan is clean, then apply a 1/8-inch bead of RTV sealant to the perimeter of the pan. Put the pan in place against the transmission and, working around the pan, tighten each bolt a little at a time to the torque listed in this Chapter's Specifications.

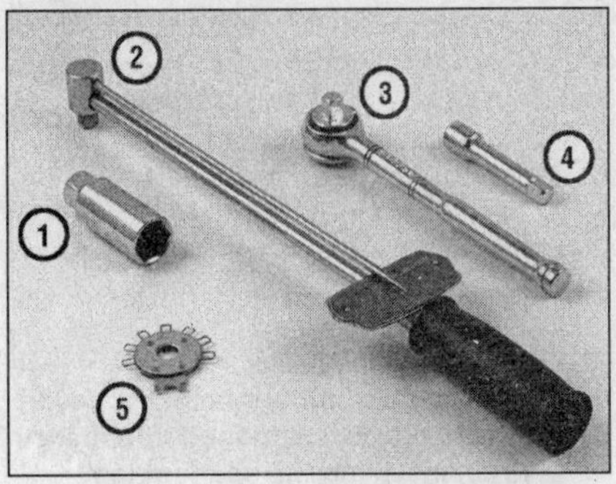

26.1 Tools required for changing spark plugs

1 ***Spark plug socket*** *- This will have special padding inside to protect the spark plug's porcelain insulator*

2 ***Torque wrench*** *- Although not mandatory, using this tool is the best way to ensure the plugs are tightened properly*

3 ***Ratchet*** *- Standard hand tool to fit the spark plug socket*

4 ***Extension*** *- Depending on model and accessories, you may need special extensions and universal joints to reach one or more of the plugs*

5 ***Spark plug gap gauge*** *- This gauge for checking the gap comes in a variety of styles. Make sure the gap for your engine is included*

12 Lower the vehicle and add approximately 4 quarts of the specified type of automatic transmission fluid through the filler tube (see Section 6).

13 With the transmission in Park and the parking brake set, run the engine for two minutes at a fast idle, but don't race it.

14 With your foot on the brakes, move the gear selector through each range and back to Park. Check the fluid level. It will probably be low. Add enough fluid to bring the level to just above the bottom hole in the transaxle dipstick.

15 Drive the vehicle for 10 miles or more to fully warm the fluid, then recheck the level and add as necessary to bring the level to the Hot area of the dipstick.

25 Air filter replacement (every 30,000 miles or 24 months)

Refer to illustration 25.3

1 At the specified intervals, the air filter element should be replaced.

2 The air filter element is located in a housing in the right front corner of the engine compartment.

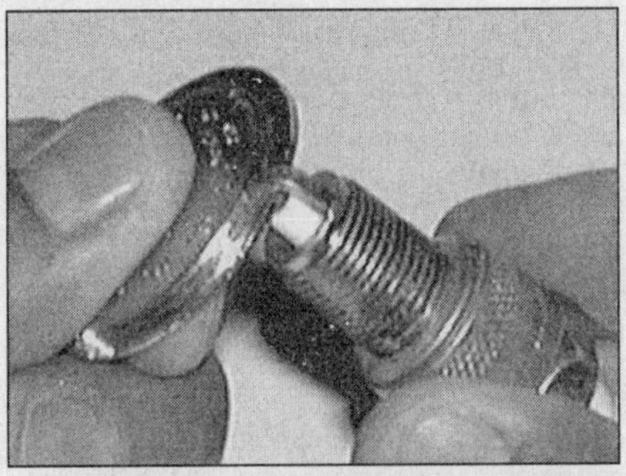

26.4a Spark plug manufacturers recommend using a tapered thickness gauge when checking the gap - slide the thin side into the gap and turn until the gauge just fills the gap, then read the thickness on the gauge - do not force the tool into the gap or use the tapered portion to widen a gap

3 Release the two clips at the front of the air filter housing, lift up the cover and remove the old filter element **(see illustration)**.

4 Be careful not to drop anything down into the air cleaner assembly. Clean the inside of the housing with a rag.

5 Place the new filter element in position and install the cover. Be sure the clips at the front of the cover are engaged into the housing.

26 Spark plug check and replacement (every 60,000 miles or 48 months)

Refer to illustrations 26.1, 26.4a and 26.4b

1 In most cases the tools necessary for spark plug replacement include a spark plug socket that fits onto a ratchet (this special socket will be padded inside to protect the porcelain insulators on the new plugs), various extensions and a gauge to check and adjust the spark plug gap **(see illustration)**. Since these engines are equipped with an aluminum cylinder head, a torque wrench should be used for tightening the spark plugs.

2 The best approach when replacing the spark plugs is to purchase the new spark plugs beforehand, adjust them to the proper gap and then replace each plug one at a time. When buying the new spark plugs, be sure to obtain the correct plug for your specific engine. This information can be found in the Specifications at the front of this Chapter, in the factory owner's manual or on the Vehicle Emissions Control Information label located under the hood. If differences exist between the sources, purchase the spark plug type specified on the VECI label as it was printed for your specific engine.

3 Allow the engine to cool completely before attempting to remove any of the plugs. During this cooling off time, each of the new spark plugs can be inspected for defects and the gaps can be checked.

4 The gap is checked by inserting a tapered thickness gauge between the electrodes at the tip of the plug **(see illustration)**.

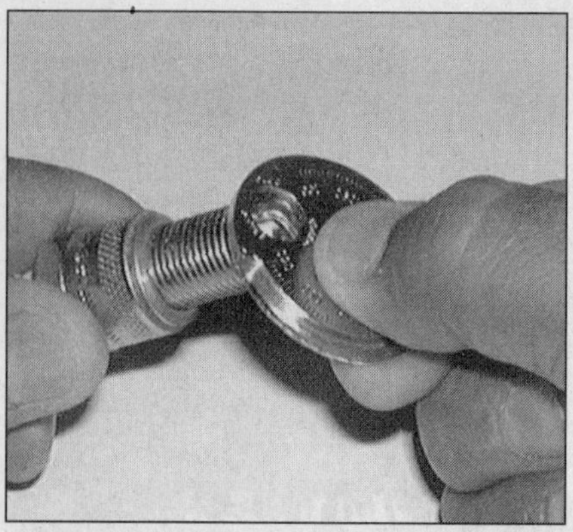

26.4b To change the gap, bend the side electrode only, using the adjuster hole in the tool, and be very careful not to crack or chip the porcelain insulator surrounding the center electrode

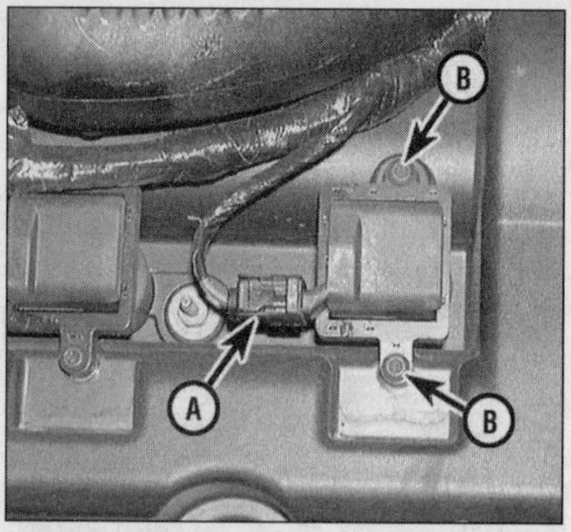

26.6 Disconnect the electrical connector (A) at the individual coil, remove the mounting bolts (B) and withdraw the coil and its boot from the spark plug

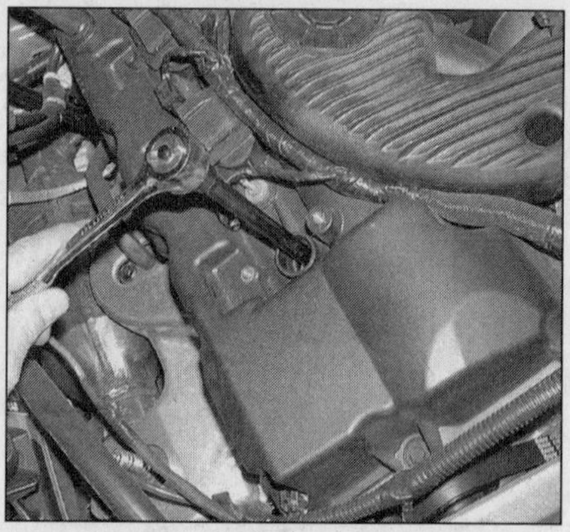

26.8 Use a ratchet and short extension to remove the spark plugs (2.7L engine shown)

The gap between the electrodes should be as specified on the VECI label in the engine compartment or as listed in this Chapter's Specifications. The tapered gauge should touch each of the electrodes, but do not force the taper in, since the factory platinum coating can be scratched, reducing spark plug life. If the gap is incorrect, use the adjuster hole on the thickness gauge body to bend the curved side electrode slightly until the proper gap is obtained **(see illustration)**. Also, at this time check for cracks in the spark plug body (if any are found, the plug should not be used). If the side electrode is not exactly over the center one, use the adjuster to align the two.

Removal

Refer to illustrations 26.6 and 26.8

5 Cover the fender to prevent damage to the paint.

6 With the engine cool, remove the spark plug coil from one spark plug. Remove the two bolts, disconnect the electrical connector and pull the coil and its plug boot out **(see illustration)**.

7 If compressed air is available, use it to blow any dirt or foreign material away from the spark plug area. The idea here is to eliminate the possibility of material falling into the cylinder through the plug hole as the spark plug is removed.

8 Now place the spark plug socket over the plug and remove it from the engine by turning it in a counterclockwise direction **(see illustration)**.

9 Compare the spark plug with the chart on the inside back cover of this manual to get an indication of the overall running condition of the engine.

Installation

Refer to illustrations 26.10 and 26.11

10 It's a good idea to lightly coat the threads of the spark plugs with anti-seize compound **(see illustration)** to insure that the spark plugs do not seize in the aluminum cylinder head.

11 It's often difficult to insert spark plugs into their holes without cross-threading them. To avoid this possibility, fit a piece of snug-fitting rubber hose over the end of the spark plug **(see illustration)**. The flexible hose acts as a universal joint to help align the plug with the plug hole. Should the plug begin to cross-thread, the hose will slip on the spark plug, preventing thread damage. Tighten the spark plug to the torque listed in this Chapter's Specifications.

12 Push down the individual coil for that plug until the boot is firmly seated on the plug, then bolt the coil down and reconnect the electrical connector.

13 Follow the above procedure for the remaining spark plugs, replacing them one at a time to prevent mixing up the coil connectors.

27 Differential lubricant change (every 60,000 miles or 48 months)

Refer to illustration 27.3

1 Raise the vehicle and support it securely on jackstands.

2 Move a drain pan, rags, newspapers and wrenches under the differential.

3 Remove the differential drain plug at the bottom of the case and allow the lubricant to drain into the pan **(see illustration)**.

4 After the lubricant has drained completely, reinstall the plug and tighten it securely.

5 Remove the fill plug from the side of the differential case (see Section 20). Using a hand pump, syringe or funnel, fill the differential with the specified lubricant until it begins to leak out through the hole. Reinstall the fill plug and tighten it securely.

6 Lower the vehicle.

7 Drive the vehicle for a short distance, then check the drain and fill plugs for leakage.

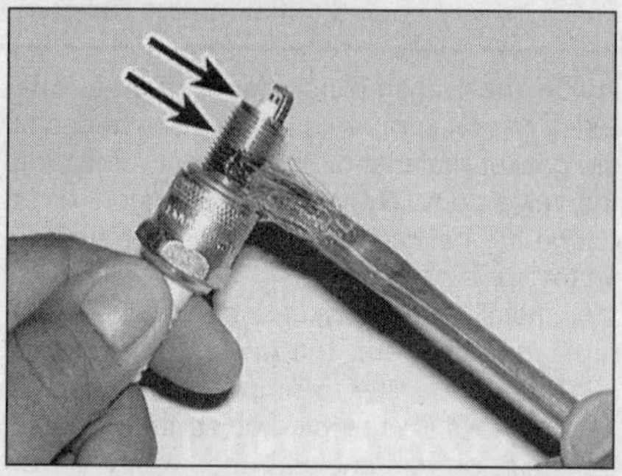

26.10 Apply a thin coat of anti-seize compound to the spark plug threads, being careful not to get any near the lower threads (arrows)

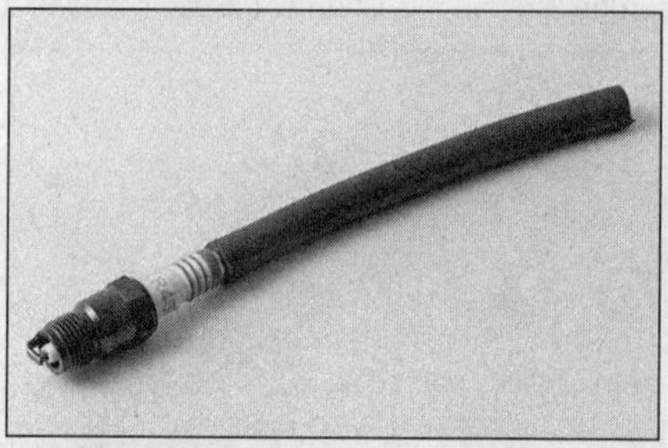

26.11 A length of rubber hose will save time and prevent damaged threads when installing the spark plugs

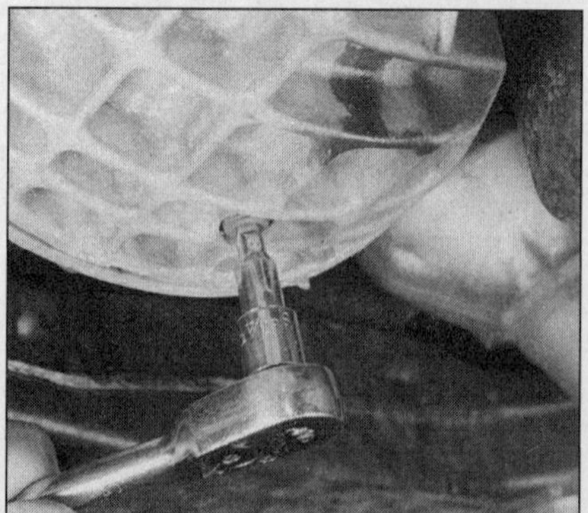

27.3 Use an Allen wrench or hex bit to remove the differential drain plug

Chapter 2 Part A
2.7L engine

Contents

Specifications

General

Displacement	167 cubic inches
Bore and stroke	3.386 x 3.091 inches
Cylinder numbers (front to rear)	
Left bank	2-4-6
Right bank	1-3-5
Firing order	1-2-3-4-5-6

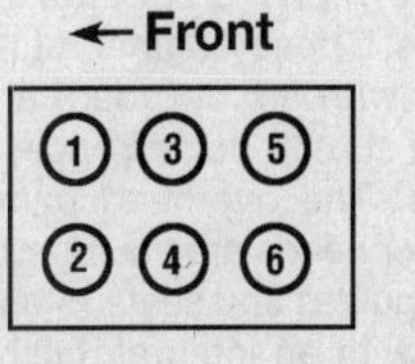

Cylinder identification diagram

Camshaft

Endplay	0.0051 to 0.011 inch
Lobe wear limit	
Standard	0.001 inch
Service limit	0.010 inch
Camshaft bearing oil clearance	
Standard	0.002 to 0.0035 inch
Service limit	0.0051 inch
Camshaft journal diameter	0.9441 to 0.9449 inch
Camshaft bore diameter	0.9469 to 0.9476 inch

Oil pump

Cover warpage limit	0.001 inch
Inner and outer rotor thickness	0.3731 to 3741 inch
Outer rotor diameter (minimum)	3.5109 inches
Outer rotor-to-housing clearance (maximum)	0.015 inch
Inner rotor-to-outer rotor lobe clearance	0.008 inch
Oil pump housing-to-rotor side clearance	0.003 inch

Torque specifications

	Ft-lbs (unless otherwise indicated)
Camshaft sprocket bolts	21
Camshaft bearing cap bolts	105 in-lbs
Camshaft timing chain tensioner bolts (secondary)	105 in-lbs
Crankshaft pulley bolt	125
Cylinder head bolts (in sequence - **see illustration 11.19**)	
Step 1 (tighten bolts 1 through 8)	35
Step 2 (tighten bolts 1 through 8)	55
Step 3 (tighten bolts 1 through 8)	55
Step 4 (tighten bolts 1 through 8)	Tighten an additional 90 degrees
Step 5 (tighten bolts 9 through 11)	21
Valve cover bolts	105 in-lbs
Driveplate bolts	70 to 75
Exhaust manifold nuts	17
Exhaust manifold heat shield bolts	105 in-lbs
Exhaust manifold V-band clamp	100 in-lbs
Engine mount to bracket bolts	45
Engine mount retaining nuts	45
Engine rear mount to frame bolts	21
Intake manifold bolts (upper and lower)	105 in-lbs
Oil pan bolts	
6-mm bolts	105 in-lbs
6-mm nuts	105 in-lbs
8-mm bolts	21
Oil pan drain plug	21
Oil pick-up tube mounting bolts	21
Oil pump mounting bolts	21
Oil pump cover screws	105 in-lbs
Timing chain cover bolts	
6-mm	105 in-lbs
10-mm	40
Timing chain guide bolts	21
Timing chain guide access plugs	15
Timing chain tensioner arm pivot bolt	21
Timing chain tensioner (primary)	40
Transaxle to oil pan support brace	40
Rear main oil seal retainer bolts	105 in-lbs
Water outlet housing	105 in-lbs

1 General information

This Part of Chapter 2 is devoted to in-vehicle repair procedures for the 2.7L V6 engine. These engines utilize an aluminum block with six cylinders arranged in a "V" shape at a 60-degree angle between the two banks. The overhead camshaft aluminum cylinder heads are equipped with replaceable valve guides and seats. Stamped steel rocker arms with an integral roller bearing actuate the valves.

All information concerning engine removal and installation and engine block and cylinder head overhaul can be found in Part C of this Chapter.

The following repair procedures are based on the assumption that the engine is installed in the vehicle. If the engine has been removed from the vehicle and mounted on a stand, many of the steps outlined in this Part of Chapter 2 will not apply.

The Specifications included in this Part of Chapter 2 apply only to the procedures contained in this Part. Part C of Chapter 2 contains the Specifications necessary for cylinder head and engine block rebuilding.

2 Repair operations possible with the engine in the vehicle

Many major repair operations can be accomplished without removing the engine from the vehicle.

Clean the engine compartment and the exterior of the engine with some type of degreaser before any work is done. It will make the job easier and help keep dirt out of the internal areas of the engine.

Depending on the components involved, it may be helpful to remove the hood to improve access to the engine as repairs are performed (refer to Chapter 11, if necessary). Cover the fenders to prevent damage to the paint. Special pads are available, but an old bedspread or blanket will also work.

If vacuum, exhaust, oil or coolant leaks develop, indicating a need for gasket or seal replacement, the repairs can generally be made with the engine in the vehicle. The intake and exhaust manifold gaskets, oil pan gasket, crankshaft oil seals and cylinder head gaskets are all accessible with the engine in place.

Exterior engine components, such as the intake and exhaust manifolds, the oil pan, the oil pump, the water pump (see Chapter 3), the starter motor, the alternator and the fuel system components (see Chapter 4) can be removed for repair with the engine in place.

Since the cylinder heads can be removed without pulling the engine, valve component servicing can also be accomplished with the engine in the vehicle. Replacement of the camshafts, timing chains and sprockets are also possible with the engine in the vehicle.

In extreme cases caused by a lack of necessary equipment, repair or replacement of piston rings, pistons, connecting rods and rod bearings is possible with the engine in the vehicle. However, this practice is not recommended because of the cleaning and preparation work that must be done to the components involved.

3 Top Dead Center (TDC) for number one piston - locating

Refer to illustration 3.5

1 Top Dead Center (TDC) is the highest point in the cylinder that each piston reaches as it travels up the cylinder bore. Each piston reaches TDC on the compression stroke and again on the exhaust stroke, but TDC generally refers to piston position on the compression stroke.

2 Positioning the piston(s) at TDC is an essential part of many procedures such as valve timing, camshaft and timing chain/sprocket removal.

3 Before beginning this procedure, be sure to place the transaxle in Neutral and apply the parking brake or block the rear wheels. Also, disable the ignition system by disconnecting the primary electrical connectors at the ignition coil packs and remove the spark plugs (see Chapter 1).

4 In order to bring any piston to TDC, the crankshaft must be turned using one of the methods outlined below. When looking at the front of the engine, normal crankshaft rotation is clockwise.

a) *The preferred method is to turn the crankshaft with a socket and ratchet attached to the bolt threaded into the front of the crankshaft. Apply pressure on the bolt in a clockwise direction only. Never turn the bolt counterclockwise.*

b) *A remote starter switch, which may save some time, can also be used. Follow the instructions included with the switch. Once the piston is close to TDC, use a socket and ratchet as described in the previous paragraph.*

c) *If an assistant is available to turn the ignition switch to the Start position in short bursts, you can get the piston close to TDC without a remote starter switch. Make sure your assistant is out of the vehicle, away from the ignition switch, then use a socket and ratchet as described in Paragraph (a) to complete the procedure.*

3.5 A compression gauge can be used in the number one plug hole to assist in finding TDC

5 Install a compression pressure gauge in the number one spark plug hole (refer to Chapter 2C). It should be a gauge with a screw-in fitting and a hose at least six inches long **(see illustration)**.

6 Rotate the crankshaft using one of the methods described above while observing for pressure on the compression gauge. The moment the gauge shows pressure indicates that the number one cylinder is on the compression stroke.

7 Once the compression stroke has begun, TDC for the compression stroke of the number one cylinder is reached by bringing the piston to the top of the cylinder.

8 Remove the compression gauge and place a long screwdriver into the number one spark plug hole until it touches the top of the piston. Use the screwdriver (as a feeler gauge) to tell where the top of the piston is located in the cylinder while slowly rotating the crankshaft. TDC for the number one cylinder is obtained when the piston reaches the top of the cylinder on the compression stroke.

9 If you go past TDC, rotate the crankshaft clockwise two revolutions until the piston is approximately one inch below TDC, then slowly rotate the crankshaft clockwise until TDC is reached.

4 Valve cover - removal and installation

Refer to illustrations 4.4a, 4.4b and 4.7

Removal

1 Disconnect the negative battery cable from the remote ground terminal (see Chapter 5).

2 Remove the upper intake manifold (see Section 9) and cover the lower intake manifold with rags to keep out dirt.

3 Remove the ignition coils from the spark plugs (see Chapter 5) and detach the electrical connector(s) from the ignition coil capacitors.

4 Pull the wire harness up from the valve cover studs and remove the valve cover studs/nuts and bolts **(see illustrations)**.

5 Detach the valve cover. **Note:** *If the cover sticks to the cylinder head, use a block of wood and a hammer to dislodge it. If the*

4.4a Remove the wire harness retaining clips (A) from the studs on the valve covers and the electrical connector from the ignition coil capacitors (B)

4.4b Valve cover mounting bolts (arrows)

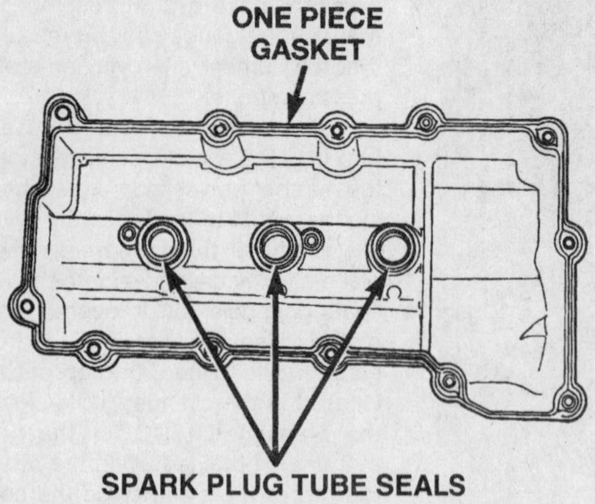

4.7 Inspect the spark plug tube seals and replace them if necessary

5.5 Using a shaft mount type valve spring compressor, depress the valve spring just enough to remove the rocker arm

5.7 Pull the lash adjuster up and out of its bore to remove it from the cylinder head

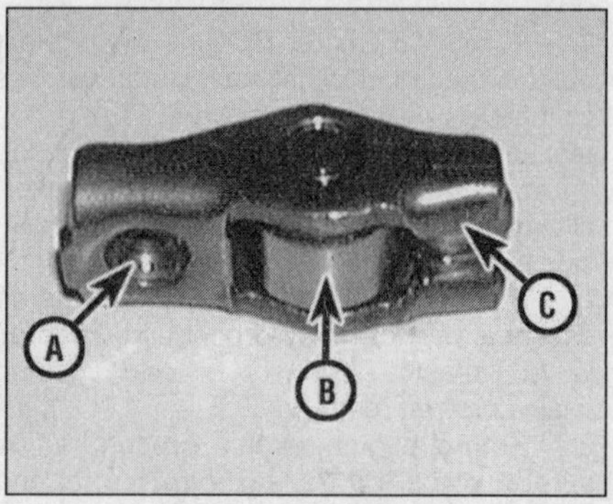

5.8 Inspect the rocker arms at the following locations

A Lash adjuster pocket
B Roller
C Valve stem seat

cover still won't come loose, pry on it carefully, but don't distort the sealing flange.

Installation

6 The mating surfaces of each cylinder head and valve cover must be perfectly clean when the covers are installed. Use a gasket scraper to remove all traces of sealant or old gasket material, then clean the mating surfaces with lacquer thinner or acetone (if there's sealant or oil on the mating surfaces when the cover is installed, oil leaks may develop). Be extra careful not to nick or gouge the mating surfaces with the scraper.

7 Inspect the spark plug tube seals **(see illustration)**. Replace them if they're cracked or flattened, or if the rubber has hardened. Make sure the spark plug tube seals are in position before installing the valve cover.

8 Clean the mounting bolt threads with a die if necessary to remove any corrosion and restore damaged threads. Use a tap to clean the threaded holes in the heads.

9 Place the valve cover and new gasket in position, then install the bolts. Tighten the bolts in several steps to the torque listed in this Chapter's Specifications.

10 Complete the installation by reversing the removal procedure. Start the engine and check carefully for oil leaks.

5 Rocker arms and hydraulic lash adjusters - removal, inspection and installation

Refer to illustrations 5.5, 5.7 and 5.8

Note: *A universal shaft-type valve spring compressor available from most aftermarket specialty tool manufacturers will be required for this procedure. The only other alternative to accomplishing this task without the use of this special tool is to remove the timing chains and the camshafts which requires major disassembly of the engine and surrounding components.*

1 Before beginning this procedure, be sure to place the transaxle in Neutral and apply the parking brake or block the rear wheels. Also, disable the ignition system by disconnecting the primary electrical connectors at the ignition coils and remove the spark plugs (see Chapter 1).

2 Remove the upper intake manifold (see Section 9) and the valve cover(s) (see Section 4).

3 Rotate the engine with a socket and ratchet attached to the crankshaft pulley bolt until the cam lobe for the rocker arm to be removed is located on its base circle. Apply pressure on the crankshaft bolt in a clockwise direction only.

4 Before the rocker arms and lash adjusters are removed, arrange to label and store them, so they can be kept separate and reinstalled on the same valve they were removed from.

5 Mount the valve spring compressor on the cylinder head. Depress the valve spring just enough to release tension on the rocker arm to be removed. Once tension on the rocker arm is relieved, the rocker arm can be removed by simply pulling it out **(see illustration)**.

6 If you're replacing or removing all of the rockers arms or lash adjusters, begin with cylinder number one and work on the rocker arms for one cylinder at a time. Move from cylinder-to-cylinder following the firing order sequence (see this Chapter's Specifications). Remember to keep the rocker arm and lash adjuster for each valve together so they can be reinstalled in the same locations

7 Once the rocker arms are removed, the lash adjusters can be pulled out of the cylinder head and stored with the corresponding rocker arm **(see illustration)**.

8 Inspect each rocker arm for wear, cracks and other damage. Make sure the

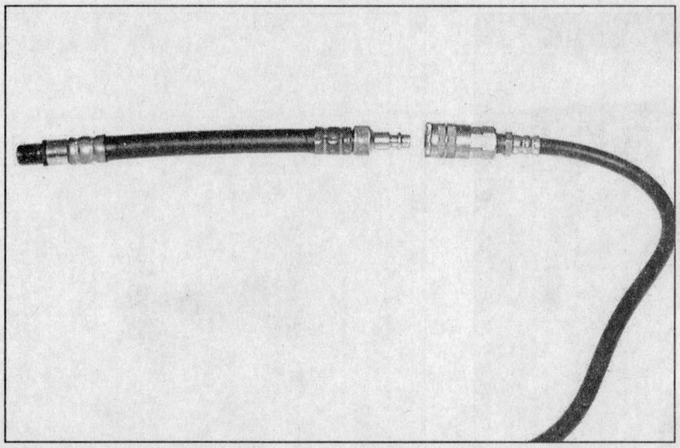

6.5 You'll need an air hose adapter this long to reach down into the spark plug tubes - they're commonly available from auto parts stores

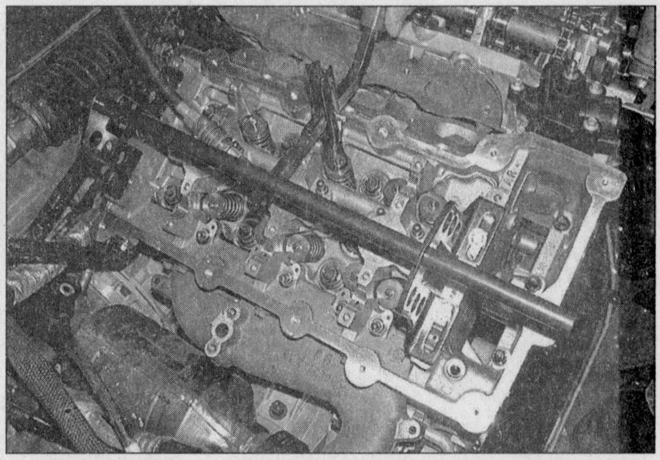

6.7a Compress the valve spring enough to release the valve stem locks . . .

rollers turn freely and show no signs of wear, also check the pivot area for wear, cracks and galling **(see illustration)**.

9 Inspect the lash adjuster contact surfaces wear or damage. Make sure the lash adjusters move up and down freely in their bores on the cylinder head without excessive side to side play.

10 Installation is the reverse of removal with the following exceptions: Always install the lash adjuster first and make sure they're at least partially full of oil before installation. This is indicated by little or no lash adjuster plunger travel.

6 Valve springs, retainers and seals - replacement

Refer to illustrations 6.5, 6.7a, 6.7b, 6.8, 6.13 and 6.15

Note: *Broken valve springs and defective valve stem seals can be replaced without removing the cylinder heads. Two special tools and a compressed air source are normally required to perform this operation, so read through this Section carefully. The universal shaft-type valve spring compressor required for the tight valve spring pockets of this vehicle may not be available at all tool rental yards, so check on the availability before beginning the job.*

1 Remove the upper intake manifold (see Section 9) and the valve cover(s) (see Section 4).

2 Refer to Section 7 and remove the primary timing chain, then remove the camshafts (see Section 8) and the rocker arms from the affected cylinder head.

3 Remove the spark plug from the cylinder that has the defective component. If all of the valve stem seals are being replaced, all of the spark plugs should be removed.

4 Turn the crankshaft until the piston in the affected cylinder is at Top Dead Center on the compression stroke (refer to Section 3). If you're replacing all of the valve stem seals, begin with cylinder number one and work on the valves for one cylinder at a time. Move from cylinder-to-cylinder following the firing order sequence (see this Chapter's Specifications).

6.7b . . . and lift them out with a magnet or needle-nose pliers

5 Thread a long adapter into the spark plug hole and connect an air hose from a compressed air source to it **(see illustration)**. Most auto parts stores can supply the air hose adapter. **Note:** *Because of the length of the spark plug tubes, it will be necessary to use a long spark plug adapter with a length of hose attached (as used on many cylinder compression gauges) utilizing a quick-disconnect fitting to hook to your air source.*

6 Apply 90 to 100 psi of compressed air to the cylinder. **Warning:** *The piston may be forced down by the compressed air, causing the crankshaft to turn suddenly. If the wrench used when positioning the number one piston at TDC is still attached to the bolt in the crankshaft nose, it could cause damage or injury when the crankshaft moves.*

7 Stuff shop rags into the cylinder head holes around the valves to prevent parts and tools from falling into the engine, then use a valve spring compressor to compress the spring. Remove the valve stem locks with small needle-nose pliers or a magnet **(see illustrations)**. **Note:** *The valves should be held in place by the air pressure. If the valve faces or seats are in poor condition, leaks may prevent air pressure from retaining the valves. If the valves cannot hold air, the cylinder head should be removed for a valve job at a machine shop.*

6.8 A pair of pliers will be required to remove the valve seal from the valve guide

8 Remove the spring retainer and valve spring, then remove the valve stem seal **(see illustration)**.

9 Wrap a rubber band or tape around the top of the valve stem so the valve won't fall into the combustion chamber, then release the air pressure.

10 Inspect the valve stem for damage. Rotate the valve in the guide and check the end for eccentric movement, which would indicate that the valve is bent.

11 Move the valve up-and-down in the guide and make sure it doesn't bind. If the valve stem binds, either the valve is bent or the guide is damaged. In either case, the head will have to be removed for repair.

12 Reapply air pressure to the cylinder to retain the valve in the closed position, then remove the tape or rubber band from the valve stem.

13 Lubricate the valve stems with engine oil and install the valve spring seat/valve seal assembly over the top of the valves stems. Using the stem of the valves as a guide, slide the seals down to the top of each valve guide. Using a hammer and a deep socket or seal installation tool, gently tap each seal into place until it's completely seated on the guide **(see illustration)**. Don't twist or cock the seals during installation or they won't seal properly on the valve stems. Make sure the garter spring is still in place around the top of the seal.

14 Install the spring and retainer in position over the valve. Compress the valve spring assembly only enough to install the keepers in the valve stem.

15 Position the keepers in the valve stem groove. Apply a small dab of grease to the inside of each keeper to hold it in place if necessary **(see illustration)**. Remove the pressure from the spring tool and make sure the keepers are seated.

16 Disconnect the air hose and remove the adapter from the spark plug hole.

17 Repeat the above procedure on the remaining cylinders, following the firing order sequence (see the Specifications). Bring each piston to top dead center on the compression stroke before applying air pressure.

18 Install the rocker arms. Refer to Section 8 and install the camshafts then refer to Section 7 and install the primary timing chain.

19 Refer to Section 4 and install the valve covers.

20 Install the spark plug(s), ignition coils and the upper intake manifold referring to the appropriate sections as necessary.

21 Start and run the engine, then check for oil leaks and unusual sounds coming from the valve cover area.

7 Timing chain and sprockets - removal, inspection and installation

Note 1: *Special tools are necessary to complete this procedure. Read through the entire procedure and obtain the special tools before beginning work.*

Note 2: *Because of work necessary to get at the timing chain and replace it, and because the water pump is in this area, it is recommended that the water pump be thoroughly inspected and replaced if necessary during this procedure* (see Chapter 3).

Note 3: *The 2.7L engine utilizes three timing chains to produce proper valve timing. The primary timing chain runs around the crankshaft sprocket, the water pump and around two intake camshaft sprockets. This chain synchronizes the valve timing with the crankshaft and pistons, while two secondary timing chains run around separate intake and exhaust camshaft sprockets to synchronize the intake and exhaust camshaft events. Refer to Step 19 for primary timing chain inspection procedures prior to timing chain removal.*

6.13 Using a deep socket and hammer, gently tap the new seals onto the valve guide only until seated

6.15 Apply a small dab of grease to each valve stem lock as shown here before installation - it will hold them in place on the valve stem as the spring is released

Removal

Refer to illustrations 7.10, 7.11, 7. 12a, 7.12b, 7.12c, 7.13a, 7.13b, 7.14a, 7.14b, 7.16a, 7.16b and 7.19

1 Disconnect the negative battery cable from the remote ground terminal (see Chapter 5).

2 Relieve the fuel system pressure (see Chapter 4) and drain the cooling system (see Chapter 1).

3 Refer to Chapter 3 and remove the upper radiator crossmember, the cooling fan assembly and the radiator.

4 Remove the accessory drivebelts (see Chapter 1).

5 Remove the crankshaft pulley (see Section 12).

6 Remove the upper intake plenum (see Section 9) and the valve covers (see Section 4).

7 Remove the spark plugs (see Chapter 1).

8 Unbolt the power steering pump and set it aside without disconnecting the fluid lines (see Chapter 10).

9 Remove the camshaft position sensor from the left cylinder head (see Chapter 6).

10 Remove the idler pulley bracket **(see illustration)**.

7.10 Idler pulley retaining bolts (arrows) - power steering pump pulley removed for clarity

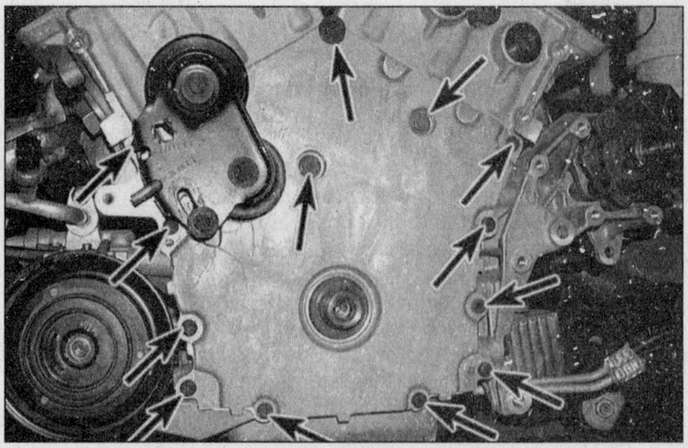

7.11 Timing cover retaining bolts (arrows)

7.12a Make sure the mark on the crankshaft sprocket (A) aligns with the colored link on the primary timing chain and the mark on the oil pump housing (B)

7.12b Also verify that the marks on the left camshaft sprocket . . .

7.12c . . . and the marks on the right camshaft sprocket align with the colored links on the primary chain

7.13a Use a wrench to loosen the primary timing chain tensioner from the right cylinder head (1999 and earlier models shown)

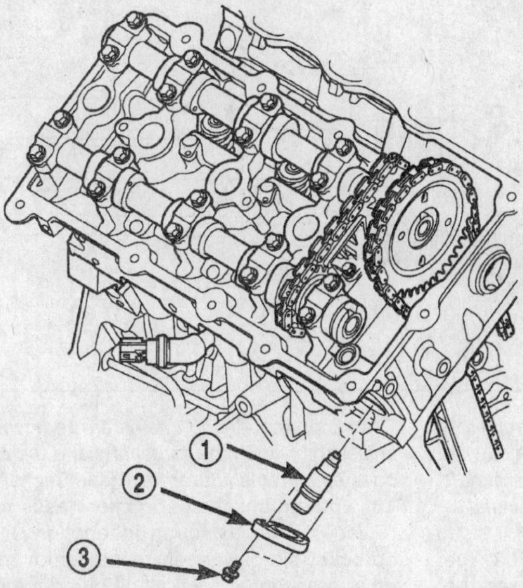

7.13b Primary timing chain tensioner mounting details (2000 and later models)

1 *Tensioner*
2 *Retaining plate*
3 *Bolt*

11 Remove the timing chain cover **(see illustration)**. Note that various types and sizes of bolts are used. They must be reinstalled in their original locations. Mark each bolt or make a sketch to help remember where they go.

12 Rotate the engine until the crankshaft sprocket timing mark is aligned with the mark on the oil pump housing and the colored links on the chain are aligned with the timing marks on the camshaft sprockets and the crankshaft sprocket **(see illustrations)**.

13 Remove the primary timing chain tensioner from the right cylinder head **(see illustrations)**.

14 Remove the retaining bolts from the primary camshaft sprockets **(see illustrations)**. **Warning:** *Pressure from the valve springs will make the camshafts rotate clockwise as the bolts are removed. Do not rotate the crankshaft or camshaft separately after the primary timing chain is loosened or removed as piston or valve damage may occur. The*

7.14a A 3/8 drive extension and ratchet inserted into the end of the camshaft hub is used as leverage while the sprocket bolts are loosened - make note of the vibration damper to camshaft sprocket alignment hole (arrow)

7.14b Left camshaft sprocket retaining bolts (arrows)

7.16a Primary timing chain guide access plugs (arrows)

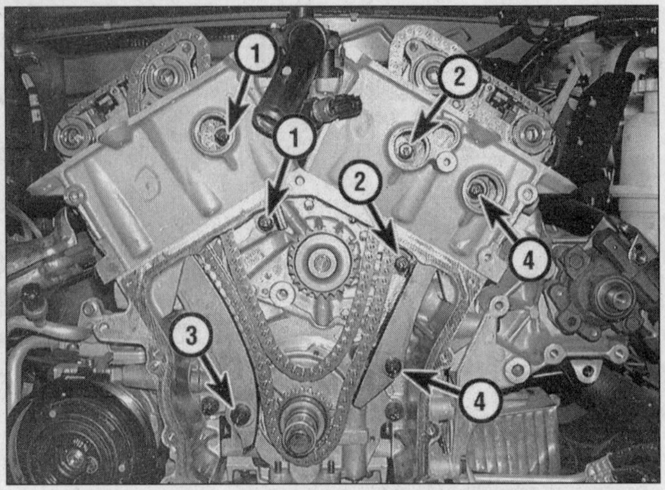

7.16b Primary timing chain guide mounting details

1 Upper right timing chain guide mounting bolts
2 Upper left timing chain guide mounting bolts
3 Tensioner arm pivot bolt
4 Lower timing chain guide mounting bolts

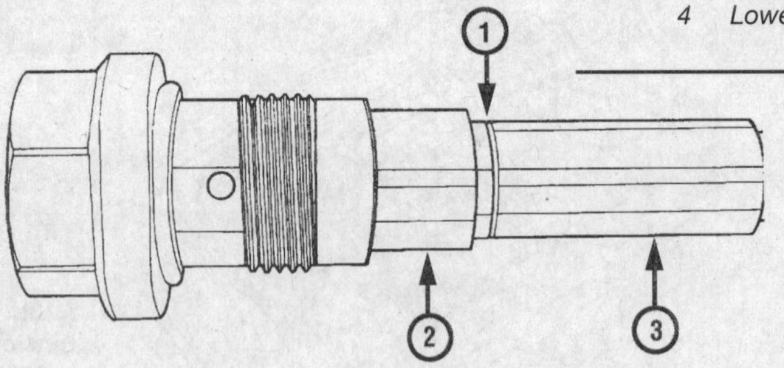

7.19 Primary timing chain tensioner

1 Maximum wear indicator groove
2 Tensioner housing (1999 and earlier models)
3 Tensioner

only exception to this rule is when the camshafts must be rotated counterclockwise slightly, to realign the primary camshaft sprockets with the camshafts during installation.

15 Pull the primary sprockets off the camshaft hubs one at a time, lower the sprocket(s) into the cylinder head opening until the chain can be displaced from around the sprocket, then remove the primary camshaft sprockets from the engine. Note that the left (primary) camshaft sprocket is identified by the camshaft position sensor ring which is mounted on the front of the sprocket by two nuts. It is not necessary to remove the sensor ring from the sprocket during this procedure unless damage to the sensor ring or sprocket has occurred. Also note that the right (primary) camshaft sprocket is identified by a vibration damper which is mounted in front of the sprocket. Make note of the alignment holes on the damper and the right (primary) sprocket as these two components will separate as the sprocket is removed from the camshaft. Always install the damper in the same position from which it was removed.

16 Remove the access plugs from the front of the cylinder heads and detach the primary timing chain guides and tensioner arm **(see illustrations)**.

17 Remove the primary timing chain. **Note:** *The secondary timing chains are removed as an assembly with the camshafts and therefore covered in camshaft removal* (see Section 8).

18 If the crankshaft sprocket needs to be replaced after thorough inspection or the sprocket simply needs to be removed for other procedures such as oil pump removal, proceed to Step 36.

Inspection

19 Inspect the camshaft, water pump and crankshaft sprockets for wear on the teeth and keyways. Inspect the chains for cracks or excessive wear of the rollers. Inspect the facing of the chain guides and tensioner arm for excessive wear. If any of the components show signs of excessive wear they must be replaced. **Note:** *Timing chain stretch can also be checked without major disassembly of the engine by removing the right valve cover and inspecting the maximum extension of the primary chain tensioner through the cylinder head opening* **(see illustration)***. If the maximum wear indicator groove on the tensioner is visible the timing drive system is worn beyond it limits and should be replaced.*

Installation

Refer to illustrations 7.26, 7.27 and 7.32

20 If removed, install the crankshaft sprocket as outlined in Step 38 and 39.

21 If you purchased a new timing chain verify that you have the correct timing chain for your vehicle by counting the number of links the chain has and comparing the new chain with the old chain. Also compare the position of the colored links in the new chain with the position of the colored links in the old chain.

22 Verify the crankshaft sprocket is still aligned with the mark on the oil pump housing **(see illustration 7.12a)** and install the upper chain guides back into position on the engine **(see illustration 7.16b)**.

23 Prepare to install the primary timing chain by aligning the left (primary) camshaft sprocket mark between the light colored links on the chain. Then lower the sprocket and chain assembly down through the opening in the left cylinder head and reposition the left camshaft sprocket over the camshaft hub.

24 Install the right (primary) camshaft sprocket, vibration damper and timing chain onto the engine by looping the chain around the crankshaft sprocket and aligning the light colored chain link with the mark on the crankshaft sprocket. Then place the chain around the water pump sprocket and install the right (primary) camshaft sprocket over the right camshaft hub making sure the colored links align with there respective marks on the sprockets **(see illustrations 7.12a, 7.12b and 7.12c)**.

25 Install the lower chain guide and tensioner arm **(see illustration 7.16b)**.

26 Separate the timing chain tensioner from the tensioner housing on 1999 and earlier models **(see illustration 7.19)**. On all models use the special tool to purge the oil from the tensioner. Place the check ball end of the tensioner into the shallow end of the tool over the pin, apply hand pressure and slowly depress the tensioner until the oil has purged itself from the tensioner **(see illustration)**.

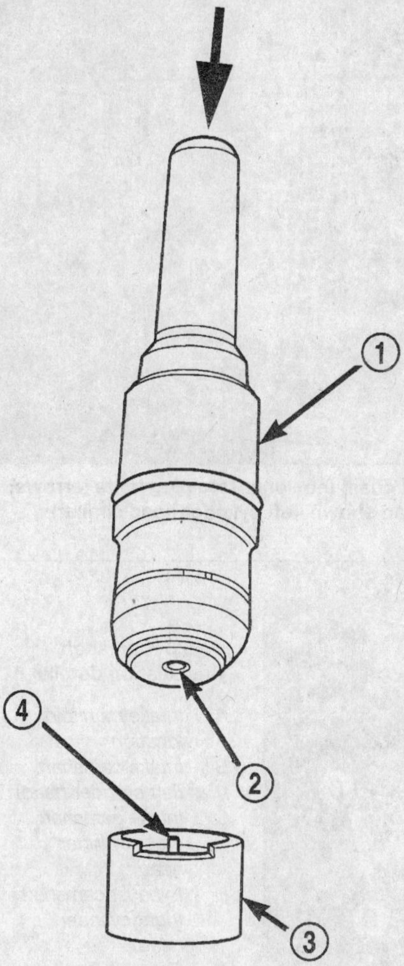

7.26 Primary timing chain tensioner - oil purging details

1. *Tensioner body*
2. *Check ball*
3. *Special tool*
4. *Pin*

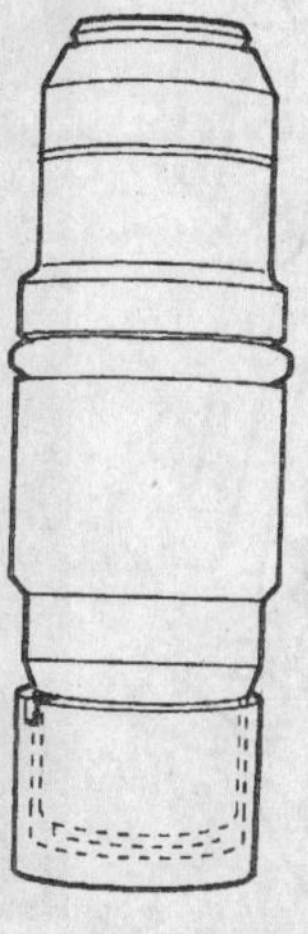

7.27 After the oil has been purged, the tensioner must be reset by inserting the tensioner plunger into the opposite (deep) end of the tool and depressing the plunger until the plunger locks into place and resets itself

27 After the oil has been purged, the tensioner must be reset before installation. Place the tensioner plunger into the deep end of the tool and depress the plunger until it locks into place and resets itself. Once the tensioner is reset it will be about 1-1/2 inches shorter **(see illustration)**.

28 Install the reset tensioner into the engine and tighten the tensioner housing (1999 and earlier models) or the tensioner retaining plate bolts (2000 and later models) to the torque listed in this Chapters Specifications. Always use a new O-ring or gasket on the tensioner housing or tensioner retaining plate.

29 Install the camshaft sprocket retaining bolts by inserting a 3/8-inch drive extension and ratchet into the primary camshaft hub and slightly rotating the camshafts counterclockwise until the camshaft sprocket bolt holes align with the camshaft hub bolt holes. Perform the procedure on the right (primary) camshaft sprocket first then proceed to the left (primary) camshaft sprocket.

30 Leaving the 3/8-inch extension and ratchet inserted into the camshaft hub as leverage tighten the camshaft sprocket bolts to torque listed in this Chapter's Specifications.

31 Rotate the engine clockwise just enough remove any slack from the left side of the timing chain.

32 Reconfirm that the timing marks on the camshaft and crankshaft sprockets are aligned with the colored links on the chain and release the primary timing chain tensioner from its reset position **(see illustration)**.

33 Remove all traces of old sealant from the timing chain cover and the cover bolts.

34 Apply a bead of RTV sealant to the timing cover gasket and sealing surfaces. Place the timing cover in position on the engine and install the bolts in their original locations and tighten the bolts to the torque listed in this Chapter's Specifications.

35 The remainder of the installation is the reverse of removal.

Crankshaft sprocket

Refer to illustrations 7.37 and 7.39

36 If the crankshaft sprocket is to be removed and installed it will require the use of several special tools, a three jaw puller, a propane torch or crankshaft sprocket installation tool and a machinist ruler or dial caliper.

37 After the primary timing chain has been removed the crankshaft sprocket can be removed with a three jaw puller **(see illustration)**.

38 To install the crankshaft sprocket it will be necessary to purchase a sprocket installation tool or a common household propane torch. If a sprocket installation tool is purchased follow the installation procedures out-

7.32 With all slack removed from the left side of the chain and the colored links on the chain aligned with their respective marks on the sprockets, engage the tensioner by pushing the tensioner arm inward slightly, then release the tensioner arm to extend the tensioner

7.37 The crankshaft sprocket can be removed with a conventional three jaw puller

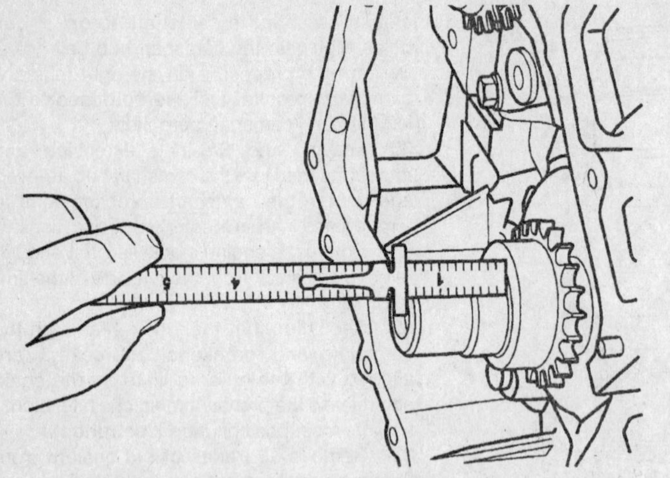

7.39 Install the crankshaft sprocket 1.537 inches from the end of the crankshaft snout

8.4 Secondary timing chain tensioner retaining bolts (arrows) (right cylinder head shown, left cylinder head similar)

8.5 Verify that the camshaft bearing caps are marked to ensure correct reinstallation

lined in the tools instructions and install the sprocket to the proper depth (see Step 39). If a propane torch is chosen simply place the sprocket in a vise and heat the sprocket hub for several minutes until the sprocket has expanded enough to slide over the crankshaft. **Caution:** *After heating the sprocket always handle the sprocket with a pair of pliers or other insulated tool to avoid serious injury and never heat an object when gasoline or other volatile chemicals are present.*

39 Using a machinist ruler or dial caliper install the sprocket on the crankshaft to the proper depth (1.537 inches plus-or-minus 0.020 inch) by measuring from the end of the crankshaft to the face of the crankshaft sprocket **(see illustration)**.

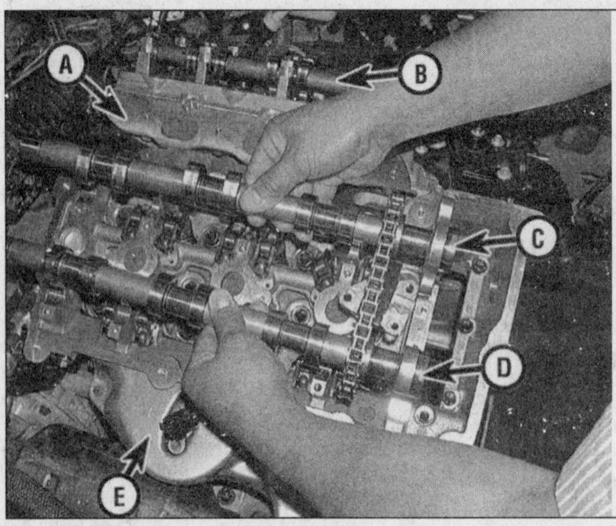

8.6 Camshaft installation details

A Intake manifold location
B Intake camshaft (left cylinder head)
C Intake camshaft (right cylinder head)
D Exhaust camshaft (right cylinder head)
E Exhaust manifold

8 Camshafts - removal and installation

Note: *The camshafts should always be thoroughly inspected before installation and camshaft endplay should always be checked prior to camshaft removal. Refer to Chapter 2C for the camshaft and lifter inspection procedures.*

Removal

Refer to illustrations 8.4, 8.5 and 8.6

1 Detach the negative battery cable from the remote ground terminal.

2 Remove the valve covers (see Section 4).

3 Remove the primary timing chain and the primary camshaft sprockets (see Section 7).

4 Remove the retaining bolts from the secondary timing chain tensioner **(see illustration)**.

5 Verify the markings on the camshaft bearing caps. the caps should be marked from 1 to 5, and with an "I" or an "E", to indicate intake or exhaust. Also verify that there are arrow marks on the caps indicating the front of the engine **(see illustration)**. Loosen the camshaft bearing caps in two or three steps, in the reverse order of the tightening sequence **(see illustration 8.15)**. **Caution:** *Keep the caps in order. They must go back in the same location they were removed from.*

6 Detach the bearing caps, then remove the camshafts, secondary timing chain and the secondary tensioner as an assembly from the cylinder head. Make a note that the intake camshafts have a flanged hub at the front and the exhaust camshafts do not. Also note that the intake camshafts are installed in the cylinder head (towards the center of the engine) next the intake manifold and the exhaust camshafts are installed (towards the sides of the engine) next the exhaust manifolds **(see illustration)**.

7 Remove the secondary tensioner and the timing chain from the camshafts.

8 Inspect the camshafts as described in Chapter 2C. Also inspect the camshaft secondary sprockets for wear on the teeth.

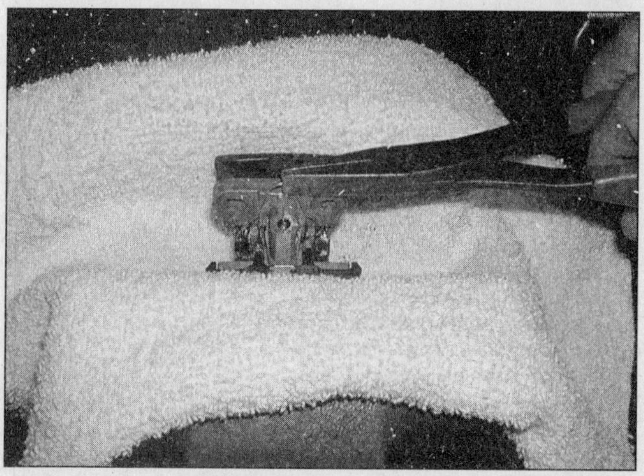

8.10a Compress the secondary tensioner in a vise until a fabricated paperclip can be inserted into the secondary tensioner locking holes

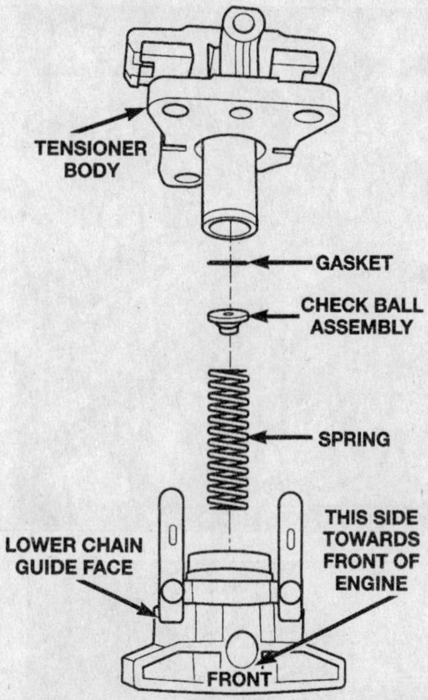

8.10b Two piece secondary tensioner - exploded view

Inspect the chains for cracks or excessive wear of the rollers. Inspect the facing of the secondary chain tensioners for excessive wear. If any of the components show signs of excessive wear they must be replaced.

Installation

Refer to illustrations 8.10a, 8.10b, 8.13 and 8.15

9 Install the secondary timing chain(s) over the camshaft sprockets while aligning the colored links on the chain with the marks on the secondary camshaft sprockets in a 12 o'clock position. **Note:** *The colored links on the chain must face outward toward the front of the engine.*

10 Using a paperclip, fabricate a U-shaped tool to use as a tensioner locking pin. Then place the secondary tensioner in a vise and compress the tensioner until the U-shaped tool can be inserted into the locking holes on the tensioner. This places the tensioner in the locked position so it can be reinstalled **(see illustration). Note:** *Some tensioners have a two piece design. On these models it will be necessary separate the tensioner halves first and drain the oil from the tensioner housing before compressing the tensioner in a vise and inserting the locking pin. Be careful not remove any of the internal tensioner components when the halves are separated* **(see illustration)**.

11 Once the tensioner is locked into place it can be installed back into the place between the camshafts and the secondary timing chain.

12 Apply moly-based engine assembly lubricant to the camshaft lobes and journals. Make sure the rocker arms are properly seated on their respective lash adjuster and the valve stem tip.

13 Install the camshafts, secondary tensioner and the timing chain as an assembly in their original position with the marks on the sprockets and the colored links on the chain facing up (90 degrees from the valve cover mating surface) and inline with the cylinder bank **(see illustration). Note:** *When installed correctly there should be 12 timing chain pins between the intake and exhaust camshaft marks.*

14 Install the bearing caps and bolts and tighten them hand tight.

15 Tighten the bearing cap bolts in several steps, to the torque listed in this Chapter's Specifications, using the proper tightening sequence **(see illustration)**.

16 Tighten the tensioner mounting bolts to the torque listed in this Chapter's Specifica-

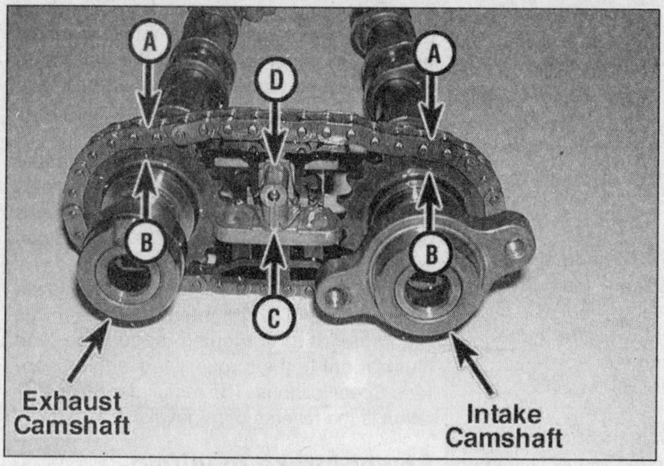

8.13 Camshaft installation details

A Secondary timing chain colored links
B Secondary camshaft sprocket marks
C Tensioner locking pin
D Secondary timing chain tensioner

8.15 Camshaft bearing cap TIGHTENING sequence

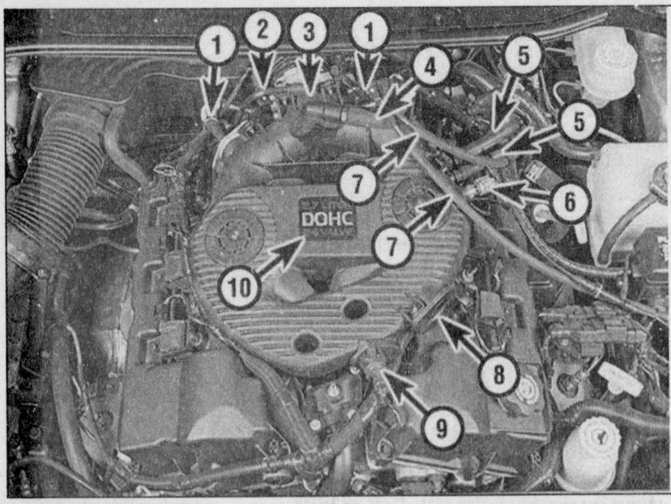

9.4 Label and disconnect the following components required for upper intake manifold removal

1. *EGR tubes*
2. *Throttle Position Sensor/Idle Air Control valve connectors*
3. *Vacuum hose (if equipped)*
4. *PCV valve hose*
5. *Vacuum hoses*
6. *Intake Air Temperature sensor*
7. *Accelerator and cruise control cables*
8. *Manifold Tuning Valve (if equipped)*
9. *Manifold Absolute Pressure sensor*
10. *Name badge*

9.5a Remove the upper intake manifold support bracket bolt (arrow) at the rear of the manifold . . .

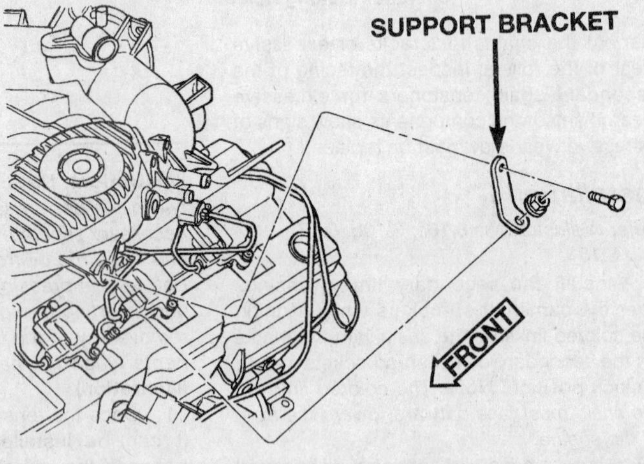

9.5b . . . and the left and right side support brackets (if equipped)

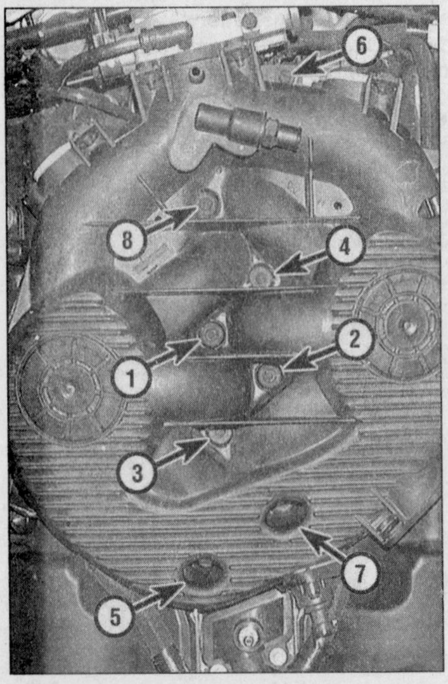

9.8 Upper plenum TIGHTENING sequence

tions and remove the tensioner locking pin.

17 Install the primary timing chain and camshaft sprockets (see Section 7).

18 The remainder of installation is the reverse of removal.

9 Intake manifold - removal and installation

Upper intake manifold (plenum)

Refer to illustrations 9.4, 9.5a, 9.5b and 9.8

1 Relieve the fuel pressure (see Chapter 4).

2 Disconnect the negative battery cable from the remote ground terminal.

3 Remove the air intake duct (see Chapter 4).

4 Label and disconnect the hoses and electrical connectors attached to the plenum and throttle body **(see illustration)**. Remove the throttle cable, throttle cable bracket and the cruise control cable from the throttle body (see Chapter 4).

5 Remove the EGR tubes **(see illustration 9.4)**. Remove the upper manifold support bracket from the rear of the upper plenum and the left and right support brackets (if equipped) **(see illustrations)**.

6 Detach the name badge from the top of plenum and loosen the upper intake manifold bolts in the reverse order of the tightening sequence **(see illustration 9.8)** and remove the upper plenum with the throttle body attached.

7 Clean and inspect the upper intake manifold to lower intake manifold sealing surfaces. Inspect the gaskets for tears or cracks replacing them if necessary. The gaskets can be reused if not damaged.

8 Install the upper plenum onto the lower intake manifold and tighten the bolts in the recommended tightening sequence **(see illustration)** to the torque listed in this Chapter's Specifications. The remainder the installation is the reverse of removal.

Lower intake manifold

Refer to illustration 9.16

9 Remove the upper intake manifold (see Steps 1 through 6).

10 Label and detach any remaining hoses which would interfere with the removal of the

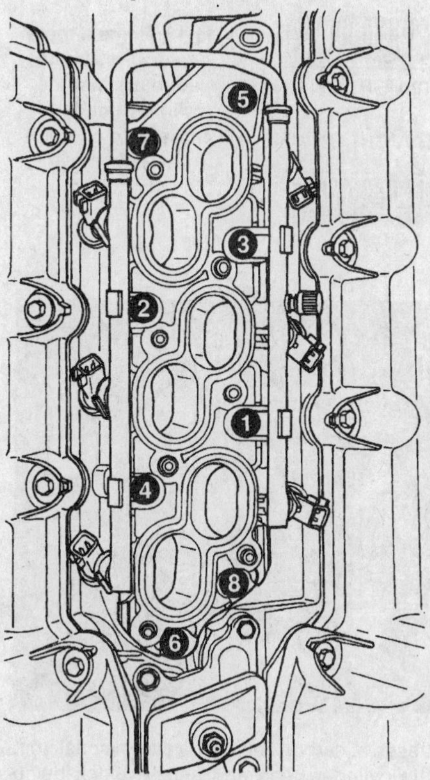

9.16 Lower intake manifold TIGHTENING sequence

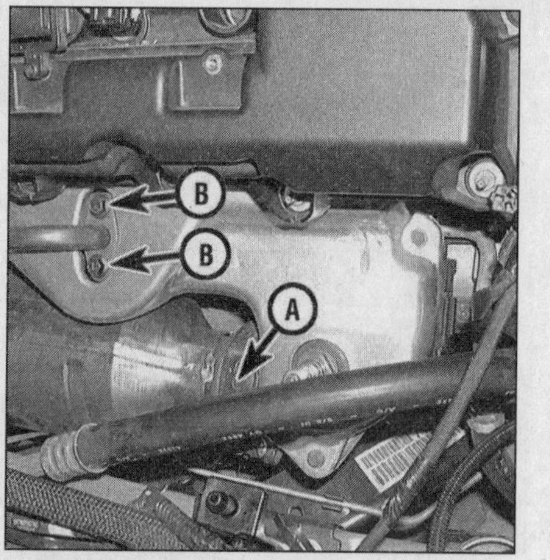

10.2 Remove the exhaust manifold to catalytic converter V-band clamp (A) - If removing the right manifold, detach the EGR tube bolts (B)

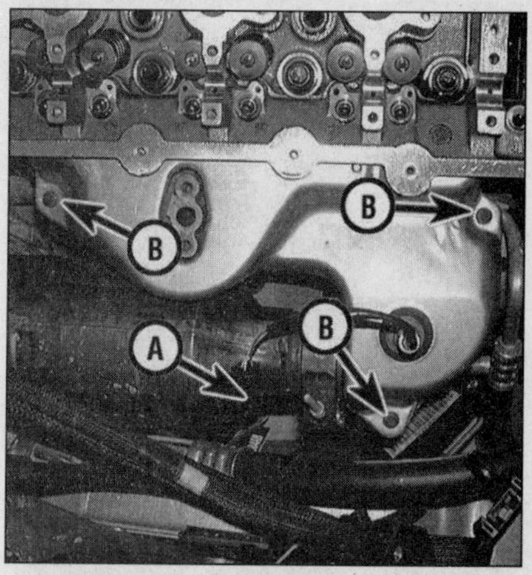

10.5 Detach the oxygen sensor electrical connector (A) and the exhaust manifold heat shield mounting bolts (B) - right exhaust manifold shown, left exhaust manifold similar

10.6 Exhaust manifold retaining bolts (arrows) (upper bolts shown, lower three bolts not visible in the photo)

lower intake manifold.

11 Loosen the manifold mounting bolts/nuts in 1/4-turn increments until they can be removed by hand In the reverse order of the tightening sequence **(see illustration 9.16)**.

12 Remove the fuel rail and injectors from the lower intake manifold (see Chapter 4).

13 The manifold will probably be stuck to the cylinder heads and force may be required to break the gasket seal. **Caution:** *Don't pry between the manifold and the heads or damage to the gasket sealing surfaces may occur, leading to vacuum leaks.*

14 Clean and inspect the lower intake manifold to cylinder head sealing surfaces. Inspect the gaskets for tears or cracks replacing them if necessary. The gaskets can be reused if not damaged.

15 Position the lower manifold on the engine making sure the gaskets and manifold are aligned correctly over the cylinder heads. Install the fuel rail and injectors onto the cylinder heads and the lower manifold. Install the fuel rail retaining bolts into the manifold loosely to ensure correct gasket/manifold alignment, then install the remaining lower intake manifold bolts.

16 Following the recommended tightening sequence, tighten the bolts, in several steps, to the torque listed in this Chapter's Specifications **(see illustration)**.

17 The remainder of the installation is the reverse of the removal procedure. Run the engine and check for fuel, vacuum and coolant leaks.

10 Exhaust manifold - removal and installation

Warning: *The engine must be completely cool before beginning this procedure.*

Removal

Refer to illustrations 10.2, 10.5 and 10.6

1 Disconnect the negative battery cable from the remote ground terminal.

2 Working in the engine compartment unbolt the catalytic converter pipes where they join the manifolds. If removing the right exhaust manifold detach the EGR tube from the top of the manifold **(see illustration)**. If removing the left manifold detach the engine wiring harness support bracket from the left cylinder head and remove the oil dipstick tube.

3 Block the rear wheels, set the parking brake, raise the front of the vehicle and support it securely on jackstands. Remove the catalytic converter/front exhaust pipes from below the vehicle (see Chapter 4). If removing the left exhaust manifold detach the transaxle dipstick tube retaining bolt and rotate the tube away from the engine while working below the vehicle.

4 Working in the engine compartment again, disconnect the oxygen sensor's electrical connector.

5 Remove the exhaust manifold upper heat shield mounting bolts **(see illustration)** and lift the heat shields from the engine.

6 Remove the mounting bolts and detach the manifold from the cylinder head **(see illustration)**. Be sure to spray penetrating lubricant onto the bolts and threads before attempting to remove them.

Installation

7 Clean the mating surfaces to remove all traces of old gasket material, then inspect the manifold for distortion and cracks. Warpage can be checked with a precision straightedge held against the mating flange. If a feeler gauge thicker than 0.030-inch can be

11.5 Remove the water outlet housing by detaching the heater supply tube retaining bolts (A), then slide the heater supply tube out of the water outlet housing and remove the water outlet housing retaining bolts (B)

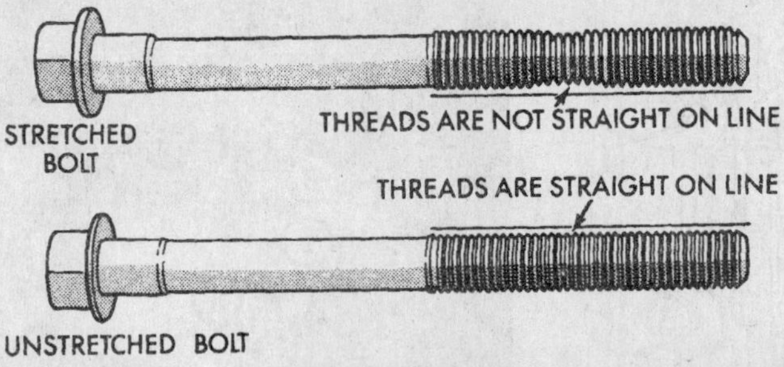

11.13 Place a metal ruler or straight edge against the cylinder head bolt threads to check if the bolts have stretched

11.19 Cylinder head TIGHTENING sequence

inserted between the straightedge and flange surface, take the manifold to an automotive machine shop for resurfacing.

8 Place the exhaust manifold in position with a new gasket (and the lower heat shields) and install the mounting bolts finger tight. **Note:** *Be sure to identify the exhaust manifold gaskets by the correct cylinder designation and the position of the exhaust ports on the gasket.*

9 Starting in the middle and working out toward the ends, tighten the mounting bolts in several increments, to the torque listed in this Chapter's Specifications.

10 Install the remaining components in the reverse order of removal. **Note:** *The manufacturer recommends replacing the exhaust V-band clamps every time the bands are removed.*

11 Start the engine and check for exhaust leaks between the manifold and cylinder head and between the manifold and exhaust pipe.

11 Cylinder head - removal and installation

Caution: *The engine must be completely cool before beginning this procedure.*

Removal

Refer to illustration 11.5

1 Refer to Section 7 Steps 1 through 17 and remove the primary timing chain and sprockets. **Caution :** *Be careful not to disturb the crankshaft from its alignment marks during the remainder of this procedure.*

2 Remove the camshafts from the cylinder head (see Section 8).

3 Remove the rocker arms and hydraulic lash adjusters from the cylinder head. Before the rocker arms and lash adjusters are removed, arrange to label and store them, so they can be kept separate and reinstalled on the same valve from which they were removed.

4 Remove the lower intake manifold (see Section 9). and the exhaust manifold V-band clamps (see Section 10).

5 Label and remove any remaining items attached to the cylinder head, such as coolant fittings, ground straps, cables, hoses, wires or brackets **(see illustration)**.

6 Using a breaker bar and the appropriate sized socket, loosen the cylinder head bolts in 1/4-turn increments until they can be removed by hand. Loosen the bolts in the reverse order of the tightening sequence **(see illustration 11.19)** to avoid warping or cracking the head.

7 Lift the cylinder head off the engine block with the exhaust manifold attached. If it's stuck, very carefully pry up at the transaxle end, beyond the gasket surface, at a casting protrusion.

8 Remove all external components from the head to allow for thorough cleaning and inspection. **Note:** *See Chapter 2, Part C, for cylinder head inspection and servicing procedures.*

Installation

Refer to illustrations 11.13 and 11.19

9 The mating surfaces of the cylinder head and block must be perfectly clean when the head is installed.

10 Use a gasket scraper to remove all traces of carbon and old gasket material from the cylinder head and engine block being careful not to gouge the aluminum, then clean the mating surfaces with lacquer thinner or acetone. If there's oil on the mating surfaces when the head is installed, the gasket may not seal correctly and leaks could develop. When working on the block, stuff the cylinders with clean shop rags to keep out debris. Use a vacuum cleaner to remove material that falls into the cylinders.

11 Check the block and head mating surfaces for nicks, deep scratches and other damage. If damage is slight, it can be removed with a file; if it's excessive, machining may be the only alternative.

12 Use a tap of the correct size to chase the threads in the head bolt holes, then clean the holes with compressed air - make sure that nothing remains in the holes. **Warning:** *Wear eye protection when using compressed air!*

13 Measure each cylinder head bolt for stretching **(see illustration)**. If the diameter of the bolt threads has necked down any where in the threaded area the bolts have exceeded the maximum amount of stretch and will need to be replaced.

14 Check the cylinder head for warpage (see Chapter 2C). Check the head gasket, intake and exhaust manifold surfaces.

15 Install the components that were removed from the head.

16 Position the new cylinder head gasket over the dowel pins on the block noting which direction on the gasket faces up.

17 Carefully set the head over the dowels on the block without disturbing the gasket.

18 Before installing the head bolts, apply a small amount of clean engine oil to the

12.4 Use strap wrench to hold the crankshaft pulley while removing the center bolt (a chain-type wrench may be used if you wrap a section of old drivebelt or rag around the crankshaft pulley first)

12.5 The use of a three jaw puller will be necessary to remove the crankshaft pulley - always place the puller jaws around the pulley hub, not the outer ring

12.6 If the sealing surface of the pulley hub has a wear groove from contact with the seal, repair sleeves are available at most auto parts stores

threads and hardened washers (if equipped). The chamfered side of the washers must face the bolt heads.

19 Install the bolts in their original locations and tighten them finger tight. Then tighten all the bolts in several steps, following the proper sequence **(see illustration)**, to the torque listed in this Chapter's Specifications.

20 Install the lash adjusters and the rocker arms in the cylinder head, then install the camshafts as described in Section 8,

21 Install the primary timing chain and sprockets as described in Section 7. The remaining installation steps are the reverse of removal.

22 Refill the cooling system, and check the engine oil adding if necessary (see Chapter 1).

23 Start the engine and check for oil and coolant leaks.

12 Crankshaft pulley - removal and installation

Refer to illustrations 12.4, 12.5 and 12.6

1 Disconnect the negative battery cable from the remote ground terminal.

2 Refer to Chapter 3 and remove the upper radiator crossmember, the cooling fan assembly and the radiator.

3 Remove the drivebelts (see Chapter 1) and position the belt tensioner away from the crankshaft pulley.

4 Use a strap wrench around the crankshaft pulley to hold it while using a breaker bar and socket to remove the crankshaft pulley center bolt **(see illustration)**.

5 Pull the damper off the crankshaft with a puller **(see illustration)**. **Caution:** *The jaws of the puller must only contact the hub of the pulley - not the outer ring.* **Note:** *A long Allen-head bolt should be inserted into the crankshaft nose for the puller's tapered tip to push against to prevent damage to the crankshaft threads.*

6 Check the surface on the pulley hub that the oil seal rides on. if the surface has been grooved from long time contact with the seal, a press on sleeve may be available to renew the sealing surface **(see illustration)**. This sleeve is pressed into place with a hammer and a block of wood and is commonly available at auto parts for various applications.

7 Lubricate the pulley hub with clean engine oil and reinstall the crankshaft pulley. Use a vibration damper installation tool to press the pulley onto the crankshaft.

8 Install the crankshaft pulley retaining bolt and tighten it to the torque listed in this Chapter's Specifications.

9 The remainder of installation is the reverse of the removal.

13 Crankshaft front oil seal - replacement

Refer to illustrations 13.2 and 13.4

1 Remove the crankshaft pulley from the engine (see Section 12).

2 Carefully pry the seal out of the cover with a seal removal tool or a large screwdriver **(see illustration)**. **Caution:** *Be careful not to scratch, gouge or distort the area that the seal fits into or an oil leak will develop.*

3 Clean the bore to remove any old seal material and corrosion. Position the new seal in the bore with the seal lip (usually the side with the spring) facing IN (toward the engine). A small amount of oil applied to the outer edge of the new seal will make installation easier - but don't overdo it!

4 Drive the seal into the bore with a large socket and hammer until it's completely seated **(see illustration)**. Select a socket that's the same outside diameter as the seal and make sure the new seal is pressed into place until it bottoms against the cover flange.

5 Lubricate the seal lips with engine oil and reinstall the crankshaft pulley.

6 The remainder of installation is the reverse of the removal. Run the engine and check for oil leaks.

13.2 Pry the seal out very carefully with a seal removal tool or screwdriver, being careful not to nick or gouge the seal bore or the crankshaft

13.4 Use a seal driver or large-diameter pipe to drive the new seal into the cover

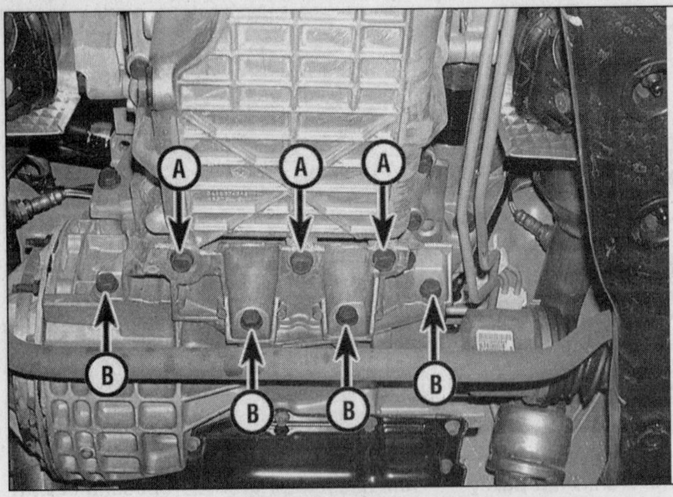

14.5 Transaxle-to-oil pan support brace

A Vertical bolts
B Horizontal bolts

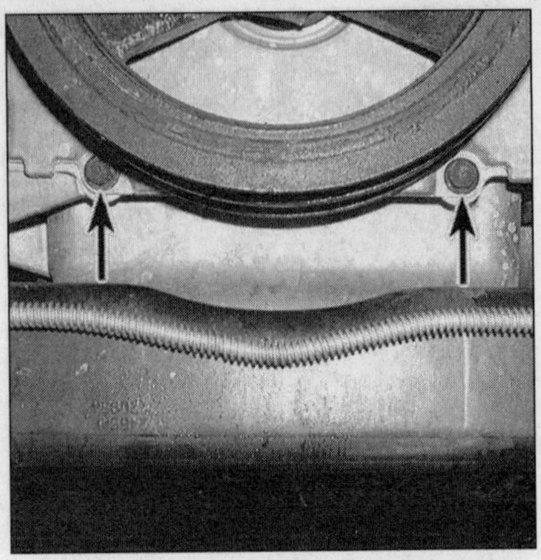

14.7a Be sure to remove the bolts (arrows) at the front of the oil pan just below the crankshaft pulley first

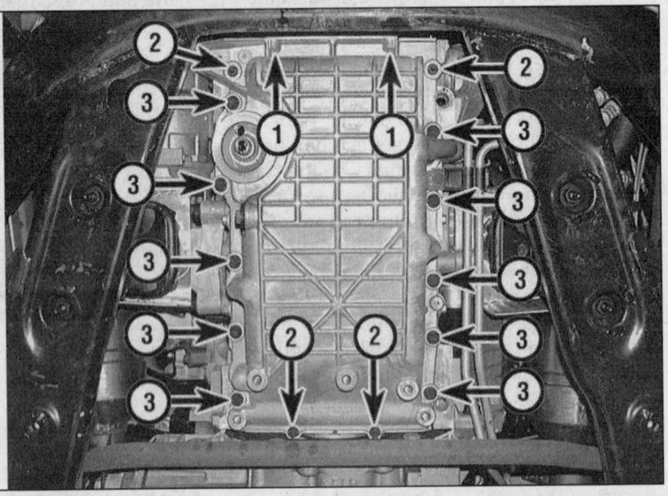

14.7b Oil pan bolt/nut identification diagram

1 Bolt 6-mm
2 Nut 6-mm
3 Bolt 8-mm

14.7c Insert a flathead screwdriver or small prybar on the casting protrusion at the front of the oil pan to break it loose

14 Oil pan - removal and installation

Removal

Refer to illustrations 14.5, 14.7a, 14.7b and 14.7c

1 Disconnect the negative battery cable from the remote ground terminal.

2 Apply the parking brake and block the rear wheels. Raise the front of the vehicle and place it securely on jackstands. Drain the engine oil and remove the oil filter (see Chapter 1).

3 Disconnect the stabilizer bar from the front suspension and move it toward the rear of the vehicle (see Chapter 10).

4 Remove the oil dipstick tube and the engine oil cooler line from the right side of the oil pan (if equipped).

5 Remove the transaxle to oil pan support brace at the rear of the pan **(see illustration)**.

6 Detach the any clips securing the transaxle oil cooler lines that would interfere with removal of the oil pan. Also remove the lower bolt securing the air conditioning compressor to the oil pan.

7 Remove the bolts and nuts **(see illustrations)**, then carefully separate the oil pan from the block. Don't pry between the block and the pan or damage to the sealing surfaces could occur and oil leaks may develop. Instead, pry at the casting protrusion at the front of the pan **(see illustration)**.

Installation

8 Clean the pan with solvent and remove all old sealant and gasket material from the block and pan mating surfaces. Clean the mating surfaces with lacquer thinner or acetone and make sure the bolt holes in the block are clear. Check the oil pan flange for distortion, particularly around the bolt holes.

9 Apply a bead of RTV sealant to the oil pan rail parting lines at the front cover and at the rear main oil seal retainer. Install the gasket on the block.

10 Place the oil pan in position on the block and install the nuts/bolts.

11 After the fasteners are installed, tighten them to the torque listed in this Chapter's Specifications. Starting at the center, follow a criss-cross pattern and work up to the final torque in three steps **(see illustration 14.7b)**.

12 Place the transaxle-to-oil pan support brace in position and install the vertically mounted bolts. Torque the vertical mounted bolts to 10 in-lbs, then install the horizontally mounted bolts. Torque the horizontal mounted bolts to 40 ft-lbs, then retorque the vertical mounted bolts to 40 ft-lbs **(see illustration 14.5)**.

13 The remaining steps are the reverse of the removal procedure.

14 Refill the engine with oil (see Chapter 1), replace the filter, run it until normal operating temperature is reached and check for leaks.

15 Oil pump - removal, inspection and installation

Removal

Refer to illustrations 15.3 and 15.4

1 Refer to Section 7 and remove the primary timing chain and the crankshaft sprocket. **Note:** *Before removing the crankshaft sprocket verify that the crankshaft sprocket marks align with the marks on the oil pump housing and do not rotate the crankshaft from this position at any time during this procedure. This position is approximately 60 degrees after TDC.*

2 Remove the oil pan (see Section 14).

15.3 Oil pump pick-up tube mounting bolts (arrows)

15.4 Oil pump housing retaining bolts (arrows)

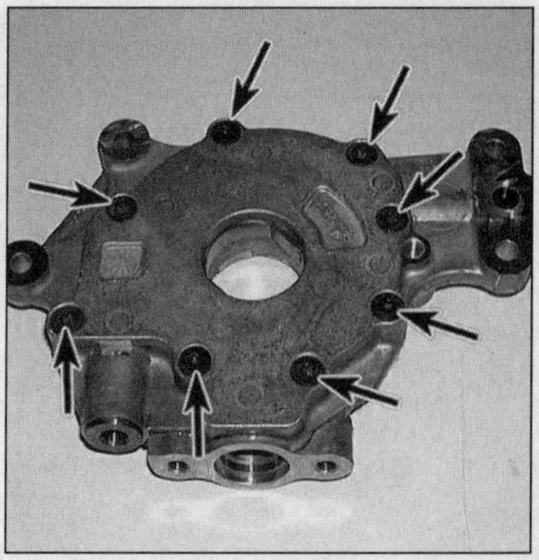

15.6 Remove the screws (arrows) and lift the cover off

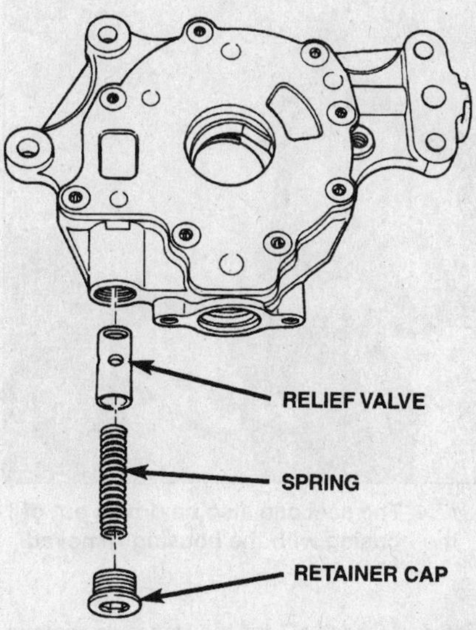

15.8 Oil pressure relief valve components

3 Remove the oil pump pick-up tube **(see illustration)**.

4 Remove the oil pump-to-engine block bolts from the front of the engine **(see illustration)**.

5 Gently pry the oil pump housing outward enough to clear the dowel pins on the engine block and remove it from the engine.

Inspection

Refer to illustrations 15.6, 15.8, 15.9a 15.9b, 15.9c, 15.9d, 15.9e and 15.9f

6 Remove the screws holding the front cover on the oil pump housing **(see illustration)**.

7 Clean all components with solvent, then inspect them for wear and damage.

8 Remove the oil pressure regulator cap, washer, spring and valve **(see illustration)**. Check the oil pressure regulator valve sliding surface and valve spring. If either the spring or the valve is damaged, they must be replaced as a set. Small burrs can be removed with 400-grit wet sandpaper and oil. The spring should measure approximately 1.95 inches long and should also have 23 to 25 pounds of pressure when compressed to 1.34 inches.

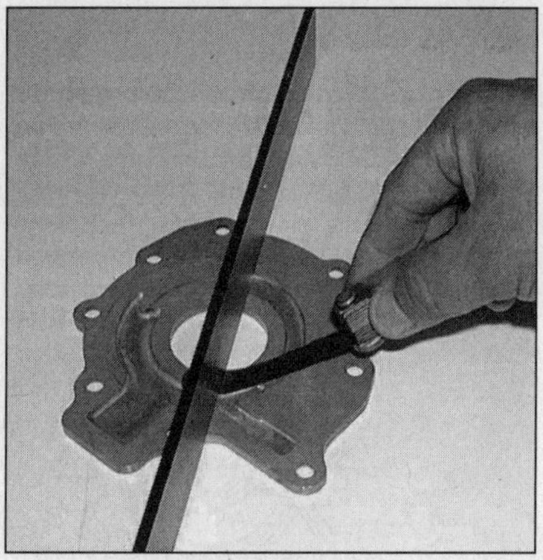

15.9a Place a straightedge across the oil pump cover and check it for warpage with a feeler gauge

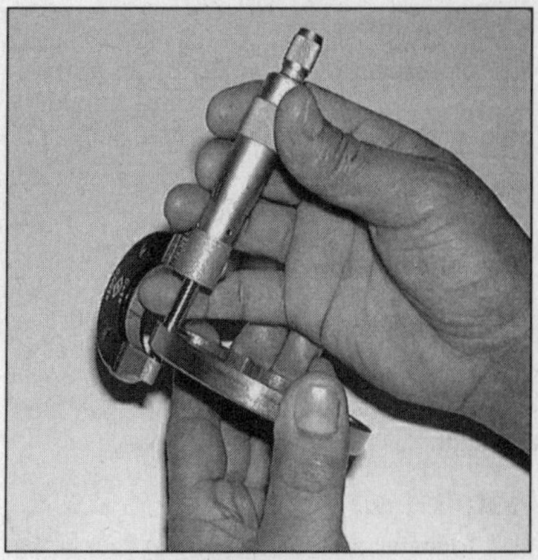

15.9b Use a micrometer or dial caliper to check the thickness and the diameter of the outer rotor

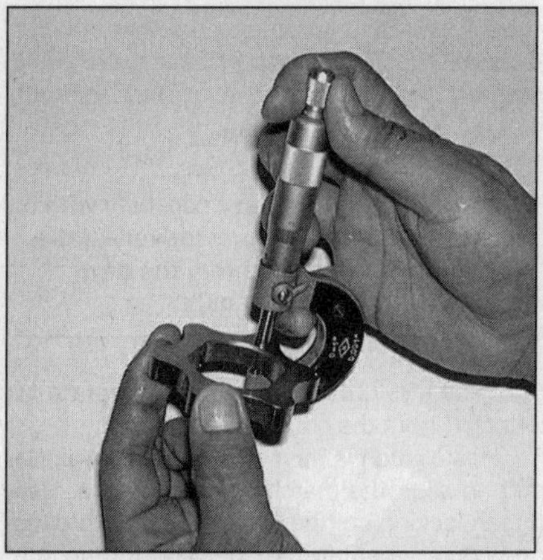

15.9c Use a micrometer or dial caliper to check the thickness of the inner rotor

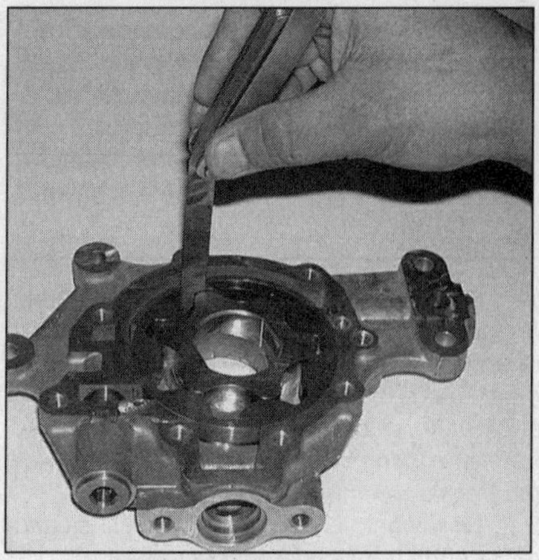

15.9d Check the outer rotor-to-housing clearance

9 Check the clearance of the following oil pump components with a feeler gauge and a micrometer or dial caliper **(see illustrations)** and compare the measurements to the clearance listed in this Chapter's Specifications:

a) Cover flatness

b) Outer rotor diameter and thickness

15.9e Check the clearance between the tips of the inner and outer rotors

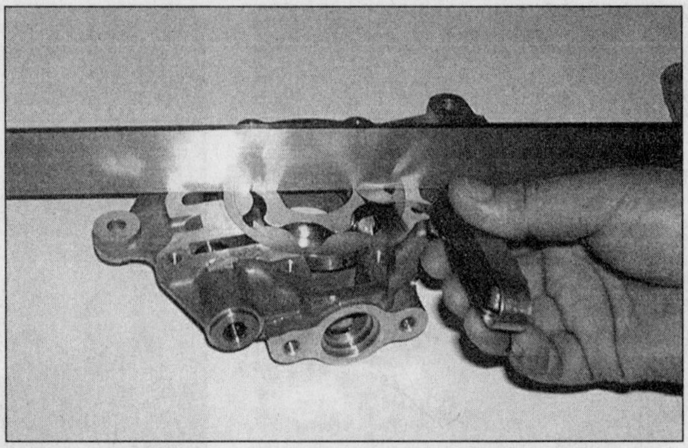

15.9f Using a straightedge and feeler gauge, check the side clearance between the surface of the oil pump and the inner and outer rotors

c) *Inner rotor thickness*
d) *Outer rotor-to-body clearance*
e) *Inner rotor to outer rotor tip clearance*
f) *Cover-to-inner rotor side clearance*
g) *Cover-to-outer rotor side clearance*

If any clearance is excessive, replace the entire oil pump assembly.

10 **Note:** *Pack the pump with petroleum jelly to prime it.* Assemble the oil pump and tighten all fasteners to the torque listed in this Chapter's Specifications. Install the oil pressure regulator valve, spring and washer, then tighten the oil pressure regulator valve cap.

Installation

11 To install the pump, turn the flats in the rotor so they align with the flats on the crankshaft.

12 Install the pump-to-block bolts and tighten them to the torque listed in this Chapter's Specifications.

13 The remainder of installation is the reverse of removal.

16 Driveplate - removal and installation

1 Raise the vehicle and support it securely on jackstands, then refer to Chapter 7 and remove the transaxle. **Warning:** *The engine must be supported from above with an engine hoist or three-bar support fixture before working underneath the vehicle with the transaxle removed.*

2 Now would be a good time to check and replace the transaxle front pump seal.

3 Use paint or a center-punch to make alignment marks on the driveplate and crankshaft to ensure correct alignment during reinstallation.

4 Remove the bolts that secure the driveplate to the crankshaft. If the crankshaft turns, jam a large screwdriver or prybar through the driveplate to keep the crankshaft from turning, then remove the mounting bolts.

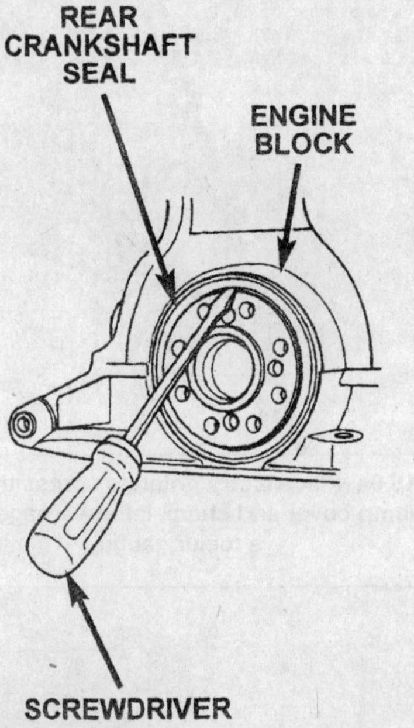

17.2 Pry the seal out very carefully with a seal removal tool or screwdriver - if the crankshaft is damaged, the new seal will leak!

5 Pull straight back on the driveplate to detach it from the crankshaft.

6 Installation is the reverse of removal. Be sure to align the matching paint marks. Use thread locking compound on the bolt threads and tighten them to the specified torque in a criss-cross pattern.

17 Rear main oil seal - replacement

Refer to illustrations 17.2, 17.4 and 17.5

1 All models use a one-piece rear main oil seal which is installed in a bolt-on housing. Replacing this seal requires removal of the transaxle, torque converter and driveplate.

17.4 The seal can also be driven out of the housing with the housing removed

Refer to Chapter 7 for the transaxle removal procedures.

2 The seal can be removed by prying it out of the housing by inserting a screwdriver, being careful not to nick the crankshaft surface **(see illustration)**. Wrap the screwdriver tip with tape to avoid damage. Be sure to note how far it's recessed into the housing bore before removal so the new seal can be installed to the same depth. Preferably, a seal installation tool is needed to press the new seal back into place. If the proper seal installation tool is unavailable, use a large socket, section of pipe or a blunt tool and carefully drive the new seal into place. The lip is stiff so carefully work it onto the seal journal of the crankshaft. Don't rush it or you may damage the seal.

3 The rear main seal housing can also be removed to change the seal, but whenever the housing is removed from the block a new seal and gasket must be installed.

4 If the housing is removed, place it on two blocks of wood and use a small punch to drive out the old seal **(see illustration)**.

5 Clean the housing thoroughly, then apply a thin coat of engine oil to the new seal.

17.5 Use a block of wood to drive the new seal into the housing

Set the seal squarely into the recess of the housing, then, using a piece of wood and a hammer, press the seal into place **(see illustration)**.

6 Carefully slide the seal over the crankshaft and bolt the seal housing to the block. Be sure to use a new gasket.

7 The remainder of installation is the reverse of the removal procedure.

18 Powertrain mounts - check and replacement

Refer to illustrations 18.8, 18.9 and 18.12

1 There are three powertrain mounts; left and right mounts attached to the engine block and to the frame and a rear mount attached to the transaxle and the frame.

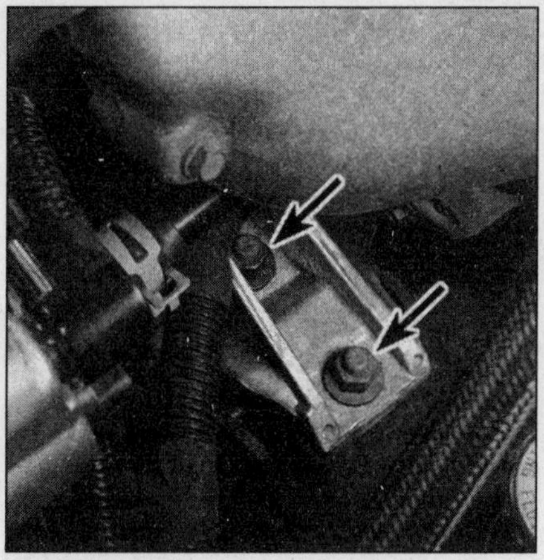

18.8 Remove the nuts (arrows) holding the mount to the engine bracket . . .

Check

2 During the check, the engine must be raised slightly to remove the weight from the mounts.

3 Raise the vehicle and support it securely on jackstands. Position two jacks, one under the crankshaft pulley and the other under the transaxle bellhousing. Place a block of wood between the jack head and the crankshaft pulley or bellhousing, then carefully raise the engine/transaxle just enough to take the weight off the mounts. **Warning:** *DO NOT place any part of your body under the engine when it's supported only by a jack!*

4 Check the mounts to see if the rubber is cracked, hardened or separated from the metal plates. Sometimes the rubber will split right down the center.

5 Check for relative movement between the mount plates and the engine or frame (use a large screwdriver or prybar to attempt to move the mounts). If movement is noted, lower the engine and tighten the mount fasteners. **Note:** *Some models have liquid-filled mounts. These should not be replaced unless there are signs the fluid has leaked out.*

6 Rubber preservative should be applied to the mounts to slow deterioration.

Replacement

7 Disconnect the negative battery cable from the remote ground terminal, then raise the vehicle and support it securely on jackstands.

Left and right mount

8 Remove the nuts holding the insulator to the engine bracket **(see illustration)**.

9 From underneath, remove the nuts holding the insulator to the frame **(see illustration)**.

10 Raise the engine with a jack and block of wood under the oil pan until the studs clear the engine bracket and the frame. remove the insulator and replace it with the new one.

11 Lower the engine and install the top and bottom nuts and torque to this Chapter's Specifications.

Rear mount

12 Remove the bolts securing the mount to the transaxle and the frame **(see illustration)**.

13 Raise the transaxle with a jack and block of wood. Remove the mount and replace it with the new one.

14 Install the bolts hand tight and lower the transaxle. Tighten the bolts to the torque listed in this Chapter's Specifications.

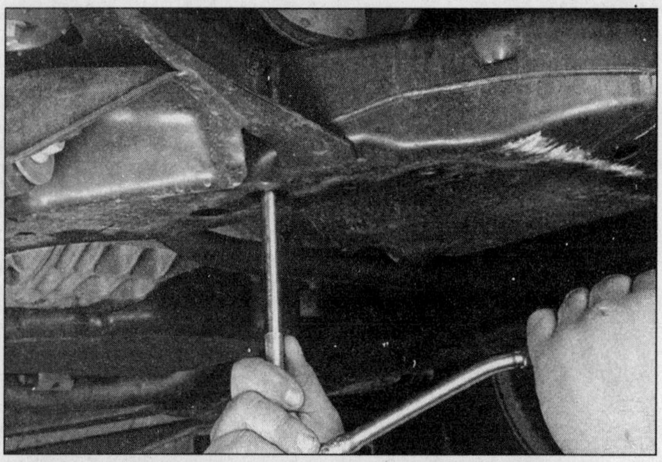

18.9 . . . then remove the nuts securing it to the frame from underneath - access to these nuts is through holes in the frame

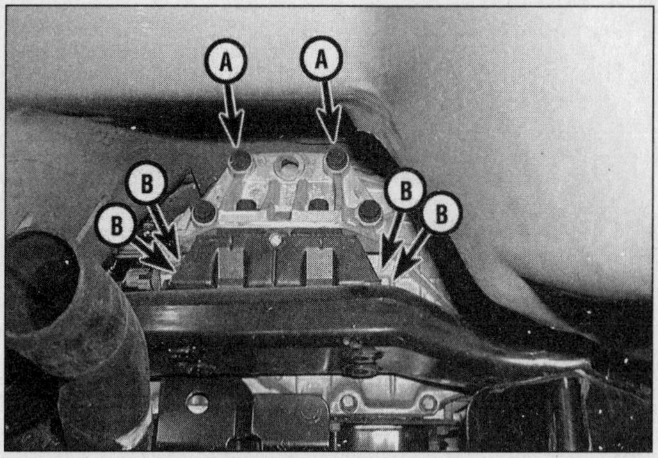

18.12 Remove the transaxle-to-rear mount bolts (A) and the rear mount-to-frame bolts (B)

Notes

Chapter 2 Part B
3.2L and 3.5L V6 engines

Contents

Specifications

General

Displacement	
3.2L V6	167 cubic inches
3.5L V6	214 cubic inches
Bore and stroke	
3.2L V6	3.622 x 3.189 inches
3.5L V6	3.780 x 3.189 inches
Cylinder numbers (front to rear)	
Left bank	2-4-6
Right bank	1-3-5
Firing order	1-2-3-4-5-6

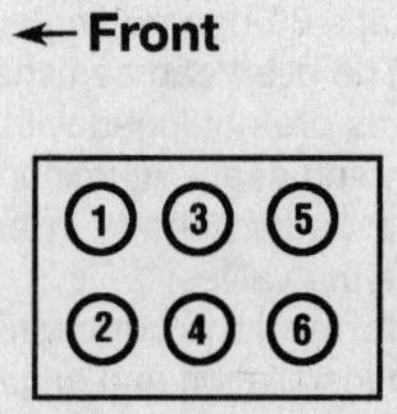

Cylinder identification diagram

Camshaft

Endplay	0.004 to 0.014 inch
Lobe wear limit	
Standard	0.001 inch
Service limit	0.010 inch
Camshaft journal diameter	1.6905 to 1.6913 inches
Camshaft bore diameter (inside)	1.6944 to 1.6952 inches
Camshaft bearing oil clearance	
Standard	0.003 to 0.0047 inch
Service limit	0.0059 inch

Oil pump

Cover warpage limit	0.001 inch
Inner and outer rotor thickness (minimum)	0.563 inch
Outer rotor diameter (minimum)	3.149 inch
Outer rotor-to-housing clearance (maximum)	0.015 inch
Inner rotor-to-outer rotor lobe clearance	0.008 inch
Oil pump housing-to-rotor side clearance	0.003 inch

Torque specifications

Torque specifications	Ft-lbs (unless otherwise indicated)
Camshaft sprocket bolts	
Right side	75 plus 1/4-turn
Left side	85 plus 1/4-turn
Camshaft thrust plate bolts	250 in-lbs
Crankshaft pulley bolt	75 to 85
Cylinder head bolts (in sequence - **see illustration 11.22**)	
First step	45
Second step	65
Third step	65
Fourth step	Additional 1/4-turn (do not use torque wrench)
Engine mount bracket-to-block bolts	45
Engine mount nuts	45
Exhaust manifold-to-cylinder head bolts	200 in-lbs
Exhaust heat shield bolts	105 in-lbs
Driveplate-to-crankshaft bolts	75
Intake manifold-to-cylinder head bolts	250 in-lbs
Upper intake manifold (plenum) to lower intake manifold	105 in-lbs
Oil pan drain plug	25
Oil pan bolts	105 in-lbs
Oil pump pick-up tube mounting bolt	250 in-lbs
Oil pump cover (plate) bolts (Torx no. 30)	105 in-lbs
Valve cover-to-cylinder head bolts	105 in-lbs
Rocker arm shaft bolts	275 in-lbs
Timing belt cover bolts	
M6	105 in-lbs
M8	250 in-lbs
M10	40
Timing belt tensioner	250 in-lbs
Rear main oil seal retainer bolts	105 in-lbs
V-band clamps to exhaust manifold	100 in-lbs

1 General information

This Part of Chapter 2 is devoted to in-vehicle repair procedures for the 3.2L and 3.5L V6 engines. These engines utilize an aluminum block with six cylinders arranged in a "V" shape at a 60-degree angle between the two banks. The overhead camshaft aluminum cylinder heads are equipped with replaceable valve guides and seats. Aluminum roller rockers mounted on two shafts in each cylinder head actuate the valves.

All information concerning engine removal and installation and engine block and cylinder head overhaul can be found in Part C of this Chapter. The following repair procedures are based on the assumption the engine is installed in the vehicle. If the engine has been removed from the vehicle and mounted on a stand, many of the steps outlined in this Part of Chapter 2 will not apply.

The Specifications included in this Part of Chapter 2 apply only to the procedures contained in this Part. Part C of Chapter 2 contains the Specifications necessary for cylinder head and engine block rebuilding.

2 Repair operations possible with the engine in the vehicle

Many major repair operations can be accomplished without removing the engine from the vehicle.

Clean the engine compartment and the exterior of the engine with some type of degreaser before any work is done. It'll make the job easier and help keep dirt out of the internal areas of the engine.

Depending on the components involved, it may be helpful to remove the hood to improve access to the engine as repairs are performed (see Chapter 11 if necessary). Cover the fenders to prevent damage to the paint. Special pads are available, but an old bedspread or blanket will also work.

If vacuum, exhaust, oil or coolant leaks develop, indicating a need for gasket or seal replacement, the repairs can generally be done with the engine in the vehicle. The intake and exhaust manifold gaskets, timing belt cover gasket, oil pan gasket, crankshaft oil seals and cylinder head gaskets are all accessible with the engine in place.

Exterior engine components, such as the intake and exhaust manifolds, the oil pan, timing belt covers (and the oil pump), the water pump, the starter motor, the alternator and the fuel system components can be removed for repair with the engine in place.

Since the cylinder heads can be removed without pulling the engine, valve component servicing can also be accomplished with the engine in the vehicle. Replacement of the camshafts, timing belt and sprockets is also possible with the engine in the vehicle, although the cylinder head must be removed from the engine to replace the camshafts.

In extreme cases caused by a lack of necessary equipment, repair or replacement of piston rings, pistons, connecting rods and rod bearings is possible with the engine in the vehicle. However, this practice is not recommended because of the cleaning and preparation work that must be done to the components involved.

3 Top Dead Center (TDC) for number one piston - locating

This procedure is essentially the same for all three V6 engines covered by this manual. Refer to Part A and follow the procedure and illustrations outlined there.

4 Valve cover(s) - removal and installation

Refer to illustrations 4.5a, 4.5b, and 4.8

Removal

1 Disconnect the negative battery cable from the remote ground terminal (see Chapter 5).

2 Remove the upper intake manifold (see Section 9) and cover the lower intake manifold with rags to keep out dirt.

3 Remove the ignition coils from the spark plugs (see Chapter 5).

4 Unbolt the air conditioning compressor and pull it away from the right cylinder head with out disconnecting the refrigerant lines (see Chapter 3).

5 Pull the wire harness up from the valve

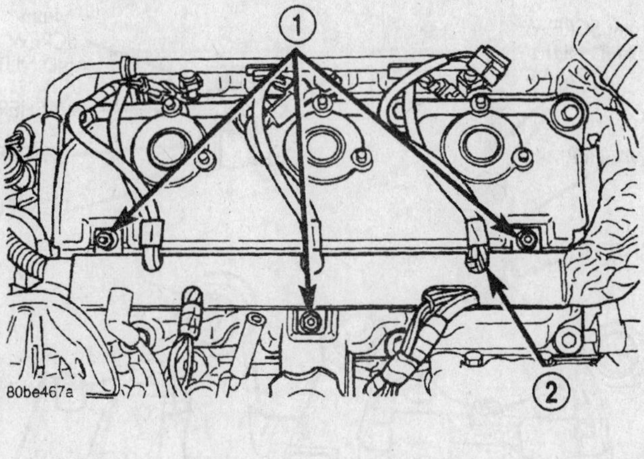

4.5a Remove the wire harness from the studs on the valve covers

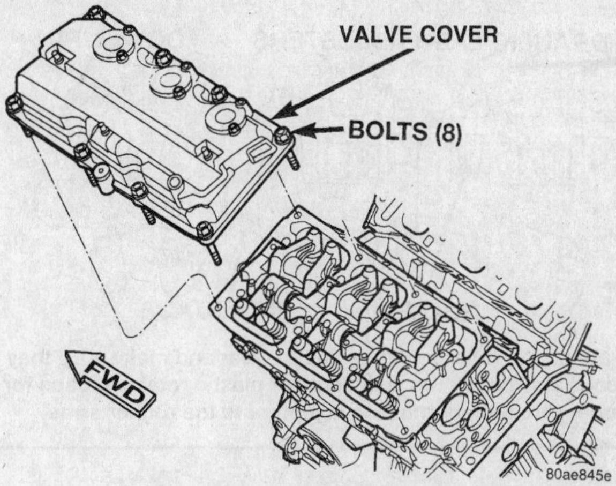

4.5b Valve cover mounting bolts

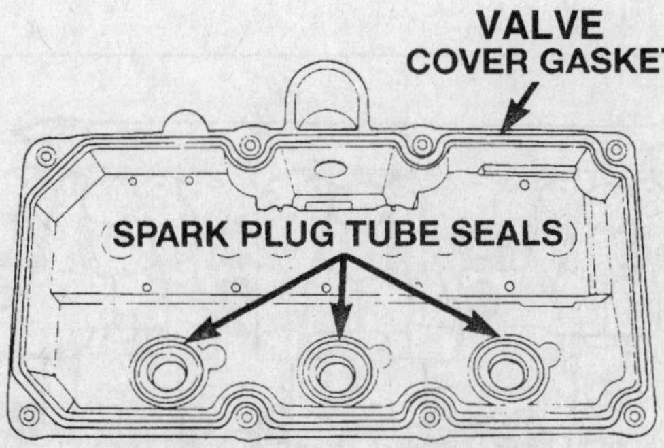

4.8 Inspect the spark plug tube seals and replace them if necessary

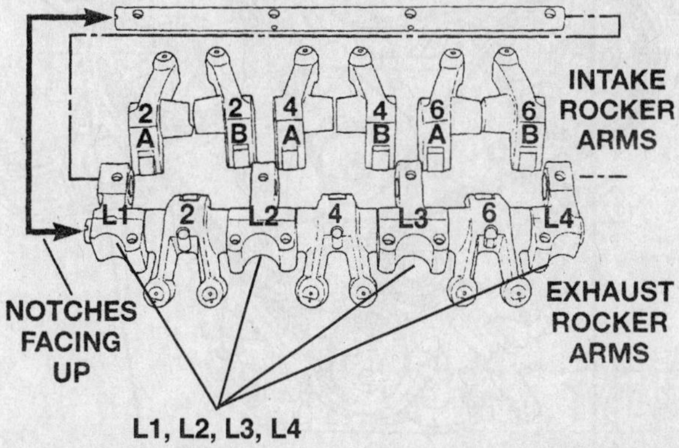

5.2 Use a permanent marker to identify each of the rocker arms and pedestals before removing them from the shaft – the rocker arm numbers represent which cylinder they operate on and the pedestal numbers represent which cylinder head and their position in relation to the front of the engine

cover studs and remove the valve cover studs/bolts **(see illustrations)**.

6 Detach the valve cover. **Note:** *If the cover sticks to the cylinder head, use a block of wood and a hammer to dislodge it. If the cover still won't come loose, pry on it carefully, but don't distort the sealing flange.*

Installation

7 The mating surfaces of each cylinder head and valve cover must be perfectly clean when the covers are installed. Use a gasket scraper to remove all traces of sealant or old gasket material, then clean the mating surfaces with lacquer thinner or acetone (if there's sealant or oil on the mating surfaces when the cover is installed, oil leaks may develop). Be extra careful not to nick or gouge the mating surfaces with the scraper.

8 Inspect the spark plug tube seals **(see illustration)**. Replace them if they're cracked or flattened, or if the rubber has hardened. Make sure the spark plug tube seals are in position before installing the valve cover.

9 Clean the mounting bolt threads with a die if necessary to remove any corrosion and restore damaged threads. Use a tap to clean the threaded holes in the heads.

10 Place the valve cover and new gasket in position, then install the bolts. Tighten the bolts in several steps to the torque listed in this Chapter's Specifications.

11 Complete the installation by reversing the removal procedure. Start the engine and check carefully for oil leaks.

5 Rocker arm assembly and hydraulic lash adjusters-removal, inspection and installation

Removal

Refer to illustrations 5.2 and 5.3

1 Remove the valve cover(s) (see Section 4).

2 Mark the rocker arms and pedestals for identification before removing them **(see illustration)**. There are four per cylinder, two intake and two exhaust.

3 Loosen each rocker arm shaft bolt a little at a time until they are all loose enough to be removed by hand. Remove the shaft and rockers as an assembly **(see illustration)**. **Caution:** *Never allow the rocker arm assembly to be placed upside down or to rest on the lash adjusters as damage may occur.*

5.3 Remove the rocker arm shaft bolts from the cylinder head - be sure to loosen them in the reverse order of the tightening sequence

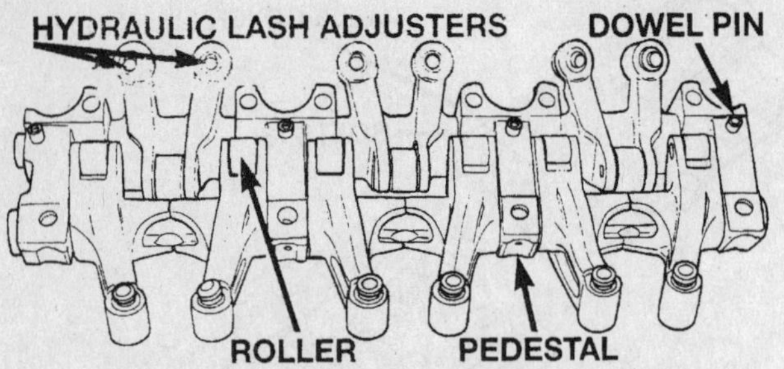

5.4 Examine the roller tips for signs of wear and make sure they turn freely; also check the lash adjuster plastic retaining caps for proper retention of the lash adjusters to the rocker arms

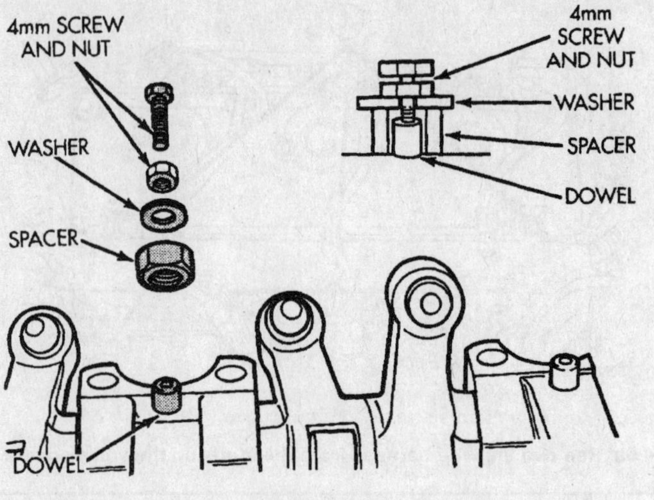

5.7 A 4mm bolt, nut, washer and spacer can be used to extract the dowel pins from the pedestals

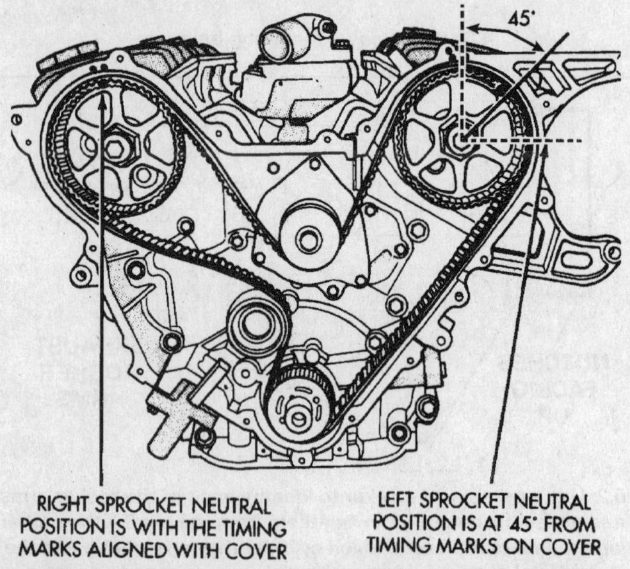

5.10a Position the camshafts in the "neutral" position before installing the rocker arm assemblies - complete the installation on the right side cylinder head first, then rotate the engine to the neutral position for the left cylinder head and complete the installation on the left side

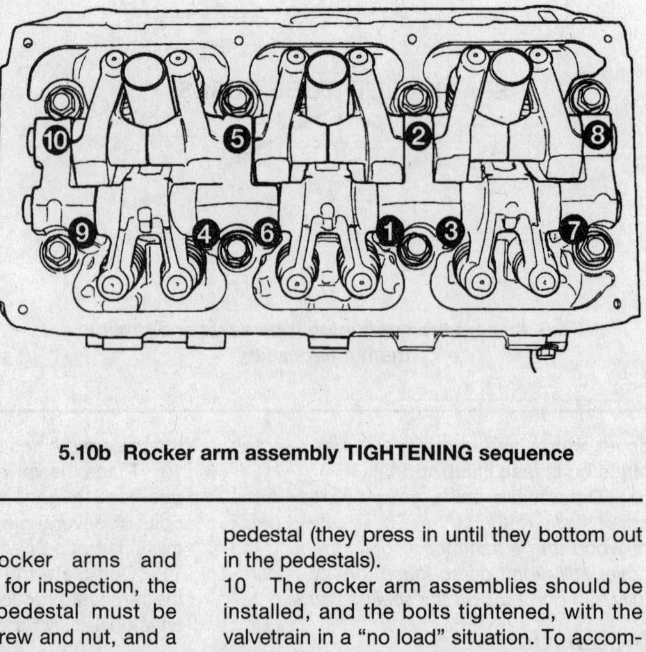

5.10b Rocker arm assembly TIGHTENING sequence

Inspection

Refer to illustrations 5.4 and 5.7

4 Inspect each rocker arm for wear, cracks and other damage. This engine uses aluminum rocker arms with steel roller tips and hydraulic lash adjusters. Make sure the rollers turn freely and show no signs of wear, also check the lash adjuster contact surfaces wear or damage. Make sure the lash adjuster retaining caps hold all of the lash adjusters securely in place on the rocker arms **(see illustration)**. **Caution:** *DO NOT at anytime remove the lash adjuster from the rocker arms or damage to the lash adjuster and the rocker arm will occur.*

5 Check each rocker arm pivot area and shaft for wear, cracks and galling. If the rocker arms or shafts are worn or damaged, replace them with new ones.

6 Make sure the axle for the roller tip is not sticking out one side more than the other, and make sure to check for wear, cracks and galling on the hydraulic lash adjuster to valve stem tip contact surface.

7 To remove the rocker arms and pedestals from the shafts for inspection, the dowel pins from each pedestal must be pulled out. Use a 4mm screw and nut, and a washer and spacer as a puller to extract the dowel pins from each pedestal **(see illustration)**. **Note:** *New dowel pins must be installed during installation.*

Installation

Refer to illustrations 5.10a and 5.10b

8 If the rockers arms or pedestals have been removed from the shafts for inspection, lubricate the shafts and install the rocker arms and pedestals in their marked order. Keep the intake rockers on the intake shaft, and exhaust rockers on the exhaust shaft. **Caution:** *The notches in the rocker arm shafts must face UP* ***when assembled or damage to the rocker arms will occur*** **(see illustration 5.2)**.

9 Reinstall new dowels pins in each pedestal (they press in until they bottom out in the pedestals).

10 The rocker arm assemblies should be installed, and the bolts tightened, with the valvetrain in a "no load" situation. To accomplish this, the camshafts must be placed in a "neutral" position. Refer to Section 7 and remove the timing belt cover. Rotate the engine until the right side camshaft timing marks align and install the right side rocker arm assembly **(see illustrations)**. Tighten the right side rocker arm assembly bolts in the proper sequence to the torque listed in this Chapter's Specifications.

11 For the left cylinder head, rotate the engine until the timing mark on the left camshaft is 45-degrees past the mark on the cover **(see illustration 5.10a)**. Install the left rocker arm assembly and tighten the bolts in the proper sequence to the torque listed in this Chapter's Specifications. **Caution:** *The notches in the left rocker arm shafts must face UP and towards the front of the engine.*

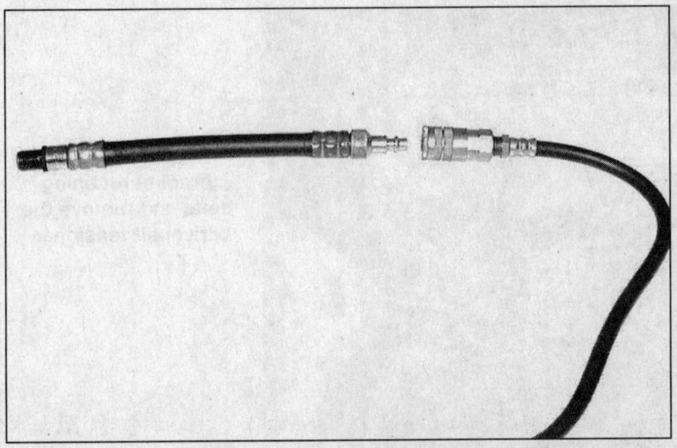

6.5 You'll need an air hose adapter this long to reach down into the spark plug tubes - they're commonly available in auto parts stores. Some compression gauge hoses will also work

6.7 Using a clamp-type spring compressor, compress the spring enough to remove the keepers with small pliers or a magnet

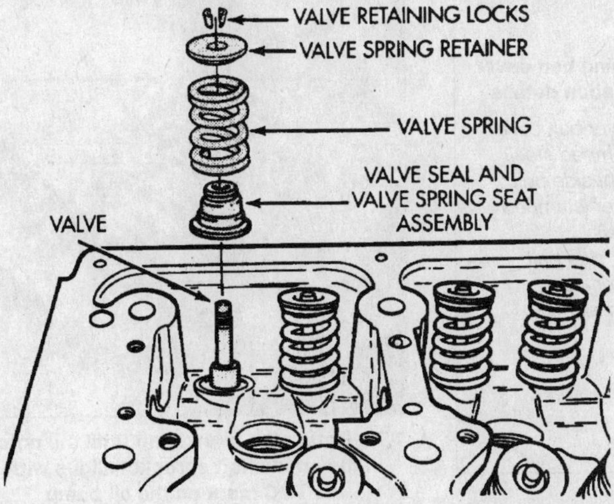

6.14 Install the new seal and valve spring seat assembly on the valve guide - do not displace the garter spring at the top of the seal

The notches in the right rocker arm shafts must face UP and towards the rear of the engine (firewall side). ***Improper oiling of the rocker arms and shafts will result if this procedure is not followed!***

12 The remainder of the installation is the reverse of the removal procedures. Start the engine and check for oil leaks.

6 Valve springs, retainers and seals - replacement

Refer to illustrations 6.5, 6.7, 6.14 and 6.17

Note: *Broken valve springs and defective valve stem seals can be replaced without removing the cylinder head. Two special tools and a compressed-air source are normally required to perform this operation, so read through this Section carefully and rent or buy the tools before beginning the job.*

1 Remove the valve covers (see Section 4).

2 Remove the spark plugs (see Chapter 1).

3 Rotate the crankshaft until the number one piston is at top dead center on the compression stroke (see Section 3).

4 Remove the rocker arm assembly (see Section 5).

5 Thread an adapter into the number 1 spark plug hole and connect an air hose from a compressed air source to it **(see illustration)**. Most auto parts stores can supply the air hose adapter. **Note:** *Many cylinder compression gauges utilize a screw-in fitting that may work with your air hose quick-disconnect fitting, and they are usually long enough to reach through the spark plug tubes on these engine.*

6 Apply 90 to 100 psi of compressed air to the cylinder. The valves should be held in place by the air pressure. If the valve faces or seats are in poor condition, leaks may prevent the air pressure from retaining the valves - valve reconditioning is indicated.

7 Stuff shop rags into the cylinder head holes around the valves to prevent parts and tools from falling into the engine, then use a valve-spring compressor to compress the spring. Remove the keepers with small needle-nose pliers or a magnet **(see illustration)**.

8 Remove the valve spring and retainer.

9 Remove the old valve stem seal and spring seat assembly.

10 Wrap a rubber band or tape around the top of the valve stem so the valve won't fall into the combustion chamber, then release the air pressure.

11 Inspect the valve stem for damage. Rotate the valve in the guide and check the end for eccentric movement, which would indicate that the valve is bent.

12 Move the valve up-and-down in the guide and make sure it doesn't bind. If the valve stem binds, either the valve is bent or the guide is damaged. In either case, the head will have to be removed for repair.

13 Reapply air pressure to the cylinder to retain the valve in the closed position, then remove the tape or rubber band from the valve stem.

14 Install the valve spring seat/valve seal assembly over the top of the valves tips by hand. Using the stem of the valves as a guide, slide the seals down to the top of each valve guide **(see illustration)**. Using a hammer and a deep socket or seal installation tool, gently tap each seal into place until it's completely seated on the guide. Don't twist or cock the seals during installation or they won't seal properly on the valve stems. Make sure the garter spring is still in place around the top of the seal.

15 Install the spring and retainer in position over the valve with the colored mark on the spring facing UP. **Caution:** *Different length springs are used on the intake and exhaust valves - accidentally installing an intake spring on an exhaust valve can cause major engine damage. The intake springs on all models are identified with a orange mark at the top. The exhaust springs on 1998 and 1999 models are identified with a green mark at the top, while 2000 and later models are identified with a yellow mark at the top.*

16 Compress the valve spring assembly only enough to install the keepers in the valve stem.

17 Position the keepers in the valve stem groove. Apply a small dab of grease to the

6.17 Apply a small dab of grease to each keeper before installation to hold it in place on the valve stem until the spring compressor is released

7.4 Detach three bracket retaining bolts and remove the drivebelt tensioner

7.5 Timing belt cover installation details

A Lower belt cover (stamped steel)
B Right side belt cover (stamped steel)
C Left side belt cover (cast aluminum)

7.7a Rotate the crankshaft until the notch in the crankshaft sprocket aligns with the TDC mark on the oil pump cover (arrow) . . .

inside of each keeper to hold it in place if necessary **(see illustration)**. Remove the pressure from the spring tool and make sure the keepers are seated.

18 Disconnect the air hose and remove the adapter from the spark plug hole.

19 Repeat the above procedure on the remaining cylinders, following the firing order sequence (see the Specifications). Bring each piston to top dead center on the compression stroke before applying air pressure.

20 Reinstall the rocker arm assemblies, valve covers and intake plenum referring to the appropriate Sections for installation procedures if necessary.

21 Start the engine, then check for oil leaks and unusual sounds coming from the valve cover area.

7 Timing belt - replacement

Refer to illustrations 7.4, 7.5, 7.7a, 7.7b, 7.7c, 7.8 and 7.9

Note 1: *The following procedure for timing belt replacement is based on the camshaft sprockets NOT being loosened or removed. If the camshaft sprockets are being removed, follow the cam timing procedure in Section 11.*

Note 2: *Because of work necessary to get at the timing belt and replace it, and because the water pump is in this area, it is recommended that the water pump be replaced at the same time as the belt (see Chapter 3). The factory recommends replacing the timing belt at 105,000 miles or 84 months.*

1 Disconnect the negative battery cable from the remote ground terminal (see Chapter 5).

2 Refer to Chapter 3 and remove the upper radiator crossmember and the cooling fan assembly.

3 Remove the accessory drivebelts (see Chapter 1).

4 Remove the crankshaft pulley (see Section 12) and the drivebelt tensioner **(see illustration)**.

5 Remove the air conditioning belt guide bracket from the top of the right timing belt cover (if equipped), then unbolt and remove the stamped steel timing belt covers **(see illustration)**.

6 Remove the cast aluminum timing belt cover from the left cylinder head.

7 Temporarily install the crankshaft pulley bolt and turn the crankshaft with the bolt to align the timing marks on the crankshaft and camshaft sprockets. The crankshaft sprocket arrow should line up with the TDC indicator on the oil pump cover and the camshaft sprocket arrows should line up between the

7.7b . . . and the camshaft sprocket timing marks align between the two marks on the rear cover (arrows)

7.7c After the timing marks have been aligned, use a permanent marker to identify the exact position of the camshaft sprockets, the timing belt and the rear covers in relationship to each other

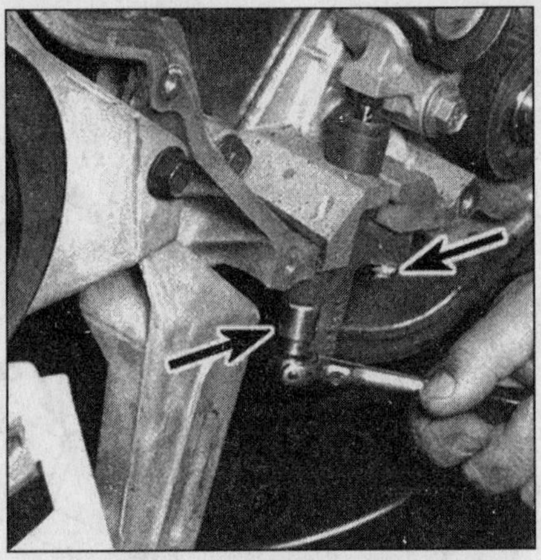

7.8 Remove the timing belt tensioner bolts (arrows), then remove the tensioner and the timing belt

7.9 Compress the plunger on the tensioner in a vise until a drill bit or Allen wrench can be inserted through the hole to retain the plunger - orient the pin in a way that won't interfere with installing the tensioner with the pin in place

marks on the top of the rear covers **(see illustrations)**.

8 Unbolt the timing belt tensioner and remove the belt **(see illustration)**.

9 Slowly compress the timing belt tensioner in a vise until a drill bit or Allen wrench can be inserted through the hole to lock it in **(see illustration)**. **Note:** *Total bleed down time of the tensioner should take approximately four to five minutes. DO NOT force tensioner to bleed down faster or damage to the tensioner may occur.*

10 Making sure that all timing marks are still aligned, start by installing the new belt at the crankshaft pulley, proceeding counterclockwise up to the left camshaft sprocket. After the belt is on the left camshaft sprocket, keep tension on the belt as it is fed under the water pump pulley, over the right camshaft sprocket, and past the tensioner. If the old timing belt is being reused, make sure to align the paint marks made in Step 7 with the camshaft sprocket marks as the belt is installed.

11 Hold the tensioner pulley against the belt and install the tensioner. Tighten the tensioner bolts to the torque listed in this Chapter's Specifications.

12 Remove the Allen key or drill bit from the tensioner, allowing it to tension the pulley on the belt.

13 Rotate the crankshaft pulley through two complete revolutions to check that the timing marks still remain aligned. If not, repeat the belt installation process.

14 The remainder of installation is the reverse of removal. **Note:** *When reinstalling the cast timing cover (which installs before the stamped steel covers), use a thin bead of RTV sealant around the perimeter. The stamped-steel cover has it's own sealant attached, which should be reusable. If there are tears or gaps in the original sealing material, fill the voids with RTV sealant.*

15 Start the engine and check for leaks. **Note:** *Noise may be present upon initial start up, due to air entering the timing chain tensioner. If this situation occurs raise the idle to 1600 to 2000 rpm for ten minutes to purge the air from the tensioner. This noise should last no longer than 15 minutes after initial start up.*

8 Camshafts - removal and installation

Note: *The camshafts should always be thoroughly inspected before installation and camshaft endplay should always be checked prior to camshaft removal. Refer to Chapter 2C for the camshaft inspection procedures.*

Removal

1 The cylinder head(s) must be removed to withdraw the camshafts from the rear of the heads. Refer to Section 11 for cylinder head removal.

2 Remove the camshaft rear cover and O-ring seal and withdraw the camshaft from the cylinder head, being careful not to nick the cam bearings or journals.

Installation

Refer to illustrations 8.3 and 8.4

3 Lubricate the camshaft bearing journals and cam lobes with camshaft installation lube **(see illustration)**.

4 Insert the camshaft carefully into the cylinder head, then install a new seal at the front of the head **(see illustration)**. Using a deep socket or section of pipe, tap the new seal in.

5 Install the camshaft cover at the back of the head with a new O-ring.

6 Install the rear timing covers and perform the camshaft sprocket timing procedure in Section 11.

7 The remainder of the installation is the reverse of removal and is covered in Sections 7 and 11.

8.3 Coat both the cam lobes and the journals with camshaft installation lube before installing the camshaft

8.4 The camshaft seal can be removed with a hook-type seal remover - use a deep socket or section of pipe to install the new seal

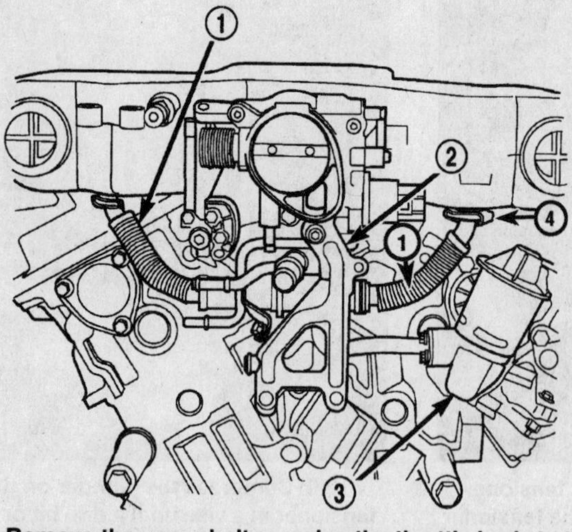

9.4 Remove the upper bolt securing the throttle body to the rear support bracket and the EGR guide tube retaining clips

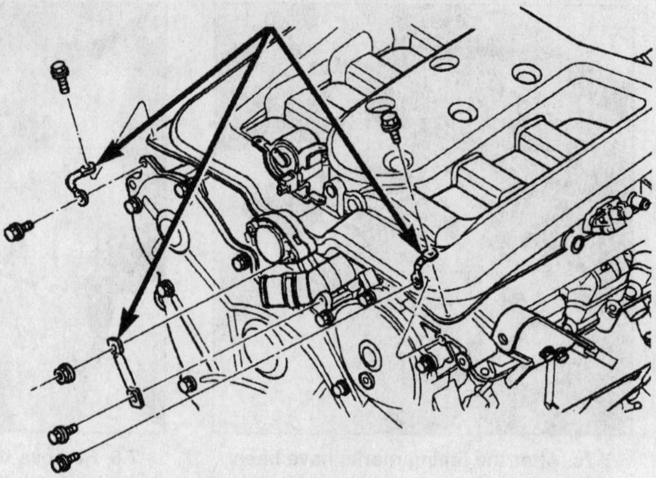
9.5a Upper intake manifold front support brackets

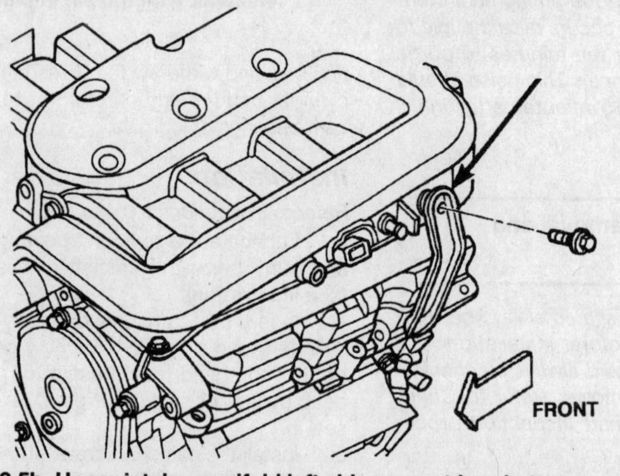

9.5b Upper intake manifold left side support bracket

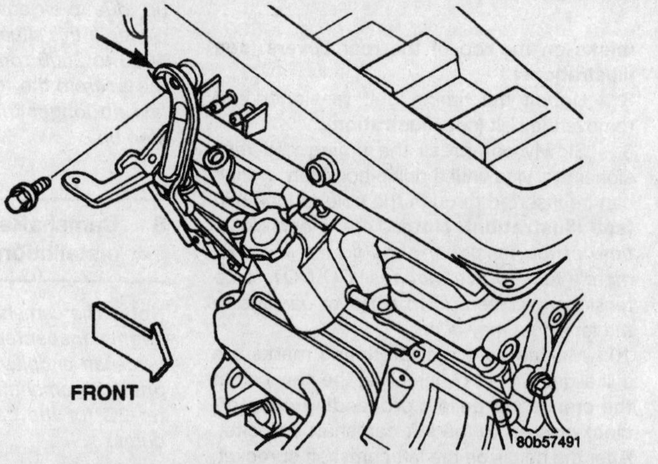

9.5c Upper intake manifold right side support bracket

9 Intake manifold - removal and installation

Upper intake manifold (plenum)

Refer to illustrations 9.4, 9.5a, 9.5b, 9.5c and 9.8

1 Disconnect the negative battery cable from the remote ground terminal (see Chapter 5).

2 Relieve the fuel system pressure. Remove the air intake duct and detach the throttle cable and the cruise control cable from the throttle body (see Chapter 4).

3 Label and disconnect the hoses and electrical connectors attached to the plenum and throttle body.

4 Remove the clips securing the EGR guide tubes to the upper plenum and the upper bolt securing the throttle body to rear support bracket **(see illustration)**.

5 Remove the remaining upper plenum support brackets **(see illustrations)**.

6 Loosen the upper intake manifold bolts in the reverse order of the tightening sequence **(see illustration 9.8)** and remove the upper plenum with the throttle body attached.

7 To install the upper manifold, clean the mounting surfaces of the intake manifold and the upper plenum with lacquer thinner and remove all traces of the old gasket material or sealant.

8 Install the new gasket over the lower intake manifold, then install the upper plenum onto the lower intake manifold and tighten the bolts in the recommended tightening sequence **(see illustration)** to the torque listed in this Chapter's Specifications. The remainder the installation is the reverse of removal.

Lower intake manifold

Refer to illustrations 9.10, 9.15 and 9.18

9 Remove the upper intake manifold (see Steps 1 through 6). Drain the cooling system (see Chapter 1).

10 Label and detach any remaining hoses which would interfere with the removal of the lower intake manifold **(see illustration)**.

11 Remove the fuel rail and injectors from the lower intake manifold (see Chapter 4).

12 Loosen the remaining manifold mounting bolts/nuts in 1/4-turn increments until they can be removed by hand.

13 The manifold will probably be stuck to the cylinder heads and force may be required to break the gasket seal. **Caution:** *Don't pry between the manifold and the heads or damage to the gasket sealing surfaces may occur, leading to vacuum leaks.*

14 Carefully use a scraper to remove all traces of old gasket material and sealant from the manifold and cylinder heads, then clean the mating surfaces with lacquer thinner or acetone.

15 Apply a bead of RTV sealant or equivalent around the front and rear cylinder head water passages before laying the new gaskets in place **(see illustration)**.

16 Install the intake manifold gaskets on the cylinder heads and apply RTV sealant to the manifold side of the gaskets, around the water passages.

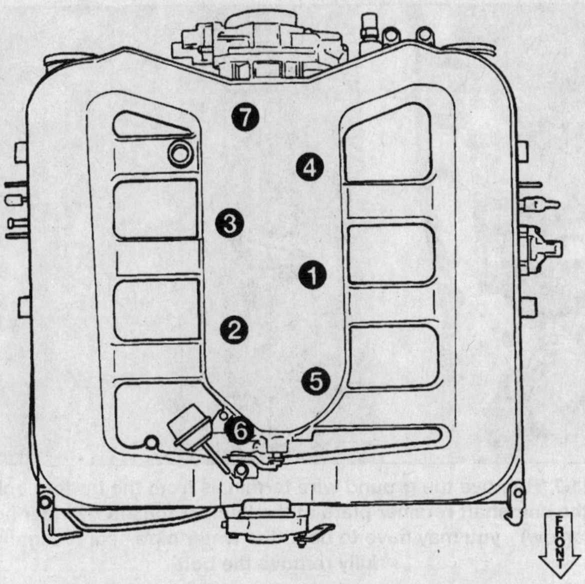

9.8 Upper intake manifold TIGHTENING sequence

9.15 Apply a small bead of RTV sealant, on either side of the gaskets, around each water passage at the ends of the heads (arrows)

17 Position the lower manifold on the engine. Making sure the gaskets and manifold are aligned over the ports in the cylinder heads. Install the fuel rail and injectors onto the lower manifold, then install the manifold mounting bolts.

18 Following the recommended tightening sequence, tighten the nuts/bolts, in several steps, to the torque listed in this Chapter's Specifications **(see illustration)**.

19 The remainder of the installation is the reverse of the removal procedure. Run the engine and check for fuel, vacuum and coolant leaks.

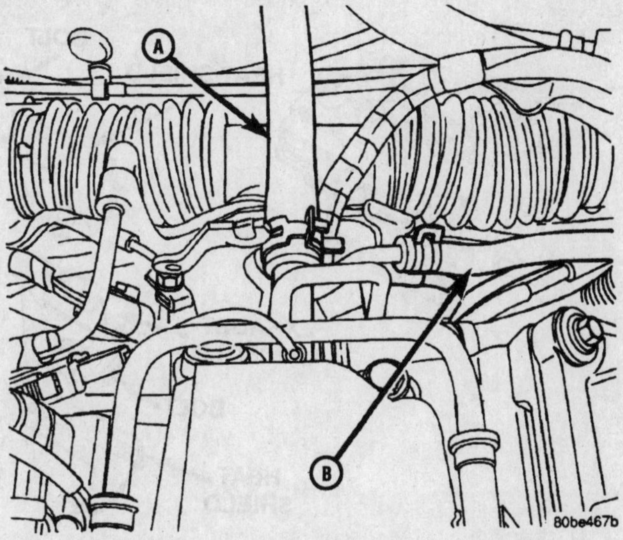

9.10 After the plenum is removed, disconnect the heater supply hose (A) and the coolant reservoir hose (B) from the rear of the manifold

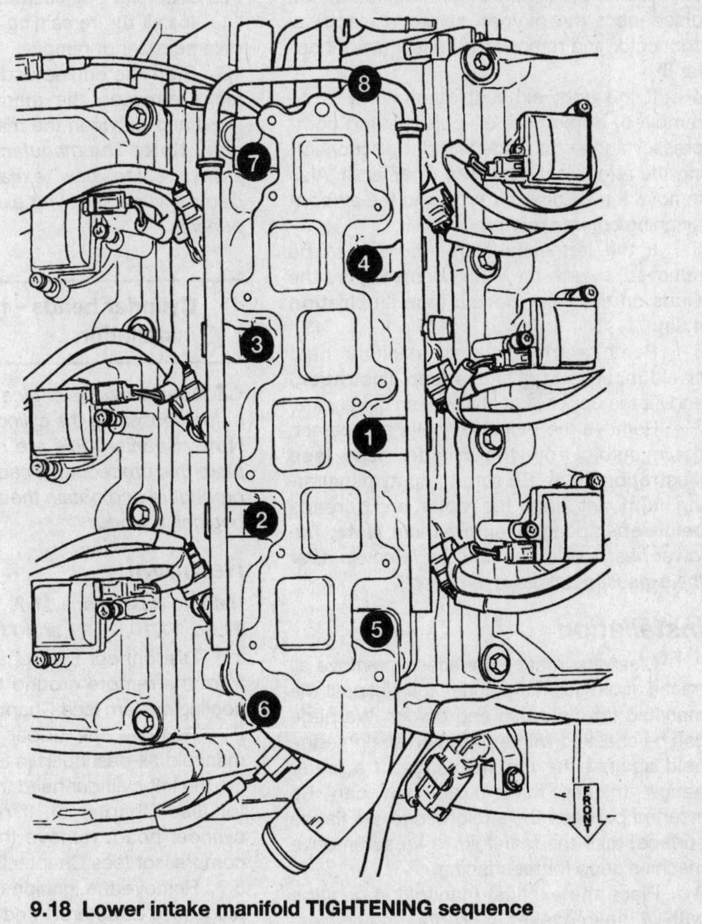

9.18 Lower intake manifold TIGHTENING sequence

10 Exhaust manifold(s) - removal and installation

Note: *The engine must be completely cool before beginning this procedure.*

Removal

Refer to illustration 10.6

1 Disconnect the negative battery cable from the remote ground terminal (see Chapter 5).

2 Raise the front of the vehicle and support it securely on jackstands. Detach the catalytic converters/front exhaust pipes from the exhaust manifolds and from the front resonator (see Chapter 6), then remove the

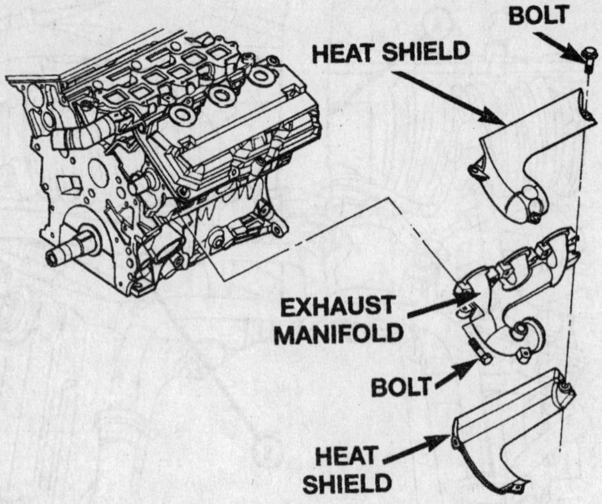

10.6 Exhaust manifold mounting details

11.7 Remove the ground wire terminals from the bottom bolt of the camshaft retainer plate at the back of the left cylinder head (arrow) - you may have to bend the water pipe near it slightly to fully remove the bolt

exhaust pipes from the vehicle.

3 Working from the engine compartment, disconnect the oxygen sensor's electrical connector and remove the sensor (see Chapter 6).

4 If the right exhaust manifold is to be removed, detach the air conditioning compressor and set it aside without disconnecting the refrigerant lines (see Chapter 3). Also remove the oil dipstick tube and the air conditioning compressor bracket.

5 If the left exhaust manifold is to be removed, detach the wiring harness from the studs on the valve covers **(see illustration 4.5a)**.

6 Remove the exhaust manifold heat shield mounting bolts/nuts **(see illustration)** and lift the upper heat shield from the engine.

7 Remove the mounting bolts and detach the manifold from the cylinder head **(see illustration 10.6)**. Be sure to spray penetrating lubricant onto the bolts and threads before attempting to remove them. **Note:** *The lower heat shield can now be removed after the exhaust manifold is removed.*

Installation

8 Clean the mating surfaces to remove all traces of old gasket material, then inspect the manifold for distortion and cracks. Warpage can be checked with a precision straightedge held against the mating flange. If a feeler gauge thicker than 0.030-inch can be inserted between the straightedge and flange surface, take the manifold to an automotive machine shop for resurfacing.

9 Place the exhaust manifold in position with a new gasket (and the lower heat shields) and install the mounting bolts finger tight. **Note:** *Be sure to identify the exhaust manifold gaskets by the correct cylinder designation and the position of the exhaust ports on the gasket.*

10 Starting in the middle and working out toward the ends, tighten the mounting bolts in several increments, to the torque listed in this Chapter's Specifications.

11 Install the remaining components in the reverse order of removal.

12 Start the engine and check for exhaust leaks between the manifold and cylinder head and between the manifold and exhaust pipe. **Note:** *The manufacturer recommends always using new exhaust system band clamps when servicing exhaust system components.*

11 Cylinder heads - removal and installation

Caution: *Allow the engine to cool completely before loosening the cylinder head bolts.*
Note: *Special tools are necessary to complete this procedure. Read through the entire procedure and obtain the special tools before beginning work.*

Removal

Refer to illustrations 11.7, 11.9a, 11.9b, 11.9c, 11.10, 11.11 and 11.15

1 Disconnect the negative battery cable from the remote ground terminal. Drain the cooling system (see Chapter 1).

2 Remove the upper and lower intake manifold as described in Section 9. If removing the left cylinder head, remove the alternator (see Chapter 5). If removing the right cylinder head, remove the air conditioning compressor (see Chapter 3).

3 Remove the ignition coils and the spark plugs (see Chapters 1 and 5, if necessary).

4 Detach the exhaust manifold from the cylinder head being removed (see Section 10).

5 Remove the valve cover(s) (see Section 4).

6 Remove the rocker arms and shafts (see Section 5).

7 Disconnect all remaining wires and vacuum hoses from the cylinder head(s) **(see illustration)**. Be sure to label them to simplify reinstallation.

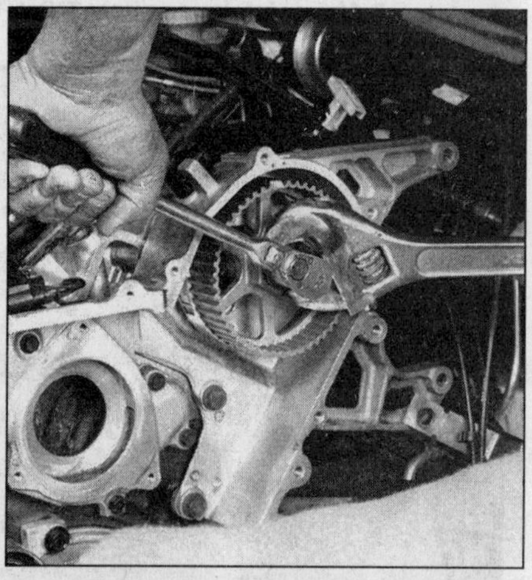

11.9a With the engine raised (or the radiator and condenser removed), hold the camshaft sprocket with a wrench while loosening the bolt with a socket and breaker bar - these bolts are very tight

8 Remove the timing belt covers, align the TDC marks and remove the timing belt (see Section 7). **Note:** *If the belt is to be reused, mark it's direction of rotation before removing it.*

9 Hold the camshaft sprocket hex with a wrench while using a socket and breaker bar to loosen the camshaft bolt, which is under considerable torque **(see illustration)**. It may be necessary to loosen the engine mounts (see Section 18) and raise the engine for sufficient clearance to withdraw the long camshaft bolt **(see illustration)**. As an alternative, remove the radiator and air conditioning condenser (see Chapter 3), it makes the job much easier and the engine does not have to be raised. **Caution:** *The two camshaft sprockets are not interchangeable, nor are the camshaft sprocket bolts. The left*

11.9b The camshaft sprocket bolts are not interchangeable - mark them "left" or "right"

11.9c The camshaft sprockets are also not interchangeable - the left sprocket has a camshaft position sensor ring (arrow) on the back

camshaft sprocket has the ignition pick-up slots **(see illustration)***, and the left sprocket bolt is longer (10 inches, vs. 8-3/8 inches long for the right bolt).*

10 The power steering pump bracket must be detached to remove the left cylinder head. Also remove the bolt at the bottom, from the power steering bracket to the block **(see illustration)**.

11 Unbolt and remove the rear timing belt cover(s) **(see illustration)**. On the left cylinder head, a steel alternator support bracket behind the rear belt cover must be removed. **Note:** *The rear cover on the right cylinder head has water-passage O-rings on the back.*

12 Make sure there are no brackets or connectors attached to the back of either cylinder head.

13 Using the new head gasket, outline the cylinders and bolt pattern on a piece of cardboard. Be sure to indicate the front of the engine for reference. Punch holes at the bolt locations.

14 Loosen each of the cylinder head mounting bolts 1/4-turn at a time until they can be removed by hand - work from bolt-to-bolt in a pattern that's the reverse of the tightening sequence **(see illustration 10.22)**. Store the bolts in the cardboard holder as they're removed. This will ensure they are reinstalled in their original locations, which is absolutely essential.

15 Lift the head(s) off the engine **(see illustration)**. If resistance is felt, don't pry between the head and block as damage to the mating surfaces will result. Recheck for head bolts that may have been overlooked, then use a hammer and block of wood to tap up on the head to break the gasket seal. Be careful because there are locating dowels in the block which position each head. As a last resort, pry each head up at the rear corner only and be careful not to damage anything. After removal, place the head on blocks of wood to prevent damage to the gasket surfaces.

16 Refer to Chapter 2C, for cylinder head disassembly, inspection and valve service procedures. **Note:** *If the camshaft is to be removed for examination or replacement, it must be done with the cylinder head* ***off*** *the engine, as it comes out the back of the cylinder head.*

11.10 Remove the two power steering pump bracket bolts (arrows) plus a hidden bolt behind the bracket

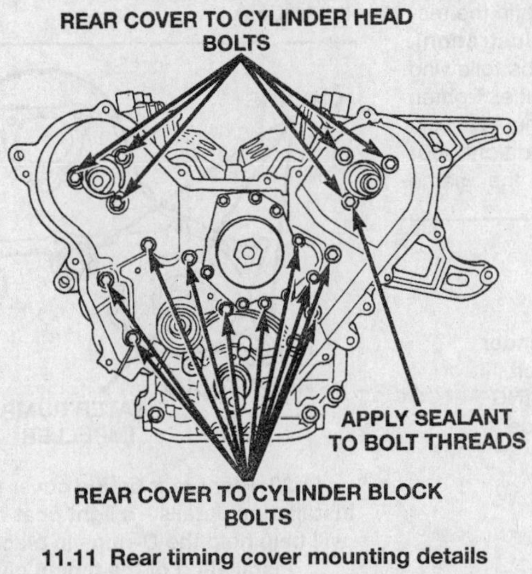

11.11 Rear timing cover mounting details

11.15 Remove the cylinder head from the engine, being careful not to damage the dowel pins in the block

11.17 Use a putty knife or gasket scraper to remove gasket material from the cylinder head and block

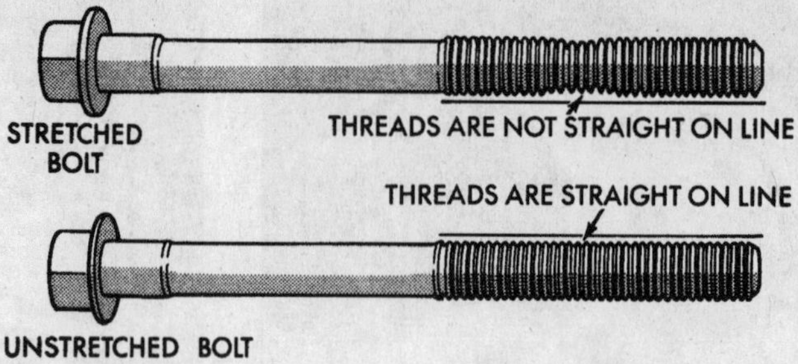

11.19 To check a cylinder head bolt for stretching, lay it against a straightedge - if any threads don't contact the straightedge, replace the bolt

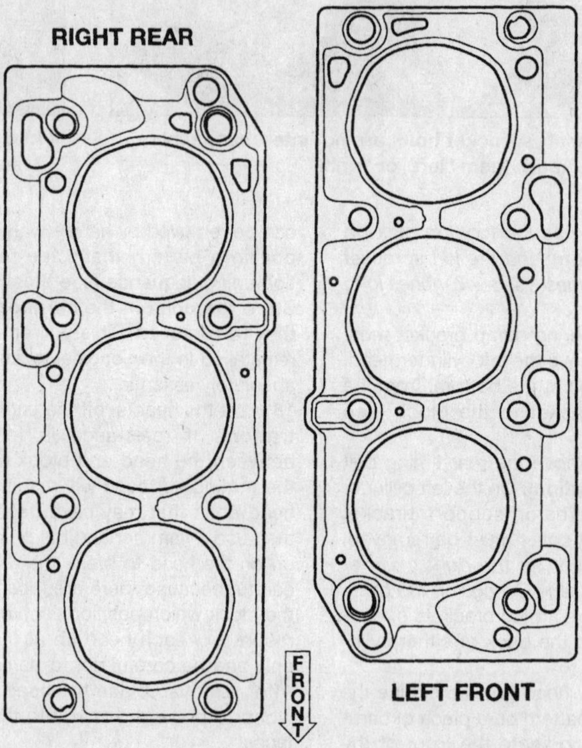

11.20 Cylinder head gasket installation details

Installation

Refer to illustrations 11.17, 11.19, 11.20, 11.22 and 11.23

17 The mating surfaces of each cylinder head and block must be perfectly clean when the head is installed. Use a gasket scraper to remove all traces of carbon and old gasket material **(see illustration)**, then clean the mating surfaces with lacquer thinner or acetone. If there's oil on the mating surfaces when the head is installed, the gasket may not seal correctly and leaks may develop. When working on the block, it's a good idea to cover the valley with shop rags to keep debris out of the engine. Use a shop rag or vacuum cleaner to remove any debris that falls into the cylinders.

18 Check the block and head mating surfaces for nicks, deep scratches and other damage. If damage is slight, it can be removed with a file; if it's excessive, machining may be the only alternative.

19 Use a tap of the correct size to chase the threads in the head bolt holes. Dirt, corrosion, sealant and damaged threads will affect torque readings. Check the cleaned head bolts for stretch by holding them next to a steel ruler **(see illustration)**. If all the threads don't touch the ruler, the bolt should be replaced.

20 Position the new gasket over the dowel pins in the block. Some gaskets are marked TOP or FRONT to ensure correct installation **(see illustration)**.

21 Make sure the camshaft is installed in the cylinder head , then carefully position the head on the block without disturbing the gasket.

22 Tighten the bolts to 45 ft-lbs in the recommended sequence **(see illustration)**. Next, tighten the bolts to 65 ft-lbs following the same recommended sequence. Tighten the bolts to 65 ft-lbs again as a double check. Finally, tighten each bolt an additional 90-degrees (1/4-turn) following the same sequence. Do not use a torque wrench for this last step.

23 Reattach the rear timing belt covers to the cylinder heads and block, making sure new O-rings are in place where used **(see illustration)**.

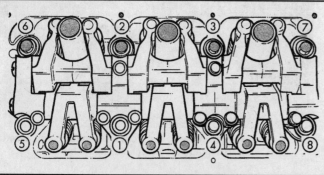

11.22 Cylinder head bolt TIGHTENING sequence

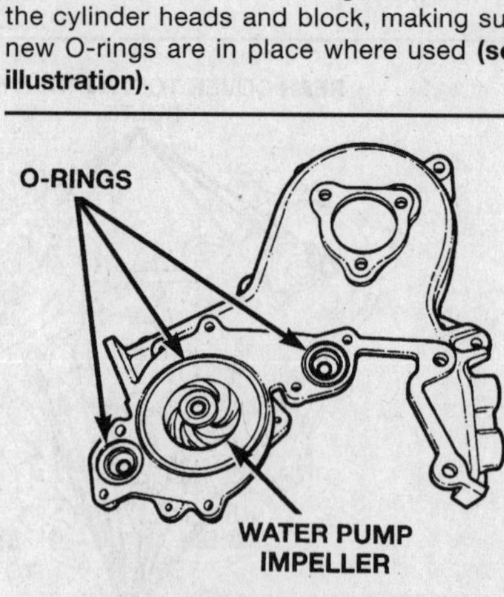

11.23 Right rear timing cover O-ring installation details – a light coat of grease will help hold the O-rings in place during installation of the timing cover

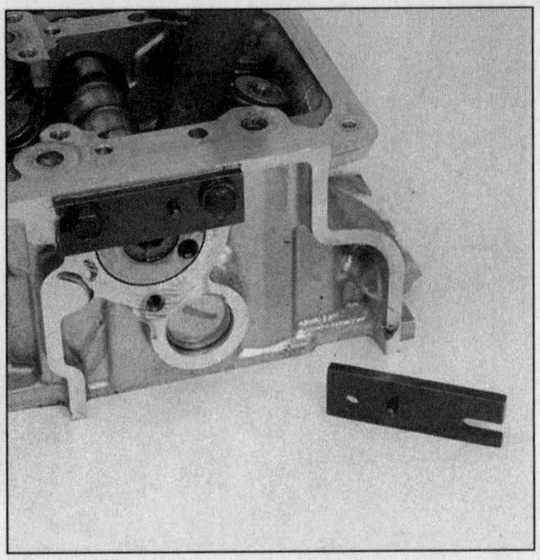

11.24 Bolt the special camshaft alignment tools to the back of each cylinder head to hold the camshafts in the TDC position

11.25 To properly index the camshaft sprockets, use a dial indicator to determine true TDC for number 1 cylinder

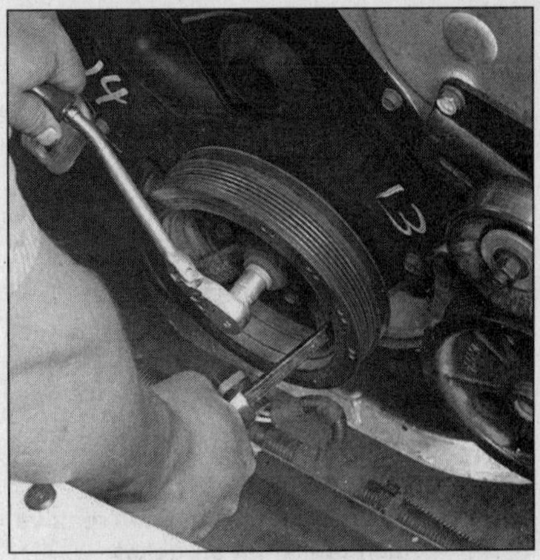

12.3 Insert a prybar or large screwdriver through the pulley to hold it while you loosen the crankshaft pulley bolt

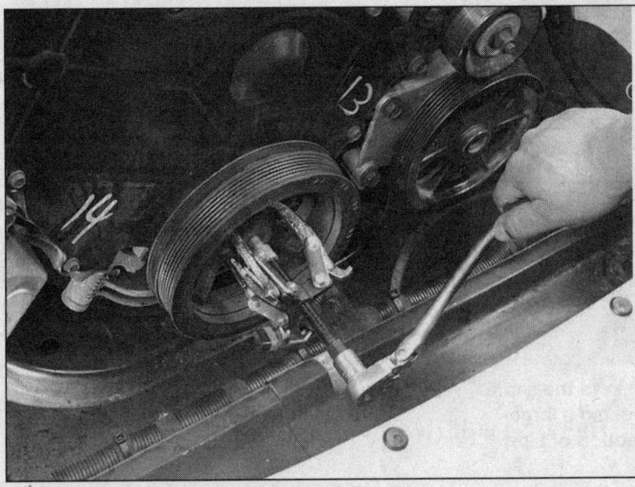

12.4 Use a three jaw puller to remove the crankshaft pulley. A long Allen bolt must be inserted into the crankshaft for the tool to push against

Camshaft sprocket timing

Refer to illustrations 11.24 and 11.25

24 At this point a special tool is required to lock the camshaft(s) into the TDC position before installing the camshaft sprockets **(see illustration)**. If you cannot obtain the tool from your local auto parts store or dealer, contact a specialty tool manufacturer. Bolt one of these tools at the back of each head, making sure the locating pin fits into the hole in the camshaft.

25 Rotate the engine clockwise until the mark on the crankshaft sprocket aligns with the TDC mark on the oil pump housing **(see illustration 7.7a)**. **Note:** *The crankshaft should already be in this position if the engine has not been rotated after the timing belt was removed.* Set up a dial indicator through the number 1 spark plug hole so that it touches the top of the piston **(see illustration)**. If you don't have a long adapter for the indicator, remove the spark plug tube with locking pliers (do not use the pliers on the threaded portion). Using the crankshaft damper bolt in the crankshaft, rotate the engine slightly back and forth until there is no piston movement indicated by the dial indicator. This will be the true TDC.

26 Each camshaft sprocket has a D-shaped hole where it fits over the camshaft, and requires precision alignment to properly time the engine. With the camshafts held at the rear by the special tools, and the crankshaft positioned at TDC for number 1 cylinder, place the camshaft sprockets in place with their respective bolts, but **do not tighten the bolts**. Use Loctite 271 sealer on the bolt threads.

27 With the engine in this position, install the timing belt and the tensioner (see Section 7, Steps 10 through 12). The timing marks on the camshaft sprockets should be within the two marks on the rear covers **(see illustration 7.7b)**.

28 Hold the hex on the camshaft sprockets with a wrench and tighten the camshaft bolts to the torque listed in this Chapter's Specifications **(see illustration 11.9a)**.

29 Remove the special camshaft aligning tools on the rear of the cylinder heads. Install the camshaft cover at the back of the head with a new O-ring.

30 After the cylinder heads have been installed and the camshaft timing procedure has been performed the remaining installation steps are the reverse of removal.

31 Change the oil and filter, refill the cooling system (see Chapter 1), run the engine and check for leaks.

12 Crankshaft pulley - removal and installation

Refer to illustrations 12.3 and 12.4

1 Disconnect the negative battery cable from the remote ground terminal. Remove the accessory drivebelts (see Chapter 1).

2 Refer to Chapter 3 and remove the upper radiator crossmember and cooling fan assembly.

3 Position a large screwdriver through the crankshaft pulley to keep the crankshaft from turning and remove the pulley-to-crankshaft bolt **(see illustration)**.

4 Pull the crankshaft pulley off the crankshaft with a puller **(see illustration)**. **Caution:** *The jaws of the puller must only contact the hub of the pulley - not the outer ring.* **Note:** *A long Allen-head bolt must be inserted into the crankshaft nose for the puller's tapered tip to push against.*

5 To install the crankshaft pulley slide the pulley onto the crankshaft as far as it will slide on, then use a vibration damper installation tool to press the pulley onto the crankshaft.

6 Install the crankshaft pulley retaining bolt and tighten it to the torque listed in this Chapter's Specifications.

7 The remainder of installation is the reverse of the removal.

13 Crankshaft front oil seal - replacement

Refer to illustrations 13.3, 13.4, 13.5 and 13.6

1 Remove the crankshaft pulley (see Section 12).

2 Remove the front timing belt covers and timing belt (see Section 7).

3 Use a two-bolt puller to remove the

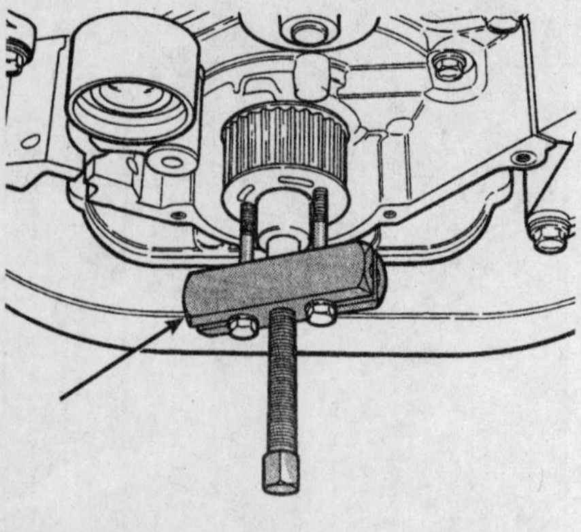

13.3 A two-bolt puller is used to remove the crankshaft sprocket

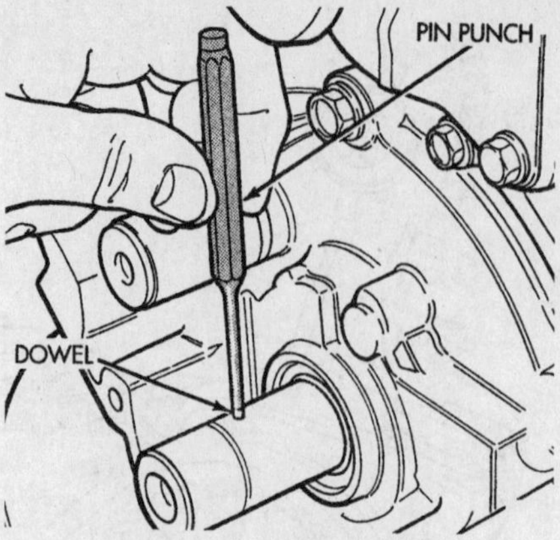

13.4 Tap the dowel pin down into the crankshaft with a punch - it can be extracted from inside the crankshaft snout with a small magnet

13.5 Using a hook-type seal remover, pry out the old seal

13.6 Drive the new seal in to the same depth as the old one, using a large-diameter socket or section of pipe

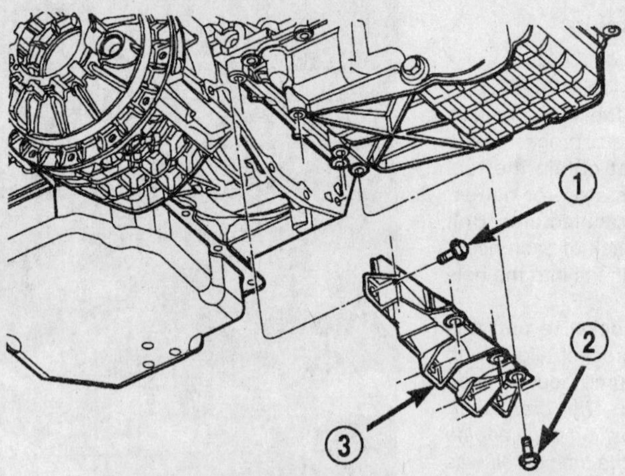

14.5 Transaxle to oil pan support brace installation details

1 *Vertical bolt*
2 *Horizontal bolt*
3 *Support brace*

crankshaft sprocket, with two bolts threaded into the sprocket **(see illustration)**.

4 With a hammer and punch, tap the dowel pin out of the crankshaft **(see illustration)**. Drive the pin into the hollow, threaded area of the crankshaft snout, where it can be extracted with a small magnet.

5 Pry the old seal out with a hook-type seal tool, being very careful not to scratch the seal surface of the crankshaft **(see illustration)**. Note how the seal is installed - the new one must be installed to the same depth and facing the same way.

6 Lubricate the inner lip of the new seal with engine oil and drive it in with a large socket or section of pipe and a hammer **(see illustration)**.

7 Installation is the reverse of removal. Tap the dowel pin back into the crankshaft, with 3/64-inch extending out.

14 Oil pan - removal and installation

Removal

Refer to illustration 14.5

1 Disconnect the negative battery cable from the remote ground terminal.

2 Raise the front of the vehicle and place it securely on jackstands. Apply the parking brake and block the rear wheels to keep the vehicle from rolling off the stands. Drain the engine oil and remove the oil filter (see Chapter 1).

3 Disconnect the stabilizer bar from the front suspension and move it toward the rear of the vehicle (see Chapter 10).

4 Remove the oil dipstick tube and the engine oil cooler line from the right side of the oil pan (if equipped).

5 Remove the transaxle to oil pan support bracket at the rear of the pan **(see illustration)**.

6 Detach the clips securing the transaxle oil cooler lines.

7 Remove the bolts and nuts, then carefully separate the oil pan from the block. Don't pry between the block and the pan or damage to the sealing surfaces could occur and oil leaks may develop. Instead, tap the pan with a soft-face hammer to break the gasket seal.

Installation

Refer to illustration 14.9

8 Clean the pan with solvent and remove all old sealant and gasket material from the block and pan mating surfaces. Clean the mating surfaces with lacquer thinner or acetone and make sure the bolt holes in the block are clear. Check the oil pan flange for distortion, particularly around the bolt holes.

9 Apply a bead of RTV sealant to the parting lines between the engine block and the oil pump housing and then to the engine block and rear main oil seal retainer. Install the gasket on the block **(see illustration)**.

10 Place the oil pan in position on the block and install the nuts/bolts.

11 After the oil pan fasteners are installed, tighten them to the torque listed in this Chapter's Specifications. Starting at the center, follow a criss-cross pattern and work up to the final torque in three steps.

12 Place the transaxle to oil pan support brace in position and install the vertical bolts. Tighten the vertical bolts to 10 in-lbs.

13 Install the horizontal bolts and tighten them to 40 ft-lbs, then re-torque the vertical bolts to 40 ft-lbs starting at the center and working outward.

14 The remaining steps are the reverse of the removal procedure.

15 Refill the engine with oil (see Chapter 1),

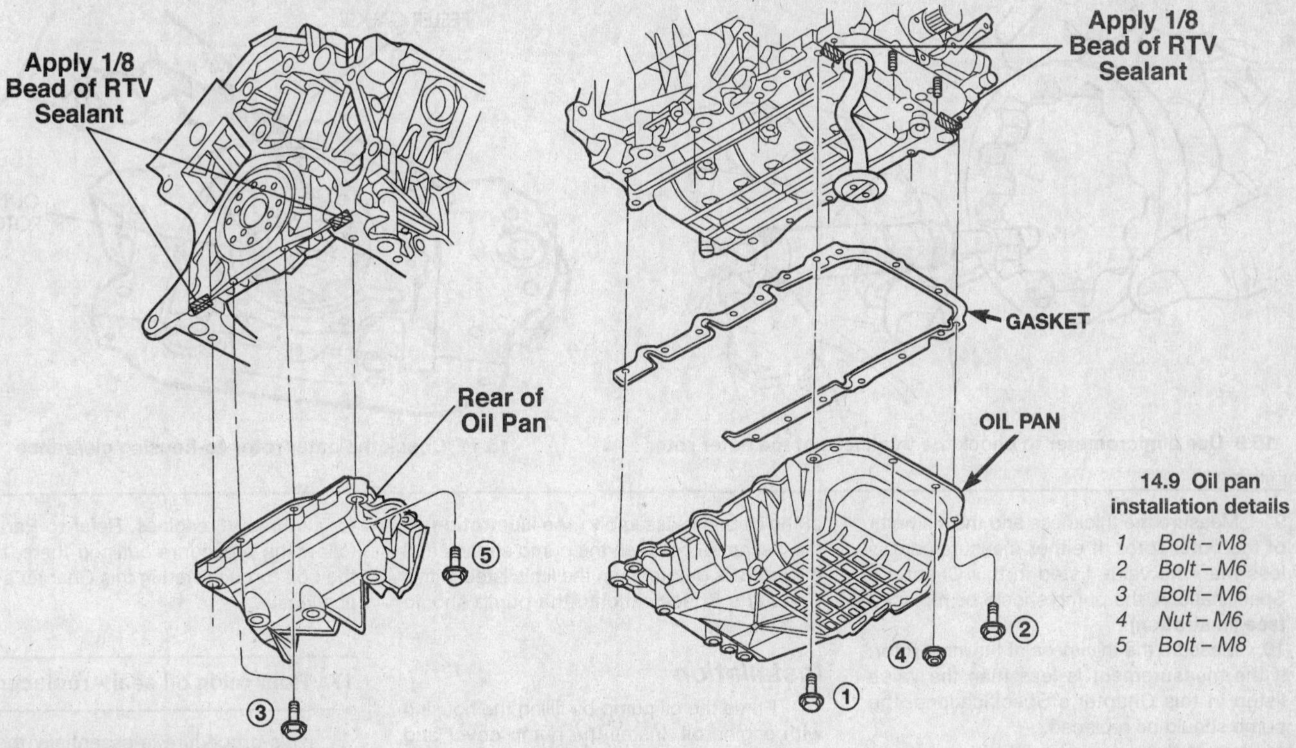

14.9 Oil pan installation details

1 Bolt – M8
2 Bolt – M6
3 Bolt – M6
4 Nut – M6
5 Bolt – M8

15.3 Oil pump housing mounting bolts (arrows) (lower two bolts not visible in this photo)

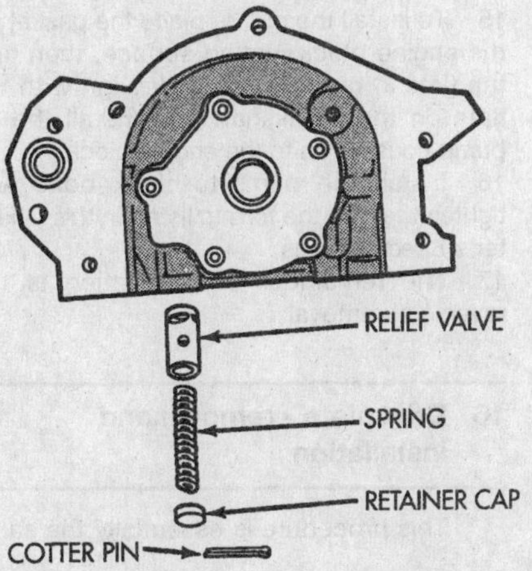

15.4 Remove the oil pressure relief valve for cleaning and inspection

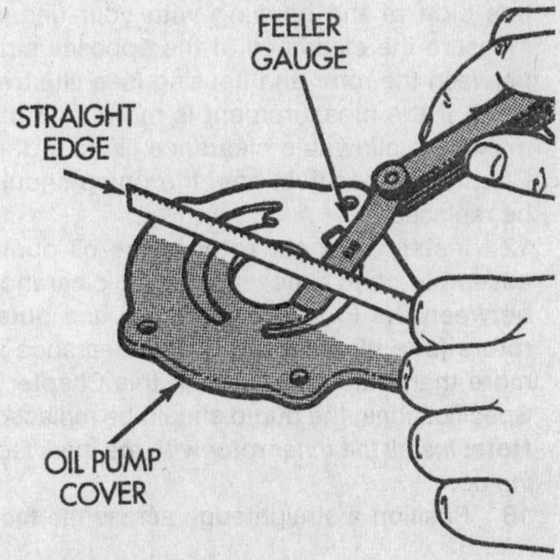

15.8 Place a straightedge across the oil pump cover and check it for warpage with a feeler gauge

replace the filter, run it until normal operating temperature is reached and check for leaks.

15 Oil pump - removal, inspection and installation

Removal

Refer to illustration 15.3

1 Remove the timing belt and crankshaft sprocket (see Sections 7 and 13).

2 Remove the oil pan, then remove oil pump pick-up tube (see Section 14).

3 Remove the oil-pump-to-block bolts and pull the oil pump from the block **(see illustration)**.

Inspection

Refer to illustrations 15.4, 15.8, 15.9, 15.11, 15.12 and 15.13

4 Remove the pressure relief valve and spring by removing the cotter pin **(see illustration)**. Drill a 1/8-inch hole in the cap and screw in a self-tapping screw. Use a vise or locking pliers to pull the cap out, allowing inspection and cleaning.

5 Unbolt the cover from the back of the oil pump housing. Remove the inner and outer rotors from the oil pump body, noting their installed direction for reassembly.

6 Clean all parts thoroughly in solvent and carefully inspect the rotors, pump cover and oil pump housing for nicks, scratches or burrs. Replace the assembly if it is damaged.

7 Clean the relief valve plunger and inspect it for wear. Small burrs can be removed with 400-grit wet sandpaper and oil. The spring should measure 1.95 inches long and it should provide 23-to 25 pounds of pressure when compressed to 1-11/32 inches.

8 Use a straightedge and measure the oil pump cover for warpage with a feeler gauge **(see illustration)**. If it's warped more than the limit listed in this Chapter's Specifications, the pump should be replaced.

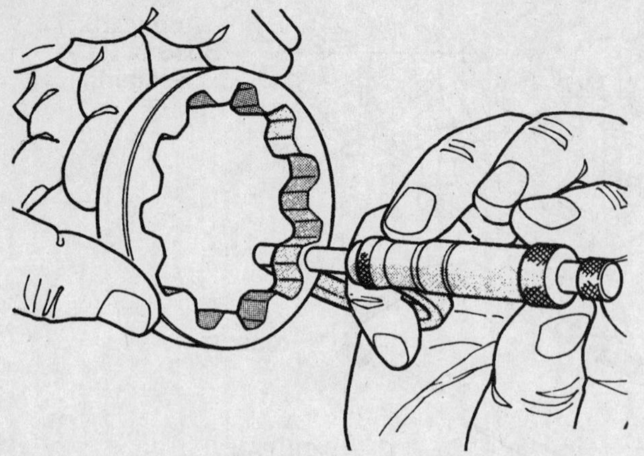

15.9 Use a micrometer to check the thickness of the outer rotor

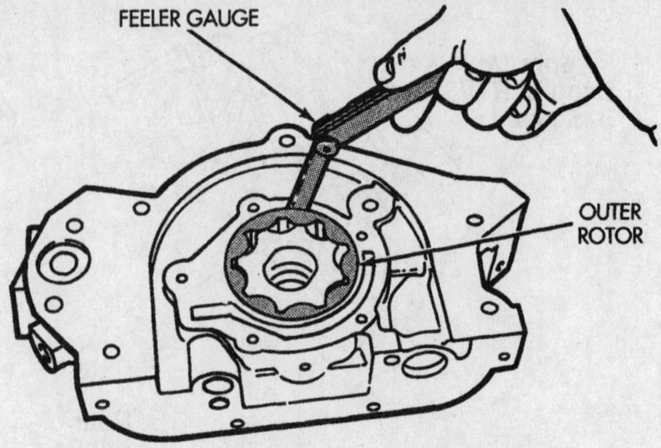

15.11 Check the outer rotor-to-housing clearance

9 Measure the thickness and the diameter of the outer rotor. If either measurement is less than the value listed in this Chapter's Specifications, the pump should be replaced **(see illustration)**.

10 Measure the thickness of the inner rotor. If the measurement is less than the value listed in this Chapter's Specifications, the pump should be replaced.

11 Insert the outer rotor into the oil pump housing and, while holding the rotor against one side of the housing with your finger, measure the clearance at the opposite side between the rotor and housing **(see illustration)**. If the measurement is more than the maximum allowable clearance listed in this Chapter's Specifications, the pump should be replaced.

12 Install the inner rotor in the oil pump assembly and measure the clearance between the lobes on the inner and outer rotors **(see illustration)**. If the clearance is more than the value listed in this Chapter's Specifications, the pump should be replaced. **Note:** *Install the inner rotor with the mark facing up.*

13 Position a straightedge across the face of the oil pump assembly **(see illustration)**. If the clearance between the pump surface and the rotors is greater than the limit listed in this Chapter's Specifications, the pump should be replaced.

Installation

14 Prime the oil pump by filling the housing with engine oil. Install the pump cover and tighten the bolts to the torque listed in this Chapter's Specifications.

15 To install the pump, place the gasket on the engine block mating surface, then turn the flats in the rotor so they align with the flats on the crankshaft and install the oil pump housing on to the engine block.

16 Install the pump-to-block bolts and tighten them to the torque listed in this Chapter's Specifications.

17 The remainder of installation is the reverse of removal.

16 Driveplate - removal and installation

This procedure is essentially the same for all three V6 engines. Refer to Part A and follow the procedure outlined there, but use the bolt torque listed in this Chapter's Specifications.

17 Rear main oil seal - replacement

This procedure is essentially the same for all three V6 engines. Refer to Part A and follow the procedure outlined there, but use the bolt torque value listed in this Chapter's Specifications.

18 Powertrain mounts - check and replacement

This procedure is essentially the same for all three V6 engines. Refer to Part A and follow the procedure and illustrations outlined there, but use the torque values listed in this Chapter's Specifications. **Note:** *Some models have liquid-filled insulators. These should not be replaced unless there are signs the fluid has leaked out.*

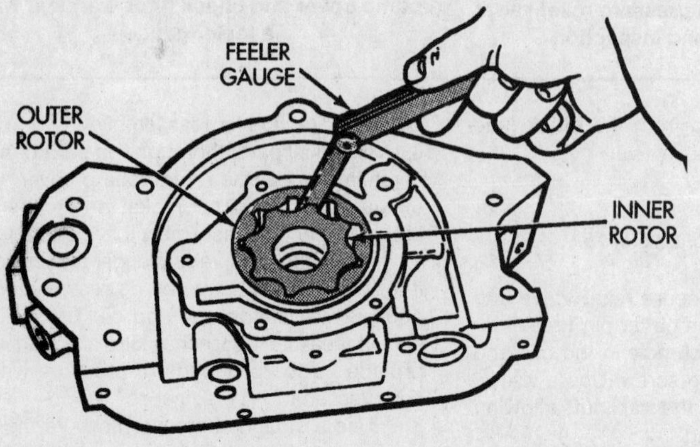

15.12 Check the clearance between the lobes of the inner and outer rotors

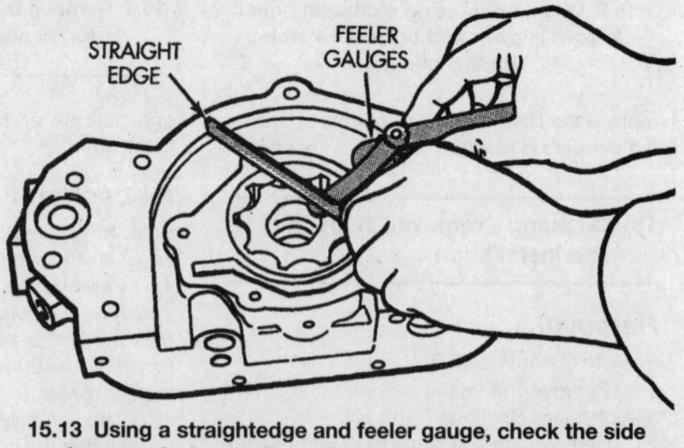

15.13 Using a straightedge and feeler gauge, check the side clearance between the surface of the oil pump housing and the rotors

Chapter 2 Part C
General engine overhaul procedures

Contents

Specifications

2.7L V6 engine

General

Displacement	167 cubic inches
Bore and stroke	3.386 x 3.091
Cylinder numbers (front to rear)	
Left bank	2-4-6
Right bank	1-3-5
Firing order	1-2-3-4-5-6
Cylinder compression pressure (minimum)	100 psi
Maximum variation between cylinders	25-percent
Oil pressure	
1998	25 to 80 psi at 3,000 rpm (5 psi minimum at idle)
1999 and 2000	25 to 105 psi at 3,000 rpm (5 psi minimum at idle)
2001 and later	45 to 105 psi at 3,000 rpm (5 psi minimum at idle)

Engine block

Cylinder bore diameter	3.3859 inches
Cylinder taper limit	0.002 inch
Cylinder out-of-round limit	0.003 inch

2.7L V6 engine (continued)

Pistons and rings

Piston to bore clearance	0.0001 to 0.0016 inch
Piston ring side clearance	
Compression rings	0.0016 to 0.0031 inch
Oil rings (steel rails)	0.0025 to 0.0082 inch
Piston ring end gap	
Top compression ring	0.008 to 0.014 inch
Second compression ring	0.0146 to 0.0249 inch
Oil ring (steel rails)	0.010 to 0.030 inch
Piston to pin clearance	0.0001 to 0.0004 inch
Piston pin to connecting rod clearance	0.0003 to 0.0008 inch

Crankshaft and connecting rods

Crankshaft endplay	0.0019 to 0.0108 inch
Main bearing journal	
Diameter	2.4997 to 2.5004 inches
Taper limit	
1998	0.0001 inch
1999 and later	0.0006 inch
Out-of-round limit	
1998	0.0002 inch
1999 and later	0.0006 inch
Connecting rod journal	
Diameter	2.1060 to 2.1067 inches
Taper limit	
1998	0.0001 inch
1999 and later	0.0006 inch
Out-of-round limit	
1998	0.0002 inch
1999 and later	0.0006 inch
Main bearing oil clearance	0.0014 to 0.0021 inch
Connecting rod bearing oil clearance	0.0010 to 0.0026 inch
Connecting rod endplay (side clearance)	0.0052 to 0.015 inch

Cylinder head and valves

Head warpage limit	0.002 inch
Valve seat angle	44 1/2 to 45 degrees
Valve face angle	45 to 45 1/2 degrees
Valve margin width (minimum)	
Intake	1/32 inch
Exhaust	3/64 inch
Valve stem diameter	
Intake	0.2337 to 0.2344 inch
Exhaust	0.2326 to 0.2333 inch
Valve stem-to-guide clearance	
Intake	0.0009 to 0.0026 inch
Exhaust	0.002 to 0.0037 inch
Valve spring free length	
Intake	1.7965 inch
Exhaust	1.7965 inch
Valve spring installed height	1-1/2 inches
Valve stem tip height	
Intake	
Standard	1.8551 inches
Allowable	1.8367 to 1.8735 inches
Exhaust	
Standard	1.9162 inches
Allowable	1.8978 to 1.9346 inches

Camshaft

Endplay	0.0051 to 0.011 inch
Lobe wear limit	
Standard	0.001 inch
Service limit	0.010 inch
Camshaft bearing oil clearance	
Standard	0.002 to 0.0035 inch
Service limit	0.0051 inch
Camshaft journal diameter	0.9441 to 0.9449 inches
Camshaft bore diameter	0.9469 to 0.9476 inches

Torque specifications*

	Ft-lbs (unless otherwise indicated)
Inner main bearing cap bolts	
Step 1	15
Step 2	Rotate an additional 1/4-turn
Outer main (windage tray) bearing cap bolts	
Step 1	20
Step 2	Rotate an additional 1/4-turn
Main bearing cap cross bolts	250 In-lbs
Connecting rod bearing cap nuts	
Step 1	20
Step 2	Rotate an additional 1/4-turn

***Note:** *Refer to Chapter 2A for additional torque specifications.*

3.2L and 3.5L V6 engines

General

Displacement	
3.2L	195 cubic inches
3.5L	214 cubic inches
Bore and stroke	
3.2L	3.622 x 3.189
3.5L	3.780 x 3.189
Cylinder numbers (front to rear)	
Left bank	2-4-6
Right bank	1-3-5
Firing order	1-2-3-4-5-6
Cylinder compression pressure (minimum)	100 psi
Maximum variation between cylinders	25-percent
Oil pressure	
1998	25 to 80 psi at 3,000 rpm (5 psi minimum at idle)
1999 and 2000	25 to 105 psi at 3,000 rpm (5 psi minimum at idle)
2001	45 to 105 psi at 3,000 rpm (5 psi minimum at idle)

Engine block

Cylinder bore diameter	
3.2L	3.622 inches
3.5L	3.780 inches
Cylinder taper limit	0.002 inch
Cylinder out-of-round limit	0.003 inch

Pistons and rings

Piston to bore clearance	0.0003 to 0.0018 inch
Piston ring side clearance	
Compression rings	
3.2L	0.0016 to 0.0031 inch
3.5L	0.0014 to 0.0034 inch
Oil rings (steel rails)	0.0015 to 0.0073 inch
Piston ring end gap	
Top compression ring	0.008 to 0.014 inch
Second compression ring	
3.2L	0.0087 to 0.0193 inch
3.5L	0.0091 to 0.0197 inch
Oil ring (steel rails)	0.010 to 0.030 inch
Piston to pin clearance	0.0002 to 0.0006 inch
Piston pin to connecting rod clearance	0.0003 to 0.0007 inch

Crankshaft and connecting rods

Crankshaft endplay	0.004 to 0.012 inch
Main bearing journal	
Diameter	2.519 to 2.520 inches
Taper limit	
1998	0.0002 inch
1999 and later	0.0006 inch
Out-of-round limit	
1998	0.0001 inch
1999 and later	0.0006 inch

3.2L and 3.5L V6 engines (continued)

Crankshaft and connecting rods (continued)

Connecting rod journal	
Diameter	2.283 to 2.284 inches
Out-of-round/taper limits	
1998	0.0001 inch
1999 and later	0.0006 inch
Main bearing oil clearance	0.0007 to 0.0030 inch
Connecting rod bearing oil clearance	0.0007 to 0.0034 inch
Connecting rod endplay (side clearance)	0.005 to 0.0157 inch

Cylinder head and valves

Head warpage limit	0.002 inch
Valve seat angle	45 to 45-1/2 degrees
Valve face angle	44-1/2 to 45 degrees
Valve margin width (minimum)	
Intake	1/32 inch
Exhaust	3/64 inch
Valve stem diameter	
Intake	0.2730 to 0.2737 inch
Exhaust	0.2719 to 0.2726 inch
Valve stem-to-guide clearance	
Intake	0.0009 to 0.0026 inch
Exhaust	0.002 to 0.0037 inch
Valve spring free length	
Intake	1.7195 inch
Exhaust	1.7448 inch
Valve spring installed height	1-1/2 inches
Valve stem tip height	
Intake	1.668 to 1.7187 inches
Exhaust	1.760 to 1.8105 inches

Camshaft

Endplay	0.004 to 0.014 inch
Lobe wear limit	
Standard	0.001 inch
Service limit	0.010 inch
Camshaft bearing oil clearance	
Standard	0.003 to 0.0047 inch
Service limit	0.0059 inch
Camshaft journal diameter	1.6905 to 1.6913 inches
Camshaft bore diameter	1.6944 to 1.6952 inches

Torque specifications*

	Ft-lbs (unless otherwise indicated)
Inner main bearing cap bolts	
Step 1	15
Step 2	Rotate an additional 1/4-turn
Outer main (windage tray) bearing cap bolts	
Step 1	20
Step 2	Rotate an additional 1/4-turn
Main bearing cap cross bolts	250 In-lbs
Connecting rod bearing cap nuts	
Step 1	40
Step 2	Rotate an additional 1/4-turn

***Note:** *Refer to Chapter 2B for additional torque specifications.*

1 General information - engine overhaul

Included in this portion of Chapter 2 are the general overhaul procedures for the cylinder head and internal engine components.

The information ranges from advice concerning preparation for an overhaul and the purchase of replacement parts to detailed, step-by-step procedures covering Removal and installation of internal engine components and the inspection of parts.

The following Sections have been written based on the assumption that the engine has been removed from the vehicle. For information concerning in-vehicle engine repair, as well as removal and installation of the external components necessary for the overhaul, see Chapter 2A or 2B.

The Specifications included in this Part are only those necessary for the inspection and overhaul procedures which follow. Refer to Chapter 2A or 2B for additional Specifications.

It's not always easy to determine when, or if, an engine should be completely overhauled, as a number of factors must be considered.

High mileage is not necessarily an indication that an overhaul is needed, while low mileage doesn't preclude the need for an overhaul. Frequency of servicing is probably

2.2a The oil pressure sending unit (arrow) on 2.7L engines is located on the lower right side of the engine block

2.2b The oil pressure sending unit (arrow) on 3.2L and 3.5L engines is located on the left side of the engine block next to the oil filter

the most important consideration. An engine that's had regular and frequent oil and filter changes, as well as other required maintenance, will most likely give many thousands of miles of reliable service. Conversely, a neglected engine may require an overhaul very early in its life.

Excessive oil consumption is an indication that piston rings, valve seals and/or valve guides are in need of attention. Make sure that oil leaks aren't responsible before deciding that the rings and/or guides are bad. Perform a cylinder compression check to determine the extent of the work required (see Section 3). Also check the vacuum readings under various conditions (see Section 4).

Loss of power, rough running, knocking or metallic engine noises, excessive valve train noise and high fuel consumption rates may also point to the need for an overhaul, especially if they're all present at the same time. If a complete tune-up doesn't remedy the situation, major mechanical work is the only solution.

An engine overhaul involves restoring the internal parts to the specifications of a new engine. During an overhaul, the piston rings are replaced and the cylinder walls are reconditioned (re-bored and/or honed). If a re-bore is done by an automotive machine shop, new oversize pistons will also be installed. The main bearings, connecting rod bearings and camshaft bearings are generally replaced with new ones and, if necessary, the crankshaft may be reground to restore the journals. Generally, the valves are serviced as well, since they're usually in less-than-perfect condition at this point. While the engine is being overhauled, other components, such as the starter, the alternator and the ignition system components can be rebuilt or replaced as well. The end result should be a like new engine that will give many trouble free miles. **Note:** *Critical cooling system components such as the hoses, drivebelts, thermostat and water pump should be replaced with new parts when an engine is overhauled. The radiator should be checked carefully to ensure that it isn't clogged or leaking* (see Chapter 3). *If you purchase a rebuilt engine or short block, some rebuilders will not warranty their engines unless the radiator has been professionally flushed. Also, we don't recommend overhauling the oil pump - always install a new one when an engine is rebuilt.*

Before beginning the engine overhaul, read through the entire procedure to familiarize yourself with the scope and requirements of the job. Overhauling an engine isn't difficult, but it is time-consuming. Plan on the vehicle being tied up for a minimum of two weeks, especially if parts must be taken to an automotive machine shop for repair or reconditioning. Check on availability of parts and make sure that any necessary special tools and equipment are obtained in advance. Most work can be done with typical hand tools, although a number of precision measuring tools are required for inspecting parts to determine if they must be replaced. Often an automotive machine shop will handle the inspection of parts and offer advice concerning reconditioning and replacement. **Note:** *Always wait until the engine has been completely disassembled and all components, especially the engine block, have been inspected before deciding what service and repair operations must be performed by an automotive machine shop.* Since the block's condition will be the major factor to consider when determining whether to overhaul the original engine or buy a rebuilt one, never purchase parts or have machine work done on other components until the block has been thoroughly inspected. As a general rule, time is the primary cost of an overhaul, so it doesn't pay to install worn or substandard parts.

As a final note, to ensure maximum life and minimum trouble from a rebuilt engine, everything must be assembled with care in a spotlessly-clean environment.

2 Oil pressure check

Refer to illustrations 2.2a and 2.2b

1 Low engine oil pressure can be a sign of an engine in need of rebuilding. A "low oil pressure" indicator (often called an "idiot light") is not a test of the oiling system. Such indicators only come on when the oil pressure is dangerously low. Even a factory oil pressure gauge in the instrument panel is only a relative indication, although much better for driver information than a warning light. A better test is with a mechanical (not electrical) oil pressure gauge. When used in conjunction with an accurate tachometer, an engine's oil pressure performance can be compared to factory Specifications for that year and model.

2 Locate the oil pressure indicator sending unit **(see illustrations)**.

3 Remove the oil pressure sending unit and install a fitting which will allow you to directly connect your hand-held, mechanical oil pressure gauge. Use Teflon tape or sealant on the threads of the adapter and the fitting on the end of your gauge's hose.

4 Connect an accurate tachometer to the engine, according to the tachometer manufacturer's instructions.

5 Check the oil pressure with the engine running (full operating temperature) at the specified engine speed, and compare it to this Chapter's Specifications. If it's extremely low, the bearings and/or oil pump are probably worn out.

3 Cylinder compression check

Refer to illustration 3.6

1 A compression check will tell you what mechanical condition the upper end of your engine (pistons, rings, valves, cylinder head gaskets) is in. Specifically, it can tell you if the compression is down due to leakage caused by worn piston rings, defective valves and seats or a blown cylinder head gasket. **Note:** *The engine must be at normal operating temperature and the battery must be fully charged for this check.*

2 Begin by cleaning the area around the spark plugs before you remove them (compressed air should be used, if available). The

3.6 A compression gauge with a threaded fitting for the spark plug hole is preferred over the type that requires hand pressure to maintain the seal

4.4 A simple vacuum gauge can be very handy in diagnosing engine condition and performance

idea is to prevent dirt from getting into the cylinders as the compression check is being done.

3 Remove all of the spark plugs from the engine (see Chapter 1).

4 Block the throttle wide open.

5 On conventional type ignition systems equipped with a distributor detach the coil wire from the center of the distributor cap and ground it on the engine block. Use a jumper wire with alligator clips on each end to ensure a good ground. On Direct Ignition Systems (DIS) or a Coil Over Plug (COP) type ignition systems disconnect electrical connector from the coil(s) to ensure that ignition system is disabled. The fuel pump circuit should also be disabled and the engine fuel system pressure relieved (see Chapter 4).

6 Install the compression gauge in the spark plug hole **(see illustration)**.

7 Crank the engine over at least seven compression strokes and watch the gauge. The compression should build up quickly in a healthy engine. Low compression on the first stroke, followed by gradually increasing pressure on successive strokes, indicates worn piston rings. A low compression reading on the first stroke, which doesn't build up during successive strokes, indicates leaking valves or a blown cylinder head gasket (a cracked cylinder head could also be the cause). Deposits on the undersides of the valve heads can also cause low compression. Record the highest gauge reading obtained.

8 Repeat the procedure for the remaining cylinders and compare the results to this Chapter's Specifications.

9 Add some engine oil (about three squirts from a plunger-type oil can) to each cylinder, through the spark plug hole, and repeat the test.

10 If the compression increases after the oil is added, the piston rings are definitely worn. If the compression doesn't increase significantly, the leakage is occurring at the valves or cylinder head gasket. Leakage past the valves may be caused by burned valve seats and/or faces or warped, cracked or bent valves.

11 If two adjacent cylinders have equally low compression, there's a strong possibility that the cylinder head gasket between them is blown. The appearance of coolant in the combustion chambers or the crankcase would verify this condition.

12 If one cylinder is slightly lower than the others, and the engine has a slightly rough idle, a worn lobe on the camshaft could be the cause.

13 If the compression is unusually high, the combustion chambers are probably coated with carbon deposits. If that's the case, the cylinder head(s) should be removed and decarbonized.

14 If compression is way down or varies greatly between cylinders, it would be a good idea to have a leak-down test performed by an automotive repair shop. This test will pinpoint exactly where the leakage is occurring and how severe it is.

4 Vacuum gauge diagnostic checks

Refer to illustrations 4.4 and 4.6

A vacuum gauge provides valuable information about what is going on in the engine at a low-cost. You can check for worn rings or cylinder walls, leaking cylinder head or intake manifold gaskets, incorrect carburetor adjustments, restricted exhaust, stuck or burned valves, weak valve springs, improper ignition or valve timing and ignition problems.

Unfortunately, vacuum gauge readings are easy to misinterpret, so they should be used in conjunction with other tests to confirm the diagnosis.

Both the absolute readings and the rate of needle movement are important for accurate interpretation. Most gauges measure vacuum in inches of mercury (in-Hg). The following references to vacuum assume the diagnosis is being performed at sea level. As elevation increases (or atmospheric pressure decreases), the reading will decrease. For every 1,000 foot increase in elevation above approximately 2000 feet, the gauge readings will decrease about one inch of mercury.

Connect the vacuum gauge directly to intake manifold vacuum, not to ported (throttle body) vacuum **(see illustration)**. Be sure no hoses are left disconnected during the test or false readings will result.

Before you begin the test, allow the engine to warm up completely. Block the wheels and set the parking brake. With the transmission in Park, start the engine and allow it to run at normal idle speed. **Warning:** *Keep your hands and the vacuum gauge clear of the fans.*

Read the vacuum gauge; an average, healthy engine should normally produce about 17 to 22 in-Hg of vacuum with a fairly steady needle **(see illustration)**. Refer to the following vacuum gauge readings and what they indicate about the engine's condition:

1 A low steady reading usually indicates a leaking gasket between the intake manifold and cylinder head(s) or throttle body, a leaky vacuum hose, late ignition timing or incorrect camshaft timing. Check ignition timing with a timing light and eliminate all other possible causes, utilizing the tests provided in this Chapter before you remove the timing chain cover to check the timing marks.

2 If the reading is three to eight inches below normal and it fluctuates at that low reading, suspect an intake manifold gasket leak at an intake port or a faulty fuel injector.

3 If the needle has regular drops of about two-to-four in-Hg at a steady rate, the valves are probably leaking. Perform a compression check or leak-down test to confirm this.

4 An irregular drop or down-flick of the needle can be caused by a sticking valve or an ignition misfire. Perform a compression check or leak-down test and read the spark plugs.

5 A rapid vibration of about four in-Hg

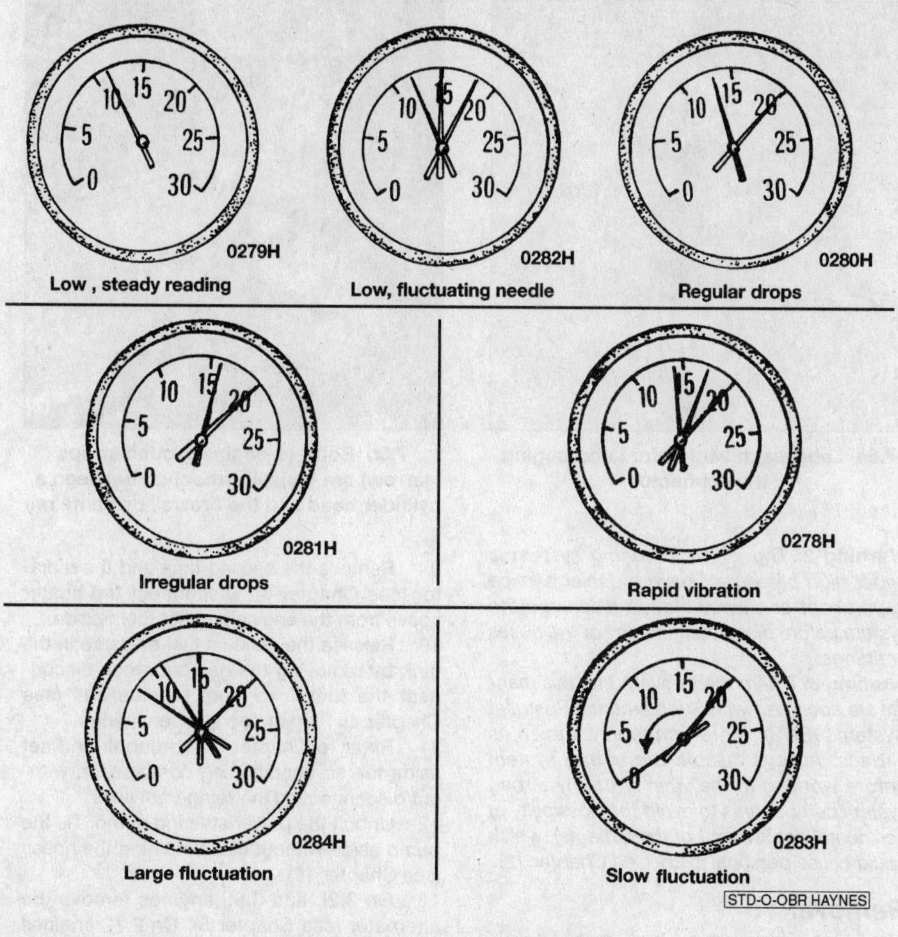

4.6 Typical vacuum gauge readings

vibration at idle combined with exhaust smoke indicates worn valve guides. Perform a leak-down test to confirm this. If the rapid vibration occurs with an increase in engine speed, check for a leaking intake manifold gasket or cylinder head gasket, weak valve springs, burned valves or ignition misfire.

6 A slight fluctuation, say one inch up and down, may mean ignition problems. Check all the usual tune-up items and, if necessary, run the engine on an ignition analyzer.

7 If there is a large fluctuation, perform a compression or leak-down test to look for a weak or dead cylinder or a blown cylinder head gasket.

8 If the needle moves slowly through a wide range, check for a clogged PCV system, incorrect idle fuel mixture, carburetor/throttle body or intake manifold gasket leaks.

9 Check for a slow return after revving the engine by quickly snapping the throttle open until the engine reaches about 2,500 rpm and let it shut. Normally the reading should drop to near zero, rise above normal idle reading (about 5 in-Hg over) and then return to the previous idle reading. If the vacuum returns slowly and doesn't peak when the throttle is snapped shut, the rings may be worn. If there is a long delay, look for a restricted exhaust system (often the muffler or catalytic converter). An easy way to check this is to temporarily disconnect the exhaust ahead of the suspected part and redo the test.

5 Engine rebuilding alternatives

The do-it-yourselfer is faced with a number of options when performing an engine overhaul. The decision to replace the engine block, piston/connecting rod assemblies and crankshaft depends on a number of factors, with the number one consideration being the condition of the block. Other considerations are cost, access to machine shop facilities, parts availability, time required to complete the project and the extent of prior mechanical experience on the part of the do-it-yourselfer.

Some of the rebuilding alternatives include:

Individual parts - If the inspection procedures reveal that the engine block and most engine components are in reusable condition, purchasing individual parts may be the most economical alternative. The block, crankshaft and piston/connecting rod assemblies should all be inspected carefully. Even if the block shows little wear, the cylinder bores should be surface-honed.

Crankshaft kit - This rebuild package consists of a reground crankshaft and a matched set of pistons and connecting rods. The pistons will already be installed on the connecting rods. Piston rings and the necessary bearings will be included in the kit. These kits are commonly available for standard cylinder bores, as well as for engine blocks which have been bored to a regular oversize.

Short block - A short block consists of an engine block with renewed crankshaft and piston/connecting rod assemblies already installed. All new bearings are incorporated and all clearances will be correct. The existing cylinder head(s), camshaft, valve train components and external parts can be bolted to the short block with little or no machine shop work necessary.

Long block - A long block consists of a short block plus an oil pump, oil pan, cylinder heads, valve covers, camshaft and valve train components, timing sprockets, timing chain and timing cover. All components are installed with new bearings, seals and gaskets incorporated throughout. The installation of manifolds and external parts is all that is necessary.

Used engine assembly - While overhaul provides the best assurance of a like-new engine, used engines available from wrecking yards and importers are often a very simple and economical solution. Many used engines come with warranties, but always give any engine a thorough diagnostic check-out before purchase. Check compression, vacuum and also for signs of oil leakage. If possible, have the seller run the engine, ether in the vehicle or on a test stand so you can be sure it runs smoothly with no knocking or other noises.

Give careful thought to which alternative is best for you and discuss the situation with local automotive machine shops, auto parts dealers or parts store countermen before ordering or purchasing replacement parts.

6 Engine removal - methods and precautions

If you've decided that an engine must be removed for overhaul or major repair work, several preliminary steps should be taken.

Locating a suitable place to work is extremely important. Adequate work space, along with storage space for the vehicle, will be needed. If a shop or garage isn't available, at the very least a flat, level, clean work surface made of concrete or asphalt is required.

Cleaning the engine compartment and engine before beginning the removal procedure will help keep tools clean and organized.

An engine hoist or A-frame will also be necessary. Make sure the equipment is rated in excess of the combined weight of the engine and transaxle. Safety is of primary importance, considering the potential hazards involved in lifting the engine out of the vehicle. The engine combinations used in the vehicles covered by this manual are intended to be removed from the top with the transaxle remaining in the vehicle.

If the engine is being removed by a novice, a helper should be available. Advice and aid from someone more experienced would also be helpful. There are many instances when one person cannot simultaneously perform all of the operations required when lifting the engine out of the vehicle.

Plan the operation ahead of time. Arrange for or obtain all of the tools and equipment you'll need prior to beginning the job. Some of the equipment necessary to perform engine removal and installation safely and with relative ease are (in addition to an engine hoist) a heavy duty floor jack, complete sets of wrenches and sockets as described in the front of this manual, wooden blocks and plenty of rags and cleaning solvent for mopping up spilled oil, coolant and gasoline. If the hoist must be rented, make sure that you arrange for it in advance and perform all of the operations possible without it beforehand. This will save you money and time.

Plan for the vehicle to be out of use for quite a while. A machine shop will be required to perform some of the work which the do-it-yourselfer can't accomplish without special equipment. These shops often have a busy schedule, so it would be a good idea to consult them before removing the engine in order to accurately estimate the amount of time required to rebuild or repair components that may need work.

Always be extremely careful when removing and installing the engine. Serious injury can result from careless actions. Plan ahead, take your time and a job of this nature, although major, can be accomplished successfully.

7 Engine - removal and installation

Warning 1: *Gasoline is extremely flammable, so take extra precautions when you work on any part of the fuel system. Don't smoke or allow open flames or bare light bulbs near the work area, and don't work in a garage where a natural gas-type appliance (such as a water heater or a clothes dryer) with a pilot light is present. Since gasoline is carcinogenic, wear latex gloves when there's a possibility of being exposed to fuel, and, if you spill any fuel on your skin, rinse it off immediately with soap and water. Mop up any spills immediately and do not store fuel-soaked rags where they could ignite. The fuel system is under constant pressure, so, if any fuel lines are to be disconnected, the fuel pressure in the system must be relieved first* (see Chapter 4). *When you perform any kind of work on the fuel system, wear safety glasses and have a Class B type fire extinguisher on hand.*

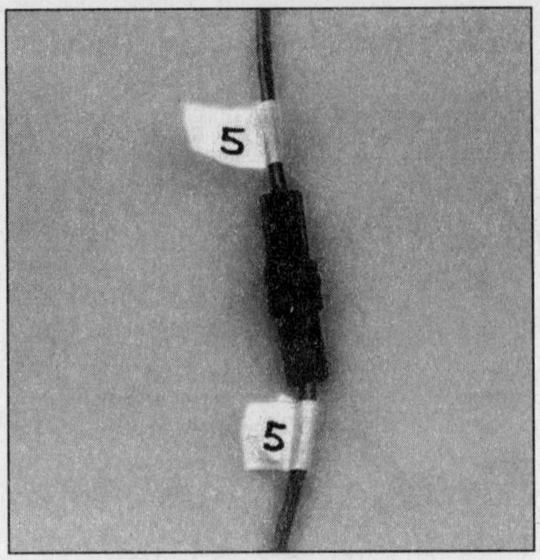

7.6a Label each wire before unplugging the connector

7.6b Body-to-engine ground straps (arrow) are typically attached between a cylinder head and the firewall or frame rail

Warning 2: *The air conditioning system is under high pressure - have a dealer service department or service station discharge the system before disconnecting any of the hoses or fittings.*

Warning 3: *The models covered by this manual are equipped with Supplemental Restraint Systems (SRS), more commonly known as airbags. Always disable the airbag system before working in the vicinity of any airbag system components to avoid the possibility of accidental deployment of the airbag(s), which could cause personal injury (see Chapter 12).*

Removal

Refer to illustrations 7.6a, 7.6b, 7.19a, 7.19b and 7.22

Note: *Read through the entire Section before beginning this procedure. The engine and transaxle are removed as a unit from below and then separated outside the vehicle.*

1 Relieve the fuel system pressure (see Chapter 4).

2 Disconnect the negative battery cable from the remote ground terminal (see Chapter 5).

3 Remove the hood, the cowl cover and the strut support brace (see Chapter 11).

4 Remove the air cleaner assembly (see Chapter 4).

5 Disconnect the throttle linkage (and speed control cable, when equipped) from the engine (see Chapter 4). Remove the upper intake manifold and the throttle body support bracket (see Chapter 2A or2B).

6 Clearly label, then disconnect all vacuum lines, emissions hoses, wiring harness connectors and ground straps. Masking tape and/or a touch up paint applicator work well for marking items **(see illustrations)**. Take instant photos or sketch the locations of components and brackets.

7 Raise the front of vehicle, support it securely on jackstands and block the rear wheels. Drain the cooling system and engine oil and remove the drivebelts (see Chapter 1).

8 Detach the hood release cable from the hood latch.

9 Remove the cooling fans and the radiator (see Chapter 3). Disconnect the heater hoses from the engine and set them aside.

10 Release the residual fuel pressure in the tank by removing the gas cap, then disconnect the fuel lines from the fuel rail (see Chapter 4). Plug or cap all open fittings.

11 Refer to Chapter 3 and unbolt and set aside the air-conditioning compressor, without disconnecting the refrigerant lines.

12 Unbolt the power steering pump. Tie the pump aside without disconnecting the hoses (see Chapter 10).

13 On 3.2L and 3.5L engines remove the alternator (see Chapter 5). On 2.7L engines remove the EGR valve assembly (see Chapter 6).

14 Remove the crankshaft and camshaft position sensors from the engine to avoid damage to the sensors during engine removal (see Chapter 6).

15 Working under the vehicle, disconnect the front exhaust pipes from the exhaust manifolds and at the front resonator, then remove the pipes from the vehicle (see Chapter 4).

16 Detach the transaxle oil cooler lines from the engine and remove the starter (see Chapter 5).

17 Remove the transaxle to oil pan support brace (see Chapter 2A or 2B), then mark the relationship of the drive plate to the torque converter and remove the torque converter mounting bolts. **Note:** *It will be necessary to place the vehicle in neutral and rotate the engine over by hand to access all of the torque converter mounting bolts. Once the bolts can be accessed it will be necessary to wedge a large screwdriver or pry bar between the torque converter ring gear and the transaxle bellhousing to hold the torque converter in place while loosening the bolts.*

18 Support the transaxle with a floor jack. Place a block of wood on the jack head to prevent damage to the transaxle and remove the remaining transaxle to engine mounting bolts. On 2.7L engines detach the transaxle shift cable bracket from the engine block.

7.19a On 2.7L engines, attach the chain or sling to the front of the left cylinder head . . .

7.19b . . . and to the rear of the right cylinder head as shown

7.22 Lift the engine off the mounts and guide it carefully around any obstacles as an assistant raises the hoist

19 Attach a lifting sling or chain to the lifting eye (if equipped) on the engine. If lifting eyes are not equipped attach the lifting sling or chain on a safe place such as the side of each cylinder head **(see illustrations)**. Position a hoist and connect the sling to it. Take up the slack until there is slight tension on the hoist.

20 Recheck to be sure nothing except the mounts are still connecting the engine to the vehicle. Disconnect anything still remaining.

21 Remove the engine mount to engine block bracket retaining nuts **(see Chapter 2A or 2B)**. **Warning:** *Do Not place any part of your body under the engine/transaxle when it's supported only by a hoist or other lifting device.*

22 Raise the engine slightly to disengage the mounts. Slowly raise the engine out of the vehicle **(see illustration)**. Check carefully to make sure nothing is hanging up as the hoist is raised.

23 Once the engine assembly is out of the vehicle, lower it to the ground and support it on wood blocks.

24 Remove the driveplate and mount the engine on an engine stand.

Installation

25 Check the engine and transaxle mounts. If they're worn or damaged, replace them.

26 Inspect the converter seal and bushing, if the seal is leaking now is the time to replace it. Before installing the torque converter, always apply a dab of grease to the nose of the converter and to the seal lips. **Caution:** *Take great care when installing the torque converter, following the procedure outlined in Chapter 7.*

27 Carefully lower the engine into the engine compartment making sure the mounts line up. Reinstall the remaining components in the reverse order of removal. Double-check to make sure everything is hooked up right. **Caution:** *DO NOT use the transaxle-to-engine bolts to force the transaxle and engine together.*

28 Add coolant, oil, power steering and transmission fluid as needed.

29 Run the engine and check for leaks and proper operation of all accessories, then install the hood and test drive the vehicle.

30 If the air conditioning system was discharged, have it evacuated, recharged and leak tested by the shop that discharged it.

8 Engine overhaul - disassembly sequence

1 It's much easier to disassemble and work on the engine if it's mounted on a portable engine stand. A stand can often be rented quite cheaply from an equipment rental yard. Before the engine is mounted on a stand, the driveplate should be removed from the engine.

2 If a stand isn't available, it's possible to disassemble the engine with it blocked up on the floor. Be extra careful not to tip or drop the engine when working without a stand.

3 If you're going to obtain a rebuilt engine, all external components must come off first, to be transferred to the replacement engine, just as they will if you're doing a complete engine overhaul yourself. These include:

Alternator and brackets
Emissions control components
Ignition coils
Valve covers
Thermostat and housing cover
EFI components
Intake/exhaust manifolds
Oil filter
Powertrain mounts
Driveplate

Note: *When removing the external components from the engine, pay close attention to details that may be helpful or important during installation. Note the installed position of gaskets, seals, spacers, pins, brackets, washers, bolts and other small items.*

4 If you're obtaining a short block, which consists of the engine block, crankshaft, pistons and connecting rods all assembled, then the cylinder heads, oil pan and oil pump will have to be removed as well. See *Engine rebuilding alternatives* for additional information regarding the different possibilities to be considered.

5 If you're planning a complete overhaul, the engine must be disassembled and the internal components removed in the following general order:

2.7L engine

Lower timing chain cover
Primary timing chain and sprockets
Water pump
Camshafts and secondary timing chains
Rocker arms and hydraulic lash adjusters
Cylinder heads
Oil pan
Oil pump and pick-up tube
Windage tray
Piston/connecting rod assemblies
Rear main oil seal retainer
Crankshaft and main bearings

3.2L and 3.5L engines

Rocker arm assemblies
Front timing belt covers
Timing belt and sprockets
Water pump

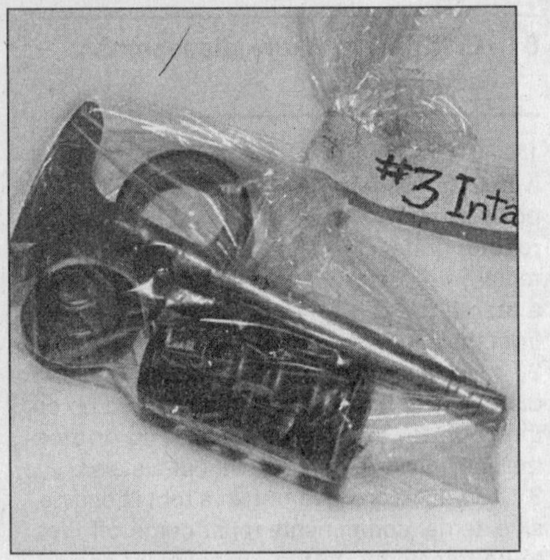

9.2 A small plastic bag, with an appropriate label, can be used to store the valve train components so they can be kept together and reinstalled in the original position

9.3 Use a valve spring compressor to compress the spring, then remove the valve stem locks from the valve stem

9.4 If the valve won't pull through the guide, deburr the edge of the stem end and the area around the top of the valve stem lock groove with a fine file or whetstone

Rear timing belt covers
Cylinder heads
Camshafts
Oil pan
Oil pump and pick-up tube
Windage tray
Piston/connecting rod assemblies
Rear main oil seal retainer
Crankshaft and main bearings

6 Before beginning the disassembly and overhaul procedures, make sure the following items are available. Also, refer to Engine overhaul - reassembly sequence for a list of tools and materials needed for engine reassembly.

Common hand tools
Small cardboard boxes or plastic bags for storing parts
Gasket scraper
Ridge reamer
Vibration damper puller
Micrometers
Telescoping gauges
Dial indicator set
Valve spring compressor
Cylinder surfacing hone
Piston ring groove cleaning tool
Electric drill motor
Tap and die set
Wire brushes
Oil gallery brushes
Cleaning solvent

9 Cylinder head - disassembly

Refer to illustrations 9.2, 9.3 and 9.4

Note: *New and rebuilt cylinder heads are commonly available for most engines at dealerships and auto parts stores. Due to the fact that some specialized tools are necessary for the disassembly and inspection procedures, and replacement parts may not be readily available, it may be more practical and economical for the home mechanic to purchase replacement heads rather than taking the time to disassemble, inspect and recondition the originals.*

1 Cylinder head disassembly involves removal of the intake and exhaust valves and related components. By now all of the rocker arm components and the camshafts should be removed from the cylinder head. If any of these components are still in place, remove them (see Chapter 2A or 2B) from the cylinder head. Label the parts or store them separately so they can be reinstalled in their original locations.

2 Before the valves are removed, arrange to label and store them, along with their related components, so they can be kept separate and reinstalled in the same valve guides they are removed from **(see illustration)**.

3 Compress the springs on the first valve with a spring compressor and remove the valve stem locks **(see illustration)**. Carefully release the valve spring compressor and remove the retainer, the spring and the spring seat (if used).

4 Pull the valve out of the cylinder head, then remove the oil seal from the guide. If the valve binds in the guide (won't pull through), push it back into the cylinder head and deburr the area around the valve stem lock groove with a fine file or whetstone **(see illustration)**.

5 Repeat the procedure for the remaining valves. Remember to keep all the parts for each valve together so they can be reinstalled in the same locations.

6 Once the valves and related components have been removed and stored in an organized manner, the cylinder head should be thoroughly cleaned and inspected. If a complete engine overhaul is being done, finish the engine disassembly procedures before beginning the cylinder head cleaning and inspection process.

10 Cylinder head - cleaning and inspection

1 Thorough cleaning of the cylinder heads and related valve train components, followed by a detailed inspection, will enable you to decide how much valve service work must be done during the engine overhaul. **Note:** *If the engine was severely overheated, the cylinder heads are probably warped (see Step 12).*

Cleaning

2 Scrape all traces of old gasket material and sealing compound off the cylinder head gasket, intake manifold and exhaust manifold sealing surfaces. Be very careful not to gouge the cylinder head. Special gasket removal solvents that soften gaskets and make removal much easier are available at auto parts stores.

3 Remove all built up scale from the coolant passages.

4 Run a stiff wire brush through the various holes to remove deposits that may have formed in them.

5 Run an appropriate-size tap into each of the threaded holes to remove corrosion and thread sealant that may be present. If compressed air is available, use it to clear the holes of debris produced by this operation. **Warning:** *Wear eye protection when using compressed air!*

6 Clean the combustion chambers with a brass wire brush and solvent if carbon has accumulated.

7 Clean the cylinder head with solvent and dry it thoroughly. Compressed air will speed the drying process and ensure that all holes and recessed areas are clean. **Note:** *Decarbonizing chemicals are available and may prove very useful when cleaning cylinder heads and valve train components. They are very caustic and should be used with caution.*

10.12 Check the cylinder head gasket surface for warpage by trying to slip a feeler gauge under the straightedge (see the Specifications for the maximum warpage allowed and use a feeler gauge of that thickness)

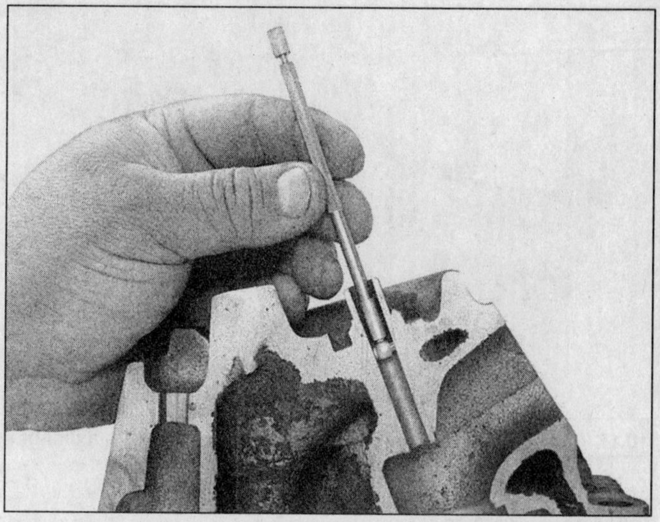

10.14 Use a small hole gauge to determine the inside diameter of the valve guides (the gauge is then measured with a micrometer)

Be sure to follow the instructions on the container.

8 Clean the rocker arms with solvent and dry them thoroughly (don't mix them up during the cleaning process). Compressed air will speed the drying process and can be used to clean out the oil passages.

9 Clean all the valve springs, spring seats, valve stem locks and retainers with solvent and dry them thoroughly. Do the components from one valve at a time to avoid mixing up the parts.

10 Scrape off any heavy deposits that may have formed on the valves, then use a motorized wire brush to remove deposits from the valve heads and stems. Again, make sure the valves don't get mixed up.

Inspection

Note: *Be sure to perform all of the following inspection procedures before concluding that machine shop work is required. Make a list of the items that need attention.*

Cylinder head

Refer to illustrations 10.12 and 10.14

11 Inspect the heads very carefully for cracks, evidence of coolant leakage and other damage. If cracks are found, check with an automotive machine shop concerning repair. If repair isn't possible, a new cylinder head should be obtained.

12 Using a straightedge and feeler gauge, check the cylinder head gasket mating surface for warpage **(see illustration)**. If the warpage exceeds the limit specified in this Chapter, it can be resurfaced at an automotive machine shop. **Note:** *The cylinder heads and the engine block have a combined total maximum resurface limit of 0.008 inch, be sure your machinist is aware of this fact!*

13 Examine the valve seats in each of the combustion chambers. If they're pitted, cracked or burned, the cylinder head will

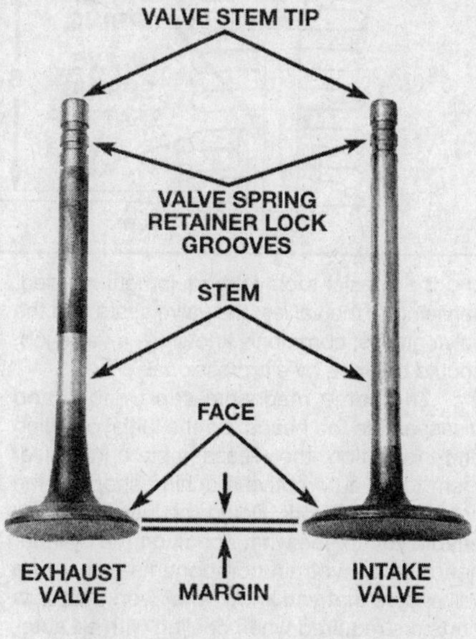

10.15 Check for valve wear at the points shown here

require valve service that's beyond the scope of the home mechanic.

14 Check the valve stem-to-guide clearance with a small hole gauge and micrometer **(see illustration)**, then measure the valve stem diameter with a micrometer and subtract it from the valve guide inside diameter to obtain the stem to guide clearance. When using a small hole gauge or telescoping snap gauge, insert the gauge to the middle portion of the valve guide (where wear should be minimal) and tighten the gauge. Move the gauge up and down in the guide. If the guide isn't worn the clearance should be equal from top to bottom. Loose areas indicate that the guide is tapered. If the measurement exceeds the stem-to-guide clearance limit found in this Chapter's Specifications, the

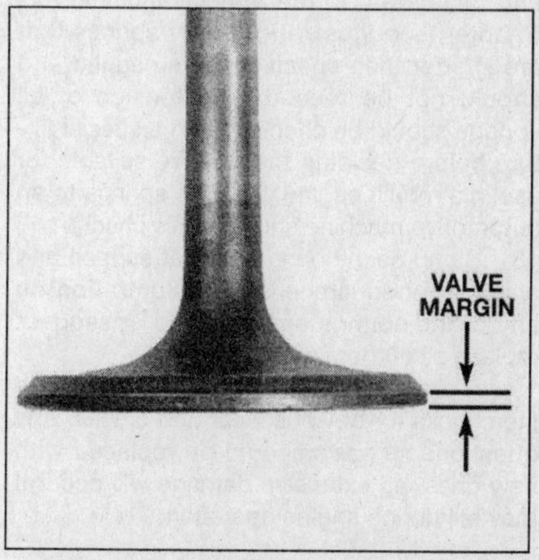

10.16 The margin width on each valve must be as specified (if no margin exists, the valve cannot be reused)

valve guides should be resized or replaced. After this is done, if there's still some doubt regarding the condition of the valve guides they should be checked by an automotive machine shop (the cost should be minimal).

Valves

Refer to illustrations 10.15 and 10.16

15 Carefully inspect each valve face for uneven wear, deformation, cracks, pits and burned areas **(see illustration)**. Check the valve stem for scuffing and galling and the neck for cracks. Rotate the valve and check for any obvious indication that it's bent. Look for pits and excessive wear on the end of the stem. The presence of any of these conditions indicates the need for valve service by an automotive machine shop.

16 Measure the margin width on each valve **(see illustration)**. Any valve with a margin narrower than specified in this Chapter will have to be replaced with a new one.

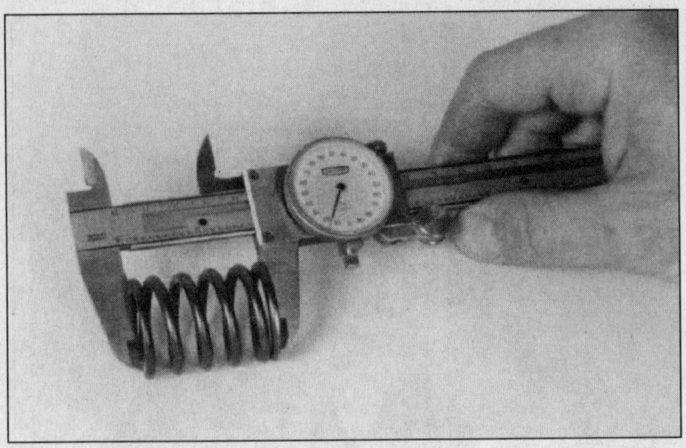

10.17 Measure the free length of each valve spring with a dial or vernier caliper

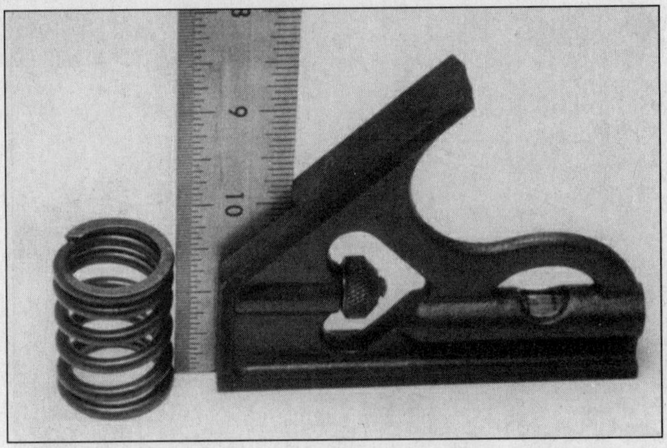

10.18 Check each valve spring for squareness

Valve components

Refer to illustrations 10.17 and 10.18

17 Check each valve spring for wear (on the ends) and pits. Measure the free length and compare it to the Specifications in this Chapter **(see illustration)**. Any springs that are shorter than specified have sagged and should not be reused. The tension of all springs should be checked with a special fixture before deciding that they're suitable for use in a rebuilt engine (take the springs to an automotive machine shop for this check).

18 Stand each spring on a flat surface and check it for squareness **(see illustration)**. If any of the springs are distorted or sagged, replace all of them with new parts.

19 Check the spring retainers and valve stem locks for obvious wear and cracks. Any questionable parts should be replaced with new ones, as extensive damage will occur if they fail during engine operation.

Camshaft, bearings, rocker arms and hydraulic lash adjusters

20 Refer to Section 21 of this Chapter for the camshaft and camshaft bearing inspection procedures. Be sure to inspect the camshaft bearing journals before the cylinder head is sent to the machine shop to have the valves serviced. If the journals are gouged or scored the cylinder head will have to be replaced regardless of the condition of the valves and related components. Inspect the rocker arms and the hydraulic lash adjusters (see Chapter 2A or 2B).

21 Any damaged or excessively worn parts must be replaced with new ones.

22 If the inspection process indicates that the valve components are in generally poor condition and worn beyond the limits specified, which is usually the case in an engine that's being overhauled, reassemble the valves in the cylinder head (see to Section 11 for valve servicing recommendations).

11 Valves - servicing

1 Because of the complex nature of the job and the special tools and equipment needed, servicing of the valves, the valve seats and the valve guides, commonly known as a valve job, should be done by a professional.

2 The home mechanic can remove and disassemble the heads, do the initial cleaning and inspection, then reassemble and deliver them to an automotive machine shop for the actual service work. Doing the inspection will enable you to see what condition the cylinder head and valvetrain components are in and will ensure that you know what work and new parts are required when dealing with an automotive machine shop.

3 The automotive machine shop, will remove the valves and springs, recondition or replace the valves and valve seats, recondition or replace the valve guides, check and replace the valve springs, spring retainers and valve stem locks (as necessary). They will also replace the valve seals with new ones, reassemble the valve components and make sure the installed spring height is correct. The cylinder head gasket surface will also be resurfaced if it's warped.

4 After the valve job has been performed by a professional, the cylinder head will be in like-new condition. When the cylinder head is returned, be sure to clean it again before installation on the engine to remove any metal particles and abrasive grit that may still be present from the valve service or cylinder head resurfacing operations. Use compressed air, if available, to blow out all the oil holes and passages.

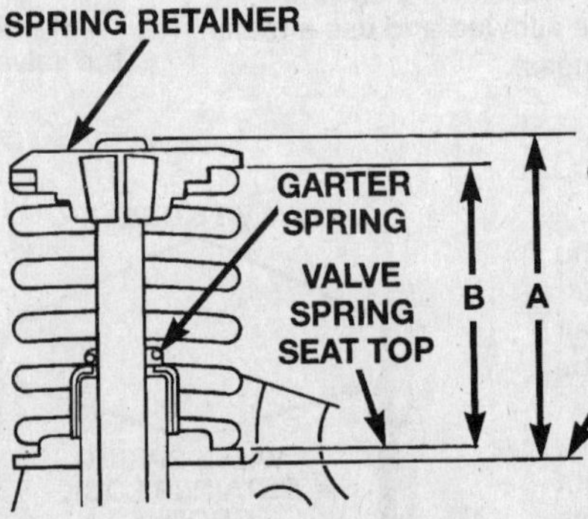

12.6 Valve stem tip height (A) is measured from the cylinder head surface to the top of the valve stem - Installed height (B) is measured from the top of the valve spring seat to the bottom of the retainer

12 Cylinder head - reassembly

Refer to illustration 12.6

1 Regardless of whether or not the cylinder head was sent to an automotive repair shop for valve servicing, make sure it is clean before beginning reassembly.

2 If the cylinder head was sent out for valve servicing, the valves and related components will already be in place. Begin the reassembly procedure with Step 6.

3 Install the valves, with light oiling on the stems into valve guides. Install the valve spring seat/valve seal assembly over the top of the valves tips by hand. Using the stem of the valves as a guide, slide the seals down to the top of each valve guide. Using a hammer and a deep socket or seal installation tool, gently tap each seal into place until it's completely seated on the guide. Don't twist or cock the seals during installation or they won't seal properly on the valve stems (see Chapter 2A or 2B).

4 Position the valve spring(s) in place on the cylinder head with the colored end facing UP and install the retainer. Compress the spring and retainer with a valve spring compressor and carefully install the keepers in the groove, then slowly release the compressor and make sure the keepers seat properly. Apply a small dab of grease to each keeper to hold it in place if necessary (see Chapter 2A or 2B). **Caution:** *Different length springs are used on the intake and exhaust*

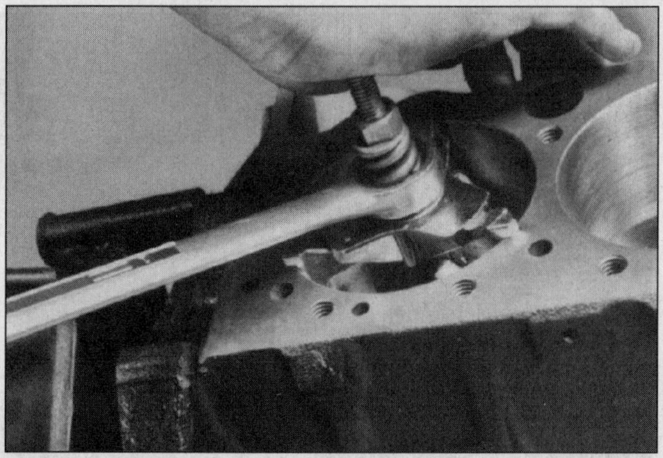

13.1 A ridge reamer is required to remove the ridge from the top of each cylinder - do this before removing the pistons!

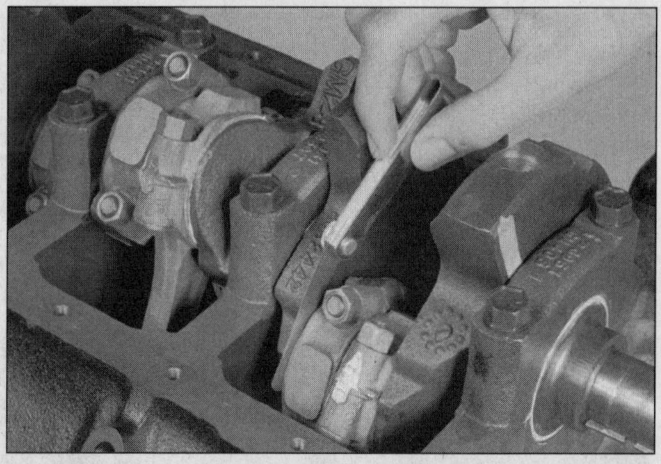

13.3 Check the connecting rod side clearance with a feeler gauge as shown

valves - accidentally installing an intake spring on an exhaust valve can cause major engine damage. The intake springs on all models are identified with a orange mark at the top. The exhaust springs on 1998 and 1999 models are identified with a green mark at the top, while 2000 and 2001 models exhaust springs are identified with a yellow mark at the top.

5 Repeat the procedure for the remaining valves. Be sure to return the components to their original locations - don't mix them up!

6 Check the installed valve spring height and the valve stem tip height with a ruler graduated in 1/32-inch increments or a dial caliper. If the head was sent out for service work, the installed height and the tip height should be correct (but don't automatically assume it is). The installed height measurement is taken from the top of each spring seat to the bottom of the retainer. If the height is greater than specified in this Chapter, shims can be added under the springs to correct it. **Caution:** *Do not, under any circumstances, shim the springs to the point where the installed height is less than specified.* The valve stem tip height measurement is taken from the cylinder head surface to the top of the valve stem **(see illustration)**. If the height is greater than specified in this Chapter, the tip of the valve can be ground to correct it. Incorrect tip height on these engines will lead to incorrect hydraulic lash adjuster preload. Too much hydraulic lash adjuster preload will result in a rough idle condition while too little preload will result in a noisy valve condition.

7 On 3.2L and 3.5L engines refer to Chapter 2B and install the camshafts, front oil seals and the rear cover plates.

8 Always install old cylinder head components in their original locations.

13 Pistons/connecting rods - removal

Refer to illustrations 13.1, 13.3 and 13.6

Note: *Prior to removing the piston/connecting rod assemblies, remove the cylinder heads, the oil pan and the oil pump pick-up by referring to the appropriate Sections in Chapter 2A or 2B, if not already removed.*

1 Use your fingernail to feel if a ridge has formed at the upper limit of ring travel (about 1/4-inch down from the top of each cylinder). If carbon deposits or cylinder wear have produced ridges, they must be completely removed with a special tool **(see illustration)**. Follow the manufacturer's instructions provided with the tool. Failure to remove the ridges before attempting to remove the piston/connecting rod assemblies may result in piston breakage.

2 After the cylinder ridges have been removed, turn the engine upside-down so the crankshaft is facing up and remove the windage tray.

3 Before the connecting rods are removed, check the side clearance (endplay) with feeler gauges. Slide them between the first connecting rod and the crankshaft throw until the play is removed **(see illustration)**. The side clearance is equal to the thickness of the feeler gauge(s). If the side clearance exceeds the service limit, new connecting rods will be required. If new rods (or a new crankshaft) are installed, the side clearance may fall under the specified minimum (if it does, the rods will have to be machined to restore it - consult an automotive machine shop for advice if necessary). Repeat the procedure for the remaining connecting rods.

4 Check the connecting rods and caps for identification marks. If they aren't plainly marked, use a small center punch to make the appropriate number of indentations on each rod and cap (1, 2, 3, etc.).

5 Loosen each of the connecting rod cap nuts 1/2-turn at a time until they can be removed by hand. Remove the number one connecting rod cap and bearing insert. Don't drop the bearing insert out of the cap.

6 Slip a short length of plastic or rubber hose over each connecting rod cap bolt to protect the crankshaft journal and cylinder wall as the piston is removed **(see illustration)**.

13.6 To prevent damage to the crankshaft journals and cylinder walls, slip sections of rubber or plastic hose over the connecting rod bolts before removing the pistons

7 Remove the bearing insert and push the connecting rod/piston assembly out through the top of the engine. Use a wooden hammer handle to push on the upper bearing surface in the connecting rod. If resistance is felt, double-check to make sure that all of the ridge was removed from the cylinder.

8 Repeat the procedure for the remaining cylinders.

9 After removal, reassemble the connecting rod caps and bearing inserts in their respective connecting rods and install the cap nuts finger tight. Leaving the old bearing inserts in place until reassembly will help prevent the connecting rod bearing surfaces from being accidentally nicked or gouged.

10 Don't separate the pistons from the connecting rods (see Section 18 for additional information).

14 Crankshaft - removal

Refer to illustrations 14.1, 14.3 and 14.4

Note: *The crankshaft can be removed only*

14.1 Checking crankshaft endplay with a dial indicator

14.3 Crankshaft endplay can also be measured with a feeler gauge at the number four main bearing

14.4 Use a center punch or number stamping dies to mark the main bearing caps to ensure installation in their original locations of the block (make the punch marks near one of the bolt heads)

15.1a The core plugs can be removed by tapping in one edge until the plug turns sideways . . .

15.1b . . . then remove the core plug with pliers

after the engine has been removed from the vehicle. It's assumed that the driveplate, crankshaft pulley, timing belt (3.2 and 3.5L engine), timing chain (2.7L engine), sprockets, oil pan, oil pump, windage tray and piston/connecting rod assemblies have already been removed. The rear main oil seal retainer must be unbolted and separated from the block before proceeding with crankshaft removal.

1 Before the crankshaft is removed, check the endplay. Mount a dial indicator with the stem in line with the crankshaft and just touching one of the crank throws **(see illustration)**.

2 Push the crankshaft all the way to the rear and zero the dial indicator. Next, pry the crankshaft to the front as far as possible and check the reading on the dial indicator. The distance that it moves is the endplay. If it's greater than specified in this Chapter, check the crankshaft thrust surfaces for wear. If no wear is evident, new main bearings should correct the endplay.

3 If a dial indicator isn't available, feeler gauges can be used. Gently pry or push the crankshaft all the way to the front of the engine. Slip feeler gauges between the crankshaft and the front face of the rear (thrust) main bearing to determine the clearance **(see illustration)**.

4 Main bearing caps typically have cast-in numbers and arrows on them, the numbers indicate the journal on which they are located and the arrows indicate the drivebelt end of the engine. Always check the main bearing caps to see if they're marked to indicate their locations. They should be numbered consecutively from the front of the engine to the rear. If they aren't, mark them with number stamping dies or a center-punch **(see illustration)**. Loosen the remaining main bearing cap bolts 1/4-turn at a time each in the reverse order of the tightening sequence (see Section 24), until the bearing caps can be removed by hand. Note if any stud bolts are used and make sure they're returned to their original locations when the crankshaft is reinstalled.

5 Gently tap the caps with a soft-face hammer, then separate it from the engine block. If necessary, use the bolts as levers to remove the cap assembly. Try not to drop the bearing inserts if they come out with the cap assembly.

6 Carefully lift the crankshaft out of the engine. It may be a good idea to have an assistant available, since the crankshaft is quite heavy. With the bearing inserts in place in the engine block and in the main bearing caps, return the caps to they're original locations on the engine block and tighten the bolts finger tight.

15 Engine block - cleaning

Refer to illustrations 15.1a, 15.1b, 15.8 and 15.10

Caution: *The core plugs (also known as freeze or soft plugs) may be difficult or impossible to retrieve if they're driven completely into the block coolant passages.*

1 Using the blunt end of a punch, tap in on the outer edge of the core plug to turn the

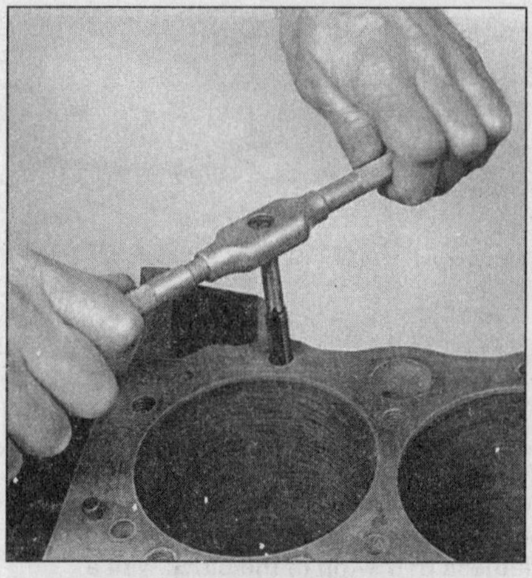

15.8 All bolt holes in the block - particularly the main bearing cap and cylinder head bolt holes - should be cleaned and restored with a tap (be sure to remove debris from the holes after this is done)

15.10 A large socket on an extension can be used to drive the new core plugs into the bores

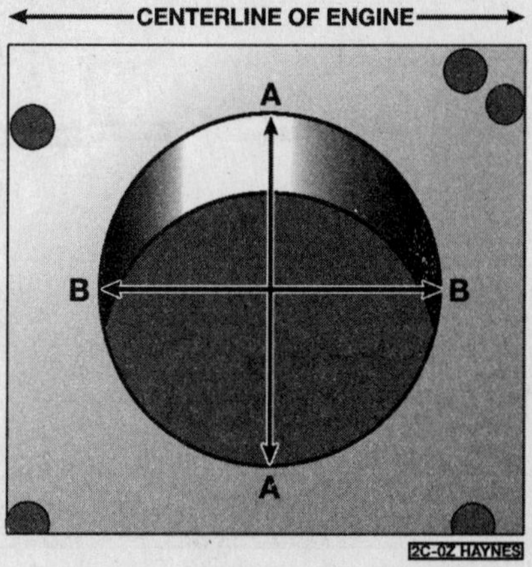

16.4a Measure the diameter of each cylinder at a right angle to the engine centerline (A), and parallel to the engine centerline (B) - out-of-round is the difference between A and B; taper is the difference between A and B at the top of the cylinder and A and B at the bottom of the cylinder

plug sideways in the bore. Then use pliers to pull the core plug from the engine block **(see illustrations)**.

2 Using a gasket scraper, remove all traces of gasket material from the engine block. Be very careful not to nick or gouge the gasket sealing surfaces.

3 Remove the main bearing cap assembly and separate the bearing inserts from the caps and the engine block. Label the bearings, indicating which cylinder they were removed from and whether they were in the cap or the block, then set them aside.

4 Remove all of the threaded oil gallery plugs from the block. The plugs are usually very tight - they may have to be drilled out and the holes retapped. Use new plugs when the engine is reassembled.

5 If the engine is extremely dirty, it should be taken to an automotive machine shop to be steam cleaned or hot tanked.

6 After the block is returned, clean all oil holes and oil galleries one more time. Brushes specifically designed for this purpose are available at most auto parts stores. Flush the passages with warm water until the water runs clear, dry the block thoroughly and wipe all machined surfaces with a light, rust-preventive oil. If you have access to compressed air, use it to speed the drying process and to blow out all the oil holes and galleries. **Warning:** *Wear eye protection when using compressed air!*

7 If the block isn't extremely dirty or sludged up, you can do an adequate cleaning job with hot soapy water and a stiff brush. Take plenty of time and do a thorough job. Regardless of the cleaning method used, be sure to clean all oil holes and galleries very thoroughly, dry the block completely and coat all machined surfaces with light oil.

8 The threaded holes in the block must be clean to ensure accurate torque readings during reassembly. Run the proper size tap into each of the holes to remove rust, corrosion, thread sealant or sludge and restore damaged threads **(see illustration)**. If possible, use compressed air to clear the holes of debris produced by this operation. Now is a good time to clean the threads on the cylinder head bolts and the main bearing cap bolts as well.

9 Reinstall the main bearing caps and tighten the bolts finger tight.

10 After coating the sealing surfaces of the new core plugs with core plug sealant, install them in the engine block **(see illustration)**. Make sure they're driven in straight and seated properly or leakage could result. Special tools are available for this purpose, but a large socket, with an outside diameter that will just slip into the core plug, a 1/2-inch drive extension and a hammer will work just as well. **Note:** *Make sure the socket only contacts the inside of the core plug, not the rim.*

11 Apply non-hardening thread sealant to the new oil gallery plugs and thread them into the holes in the block. Make sure they're tightened securely.

12 If the engine isn't going to be reassembled right away, cover it with a large plastic trash bag to keep it clean.

16 Engine block - inspection

Refer to illustrations 16.4a, 16.4b, 16.4c and 16.11

1 Before the block is inspected, it should be cleaned (see Section 15).

2 Visually check the block for cracks, rust and corrosion. Look for stripped threads in the threaded holes. It's also a good idea to have the block checked for hidden cracks by an automotive machine shop that has the special equipment to do this type of work. If defects are found, have the block repaired, if possible, or replaced.

3 Check the cylinder bores for scuffing and scoring.

4 Check the cylinders for taper and out-of-round conditions as follows **(see illustrations)**:

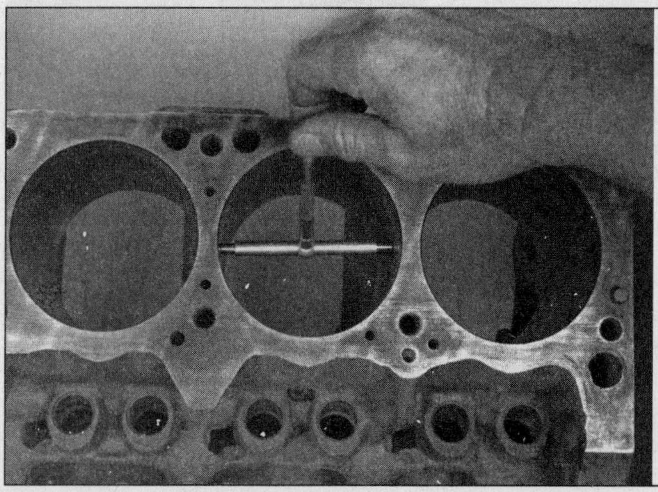

16.4b Use a telescoping gauge to measure the bore - the ability to "feel" when it is at the correct point will be developed over time, so work slowly and repeat the check until you're satisfied the bore measurement is accurate

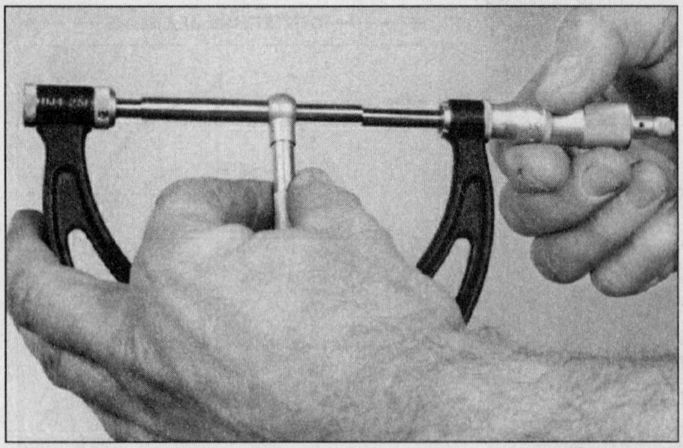

16.4c The gauge is then measured with a micrometer to determine the bore size

16.8 Check the flatness of the top of the block with a straightedge and feeler gauge - if distortion exceeds Specifications, the block deck will have to be machined

a) *Measure the diameter of each cylinder at the top (just under the ridge area), center and bottom of the cylinder bore, parallel to the crankshaft axis.*
b) *Next measure each cylinder's diameter at the same three locations perpendicular to the crankshaft axis.*
c) *The taper of the cylinder is the difference between the bore diameter at the top of the cylinder and the diameter at the bottom. The out-of-round specification of the cylinder bore is the difference between the parallel and perpendicular readings. Compare your results to those listed in this Chapter's Specifications.*

5 Repeat the procedure for the remaining pistons and cylinders.

6 If the cylinder walls are badly scuffed or scored, or if they're out-of-round or tapered beyond the limits given in this Chapter's Specifications, have the engine block rebored and honed at an automotive machine shop. If a rebore is done, oversize pistons and rings will be required.

7 If the cylinders are in reasonably good condition and not worn to the outside of the limits, and if the piston-to-cylinder clearances can be maintained properly, then they don't have to be rebored. Honing is all that's necessary (see Section 17).

8 Using a precision straightedge and feeler gauge, check the block deck (the surface that mates with the cylinder head) for distortion **(see illustration)**. **Note:** *The cylinder heads and the engine block have a combined total maximum resurface limit of 0.008 inch, be sure your machinist is aware of this fact!*

17 Cylinder honing

Refer to illustrations 17.3a and 17.3b

1 Prior to engine reassembly, the cylinder bores must be honed so the new piston rings will seat correctly and provide the best possible combustion chamber seal. **Note:** *If you don't have the tools or don't want to tackle the honing operation, most automotive machine shops will do it for a reasonable fee.*

2 Before honing the cylinders, install the main bearing caps and tighten the bolts to the torque specified in this Chapter.

3 Two types of cylinder hones are commonly available - the flex hone or "bottle brush" type and the more traditional surfacing hone with spring-loaded stones. Both will do the job, but for the less experienced mechanic the "bottle brush" hone will probably be easier to use. You'll also need some kerosene or honing oil, rags and an electric drill motor. Proceed as follows:

a) *Mount the hone in the drill motor, compress the stones and slip it into the first cylinder* **(see illustration)**. *Be sure to wear safety goggles or a face shield!*
b) *Lubricate the cylinder with plenty of honing oil, turn on the drill and move the hone up-and-down in the cylinder at a pace that will produce a fine crosshatch pattern on the cylinder walls. Ideally, the crosshatch lines should intersect at approximately a 60-degree angle* **(see illustration)**. *Be sure to use plenty of lubricant and don't take off any more material than is absolutely necessary to produce the desired finish.* **Note:** *Piston ring manufacturers may specify a smaller crosshatch angle than the traditional 60-degrees - read and follow any instructions included with the new rings.*
c) *Don't withdraw the hone from the cylinder while it's running. Instead, shut off the drill and continue moving the hone up-and-down in the cylinder until it comes to a complete stop, then compress the stones and withdraw the hone. If you're using a "bottle brush" type hone, stop the drill motor, then turn the chuck in the normal direction of rotation while withdrawing the hone from the cylinder.*
d) *Wipe the oil out of the cylinder and repeat the procedure for the remaining cylinders.*

4 After the honing job is complete, chamfer the top edges of the cylinder bores with a small file so the rings won't catch when the pistons are installed. Be very careful not to

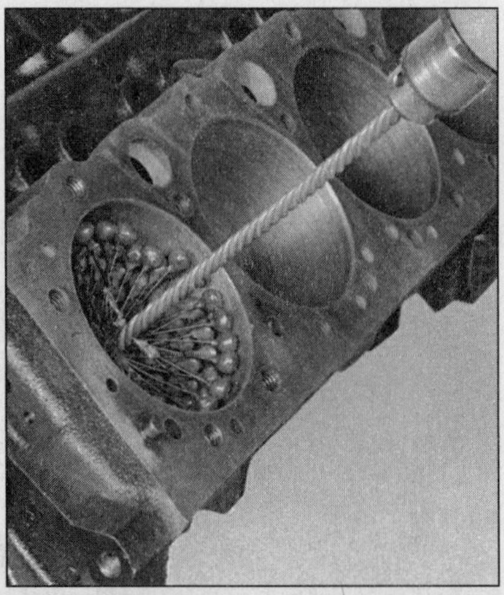

17.3a A "bottle brush" hone is the easiest type to use

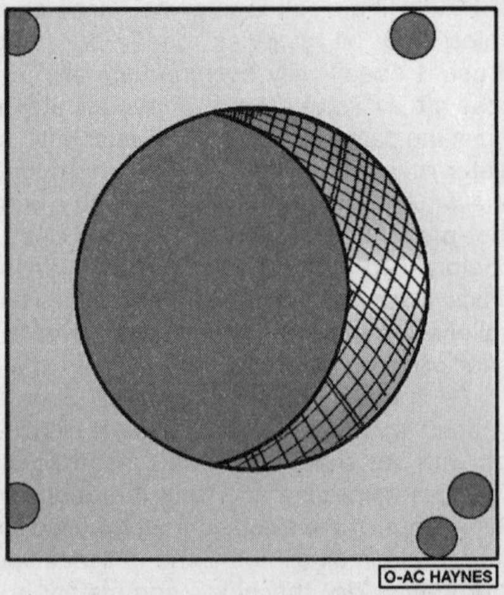

17.3b The cylinder hone should leave a smooth, crosshatch pattern with the lines intersecting at approximately a 60-degree angle

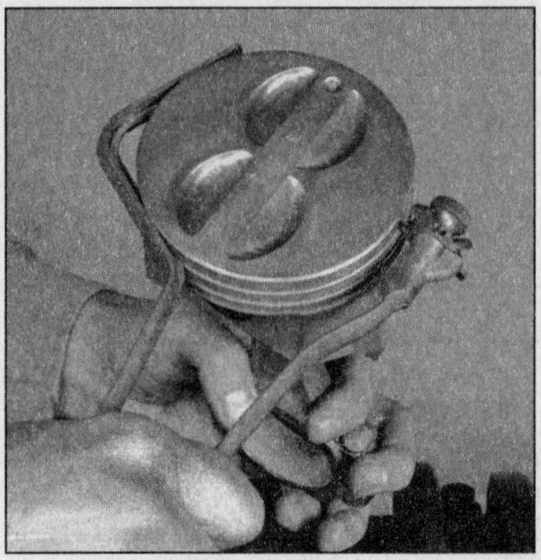

18.4a The piston ring grooves can be cleaned with a special tool, as shown here . . .

18.4b . . . or a section of a broken ring

nick the cylinder walls with the end of the file.

5 The entire engine block must be washed again very thoroughly with warm, soapy water to remove all traces of the abrasive grit produced during the honing operation. **Note:** *The bores can be considered clean when a lint-free white cloth - dampened with clean engine oil - used to wipe them out doesn't pick up any more honing residue, which will show up as gray areas on the cloth. Be sure to run a brush through all oil holes and galleries and flush them with running water.*

6 After rinsing, dry the block and apply a coat of light rust-preventive oil to all machined surfaces. Wrap the block in a plastic trash bag to keep it clean and set it aside until reassembly.

18 Pistons/connecting rods - inspection

Refer to illustrations 18.4a, 18.4b, 18.10, 18.11a, 18.11b and 18.14

1 Before the inspection process can be carried out, the piston/connecting rod assemblies must be cleaned and the original piston rings removed from the pistons. **Note:** *Always use new piston rings when the engine is reassembled.*

2 Using a piston ring installation tool, carefully remove the rings from the pistons. Be careful not to nick or gouge the pistons in the process.

3 Scrape all traces of carbon from the top of the piston. A hand-held brass wire brush or a piece of fine emery cloth can be used (with solvent) once the majority of the deposits have been scraped away. Do not, under any circumstances, use a wire brush mounted in a drill motor to remove deposits from the pistons. The piston material is soft and may be eroded away by the wire brush.

4 Use a piston ring groove-cleaning tool to remove carbon deposits from the ring grooves. If a tool isn't available, a piece broken off the old ring will do the job. Be very careful to remove only the carbon deposits - don't remove any metal and do not nick or scratch the sides of the ring grooves **(see illustrations)**.

5 Once the deposits have been removed, clean the piston/rod assemblies with solvent and dry them with compressed air (if available). Make sure the oil return holes in the back sides of the ring grooves are clear.

6 If the pistons and cylinder walls aren't damaged or worn excessively, and if the engine block is not rebored, new pistons won't be necessary. Normal piston wear appears as even vertical wear on the piston thrust surfaces and slight looseness of the top ring in its groove. New piston rings, however, should always be used when an engine is rebuilt.

7 Carefully inspect each piston for cracks around the skirt, at the pin bosses and at the ring lands.

8 Look for scoring and scuffing on the thrust faces of the skirt, holes in the piston crown and burned areas at the edge of the crown. If the skirt is scored or scuffed, the engine may have been suffering from overheating and/or abnormal combustion, which caused excessively high operating temperatures. The cooling and lubrication systems should be checked thoroughly. A hole in the piston crown is an indication that abnormal combustion (preignition) was occurring. Burned areas at the edge of the piston crown are usually evidence of spark knock (detonation). If any of the above problems exist, the causes must be corrected or the damage will occur again. The causes may include intake air leaks, incorrect fuel/air mixture, incorrect ignition timing and EGR system malfunctions.

9 Corrosion of the piston, in the form of small pits, indicates that coolant is leaking into the combustion chamber and/or the crankcase. Again, the cause must be corrected or the problem may persist in the rebuilt engine.

10 Measure the piston ring side clearance by laying a new piston ring in each ring groove and slipping a feeler gauge in beside it **(see illustration)**. Check the clearance at three or four locations around each groove. Be sure to use the correct ring for each groove - they are different. If the side clearance is greater than specified in this Chapter, new pistons will have to be used.

11 Check the piston-to-bore clearance by

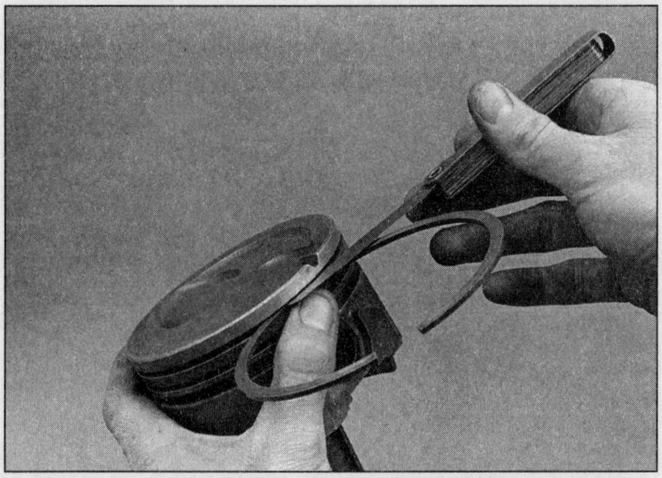

18.10 Check the ring side clearance with a feeler gauge at several points around the groove

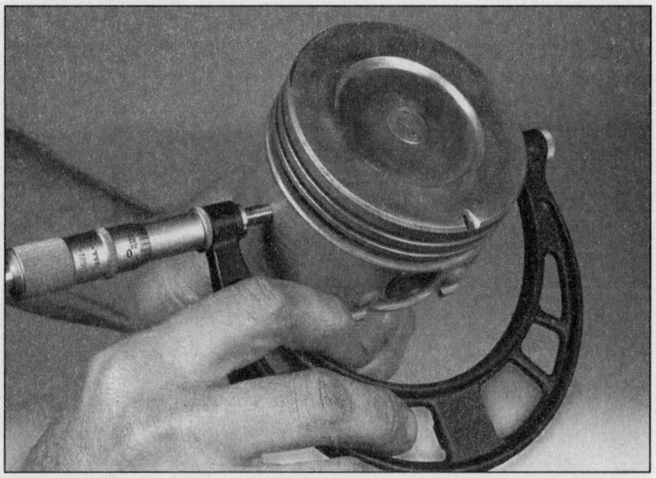

18.11a Measure the piston diameter at a 90-degree angle to the piston pin . . .

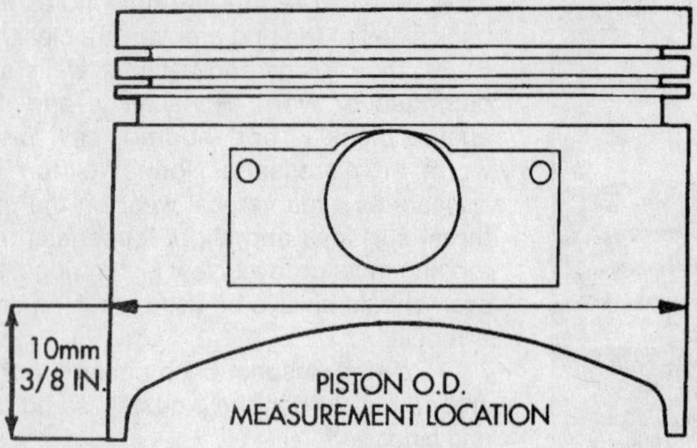

18.11b . . . and at the measurement shown

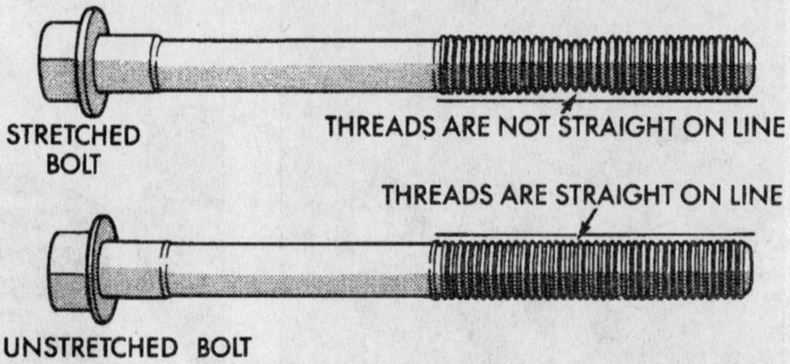

18.14 Place the straight edge of a ruler along the bolt threads to identify stretched bolts

measuring the bore (see Section 16) and the piston diameter. Make sure the pistons and bores are correctly matched. Measure the piston across the skirt, at a 90-degree angle to the piston pin at the specified distance from the bottom of the piston **(see illustrations)**. Subtract the piston diameter from the bore diameter to obtain the clearance. If it's greater than specified in this Chapter, the block will have to be rebored and new pistons and rings installed.

19.1 The oil holes should be chamfered so sharp edges don't gouge or scratch the new bearings

12 Check the piston pin-to-rod clearance by twisting the piston and rod in opposite directions. Any noticeable play indicates excessive wear, which must be corrected. The piston/connecting rod assemblies should be taken to an automotive machine shop to have the pistons and rods resized and new pins installed.

13 If the pistons must be removed from the connecting rods for any reason, they should be taken to an automotive machine shop. While they are there have the connecting rods checked for bend and twist, since automotive machine shops have special equipment for this purpose. **Note:** *Unless new pistons and/or connecting rods must be installed, do not disassemble the pistons and connecting rods.*

14 Check the connecting rods for cracks and other damage. Temporarily remove the rod caps, lift out the old bearing inserts, wipe the rod and cap bearing surfaces clean and inspect them for nicks, gouges and scratches.

Also inspect the rod bolts for stretch **(see illustration)**. If the bolts have stretched they must be taken to an automotive machine shop to have new bolts pressed in. After checking the rods, replace the old bearings, slip the caps into place and tighten the nuts finger tight. **Note:** *If the engine is being rebuilt because of a connecting rod knock, be sure to install new or rebuilt rods.*

19 Crankshaft - inspection

Refer to illustrations 19.1, 19.2, 19.5 and 19.7

1 Remove all burrs from the crankshaft oil holes with a stone, file or scraper **(see illustration)**.

2 Clean the crankshaft with solvent and dry it with compressed air (if available). Be sure to clean the oil holes with a stiff brush **(see illustration)** and flush them with solvent.

3 Check the main and connecting rod bearing journals for uneven wear, scoring, pits and cracks.

4 Check the rest of the crankshaft for cracks and other damage. It should be magnafluxed to reveal hidden cracks - an automotive machine shop will handle the procedure.

5 Using a micrometer, measure the diameter of the main and connecting rod journals **(see illustration)** and compare the results to the Specifications in this Chapter. By measuring the diameter at a number of points around each journal's circumference, you'll be able to determine whether or not the jour-

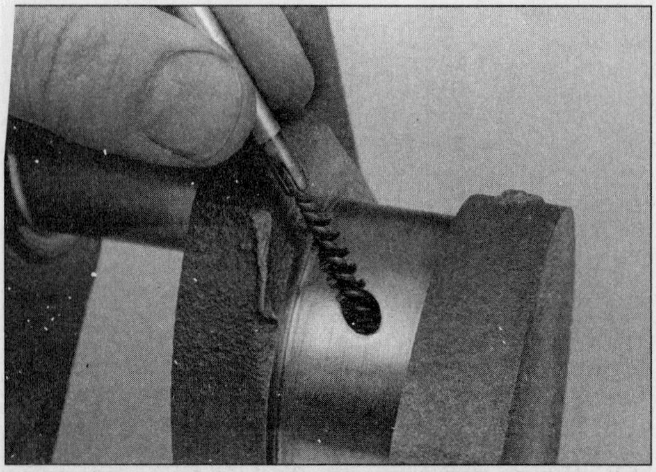

19.2 Use a wire or stiff plastic bristle brush to clean the oil passages in the crankshaft

19.5 Measure the diameter of each crankshaft journal at several points to detect taper and out-of-round conditions

19.7 If the seals have worn grooves in the crankshaft journals, or if the seal contact surfaces are nicked or scratched, the new seals will leak

nal is out-of-round. Take the measurement at each end of the journal, near the crank throws, to determine if the journal is tapered.

6 If the crankshaft journals are damaged, tapered, out-of-round or worn beyond the limits given in the Specifications in this Chapter, have the crankshaft reground by an automotive machine shop. Be sure to use the correct size bearing inserts if the crankshaft is reconditioned.

7 Check the oil seal journals at each end of the crankshaft for wear and damage. If the seal has worn a groove in the journal, or if it's nicked or scratched **(see illustration)**, the new seal may leak when the engine is reassembled. In some cases, an automotive machine shop may be able to repair the journal by pressing on a thin sleeve. If repair isn't feasible, a new or different crankshaft should be installed.

8 Refer to Section 20 and examine the main and rod bearing inserts.

20 Main and connecting rod bearings - inspection and selection

Inspection

Refer to illustration 20.1

1 Even though the main and connecting rod bearings should be replaced with new ones during the engine overhaul, the old bearings should be retained for close examination, as they may reveal valuable information about the condition of the engine **(see illustration)**.

2 Bearing failure occurs because of lack of lubrication, the presence of dirt or other foreign particles, overloading the engine and corrosion. Regardless of the cause of bearing failure, it must be corrected before the engine is reassembled to prevent it from happening again.

3 When examining the bearings, remove them from the engine block, the main bearing caps, the connecting rods and the rod caps and lay them out on a clean surface in the same general position as their location in the engine. This will enable you to match any bearing problems with the corresponding crankshaft journal.

4 Dirt and other foreign particles get into the engine in a variety of ways. It may be left in the engine during assembly, or it may pass through filters or the PCV system. It may get into the oil, and from there into the bearings. Metal chips from machining operations and normal engine wear are often present. Abrasives are sometimes left in engine components after reconditioning, especially when parts are not thoroughly cleaned using the proper cleaning methods. Whatever the source, these foreign objects often end up embedded in the soft bearing material and are easily recognized. Large particles will not embed in the bearing and will score or gouge the bearing and journal. The best prevention for this cause of bearing failure is to clean all parts thoroughly and keep everything spotlessly clean during engine assembly. Frequent and regular engine oil and filter changes are also recommended.

5 Lack of lubrication (or lubrication breakdown) has a number of interrelated causes. Excessive heat (which thins the oil), overloading (which squeezes the oil from the bearing face) and oil leakage or throw off (from excessive bearing clearances, worn oil pump or high engine speeds) all contribute to lubrication breakdown. Blocked oil passages, which usually are the result of misaligned oil holes in a bearing shell, will also oil starve a bearing and destroy it. When lack of lubrication is the cause of bearing failure, the bearing material is wiped or extruded from the steel backing of the bearing. Temperatures may increase to the point where the steel backing turns blue from overheating.

6 Driving habits can have a definite effect on bearing life. Low-speed operation in too-high a gear (lugging the engine) puts very high loads on bearings, which tends to squeeze out the oil film. These loads cause

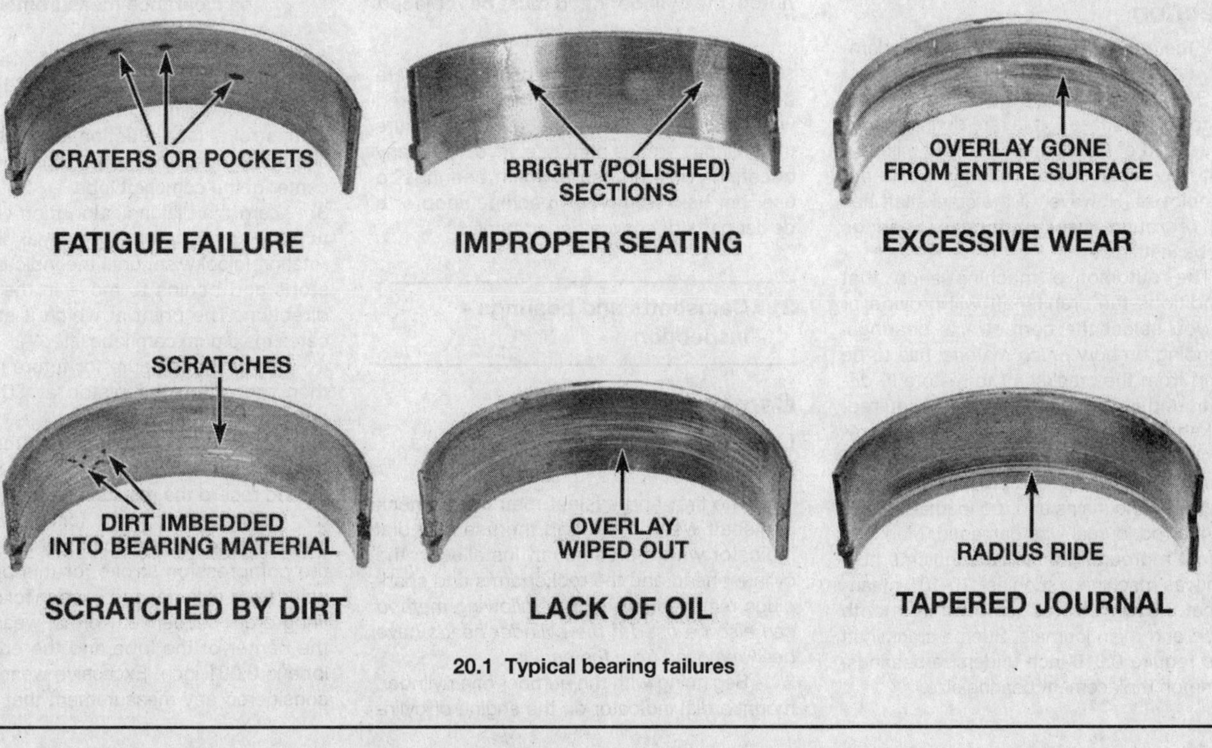

20.1 Typical bearing failures

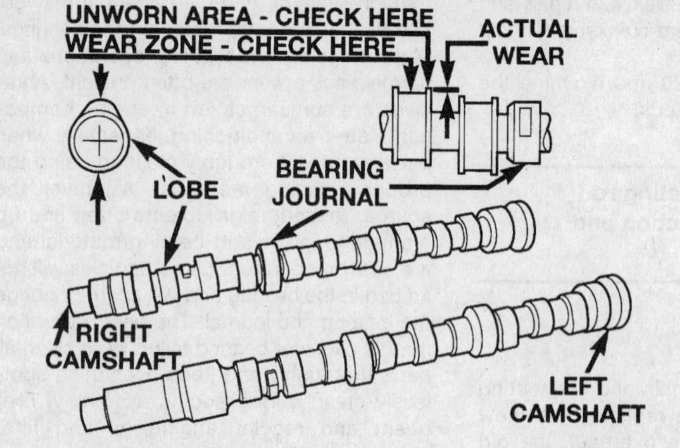

21.6 Camshaft lobe wear is the difference between the worn area (center of the lobe) and the unworn area (edge of the lobe)

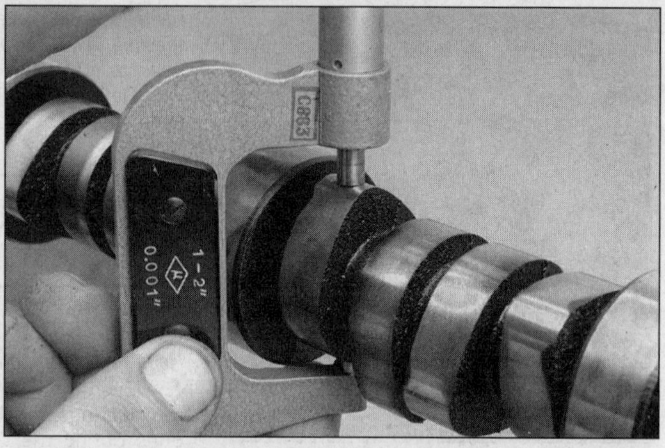

21.8 Measuring cam lobe wear with a micrometer - make sure you move the micrometer to get the highest reading at the center and at the edge of the lobe

the bearings to flex, which produces fine cracks in the bearing face (fatigue failure). Eventually the bearing material will loosen in pieces and tear away from the steel backing. Short-trip driving leads to corrosion of bearings because insufficient engine heat is produced to drive off the condensed water and corrosive gases. These products collect in the engine oil, forming acid and sludge. As the oil is carried to the engine bearings, the acid attacks and corrodes the bearing material.

7 Incorrect bearing installation during engine assembly will lead to bearing failure as well. Tight-fitting bearings leave insufficient bearing oil clearance and will result in oil starvation. Dirt or foreign particles trapped behind a bearing insert result in high spots on the bearing which lead to failure.

Selection

8 If the original bearings are worn or damaged, or if the oil clearances are incorrect (see Sections 24 or 26), new bearings will have to be purchased. It is rare during a thorough rebuild of an engine with many miles on it that new replacement bearings would not be employed. However, if the crankshaft has been reground, new **undersize** bearings must be installed.

9 The automotive machine shop that reconditions the crankshaft will provide or help you select the correct size bearings. Depending on how much material has to be ground from the crankshaft to restore it, different undersize bearings are required. Crankshafts are normally ground in increments of 0.010-inch. Sometimes the amount of material machined on a crankshaft will differ between the mains and rod journals, especially if a rod journal was damaged. Markings on most reground crankshafts indicate how much was machined, such as "10-10", meaning that 0.010-inch was removed from both the rod and main journals. Such a crankshaft would require 0.010-inch undersize bearings, a common replacement bearing size.

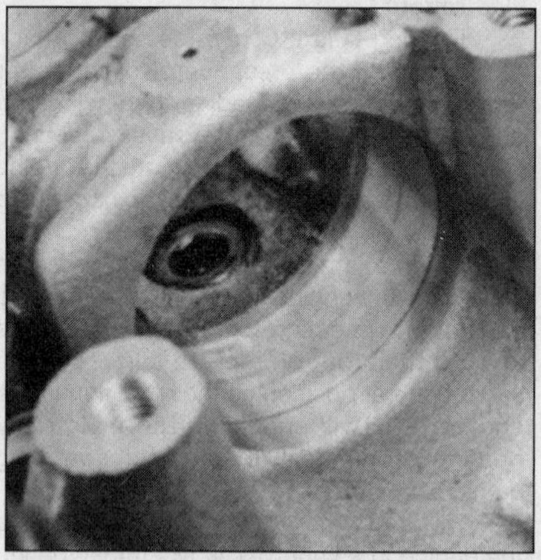

21.11 Inspect the cam bearing surfaces in each cylinder head for pits, score marks and abnormal wear - if wear or damage is noted, the cylinder head must be replaced

21.12 Measure the outside diameter of each camshaft journal and the inside diameter of each bearing to determine the oil clearance measurement

10 Regardless of how the bearing sizes are determined, use the oil clearance, measured with Plastigage, as the final guide to ensure the bearings are the right size. If you have any questions or are unsure which bearings to use, get help from your machine shop or a dealer parts or service department.

21 Camshafts and bearings - inspection

Camshaft

Lobe wear check

Refer to illustrations 21.6 and 21.8

1 The first and easiest method to check camshaft wear is through the use of a dial indicator with the camshaft installed in the cylinder head and the rocker arms and spark plugs removed. **Note:** *The following method can also be used if the cylinder heads have been removed from the engine.*

2 Beginning with the number one cylinder, mount a dial indicator on the engine or cylinder head and position the plunger against the center of the camshaft lobe. Position the number one cylinder at TDC on the compression stroke (see Section 3). The plunger should be directly above and in line with the center of the camshaft lobe.

3 Zero the dial indicator, then very slowly turn the crankshaft in the normal direction of rotation (clockwise) until the indicator needle stops and begins to move in the opposite direction. The point at which it stops indicates maximum cam lobe lift.

4 Record this figure for future reference, then reposition the piston at TDC on the compression stroke again.

5 Move the dial indicator to the edge of the camshaft lobe and repeat the check. Be sure to record the results for each valve.

6 Repeat the check for the remaining valves. Since each piston must be at TDC on the compression stroke for this procedure, work from cylinder-to-cylinder following the firing order sequence. Normal wear between the center of the lobe and the edge of the lobe is 0.001 inch. Excessive wear would be considered any measurement that is greater

than 0.010 inch between the center of the lobe and the edge of the lobe **(see illustration)**.

7 The second method for measuring camshaft lobe wear is obtained through the use of a micrometer with the camshaft removed from the engine.

8 Using this method, measure the camshaft lobe height at the center and at the edge of the cam lobe **(see illustration)**. The difference between the two measurements is the lobe wear measurement. Record this figure for future reference and repeat the check on the remaining camshaft lobes.

9 If the lobe wear is 0.010 inch or greater between the center of the lobe and the edge of the lobe, cam lobe wear has occurred and a new camshaft should be installed.

Bearing journals, lobes and bearings

Refer to illustrations 21.11 and 21.12

10 After the camshaft has been removed from the engine, cleaned with solvent and dried, inspect the bearing journals for uneven wear, pitting and evidence of seizure. Check the camshaft lobes for heat discoloration, score marks, chipped areas, pitting and uneven wear. If the lobes and journals are in good condition and if the lobe wear measurements recorded earlier are as specified, the camshaft can be reused.

11 Visually check the camshaft bearing surfaces in the cylinder head for pitting, score marks, galling and abnormal wear **(see illustration)**. If the journals and the bearings are damaged, both the camshaft and the cylinder head will have to be replaced.

12 Measure the outside diameter of each camshaft bearing journals and record your measurements **(see illustration)**. Compare them to the journal outside diameter specified in this Chapter, then measure the inside diameter of each corresponding camshaft bearing and record the measurements. Subtract each cam journal outside diameter from its respective cam bearing bore inside diameter to determine the oil clearance for each bearing. Compare the results to the specified journal-to-bearing clearance. If any of the measurements fall outside the standard specified wear limits in this Chapter, either the camshaft or the cylinder head, or both, must be replaced.

13 Check camshaft runout by placing the camshaft between two V-blocks or back into the cylinder head and set up a dial indicator on the center journal. Zero the dial indicator. Turn the camshaft slowly and note the dial indicator readings. If the measured runout exceeds 0.005 inch, replace the camshaft.

22 Engine overhaul - reassembly sequence

1 Before beginning engine reassembly, make sure you have all the necessary new parts (including new cylinder head bolts), gaskets and seals as well as the following items on hand:

Common hand tools
A 1/2-inch drive torque wrench
Piston ring installation tool
Piston ring compressor
Short lengths of rubber or plastic hose to fit over connecting rod bolts
Plastigage
Feeler gauges
A fine-tooth file
New engine oil
Engine assembly lube or moly-base grease
Gasket sealant
Thread locking compound

2 In order to save time and avoid problems, engine reassembly must be done in the following general order:

2.7L engine

Piston rings
Crankshaft and main bearings
Piston/connecting rod assemblies
Windage tray
Rear main oil seal and retainer
Oil pump and pick up tube
Oil pan
Cylinder heads
Hydraulic lash adjusters and rocker arms
Camshafts and secondary timing chain assemblies
Water pump
Primary timing chain and sprockets
Front timing cover
Crankshaft pulley
Valve covers
Intake and exhaust manifolds
Driveplate

3.2L and 3.5L engines

Piston rings
Crankshaft and main bearings
Piston/connecting rod assemblies
Windage tray
Rear main oil seal and retainer
Oil pump and pick up tube
Oil pan
Cylinder heads and camshafts
Rear timing belt covers
Water pump
Timing belt and sprockets
Rocker arms and valve covers
Front timing belt covers
Crankshaft pulley
Intake and exhaust manifolds
Driveplate

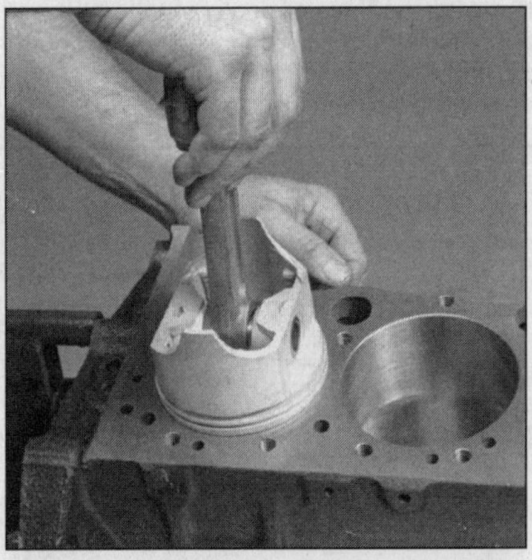

23.3 When checking piston ring end gap, the ring must be square in the cylinder bore (this is done by pushing the ring down with the top of a piston as shown)

23 Piston rings - installation

Refer to illustrations 23.3, 23.4, 23.5, 23.9a, 23.9b, 23.12, 23.13a and 23.13b

1 Before installing the new piston rings, the ring end gaps must be checked. It's assumed that the piston ring side clearance has been checked and verified correct (see Section 18).

2 Lay out the piston/connecting rod assemblies and the new ring sets so the ring sets will be matched with the same piston and cylinder during the end gap measurement and engine assembly.

3 Insert the top (number one) ring into the first cylinder and square it up with the cylinder walls by pushing it in with the top of the piston **(see illustration)**. The ring should be near the bottom of the cylinder, at the lower limit of ring travel.

4 To measure the end gap, slip feeler gauges between the ends of the ring until a gauge equal to the gap width is found **(see illustration)**. The feeler gauge should slide between the ring ends with a slight amount of drag. Compare the measurement to the Specifications in this Chapter. If the gap is larger or smaller than specified, double-check to make sure you have the correct rings before proceeding.

5 If the gap is too small, it must be enlarged or the ring ends may come in contact with each other during engine operation, which can cause serious engine damage. The end gap can be increased by filing the ring

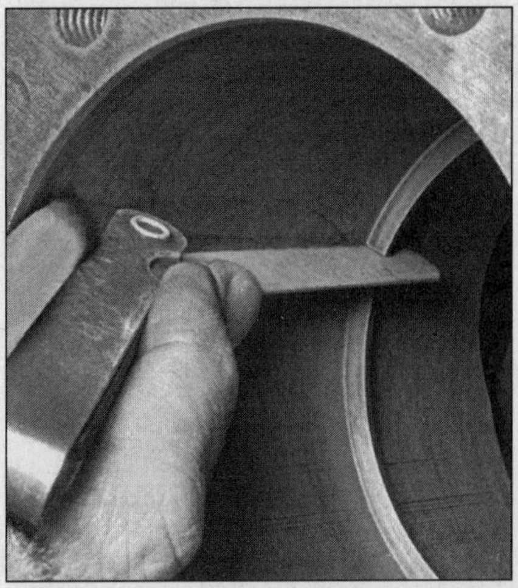

23.4 With the ring square in the cylinder, measure the end gap with a feeler gauge

23.5 If the end gap is too small, clamp a file in a vise and file the ring ends (from the outside in only) to enlarge the gap slightly

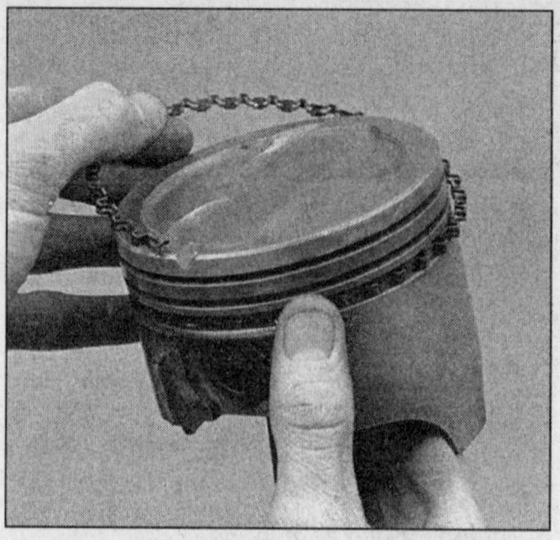

23.9a Installing the spacer/expander in the oil control ring groove

23.9b DO NOT use a piston ring installation tool when installing the oil ring side rails

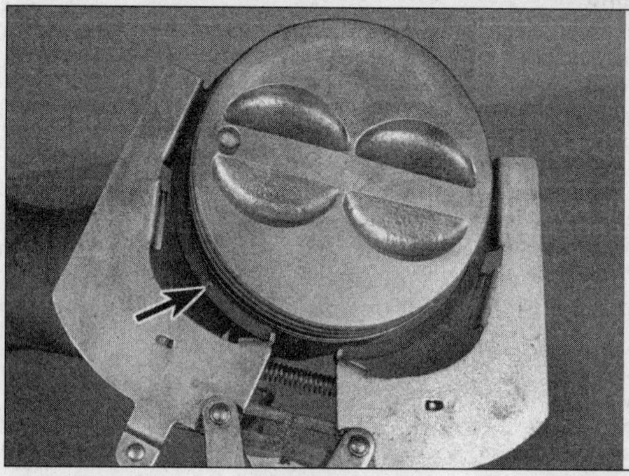

23.12 Installing the compression rings with a ring expander - the mark (arrow) must face up

ends very carefully with a fine file. Mount the file in a vise equipped with soft jaws, slip the ring over the file with the ends contacting the file teeth and slowly move the ring to remove material from the ends. When performing this operation, file only from the outside in **(see illustration)**.

6 Excess end gap isn't as critical as too little gap, unless the gap is greater than 0.040-inch. Compare your measurements to this Chapter's Specifications for maximum end gap. Again, double-check to make sure you have the correct rings for your engine. If you do file the ring gaps, recheck that ring's end gap in the bore before filing any more. When the correct gap is achieved, use a whetstone or fine file to deburr the edges that have been filed.

7 Repeat the procedure for each ring that will be installed in the first cylinder and for each ring in the remaining cylinders. Remember to keep rings, pistons and cylinders matched up.

8 Once the ring end gaps have been checked/corrected, the rings can be installed on the pistons.

9 The oil control ring (lowest one on the piston) is usually installed first. It's composed of three separate components. Slip the spacer/expander into the groove **(see illustration)**. If an anti-rotation tang is used, make sure it's inserted into the drilled hole in the ring groove. Next, install the lower side rail. Don't use a piston ring installation tool on the oil ring side rails, as they may be damaged. Instead, place one end of the side rail into the groove between the spacer/expander and the ring land, hold it firmly in place and slide a finger around the piston while pushing the rail into the groove **(see illustration)**. Next, install the upper side rail in the same manner.

10 After the three oil ring components have been installed, check to make sure that both the upper and lower side rails can be turned smoothly in the ring groove.

11 The number two (middle) ring is installed next. It's usually stamped with a mark which must face up, toward the top of the piston. **Note:** *Always follow the instructions printed on the ring package or box - different manufacturers may require different approaches. Do not mix up the top and middle rings, as they have different cross sections.*

12 Use a piston ring installation tool and make sure the identification mark is facing the top of the piston, then slip the ring into the middle groove on the piston **(see illustration)**. Don't expand the ring any more than necessary to slide it over the piston.

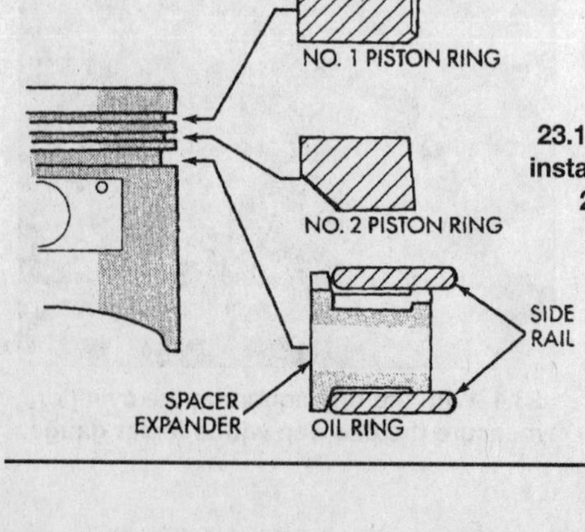

23.13a Piston ring installation details - 2.7L engine

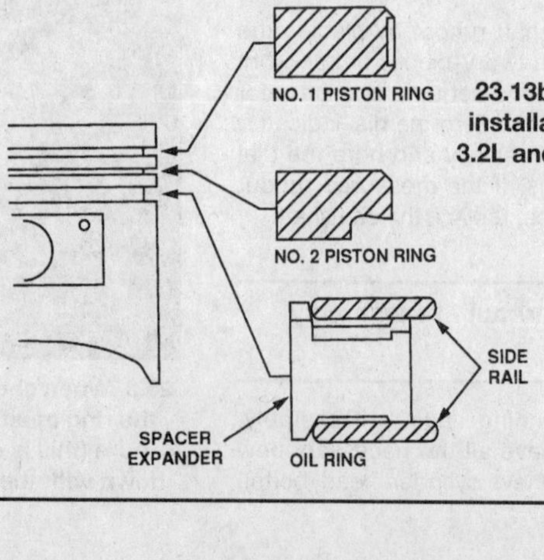

23.13b Piston ring installation details - 3.2L and 3.5L engines

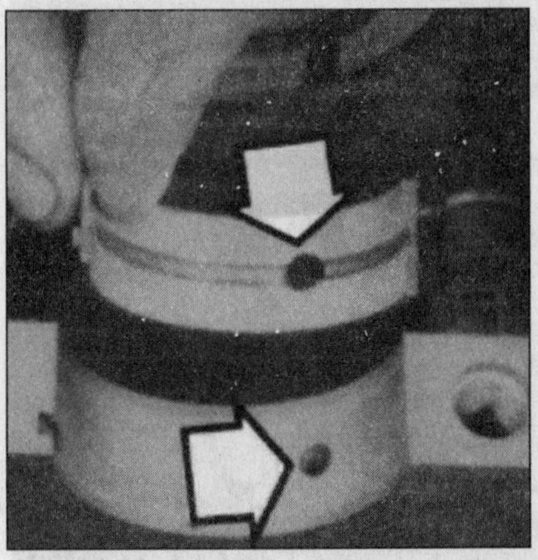

24.5 Make sure the oil holes in the bearings are aligned with the oil holes in the block (arrows)

13 Install the number one (top) ring in the same manner. Make sure the mark is facing up. Be careful not to confuse the number one and number two rings **(see illustrations)**.

14 Repeat the procedure for the remaining pistons and rings.

24 Crankshaft - installation and main bearing oil clearance check

Refer to illustrations 24.5, 24.6, 24.11, 24.15, 24.23 and 24.28

Note: *Always apply a thin coat of engine oil to the bolt threads before tightening the main bearing cap bolts to Specifications.*

1 Crankshaft installation is the first step in engine reassembly. It's assumed at this point that the engine block and crankshaft have been cleaned, inspected and repaired or reconditioned.

2 Position the engine on the stand with the crankcase facing up.

3 Remove the main bearing cap bolts and lift out the bearing caps.

4 If they're still in place, remove the original bearing inserts from the block and the main bearing caps. Wipe the bearing surfaces of the block and caps with a clean, lint-free cloth. They must be kept spotlessly clean.

Main bearing oil clearance check

5 Clean the back sides of the new main bearing inserts and lay one in each main bearing saddle in the block. If any of the bearing inserts have a large groove in it, make sure the grooved inserts are installed in the block. Lay the other bearings from the set in the corresponding main bearing caps. Make sure the tab on the bearing insert fits into the recess in the block or cap. **Caution:** *The oil holes in the block must line up with the oil holes in the bearing inserts* **(see illustration)**. *Do not hammer the bearing into place and don't nick or gouge the bearing faces. No lubrication should be used at this time.*

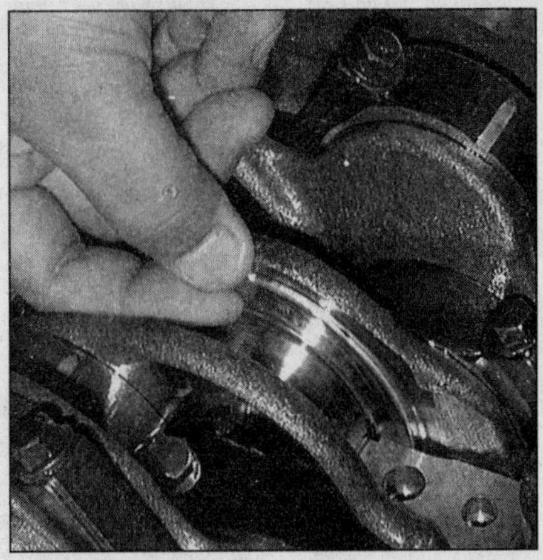

24.6 Insert the thrust bearing into the machined surface between the crankshaft and the upper bearing saddle then rotate it down into the block until it's flush with the parting line of the main bearing cap - make sure the coated side of the thrust bearing faces the crankshaft

6 The thrust bearings on these engines are a two piece design which must be installed in the machined surfaces of the upper bearing saddle in the engine block. **Note:** *There are front and rear crankshaft thrust bearings on all engines covered by this manual and they're installed in the number three bearing saddle on 2.7L engines or the number two bearing saddle on 3.2L and 3.5L engines*. Pry the crankshaft forward and install the front thrust bearing into the machined surface of the upper bearing saddle in the engine block **(see illustration)**. Next pry the crankshaft toward the rear of the engine and install the rear thrust bearing into the machined surface of the upper bearing saddle in the engine block. **Note:** *Be sure to install the thrust bearing with the coated side facing the crankshaft.*

7 Clean the faces of the bearings in the block and the crankshaft main bearing journals with a clean, lint-free cloth.

8 Check or clean the oil holes in the crankshaft, as any dirt here can go only one way - straight through the new bearings.

9 Once you're certain the crankshaft is clean, carefully lay it in position in the main bearings. Do not lubricate the crankshaft with oil at this time.

10 Before the crankshaft can be permanently installed, the main bearing oil clearance must be checked.

11 Cut several pieces of the appropriate size Plastigage (they must be slightly shorter than the width of the main bearings) and place one piece on each crankshaft main bearing journal, parallel with the journal axis **(see illustration)**.

12 Clean the faces of the bearings in the cap and install the bearing caps and brace assembly with the arrows pointing toward the drivebelt end of the engine. Don't disturb the Plastigage.

13 Starting with the center mains and working out toward the ends **(see illustration 24.23)**, tighten the inner main bearing cap bolts, in several steps, to the torque specified in this Chapter. Don't rotate the crankshaft at any time during this operation.

24.11 Lay the Plastigage strips (arrow) on the main bearing journals, parallel to the crankshaft centerline

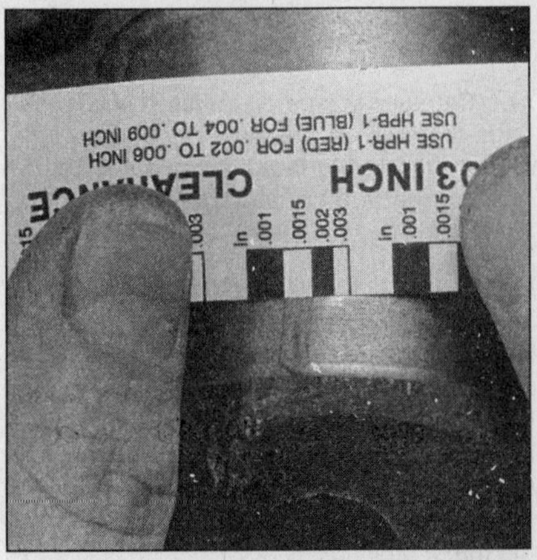

24.15 Compare the width of the crushed Plastigage to the scale on the envelope to determine the main bearing oil clearance (always take the measurement at the widest point of the Plastigage); be sure to use the correct scale - standard and metric ones are included

14 Remove the bolts and carefully lift off the main bearing caps. Don't disturb the Plastigage or rotate the crankshaft.

15 Compare the width of the crushed Plastigage on each journal to the scale printed on the Plastigage envelope to obtain the main bearing oil clearance **(see illustration)**. Check the Specifications in this Chapter to make sure it's correct.

16 If the clearance is not as specified, the bearing inserts may be the wrong size (which means different ones will be required). Before deciding that different inserts are needed, make sure that no dirt or oil was between the bearing inserts and the caps or block when the clearance was measured. If the Plastigage was wider at one end than the other, the journal may be tapered (see Section 19).

24.23 Inner main bearing cap bolt TIGHTENING sequence

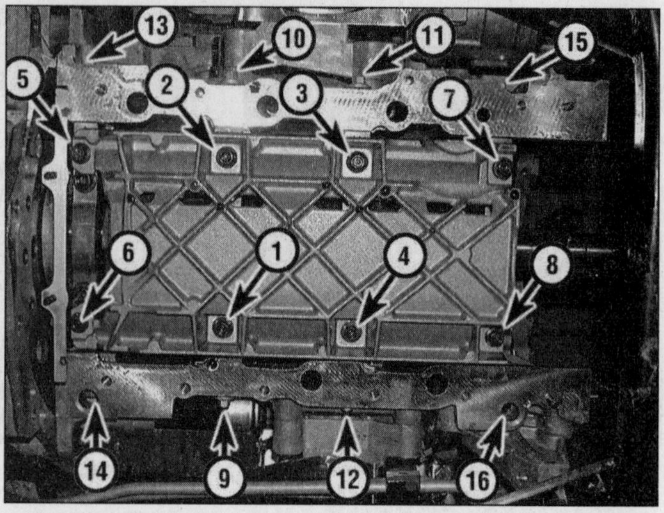

24.28 Outer main bearing cap bolt and main bearing cap cross bolt TIGHTENING sequence - 2.7L engine shown; 3.2L and 3.5L engines look slightly different but use this same sequence

17 Carefully scrape all traces of the Plastigage material off the main bearing journals and/or the bearing faces. Use your fingernail or the edge of a credit card - don't nick or scratch the bearing faces.

Final crankshaft installation

18 Carefully lift the crankshaft out of the engine.

19 Clean the bearing faces in the block, then apply a thin, uniform layer of moly-base grease or engine assembly lube to each of the bearing surfaces. Be sure to coat the thrust bearings as well as the journal face of the thrust bearing.

20 Make sure the crankshaft journals are clean, then lay the crankshaft back in place in the block. If the thrust bearings came out of the block when the crankshaft was removed, install the thrust bearings as described in Step 6.

21 Clean the faces of the bearings in the caps, then apply lubricant to them.

22 Install the bearing caps in their original locations with the arrows pointing toward the drivebelt end of the engine.

23 Tighten the inner main bearing cap bolts in the proper sequence to torque listed in this Chapter's Specifications **(see illustration)**.

24 Gently tap the ends of the crankshaft forward and backward with a lead or brass hammer to line up the main bearing and crankshaft thrust surfaces.

25 Rotate the crankshaft a number of times by hand to check for any obvious binding.

26 Check the crankshaft endplay with a feeler gauge or a dial indicator (see Section 14). The endplay should be correct if the crankshaft thrust faces aren't worn or damaged and new bearings have been installed.

27 Install the piston and connecting rod assemblies (see Section 26).

28 Position the windage tray in place and install the outer main bearing cap bolts hand tight, then install the main bearing cap cross bolts and washers through the side of the block and into the main caps hand tight. Tighten the outer main bearing cap bolts and the main bearing cap cross bolts in the proper sequence to torque listed in this Chapter's Specifications **(see illustration)**.

29 Install the rear new seal, then bolt the retainer to the block (see Section 25).

25 Rear main oil seal installation

Refer to illustrations 25.3 and 25.4

1 All models are equipped with a one-piece seal that fits into a housing (retainer) attached to the transaxle end of the block. The crankshaft must be installed first and the main bearing caps bolted in place, then the new seal should be installed in the retainer and the retainer bolted to the block.

2 Check the seal contact surface very carefully for scratches and nicks that could damage the new seal lip and cause oil leaks. If the crankshaft is damaged, the only alternative is a new or different crankshaft.

25.3 Place the retainer between two blocks of wood and drive the seal out of the retainer from the rear

3 The old seal can be removed from the retainer with a hammer and punch by driving it out from the back side **(see illustration)**. Be sure to note how far it's recessed into the retainer bore before removing it; the new seal will have to be recessed an equal amount. Be very careful not to scratch or otherwise damage the bore in the retainer or oil leaks could develop.

4 Make sure the retainer is clean, then apply a thin coat of engine oil to the outer edge of the new seal. The seal must be pressed squarely into the retainer bore, so hammering it into place is not recommended. If you don't have access to a press, sandwich the retainer and seal between two smooth pieces of wood and press the seal into place with the jaws of a large vise. The pieces of wood must be thick enough to distribute the force evenly around the entire circumference of the seal. Work slowly and make sure the seal enters the bore squarely **(see illustration)**.

5 Apply small amount RTV sealant on the retainer to block gasket and install the gasket on the retainer. Lubricate the seal lip with

25.4 Drive the new seal into the retainer with a block of wood or a section of pipe - make sure that you don't cock the seal in the bore

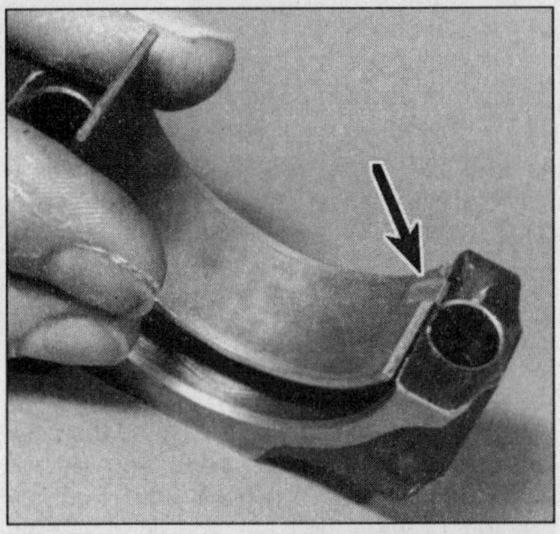

26.4 The tab on the bearing insert (arrow) must fit into the cap recess so the bearing will seat properly

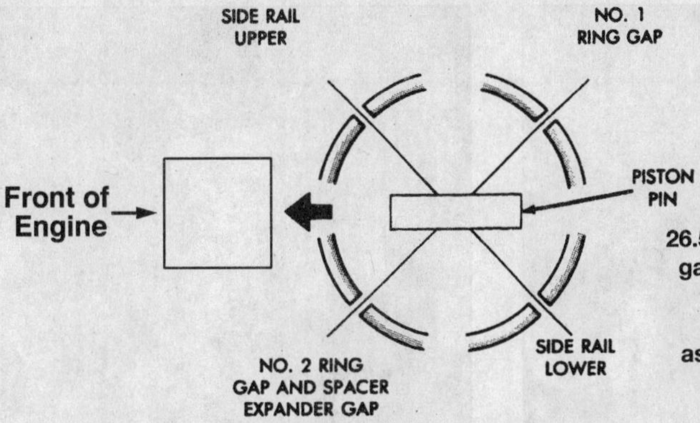

26.5 Stagger the ring end gaps as shown here before installing the piston/connecting rod assemblies into the engine

clean engine oil or multi purpose grease, then slip the seal/retainer over the crankshaft. making sure the dowel pins (if equipped) are in place before installing the retainer.

6 Verify that the crankshaft seal is centered over the crankshaft journal and tighten the screws a little at a time until the torque specified in this Chapter is reached.

26 Pistons/connecting rods - installation and rod bearing oil clearance check

Refer to illustrations 26.4, 26.5, 26.9, 26.11, 26.13 and 26.17

1 Before installing the piston/connecting rod assemblies, the cylinder walls must be perfectly clean, the top edge of each cylinder must be chamfered, and the crankshaft must be in place.

2 Remove the cap from the end of the number one connecting rod (refer to the marks made during removal). Remove the original bearing inserts and wipe the bearing surfaces of the connecting rod and cap with a clean, lint-free cloth. They must be kept spotlessly clean.

Connecting rod bearing oil clearance check

3 Clean the back side of the new upper bearing insert, then lay it in place in the connecting rod. Make sure the tab on the bearing fits into the recess in the rod. Don't hammer the bearing insert into place and be very careful not to nick or gouge the bearing face. Don't lubricate the bearing at this time.

4 Clean the back side of the other bearing insert and install it in the rod cap. Again, make sure the tab on the bearing fits into the recess in the cap **(see illustration)**, and don't apply any lubricant. It's critically important that the mating surfaces of the bearing and connecting rod are perfectly clean and oil free when they're assembled for clearance checking.

5 Position the piston ring gaps at the specified intervals around the piston **(see illustration)**.

6 Slip a section of plastic or rubber hose over each connecting rod cap bolt.

7 Lubricate the piston and rings with clean engine oil and attach a piston ring compressor to the piston. Leave the skirt protruding about 1/4-inch to guide the piston into the cylinder. The rings must be compressed until they're flush with the piston.

8 Rotate the crankshaft until the number one connecting rod journal is at BDC (bottom dead center) and apply a coat of engine oil to the cylinder walls.

9 With the notch on top of the piston facing the front of the engine and the connecting rod oil holes facing the right (thrust) side of the engine **(see illustration)**, gently insert the piston/connecting rod assembly into the number one cylinder bore and rest the bottom edge of the ring compressor on the engine block.

10 Tap the top edge of the ring compressor to make sure it's contacting the block around its entire circumference.

11 Gently tap on the top of the piston with the end of a wooden hammer handle **(see**

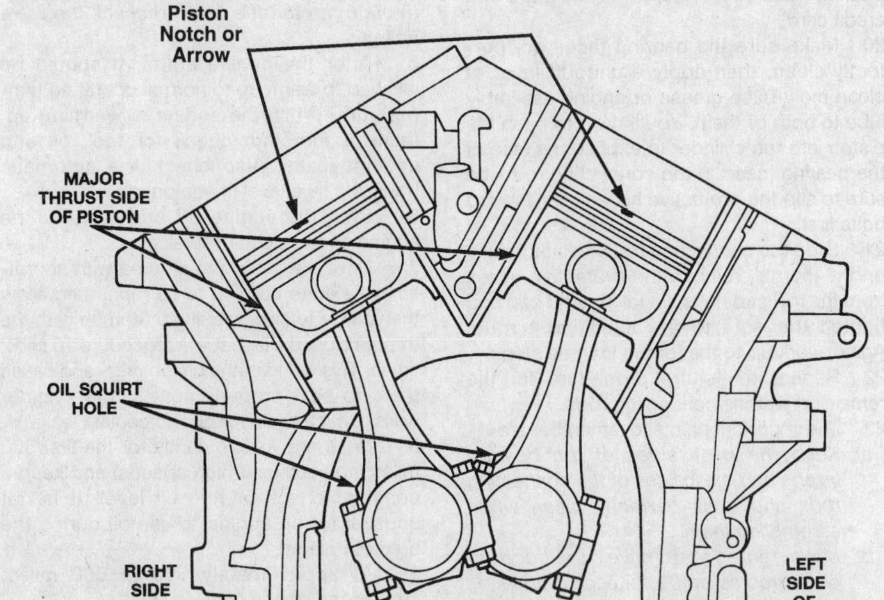

26.9 Make sure the connecting rod oil holes line up with the piston notches as shown here or the cylinder walls will not receive the proper amount of oil during engine operation

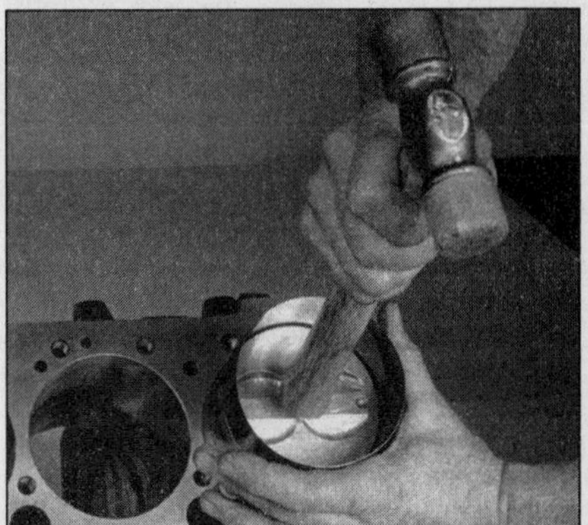

26.11 The piston can be driven (gently) into the cylinder bore with the end of a wooden hammer handle

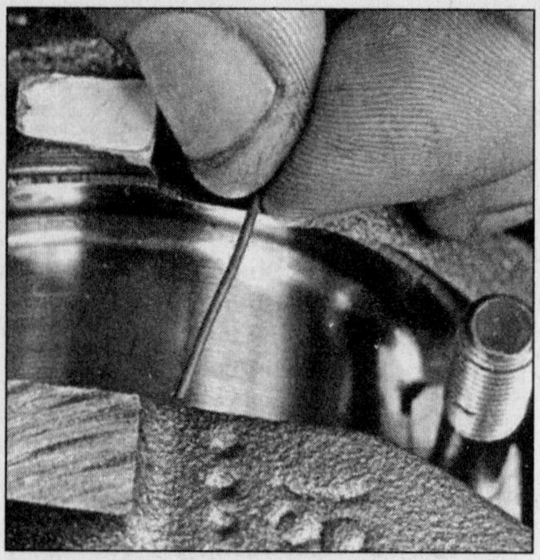

26.13 Lay the Plastigage strips on each rod bearing journal, parallel to the crankshaft centerline

26.17 Measure the width of the crushed Plastigage to determine the rod bearing oil clearance (be sure to use the correct scale - standard and metric ones are included)

illustration) while guiding the end of the connecting rod into place on the crankshaft journal. The piston rings may try to pop out of the ring compressor just before entering the cylinder bore, so keep some downward pressure on the ring compressor. Work slowly, and if any resistance is felt as the piston enters the cylinder, stop immediately. Find out what's hanging up and fix it before proceeding. Do not, for any reason, force the piston into the cylinder - you might break a ring and/or the piston.

12 Once the piston/connecting rod assembly is installed, the connecting rod bearing oil clearance must be checked before the rod cap is permanently bolted in place.

13 Cut a piece of the appropriate size Plastigage slightly shorter than the width of the connecting rod bearing and lay it in place on the number one connecting rod journal, parallel with the journal axis **(see illustration)**.

14 Clean the connecting rod cap bearing face, remove the protective hoses from the connecting rod bolts and install the rod cap. Make sure the mating mark on the cap is on the same side as the mark on the connecting rod.

15 Install the nuts and tighten them to the torque specified in this Chapter (work up to it in three steps). **Note:** *Use a thin-wall socket to avoid erroneous torque readings that can result if the socket is wedged between the rod cap and nut. If the socket tends to wedge itself between the nut and the cap, lift up on it slightly until it no longer contacts the cap. Do not rotate the crankshaft at any time during this operation.*

16 Remove the nuts and detach the rod cap, being very careful not to disturb the Plastigage.

17 Compare the width of the crushed Plastigage to the scale printed on the Plastigage envelope to obtain the oil clearance **(see illustration)**. Compare it to the Specifications in this Chapter to make sure the clearance is correct.

18 If the clearance is not as specified, the bearing inserts may be the wrong size (which means different ones will be required). Before deciding that different inserts are needed, make sure that no dirt or oil was between the bearing inserts and the connecting rod or cap when the clearance was measured. Also, recheck the journal diameter. If the Plastigage was wider at one end than the other, the journal may be tapered (see Section 19).

Final connecting rod installation

19 Carefully scrape all traces of the Plastigage material off the rod journal and/or bearing face. Be very careful not to scratch the bearing - use your fingernail or the edge of a credit card.

20 Make sure the bearing faces are perfectly clean, then apply a uniform layer of clean moly-base grease or engine assembly lube to both of them. You'll have to push the piston into the cylinder to expose the face of the bearing insert in the connecting rod - be sure to slip the protective hoses over the rod bolts first.

21 Slide the connecting rod back into place on the journal, remove the protective hoses from the rod cap bolts, install the rod cap and tighten the nuts to the specified torque. Again, work up to the torque in three steps.

22 Repeat the entire procedure for the remaining pistons/connecting rods.

23 The important points to remember are . . .

a) *Keep the back sides of the bearing inserts and the insides of the connecting rods and caps perfectly clean when assembling them.*
b) *Make sure you have the correct piston/rod assembly for each cylinder.*
c) *The notch on the top of the piston must face the front of the engine and the connecting rod oil holes must face the right (thrust) side of the engine.*
d) *Lubricate the cylinder walls with clean oil.*
e) *Lubricate the bearing faces when installing the rod caps after the oil clearance has been checked.*

24 After all the piston/connecting rod assemblies have been properly installed, rotate the crankshaft a number of times by hand to check for any obvious binding.

25 As a final step, the connecting rod endplay must be checked. Refer to Section 13 for this procedure.

26 Compare the measured endplay to the Specifications to make sure it's correct. If it was correct before disassembly and the original crankshaft and rods were reinstalled, it should still be right. If new rods or a new crankshaft were installed, the endplay may be inadequate. If so, the rods will have to be removed and taken to an automotive machine shop for resizing. If the endplay is too great, new rods may be required.

27 Initial start-up and break-in after overhaul

Warning: *Have a fire extinguisher ready when starting the engine for the first time.*

1 Once the engine has been installed in the vehicle, double-check the engine oil and coolant levels.

2 With the spark plugs out of the engine and the ignition system disabled (see Section 3), crank the engine until oil pressure registers on the gauge.

3 Install the spark plugs, and restore the ignition system functions.

4 Start the engine. It may take a few moments for the fuel system to build up pressure, but the engine should start without a great deal of effort. **Note:** *If backfiring occurs through the throttle body, recheck the valve timing.*

5 After the engine starts, it should be allowed to warm up to normal operating temperature. While the engine is warming up, make a thorough check for fuel, oil and coolant leaks. Also check the automatic transaxle fluid level (if equipped).

6 Shut the engine off and recheck the engine oil and coolant levels.

7 Drive the vehicle to an area with no traffic, accelerate from 30 to 50 mph, then allow the vehicle to slow rapidly to 30 mph with the throttle closed. Repeat the procedure 10 or 12 times. This will load the piston rings and cause them to seat properly against the cylinder walls. Check again for oil and coolant leaks.

8 Drive the vehicle gently for the first 500 miles (no sustained high speeds) and keep a constant check on the oil level. It is not unusual for an engine to use oil during the break-in period.

9 At approximately 500 to 600 miles, change the oil and filter.

10 For the next few hundred miles, drive the vehicle normally. Do not pamper it or abuse it.

11 After 2000 miles, change the oil and filter again and consider the engine broken in.

Chapter 3 Cooling, heating and air conditioning systems

Contents

Specifications

General

Radiator cap pressure rating	14 to 18 psi
Thermostat rating (opening temperature)	195-degrees F
Cooling system capacity	See Chapter 1

Torque specifications

	Ft-lbs (unless otherwise indicated)
Air conditioning condenser to radiator screws	45 in-lbs
Cooling system bleeder screws	
2.7L engine	110 in-lbs
3.2L and 3.5L engines	70 in-lbs
Cooling fan to radiator screws	45 in-lbs
Cooling fan blade to motor nut	45 in-lbs
Cooling fan motor to shroud	25 in-lbs
Thermostat housing bolts/nuts	105 in-lbs
Water pump mounting bolts (all models)	105 in-lbs
Water outlet housing	105 in-lbs

1 General information

Engine cooling system

All vehicles covered by this manual employ a pressurized engine cooling system with thermostatically controlled coolant circulation. An impeller-type water pump mounted on the front of the engine pumps coolant through the engine. The pump mounts directly to the engine block on 2.7L engines or to the right rear timing belt cover on the 3.2L and 3.5L engines. The coolant flows around the combustion chambers and toward the rear of the engine. Cast-in coolant passages direct coolant near the intake ports, exhaust ports, and spark plug areas.

A wax pellet-type thermostat is located in a housing near the front of the engine. During warm-up, the closed thermostat prevents coolant from circulating through the radiator. As the engine nears normal operating temperature, the thermostat opens and allows hot coolant to travel through the radiator, where it's cooled before returning to the engine.

The coolant reservoir does double duty as both the point at which fresh coolant is added to the cooling system to maintain the proper fluid level and as a holding tank for overheated coolant. This type of cooling system is known as a closed design because coolant that escapes past the pressure cap is saved and reused. Unlike most conventional coolant recovery tanks, these models have a *pressurized* section and an *overflow* section in the coolant recovery tank. The pressure chamber of the tank is used to add fluid and disperse trapped air and the overflow chamber of the tank is used to collect overheated coolant. The location of the tank compared to the radiator makes it the highest point in the system.

The cooling system is sealed by a pressure-type cap on the coolant recovery tank, which raises the boiling point of the coolant and increases the cooling efficiency of the system. If the system pressure exceeds the cap pressure relief value, the excess pressure in the system forces the spring-loaded valve inside the cap off its seat and allows the coolant to escape from the pressure chamber of the recovery tank to the chamber. When the system cools the excess coolant from the overflow chamber is automatically drawn back into the pressure chamber and into the radiator.

Heating system

The heating system consists of a blower fan and heater core located in the heater box, with hoses connecting the heater core to the engine cooling system. Hot engine coolant is circulated through the heater core. When the heater mode on the heater/air conditioning control head on the dashboard is activated, a flap door opens to expose the heater box to the passenger compartment. A fan switch on the control head activates the blower motor, which forces air through the core, heating the air.

2.4 An inexpensive hydrometer can be used to test the level of anti-freeze protection in your coolant

Air conditioning system

The air conditioning system consists of a condenser mounted in front of the radiator, an evaporator mounted adjacent to the heater core, a compressor mounted on the engine, which contains a high pressure relief valve, a receiver/drier and the plumbing connecting all of the above components.

A blower fan forces the warmer air of the passenger compartment through the evaporator core, transferring the heat from the air to the refrigerant (sort of a "radiator in reverse"). The liquid refrigerant boils off into low pressure vapor, taking the heat with it when it leaves the evaporator.

2 Antifreeze - general information

Refer to illustration 2.4

Warning: *Do not allow antifreeze to come in contact with your skin or painted surfaces of the vehicle. Rinse off spills immediately with plenty of water. Antifreeze is highly toxic if ingested. Never leave antifreeze lying around in an open container or in puddles on the floor; children and pets are attracted by it's sweet smell and may drink it. Antifreeze is also flammable, so don't store or use it near open flames. Check with local authorities about disposing of used antifreeze. Many communities have collection centers which will see that antifreeze is disposed of safely. Never dump used anti-freeze on the ground or into drains.*

Note: *Non-Toxic coolant is available at local auto parts stores. Although the coolant is non-toxic when fresh, proper disposal is still required.*

The cooling system should be filled with a water/ethylene glycol based antifreeze solution, which will prevent freezing down to at least minus 20-degrees F, or lower if local climate requires it. It also provides protection against corrosion and increases the coolant boiling point.

The cooling system should be drained, flushed and refilled at the specified intervals (see Chapter 1). Old or contaminated antifreeze solutions are likely to cause damage and encourage the formation of rust and scale in the system. Use distilled water with the antifreeze.

Before adding antifreeze, check all hose connections, because antifreeze tends to leak through very minute openings. Engines don't normally consume coolant, so if the level goes down, find the cause and correct it.

The exact mixture of antifreeze-to-water which you should use depends on the relative weather conditions. The mixture should contain at least 50-percent antifreeze, but should never contain more than 70 percent antifreeze. Consult the mixture ratio chart on the antifreeze container before adding coolant. Hydrometers are available at most auto parts stores to test the coolant **(see illustration)**. Use antifreeze that meets the vehicle manufacturer's specifications.

3 Thermostat - check and replacement

Warning: *Do not remove the coolant reservoir tank cap, drain the coolant or replace the thermostat until the engine has cooled completely.*

Check

Refer to illustration 3.7

1 Before assuming the thermostat is responsible for a cooling system problem, check the coolant level (see Chapter 1), drivebelt tension (see Chapter 1) and temperature gauge (or light) operation.

2 If the engine takes a long time to warm up (as indicated by the temperature gauge or heater operation), the thermostat is probably stuck open. Replace the thermostat with a new one.

3 If the engine runs hot, use your hand to check the temperature of the lower radiator hose. If the hose is not hot, but the engine is,

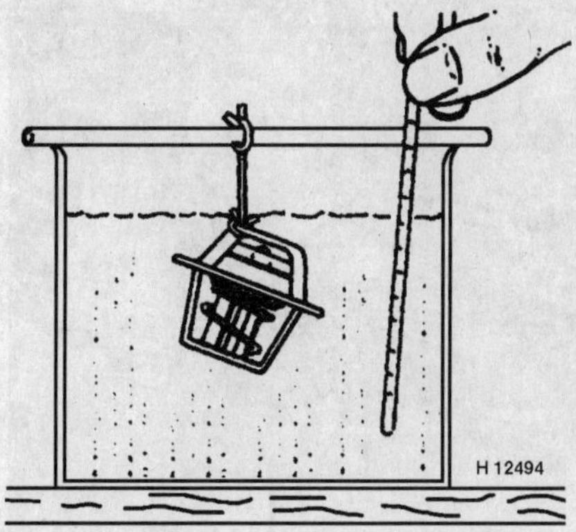

3.7 A thermostat can be accurately checked by heating it in a container of water with a thermostat and observing the opening and fully open temperature

the thermostat is probably stuck in the closed position, preventing the coolant inside the radiator from traveling through the engine. Replace the thermostat. **Caution:** *Do not drive the vehicle without a thermostat. The computer may stay in open loop and emissions and fuel economy will suffer.*

4 If the lower radiator hose is medium to hot temperature, it means that the coolant is flowing and the thermostat is open. Consult the *Troubleshooting* Section at the front of this manual for further diagnosis.

5 A more thorough test of the thermostat can only be made when it is removed from the vehicle (see below). If the thermostat remains in the open position at room temperature, it is faulty and must be replaced.

6 To test it fully, suspend the (closed) thermostat on a length of string or wire in a container of cold water, with a thermometer (cooking type that reads beyond 212 degrees F).

7 Heat the water on a stove while observing the temperature and the thermostat. Neither should contact the sides of the container **(see illustration)**.

8 Note the temperature when the thermostat begins to open and when it is fully open. The number stamped into the thermostat is generally the fully open temperature.

9 If the thermostat doesn't open and close, or sticks in any position, replace it.

3.13 Remove the hose clamps (arrows) and hoses from the thermostat housing (2.7L engine shown, 3.2L and 3.5L engines similar)

Replacement

Refer to illustrations 3.13, 3.15a and 3.15b

10 Disconnect the negative battery cable from the remote ground terminal (see Chapter 5).

11 Drain the cooling system (see Chapter 1). If the coolant is relatively new or in good condition, save it and reuse it. On 2.7L engines (see Chapter 5) and remove the alternator.

12 Follow the lower radiator hose to the engine to locate the thermostat housing.

13 Using radiator hose clamp pliers, remove the hose clamp, then detach the hoses from the thermostat housing **(see illustration)**. If the hoses are stuck, grasp them near the end with a pair of adjustable pliers and twist it to break the seal, then pull it off. If the hose is old or deteriorated, cut it off and install a new one.

14 If the hose fittings on the thermostat housing are deteriorated (corroded, pitted, etc.) they may be damaged further by hose removal. If it is, the thermostat housing will have to be replaced.

15 Remove the fasteners and detach the housing **(see illustrations)**. If the housing is stuck, tap it with a soft-face hammer to jar it loose. Be prepared for some coolant to spill as the gasket seal is broken.

16 Note how it's installed (which end is facing up), then remove the thermostat.

17 Remove all traces of old gasket material and sealant from the housing and cover with a gasket scraper.

18 Install the thermostat and gasket into the housing with the air bleed hole facing up.

19 Install the housing and fasteners to the engine block. Tighten the fasteners to the torque listed in this Chapter's Specifications.

20 Reattach the hoses to the thermostat housing and replace the hose clamps.

21 Refill the cooling system (see Chapter 1).

22 Start the engine and allow it to reach normal operating temperature, then check for leaks and proper thermostat operation (as described in Steps 2 through 4). See Chapter 1 for cooling system air-bleeding procedure.

4 Engine cooling fans and circuit - check and component replacement

Warning: *Do not work with your hands near the fans at any time that the engine is running or the key is ON. With the key ON, (even with the engine not running) the fan can start at any time, since it is controlled by coolant temperature.*

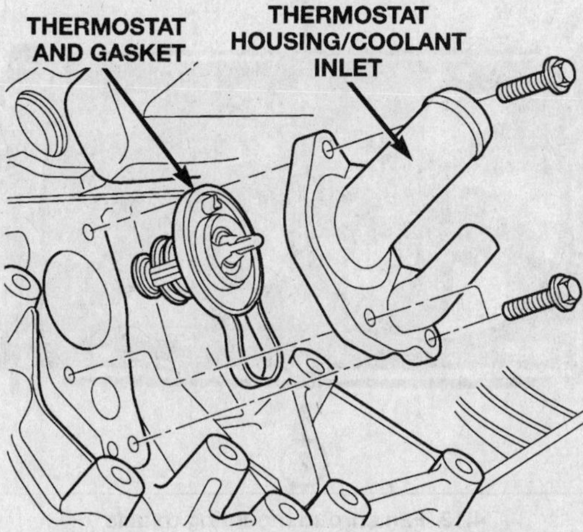

3.15a Thermostat mounting details (2.7L engine)

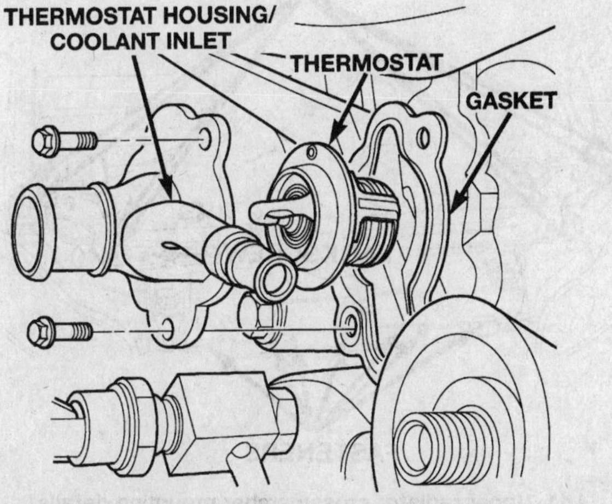

3.15b Thermostat mounting details (3.2L and 3.5L engines)

4.2 The high-speed and low-speed fan relays are mounted in the power distribution center in the engine compartment

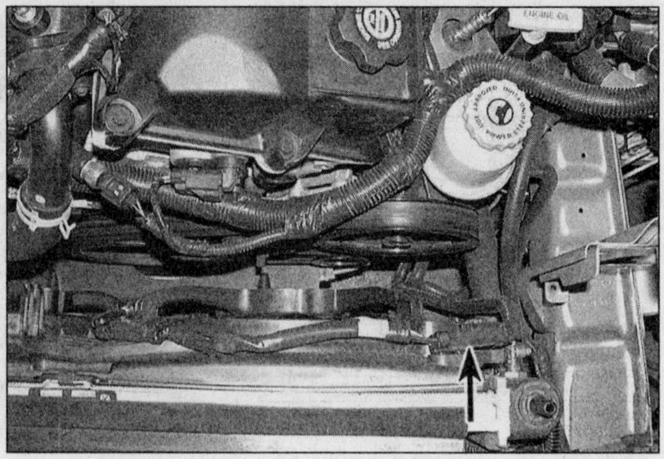

4.4 Disconnect the fan connector (arrow) and try operating the fan with a fused battery-voltage jumper wire and a ground wire

Check

Refer to illustrations 4.2 and 4.4

1 All models have a two-speed electric fan mounted in a plastic shroud attached to the back of the radiator.

2 Fan operation is controlled both by the PCM and the high and low-speed fan relays **(see illustration)**. The PCM receives signals from various sensors such as the coolant temperature sensor, the air intake temperature sensor, the vehicle speed sensor, the air conditioning pressure transducer and the transaxle temperature sensor. These sensors signal the PCM of engine temperature and varying engine conditions then the PCM turns on the appropriate relay(s). When the engine reaches operating temperature, the PCM turns both fans on at low speed. When coolant temperature reaches 230 degrees F, the PCM turns the high-speed relay on, causing both fans to run at high speed.

3 Warm the engine up until the gauge on the instrument panel indicates the high side of NORMAL. The fan should come on. If not, check the cooling system fan control fuses in the engine compartment fuse panel and in the interior fuse panel (see Chapter 12 for fuse locations).

4 If the fuses checked OK, disconnect the electrical connector from the electric fan motor **(see illustration)**. Attach a fused jumper wire with battery voltage to either of the two power terminals on the fan, and a second jumper wire to chassis-ground and the black wire terminal on the fan (see the wiring diagrams in Chapter 12). If the fan doesn't operate, it should be replaced.

5 If it does operate with jumper wires, but doesn't under normal driving conditions, connect a voltmeter to a chassis ground and probe the power terminals of the fan connector on the harness side. If the engine is hot and the temperature gauge shows above NORMAL, there should be battery voltage at one of these terminals.

6 Check the ground side of the circuit by switching your meter to the ohms scale. Ground one side of the meter and probe the other side at the black wire terminal of the fan connector. Resistance should be no more than 5 ohms. If resistance is high, trace the ground wire circuit to the chassis.

7 If there was no power at the terminals in Step 5, check that power is being supplied to the low-speed fan relay. One of its sockets on the relay panel should exhibit battery voltage at all times, and one only when the key is in the On or Start position.

8 If power at the fan relay exists, refer to Chapter 12 for checking continuity within the relays themselves.

9 If the fan operates continuously, the fault could be the coolant temperature sensor or the relays. To diagnose the various sensors, see Chapter 6, or to diagnose the relays see Chapter 12.

Replacement

Refer to illustrations 4.11, 4.12, 4.13 and 4.15

10 Disconnect the electrical connector from the fan motor.

11 Partially drain the cooling system (see Chapter 1) and disconnect the upper radiator hose at the radiator. Remove the windshield

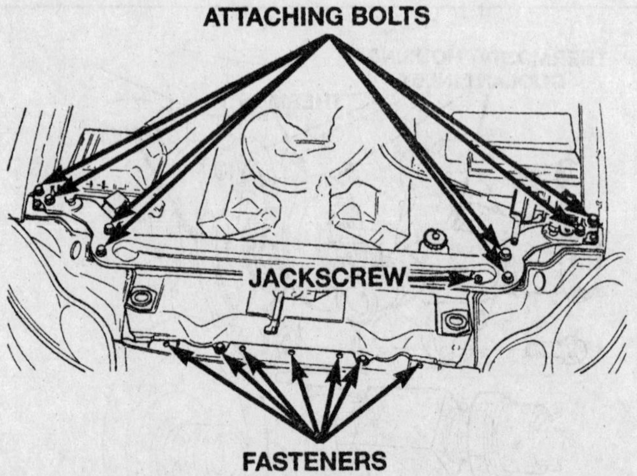

4.11 Upper radiator crossmember mounting details

4.12 Fan shroud mounting details

1 Mounting bolts
2 Retaining clips

4.13 Fan blade retaining nut (arrow)

washer bottle and the cruise control servo (if equipped) from the upper radiator crossmember. Disconnect the hood latch cable from the hood latch (see Chapter 11). Remove the upper radiator crossmember retaining bolts, clips and the headlight jack screws and remove the crossmember from the vehicle **(see illustration)**.

12 Remove the fan shroud retaining bolts and clips and remove the fan/shroud assembly **(see illustration)**.

13 Remove the nut retaining the fan to the motor shaft **(see illustration)**.

14 With an assistant retaining the fan, hit the shaft of the motor with a hammer and blunt punch to separate the fan from the motor.

15 Remove the screws retaining the motor to the shroud **(see illustration)**.

16 Installation is the reverse of removal.

5 Radiator and coolant recovery tank - removal and installation

Warning: *Wait until the engine is completely cool before beginning this procedure.*

5.6b . . . and the transaxle auxiliary oil cooler lines (arrows) from below the vehicle

4.15 To remove the fan motor from the shroud, remove the screws (arrows)

Radiator

Refer to illustrations 5.4, 5.6a, 5.6b, 5.8 and 5.9

1 Disconnect the negative battery cable from the remote ground terminal (see Chapter 5).

2 Drain the cooling system (see Chapter 1). If the coolant is relatively new and in good condition, save it and reuse it.

3 Remove the upper radiator crossmember and cooling fan assembly (see Section 4).

4 Using radiator hose clamp pliers, remove the hose clamps then detach the upper and lower coolant hoses from the radiator **(see illustration)**. If they're stuck, grasp each hose near the end with a pair of adjustable pliers and twist it to break the seal, then pull it off - be careful not to distort the radiator fittings! If the hoses are old or deteriorated, cut them off and install new ones.

5 Disconnect the engine oil cooler lines (if equipped) from the right side of the radiator.

6 Disconnect and plug the transaxle oil cooler lines **(see illustrations)**.

7 At this point, if the vehicle is equipped with air conditioning, there are two ways to remove the radiator. If the condenser is staying in the vehicle, remove the two condenser-to-radiator mounting screws (accessible through the lower openings in the front of the body) and the one screw for the transaxle auxiliary oil cooler, and the radiator can be pulled up.

8 The alternative to Step 7 (if the condenser is being removed and the air conditioning system has already been discharged of refrigerant) is to disconnect the condenser lines (see Section 15) and remove the radia-

5.4 Most of the coolant hoses on these models have spring type hose clamps which require a pair of hose clamp pliers to remove them - squeeze the clamp and slide it back away from the hose fitting

5.6a Detach the transaxle oil cooler line (arrow) from the top of the left radiator tank . . .

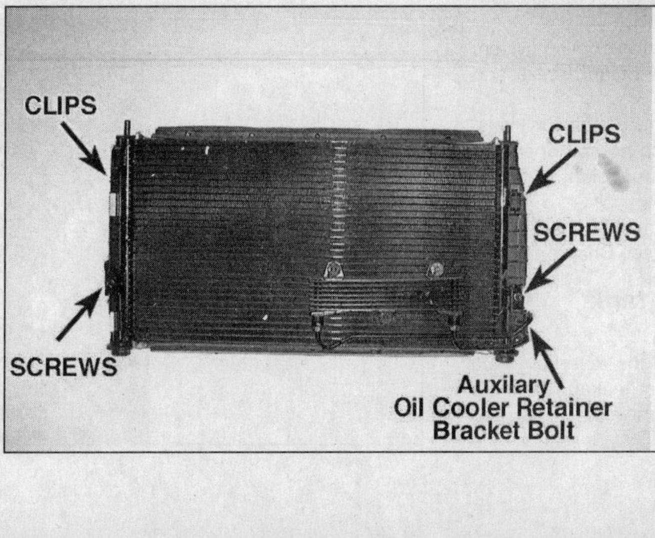

5.8 To remove the condenser and the auxiliary oil cooler from the radiator, remove the oil cooler bracket screw and the condenser retaining screws, then lift the condenser up and out of the retaining clips

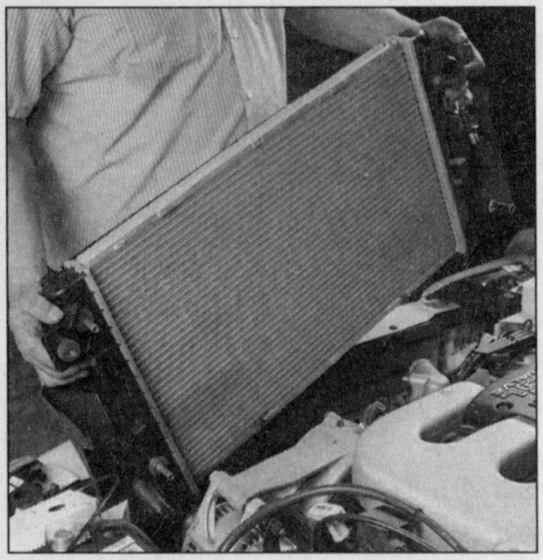

5.9 Carefully lift the radiator out of the engine compartment - it can be removed with the condenser either attached or left in the vehicle

5.18 Detach the hose (A) from the recovery tank, and remove the mounting bolts (B)

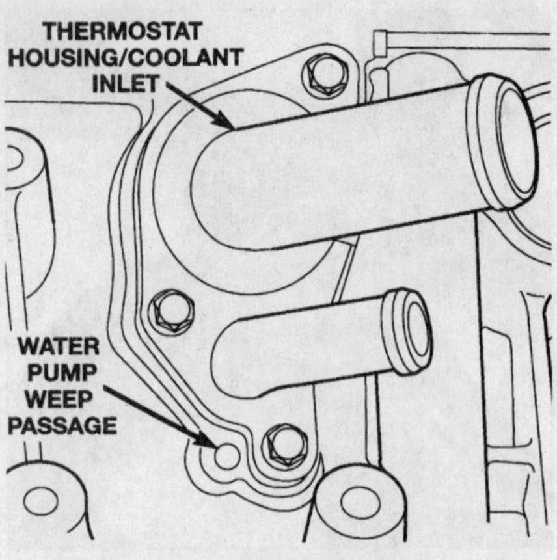

6.3 A failed front water pump seal on 2.7L engines will direct coolant out a weep hole on side of the block

tor, the condenser and the auxiliary oil cooler as a unit, separating the two components outside of the vehicle where the fasteners are easier to get at **(see illustration)**. **Warning:** *The air conditioning system is under high pressure. Do not loosen any hose fittings or remove any components until after the system has been discharged. Air conditioning refrigerant should be properly discharged into an EPA-approved recovery/recycling unit at a dealer service department or an automotive air conditioning repair facility. Always wear eye protection when disconnecting air conditioning system fittings.*

9 Carefully lift out the radiator. Don't spill coolant on the vehicle or scratch the paint **(see illustration)**.

10 Check the radiator for leaks and damage. If it needs repair, have a radiator shop or dealer service department perform the work, as special techniques are required.

11 Remove bugs and dirt from the radiator with compressed air and a soft brush (don't bend the cooling fins).

12 Inspect the radiator mounts for deterioration and make sure there's no dirt or gravel in them when the radiator is installed.

13 Installation is the reverse of the removal procedure. Make sure the radiator is properly seated on the lower mounting insulators before fastening the upper radiator crossmember.

14 After installation, fill the cooling system with the proper mixture of antifreeze and water (see Chapter 1).

15 Start the engine and check for leaks. Allow the engine to reach normal operating temperature. Recheck the coolant level and add more, if required.

16 Also check the automatic transaxle fluid and add fluid as needed (see Chapter 1).

Coolant recovery tank

Refer to illustration 5.18

17 Detach the hose at the reservoir. Plug the hose fitting to prevent leakage from the reservoir as the tank is removed.

18 Remove the reservoir retaining bolts and lift the reservoir out of the engine compartment **(see illustration)**.

19 Installation is the reverse of removal. While the tank is off the vehicle, it should be cleaned with soapy water and a brush to remove any deposits inside.

6 Water pump - check and replacement

Warning: *Wait until the engine is completely cool before beginning this procedure.*

Check

Refer to illustration 6.3

1 A failure in the water pump can cause serious engine damage due to overheating.

2 There are three ways to check the operation of the water pump while it's installed on the engine. If the pump is defective, it should be replaced with a new or rebuilt unit.

3 Water pumps are usually equipped with weep or vent holes **(see illustration)**. If a failure occurs in the pump seal, coolant will leak from the hole. In most cases you'll need a flashlight to find the hole on the water pump from underneath to check for leaks. **Note:** *Some small black staining around the weep hole is normal. If the stain is heavy brown or actual coolant is evident, replace the pump.*

4 If the water pump shaft bearings fail there may be a howling sound at the front of the engine while it's running. With the engine off, shaft wear can be felt if the water pump pulley or sprocket is rocked up-and-down. **Note:** *Checking shaft wear on these engines will require removal of the timing cover(s) and relieving tension on the timing chain (2.7L engine) or the timing belt (3.2L and 3.5L engines) (see Chapter 2A or 2B).* In either case don't mistake drivebelt slippage, which causes a squealing sound, for water pump bearing failure.

5 Even a pump that exhibits no outward signs of a problem, such as noise or leakage, can still be due for replacement. Removal for close examination is the only sure way to tell. Sometimes the fins on the back of the impeller can corrode to the point that cooling efficiency is hampered.

Replacement

Refer to illustrations 6.10a, 6.10b, 6.11a and 6.11b

6 Disconnect the negative battery cable from the remote ground terminal (see Chapter 5).

7 Drain the cooling system (see Chapter 1). If the coolant is relatively new or in

6.10a Remove the water pump retaining bolts (B) and the upper timing chain guide bolts (A) (2.7L engine)

6.10b Remove the water pump mounting bolts (3.2L and 3.5L engines)

6.11a Water pump O-ring installation details (2.7L engine)

good condition, save and reuse it.

8 Remove the upper radiator crossmember and the cooling fan assembly (see Section 4).

9 The water pump on these engines is driven by the timing chain (2.7L engine) or the timing belt (3.2L and 3.5L engines). Refer to Chapter 2A or 2B and remove the timing chain or belt. On 2.7L models, remove the chain guides. **Caution:** *Do not turn the crankshaft or camshafts while the chain or belt is disconnected, or camshaft timing will be disturbed*.

10 Remove the water pump bolts and remove the pump from the engine **(see illustrations)**.

11 Install a new O-ring, wetting it with coolant for easier installation in the groove **(see illustrations)**. Install the pump, tightening the bolts to the torque listed in this Chapter's Specifications

12 Reinstall the timing chain or timing belt (see Chapter 2A or 2B). The remainder of the installation is the reverse of removal.

13 Refill the cooling system and operate the engine to check for leaks.

7 Coolant temperature gauge sending unit - check and replacement

The coolant temperature indicator system is composed of a light or temperature gauge mounted in the dash and a coolant temperature sending unit mounted on the engine. In the models covered by this manual, there is only one coolant temperature sensor, which functions as indicator to both the PCM and the instrument panel. Refer to the procedures outlined in Chapter 6 for the checking and replacement of this sensor.

8 Blower motor circuit - check

Refer to illustrations 8.3, 8.4 and 8.12

Warning: *The models covered by this manual are equipped with Supplemental Restraint Systems (SRS), more commonly known as airbags. Always disable the airbag system before working in the vicinity of any airbag system components to avoid the possibility of accidental deployment of the airbag(s), which could cause personal injury (see Chapter 12).* **Note:** *This procedure applies to vehicles equipped with manual heating and air conditioning systems only. Vehicles equipped with automatic heating and air conditioning systems are very complex and considered beyond the scope of the home mechanic. All Vehicles equipped with automatic heating and air conditioning systems should be taken to dealer service department or other qualified repair facility because of the specialized tools and equipment required to perform the work, however see Section 12 for self diagnostic procedures requiring specialized tools.*

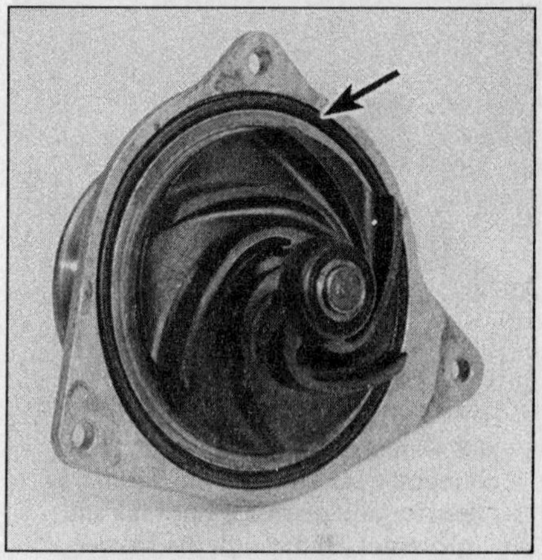

6.11b Water pump O-ring installation details (3.2L and 3.5L engines)

1 If the blower motor speed does not correspond to the setting selected on the blower switch, or the blower motor does not operate at all, the problem could be a bad fuse, switch, blower motor resistor, blower motor or blower motor circuit wiring.

2 Before checking the blower motor or circuit, always check the fuse and relay (if equipped) first (see Chapter 12).

3 Remove the lower right air duct (below the glove box) to gain access to the heater case and blower motor **(see illustration)**.

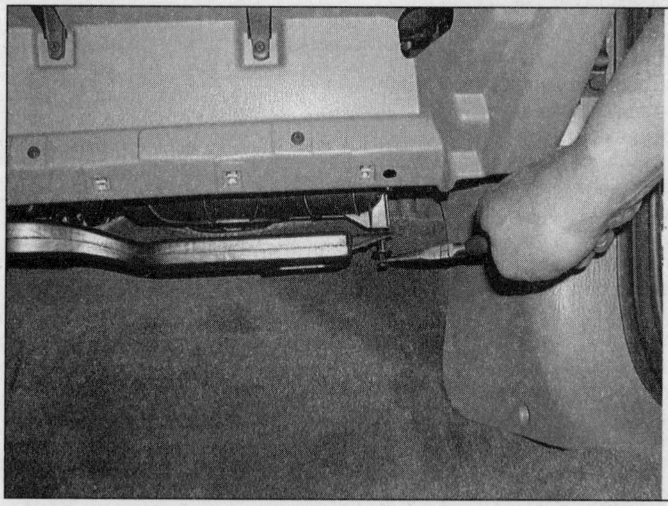

8.3 The lower right air duct is fastened to the heater case with plastic clips

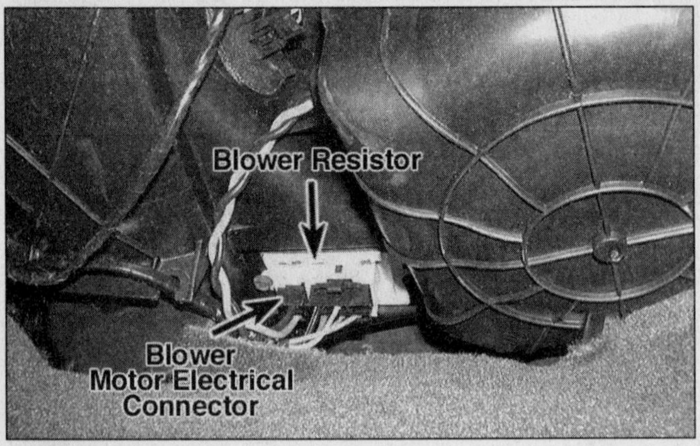

8.4 Test for voltage at the blower motor electrical connector

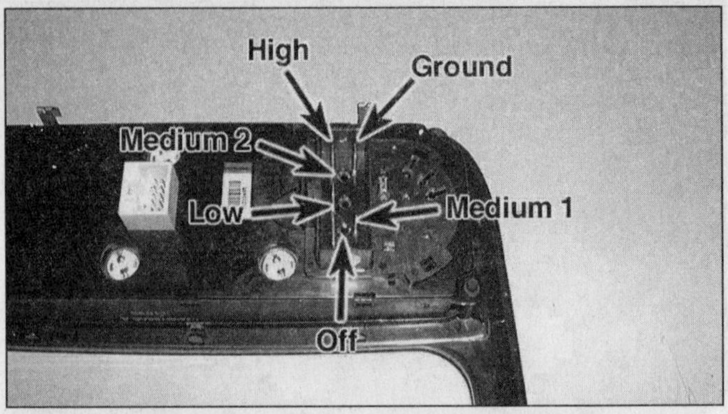

8.12 Blower motor speed switch terminal identification - there should be continuity between the switch terminal and the ground terminal with the switch in the proper position

9.3 Disconnect the blower harness connector (A) from the blower motor resistor and push the harness and grommet (B) through the blower motor cover

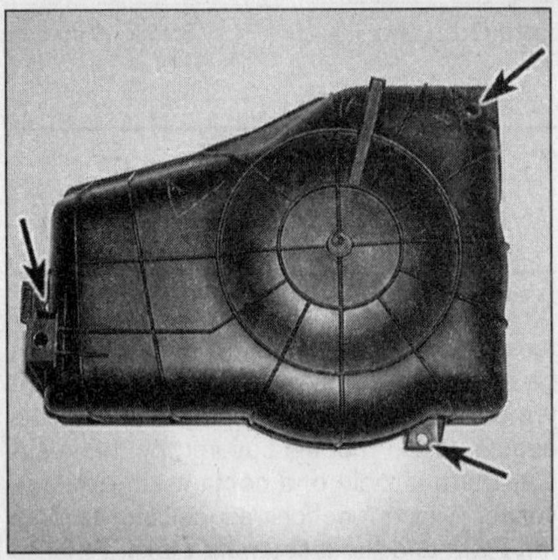

9.4 Remove the screws (arrows) and remove the blower motor cover (cover removed for clarity)

9.5 Blower motor retaining screws (arrows)

4 With the ignition key in the ON position, turn the blower switch to the faulty position(s) and, using a test light or voltmeter, check the voltage at the motor electrical connector **(see illustration)**. If the motor is receiving voltage but not operating, either the motor ground is bad (on these models the blower switch and resistor are part of the ground circuit) or the motor itself is faulty or the fan is binding.

5 To check the blower motor, disconnect the electrical connector from the blower motor, connect a jumper wire between the ground wire terminal on the blower motor and a good ground, then connect a fused jumper wire between the positive terminal of the battery and the positive terminal on the blower motor. If the motor now operates properly, the ground circuit or resistor is bad. If the motor does not operate, the fan is either binding or the motor is faulty.

6 If you suspect the blower motor fan is binding, remove the blower motor (see Section 9) to check for free operation of the fan.

7 If the ground circuit to the motor is bad check the blower resistor , the blower switch and the associated wiring for proper operation. The blower motor resistor is mounted near the blower motor to the heater/AC housing **(see illustration 8.4)**.

8 Refer to the wiring diagrams at the end of this manual and probe the wires at the resistor leading from the blower switch. Using an ohmmeter, check for continuity to ground at the resistor electrical connector while the blower switch is rotated through all the switch position(s). Continuity to ground should be present at one of the terminals in each of the switch positions except Off.

9 If a ground signal does not exist at the blower resistor connector repair the blower motor switch and or the circuit leading to the switch.

10 If a ground signal from the switch does exist at the blower resistor connector, check the blower resistor for continuity between the terminals. Continuity should exist, with varying resistance, between each of the terminals. If any checks indicate infinite resistance replace the blower resistor.

11 To check the blower speed switch refer to Section 10 and pull the heater/ air conditioning control unit out from the dash enough to access the rear of the fan switch.

12 Unplug the electrical connector from the blower switch and check for continuity between the ground terminal and each of the indicated switch terminals with an ohmmeter **(see illustration)**. Example: If the switch is placed in the LOW position there should be continuity between the ground terminal and the low speed terminal, If the switch is placed in the HIGH position there should be continuity between the ground terminal and the high speed terminal.

13 If continuity isn't as specified, replace the switch.

9 Blower motor - removal and installation

Refer to illustrations 9.3, 9.4 and 9.5

1 Disconnect the battery negative cable from the remote ground terminal (see Chapter 5).

2 Remove the lower right air duct (below the glove box) to gain access to the heater case and blower motor **(see illustration 8.3)**.

3 Disconnect the wiring plug at the blower motor resistor and push the harness grommet through the blower motor cover **(see illustration)**.

4 Remove the screws holding the blower motor cover **(see illustration)**. Some of these screws are difficult to access and may require the use of a swivel adapter and a socket to remove.

5 Remove the three screws and pull out the blower motor and fan assembly **(see illustration)**.

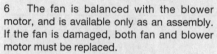

10.3 Detach the center instrument panel bezel and disconnect the electrical connectors (arrows) from the heater/air conditioning control unit

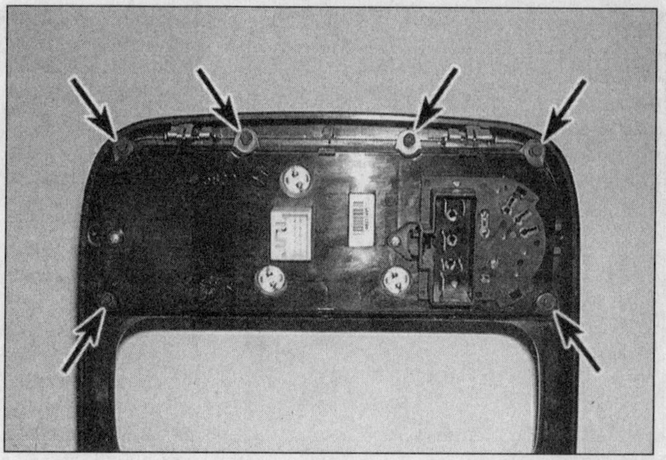

10.4 Remove the retaining screws (arrows) to detach the heater/air conditioning control unit from the instrument panel center bezel

6 The fan is balanced with the blower motor, and is available only as an assembly. If the fan is damaged, both fan and blower motor must be replaced.

7 Installation is the reverse of removal.

10 Heater and air conditioning control assembly - removal and installation

Refer to illustrations 10.3 and 10.4

Warning: *The models covered by this manual are equipped with Supplemental Restraint Systems (SRS), more commonly known as airbags. Always disable the airbag system before working in the vicinity of any airbag system components to avoid the possibility of accidental deployment of the airbag(s), which could cause personal injury (see Chapter 12).*

1 Disconnect the negative battery cable from the remote ground terminal (see Chapter 5).

2 Carefully pry the instrument panel center bezel out (see Chapter 11).

3 Pull the control assembly back and disconnect the electrical connectors **(see illustration)**, then remove the bezel and control unit as an assembly from the instrument panel.

4 Remove the control unit to bezel mounting screws and detach the control unit from the bezel **(see illustration)**.

5 Installation is the reverse of removal. Be sure align the bezel retaining clips with their respective holes before snapping the bezel into place.

11 Heater core - replacement

Refer to illustrations 11.4a, 11.4b,11.6a, 11.6b, 11.9, 11.11, 11.12a and 11.12b

Warning 1: *The air conditioning system is under high pressure. Do not loosen any hose fittings or remove any components until after the system has been discharged. Air conditioning refrigerant should be properly discharged into an EPA-approved recovery/recycling unit at a dealer service department or an automotive air conditioning repair facility. Always wear eye protection when disconnecting air conditioning system fittings.*

Warning 2: *The models covered by this manual are equipped with Supplemental Restraint Systems (SRS), more commonly known as airbags. Always disable the airbag system before working in the vicinity of any airbag system components to avoid the possibility of accidental deployment of the airbag(s), which could cause personal injury (see Chapter 12).*

1 Replacement of the heater core is difficult procedure for the home mechanic, involving removal of the entire dashboard, floor console and many wiring connectors. If you attempt this procedure at home, keep track of the assemblies by taking notes and keeping screws and other hardware in small, marked plastic bags for reassembly.

2 Have the air conditioning system discharged at a dealer service department or automotive air conditioning repair facility, drain the cooling system (see Chapter 1) and disconnect the negative battery cable from the remote ground terminal (see Chapter 5). If the coolant is relatively new, or tests in good condition (see Section 2), save it and re-use it. **Warning:** *Do not allow antifreeze to come in contact with your skin or painted surfaces of the vehicle. Rinse off spills immediately with plenty of water. Antifreeze is highly toxic if ingested. Never leave antifreeze lying around in an open container or in puddles on the floor; children and pets are attracted by it's sweet smell and may drink it. Check with local authorities about disposing of used antifreeze. Many communities have collection centers which will see that antifreeze is disposed of safely. Never dump used anti-freeze on the ground or into drains.*

3 Remove the air intake duct from the throttle body and the air cleaner housing (see Chapter 4).

4 Disconnect the heater hoses at the firewall and unbolt the air conditioning lines from the expansion valve **(see illustrations). Caution:** *Plug the air conditioning lines to prevent the entry of air into the system, since the lubricant absorbs air.*

5 Remove the receiver-drier (see Section 13).

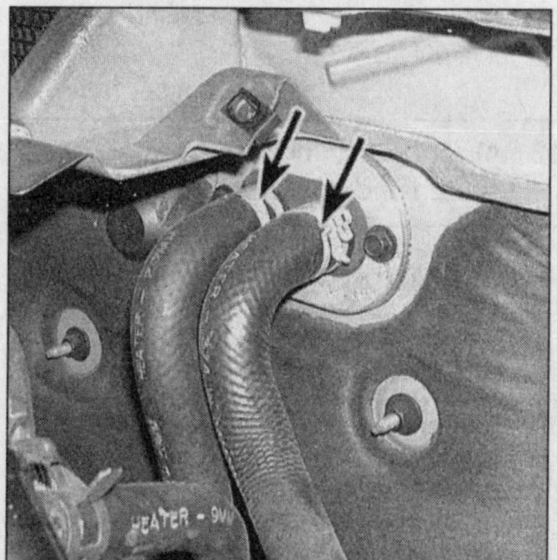

11.4a Disconnect the heater hoses at the firewall (arrows)

11.4b Unbolt the air conditioning lines (arrow) from the expansion valve

11.6a Remove the heater/air conditioning housing nuts (arrows) and the rubber grommets where the heater core tubes go through the firewall

11.6b The third heater/air conditioning housing nut (arrow) is accessible after removing the receiver-drier

11.9 Defroster air duct retaining screws (arrows)

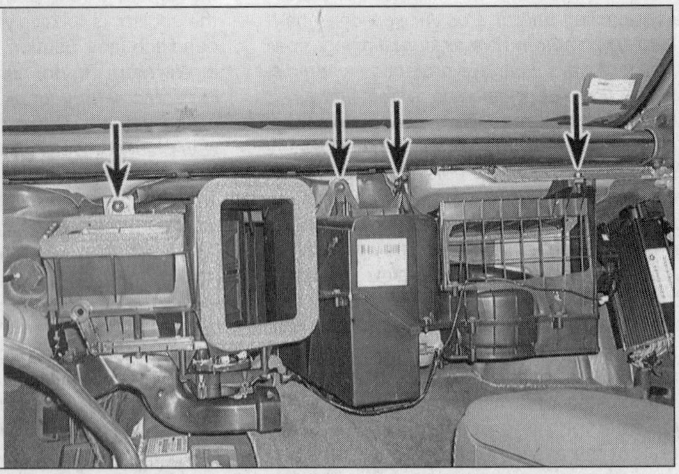

11.11 Heater/air conditioning housing to cowl bolts and nuts (arrows)

11.12a Remove the heater core retaining screws (arrows) . . .

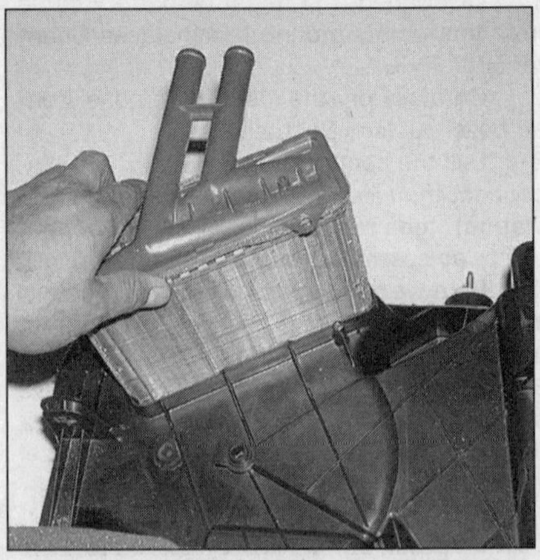

11.12b . . . and pull the heater core out of the housing

6 Remove three heater/air conditioning housing nuts from the studs protruding through the firewall into the engine compartment and the rubber grommets where the heater core tubes go through the firewall **(see illustrations)**.

7 Plug the heater core tubes to prevent coolant spillage in the interior of the vehicle as the heater/air conditioning housing is removed.

8 Lower the steering column and remove the entire instrument panel (see Chapter 11). **Note:** *Instrument panel removal is very difficult. Take your time and don't use excessive force - there may be fasteners you haven't found yet.*

9 Remove the defroster air duct from the top heater/air conditioning housing **(see illustration)**.

10 Remove the floor heater ducting and any remaining electrical connectors attached to the heater/air conditioning housing.

11 Remove the bolts which hold the heater/air conditioning housing to the cowl, and carefully pull the housing out and down to remove it **(see illustration)**.

12 Remove the retaining screws and pull the heater core from the housing **(see illustrations)**.

13 Installation is the reverse of removal. Be sure to refill the cooling system (see Chapter 1) and recharge the air conditioning system. **Note:** *Since the heater core replacement is so difficult, it is recommended that once the housing is removed from the vehicle, the heater core should be replaced with a new unit, not repaired.*

12 Air conditioning and heating system - check and maintenance

Air conditioning system

Refer to illustration 12.1

Warning: *The air conditioning system is under high pressure. Do not loosen any hose fittings or remove any components until after the system has been discharged. Air conditioning refrigerant should be properly discharged into an EPA-approved recovery/recycling unit at a dealer service department or an automotive air conditioning repair facility. Always wear eye protection when disconnecting air conditioning system fittings.*

Caution 1: *All models covered by this manual use environmentally friendly R-134a. This refrigerant (and its appropriate refrigerant oils) are not compatible R-12 refrigerant system components and must never be mixed or the components will be damaged.*

Caution 2: *When replacing entire compo-*

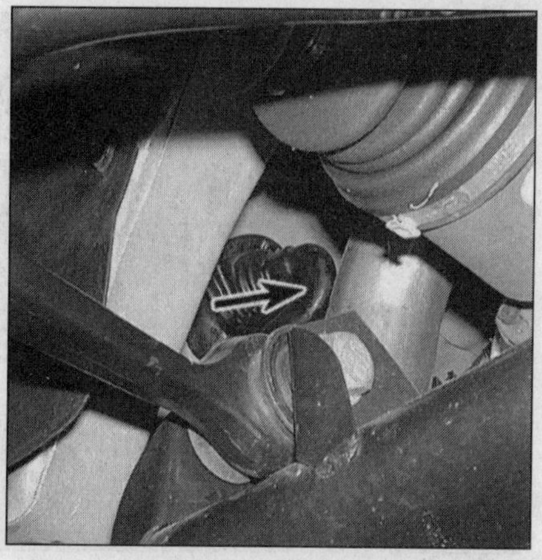

12.1 Check that the evaporator housing drain tube (arrow) at the firewall is clear of any blockage – the view here is through the passenger side wheelwell housing

nents, additional refrigerant oil should be added equal to the amount that is removed with the component being replaced. Be sure to read the can before adding any oil to the system, to make sure it is compatible with the R-134a system.

1 The following maintenance checks should be performed on a regular basis to ensure that the air conditioning continues to operate at peak efficiency.

a) *Inspect the condition of the compressor drivebelt. If it is worn or deteriorated, replace it* (see Chapter 1).
b) *Check the drivebelt tension and, if necessary, adjust it* (see Chapter 1).
c) *Inspect the system hoses. Look for cracks, bubbles, hardening and deterioration. Inspect the hoses and all fittings for oil bubbles or seepage. If there is any evidence of wear, damage or leakage, replace the hose(s).*
d) *Inspect the condenser fins for leaves, bugs and any other foreign material that may have embedded itself in the fins. Use a "fin comb" or compressed air to remove debris from the condenser.*
e) *Make sure the system has the correct refrigerant charge.*
f) *If you hear water sloshing around in the dash area or have water dripping on the carpet, check the evaporator housing drain tube* **(see illustration)** *and insert a piece of wire into the opening to check for blockage.*

2 It's a good idea to operate the system for about ten minutes at least once a month. This is particularly important during the winter months because long term non-use can cause hardening, and subsequent failure, of the seals. Note that using the Defrost function operates the compressor.

3 If the air conditioning system is not working properly, proceed to Step 6 and perform the general checks outlined below.

4 Because of the complexity of the air conditioning system and the special equipment necessary to service it, in-depth troubleshooting and repairs beyond checking the refrigerant charge and the compressor clutch operation are not included in this manual. However, simple checks and component replacement procedures are provided in this Chapter. For more complete information on the air conditioning system, refer to the *Haynes Automotive Heating and Air Conditioning Manual*.

12.9 Insert a thermometer in the center duct while operating the air conditioning system - the output air should be 35-40 degrees F less than the ambient temperature, depending on humidity (but not lower than 40-degrees F)

5 The most common cause of poor cooling is simply a low system refrigerant charge. If a noticeable drop in system cooling ability occurs, one of the following quick checks will help you determine whether the refrigerant level is low. Should the system lose its cooling ability, the following procedure will help you pinpoint the cause.

Check

Refer to illustration 12.9

6 Warm the engine up to normal operating temperature.

7 Place the air conditioning temperature selector at the coldest setting and put the blower at the highest setting. Open the doors (to make sure the air conditioning system doesn't cycle off as soon as it cools the passenger compartment).

8 After the system reaches operating temperature, feel the two pipes connected to the evaporator at the firewall.

9 The evaporator inlet pipe (thinner tubing leading from the condenser outlet to the evaporator) should be cold, and the evaporator outlet line (the thicker tubing that leads back to the compressor) should be slightly colder (3 to 10 degrees F colder). If the evaporator outlet is considerably warmer than the inlet, the system needs a charge. Insert a thermometer in the center air distribution duct **(see illustration)** while operating the air conditioning system at its maximum setting - the temperature of the output air should be 35 to 40 degrees F below the ambient air temperature (down to approximately 40 degrees F). If the ambient (outside) air temperature is very high, say 110 degrees F, the duct air temperature may be as high as 60 degrees F, but generally the air conditioning is 35 to 40 degrees F cooler than the ambient air.

10 If the air isn't as cold as it used to be, the system probably needs a charge.

11 If the air is warm and the system doesn't seem to be operating properly check the operation of the compressor clutch.

12 Have an assistant switch the air conditioning On while you observe the front of the compressor. The clutch will make an audible click and the center of the clutch should rotate. If it doesn't, shut the engine off and disconnect the air conditioning system pressure switch **(see illustration 12.22)**. Bridge the terminals of the connector with a jumper wire and turn the air conditioning On again. If it works now, the system pressure is too high or too low. Have your system tested by a dealer service department or air conditioning shop.

13 If the clutch still didn't operate, check the appropriate fuses. Inspect the fuses in the interior fuse panel.

14 Remove the compressor clutch (AC) relay from the engine compartment relay panel and test it (see Chapter 12). With the relay out and the ignition On, check for battery power at two of the relay terminals (refer to the wiring diagrams for wire color designations to determine which terminals to check). There should be battery power with the key On, at the terminals for the relay control and power circuits.

15 Using a jumper wire, connect the terminals in the relay box from the relay power circuit to the terminal that leads to the compressor clutch (refer to the wiring diagrams for wire color designations to determine which terminals to connect). Listen for the clutch to click as you make the connection. If the clutch doesn't respond, disconnect the clutch connector at the compressor and check for battery voltage at the compressor clutch connector. Check for continuity to ground on the black wire terminal of the compressor clutch connector. If power and ground are available and the clutch doesn't operate when connected, the compressor clutch is defective.

16 If the compressor clutch, relay and related circuits are good and the system is fully charged with refrigerant and the compressor does not operate under normal conditions, have the PCM and related circuits checked by a dealer service department or other properly equipped repair facility.

17 Further inspection or testing of the system is beyond the scope of the home mechanic and should be left to a professional.

Adding refrigerant

Refer to illustrations 12.18, 12.21a, 12.21b, 12.22a and 12.22b

Caution: *Make sure any refrigerant, refrigerant oil or replacement component your purchase is designated as compatible with environmentally friendly R-134a systems.*

12.18 A basic charging kit for 134a systems is available at most auto parts stores - it must say 134a (not R-12) and so should the can of refrigerant

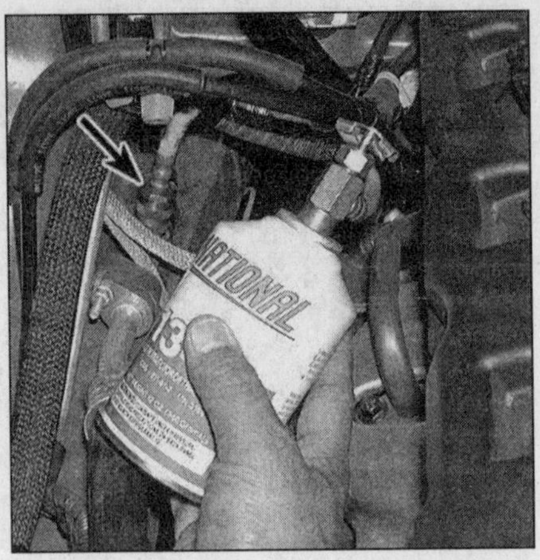
12.21a The low-side charging port (arrow) on 2.7L engines is near the right shock tower - the cap should be marked with an "L"

12.21b The low-side charging port (arrow) on 3.2L and 3.5L engines is on top of the compressor - the cap should be marked with an "L"

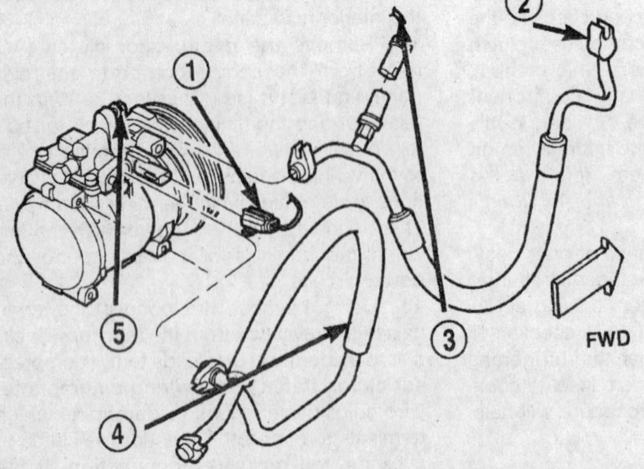

12.22a A/C compressor refrigerant lines and related components (2.7L engine)

1 *Compressor clutch electrical connector*
2 *Discharge line*
3 *A/C pressure switch and connector*
4 *Suction line*
5 *A/C compressor*

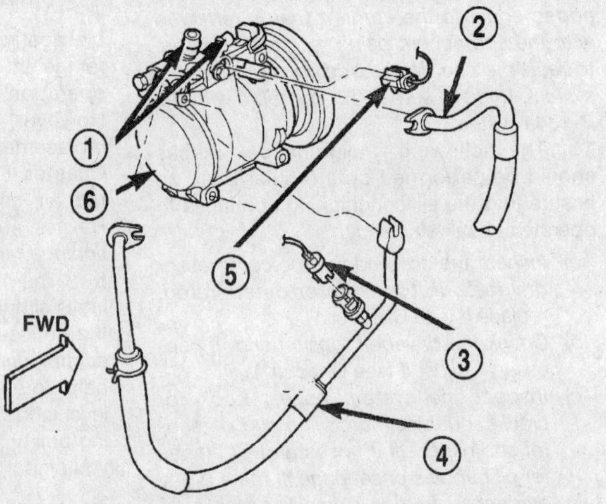

12.22b AC compressor refrigerant lines and related components (3.2L and 3.5L engines)

1 *Service ports*
2 *Suction line*
3 *A/C pressure switch and connector*
4 *Discharge line*
5 *Compressor clutch electrical connector*
6 *A/C compressor*

18 Purchase a R-134a automotive charging kit at an auto parts store **(see illustration)**. A charging kit includes a 12-ounce can of refrigerant, a tap valve and a short section of hose that can be attached between the tap valve and the system low side service valve. Because one can of refrigerant may not be sufficient to bring the system charge up to the proper level, it's a good idea to buy an additional can. **Warning:** *Never add more than two cans of refrigerant to the system.*

19 Hook up the charging kit by following the manufacturer's instructions. **Warning:** *DO NOT hook the charging kit hose to the system high side!* The fittings on the charging kit are designed to fit only on the low side of the system.

20 Back off the valve handle on the charging kit and screw the kit onto the refrigerant can, making sure first that the O-ring or rubber seal inside the threaded portion of the kit is in place. **Warning:** *Wear protective eyewear when dealing with pressurized refrigerant cans.*

21 Remove the dust cap from the low-side charging and attach the quick-connect fitting on the kit hose **(see illustrations)**.

22 Warm up the engine and turn On the air conditioning. Keep the charging kit hose away from the fan and other moving parts. **Note:** *The charging process requires the compressor to be running. Put the air conditioning switch on High and leave the car doors open to keep the clutch on and compressor working. If the compressor cycles off, the compressor can be kept on during the charging by removing the connector from the low-pressure switch and attaching a jumper wire to the connector during the procedure* **(see illustrations)**. *Refer to the wiring diagrams for wire color designations to determine which terminals to connect.*

23 Turn the valve handle on the kit until the stem pierces the can, then back the handle out to release the refrigerant. You should be able to hear the rush of gas. Add refrigerant to the low side of the system, keeping the can upright at all times, but shaking it occasionally. Allow stabilization time between each addition. **Note:** *The charging process will go faster if you wrap the can with a hot-water-soaked shop rag to keep the can from freezing up.*

24 If you have an accurate thermometer, place it in the center air conditioning duct inside the vehicle and keep track of the output air temperature **(see illustration 12.9)**. A charged system that is working properly should cool down to approximately 40-degrees F. If the ambient (outside) air temper-

CODE	DESCRIPTION
23	BLEND DOOR ACTUATOR FEEDBACK FAILURE
24	MODE DOOR ACTUATOR FEEDBACK FAILURE
25	AMBIENT SENSOR
26	ATC IN-CAR TEMPERATURE THERMISTER FAILURE
27	ATC IN-CAR SENSOR FAILURE
31	RECIRCULATION DOOR ACTUATOR STALL FAILURE
32	BLEND DOOR ACTUATOR STALL FAILURE
33	MODE DOOR ACTUATOR STALL FAILURE
34	ENGINE TEMPERATURE MESSAGE NOT RECEIVED
35	EVAPORATOR SENSOR FAILURE
36	ATC CONTROL COMMUNICATION FAILURE
37	BLEND DOOR ACTUATOR OUTPUT SHORTED TO BATTERY
38	BLEND DOOR ACTUATOR OUTPUT SHORTED TO GROUND
39	MODE DOOR ACTUATOR OUTPUT SHORTED TO BATTERY

CODE	DESCRIPTION
40	MODE DOOR ACTUATOR OUTPUT SHORTED TO GROUND
41	RECIRC DOOR ACTUATOR OUPUT SHORTED TO BATTERY
42	RECIRC DOOR ACTUATOR OUTPUT SHORTED TO GROUND
43	COMMON DOOR OUTPUT SHORTED TO BATTERY
44	COMMON DOOR OUTPUT SHORTED TO GROUND
45	A/C CONTROL BLEND DOOR INPUT OPEN OR SHORTED TO GROUND
46	A/C CONTROL BLEND DOOR SHORTED TO BATTERY
47	A/C CONTROL - A/C SWITCH FAILURE
48	A/C CONTROL MODE DOOR INPUT SHORTED TO GROUND
49	A/C CONTROL MODE DOOR INPUT SHORTED TO BATTERY
50	A/C CONTROL ELECTRIC BACKLITE (EBL) SWITCH FAILURE
51	SYSTEM VOLTAGE TOO LOW FOR DOOR CALIBRATION

12.38 Manual and automatic heating and air conditioning system diagnostic trouble codes

ature is very high, say 110 degrees F, the duct air temperature may be as high as 60 degrees F, but generally the air conditioning is 30 to 40 degrees F cooler than the ambient air.

25 When the can is empty, turn the valve handle to the closed position and release the connection from the low-side port. Replace the dust cap.

26 Remove the charging kit from the can and store the kit for future use with the piercing valve in the UP position, to prevent inadvertently piercing the can on the next use.

Heating systems

27 If the carpet under the heater core is damp, or if antifreeze vapor or steam is coming through the vents, the heater core is leaking. Remove it (see Section 11) and install a new unit (most radiator shops will not repair a leaking heater core).

28 If the air coming out of the heater vents isn't hot, the problem could stem from any of the following causes:

a) *The thermostat is stuck open, preventing the engine coolant from warming up enough to carry heat to the heater core. Replace the thermostat (see Section 3).*
b) *There is a blockage in the system, preventing the flow of coolant through the heater core. Feel both heater hoses at the firewall. They should be hot. If one of them is cold, there is an obstruction in one of the hoses or in the heater core, or the heater control valve is shut. Detach the hoses and back flush the heater core with a water hose. If the heater core is clear but circulation is impeded, remove the two hoses and flush them out with a water hose.*
c) *If flushing fails to remove the blockage from the heater core, the core must be replaced (see Section 11).*

Eliminating air conditioning odors

29 Unpleasant odors that often develop in air conditioning systems are caused by the growth of a fungus, usually on the surface of the evaporator core. The warm, humid environment there is a perfect breeding ground for mildew to develop.

30 The evaporator core on most vehicles is difficult to access, and factory dealerships have a lengthy, expensive process for eliminating the fungus by opening up the evaporator case and using a powerful disinfectant and rinse on the core until the fungus is gone. You can service your own system at home, but it takes something much stronger than basic household germ-killers or deodorizers.

30 Aerosol disinfectants for automotive air conditioning systems are available in most auto parts stores, but remember when shopping for them that the most effective treatments are also the most expensive. The basic procedure for using these sprays is to start by running the system in the RECIRC mode for ten minutes with the blower on its highest speed. Use the highest heat mode to dry out the system and keep the compressor from engaging by disconnecting the wiring connector at the compressor (see Section 14).

32 The disinfectant can usually comes with a long spray hose. Remove the blower motor resistor (see Section 8), point the nozzle inside the hole and to the left towards the evaporator core, and spray according to the manufacturer's recommendations. Try to cover the whole surface of the evaporator core, by aiming the spray up, down and sideways. Follow the manufacturer's recommendations for the length of spray and waiting time between applications.

33 Once the evaporator has been cleaned, the best way to prevent the mildew from coming back again is to make sure your evaporator housing drain tube is clear **(see illustration 12.1)**.

Self-diagnostic checks

Manual heater/air conditioning

Refer to illustration 12.38

34 On manual (non-ATC) systems, the diagnostic trouble codes will appear on the odometer display.

35 To begin the diagnostic mode, run the vehicle at idle with the controls set as follows: the blower speed knob should be on any position other than OFF, the temperature knob should be in full COOL, and the right knob should be in the DEFROST mode.

36 To enter the diagnostic mode, press the "EBL" button (rear window defogger), until the instrument cluster display reads "AC00". The body control module will then chime once and the LED on the A/C button will begin to blink. Release the "EBL" button and wait until the A/C button stops blinking. It will continue to blink for about 30 seconds while the unit calibrates.

37 After the A/C button LED goes out and the unit calibration is completed, diagnostic codes will be displayed in numerical order on the odometer display.

38 The odometer will display the letters "AC" which designates the beginning of the air conditioning codes followed by two-digit trouble codes, if any are present. The codes range from 23 to 51 **(see illustration)**.

40 Only one code can be displayed at a

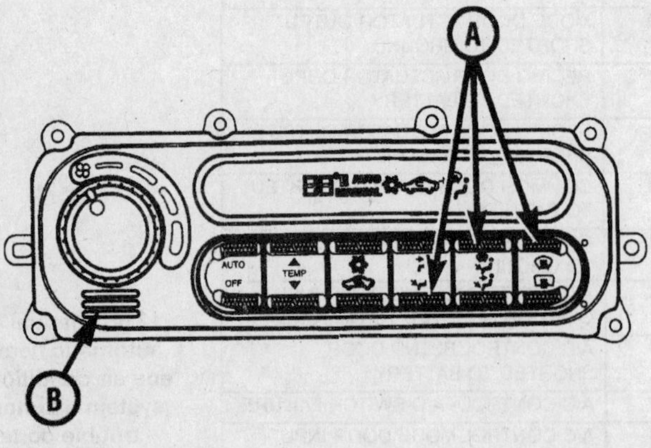

12.43 With ATC systems, set the display for 75 degrees and depress these three buttons (A) until the display blinks - (B) is the location of the ambient temperature sensor

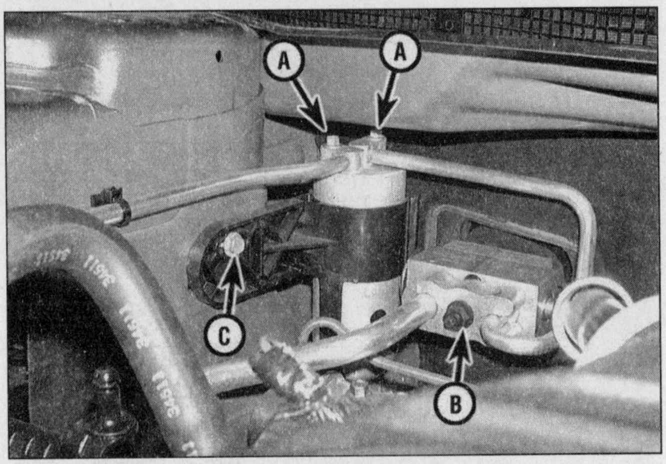

13.4 Remove the refrigerant lines at the receiver-drier (A) and at the expansion valve (B), then remove the bracket retaining bolt (C)

time, but pressing and releasing the A/C button will display the next code, if present. Be careful not push any other buttons except the A/C button while in self diagnostic mode or the computer will leave the self diagnostic mode without showing the remaining codes.

41 To get out of the self-diagnostic mode, turn the blower Off.

42 To clear the codes disconnect the negative battery cable from the remote ground terminal for 10 minutes.

Automatic Temperature Control (ATC)

Refer to illustration 12.43

43 To use the diagnostic mode on Automatic Temperature Control models, have the engine idling, set the temperature on the panel to 75 degrees and push in and hold the Floor, Mix and Defrost buttons all at the same time until the display section blinks, then release the buttons **(see illustration)**.

44 The control display will continue to blink, and then show two-digit trouble codes, if any are present. The codes range from 23 to 51 **(see illustration 12.38)**.

45 Only one code can be displayed at a time, but pressing and releasing the Panel button will display the next code, if present.

46 If there is a code indicating the problem is with the in-car ambient temperature sensor, test the sensor's fan by turning on the system and placing a small section of a tissue over the grille opening on the A/C control unit which incorporates a small fan that circulates interior air past the sensor. If the tissue stays in place over the name-plate, the fan is working.

47 If the tissue won't stay in place, the fan is not running, and the sensor/fan assembly needs to be replaced. Remove the heater/air conditioning control assembly (see Section 10).

48 To clear the codes disconnect the negative battery cable from the remote ground terminal for 10 minutes.

13 Air conditioning receiver-drier - removal and installation

Refer to illustration 13.4

Warning: *The air conditioning system is under high pressure. Do not loosen any hose fittings or remove any components until after the system has been discharged. Air conditioning refrigerant should be properly discharged into an EPA-approved recovery/recycling unit at a dealer service department or an automotive air conditioning repair facility. Always wear eye protection when disconnecting air conditioning system fittings.*

Caution: *Replacement receiver-drier units are so effective at absorbing moisture that they can quickly saturate upon exposure to the atmosphere. When installing a new unit, have all tools and supplies ready for quick reassembly to avoid having the system open any longer than necessary.*

1 Have the air conditioning system discharged at a dealer service department or automotive air conditioning repair facility.

2 The receiver-drier acts as a reservoir for the system refrigerant. It's located on the right side of the engine compartment, next to the strut tower.

3 Disconnect the negative battery cable from the remote ground terminal (see Chapter 5). Remove the air intake duct from the throttle body and the air cleaner housing (see Chapter 4).

4 Disconnect the refrigerant lines from the receiver-drier and the expansion valve **(see illustration)**. Use a back-up wrench to prevent twisting the tubing where it joins the receiver-drier.

5 Plug the open fittings to prevent entry of dirt and moisture.

6 Detach the bracket retaining bolt and remove receiver-drier and bracket together.

7 Installation is the reverse of removal. If a new receiver-drier is being installed add one ounce of refrigerant oil to it before installation.

8 Take the vehicle back to the shop that discharged it. Have the system evacuated, recharged and leak tested.

14 Air conditioning compressor - removal and installation

Refer to illustration 14.6

Warning: *The air conditioning system is under high pressure. Do not loosen any hose fittings or remove any components until after the system has been discharged. Air conditioning refrigerant should be properly discharged into an EPA-approved recovery/recycling unit at a dealer service department or an automotive air conditioning repair facility. Always wear eye protection when disconnecting air conditioning system fittings.*

Note: *The receiver-drier should be replaced whenever the compressor is replaced (see Section 13).*

1 Have the air conditioning system discharged at a dealer service department or automotive air conditioning repair facility.

2 Disconnect the negative battery cable from the remote ground terminal (see Chapter 5).

3 Unplug the electrical connector from the compressor clutch.

4 Remove the drivebelt (see Chapter 1).

5 Disconnect the refrigerant lines from the compressor **(see illustrations 12.22a and 12.22b)**. Plug the open fittings to prevent entry of dirt and moisture.

6 Unbolt the compressor from the mounting bracket **(see illustration)** and lift it out of the vehicle.

7 If a new compressor is being installed, pour out the oil from the old compressor into a graduated container and add that amount of new refrigerant oil to the new compressor. Also follow any directions included with the new compressor.

8 The clutch may have to be transferred from the original to the new compressor.

9 Installation is the reverse of removal. Replace all O-rings with new ones specifically made for use with R-134a refrigerant

14.6 Air conditioning compressor mounting bolts (2.7L engine shown, 3.2L and 3.5L similar)

15.4 Disconnect the refrigerant lines (arrows) from the condenser

and lubricate them with R-134a-compatible refrigerant oil.

10 Have the system evacuated, recharged and leak tested by the shop that discharged it.

15 Air conditioning condenser - removal and installation

Refer to illustration 15.4

Warning: *The air conditioning system is under high pressure. Do not loosen any hose fittings or remove any components until after the system has been discharged. Air conditioning refrigerant should be properly discharged into an EPA-approved recovery/recycling unit at a dealer service department or an automotive air conditioning repair facility. Always wear eye protection when disconnecting air conditioning system fittings.*

Note: *The receiver-drier should be replaced whenever the condenser is replaced* (see Section 13).

1 Have the air conditioning system discharged at a dealer service department or automotive air conditioning repair facility.

2 Disconnect the negative battery cable from the remote ground terminal (see Chapter 5).

3 Remove the front bumper fascia (see Chapter 11), then remove the right headlight housing (see Chapter 12).

4 Disconnect the refrigerant lines from the condenser **(see illustration)**.

5 Drain the cooling system and remove the fan assembly and radiator with the condenser attached (see Sections 4 and 5), then remove the condenser to radiator retaining screws and the transaxle auxiliary oil cooler mounting screw to separate the condenser from the radiator **(see illustration 5.8)**. Plug the open ends of the condenser and the disconnected refrigerant lines to prevent entry of dirt or moisture.

6 Inspect the rubber insulator pads (on the lower crossmember) on which the radiator sits. Replace them if they're dried or cracked.

7 If the original condenser will be reinstalled, store it with the line fittings on top to prevent oil from draining out. If a new condenser is being installed, pour one ounce of R-134a-compatible refrigerant oil into it prior to installation.

8 Reinstall the components in the reverse order of removal. Be sure the rubber pads are in place under the condenser.

9 Have the system evacuated, recharged and leak tested by the shop that discharged it.

Notes

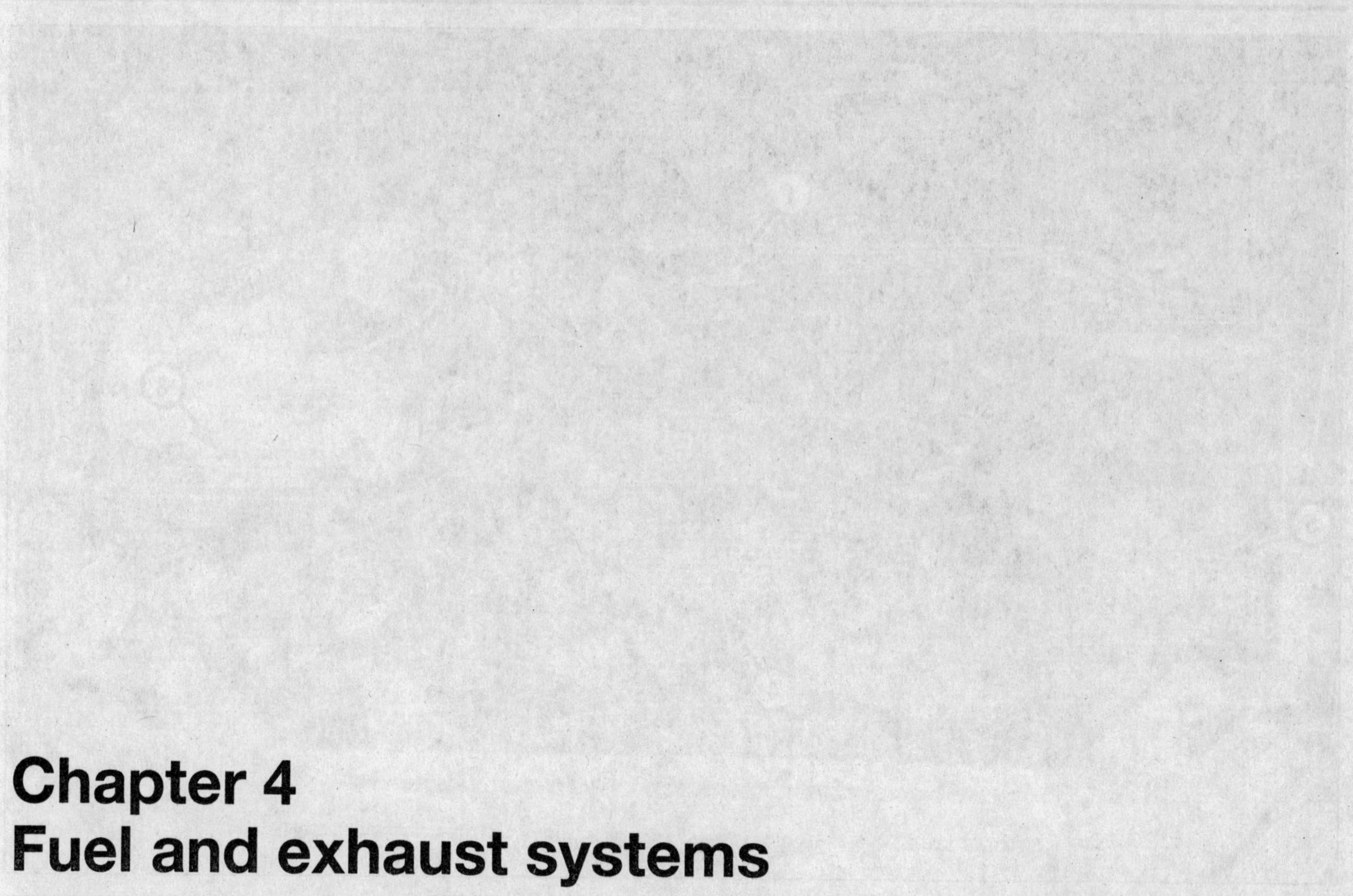

Chapter 4
Fuel and exhaust systems

Contents

Specifications

General

Fuel pressure	44 to 54 psi
Fuel injector resistance	10.8 to 13.2 ohms @ 68-degrees F
Fuel level sending unit resistance	
Empty	1040 to 1060 ohms
1/2	520 to 580 ohms
Full	50 to 70 ohms

Torque specifications

Throttle body mounting bolts	
1998 and 1999	19 ft-lbs
2000 and 2001	105 in-lbs
Fuel rail mounting bolts	100 in-lbs
Fuel tank mounting strap bolts	44 ft-lbs

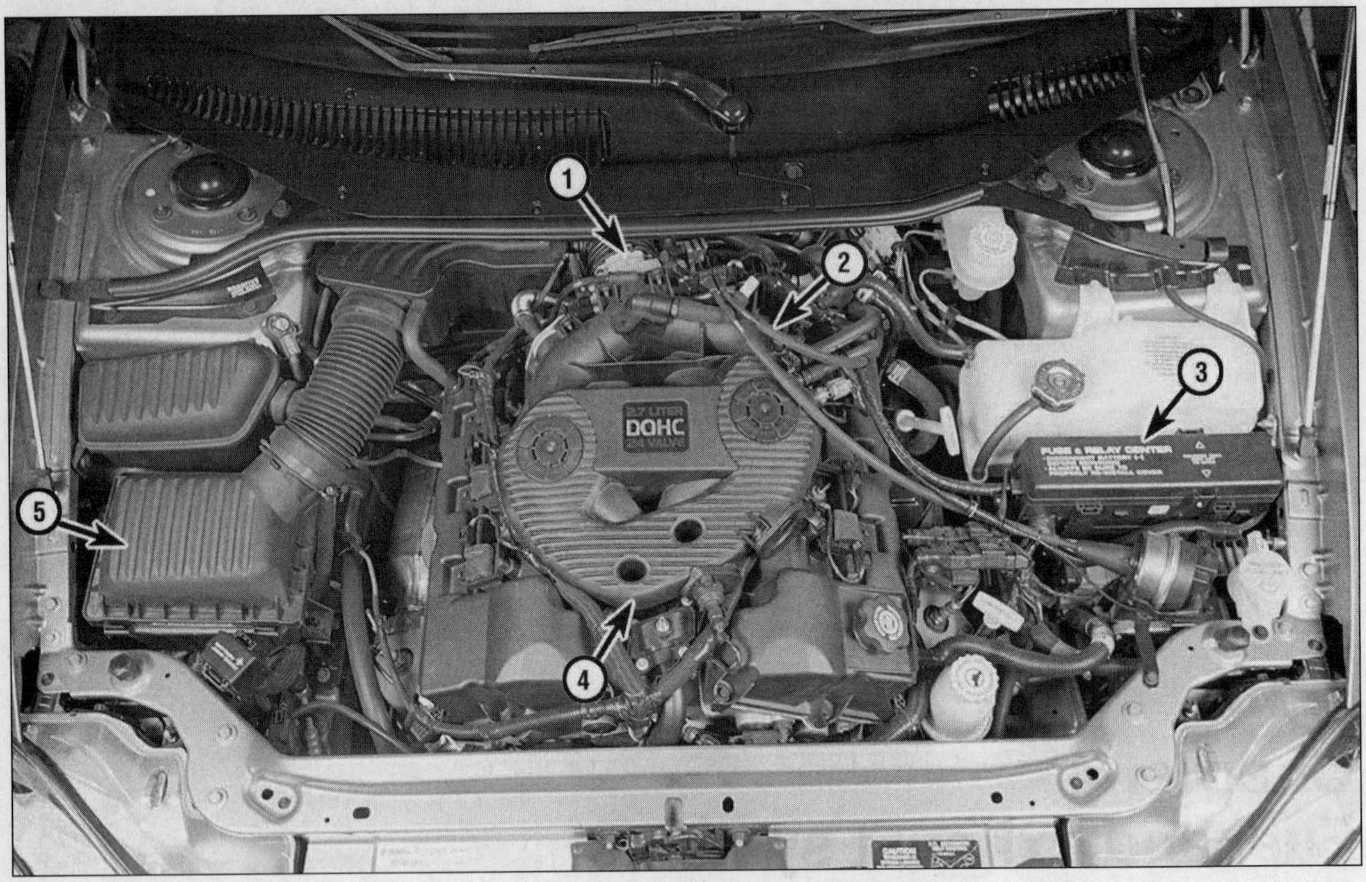

1.1 Typical fuel system components - 2.7L engine

1. *Throttle body*
2. *Accelerator cable*
3. *Fuel pump relay (inside Power Distribution Center)*
4. *Fuel rail and injectors (under upper intake manifold plenum)*
5. *Air filter housing*

1 General information

Refer to illustration 1.1

All models covered by this manual are equipped with a sequential Multi Port Fuel Injection (MPFI) system **(see Illustration)**. This system uses timed impulses to sequentially inject the fuel directly into the intake ports of each cylinder. The injectors are controlled by the Powertrain Control Module (PCM). The PCM monitors various engine parameters and delivers the exact amount of fuel, in the correct sequence, into the intake ports.

All models are equipped with an electric fuel pump, mounted in the fuel tank. It is necessary to remove the fuel tank for access to the fuel pump. The fuel level sending unit is an integral component of the fuel pump and it must be removed from the fuel tank in the same manner. These vehicles are equipped with a "returnless" fuel system. The fuel pressure regulator is mounted on top of the fuel pump/fuel level sending unit module. Regulated fuel is sent to the fuel rail and excess fuel is bled off into the tank.

The exhaust system consists of exhaust manifolds, catalytic converters, an exhaust pipe and a muffler. Each of these components is replaceable. For further information regarding the catalytic converter, refer to Chapter 6.

2 Fuel pressure relief procedure

Warning: *Gasoline is extremely flammable, so take extra precautions when you work on any part of the fuel system. Don't smoke or allow open flames or bare light bulbs near the work area, and don't work in a garage where a natural gas-type appliance (such as a water heater or a clothes dryer) with a pilot light is present. Since gasoline is carcinogenic, wear latex gloves when there's a possibility of being exposed to fuel, and, if you spill any fuel on your skin, rinse it off immediately with soap and water. Mop up any spills immediately and do not store fuel-soaked rags where they could ignite. The fuel system is under constant pressure, so, if any fuel lines are to be disconnected, the fuel pressure in the system must be relieved first. When you perform any kind of work on the fuel system, wear safety glasses and have a Class B type fire extinguisher on hand.*

1 Remove the fuel filler cap (this will relieve any pressure that has built-up in the tank).

2 Remove the fuel pump relay from the Power Distribution Center in the engine compartment (you can identify the relays by looking at the underside of the Power Distribution Center cover).

3 Start the engine and let it run until it dies. Crank the engine for several seconds.

4 Turn the ignition key to the Off position. Install the fuel pump relay.

5 Disconnect the negative battery cable from the remote ground terminal (see Chapter 5) before beginning work on the fuel system.

6 **Note:** *Cranking the engine over with the fuel pump relay removed may set a trouble code. Refer to Chapter 6 for the trouble code clearing procedure.*

3 Fuel pump/fuel pressure - check

Warning: *Gasoline is extremely flammable, so take extra precautions when you work on any part of the fuel system. Don't smoke or allow open flames or bare light bulbs near the work area, and don't work in a garage where a natural gas-type appliance (such as a water heater or a clothes dryer) with a pilot light is present. Since gasoline is carcinogenic, wear latex gloves when there's a possibility of being exposed to fuel, and, if you spill any*

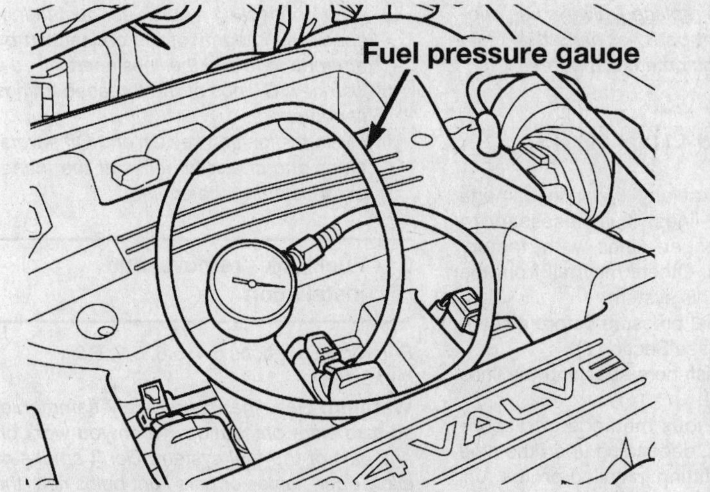

3.6a On 3.2L/3.5L models, the fuel pressure test port is located on the fuel rail

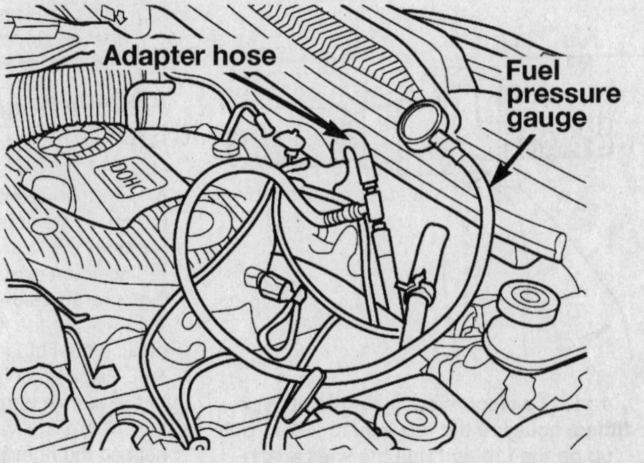

3.6b On 2.7L models, a special adapter hose will be required to attach a fuel pressure gauge (the fuel rail isn't equipped with a test port) - the adapter will be required for the leakdown test on all models

fuel on your skin, rinse it off immediately with soap and water. Mop up any spills immediately and do not store fuel-soaked rags where they could ignite. The fuel system is under constant pressure, so, if any fuel lines are to be disconnected, the fuel pressure in the system must be relieved first (see Section 2 for more information). *When you perform any kind of work on the fuel system, wear safety glasses and have a Class B type fire extinguisher on hand.*

Note: *On all models, the fuel pump is located inside the fuel tank (see Section 7).*

Preliminary check

1 If you suspect insufficient fuel delivery, first inspect all fuel lines to ensure that the problem is not simply a leak in a line.

2 Set the parking brake and have an assistant turn the ignition switch to the ON position while you listen to the fuel pump (inside the fuel tank). You should hear a "whirring" sound, lasting for a couple of seconds indicating the fuel pump is operating. If the fuel pump is operating, proceed to the pressure check.

3 If there is no sound, check the fuel pump circuit (see Chapter 12) and the wiring diagrams. Check the related fuses, the fuel pump relay and the related wiring to ensure power is reaching the fuel pump connector. Check the ground circuit for continuity.

4 If the power and ground circuits are good and the fuel pump does not operate, replace the fuel pump (see Section 7).

Pressure check

Refer to illustrations 3.6a and 3.6b

Note: *In order to perform the fuel pressure test, you will need a fuel pressure gauge capable of measuring high fuel pressure. The fuel gauge must be equipped with the proper fittings or adapters required to attach it to the fuel line or fuel rail.*

5 Relieve the fuel pressure (see Section 2).

6 Remove the cap from the fuel pressure test port (if equipped) on the fuel rail and attach a fuel pressure gauge **(see illustration)**. If the fuel rail is not equipped with a test port, disconnect the fuel line from the fuel rail and connect a fuel pressure gauge using a special adapter **(see illustration)**.

7 Start the engine and check the pressure on the gauge, comparing your reading with the pressure listed in this Chapter's Specifications.

8 If the fuel pressure is lower than specified, check the fuel lines and the fuel filter for restrictions. **Note:** *The fuel filter and pressure regulator are not separable - they must be replaced as a unit.* If no restriction is found, replace the fuel pump (see Section 7).

9 If fuel pressure is higher than specified, replace the fuel pressure regulator/fuel filter (see Section 14).

10 If the fuel pressure is within specifications, turn the engine off and monitor the fuel pressure for five minutes. The fuel pressure should not drop below 30 psi within five minutes. If it does, there is a leak in the fuel line, a fuel injector is leaking or the fuel pump module check valve is defective. To determine the problem area, perform the following: **Note:** *A special fuel gauge adapter hose with a T-fitting is required for the following tests, regardless of which engine your vehicle has* **(see illustration 3.6b)**.

11 Install the adapter hose, then turn on the ignition key to power-up the fuel system. Clamp off the adapter hose between the T-fitting and the line to the fuel pump, then turn the ignition key off. If the pressure drops below 30 psi within five minutes, a fuel injector (or injectors) is leaking (or the fuel rail may be leaking, but such a leak would be very apparent).

12 With the adapter hose installed, clamp off the adapter hose between the T-fitting and the fuel rail. Turn the ignition key on to energize the fuel pump, then turn the key Off. If the pressure drops below 30 psi within five minutes, the fuel line is leaking, the check valve in the fuel pressure regulator is defective or the fuel pump is defective.

- a) *Check the entire length of the fuel line for leaks.*
- b) *If no leaks are found in the fuel line and the pressure dropped quickly, replace the fuel pressure regulator/fuel filter.*
- c) *If no leaks are found in the fuel line and the pressure dropped slowly, replace the fuel pump.*

4 Fuel lines and fittings - repair and replacement

Warning: *Gasoline is extremely flammable, so take extra precautions when you work on any part of the fuel system. Don't smoke or allow open flames or bare light bulbs near the work area, and don't work in a garage where a natural gas-type appliance (such as a water heater or a clothes dryer) with a pilot light is present. Since gasoline is carcinogenic, wear latex gloves when there's a possibility of being exposed to fuel, and, if you spill any fuel on your skin, rinse it off immediately with soap and water. Mop up any spills immediately and do not store fuel-soaked rags where they could ignite. The fuel system is under constant pressure, so, if any fuel lines are to be disconnected, the fuel pressure in the system must be relieved first* (see Section 2). *When you perform any kind of work on the fuel system, wear safety glasses and have a Class B type fire extinguisher on hand.*

1 Always relieve the fuel pressure before servicing fuel lines or fittings (see Section 2).

2 The fuel feed and vapor lines extend from the fuel tank to the engine compartment. The lines are secured to the underbody with clip and screw assemblies. These lines must be occasionally inspected for leaks, kinks and dents.

3 If evidence of dirt is found in the system or fuel filter during disassembly, the line should be disconnected and blown out. Check the fuel strainer on the fuel pump module for damage and deterioration.

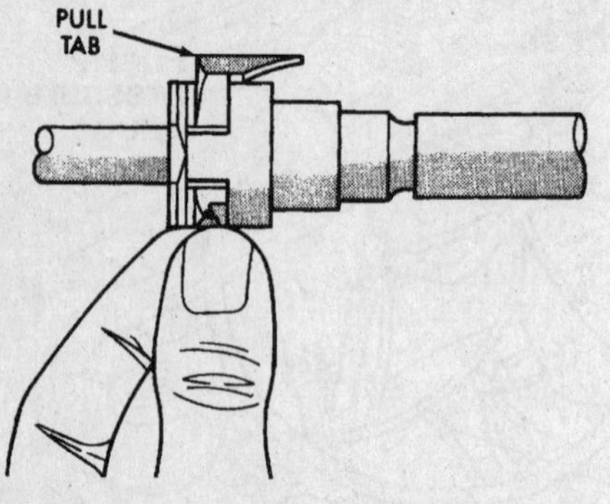

4.11a To disconnect a single-tab type fitting, squeeze the tab legs together, pull up on the tab and pull the lines apart - discard the tab and obtain a new one for reassembly

Steel tubing

4 If replacement of a fuel line or emission line is called for, use tubes/hoses meeting the manufacturers specification.

5 Don't use copper or aluminum tubing to replace steel tubing. These materials cannot withstand normal vehicle vibration.

6 Because fuel lines used on fuel-injected vehicles are under high pressure, they require special consideration.

7 Some fuel lines have threaded fittings with O-rings. Any time the fittings are loosened to service or replace components:

a) *Use a backup wrench while loosening and tightening the fittings.*
b) *Check all O-rings for cuts, cracks and deterioration. Replace any that appear hardened, worn or damaged.*
c) *If the lines are replaced, always use original equipment parts, or parts that meet the original equipment standards.*

Flexible hose

Refer to illustrations 4.11a, 4.11b, 4.11c and 4.11d

8 In the event of any fuel line damage (metal or flexible lines) it is necessary to replace the damaged lines with factory replacement parts. Others may fail from the high pressures of this system.

9 Relieve the fuel pressure before disconnecting the fitting (see Section 2).

10 Remove all fasteners attaching the lines to the vehicle body.

11 There are various methods of disconnecting the fittings, depending upon the type of quick-connect fitting installed on the fuel line **(see illustrations)**. Clean any debris from around the fitting. Disconnect the fitting and carefully remove the fuel line from the vehicle.

Caution: *The quick-connect fittings are not serviced separately. Do not attempt to repair these types of fuel lines in the event the fitting or line becomes damaged. Replace the entire fuel line as an assembly.*

12 Don't route fuel hose within four inches of any part of the exhaust system or within ten inches of the catalytic converter. Metal lines and rubber hoses must never be allowed to chafe against the frame. A minimum of 1/4-inch clearance must be maintained around a line or hose to prevent contact with the frame.

13 Installation is the reverse of removal with the following additions:

a) *Clean the quick-connect fittings with a lint-free cloth and apply clean engine oil the fittings.*
b) *After connecting a quick-connect fitting, check the integrity of the connection by attempting to pull the lines apart.*
c) *Use new O-rings at the threaded fittings (if equipped).*
d) *Cycle the ignition key On and Off several times and check for leaks at the fitting, before starting the engine.*

5 Fuel tank - removal and installation

Refer to illustrations 5.4, 5.6, 5.8, 5.9 and 5.10

Warning: *Gasoline is extremely flammable, so take extra precautions when you work on any part of the fuel system. Don't smoke or allow open flames or bare light bulbs near the work area, and don't work in a garage where a natural gas-type appliance (such as a water heater or a clothes dryer) with a pilot light is present. Since gasoline is carcinogenic, wear latex gloves when there's a possibility of being exposed to fuel, and, if you spill any fuel on your skin, rinse it off immediately with soap and water. Mop up any spills immediately and do not store fuel-soaked rags where they could ignite. The fuel system is under constant pressure, so, if any fuel lines are to be disconnected, the fuel pressure in the system must be relieved first* (see Section 2 for more information). *When you perform any kind of work on the fuel system, wear safety glasses and have a Class B type fire extinguisher on hand.*

1 Remove the fuel tank filler cap to relieve fuel tank pressure.

2 Relieve the fuel system pressure (see Section 2).

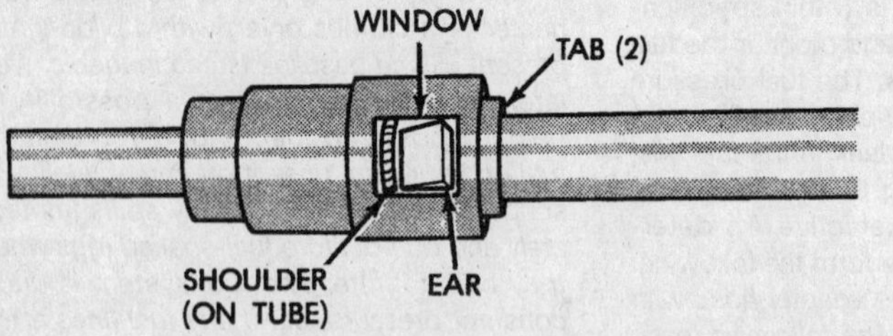

4.11b To disconnect a two-tab type fitting, squeeze the two tabs together and pull the lines apart

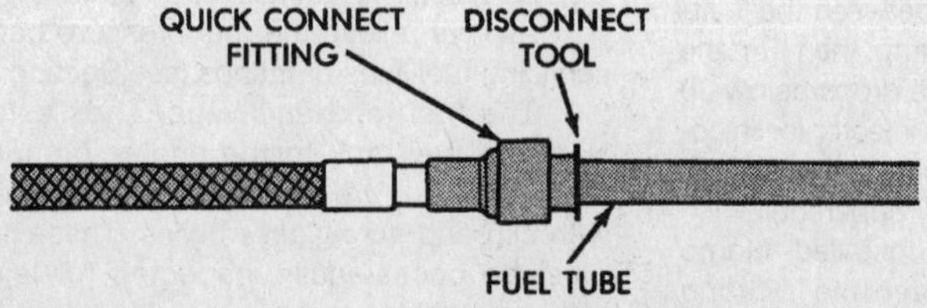

4.11d A special tool (available at most auto parts stores) is required to disconnect this type of metal fitting - remove the tethered clip, place the tool over the fuel line, insert it squarely into the fitting and pull the lines apart (the tool is not required to connect the lines)

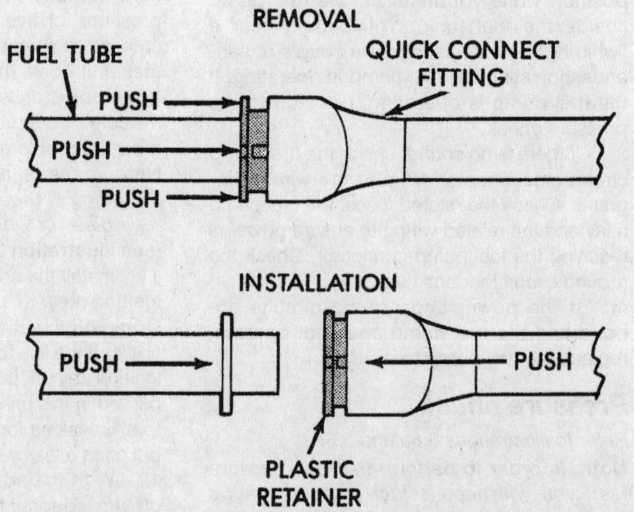

4.11c To disconnect a plastic ring type fitting, push the fuel lines together, push the retainer ring squarely into the fitting and pull the lines apart

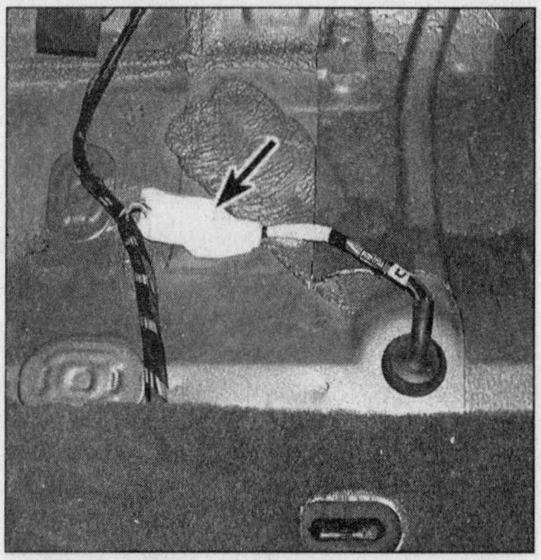

5.4 Remove the rear seat cushion and disconnect the electrical connector for the fuel pump/fuel level sending unit

5.6 The fuel tank is equipped with a drain plug - be sure to drain and store the fuel in an approved gasoline container

5.8 Loosen the hose clamp and disconnect the fuel filler hose (A) from the fuel tank - disconnect the vent hose from the rubber coupling (B)

3 Disconnect the negative battery cable from the remote ground terminal (see Chapter 5).

4 Remove the rear seat cushion (see Chapter 11) and disconnect the electrical connector for the fuel pump/fuel level sending unit **(see illustration)**. Push the grommet and the wiring harness through the body opening.

5 Raise the vehicle and support it securely on jackstands.

6 Drain the fuel into an approved gasoline container **(see illustration)**.

7 Remove the rear stabilizer bar bushing brackets and swing the stabilizer bar to the rear.

8 Loosen the hose clamp and disconnect the fuel filler hose from the fuel tank **(see illustration)**. Separate the vent hose from the rubber hose coupling.

9 Disconnect the fuel line (see Section 4) and the EVAP hoses from the metal lines **(see illustration)**.

10 Position a transmission jack under the fuel tank. Remove the fuel tank strap bolts and remove the straps **(see illustration)**.

11 Lower the jack and remove the tank from the vehicle.

12 Installation is the reverse of removal.

6 Fuel tank cleaning and repair - general information

1 The fuel tanks installed in the vehicles covered by this manual are made of plastic and are not repairable. If the fuel tank becomes damaged, it must be replaced.

2 Cleaning the fuel tank (due to fuel contamination) should be performed by a professional with the proper training to carry out this critical and potentially dangerous work. Even after cleaning and flushing, explosive fumes may remain inside the fuel tank.

3 If the fuel tank is removed from the vehicle, it should not be placed in an area where sparks or open flames could ignite the fumes coming out of the tank. Be especially careful inside a garage where a natural gas-type appliance is located, because the pilot light could cause an explosion.

7 Fuel pump - removal and installation

Refer to illustrations 7.4, 7.5, 7.6 and 7.9

Warning: *Gasoline is extremely flammable, so take extra precautions when you work on any part of the fuel system. Don't smoke or allow open flames or bare light bulbs near the work area, and don't work in a garage where a natural gas-type appliance (such as a water heater or a clothes dryer) with a pilot light is present. Since gasoline is carcinogenic, wear latex gloves when there's a possibility of being exposed to fuel, and, if you spill any fuel on your skin, rinse it off immediately with soap and water. Mop up any spills immediately and do not store fuel-soaked rags where they could ignite. The fuel system is under constant pressure, so, if any fuel lines are to be disconnected, the fuel pressure in the system must be relieved first* (see Section 2) *for more information). When you perform any kind of work on the fuel system, wear safety glasses and have a Class B type fire extin-*

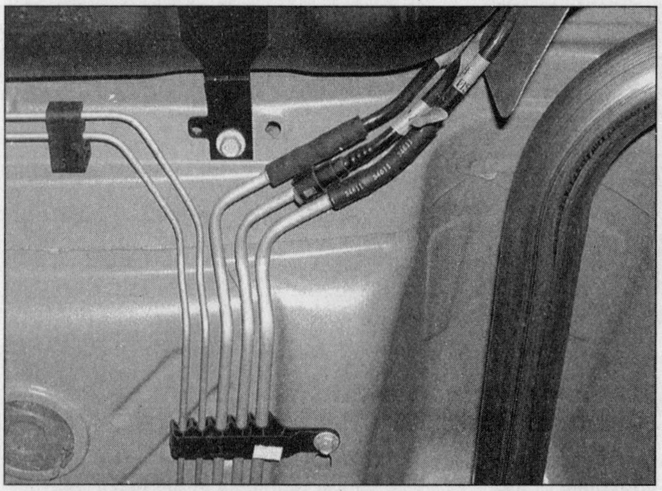

5.9 Disconnect the fuel line and the EVAP hoses from the metal lines

5.10 Remove the fuel tank strap bolts (arrows) and remove the straps

guisher on hand.

1 Relieve the fuel system pressure (see Section 2).

2 Disconnect the negative battery cable from the remote ground terminal (see Chapter 5).

3 Remove the fuel tank from the vehicle (see Section 5).

4 Disconnect the electrical connector and the fuel hose (see Section 4) from the fuel pump module **(see illustration)**.

5 Turn the fuel pump module locknut counterclockwise and remove it **(see illustration)**. If the locknut is difficult to turn, use a large pair of adjustable pliers to loosen it.

6 Remove the fuel pump module from the tank **(see illustration)**. Angle the assembly slightly to avoid damaging the fuel level sending unit float. **Warning:** *Some fuel may remain the module reservoir and spill as the module is removed. Have several shop towels ready and a drain pan near by to place the module in.*

7 The electric fuel pump is not serviced separately. In the event of failure, the complete assembly must be replaced. Transfer the fuel level sending unit to the new fuel pump module assembly, if necessary (see Section 8).

8 Clean the fuel tank sealing surface and install a new seal.

9 Install the fuel pump module aligning the tabs on the underside of the module with the notches in the fuel tank **(see illustration)**.

10 Tighten the fuel pump module locknut securely (approximately 40 ft-lbs). **Caution:** *Do not overtighten the locknut or a fuel leak may develop.*

11 The remainder of installation is the reverse of removal.

7.4 Disconnect the fuel line and electrical connectors from the fuel pump module

7.5 Loosen the fuel pump module locknut by turning it counterclockwise

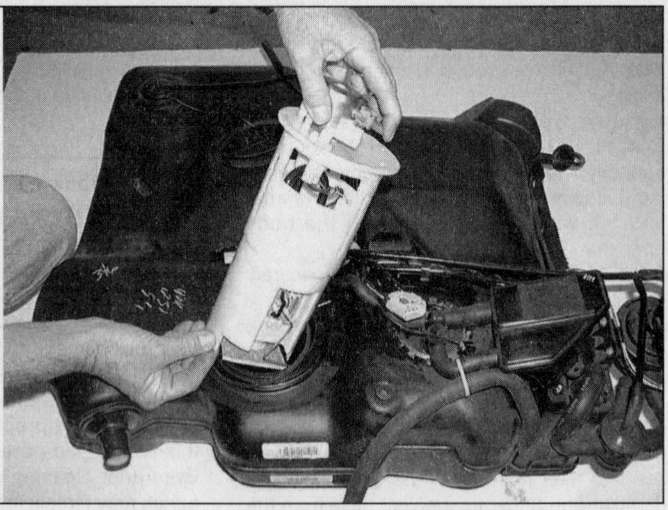

7.6 Carefully remove the fuel pump module from the tank

8 Fuel level sending unit - check and replacement

Warning: *Gasoline is extremely flammable, so take extra precautions when you work on any part of the fuel system. Don't smoke or allow open flames or bare light bulbs near the work area, and don't work in a garage where a natural gas-type appliance (such as a water heater or a clothes dryer) with a pilot light is present. Since gasoline is carcinogenic, wear latex gloves when there's a possibility of being exposed to fuel, and, if you spill any fuel on your skin, rinse it off immediately with soap and water. Mop up any spills immediately and do not store fuel-soaked rags where they could ignite. The fuel system is under constant pressure, so, if any fuel lines are to be disconnected, the fuel pressure in the system must be relieved first* (see Section 2). *When you perform any kind of work on the fuel system, wear safety glasses and have a Class B type fire extinguisher on hand.*

Check

Refer to illustrations 8.2 and 8.3

1 Remove the fuel tank and the fuel pump module (see Sections 5 and 7).

2 Connect the probes of an ohmmeter to the two center terminals of the fuel pump module electrical connector **(see illustration)**.

3 Position the float in the down (empty) position **(see illustration)**. Measure the resistance and compare it to the values listed in this Chapter's Specifications.

4 Move the float up to the full position. Measure the resistance and compare it to the values listed in this Chapter's Specifications.

5 If the fuel level sending unit resistance is incorrect or if the resistance does not change

7.9 When installing the fuel pump module, align the tabs on the underside of the module with the notches (arrows) in the fuel tank

8.2 Connect an ohmmeter to the two center terminals of the fuel pump module connector

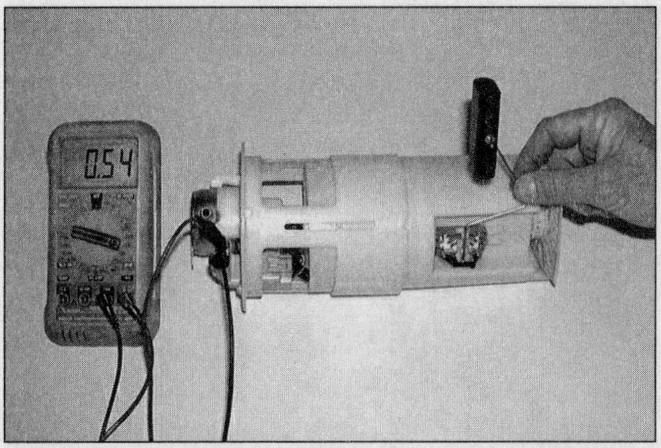

8.3 Measure the resistance of the fuel level sending unit with the float lowered (empty tank) and then with the float raised (full tank)

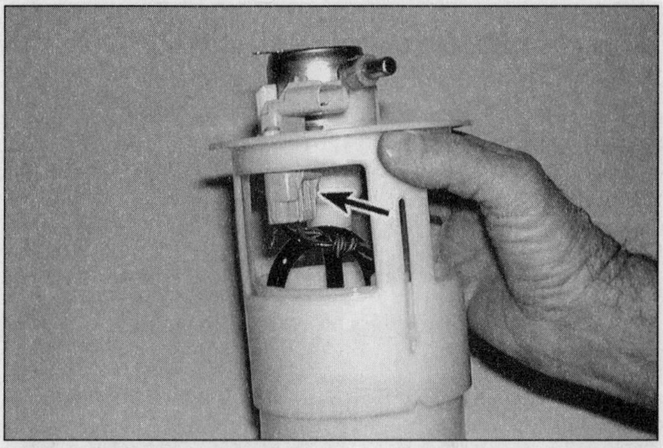

8.7 Disconnect the fuel pump/fuel level sending unit electrical connector from the fuel pump module

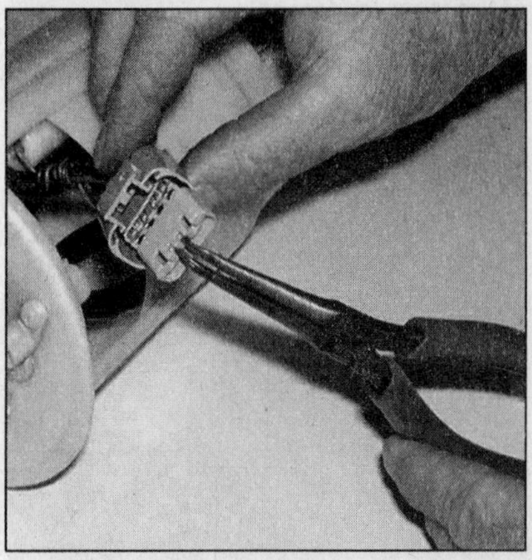

8.8a Carefully remove the locking collar from the connector

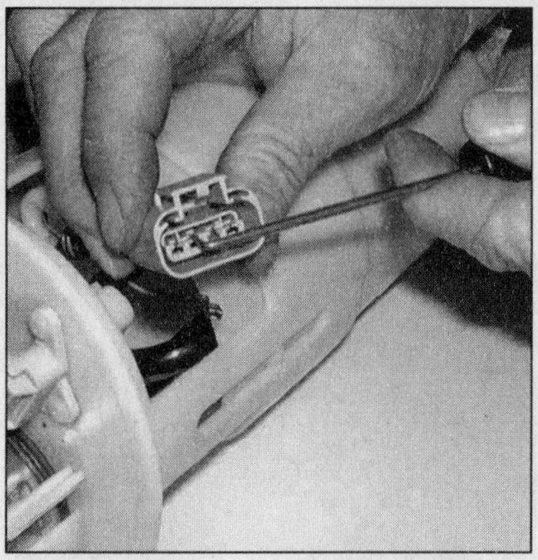

8.8b Using a small pick, depress the terminal locking finger and push the terminal into the connector

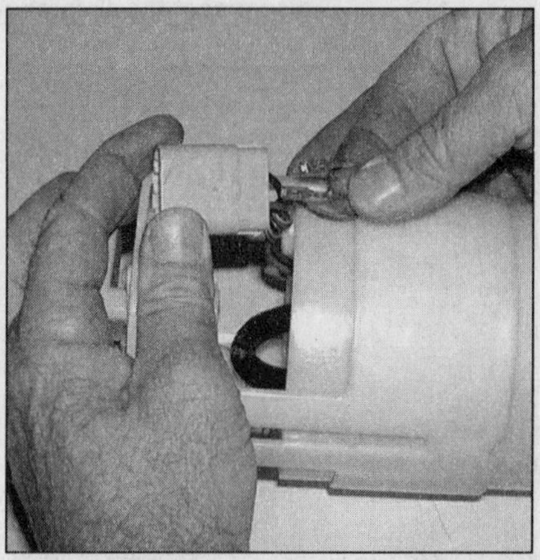

8.8c Pull the two fuel level sending unit wires and terminals out of the connector

smoothly as the float travels from empty to full, replace the fuel level sending unit assembly.

Replacement

Refer to illustrations 8.7, 8.8a, 8.8b, 8.8c, 8.8d and 8.9

6 Remove the fuel tank and the fuel pump module (see Sections 5 and 7).

7 Disconnect the electrical connector inside the module **(see illustration)**.

8 Separate the fuel level sending unit wire terminals from the module connector as follows **(see illustrations)**:

- a) *Note the position of the wires, by wire color, in the connector. They must be installed in the original positions.*
- b) *Remove the locking collar from inside the connector.*
- c) *Using a small pick, depress the locking finger on the terminal and push the terminal in.*
- d) *Pull the wire and terminal out of the connector from the backside.*
- e) *Unwrap the sending unit wires from the fuel pump wires*

9 Using a small screwdriver or pick, pry the lock tab out of the notch and slide the fuel level sending unit down the tracks **(see illustration)**. Note the routing of the wiring for installation.

10 Insert the wires through the standpipe and slide the level sending unit onto the tracks until the lock tab engages with the notch. Route the wiring as originally installed.

11 Insert the wire terminals into the connector in their original positions and install the locking collar. Make sure the wire terminals are locked in place by attempting to pull them out from the backside. If necessary carefully bend the locking fingers out before inserting them into the connector.

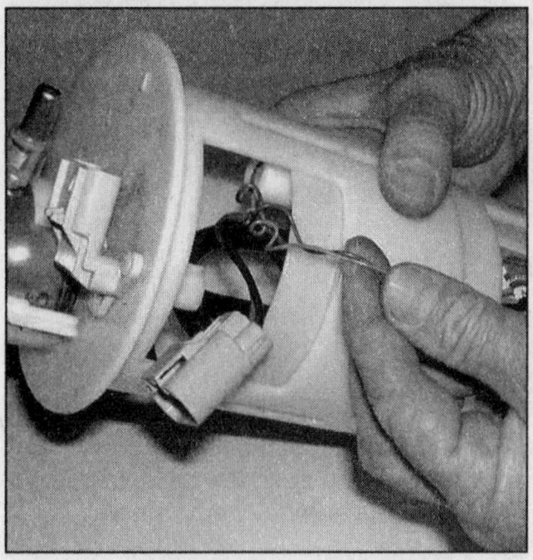

8.8d Unwrap the sending unit wires from around the fuel pump wires

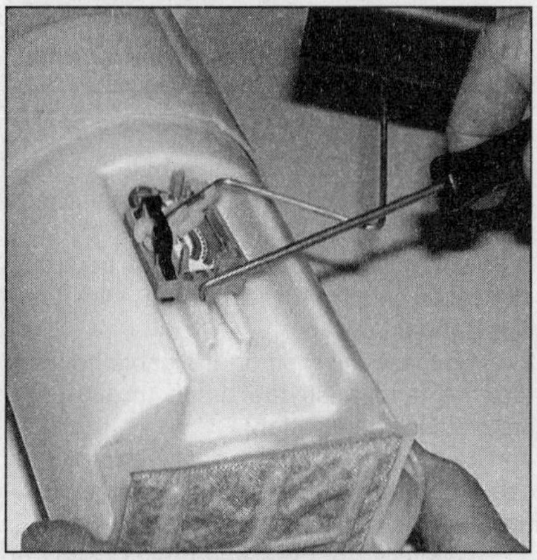

8.9 Pry the lock tab out of the notch and slide the fuel level sending unit down the tracks

9.2 Detach the latches (arrows) from the air filter cover and disconnect the air intake duct

9.3 Lift the air filter housing up off the mounting pin and pull it out of the inner fender

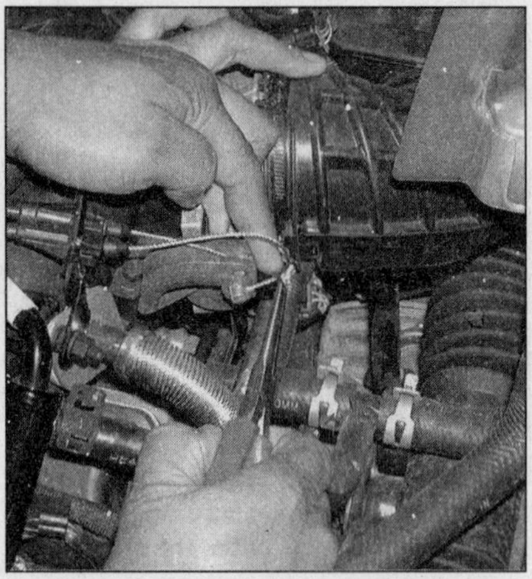

10.2 Rotate the throttle lever and detach the cable from the throttle lever

10.3 Depress the locking tabs and remove the cable from the bracket

10.4 Pull the accelerator cable out of the grommet and detach the cable retainer (arrow)

12 Connect the electrical connector to the fuel pump module and install the module in the fuel tank (see Section 7).

13 The remainder of installation is the reverse of removal.

9 Air filter housing - removal and installation

Refer to illustrations 9.2 and 9.3

1 Disconnect the negative battery cable from the remote ground terminal (see Chapter 5).

2 Loosen the hose clamp from the air intake duct and detach the latches from the air filter cover **(see illustration)**. Remove the cover and the air filter element.

3 Lift the housing up, detach the housing from the mounting pin and pull the housing from the inner fender **(see illustration)**. Remove the assembly from the engine compartment.

4 If necessary, loosen the hose clamps, detach the fasteners and separate the air intake duct and resonator assembly from the throttle body.

5 Installation is the reverse of removal.

10 Accelerator cable - replacement

Refer to illustrations 10.2, 10.3, 10.4 and 10.5

1 Disconnect the negative battery cable from the remote ground terminal (see Chapter 5).

2 Rotate the throttle lever and separate the cable end from the throttle lever **(see illustration)**.

3 Squeeze the tabs on the cable housing together and push the cable through the bracket **(see illustration)**.

4 Working under the dash, detach the cable from the accelerator pedal **(see illustration)**.

5 Carefully pry the cable retainer clip out of the cable and firewall grommet **(see illustration)**. Push the cable through the firewall grommet and into the engine compartment.

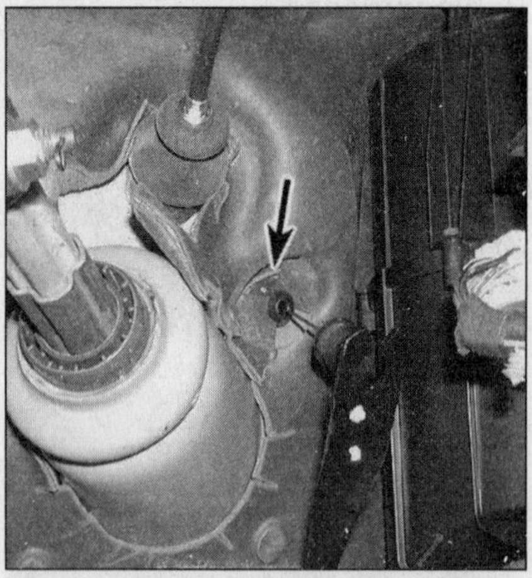

10.5 Remove the cable housing retaining clip (arrow) and push the cable housing into the engine compartment

6 Remove the cable from the engine compartment.

7 Installation is the reverse of removal.

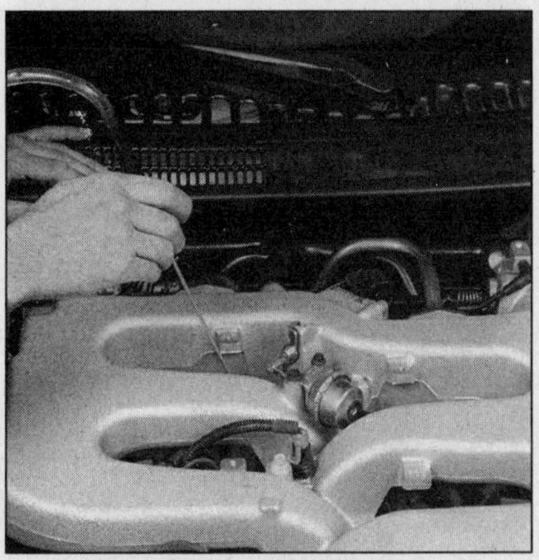

12.7 Use a stethoscope to determine if the injectors are working properly - they should make a steady clicking sound that rises and falls with engine speed changes

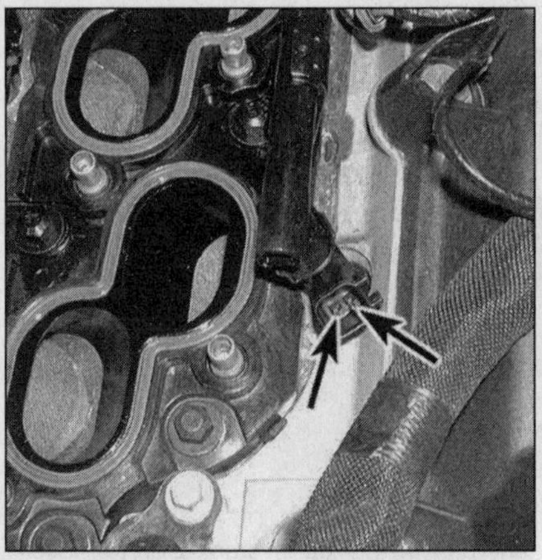

12.8 Measure the resistance of each injector across the two terminals of the injector

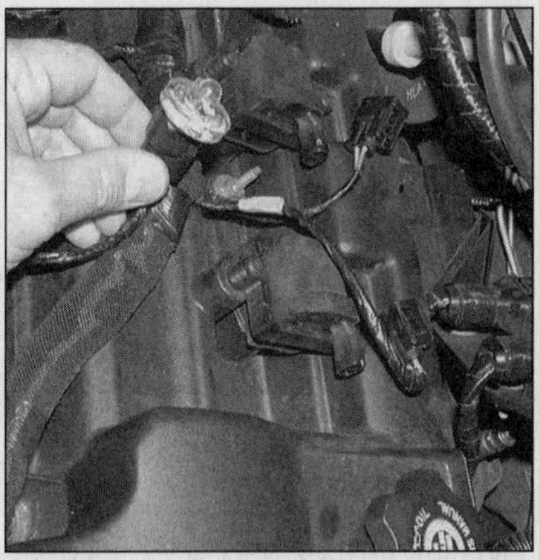

12.10 Install the "noid" light (available at most auto parts stores) into each injector electrical connector and confirm that it blinks when the engine is cranking

11 Fuel injection system - general information

The sequential Multi Port Fuel Injection (MPFI) system consists of three sub-systems: air intake, engine control and fuel delivery. The system uses a Powertrain Control Module (PCM) along with the sensors (coolant temperature sensor, throttle position sensor, manifold absolute pressure sensor, oxygen sensor, etc.) to determine the proper air/fuel ratio under all operating conditions.

The fuel injection system and the engine control system are closely linked in function and design. For additional information, refer to Chapter 6.

Air intake system

The air intake system consists of the air filter, the air intake ducts, the throttle body, the air intake plenum and the intake manifold.

When the engine is idling, the air/fuel ratio is controlled by the idle air control system, which consists of the Powertrain Control Module (PCM) and the idle air control valve. The idle air control valve is controlled by the PCM and is opened and closed depending upon the running conditions of the engine (air conditioning system, power steering, cold and warm running etc.). This idle air control regulates the amount of airflow past the throttle plate and into the intake manifold, thus increasing or decreasing the engine idle speed. The PCM receives information from the sensors (vehicle speed, coolant temperature, air conditioning, power steering mode etc.) and adjusts the idle according to the demands of the engine and driver. Refer to Chapter 6 for information on the idle air control valve.

Emissions and engine control system

The emissions and engine control system is described in detail in Chapter 6.

Fuel delivery system

The fuel delivery system consists of these components: the fuel pump, the fuel pressure regulator/fuel filter, the fuel rail and the fuel injectors.

The fuel pump is an electric type. Fuel is drawn through an inlet screen into the pump, flows through the one-way valve, passes through the fuel pressure regulator/filter and is delivered to the fuel rail and injectors.

The pressure regulator maintains a constant fuel pressure to the injectors. Excess fuel is routed back to the fuel tank through the fuel pressure regulator. **Note:** *The fuel pressure regulator is mounted on top of the fuel pump module.*

The injectors are solenoid-actuated pintle types consisting of a solenoid, plunger, needle valve and housing. When current is applied to the solenoid coil, the needle valve raises and pressurized fuel sprays out the nozzle. The injection quantity is determined by the length of time the valve is open (the length of time during which current is supplied to the solenoid coils).

The Automatic Shutdown (ASD) relay and the fuel pump relay are contained within the Power Distribution Center, which is located in the engine compartment. The ASD relay connects battery voltage to the fuel injectors and the ignition coils while the fuel pump relay connects battery voltage only to the fuel pump. If the PCM senses there is NO signal from the camshaft or crankshaft sensors (as with the engine not running or cranking), the PCM will de-energize both relays.

12 Fuel injection system - check

Refer to illustrations 12.7, 12.8 and 12.10

Note: *The following procedure is based on the assumption that the fuel pressure is adequate* (see Section 3).

1 Check all electrical connectors that are related to the system. Check the ground wire connections on the intake manifold for tightness. Loose connectors and poor grounds can cause many problems that resemble more serious malfunctions.

2 Check to see that the battery is fully charged, as the control unit and sensors depend on an accurate supply voltage in order to properly meter the fuel.

3 Check the air filter element - a dirty or partially blocked filter will severely impede performance and economy (see Chapter 1).

4 Check the related fuses. If a blown fuse is found, replace it and see if it blows again. If it does, search for a wire shorted to ground in the harness.

5 Check the air intake duct to the intake manifold for leaks, which will result in an excessively lean mixture. Also check the condition of all vacuum hoses connected to the intake manifold and/or throttle body.

6 Remove the air intake duct from the throttle body and check for dirt, carbon or other residue build-up. If it's dirty, clean it with carburetor cleaner spray and a toothbrush.

7 With the engine running, place an automotive stethoscope against each injector, one at a time, and listen for a clicking sound, indicating operation **(see illustration)**. If you don't have a stethoscope, place the tip of a screwdriver against the injector and listen through the handle. **Note:** *This test can't be performed on the 2.7L engine.*

8 Disconnect the injector electrical connectors and measure the resistance of each injector **(see illustration)**. Compare the measurements with the resistance values listed in this Chapter's Specifications. **Note:** *On 2.7L models it is necessary to remove the upper intake manifold to access the injectors.*

9 Turn the ignition key On and check for battery voltage at the dark green wire terminal of one of the injector harness connectors. If battery voltage is not present, check the ASD relay and related wiring (see Chapter 12).

10 Remove the fuel pump relay **(see illustration 1.1)**. Install an injector test light ("noid" light) into each injector electrical connector, one at a time **(see illustration)**. Crank

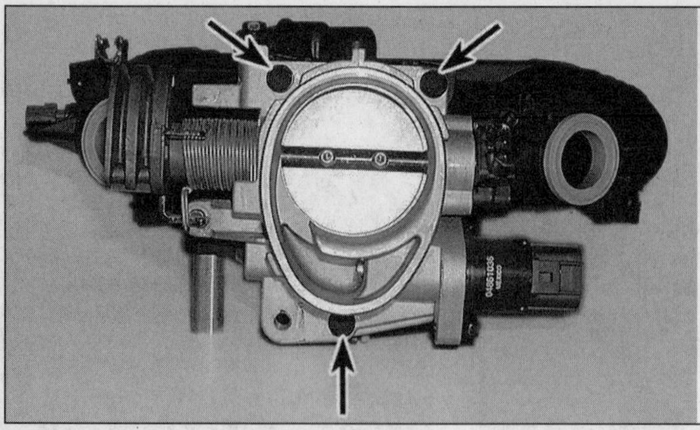

13.6 Remove the bolts (arrows) and separate the throttle body from the upper intake manifold

the engine over. Confirm that the light flashes evenly on each connector. This tests the PCM control of the injectors. If the light does not flash, have the PCM checked at a dealer service department or other properly equipped repair facility. **Caution:** *On 2.7L models it is necessary to remove the upper intake manifold to access the injectors. Be very careful not to drop anything into the intake ports and cover the intake ports with screen (NOT a cloth) before cranking the engine.*

11 The remainder of the engine control system checks can be found in Chapter 6.

13 Throttle body - removal and installation

Refer to illustration 13.6

Warning: *Wait until the engine is completely cool before beginning this procedure.*

1 Disconnect the negative battery cable from the remote ground terminal (see Chapter 5).

2 Remove the air intake duct.

3 Disconnect the electrical connectors from the throttle body.

4 Label and detach the vacuum hoses from the throttle body.

5 Detach the accelerator cable (see Section 10) and if equipped, the cruise control cable.

6 Remove the mounting bolts/nuts and remove the throttle body and gasket **(see illustration)**.

7 Remove all traces of old gasket material from the throttle body and intake manifold and install a new gasket.

8 Install the throttle body and tighten the bolts to the torque listed in this Chapter's Specifications.

9 The remainder of installation is the reverse of removal.

14 Fuel pressure regulator/fuel filter - replacement

Refer to illustration 14.5

Warning: *Gasoline is extremely flammable, so take extra precautions when you work on any part of the fuel system. Don't smoke or allow open flames or bare light bulbs near the work area, and don't work in a garage where a natural gas-type appliance (such as a water heater or a clothes dryer) with a pilot light is present. Since gasoline is carcinogenic, wear latex gloves when there's a possibility of being exposed to fuel, and, if you spill any fuel on your skin, rinse it off immediately with soap and water. Mop up any spills immediately and do not store fuel-soaked rags where they could ignite. The fuel system is under constant pressure, so, if any fuel lines are to be disconnected, the fuel pressure in the system must be relieved first* (see Section 2). *When you perform any kind of work on the fuel system, wear safety glasses and have a Class B type fire extinguisher on hand.*

Note: *The fuel filter requires service only when a fuel contamination problem is suspected.*

1 Relieve the fuel system pressure (see Section 2).

2 Disconnect the negative battery cable from the remote ground terminal (see Chapter 5).

3 Remove the fuel tank (see Section 5).

4 Remove the fuel line and ground terminal from the fuel pressure regulator (see Section 4).

5 Press the locking tab in, turn the fuel pressure regulator/fuel filter counterclockwise and pull the unit straight up **(see illustration)**.

6 Press the fuel pressure regulator/fuel filter assembly into the fuel pump module and lock it into place. Make sure the locking tab is seated in the slot.

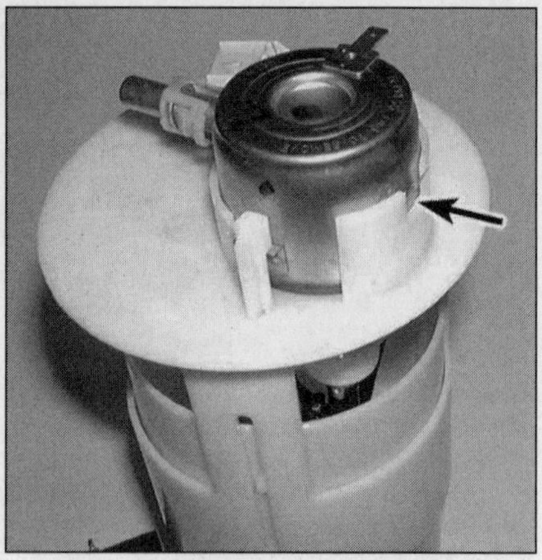

14.5 To remove the fuel pressure regulator/fuel filter, depress the locking tab (arrow), turn the assembly counterclockwise and pull it up

7 The remainder of installation is the reverse of removal.

15 Fuel rail and injectors - removal and installation

Warning: *Gasoline is extremely flammable, so take extra precautions when you work on any part of the fuel system. Don't smoke or allow open flames or bare light bulbs near the work area, and don't work in a garage where a natural gas-type appliance (such as a water heater or a clothes dryer) with a pilot light is present. Since gasoline is carcinogenic, wear latex gloves when there's a possibility of being exposed to fuel, and, if you spill any fuel on your skin, rinse it off immediately with soap and water. Mop up any spills immediately and do not store fuel-soaked rags where they could ignite. The fuel system is under constant pressure, so, if any fuel lines are to be disconnected, the fuel pressure in the system must be relieved first* (see Section 2). *When you perform any kind of work on the*

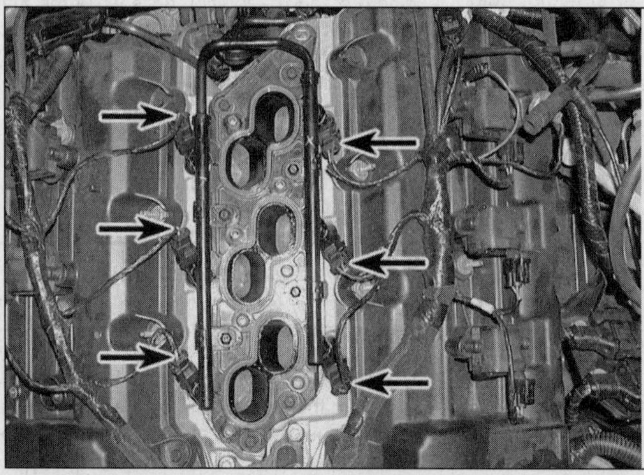

15.5 Disconnect the electrical connectors from the injectors - apply numbered tags on the wiring harness corresponding to the cylinder numbers

15.6 Disconnect the fuel line quick-connect fitting from the fuel rail

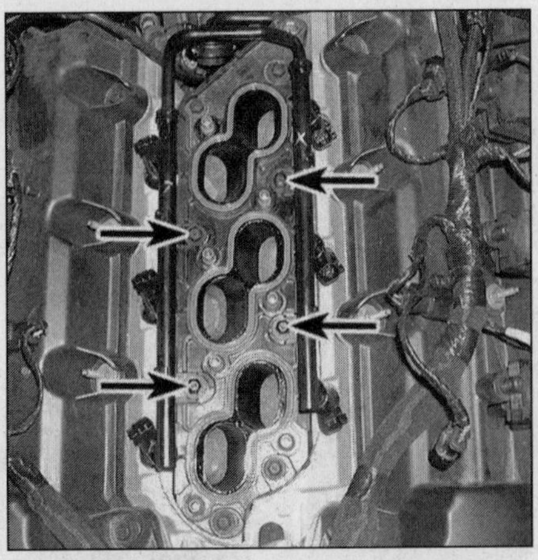

15.7 Remove the bolts (arrows) securing the fuel rail to the intake manifold

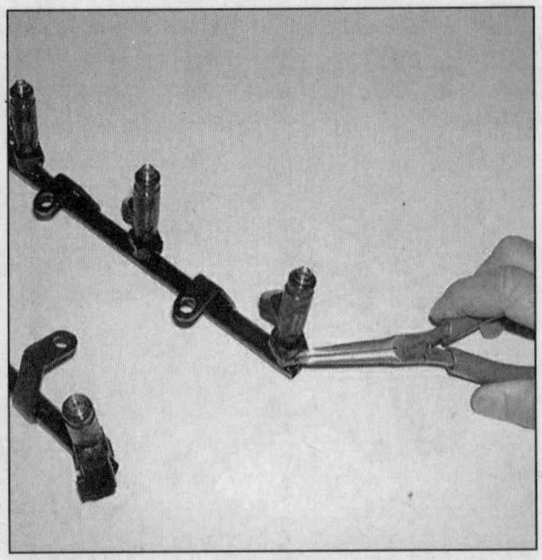

15.8a Remove the injector retaining clip and pull the injector off the fuel rail

fuel system, wear safety glasses and have a Class B type fire extinguisher on hand.

Removal

Refer to illustrations 15.5, 15.6, 15.7, 15.8a and 15.8b

1 Relieve the fuel pressure (see Section 2).

2 Disconnect the negative battery cable from the remote ground terminal (see Chapter 5).

3 Remove the upper intake manifold (see Chapter 2A or 2B). Cover the lower intake manifold ports to prevent any foreign objects from entering the engine.

4 Clearly label and remove any vacuum hoses or electrical wiring that will interfere with the fuel rail removal. Detach any wiring harness retainers from the fuel rail.

5 Disconnect the fuel injector electrical connectors and position the harness aside **(see illustration)**. **Note:** *Each connector should be numbered with the corresponding cylinder number. If the number tag is obscured or missing, renumber the connectors.*

6 Refer to Section 4 and disconnect the fuel line from the fuel rail **(see illustration)**.

7 Clean any debris from around the injectors. Remove the fuel rail mounting nuts/bolts **(see illustration).** Gently rock the fuel rail and injectors to loosen the injectors and remove the fuel rail and fuel injectors as an assembly. **Caution:** *Do not attempt to separate the left and right fuel rails. Both sides are serviced together as an assembly.*

8 Remove the retaining clip and remove the injector(s) from the fuel rail assembly **(see illustrations)**. Remove and discard the O-rings. **Note:** *Whether you're replacing an injector or a leaking O-ring, it's a good idea to remove all the injectors from the fuel rail and replace all the O-rings.*

Installation

9 Coat the new seal rings with clean engine oil and slide them onto the injectors.

10 Coat the new O-rings with clean engine oil and install them on the injector(s), then insert each injector into its corresponding

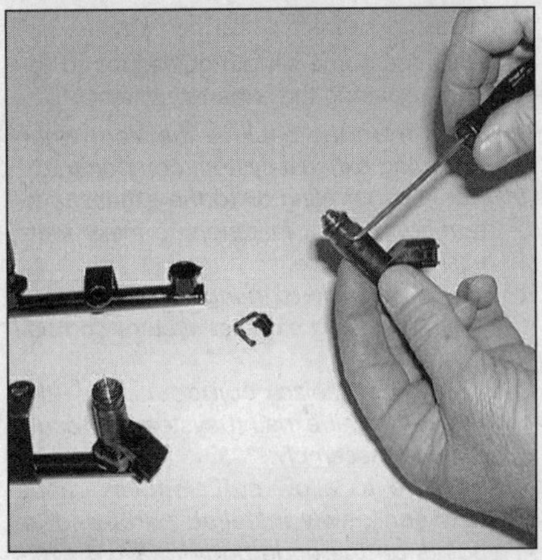

15.8b Carefully remove the O-rings from the injector

bore in the fuel rail. Install the injector retaining clip.

11 Install the injector and fuel rail assembly on the intake manifold. Make sure the injectors are fully seated, then tighten the fuel rail mounting nuts to the torque listed in this Chapter's Specifications.

12 Connect the fuel line and make sure its securely installed.

13 Connect the electrical connectors to each injector, referring to the numbered tags.

14 The remainder of installation is the reverse of removal.

15 After the injector/fuel rail assembly installation is complete, turn the ignition switch to On, but don't operate the starter (this activates the fuel pump for about two seconds, which builds up fuel pressure in the fuel lines and the fuel rail). Repeat this about two or three times, then check the fuel lines, fuel rail and injectors for fuel leakage.

16 Exhaust system servicing - general information

Warning: *Inspection and repair of exhaust system components should be done only*

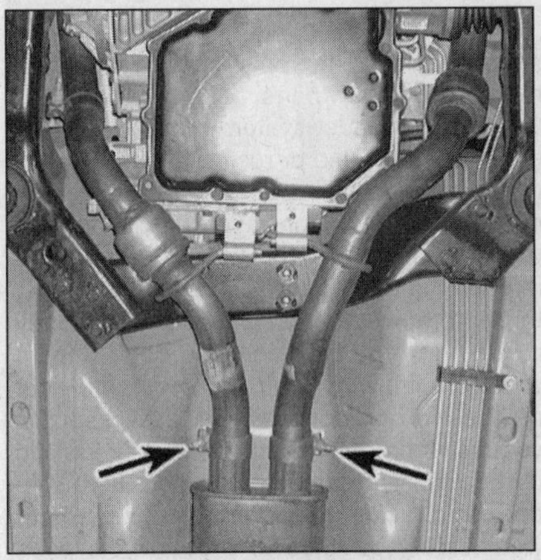

16.2a Inspect the exhaust system connections for leakage

after enough time has elapsed after driving the vehicle to allow the system components to cool completely. Also, when working under the vehicle, make sure it is securely supported on jackstands.

1 The exhaust system consists of the exhaust manifolds, two catalytic converters (one at each manifold), the muffler, resonators, the tailpipe and all connecting pipes, brackets, hangers and clamps. The exhaust system is attached to the body with mounting brackets and rubber hangers. If any of the parts are improperly installed, excessive noise and vibration will be transmitted to the body.

Muffler and pipes

Refer to illustrations 16.2a and 16.2b

2 Conduct regular inspections of the exhaust system to keep it safe and quiet. Look for any damaged or bent parts, open seams, holes, loose connections, excessive corrosion or other defects which could allow exhaust fumes to enter the vehicle **(see illustrations)**. Also check the catalytic converter when you inspect the exhaust system (see below). Deteriorated exhaust system compo-

16.2b Inspect the rubber insulators for damage

16.6 Inspect the catalytic converter and heat shield for damage

nents should not be repaired; they should be replaced with new parts.

3 If the exhaust system components are extremely corroded or rusted together, welding equipment will probably be required to remove them. The convenient way to accomplish this is to have a muffler repair shop remove the corroded sections with a cutting torch. If, however, you want to save money by doing it yourself (and you don't have a welding outfit with a cutting torch), simply cut off the old components with a hacksaw. If you have compressed air, special pneumatic cutting chisels can also be used. If you do decide to tackle the job at home, be sure to wear safety goggles to protect your eyes from metal chips and work gloves to protect your hands.

4 Here are some simple guidelines to follow when repairing the exhaust system:

a) *Work from the back to the front when removing exhaust system components.*
b) *Apply penetrating oil to the exhaust system component fasteners to make them easier to remove.*
c) *Use new gaskets, hangers and clamps when installing exhaust system components.*
d) *Apply anti-seize compound to the threads of all exhaust system fasteners during reassembly.*
e) *Be sure to allow sufficient clearance between newly installed parts and all points on the underbody to avoid overheating the floor pan and possibly damaging the interior carpet and insulation. Pay particularly close attention to the catalytic converter and heat shield.*

Catalytic converter

Refer to illustration 16.6

Warning: *The converter gets very hot during operation. Make sure it has cooled down before you touch it.*

Note: *See Chapter 6 for additional information on the catalytic converter.*

5 Periodically inspect the heat shield for cracks, dents and loose or missing fasteners.

6 Inspect the converter for cracks or other damage **(see illustration)**.

7 If the catalytic converter requires replacement, refer to Chapter 6.

Chapter 5
Engine electrical systems

Contents

Specifications

General

Battery voltage	
Engine off	12.0 to 12.6 volts
Engine running	13.5 to 14.5 volts

Torque specifications

	Ft-lbs
Alternator mounting bolts	
8 mm bolt	30
10 mm bolts	40
Starter mounting bolts	40

1.1 Typical engine electrical system components

1. *Remote battery cable terminal (positive)*
2. *Remote battery cable terminal (negative)*
3. *Power Distribution Center*
4. *Alternator*
5. *Ignition coil*
6. *Battery (under air filter housing)*

1 General information, precautions and battery disconnection

General information

Refer to illustration 1.1

The engine electrical systems include all ignition, charging and starting components **(see illustration)**. Because of their engine-related functions, these components are discussed separately from body electrical devices such as the lights, the instruments, etc. (which are included in Chapter 12).

Precautions

Always observe the following precautions when working on the electrical system:

(a) *Be extremely careful when servicing engine electrical components. They are easily damaged if checked, connected or handled improperly.*
(b) *Never leave the ignition switched on for long periods of time when the engine is not running.*
(c) *Never disconnect the battery cables while the engine is running.*
(d) *Maintain correct polarity when connecting battery cables from another vehicle during jump starting - see the "Booster battery (jump) starting" section at the front of this manual.*
(e) *Always disconnect the negative battery cable from the remote ground terminal before working on the electrical system.*

It's also a good idea to review the safety-related information regarding the engine electrical systems located in the *"Safety first!"* section at the front of this manual, before beginning any operation included in this Chapter.

Battery disconnection

Refer to illustration 1.4

The battery on these vehicles is located behind the right fender, in front of the right front wheel. Since the battery terminals cannot be easily accessed, the manufacturer has provided a remote ground terminal on the right strut tower and also a remote positive terminal for jump starting purposes. To disconnect the battery for service procedures requiring power to be cut from the vehicle, remove the nut and detach the negative cable from the ground stud on the strut tower, then press the hole in the side of the cable insulator over the stud **(see illustration)**. This will isolate the cable end and pre-

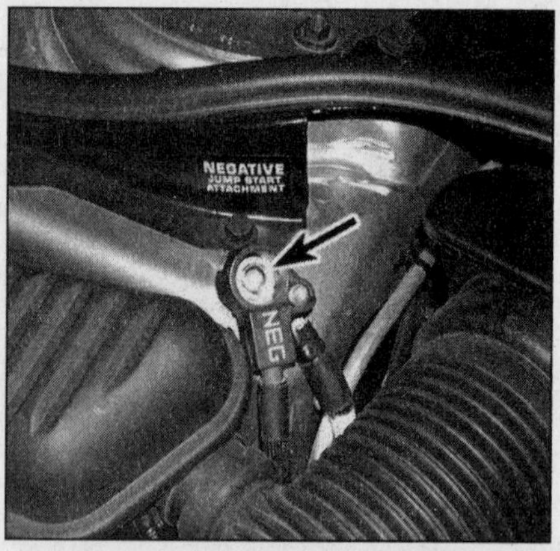

1.4 To disconnect battery power from the vehicle, remove the nut from the ground stud on the right strut tower, remove the cable terminal from the stud and place it back on the stud using the hole in the terminal insulator (arrow)

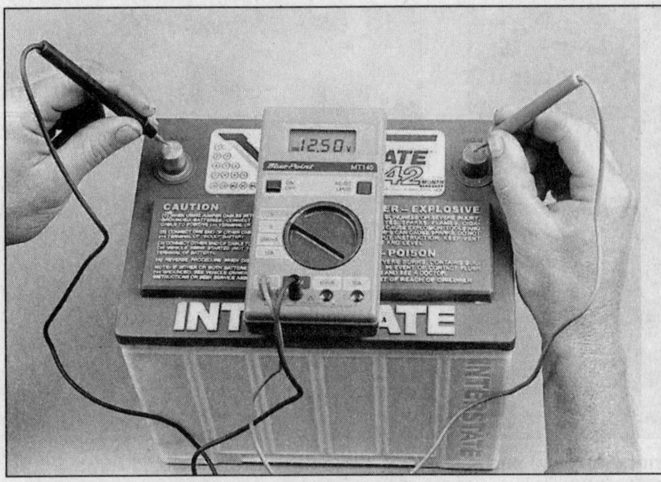

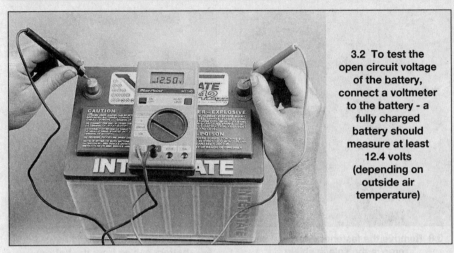

3.2 To test the open circuit voltage of the battery, connect a voltmeter to the battery - a fully charged battery should measure at least 12.4 volts (depending on outside air temperature)

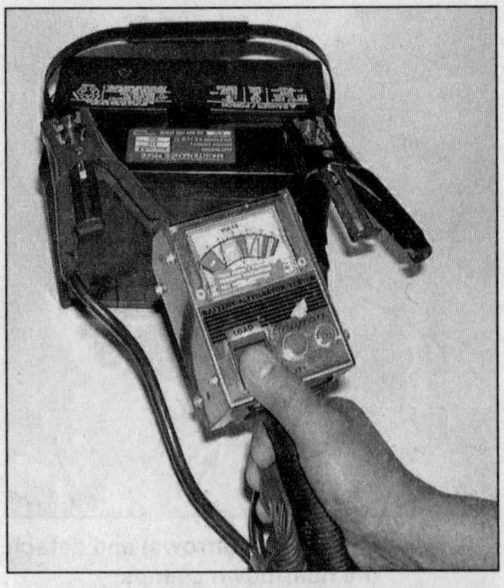

3.3 Connect a battery load tester to the battery and check the battery condition under load following the tool manufacturers instructions

vent it from accidentally coming into contact with ground.

Several systems on the vehicle require battery power to be available at all times, either to ensure their continued operation (such as the clock) or to maintain control unit memories (such as that in the engine management system's Powertrain Control Module [PCM]) which would be wiped out if the battery were to be disconnected. Therefore, whenever the battery is to be disconnected, first note the following to ensure that there are no unforeseen consequences of this action:

(a) *First, on any vehicle with power door locks, it is a wise precaution to remove the key from the ignition and to keep it with you, so that it does not get locked inside if the power door locks should engage accidentally when the battery is reconnected!*

(b) *The engine management system's PCM will lose the information stored in its memory when the battery is disconnected. This includes idling and operating values, and any fault codes detected (see Chapter 6). Whenever the battery is disconnected, the information relating to idle speed control and other operating values will have to be re-programmed into the unit's memory. The PCM does this by itself, but until then, there may be surging, hesitation, erratic idle and a generally inferior level of performance. To allow the PCM to relearn these values, start the engine and run it as close to idle speed as possible until it reaches its normal operating temperature, then run it for approximately two minutes at 1200 rpm. Next, drive the vehicle as far as necessary - approximately 5 miles of varied driving conditions is usually sufficient - to complete the relearning process.*

Devices known as "memory-savers" can be used to avoid some of the above problems. Precise details vary according to the device used. Typically, it is plugged into the cigarette lighter, and is connected by its own wires to a spare battery; the vehicle's own battery is then disconnected from the electrical system, leaving the "memory-saver" to pass sufficient current to maintain audio unit security codes and PCM memory values, and also to run permanently live circuits such as the clock, all the while isolating the battery in the event of a short-circuit occurring while work is carried out.

Warning: *Some of these devices allow a considerable amount of current to pass, which can mean that many of the vehicle's systems are still operational when the main battery is disconnected. If a "memory-saver" is used, ensure that the circuit concerned is actually "dead" before carrying out any work on it!*

2 Battery - emergency jump starting

Refer to the *Booster battery (jump) starting* procedure at the front of this manual.

3 Battery - check, removal and installation

Warning: *Hydrogen gas is produced by the battery, so keep open flames and lighted cigarettes away from it at all times. Always wear eye protection when working around a battery. Rinse off spilled electrolyte immediately with large amounts of water.*

Note: *The battery is located in the fender, ahead of the right front tire. The battery can be removed without removing the right front tire, but removing the tire improves access.*

Check

Refer to illustrations 3.2 and 3.3

1 The battery's surface charge must be removed before accurate voltage measurements can be made. Turn On the high beams for ten seconds, then turn them Off, let the vehicle stand for two minutes. Remove the battery from the vehicle (see Steps 4 through 10).

2 Check the battery state of charge. Visually inspect the indicator eye on the top of the battery, if the indicator eye is clear, charge the battery as described in Chapter 1. Next perform an open voltage circuit test using a digital voltmeter **(see illustration)**. With the engine and all accessories Off, touch the negative probe of the voltmeter to the negative terminal of the battery and the positive probe to the positive terminal of the battery. The battery voltage should be 12.4 volts or more. If the battery is less than the specified voltage, charge the battery before proceeding to the next test. Do not proceed with the battery load test unless the battery charge is correct.

3 Perform a battery load test. An accurate check of the battery condition can only be performed with a load tester (available at most auto parts stores). This test evaluates the ability of the battery to operate the starter and other accessories during periods of heavy amperage draw (load). Install a special battery load testing tool onto the terminals **(see illustration)**. Load test the battery according to the tool manufacturer's instructions. This tool utilizes a carbon pile to increase the load demand (amperage draw) on the battery. Maintain the load on the battery for 15 seconds or less and observe that the battery voltage does not drop below 9.6 volts. If the battery condition is weak or defective, the tool will indicate this condition immediately. **Note:** *Cold temperatures will cause the minimum voltage requirements to drop slightly. Follow the chart given in the tool manufacturer's instructions to compensate for cold climates. Minimum load voltage for freezing temperatures (32 degrees F) should be approximately 9.1 volts.*

Replacement

Refer to illustrations 3.6, 3.8 and 3.9

4 Disconnect the negative battery cable from the remote ground terminal (see Section 1).

5 Remove the air filter housing (see Chapter 4).

3.6 Remove the bolts (arrows) and detach the hold-down clamps

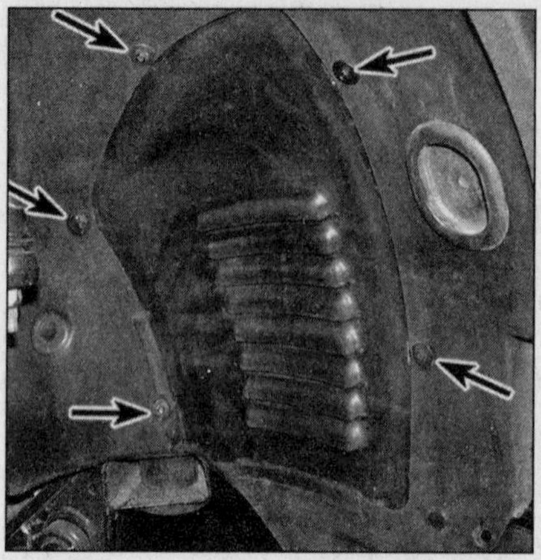

3.8 Remove the fasteners (arrows) and remove the splash shield

3.9 Slide the battery out and remove the battery cables from the battery

6 Remove the two battery hold-down clamp bolts and remove the clamps **(see Illustration)**.

7 Loosen the right front wheel lug nuts, raise the right front corner of the vehicle and support it securely on a jackstand. Remove the wheel.

8 Remove the battery cover/splash shield from the wheel well **(see illustration)**.

9 Slide the battery toward the rear of the vehicle and disconnect the battery cables from the battery **(see illustration)**.

10 Remove the battery through the wheel opening. Be careful - it's heavy. **Note:** *Battery handling tools are available at most auto parts stores for a reasonable price. They make it easier to remove and carry the battery.*

11 While the battery is removed, inspect the tray, hold-down brackets and related fasteners for corrosion or damage.

12 If corrosion is evident on the battery tray, use a baking soda/water solution to clean the corroded area to prevent further oxidation. Repaint the area as necessary using rust resistant paint.

13 Clean and service the battery and cables (see Chapter 1).

14 If you are replacing the battery, make sure you purchase one that is identical to yours, with the same dimensions, amperage rating, cold cranking amps rating, etc. Make sure it is fully charged prior to installation in the vehicle.

15 Installation is the reverse of removal. Connect the negative cable to the remote ground terminal last.

16 After connecting the cables to the battery, apply a light coating of petroleum jelly or grease to the connections to help prevent corrosion.

17 Install the wheel and tighten the wheel lug nuts to the torque given in the Chapter 1 Specifications.

4 Battery cables - replacement

Refer to illustrations 4.4a and 4.4b

1 Periodically inspect the entire length of each battery cable for damage, cracked or burned insulation and corrosion. Poor battery cable connections can cause starting problems and decreased engine performance.

2 Check the cable-to-terminal connections at the ends of the cables for cracks, loose wire strands and corrosion. The presence of white, fluffy deposits under the insulation at the cable terminal connection is a sign that the cable is corroded and should be replaced. Check the terminals for distortion, missing mounting bolts and corrosion.

3 When removing the cables, always disconnect the negative cable from the remote ground terminal first and hook it up last or the battery may be shorted by the tool used to loosen the cable clamps. Even if only the positive cable is being replaced, be sure to disconnect the negative cable from the remote ground terminal first (see Chapter 1 for further information regarding battery cable maintenance).

4 Disconnect the old cables from the battery, then disconnect them from the remote jumper terminal at the opposite end. Detach the cables from the starter solenoid, power distribution center and ground terminals, as necessary **(see illustrations)**. Note the routing of each cable to ensure correct installation.

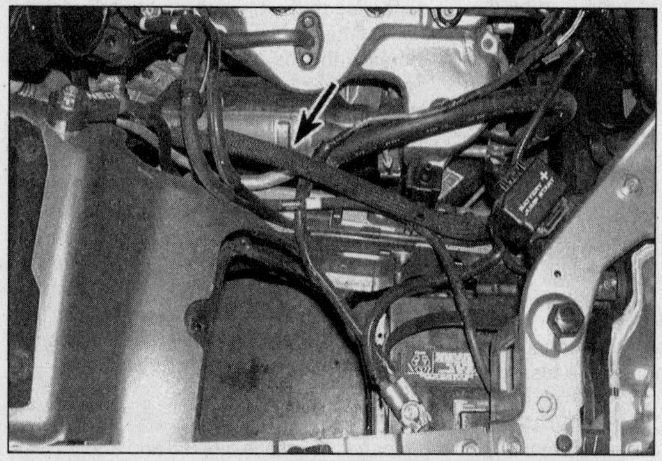

4.4a The battery cables are connected to the remote jumper terminals, then are routed through the protective sheathing (arrow) to the power distribution center, starter solenoid and main engine ground point

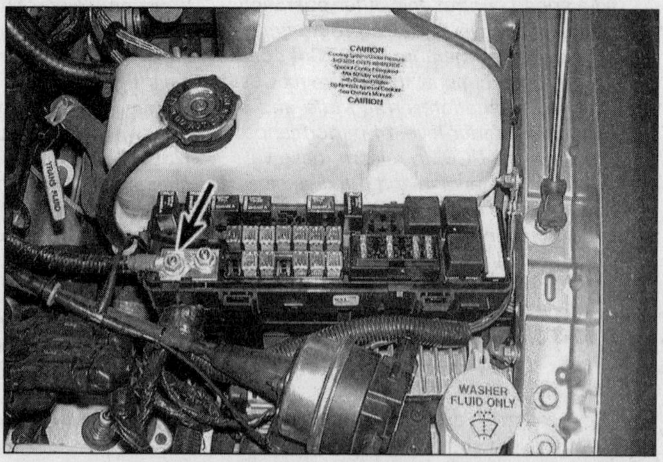

4.4b One branch of the positive cable is connected to the power distribution center

6.2 To use a calibrated ignition tester, remove an ignition coil, connect the tester to the spark plug boot, clip the tester to a convenient ground and crank the engine over - if there's enough power to fire the plug, bright blue sparks will be visible between the electrode tip and the tester body (weak sparks or intermittent sparks are the same as no sparks)

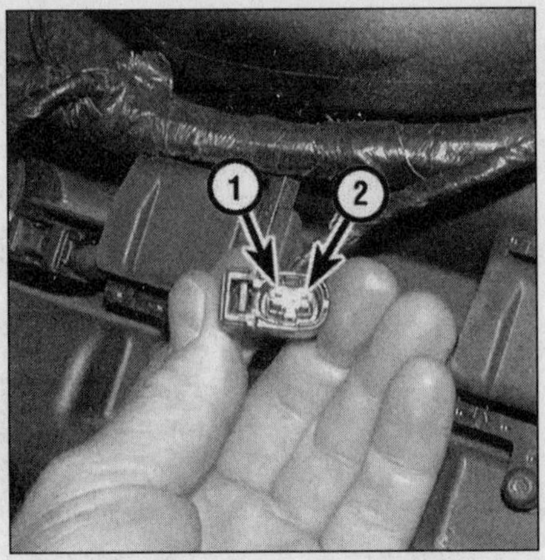

6.4 Ignition coil electrical connector terminal identification

1 Power feed (from ASD relay)
2 Coil driver

7.3 Remove the ignition coil mounting screws and pull the coil straight up

5 If you are replacing either or both of the battery cables, take them with you when buying new cables. It is vitally important that you replace the cables with identical parts. Cables have characteristics that make them easy to identify: positive cables are usually red and larger in cross-section; ground cables are usually black and smaller in cross-section.

6 Clean the threads of the remote terminal, starter solenoid or ground connection with a wire brush to remove rust and corrosion. Apply a light coat of battery terminal corrosion inhibitor or petroleum jelly to the threads to prevent future corrosion.

7 Attach the cable to the terminal and tighten the mounting nut/bolt securely.

8 Before connecting a new cable to the battery, make sure that it reaches the battery post without having to be stretched.

9 After connecting the cables to the battery and installing the battery, connect the negative cable to the remote ground terminal.

5 Ignition system - general information

All models are equipped with a distributorless ignition system (DIS). The ignition system consists of the battery, ignition coils, spark plugs, camshaft position sensor, crankshaft position sensor and the Powertrain Control Module (PCM). The PCM controls the ignition timing and spark advance characteristics for the engine. The ignition timing is not adjustable.

The crankshaft and camshaft position sensors are both Hall Effect sensors. The sensors generate pulses that are input to the Powertrain Control Module. The PCM determines crankshaft position and engine speed from these two sensors. The PCM calculates injector sequence and ignition timing from the crankshaft position. Refer to Chapter 6 for testing and replacement procedures for the crankshaft sensor and camshaft sensor.

The Automatic Shutdown Relay (ASD) supplies battery voltage to the ignition coil packs. The PCM controls the ground circuit for the ASD relay.

The PCM controls the ignition system by opening and closing the ignition coil ground circuit. The computerized ignition system provides complete control of the ignition timing by determining the optimum timing in response to engine speed, coolant temperature, throttle position and vacuum pressure in the intake manifold. These parameters are relayed to the PCM by the camshaft position sensor, crankshaft position sensor, throttle position sensor, coolant temperature sensor and manifold absolute pressure sensor. Refer to Chapter 6 for additional information on the various sensors.

6 Ignition system - check

Refer to illustrations 6.2 and 6.4

Warning: *Because of the high voltage generated by the ignition system, extreme care should be taken whenever an operation is performed involving ignition components. This not only includes the ignition coil, but related components and test equipment.*

1 If a malfunction occurs and the vehicle won't start, do not immediately assume that the ignition system is causing the problem. First, check the following items:

a) *Make sure the battery cable clamps, where they connect to the battery, are clean and tight.*
b) *Test the condition of the battery (see Section 3). If it does not pass all the tests, replace it with a new battery.*
c) *Check the external ignition coil wiring and connections.*
d) *Check the related fuses inside the power distribution center (see Chapter 12). If they're burned, determine the cause and repair the circuit*

2 If the engine turns over but won't start, make sure there is sufficient secondary ignition voltage to fire the spark plug. Remove an ignition coil (see Section 7) and attach a calibrated ignition system tester (available at most auto parts stores) to the spark plug boot (be sure to reconnect the electrical connector to the coil). Connect the clip on the tester to a bolt or metal bracket on the engine **(see illustration)**. Crank the engine and watch the end of the tester to see if a bright blue, well-defined spark occurs (weak spark or intermittent spark is the same as no spark).

3 If spark occurs, sufficient voltage is reaching the plug to fire it (repeat the check at the remaining ignition coils to verify that the ignition coils are good). However, the plugs themselves may be fouled, so remove and check them as described in Chapter 1.

4 If no spark occurs, remove the spark plug boot and check the terminals for damage. Using an ohmmeter, check the boot for an open or high resistance. Check for battery voltage to the ignition coil from the ignition switch with the ignition key On (engine not running). Attach a 12 volt test light to the battery negative (-) terminal or other good ground. Disconnect the coil electrical connector and check for power at the dark green wire terminal **(see illustration)**. Battery voltage should be available with the ignition key On. If there is no battery voltage present, check the wiring and/or circuit between the battery, ASD relay and ignition coil (don't forget to check the fuses). Also check the ASD control circuit from the ASD relay to the PCM for continuity. **Note:** *Refer to the wiring diagrams at the end of Chapter 12 for wire color identification for testing and additional information on the circuits.*

5 If battery voltage is available to the ignition coil, attach an LED test light to the battery positive (+) terminal. Connect the test light probe to the tan wire terminal of the coil

harness connector (vehicle harness side), then crank the engine. Confirm that the test light flashes. This test checks for the trigger signal (ground) from the computer. If a trigger signal is present at the coil, the computer and crankshaft position sensors are functioning properly. **Caution:** *Use only an LED test light to avoid damaging the PCM.*

6 If a trigger signal is not present at the ignition coil, refer to Chapter 6 and check the camshaft position sensor and crankshaft position sensor.

7 If battery voltage and a trigger signal exist at the ignition coil and there is no spark, replace the ignition coil.

8 If all the components are good and there is no spark, have the PCM checked by a dealer service department or other qualified repair shop.

7 Ignition coil - replacement

Refer to illustration 7.3

1 Disconnect the negative battery cable from the remote ground terminal (see Section 1).

2 Disconnect the electrical connector from the ignition coil.

3 Remove the ignition coil mounting screws and pull the coil straight up and out of the cylinder head **(see illustration)**. **Note:** *On 3.2L/3.5L models, loosen the screws slowly, alternating back-and-forth between the two screws. Be careful not to lose the spacers.*

4 Installation is the reverse of removal.

8 Charging system - general information and precautions

The charging system includes the alternator, a charge indicator light, the battery, the Powertrain Control Module (PCM), a fusible link and the wiring between all the components. The charging system supplies electrical power for the ignition system, the lights, the radio, etc. The alternator is driven by a serpentine drivebelt at the front of the engine.

The alternator voltage regulator control system within the PCM regulates the DC current output of the alternator in accordance with driving conditions. Depending upon electric load, vehicle speed, battery temperature and accessories (air conditioning system, radio, cruise control etc.), the system will adjust the amount of DC current generated, creating less load on the engine.

The purpose of the voltage regulator is to limit the alternator voltage output to a preset value. This prevents power surges, circuit overloads, etc., during peak voltage output. The voltage regulator is contained within the PCM and in the event of failure, the PCM must be replaced as a single unit.

The charging system doesn't ordinarily require periodic maintenance. However, the drivebelt, battery, harness wires and connections should be inspected at the intervals outlined in Chapter 1.

9.2 To measure battery voltage, attach the voltmeter leads to the remote battery terminals (engine OFF) - to measure charging voltage, start the engine

The dashboard warning light should come ON when the ignition key is turned to ON, but it should go off immediately after the engine is started. If it remains on, there is a malfunction in the charging system. Some vehicles are also equipped with a voltmeter. If the voltmeter indicates abnormally high or low voltage, check the charging system (see Section 9).

Be very careful when making electrical circuit connections to a vehicle equipped with an alternator and note the following:

a) When reconnecting wires to the alternator from the battery, be sure to note the polarity.
b) Before using arc welding equipment to repair any part of the vehicle, disconnect the wires from the alternator and the battery terminals.
c) Never start the engine with a battery charger connected.
d) Always disconnect both battery cables before using a battery charger.
e) The alternator is turned by an engine drivebelt which could cause serious injury if your hands, hair or clothes become entangled in it with the engine running.
f) Because the alternator is connected directly to the battery, it could arc or cause a fire if overloaded or shorted out.
g) Wrap a plastic bag over the alternator and secure it with rubber bands before steam-cleaning the engine.

9 Charging system - check

Refer to illustration 9.2

Note: *These vehicles are equipped with an On-Board Diagnostic (OBD) system that is useful for detecting charging system problems. Refer to Chapter 6 for the list of diagnostic codes and procedures for obtaining the codes.*

1 If a malfunction occurs in the charging circuit, do not immediately assume that the alternator is causing the problem. First check the following items:

a) The battery cables where they connect to the battery. Make sure the connections are clean and tight.
b) The battery electrolyte specific gravity (by observing the charge indicator on the battery). If it is low, charge the battery.
c) Check the external alternator wiring and connections.
d) Check the drivebelt condition and tension (see Chapter 1).
e) Check the alternator mounting bolts for tightness.
f) Run the engine and check the alternator for abnormal noise.

2 Connect a voltmeter to the positive and negative remote jumper terminals **(see illustration)**. Check the battery voltage with the engine off. It should be approximately 12.4 to 12.6 volts if the battery is fully charged.

3 Start the engine and check the battery voltage again. It should now be greater than the voltage recorded in Step 2, but not more than 14.5 volts.

4 If the indicated voltage reading is less or more than the specified charging voltage, have the charging system checked at a dealer service department or other properly equipped repair facility. The voltage regulator on these models is contained within the PCM and it cannot be adjusted, removed or tampered with in any way.

10 Alternator - removal and installation

Refer to illustrations 10.4a, 10.4b, 10.5 and 10.6

1 Disconnect the negative battery cable from the remote ground terminal (see Section 1).

2 Loosen the tensioner pulley, then detach the alternator drivebelt (see Chapter 1).

3 On 3.2/3.5L models, remove the alternator brace.

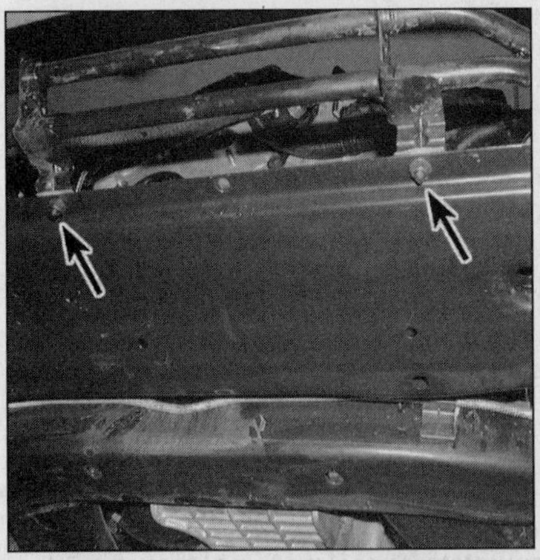

10.4a Remove the nuts (arrows) and detach the power steering fluid cooler from the lower radiator support

10.4b Remove the bolts (two at each end) and remove the radiator support crossmember

10.5 Disconnect the alternator electrical connections (arrows)

4 On 2.7L models, raise the vehicle, support it securely on jackstands and perform the following **(see illustrations)**:

a) *Remove the plastic splash shield from under the front of the engine.*

b) *Detach the power steering fluid cooler and position the cooler aside.*

c) *Remove the lower radiator support crossmember. Support the radiator with a jackstand.*

5 Disconnect the output wire and the field terminal connector from the alternator **(see illustration)**.

6 Remove the mounting bolts and remove the alternator from the engine **(see illustration)**.

7 If you are replacing the alternator, take the old one with you when purchasing a replacement unit. Make sure the new/rebuilt unit looks identical to the old alternator. Look at the terminals - they should be the same in number, size and location as the terminals on the old alternator. Finally, look at the identification numbers - they will be stamped into the housing or printed on a tag attached to the housing. Make sure the numbers are the same on both alternators.

8 Many new/rebuilt alternators do not have a pulley installed, so you may have to switch the pulley from the old unit to the new/rebuilt one. When buying an alternator, find out the shop's policy regarding pulleys; some shops will perform this service free of charge.

9 Installation is the reverse of removal. Tighten the mounting bolts to the torque listed in this Chapter's Specifications.

10 Install the drivebelt (see Chapter 1).

11 Check the charging voltage to verify proper operation of the alternator (see Section 9).

11 Starting system - general information and precautions

The starter motor assembly installed on the 2.7L engine is a permanent magnet, planetary gear drive starter motor. The starter motor assembly installed on 3.2L/3.5L engines is a field coil, offset gear drive starter motor. The starter motor assembly is serviced as a complete unit. If any component of the starter motor fails, including the solenoid, the entire assembly must be replaced.

The sole function of the starting system is to turn over the engine quickly enough to allow it to start. The starting system consists of the battery, starter relay, starter motor assembly and the wiring connecting the components.

The starter motor assembly is installed on the lower part of the engine, bolted to the transmission bellhousing.

When the ignition key is turned to the START position, the starter solenoid is actuated through the starter control circuit which includes a starter relay located in the Power Distribution Center. The starter solenoid then connects the battery to the starter motor. The battery supplies the electrical energy to the starter motor, which does the actual work of cranking the engine.

Always observe the following precautions when working on the starting system:

a) *Excessive cranking of the starter motor can overheat it and cause serious damage. Never operate the starter motor for more than 15 seconds at a time without pausing to allow it to cool for at least two minutes.*

b) *The starter is connected directly to the battery and could arc or cause a fire if mishandled, overloaded or shorted.*

c) *Always detach the cable from the negative terminal of the battery before working on the starting system.*

12 Starter motor and circuit-check

Refer to illustration 12.4

1 If a malfunction occurs in the starting circuit, do not immediately assume that the starter is causing the problem. First, check the following items:

10.6 Remove the alternator mounting bolts (arrows)

a) *Make sure the battery cable clamps, where they connect to the battery, are clean and tight.*

b) *Check the condition of the battery cables* (see Section 4). *Replace any defective battery cables with new parts.*

c) *Test the condition of the battery* (see Section 3). *If it does not pass all the tests, replace it with a new battery.*

d) *Check the starter motor wiring and connections.*

e) *Check the starter motor mounting bolts for tightness.*

f) *Check the related fuses in the engine compartment fuse box* (see Chapter 12). *If they're blown, determine the cause and repair the circuit.*

g) *Check the ignition switch circuit for correct operation* (see Chapter 12).

h) *Check the starter relay* (see Chapter 12).

i) *Check the operation of the Park/Neutral position switch* (see Chapter 7). *These systems must operate correctly to provide battery voltage to the starter solenoid.*

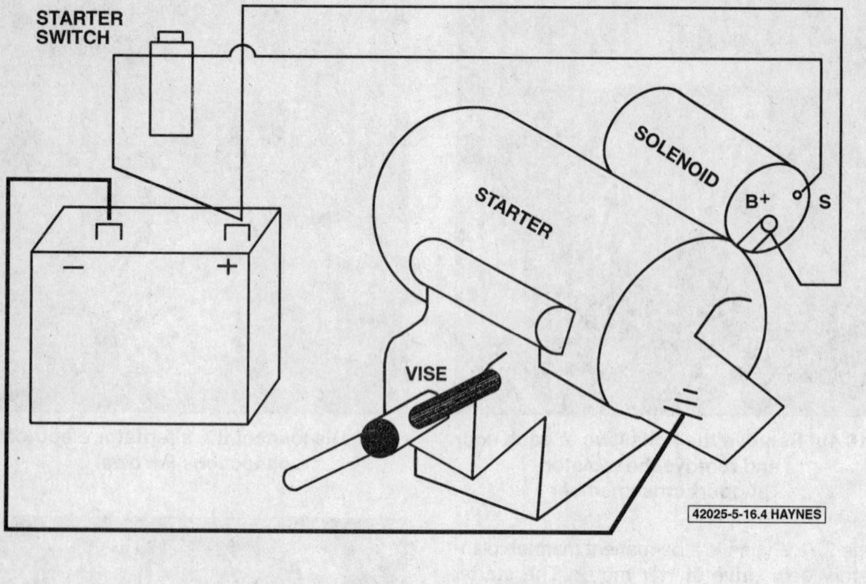

12.4 Starter motor bench testing details

2 If the starter does not activate when the ignition switch is turned to the start position, check for battery voltage to the starter solenoid. This will determine if the solenoid is receiving the correct voltage from the ignition switch. Install a 12-volt test light or a voltmeter to the starter solenoid terminal. While an assistant turns the ignition switch to the start position, observe the test light or voltmeter. The test light should shine brightly or battery voltage should be indicated on the voltmeter. If voltage is not available to the starter solenoid, refer to the wiring diagrams in Chapter 12 and check the fuses and starter relay in series with the starting system. If voltage is available but there is no movement from the starter motor, remove the starter from the engine (see Section 14) and bench test the starter (see Step 4).

3 If the starter turns over slowly, check the starter cranking voltage and the current draw from the battery. This test must be performed with the starter assembly on the engine. Crank the engine over (for 10 seconds or less) and observe the battery voltage. It should not drop below 8.5 volts. Also, observe the current draw using an ammeter. Typically a starter amperage draw should not exceed 300 amps. If the starter motor amperage draw is excessive, have it tested by a dealer service department or other qualified repair shop. There are several conditions that may affect the starter cranking potential. The battery must be in good condition and the battery cold-cranking rating must not be under-rated for the particular application. Be sure to check the battery specifications carefully. The battery terminals and cables must be clean and not corroded. Also, in cases of extreme cold temperatures, make sure the battery and/or engine block is warmed before performing the tests.

4 If the starter is receiving voltage but does not activate, remove and check the starter motor assembly on the bench. Most likely the starter motor or solenoid is defective. In some rare cases, the engine may be seized so be sure to try and rotate the crankshaft pulley (see Chapter 2A or 2B) before proceeding. With the starter assembly mounted in a vise on the bench, install one jumper cable from the positive terminal of a test battery to the B+ terminal on the starter. Install another jumper cable from the negative terminal of the battery to the body of the starter **(see illustration)**. Install a starter switch and apply battery voltage to the solenoid S terminal (for 10 seconds or less); the solenoid plunger, shift lever and overrunning clutch should extend and rotate the pinion drive. If the pinion drive extends but does not rotate, the solenoid is operating but the starter motor is defective. If there is no movement but the solenoid clicks, the solenoid and/or the starter motor is defective. If the solenoid plunger extends and rotates the pinion drive, the starter assembly is operating properly.

13 Starter motor - removal and installation

Refer to illustrations 13.4 and 13.5

1 Disconnect the negative battery cable from the remote ground terminal (see Chapter 5).

2 Raise the vehicle and support it securely on jackstands.

3 Remove the starter heat shield, if equipped.

4 Remove the starter mounting bolts **(see illustration)**.

5 Lower the starter and disconnect the wires from the terminals on the starter motor solenoid **(see illustration)**.

6 Withdraw the starter from between the catalytic converter and the motor mount. **Note:** *If necessary, remove the left engine mount bolts and raise the engine slightly with a floor jack to provide additional clearance.*

7 Installation is the reverse of removal.

13.4 Remove the starter mounting bolts (arrows)

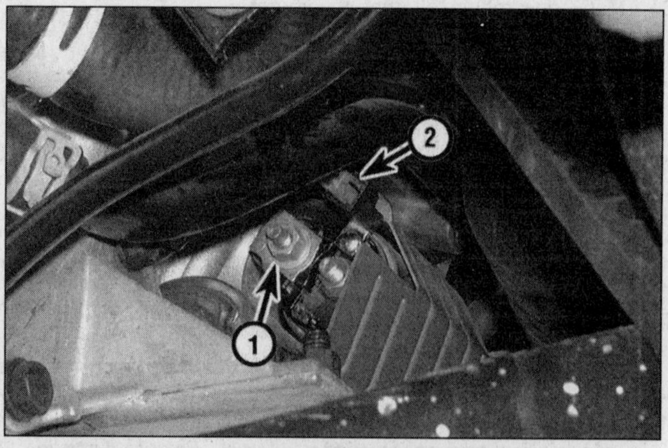

13.5 Remove the nut (1) and disconnect the battery cable from the starter motor - disconnect the connector (2) from the starter solenoid

Chapter 6
Emissions and engine control systems

Contents

1 General information

Refer to illustrations 1.1a, 1.1b and 1.7

To prevent pollution of the atmosphere from incompletely burned and evaporating gases, and to maintain good driveability and fuel economy, a number of emission control systems are incorporated **(see illustrations)**. They include the:

Electronic engine control system
Positive crankcase ventilation system
Exhaust gas recirculation system
Evaporative emissions control system
Catalytic converter

All of these systems are linked, directly or indirectly, to the emission control system.

The Sections in this Chapter include general descriptions, checking procedures within the scope of the home mechanic and component replacement procedures (when possible) for each of the systems listed above.

Before assuming that an emissions control system is malfunctioning, check the fuel and ignition systems carefully. The diagnosis of some emission control devices requires

1.1a Typical emission and engine control system components - 2.7L models

1 EGR tube
2 Throttle position sensor and idle air control valve (on side of throttle body)
3 PCV valve
4 Intake air temperature sensor
5 Powertrain Control Module
6 Oxygen sensor
7 Manifold absolute pressure sensor
8 Camshaft position sensor
9 Engine coolant temperature sensor
10 EVAP purge solenoid
11 Catalytic converter

1.1b Typical emission and engine control system components - 3.2L/3.5L models

1. *Throttle position sensor and idle air control valve (on side of throttle body)*
2. *PCV valve*
3. *Manifold absolute pressure sensor and intake air temperature sensor*
4. *Powertrain Control Module*
5. *Camshaft position sensor*
6. *Engine coolant temperature sensor (under upper intake manifold)*
7. *Manifold tuning valve*
8. *Short runner valve actuator*
9. *EVAP purge solenoid*

specialized tools, equipment and training. If checking and servicing become too difficult or if a procedure is beyond your ability, consult a dealer service department. Remember, the most frequent cause of emissions problems is simply a loose or broken vacuum hose or wire, so always check the hose and wiring connections first.

This doesn't mean, however, that emission control systems are particularly difficult to maintain and repair. You can quickly and easily perform many checks and do most of the regular maintenance at home with common tune-up and hand tools. **Note:** *Because of a Federally mandated warranty which covers the emission control system components, check with your dealer about warranty coverage before working on any emissions-related systems. Once the warranty has expired, you may wish to perform some of the component checks and/or replacement procedures in this Chapter to save money.*

Pay close attention to any special precautions outlined in this Chapter. It should be noted that the illustrations of the various systems may not exactly match the system installed on the vehicle you're working on because of changes made by the manufacturer during production or from year-to-year.

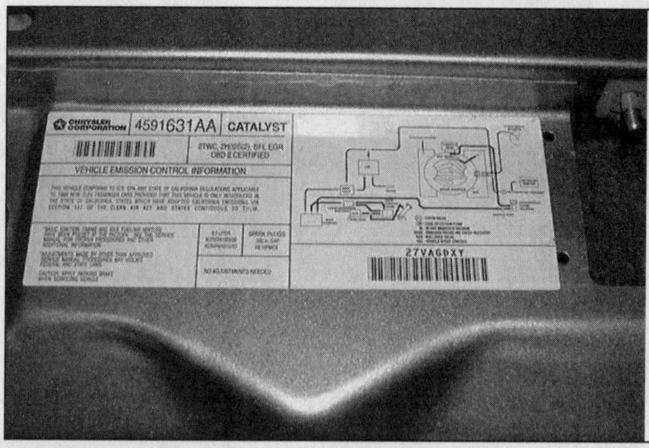

1.7 The Vehicle Emission Control Information (VECI) label is located in the engine compartment and contains information on the emission devices on your vehicle, vacuum line routing, etc.

A Vehicle Emissions Control Information (VECI) label is located in the engine compartment **(see illustration)**. This label contains important emissions specifications and adjustment information, as well as a vacuum hose schematic with emissions components identified. When servicing the engine or emissions systems, the VECI label in your particular vehicle should always be checked for up-to-date information.

2 On-Board Diagnosis system and trouble codes

Diagnostic tool information

Refer to illustrations 2.1 and 2.2

1 A digital multimeter is necessary for checking fuel injection and emission related components **(see illustration)**. A digital volt-ohmmeter is preferred over the older style

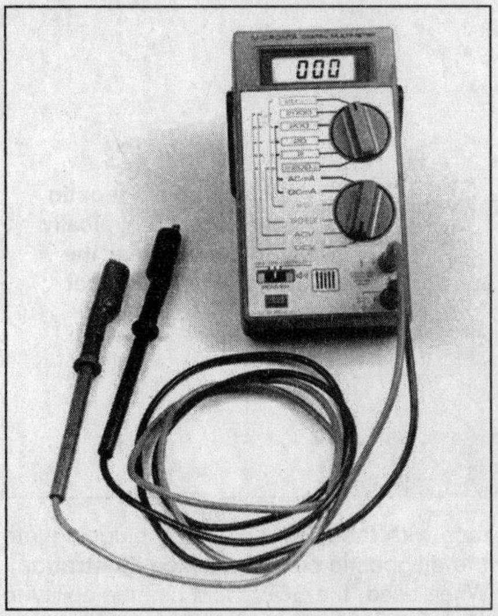

2.1 Digital multimeters can be used for testing all types of circuits; because of their high impedance, they are much more accurate than analog meters for measuring low-voltage computer circuits

2.2 Scanners like the Actron Scantool and the AutoXray XP240 are powerful diagnostic aids - programmed with comprehensive diagnostic information, they can tell you just about anything you want to know about your engine management system

analog multimeter for several reasons. The analog multimeter cannot display the volts-ohms or amps measurement in hundredths and thousandths increments. When working with electronic circuits which are often very low voltage, this accurate reading is most important. Another good reason for the digital multimeter is the high impedance circuit. The digital multimeter is equipped with a high resistance internal circuitry (10 million ohms). Because a voltmeter is hooked up in parallel with the circuit when testing, it is vital that none of the voltage being measured should be allowed to travel the parallel path set up by the meter itself. This dilemma does not show itself when measuring larger amounts of voltage (9 to 12 volt circuits) but if you are measuring a low voltage circuit such as the oxygen sensor signal voltage, a fraction of a volt may be a significant amount when diagnosing a problem. However, there are several exceptions where using an analog voltmeter may be necessary to test certain sensors.

2 Hand-held scanners are the most powerful and versatile tools for analyzing engine management systems used on later model vehicles **(see illustration)**. Each brand scan tool must be examined carefully to match the year, make and model of the vehicle you are working on. Often interchangeable cartridges are available to access the particular manufacturer (Ford, GM, Chrysler, etc.). Some manufacturers will specify by continent (Asia, Europe, USA, etc.).

3 With the arrival of the Federally mandated emission control system (OBD-II), a specially designed scanner has been developed. Several tool manufacturers have released OBD-II scan tools for the home mechanic. Ask the parts salesman at a local auto parts store for additional information concerning availability and cost.

On-Board Diagnostic system general description

4 All models described in this manual are equipped with the second generation On-Board Diagnostic (OBD-II) system. The system consists of an onboard computer, known as the Powertrain Control Module (PCM), information sensors and output actuators.

5 The information sensors monitor various functions of the engine and send data to the PCM. Based on the data and the information programmed into the computer's memory, the PCM generates output signals to control various engine functions via control relays, solenoids and other output actuators. The PCM is specifically calibrated to optimize the emissions, fuel economy and driveability of the vehicle.

6 Because of a Federally mandated warranty which covers the emissions system components and because any owner-induced damage to the PCM, the sensors and/or the control devices may void the warranty, it isn't a good idea to attempt diagnosis or replacement of the PCM at home while the vehicle is under warranty. Take the vehicle to a dealer service department if the PCM or a system component malfunctions.

Information sensors

7 **Battery temperature sensor** - The PCM monitors the ambient temperature sensor used for the air conditioning system to determine the temperature of the battery. The PCM uses this information in controlling the voltage output of the alternator.

8 **Camshaft position sensor** - The camshaft position sensor provides information on camshaft position. The PCM uses this information, along with the crankshaft position sensor information, to control fuel injection synchronization.

9 **Crankshaft position sensor** - The crankshaft position sensor senses crankshaft position (TDC) during each engine revolution. The PCM uses this information to control ignition timing and fuel injection synchronization.

10 **Engine coolant temperature sensor** - The engine coolant temperature sensor senses engine coolant temperature. The PCM uses this information to control fuel injection duration and ignition timing.

11 **Intake air temperature sensor** - The intake air temperature senses the temperature of the air entering the intake manifold. The PCM uses this information to control fuel injection duration.

12 **Knock sensor** - The knock sensor is a piezoelectric element that detects the sound of engine detonation, or "pinging". The PCM uses the input signal from the knock sensor to recognize detonation and retard spark advance to avoid engine damage.

13 **Manifold absolute pressure sensor** - The manifold absolute pressure monitors intake manifold pressure and ambient barometric pressure. The PCM uses this input signal to determine engine load and adjusts fuel injection duration accordingly.

14 **Oxygen sensor** - The oxygen sensors generate a voltage signal that varies with the difference between the oxygen content of the exhaust and the oxygen in the surrounding air. The PCM uses this information to determine if the fuel system is running rich or lean.

15 **Power steering pressure switch** - The power steering pressure switch is used to detect high line pressure in the power steering system. The PCM uses this input signal to adjust the idle speed under increased engine loads during low-speed vehicle maneuvers.

16 **Throttle position sensor** - The throttle position sensor senses throttle movement and position. This signal enables the PCM to determine when the throttle is closed, in a cruise position, or wide open. The PCM uses this information to control fuel delivery and ignition timing.

17 **Vehicle speed sensor** - The vehicle speed sensor provides information to the PCM to indicate vehicle speed.

18 **Miscellaneous PCM inputs** - In addition to the various sensors, the PCM monitors various switches and circuits to determine vehicle operating conditions. The

switches and circuits include:

a) *Air conditioning system*
b) *Auto shutdown relay*
c) *Battery voltage*
d) *Brake On/Off switch*
e) *Cruise control system*
f) *EGR valve position*
g) *EVAP leak detection pump operation*
h) *Ignition switch*
i) *Park/neutral position switch*
j) *Sensor signal and ground circuits*
k) *Transaxle control module*

Output actuators

19 **Air conditioning clutch relay** - The PCM controls the operation of the air conditioning compressor clutch with the air conditioning clutch relay.

20 **Automatic shutdown relay** - The automatic shut down relay supplies battery power to the fuel injectors, ignition coil and oxygen sensor heaters. The PCM controls the operation of the automatic shutdown relay.

21 **Check Engine light** - The PCM will illuminate the Check Engine light if a malfunction in the electronic engine control system occurs.

22 **Cruise control vacuum and vent solenoids** - The cruise control system operation is controlled by the PCM.

23 **Engine cooling fan relay** - The engine cooling fan is controlled by the PCM according to information received from the engine coolant temperature sensor.

24 **EGR valve** - The electronic EGR valve is controlled by the PCM. Ideal EGR flow is determined by the PCM and the EGR valve pintle position is adjusted accordingly.

25 **EVAP canister purge solenoid** - The evaporative emission canister purge solenoid is a solenoid valve, operated by the PCM to purge the fuel vapor canister and route fuel vapor to the intake manifold for combustion.

26 **EVAP leak detection pump** - The EVAP system is equipped with a self-diagnostic EVAP leak detection system. The system checks the integrity of the EVAP system when the engine is started cold. The PCM controls the operation of the EVAP leak detection pump.

27 **Fuel injectors** - The PCM opens the fuel injectors individually in firing order sequence. The PCM also controls the time the injector is held open (pulse width). The pulse width of the injector (measured in milliseconds) determines the amount of fuel delivered. For more information on the fuel delivery system and the fuel injectors, including injector replacement, refer to Chapter 4.

28 **Fuel pump relay** - The fuel pump relay is activated by the PCM with the ignition switch in the Start or Run position. When the ignition switch is turned on, the relay is activated to supply initial line pressure to the system. For more information on fuel pump check and replacement, refer to Chapter 4.

29 **Idle air control valve** - The idle air control valve controls the amount of air allowed to bypass the throttle plate when the throttle valve is closed or at idle position. The more

2.36 The diagnostic connector is typically located under the instrument panel

air allowed to bypass the throttle plate, the higher the idle speed. The idle air control valve opening and the resulting idle speed is controlled by the PCM.

30 **Ignition coils** - The PCM controls the ignition coils by grounding the primary circuit to the ignition coil which generates high voltage in the secondary circuit to the spark plug. The PCM controls ignition timing depending on engine operation conditions. Refer to Chapter 5 for more information on the ignition coil.

31 **Intake manifold tuning valves (3.2L/3.5L models)** - The PCM controls the operation of the manifold tuning valve and the short runner valve to obtain maximum engine performance throughout the rpm range.

32 **Tachometer** - The PCM operates the tachometer from the information received from the crankshaft position sensor.

33 **Voltage regulator** - The PCM controls the charging system voltage by grounding the alternator field driver circuit depending on electrical load requirements. The voltage regulator circuitry is fully contained within the PCM. Any failure in the voltage regulator circuitry requires replacement of the PCM.

Obtaining diagnostic trouble codes

Refer to illustration 2.36

Note: *The diagnostic trouble codes on all models can only be extracted from the Powertrain Control Module (PCM) using a specialized SCAN tool, have the vehicle diagnosed by a dealer service department or other qualified automotive repair facility if the proper SCAN tool is not available.*

34 The PCM will illuminate the CHECK ENGINE light (also known as the Malfunction Indicator Lamp) on the dash if it recognizes a fault in the system. The light will remain illuminated until the problem is repaired and the code is cleared or the PCM does not detect any malfunction for several consecutive drive cycles.

35 The diagnostic codes for the On-Board Diagnostic (OBD) system can be extracted from the PCM using a SCAN tool on all models.

36 The SCAN tool is programmed to interface with the OBD system by plugging into the diagnostic connector **(see illustration)**. When used, the SCAN tool has the ability to diagnose in-depth driveability problems and it allows freeze frame data to be retrieved from the PCM stored memory. Freeze frame data is an OBD II PCM feature that records all related sensor and actuator activity on the PCM data stream whenever an engine control or emissions fault is detected and a trouble code is set. This ability to look at the circuit conditions and values when the malfunction occurs provides a valuable tool when trying to diagnose intermittent driveability problems. If the tool is not available and intermittent driveability problems exist, have the vehicle checked at a dealer service department or other qualified repair shop. **Note:** *The SCAN tool trouble code designation is referred to as a P0 or P1 code. Refer to the "Generic Scan Tool Code" column of the trouble code chart for the code identification.*

Clearing diagnostic trouble codes

37 After the system has been repaired, the codes must be cleared from the PCM memory using a SCAN tool. **Caution:** *Do not disconnect the battery from the vehicle in an attempt to clear the codes. If necessary, have the codes cleared by a dealer service department or other qualified repair facility.*

38 Always clear the codes from the PCM before starting the engine after a new electronic emission control component is installed onto the engine. The PCM stores the operating parameters of each sensor. The PCM may set a trouble code if a new sensor is allowed to operate before the parameters from the old sensor have been erased.

Diagnostic trouble code identification

Refer to illustration 2.39

39 The accompanying list of diagnostic trouble codes is a compilation of all the codes that may be encountered **(see Illustration)**. Not all codes pertain to all models and not all codes will illuminate the Check Engine light when set. All models require a SCAN tool to access the diagnostic trouble codes.

DIAGNOSTIC TROUBLE CODE DESCRIPTIONS

(M) Check Engine Lamp (MIL) will illuminate during engine operation if this Diagnostic Trouble Code was recorded.

(G) Generator Lamp Illuminated

GENERIC SCAN TOOL CODE	DRB SCAN TOOL DISPLAY	DESCRIPTION OF DIAGNOSTIC TROUBLE CODE
P0030	1/1 O^2 Sensor Heater Relay Circuit	Problem in O^2 sensor relay circuit.
P0036	1/2 O^2 Sensor Heater Relay Circuit	Problem in O^2 sensor relay circuit.
P0106 (M)	Barometric Pressure Out of Range	MAP sensor input voltage out of an acceptable range detected during reading of barometric pressure at key-on.
P0107 (M)	Map Sensor Voltage Too Low	MAP sensor input below minimum acceptable voltage.
P0108 (M)	Map Sensor Voltage Too High	MAP sensor input above maximum acceptable voltage.
P0112 (M)	Intake Air Temp Sensor Voltage Low	Intake air (charge) temperature sensor input below the minimum acceptable voltage.
P0113 (M)	Intake Air Temp Sensor Voltage High	Intake air (charge) temperature sensor input above the maximum acceptable voltage.
P0116	Coolant temperature sensor	A rationatilty error has been detected in the coolant temp sensor.
P0117 (M)	ECT Sensor Voltage Too Low	Engine coolant temperature sensor input below the minimum acceptable voltage.
P0118 (M)	ECT Sensor Voltage Too High	Engine coolant temperature sensor input above the maximum acceptable voltage.
P0121 (M)	TPS Voltage Does Not Agree With MAP	TPS signal does not correlate to MAP sensor signal.
P0122 (M)	Throttle Position Sensor Voltage Low	Throttle position sensor input below the acceptable voltage range.
P0123 (M)	Throttle Position Sensor Voltage High	Throttle position sensor input above the maximum acceptable voltage.
P0125 (M)	Closed Loop Temp Not Reached	Time to enter Closed Loop Operation (Fuel Control) is excessive.
P0131 (M)	1/1 O^2 Sensor Shorted To Ground	Oxygen sensor input voltage maintained below normal operating range.
P0132 (M)	1/1 O^2 Sensor Shorted To Voltage	Oxygen sensor input voltage maintained above normal operating range.
P0133 (M)	1/1 O^2 Sensor Slow Response	Oxygen sensor response slower than minimum required switching frequency.
P0134 (M)	1/1 O^2 Sensor Stays at Center	Neither rich or lean condition is detected from the oxygen sensor input.
P0135 (M)	1/1 O^2 Sensor Heater Failure	Oxygen sensor heater element malfunction.
P0136	1/2 O^2 sensor heater relay circuit open or shorted	Short to ground or open in the circuit for the oxygen sensor heater on the No. 1 or No. 2 sensor.
P0137 (M)	1/2 O^2 Sensor Shorted To Ground	Oxygen sensor input voltage maintained below normal operating range.

2.39 Diagnostic Trouble Code Identification Chart (1 of 9)

(M) Check Engine Lamp (MIL) will illuminate during engine operation if this Diagnostic Trouble Code was recorded.		
(G) Generator Lamp Illuminated		
P0138 (M)	1/2 O^2 Sensor Shorted To Voltage	Oxygen sensor input voltage maintained above normal operating range.
P0139 (M)	1/2 O^2 Sensor Slow Response	Oxygen sensor response not as expected.
P0140 (M)	1/2 O^2 Sensor Stays at Center	Neither rich or lean condition is detected from the oxygen sensor.
P0141 (M)	1/2 O^2 Sensor Heater Failure	Oxygen sensor heater element malfunction.
P0143	1/3 O^2 Sensor Shorted To Ground	Oxygen sensor input voltage maintained below normal operating range.
P0144	1/3 O^2 Sensor Shorted To Voltage	Oxygen sensor input voltage maintained above normal operating range.
P0145	1/3 O^2 Sensor Slow Response	Oxygen sensor response slower than minimum required switching frequency.
P0146	1/3 O^2 Sensor Stays at Center	Neither rich or lean condition is detected from the oxygen sensor.
P0147	1/3 O^2 Sensor Heater Failure	Oxygen sensor heater element malfunction.
P0151 (M)	2/1 O^2 Sensor Shorted To Ground	Oxygen sensor input voltage maintained below normal operating range.
P0152 (M)	2/1 O^2 Sensor Shorted To Voltage	Oxygen sensor input voltage sustained above normal operating range.
P0153 (M)	2/1 O^2 Sensor Slow Response	Oxygen sensor response slower than minimum required switching frequency.
P0154 (M)	2/1 O^2 Sensor Stays at Center	Neither rich or lean condition is detected from the oxygen sensor.
P0155 (M)	2/1 O^2 Sensor Heater Failure	Oxygen sensor heater element malfunction.
P0157 (M)	2/2 O^2 Sensor Shorted To Ground	Oxygen sensor input voltage maintained below normal operating range.
P0158 (M)	2/2 O^2 Sensor Shorted To Voltage	Oxygen sensor input voltage maintained above normal operating range.
P0159	2/2 O^2 Sensor Slow Response	Oxygen sensor response slower than minimum required switching frequency.
P0160 (M)	2/2 O^2 Sensor Stays at Center	Neither rich or lean condition is detected from the oxygen sensor.
P0161 (M)	2/2 O^2 Sensor Heater Failure	Oxygen sensor heater element malfunction.
P0165	Starter Relay Control Circuit	An open or shorted condition detected in the starter relay control circuit.
P0171 (M)	1/1 Fuel System Lean	A lean air/fuel mixture has been indicated by an abnormally rich correction factor.
P0172 (M)	1/1 Fuel System Rich	A rich air/fuel mixture has been indicated by an abnormally lean correction factor.
P0174 (M)	2/1 Fuel System Lean	A lean air/fuel mixture has been indicated by an abnormally rich correction factor.
P0175 (M)	2/1 Fuel System Rich	A rich air/fuel mixture has been indicated by an abnormally lean correction factor.
P0178	Water in Fuel Sensor Voltage Too Low	Flex fuel sensor input below minimum acceptable voltage.

2.39 Diagnostic Trouble Code Identification Chart (2 of 9)

(M) Check Engine Lamp (MIL) will illuminate during engine operation if this Diagnostic Trouble Code was recorded.		
(G) Generator Lamp Illuminated		
P0179	Flex Fuel Sensor Volts Too High	Flex fuel sensor input above maximum acceptable voltage.
P0182	CNG Temp Sensor Voltage Too Low	Compressed natural gas temperature sensor voltage below acceptable voltage.
P0183	CNG Temp Sensor Voltage Too High	Compressed natural gas temperature sensor voltage above acceptable voltage.
P0201 (M)	Injector #1 Control Circuit	An open or shorted condition detected in control circuit for injector #1 or the INJ 1 injector bank.
P0202 (M)	Injector #2 Control Circuit	An open or shorted condition detected in control circuit for injector #2 or the INJ 2 injector bank.
P0203 (M)	Injector #3 Control Circuit	An open or shorted condition detected in control circuit for injector #3 or the INJ 3 injector bank.
P0204 (M)	Injector #4 Control Circuit	Injector #4 or INJ 4 injector bank output driver stage does not respond properly to the control signal.
P0205 (M)	Injector #5 Control Circuit	Injector #5 output driver stage does not respond properly to the control signal.
P0206 (M)	Injector #6 Control Circuit	Injector #6 output driver stage does not respond properly to the control signal.
P0207	Injector #7 Control Circuit	Injector #7 output driver stage does not respond properly to the control signal.
P0208	Injector #8 Control Circuit	Injector #8 output driver stage does not respond properly to the control signal.
P0209	Injector #9 Control Circuit	Injector #9 output driver stage does not respond properly to the control signal.
P0210	Injector #10 Control Circuit	Injector #10 output driver stage does not respond properly to the control signal.
P0300 (M)	Multiple Cylinder Mis-fire	Misfire detected in multiple cylinders.
P0301 (M)	CYLINDER #1 MISFIRE	Misfire detected in cylinder #1.
P0302 (M)	CYLINDER #2 MISFIRE	Misfire detected in cylinder #2.
P0303 (M)	CYLINDER #3 MISFIRE	Misfire detected in cylinder #3.
P0304 (M)	CYLINDER #4 MISFIRE	Misfire detected in cylinder #4.
P0305 (M)	CYLINDER #5 MISFIRE	Misfire detected in cylinder #5.
P0306 (M)	CYLINDER #6 MISFIRE	Misfire detected in cylinder #6.
P0307 (M)	CYLINDER #7 MISFIRE	Misfire detected in cylinder #7
P0308 (M)	CYLINDER #8 MISFIRE	Misfire detected in cylinder #8.
P0309 (M)	CYLINDER #9 MISFIRE	Misfire detected in cylinder #9.
P0310 (M)	CYLINDER #10 MISFIRE	Misfire detected in cylinder #10.
P0320	No Crank Referance Signal at PCM	No reference signal (crankshaft position sensor) detected during engine cranking.
P0325	Knock Sensor #1 Circuit	Knock sensor (#1) signal above or below minimum acceptable threshold voltage at particular engine speeds.
P0330	Knock Sensor #2 Circuit	Knock sensor (#2) signal above or below minimum acceptable threshold voltage at particular engine speeds.
P0340 (M)	No Cam Signal At PCM	No fuel sync

2.39 Diagnostic Trouble Code Identification Chart (3 of 9)

(M) Check Engine Lamp (MIL) will illuminate during engine operation if this Diagnostic Trouble Code was recorded.		
(G) Generator Lamp Illuminated		
P0350	Ignition Coil Draws Too Much Current	A coil (1-5) is drawing too much current.
P0351 (M)	Ignition Coil # 1 Primary Circuit	Peak primary circuit current not achieved with maximum dwell time.
P0352 (M)	Ignition Coil # 2 Primary Circuit	Peak primary circuit current not achieved with maximum dwell time.
P0353 (M)	Ignition Coil # 3 Primary Circuit	Peak primary circuit current not achieved with maximum dwell time.
P0354 (M)	Ignition Coil # 4 Primary Circuit	Peak primary circuit current not achieved with maximum dwell time (High Impedance).
P0355 (M)	Ignition Coil # 5 Primary Circuit	Peak primary circuit current not achieved with maximum dwell time (High Impedance).
P0356 (M)	Ignition Coil # 6 Primary Circuit	Peak primary circuit current not achieved with maximum dwell time (high impedance).
P0357	Ignition Coil # 7 Primary Circuit	Peak primary circuit current not achieved with maximum dwell time (high impedance).
P0358	Ignition Coil # 8 Primary Circuit	Peak primary circuit current not achieved with maximum dwell time (high impedance).
P0401 (M)	EGR System Failure	Required change in air/fuel ration not detected during diagnostic test.
P0403 (M)	EGR Solenoid Circuit	An open or shorted condition detected in the EGR solenoid control circuit.
P0404 (M)	EGR Position Sensor Rationality	EGR position sensor signal does not correlate to EGR duty cycle.
P0405 (M)	EGR Position Sensor Volts Too Low	EGR position sensor input below the acceptable voltage range.
P0406 (M)	EGR Position Sensor Volts Too High	EGR position sensor input above the acceptable voltage range.
P0412	Secondary Air Solenoid Circuit	An open or shorted condition detected in the secondary air (air switching/aspirator) solenoid control circuit.
P0420 (M)	1/1 Catalytic Converter Efficiency	Catalyst 1/1 efficiency below required level.
P0432 (M)	1/2 Catalytic Converter Efficiency	Catalyst 2/1 efficiency below required level.
P0441 (M)	Evap Purge Flow Monitor	Insufficient or excessive vapor flow detected during evaporative emission system operation.
P0442 (M)	Evap Leak Monitor Medium Leak Detected	A small leak has been detected in the evaporative system.
P0443 (M)	Evap Purge Solenoid Circuit	An open or shorted condition detected in the EVAP purge solenoid control circuit.
P0455 (M)	Evap Leak Monitor Large Leak Detected	A large leak has been detected in the evaporative system.
P0456	Evap Leak Monitor Small Leak Detected	
P0460	Fuel Level Unit No Change Over Miles	No movement of fuel level sender detected.
P0461	Fuel Level Unit No Changeover Time	No level of fuel level sender detected.

2.39 Diagnostic Trouble Code Identification Chart (4 of 9)

(M) Check Engine Lamp (MIL) will illuminate during engine operation if this Diagnostic Trouble Code was recorded.		
(G) Generator Lamp Illuminated		
P0462	Fuel Level Sending Unit Volts Too Low	Fuel level sensor input below acceptable voltage.
P0463	Fuel Level Sending Unit Volts Too High	Fuel level sensor input above acceptable voltage.
P0500 (M)	No Vehicle Speed Sensor Signal	No vehicle speed sensor signal detected during road load conditions.
P0505 (M)	Idle Air Control Motor Circuits	Replace
P0522	Oil Pressure Sens Low	Oil pressure sensor input below acceptable voltage.
P0523	Oil Pressure Sens High	Oil pressure sensor input above acceptable voltage.
P0551 (M)	Power Steering Switch Failure	Incorrect input state detected for the power steering switch circuit. PL: High pressure seen at high speed.
P0600 (M)	PCM Failure SPI Communications	No communication detected between co-processors in the control module.
P0601 (M)	Internal Controller Failure	Internal control module fault condition (check sum) detected.
P0604		Transmission control module RAM self test fault detected. -Aisin transmission.
P0605		Transmission control module ROM self test fault detected -Aisin transmission.
P0622 (G)	Generator Field Not Switching Properly	An open or shorted condition detected in the generator field control circuit.
P0645	A/C Clutch Relay Circuit	An open or shorted condition detected in the A/C clutch relay control circuit.
P0700 (M)	EATX Controller DTC Present	This SBEC III or JTEC DTC indicates that the EATX or Aisin controller has an active fault and has illuminated the MIL via a CCD (EATX) or SCI (Aisin) message. The specific fault must be acquired from the EATX via CCD or from the Aisin via ISO-9141.
P0703 (M)	Brake Switch Stuck Pressed or Released	Incorrect input state detected in the brake switch circuit. (Changed from P1595).
P0711	Trans Temp Sensor, No Temp Rise After Start	Relationship between the transmission temperature and overdrive operation and/or TCC operation indicates a failure of the Transmission Temperature Sensor. OBD II Rationality.
P0712	Trans Temp Sensor Voltage Too Low	Transmission fluid temperature sensor input below acceptable voltage.
P0713	Trans Temp Sensor Voltage Too High	Transmission fluid temperature sensor input above acceptable voltage.
P0720	Low Output SPD Sensor RPM, Above 15 MPH	The relationship between the Output Shaft Speed Sensor and vehicle speed is not within acceptable limits.
P0740 (M)	Torq Con Clu, No RPM Drop at Lockup	Relationship between engine and vehicle speeds indicated failure of torque convertor clutch lock-up system (TCC/PTU sol).
P0743	Torque Converter Clutch Solenoid/ Trans Relay Circuits	An open or shorted condition detected in the torque converter clutch (part throttle unlock) solenoid control circuit. Shift solenoid C electrical fault - Aisin transmission

2.39 Diagnostic Trouble Code Identification Chart (5 of 9)

(M) Check Engine Lamp (MIL) will illuminate during engine operation if this Diagnostic Trouble Code was recorded.		
(G) Generator Lamp Illuminated		
P0748	Governor Pressur Sol Control/Trans Relay Circuits	An open or shorted condition detected in the Governor Pressure Solenoid circuit or Trans Relay Circuit in JTEC RE transmissions.
P0751	O/D Switch Pressed (Lo) More Than 5 Minutes	Overdrive override switch input is in a prolonged depressed state.
P0753	Trans 3-4 Shift Sol/Trans Relay Circuits	An open or shorted condition detected in the overdrive solenoid control circuit or Trans Relay Circuit in JTEC RE transmissions.
P0756	AW4 Shift Sol B (2-3) Functional Failure	Shift solenoid B (2-3) functional fault - Aisin transmission
P0783	3-4 Shift Sol, No RPM Drop at Lockup	The overdrive solenoid is unable to engage the gear change from 3rd gear to the overdrive gear.
P0801	Reverse Gear Lockout Circuit Open or Short	An open or shorted condition detected in the transmission reverse gear lock-out solenoid control circuit.
P01192	IAT circuit low	**Intake Air Temperature sensor circuit indicates low.**
P01193	IAT circuit high	**Intake Air Temperature sensor circuit indicates high.**
P1195 (M)	1/1 O^2 Sensor Slow During Catalyst Monitor	A slow switching oxygen sensor has been detected in bank 1/1 during catalyst monitor test. (was P0133)
P1196 (M)	2/1 O^2 Sensor Slow During Catalyst Monitor	A slow switching oxygen sensor has been detected in bank 2/1 during catalyst monitor test. (was P0153)
P1197	1/2 O^2 Sensor Slow During Catalyst Monitor	A slow switching oxygen sensor has been detected in bank 1/2 during catalyst monitor test. (was P0139)
P1198	Radiator Temperature Sensor Volts Too High	Radiator coolant temperature sensor input above the maximum acceptable voltage.
P1199	Radiator Temperature Sensor Volts Too Low	Radiator coolant temperature sensor input below the minimum acceptable voltage.
P1281	Engine is Cold Too Long	Engine coolant temperature remains below normal operating temperatures during vehicle travel (Thermostat).
P1282	Fuel Pump Relay Control Circuit	An open or shorted condition detected in the fuel pump relay control circuit.
P1288	Intake Manifold Short Runner Solenoid Circuit	An open or shorted condition detected in the short runner tuning valve circuit.
P1289	Manifold Tune Valve Solenoid Circuit	An open or shorted condition detected in the manifold tuning valve solenoid control circuit.
P1290	CNG Fuel System Pressure Too High	Compressed natural gas system pressure above normal operating range.
P1291	No Temp Rise Seen From Intake Heaters	Energizing Heated Air Intake does not change intake air temperature sensor an acceptable amount.
P1292	CNG Pressure Sensor Voltage Too High	Compressed natural gas pressure sensor reading above acceptable voltage.
P1293	CNG Pressure Sensor Voltage Too Low	Compressed natural gas pressure sensor reading below acceptable voltage.
P1294 (M)	Target Idle Not Reached	Target RPM not achieved during drive idle condition. Possible vacuum leak or IAC (AIS) lost steps.
P1295	No 5 Volts to TP Sensor	Loss of a 5 volt feed to the Throttle Position Sensor has been detected.
P1296	No 5 Volts to MAP Sensor	Loss of a 5 volt feed to the MAP Sensor has been detected.

2.39 Diagnostic Trouble Code Identification Chart (6 of 9)

(M) Check Engine Lamp (MIL) will illuminate during engine operation if this Diagnostic Trouble Code was recorded.		
(G) Generator Lamp Illuminated		
P1297 (M)	No Change in MAP From Start To Run	No difference is recognized between the MAP reading at engine idle and the stored barometric pressure reading.
P1298	Lean Operation at Wide Open Throttle	A prolonged lean condition is detected during Wide Open Throttle.
P1299 (M)	Vacuum Leak Found (IAC Fully Seated)	MAP Sensor signal does not correlate to Throttle Position Sensor signal. Possible vacuum leak.
P1388	Auto Shutdown Relay Control Circuit	An open or shorted condition detected in the ASD or CNG shutoff relay control ckt.
P1389	No ASD Relay Output Voltage At PCM	No Z1 or Z2 voltage sensed when the auto shutdown relay is energized.
P1390 (M)	Timing Belt Skipped 1 Tooth or More	Relationship between Cam and Crank signals not correct.
P1391 (M)	Intermittent Loss of CMP or CKP	Loss of the Cam Position Sensor or Crank Position sensor has occurred. For PL 2.0L
P1398 (M)	Mis-Fire Adaptive Numerator at Limit	PCM is unable to learn the Crank Sensor's signal in preparation for Misfire Diagnostics. Probable defective Crank Sensor.
P1399	Wait To Start Lamp Cicuit	An open or shorted condition detected in the Wait to Start Lamp circuit.
P1403		Loss of 5v feed to the EGR position sensor.
P1476	Too Little Secondary Air	Insufficient flow of secondary air injection detected during aspirator test.(was P0411)
P1477	Too Much Secondary Air	Excessive flow of secondary air injection detected during aspirator test (was P0411).
P1478 (M)	Battery Temp Sensor Volts Out of Limit	Internal temperature sensor input voltage out of an acceptable range.
P1479	Transmission Fan Relay Circuit	An open or shorted condition detected in the transmission fan relay circuit.
P1480	PCV Solenoid Circuit	An open or shorted condition detected in the PCV solenoid circuit.
P1481		EATX RPM pulse generator signal for misfire detection does not correlate with expected value.
P1482	Catalyst Temperature Sensor Circuit Shorted Low	Catalyst temperature sensor circuit shorted low.
P1483	Catalyst Temperature Sensor Circuit Shorted High.	Catalyst temperature sensor circuit shorted high.
P1484	Catalytic Converter Overheat Detected	A catalyst overheat condition has been detected by the catalyst temperature sensor.
P1485	Air Injection Solenoid Circuit	An open or shorted condition detected in the air assist solenoid circuit.
P1486 (M)	Evap Leak Monitor Pinched Hose Found	LDP has detected a pinched hose in the evaporative hose system.
P1487	Hi Speed Rad Fan CTRL Relay Circuit	An open or shorted condition detected in the control circuit of the #2 high speed radiator fan control relay.
P1488	Auxiliary 5 Volt Supply Output Too Low	Auxiliary 5 volt sensor feed is sensed to be below an acceptable limit.

2.39 Diagnostic Trouble Code Identification Chart (7 of 9)

(M) Check Engine Lamp (MIL) will illuminate during engine operation if this Diagnostic Trouble Code was recorded.		
(G) Generator Lamp Illuminated		
P1489 (M)	High Speed Fan CTRL Relay Circuit	An open or shorted condition detected in the control circuit of the high speed radiator fan control relay.
P1490 (M)	Low Speed Fan CTRL Relay Circuit	An open or shorted condition detected in control circuit of the low speed radiator fan control relay.
P1491	Rad Fan Control Relay Circuit	An open or shorted condition detected in the radiator fan control relay control circuit. This includes PWM solid state relays.
P1492 (M,G)	Ambient/Batt Temp Sen Volts Too High	External temperature sensor input above acceptable voltage.
P1493 (M,G)	Ambient/Batt Temp Sen Volts Too Low	External temperature sensor input below acceptable voltage.
P1494 (M)	Leak Detection Pump Sw or Mechanical Fault	Incorrect input state detected for the Leak Detection Pump (LDP) pressure switch.
P1495 (M)	Leak Detection Pump Solenoid Circuit	An open or shorted condition detected in the Leak Detection Pump (LDP) solenoid circuit.
P1496 (M)	5 Volt Supply, Output Too Low	5 volt sensor feed is sensed to be below an acceptable limit. (< 4v for 4 sec).
P1498	High Speed Rad Fan Ground CTRL Rly Circuit	An open or shorted condition detected in the control circuit of the #3 high speed radiator fan control relay.
P1594 (G)	Charging System Voltage Too High	Battery voltage sense input above target charging voltage during engine operation.
P1595	Speed Control Solenoid Circuits	An open or shorted condition detected in either of the speed control vacuum or vent solenoid control circuits.
P1596	Speed Control Switch Always High	Speed control switch input above maximum acceptable voltage.
P1597	Speed Control Switch Always Low	Speed control switch input below minimum acceptable voltage.
P1598	A/C Pressure Sensor Volts Too High	A/C pressure sensor input above maximum acceptable voltage.
P1599	A/C Pressure Sensor Volts Too Low	A/C pressure sensor input below minimum acceptable voltage.
P1680	Clutch Released Switch Circuit	
P1681	No I/P Cluster CCD/J1850 Messages Received	No CCD/J1850 messages received from the cluster control module.
P1682 (G)	Charging System Voltage Too Low	Battery voltage sense input below target charging voltage during engine operation and no significant change in voltage detected during active test of generator output circuit.
P1683	SPD CTRL PWR Relay; or S/C 12v Driver CKT	An open or shorted condition detected in the speed control servo power control circuit. (SBECII: ext relay).
P1684		The battery has been disconnected within the last 50 starts.
P1685	Skim Invalid Key	The engine controler has received an invalid key from the SKIM.
P1686	No SKIM BUS Messages Received	No CCD/J1850 messages received from the Smart Key Immobilizer Module (SKIM).

2.39 Diagnostic Trouble Code Identification Chart (8 of 9)

(M) Check Engine Lamp (MIL) will illuminate during engine operation if this Diagnostic Trouble Code was recorded.		
(G) Generator Lamp Illuminated		
P1687	No MIC BUS Message	No CCD/J1850 messages received from the Mechanical Instrument Cluster (MIC) module.
P1693	DTC Detected in Companion Module	A fault has been generated in the companion engine control module.
P1694	Fault In Companion Module	No CCD/J1850 messages received from the powertrain control module-Aisin transmission.
P1695	No CCD/J1850 Message From Body Control Module	No CCD/J1850 messages received from the body control module.
P1696 (M)	PCM Failure EEPROM Write Denied	Unsuccessful attempt to write to an EEPROM location by the control module.
P1697 (M)	PCM Failure SRI Mile Not Stored	Unsuccessful attempt to update Service Reminder Indicator (SRI or EMR) mileage in the control module EEPROM.
P1698 (M)	No CCD/J1850 Message From TCM	No CCD/J1850 messages received from the electronic transmission control module (EATX) or the Aisin transmission controller.
P1719	Skip Shift Solenoid Circuit	An open or shorted condition detected in the transmission 2-3 gear lock-out solenoid control circuit.
P1740		A rationality error has been detected in either the tcc solenoid or overdrive solenoid systems.
P1756	GOV Press Not Equal to Target @ 15-20 PSI	The requested pressure and the actual pressure are not within a tolerance band for the Governor Control System which is used to regulate governor pressure to control shifts for 1st, 2nd, and 3rd gear. (Mid Pressure Malfunction)
P1757	GOV Press Not Equal to Target @ 15-20 PSI	The requested pressure and the actual pressure are not within a tolerance band for the Governor Control System which is used to regulate governor pressure to control shifts for 1st, 2nd, and 3rd gear (Zero Pressure Malfunction)
P1762	Gov Press Sen Offset Volts Too Lo or High	The Governor Pressure Sensor input is greater than a calibration limit or is less than a calibration limit for 3 consecutive park/neutral calibrations.
P1763	Governor Pressure Sensor Volts Too Hi	The Governor Pressure Sensor input is above an acceptable voltage level.
P1764	Governor Pressure Sensor Volts Too Low	The Governor Pressure Sensor input is below an acceptable voltage level.
P1765	Trans 12 Volt Supply Relay CTRL Circuit	An open or shorted condition is detected in the Transmission Relay control circuit. This relay supplies power to the TCC
P1899 (M)	P/N Switch Stuck in Park or in Gear	Incorrect input state detected for the Park/Neutral switch.

2.39 Diagnostic Trouble Code Identification Chart (9 of 9)

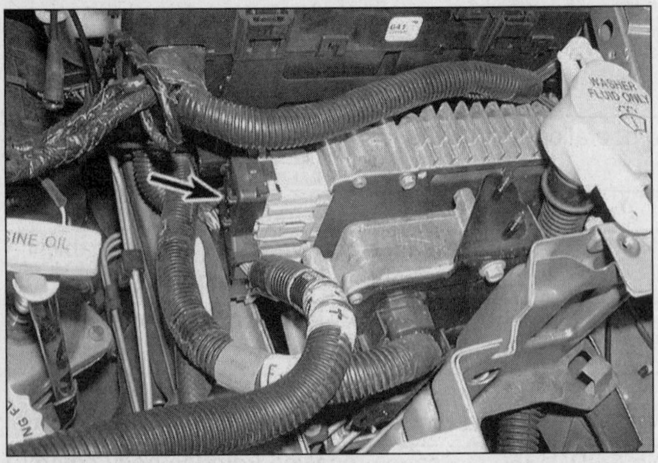

3.5a Disconnect the electrical connectors (arrow) from the PCM

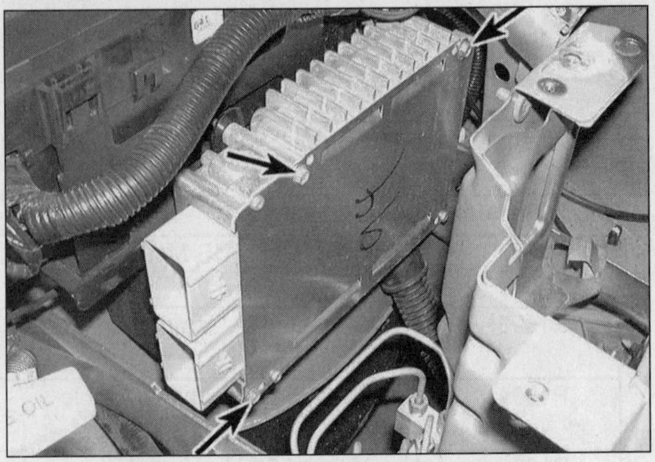

3.5b Remove the PCM mounting bolts (arrows)

4.2 The TPS (arrow) is located on the side of the throttle body

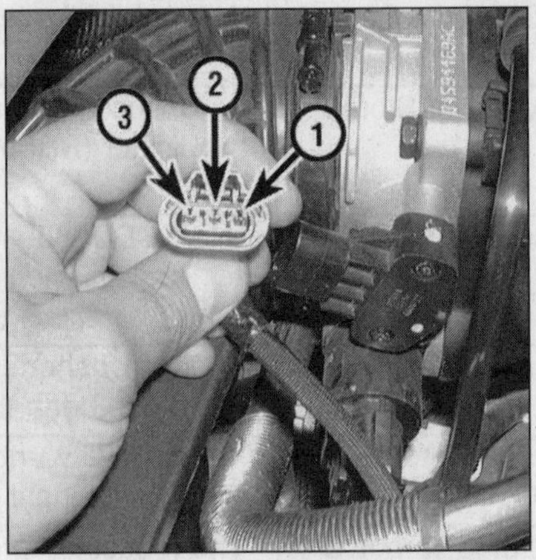

4.3a Disconnect the electrical connector from the TPS and check the voltage supply and ground circuits from the PCM at the harness connector - 2.7L model

1 *5-volt supply*
2 *Throttle position sensor signal*
3 *Sensor ground*

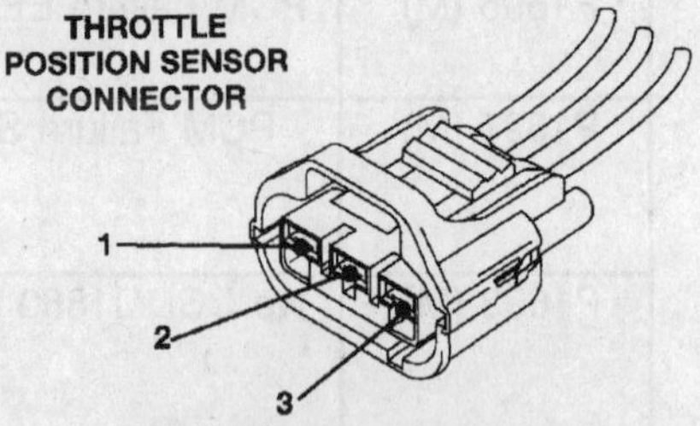

CAV	COLOR	FUNCTION
1	VT/WT	5-VOLT SUPPLY
2	OR/DB	TP SENSOR SIGNAL
3	BK/LB	SENSOR GROUND

4.3b Throttle position sensor harness connector terminal identification - 3.2L/3.5L models

3 Powertrain Control Module - removal and installation

Refer to illustrations 3.5a and 3.5b

Caution: *Avoid static electricity damage to the Powertrain Control Module (PCM) by grounding yourself to the body of the vehicle before touching the PCM and using a special anti-static pad to store the PCM on, once it is removed.*

Note 1: *Anytime the battery is disconnected stored operating parameters may be lost from the PCM causing the engine to run rough for sometime while the PCM relearns the information.*

Note 2: *Anytime the PCM is replaced with a new unit the Vehicle Identification Number and current mileage must be programmed into the new PCM with a Scan tool, if this is not done a diagnostic trouble code will be set. On models equipped with a Sentry Key Immobilizer System, the PCM must be programmed to accept the ignition keys or the engine will not start.*

1 Disconnect the negative battery cable from the remote ground terminal (see Chapter 5).

2 Remove the cruise control servo and bracket and position the unit aside.

3 Remove the windshield washer bottle filler neck.

4 Remove the Transmission Control Module and position the unit and wiring harness aside.

5 Disconnect the electrical connectors from the PCM. Remove the bolts that retain the PCM to the mounting bracket and remove the unit from the engine compartment **(see illustrations)**.

6 Installation is the reverse of removal.

4 Throttle position sensor - check and replacement

1 The Throttle Position Sensor (TPS) is a variable potentiometer connected to the end of the throttle shaft on the throttle body. By monitoring the output voltage from the TPS, the PCM can determine fuel delivery based on throttle valve angle (driver demand). A broken or loose TPS can cause intermittent bursts of fuel from the injectors and an unstable idle because the PCM thinks the throttle is moving.

Check

Refer to illustrations 4.2, 4.3a, 4.3b and 4.4

Note: *Performing the following test will set a diagnostic trouble code and illuminate the Check Engine light. Be prepared to clear the diagnostic trouble code after performing the tests and making the necessary repairs (see Section 2).*

2 The Throttle Position Sensor (TPS) is located on the side of the throttle body **(see illustration)**. Check the terminals in the connector and the wires leading to the sensor for looseness and breaks. Repair as required.

3 Before checking the TPS, check the voltage supply and ground circuits from the PCM. Disconnect the electrical connector from the TPS and connect the positive lead of a voltmeter to the violet/white wire terminal and the negative lead to the black/light blue wire terminal at the harness connector **(see illustrations)**. Turn the ignition key On - the voltage should read approximately 5.0 volts. If the voltage is incorrect, check the wiring

4.4 To check the TPS, backprobe the center wire terminal of the TPS connector with a voltmeter

4.6 Remove the TPS mounting screws (arrows)

5.2a The MAP sensor is located on the upper intake manifold - 2.7L models

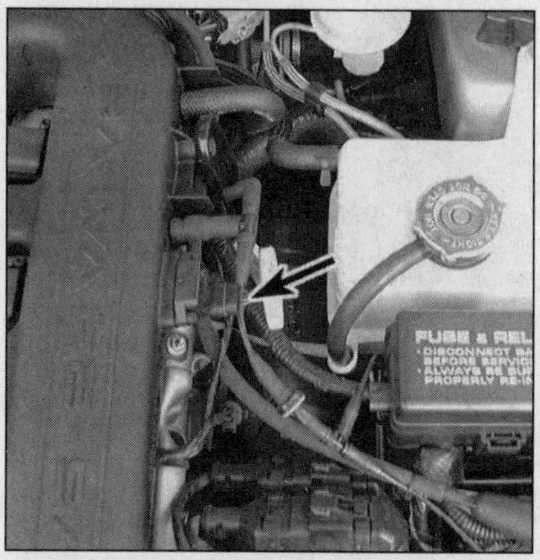

5.2b The MAP/IAT sensor is located on the side of the upper intake manifold - 3.2L/3.5L models

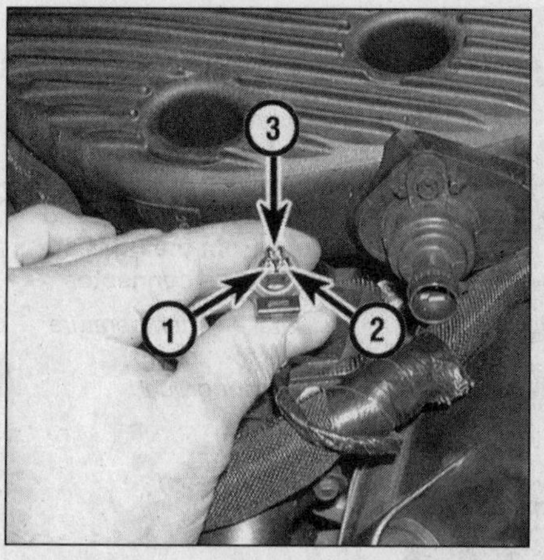

5.3a Disconnect the electrical connector from the MAP and check the voltage supply and ground circuits from the PCM at the harness connector - 2.7L model

1 *Sensor ground*
2 *5-volt supply*
3 *MAP sensor signal*

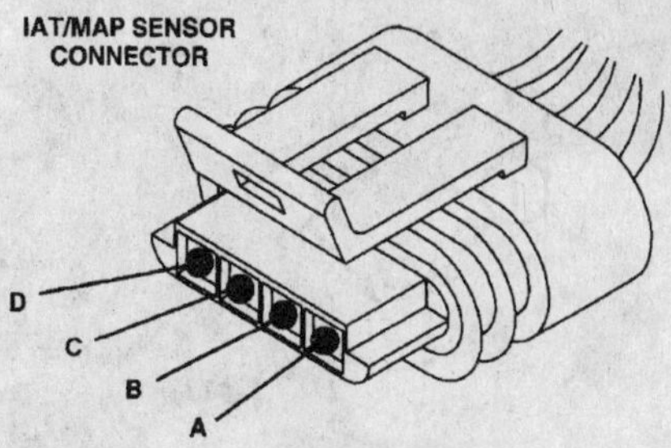

CAV	COLOR	FUNCTION
A	BK/LB	SENSOR GROUND
B	BK/RD	INTAKE AIR TEMP SENSOR SIGNAL
C	VT/WT	5V SUPPLY
D	DG/RD	MAP SENSOR SIGNAL

5.3b MAP/IAT sensor harness connector terminal identification - 3.2L/3.5L models

from the TPS to the PCM. If the circuits are good, have the PCM checked at a dealer service department or other properly equipped repair facility.

4 To check the TPS operation, reconnect the connector to the TPS and using a suitable probe, backprobe the center wire terminal of the TPS connector **(see Illustration)** (see Chapter 12 for additional information on how to backprobe a connector). Connect the positive lead of a voltmeter to the probe and the negative lead to a good engine ground point. Turn the ignition key On - with the throttle fully closed the voltage should read approximately 0.6 volts. Gradually open the throttle - the voltage should increase smoothly to approximately 4.5 volts at wide-open throttle. If the test results are incorrect, replace the TPS.

Replacement

Refer to illustration 4.6

5 Disconnect the electrical connector from the TPS.

6 Remove the TPS mounting screws and remove the TPS from the throttle body **(see illustration).**

7 When installing the TPS, align the socket locating tabs on the TPS with the throttle shaft in the throttle body and rotate the TPS slightly clockwise to align the mounting holes. If the TPS is difficult to rotate or the throttle plate opens, pull the TPS back and align the throttle shaft on the other side of the locating tabs.

8 Installation is the reverse of removal.

5 Manifold absolute pressure sensor - check and replacement

1 The Manifold Absolute Pressure (MAP) sensor monitors the intake manifold pressure changes resulting from changes in engine load and speed and converts the information into a voltage output. The PCM uses the MAP sensor to control fuel delivery and ignition timing. The PCM receives information as a voltage signal varying from 0.5 to 1.8 volts at closed throttle (high vacuum) and 3.9 to 4.8 volts at wide open throttle (low vacuum).

Check

Refer to illustrations 5.2a, 5.2b, 5.3a, 5.3b and 5.4

Note: *Performing the following test will set a diagnostic trouble code and illuminate the Check Engine light. Be prepared to clear the diagnostic trouble code after performing the tests and making the necessary repairs (see Section 2).*

2 The MAP sensor is located on the left (drivers) side of the upper intake manifold plenum **(see Illustrations)**. Check the terminals in the connector and the wires leading to the sensor for looseness and breaks. Repair as required.

3 Before checking the MAP sensor, check the voltage supply and ground circuits from the PCM. Disconnect the electrical connector from the MAP sensor and connect the positive lead of a voltmeter to the violet/white wire terminal and the negative lead to the black/light blue wire terminal at the harness connector **(see illustrations)**. Turn the ignition key On - the voltage should read approx-

5.4 To check the MAP sensor, backprobe the dark green/red wire terminal of the MAP sensor connector with a voltmeter

5.6 Remove the MAP sensor mounting screws (arrows)

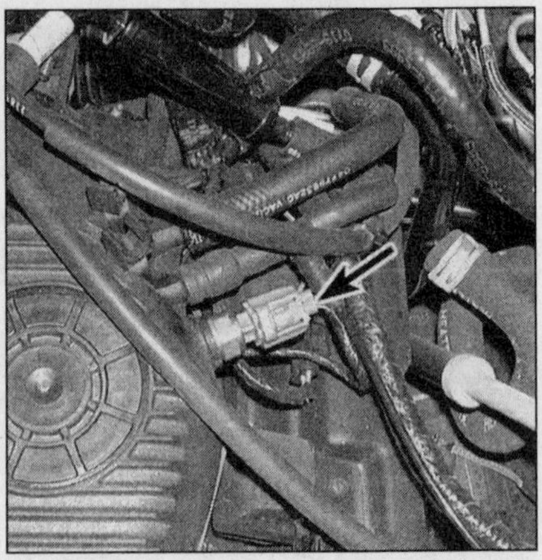

6.2 Intake air temperature sensor location - 2.7L models

6.3 Disconnect the electrical connector from the intake air temperature sensor and check the voltage supply and ground circuits from the PCM at the harness connector

1 *Intake air temperature sensor signal*
2 *Sensor ground*

6.4a MAP/IAT sensor terminal identification - 3.2L/3.5L models

A *Sensor ground*
B *Intake air temperature sensor signal*
C *5-volt supply*
D *MAP sensor signal*

imately 5.0 volts. If the voltage is incorrect, check the wiring from the MAP sensor to the PCM. If the circuits are good, have the PCM checked at a dealer service department or other properly equipped repair facility.

4 To check the MAP sensor operation, reconnect the connector to the MAP sensor and using a suitable probe, backprobe the dark green/red wire terminal of the MAP sensor connector **(see Illustration)** (see Chapter 12 for additional information on how to backprobe a connector). Connect the positive lead of a voltmeter to the probe and the negative lead to a good engine ground point. Turn the ignition key On - with the engine <u>not</u> running the voltage should read 4.0 to 5.0 volts. Start the engine and allow it to idle - the voltage should decrease to approximately 0.5 to 2.0 volts. If the test results are incorrect, replace the MAP sensor.

Replacement

Refer to illustration 5.6

5 Disconnect the electrical connector from the MAP sensor.

6 Remove the screws that retain the MAP sensor to the upper intake manifold plenum **(see illustration)**. Remove the MAP sensor.

7 Installation is the reverse of removal.

6 Intake air temperature sensor - check and replacement

1 The intake air temperature sensor is a thermistor (a resistor which varies the value of its resistance in accordance with temperature changes). The change in the resistance values will directly affect the voltage signal from the sensor to the PCM. As the sensor temperature INCREASES, the resistance values will DECREASE. As the sensor temperature DECREASES, the resistance values will INCREASE.

Check

Refer to illustrations 6.2, 6.3a, 6.3b, 6.4a and 6.4b

Note: *Performing the following test will set a diagnostic trouble code and illuminate the Check Engine light. Be prepared to clear the diagnostic trouble code after performing the tests and making the necessary repairs (see Section 2).*

2 On 2.7L models, the intake air temperature sensor is located on the left (drivers) side of the intake manifold plenum **(see Illustration)**. On 3.2L/3.5L models, the intake air temperature sensor is incorporated within the MAP sensor (see Section 5). Check the terminals in the connector and the wires leading to the sensor for looseness and breaks. Repair as required.

3 Before checking the intake air temperature sensor, check the voltage supply and ground circuits from the PCM. Disconnect the electrical connector from the intake air temperature sensor (2.7L) or manifold absolute pressure sensor (3.2L/3.5L) and connect the positive lead a voltmeter to the black/red wire terminal and the negative lead to the black/light blue wire terminal at the harness connector **(see the accompanying illustration and illustration 5.3b)**. Turn the ignition key On - the voltage should read approximately 5.0 volts. If the voltage is incorrect, check the wiring from the sensor to the PCM. If the circuits are good, have the PCM checked at a dealer service department or other properly equipped repair facility.

4 With the ignition switch OFF, disconnect the electrical connector from the intake air temperature sensor (2.7L) or manifold absolute

TEMPERATURE		RESISTANCE (OHMS)	
C	F	MIN	MAX
-40	-40	291,490	381,710
-20	-4	85,850	108,390
-10	14	49,250	61,430
0	32	29,330	35,990
10	50	17,990	21,810
20	68	11,370	13,610
25	77	9,120	10,880
30	86	7,370	8,750
40	104	4,900	5,750
50	122	3,330	3,880
60	140	2,310	2,670
70	158	1,630	1,870
80	176	1,170	1,340
90	194	860	970
100	212	640	720
110	230	480	540
120	248	370	410

6.4b Intake air temperature sensor and engine coolant temperature sensor approximate temperature vs. resistance values

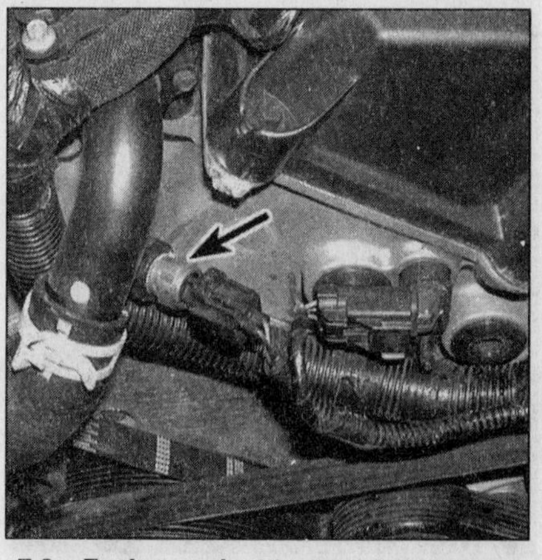

7.2a Engine coolant temperature sensor location - 2.7L models

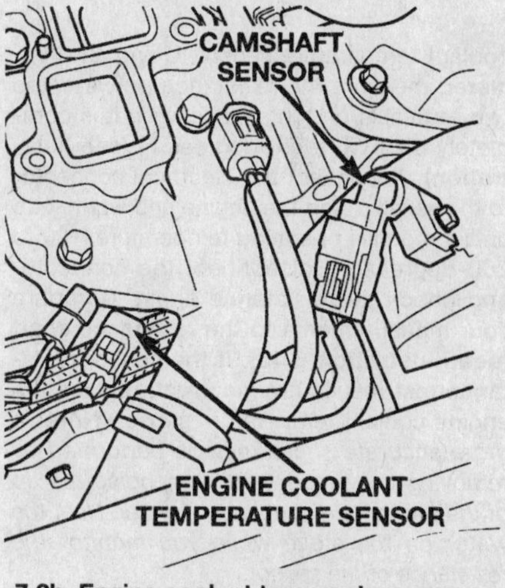

7.2b Engine coolant temperature sensor location - 3.2L/3.5L models

pressure sensor (3.2L/3.5L). Using an ohmmeter, measure the resistance between the two intake air temperature sensor terminals on the sensor while it is completely cold (50 to 80-degrees F) **(see Illustration)**. Reconnect the electrical connector to the sensor, start the engine and warm it up until it reaches operating temperature (180 to 200-degrees F), disconnect the connector and check the resistance again. Compare your measurements to the resistance chart **(see Illustration)**. If the sensor resistance test results are incorrect, replace the intake air temperature sensor. **Note:** *A more accurate check may be performed by removing the sensor and suspending the tip of the sensor in a container of water. Heat the water on the stove while you monitor the resistance of the sensor.*

Replacement

5 Disconnect the electrical connector from the sensor.

6 On 2.7L models, unscrew the sensor from the intake manifold and remove the intake air temperature sensor.

7 On 3.2L/3.5L models, replace the manifold absolute pressure sensor (see Section 5).

8 Installation is the reverse of removal.

7 Engine coolant temperature sensor - check and replacement

1 The engine coolant temperature sensor is a thermistor (a resistor which varies the value of its resistance in accordance with temperature changes). The change in the resistance values will directly affect the voltage signal from the sensor to the PCM. As the sensor temperature INCREASES, the resistance values will DECREASE. As the sensor temperature DECREASES, the resistance values will INCREASE.

Check

Refer to illustrations 7.2a, 7.2b, 7.3 and 7.4

Note: *Performing the following test will set a diagnostic trouble code and illuminate the Check Engine light. Be prepared to clear the diagnostic trouble code after performing the tests and making the necessary repairs (see Section 2).*

2 The engine coolant temperature sensor threads into a coolant passage near the coolant outlet at the intake manifold **(see Illustrations)**. Check the terminals in the connector and the wires leading to the sensor for looseness and breaks. Repair as required.

3 Before checking the engine coolant temperature sensor, check the voltage supply and ground circuits from the PCM. Disconnect the electrical connector from the engine coolant temperature sensor and connect a voltmeter to the two terminals of the harness connector **(see illustration)**. Turn the ignition key On - the voltage should read approximately 5.0 volts. If the voltage is incorrect, check the wiring from the engine coolant temperature sensor to the PCM. If the circuits are good, have the PCM checked at a dealer service department or other properly equipped repair facility.

4 With the ignition switch OFF, disconnect the electrical connector from the engine

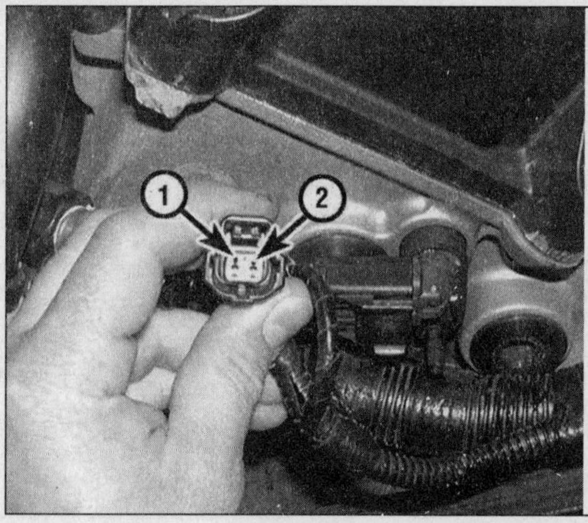

7.3 Disconnect the electrical connector from the engine coolant air temperature sensor and check the voltage supply and ground circuits from the PCM at the harness connector

1 *Engine coolant temperature sensor signal*

2 *Sensor ground*

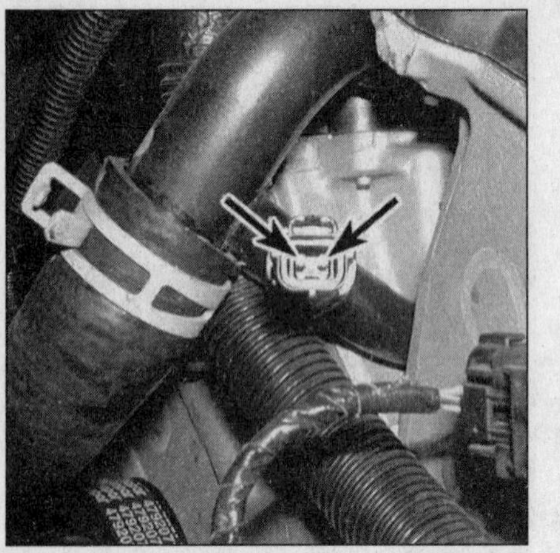

7.4 Measure the resistance of the coolant temperature sensor across the two terminals of the sensor

8.2 The crankshaft position sensor is located at the right (passenger) side of the transaxle bellhousing

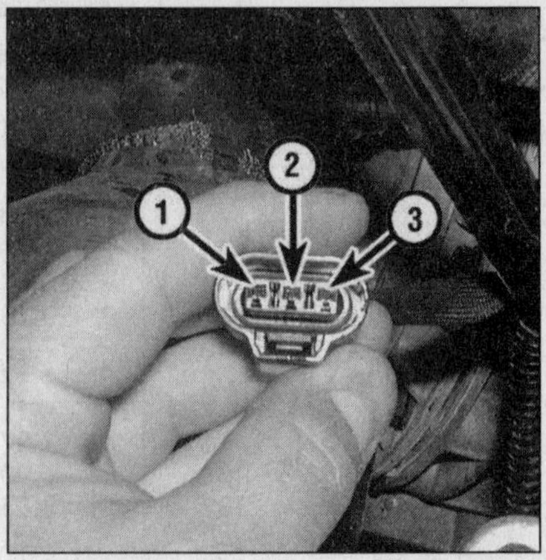

8.3 Disconnect the electrical connector from the crankshaft position sensor and check the voltage supply and ground circuits at the harness connector

1 Crankshaft position sensor signal
2 Sensor ground
3 8-volt supply

coolant temperature sensor. Using an ohmmeter, measure the resistance between the two terminals on the sensor while it is completely cold (50 to 80-degrees F) **(see Illustration)**. Reconnect the electrical connector to the sensor, start the engine and warm it up until it reaches operating temperature (180 to 200-degrees F), disconnect the connector and check the resistance again. Compare your measurements to the resistance chart **(see Illustration 6.4a)**. If the sensor resistance test results are incorrect, replace the engine coolant temperature sensor. **Note:** *A more accurate check may be performed by removing the sensor and suspending the tip of the sensor in a container of water. Heat the water on the stove while you monitor the resistance of the sensor.*

Replacement

Warning: *Wait until the engine is completely cool before beginning this procedure.*

5 Partially drain the cooling system (see Chapter 1).

6 Disconnect the electrical connector from the sensor and carefully unscrew the sensor. **Caution:** *Handle the coolant sensor with care. Damage to this sensor will affect the operation of the entire fuel injection system.*

7 Before installing the new sensor, wrap the threads with Teflon sealing tape to prevent leakage and thread corrosion.

8 Installation is the reverse of removal.

8 Crankshaft position sensor - check and replacement

1 The crankshaft position sensor determines the timing for the fuel injection and ignition on each cylinder. It also detects engine RPM. The crankshaft position sensor is a Hall-Effect device triggered by slots cut into the transaxle driveplate. The ignition system will not operate if the PCM does not receive a crankshaft position sensor input.

Check

Refer to illustrations 8.2, 8.3 and 8.4

Note 1: *Performing the following test will set a diagnostic trouble code and illuminate the Check Engine light. Be prepared to clear the diagnostic trouble code after performing the tests and making the necessary repairs (see Section 2).*

Note 2: *An analog (non-digital) voltmeter is required to check the crankshaft position sensor operation.*

2 The crankshaft position sensor is located at the right (passenger) side of the transaxle bellhousing **(see Illustration)**. Check the terminals in the connector and the wires leading to the sensor for looseness and breaks. Repair as required.

3 Before checking the crankshaft position sensor, check the voltage supply and ground circuits from the PCM. Disconnect the electrical connector and connect the positive lead of a voltmeter to the orange wire terminal and the negative lead to the black/light blue wire terminal at the harness connector **(see Illustration)**. Turn the ignition key On - the voltage should read approximately 8.0 volts. If the voltage is incorrect, check the wiring from the crankshaft position sensor to the PCM. If the circuits are good, have the PCM checked at a dealer service department or other properly equipped repair facility.

4 To check the crankshaft position sensor operation, reconnect the connector to the crankshaft position sensor and using a suitable probe, backprobe the gray/black wire terminal of the crankshaft position sensor connector (see Chapter 12 for additional information on how to backprobe a connector). Connect the positive lead of an analog voltmeter to the probe and the negative lead to a good engine ground point. Turn the ignition key On. Rotate the engine slowly with a breaker bar and socket attached to the crankshaft pulley center bolt while watching the meter. The voltage should fluctuate between 0.0 and 5.0 volts as the slots in the driveplate pass the sensor **(see Illustration)**. If the test results are incorrect, replace the crankshaft position sensor. **Note:** *Rotate the engine slowly through at least one complete*

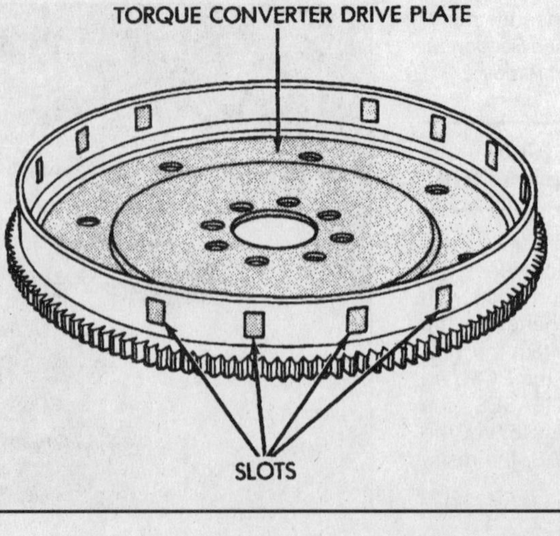

8.4 The crankshaft position sensor detects slots in the driveplate

8.6 Remove the crankshaft position sensor mounting bolt (arrow)

9.2 The camshaft position sensor is located at the left (driver's) side of the timing cover - 2.7L model

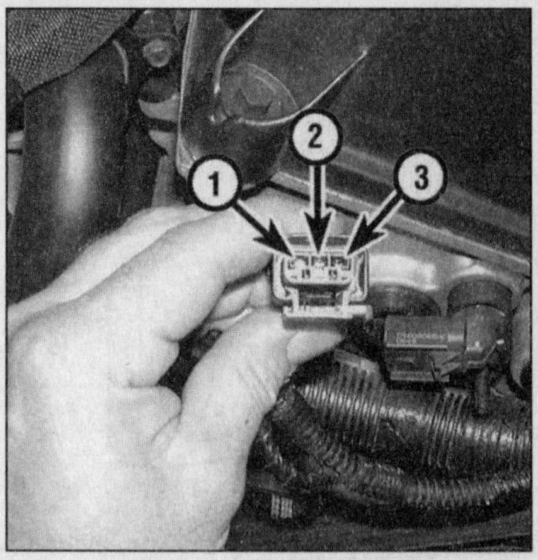

9.3 Disconnect the electrical connector from the camshaft position sensor and check the voltage supply and ground circuits at the harness connector

1. *8-volt supply*
2. *Sensor ground*
3. *Camshaft position sensor signal*

revolution. Removing the spark plugs from the engine will make the crankshaft much easier to turn.

Replacement

Refer to illustration 8.6

5 Disconnect the crankshaft sensor wiring harness connector.

6 Remove the crankshaft sensor mounting bolt and withdraw the sensor from the transaxle bellhousing **(see Illustration)**.

7 Installation is the reverse of removal. Tighten the mounting bolt to 105 in-lbs.

9 Camshaft position sensor - check and replacement

1 The camshaft position sensor, in conjunction with the crankshaft position sensor, determines the timing for the fuel injection on each cylinder. The camshaft position sensor is a Hall-Effect device triggered by notches in the camshaft sprocket.

Check

Refer to illustrations 9.2, 9.3 and 9.4

Note 1: *Performing the following test will set a diagnostic trouble code and illuminate the Check Engine light. Be prepared to clear the diagnostic trouble code after performing the tests and making the necessary repairs (see Section 2).*

Note 2: *An analog (non-digital) voltmeter is required to check the camshaft position sensor operation.*

2 The camshaft position sensor is located at the left (drivers) side of the timing cover **(see the accompanying Illustration and illustration 7.2b)**. Check the terminals in the connector and the wires leading to the sensor for looseness and breaks. Repair as required.

3 Before checking the camshaft position sensor, check the voltage supply and ground circuits from the PCM. Disconnect the electrical connector from the camshaft position sensor and connect the positive lead of a voltmeter to the orange wire terminal and the

9.4 To check the camshaft position sensor, backprobe the tan/yellow wire terminal of the sensor connector with a voltmeter

negative lead to the black/light blue wire terminal at the harness connector **(see illustration)**. Turn the ignition key On - the voltage should read approximately 8.0 volts. If the voltage is incorrect, check the wiring from the camshaft position sensor to the PCM. If the circuits are good, have the PCM checked at a dealer service department or other properly equipped repair facility.

4 To check the camshaft position sensor operation, reconnect the connector to the camshaft position sensor and using a suitable probe, backprobe the tan/yellow wire terminal of the camshaft position sensor connector **(see Illustration)** (see Chapter 12 for additional information on how to backprobe a connector). Connect the positive lead of an analog voltmeter to the probe and the negative lead to a good engine ground point. Turn the ignition key On. Rotate the engine slowly with a breaker bar and socket attached to the crankshaft pulley center bolt while watching the meter. The voltage should fluctuate between 0.0 and 5.0 volts as the notches in the camshaft sprocket pass the sensor **(see Illustration)**. If the test results are incorrect,

9.6 Remove the camshaft position sensor mounting bolt (arrow)

replace the camshaft position sensor. **Note:** *Rotate the engine slowly through at least two complete revolutions. Removing the spark plugs from the engine will make the crankshaft much easier to turn.*

Replacement

2.7L models

Refer to illustration 9.6

5 Disconnect the electrical connector from the camshaft position sensor.

6 Remove the camshaft position sensor mounting bolt and withdraw the sensor from the timing cover **(see illustration)**.

7 Installation is the reverse of removal. Tighten the mounting bolt to 105 in-lbs.

3.2L and 3.5L models

Refer to illustration 9.10

8 Remove the upper intake manifold (see Chapter 2B).

9 Remove the camshaft position sensor mounting bolt and withdraw the sensor from

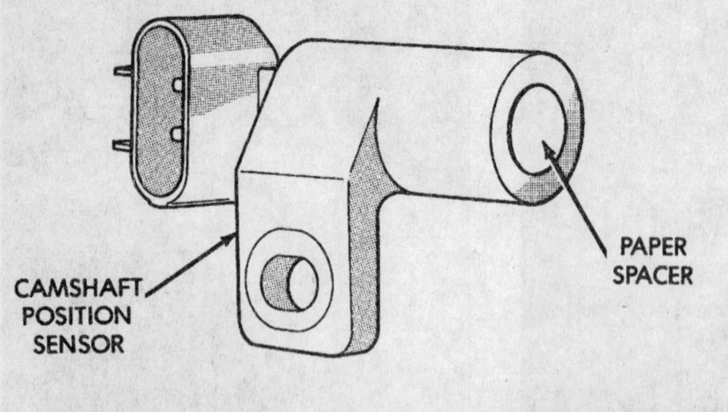

9.10 Before installing a new camshaft position sensor on a 3.2L/3.5L model, make sure the paper spacer is in place

10.3 The power steering pressure switch (arrow) is located in the high pressure line

the timing cover.

10 Before installing a new sensor, make sure the paper spacer is in place **(see illustration)**. If installing the original sensor, scrape off the original paper spacer and install a new paper spacer. **Caution:** *Failure to install the sensor with a paper spacer will result in damage to the sensor.*

11 Install the sensor in the timing cover and loosely install the mounting bolt. Lightly press the sensor in until the paper spacer contacts the camshaft sprocket and tighten the mounting bolt to 105 in-lbs.

12 The remainder of installation is the reverse of removal.

10 Power steering pressure switch - check and replacement

1 The power steering pressure switch is a normally closed switch, mounted in the pressure line between the steering gear and the power steering pump. When steering system pressure reaches a high-pressure setpoint, the switch opens and sends a signal to the PCM. The PCM uses the signal to maintain engine idle speed during parking maneuvers.

2 Check the operation of the power steering pressure switch if the engine stalls during parking or if the engine idles continuously at high rpm.

Check

Refer to illustration 10.3

3 Disconnect the power steering pressure switch connector and connect an ohmmeter to the terminals on the switch body **(see illustration)**.

4 Start the engine and allow it idle. **Warning:** *Make sure that the meter leads, loose clothing, long hair, etc. are away from the moving parts of the engine (drivebelt, cooling fan, etc.) before starting the engine.*

5 Turn the steering wheel to point the front wheels straight ahead and read the ohmmeter. It should indicate continuity (zero resistance).

6 Turn the steering wheel to either side and watch the ohmmeter. The power steering pressure switch should open as the wheel nears the steering stop on either side, and the meter should indicate no continuity (infinite resistance).

7 If the switch fails either test, replace it.

Replacement

8 Disconnect the electrical connector from the switch. Place a suitable drain pan under the power steering high pressure line.

9 Unscrew the switch from the high pressure line. Use a back-up wrench of the line block to prevent twisting the line.

10 Install and connect the new switch. Refer to Chapter 10 and bleed air from the power steering system. Add fluid as required (see Chapter 1).

11 Oxygen sensor - check and replacement

1 The oxygen in the exhaust reacts with the elements inside the oxygen sensor to produce a voltage output that varies from 0.1 volt (high oxygen, lean mixture) to 0.9 volt (low oxygen, rich mixture). The upstream oxygen sensor (mounted in the exhaust system before the catalytic converter) provides a feedback signal to the PCM that indicates the amount of leftover oxygen in the exhaust. The PCM monitors this variable voltage continuously to determine the required fuel injector pulse width and to control the engine air/fuel ratio. A mixture ratio of 14.7 parts air to 1 part fuel is the ideal ratio for minimum exhaust emissions, as well as the best combination of fuel economy and engine performance. Based on oxygen sensor signals, the PCM tries to maintain this air/fuel ratio of 14.7:1 at all times.

2 The downstream oxygen sensor (mounted in the exhaust system after the catalytic converter) has no effect on PCM control of the air/fuel ratio. However, the downstream sensor is identical to the upstream sensor and operates in the same way. The PCM uses the downstream signal to monitor the efficiency of the catalytic converter. A downstream oxygen sensor will produce a slower fluctuating voltage signal that reflects the lower oxygen content in the post-catalyst exhaust. **Note:** *All models are equipped with four oxygen sensors; two upstream oxygen sensors (one for each cylinder bank) and two downstream oxygen sensors (one for each catalytic converter).*

3 An oxygen sensor produces no voltage when it is below its normal operating temperature of about 600-degrees F. During this warm-up period, the PCM operates in an open-loop fuel control mode. It does not use the oxygen sensor signal as a feedback indication of residual oxygen in the exhaust. Instead, the PCM controls fuel metering based on the inputs of other sensors and its own programs.

4 Proper operation of an oxygen sensor depends on four conditions:

a) **Electrical** - *The low voltages generated by the sensor require good, clean connections which should be checked whenever a sensor problem is suspected or indicated.*

b) **Outside air supply** - *The sensor needs air circulation to the internal portion of the sensor. Whenever the sensor is installed, make sure the air passages are not restricted.*

c) **Proper operating temperature** - *The PCM will not react to the sensor signal until the sensor reaches approximately 600-degrees F. This factor must be considered when evaluating the performance of the sensor.*

d) **Unleaded fuel** - *Unleaded fuel is essential for proper operation of the sensor.*

5 The PCM can detect several different oxygen sensor problems and set diagnostic trouble codes to indicate the specific fault (see Section 2). When an oxygen sensor fault occurs, the PCM will disregard the oxygen sensor signal voltage and revert to open-loop fuel control as described previously.

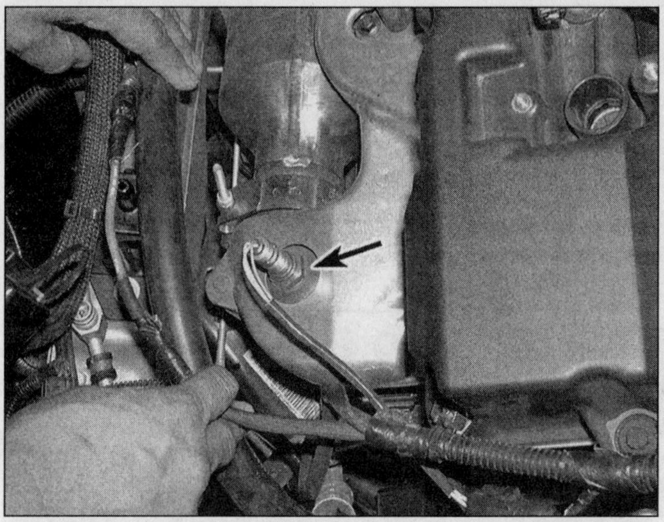

11.6a The upstream oxygen sensors (arrow) are located in the exhaust manifolds just ahead of the catalytic converters

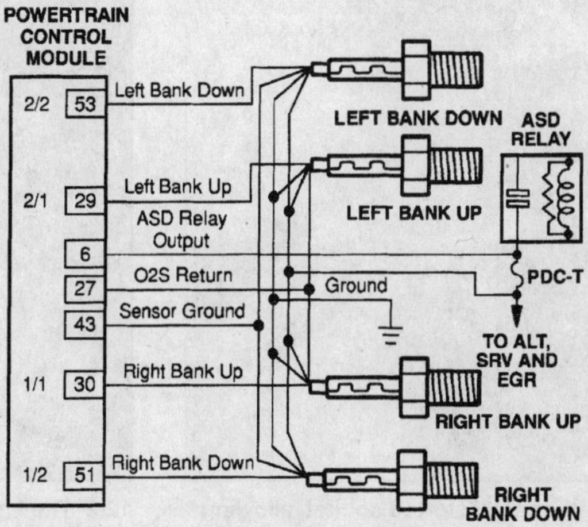

11.6b Typical oxygen sensor circuit - refer to the wiring diagrams to determine the exact wire colors for testing on your particular model

Check

Refer to illustrations 11.6a, 11.6b and 11.8

Caution: *The oxygen sensor is very sensitive to excessive circuit loads and circuit damage of any kind. For safest testing, disconnect the oxygen sensor connector, install jumper wires between the two connectors and connect your voltmeter to the jumper wires. If jumper wires aren't available, carefully backprobe the wires in the connector shell with suitable probes (such as T-pins). Do not puncture the oxygen sensor wires or try to backprobe the sensor itself. Use only a digital voltmeter to test an oxygen sensor.*

Note: *Performing the following test will set a diagnostic trouble code and illuminate the Check Engine light. Be prepared to clear the diagnostic trouble code after performing the tests and making the necessary repairs (see Section 2).*

6 Turn the ignition ON but do not start the engine. Connect your voltmeter negative (-) lead to a good ground and the positive (+) lead to the oxygen sensor signal wire at the oxygen sensor connector **(see illustrations)**. The meter should read approximately 400 to 450 millivolts (0.40 to 0.45 volt). If it doesn't, trace and repair the circuit from the sensor to the PCM. **Note:** *Refer to the wiring diagrams at the end of Chapter 12 to identify the signal wire by the color code.*

7 Start the engine and let it warm up to normal operating temperature; again check the oxygen sensor signal voltage.

a) *Voltage from an upstream sensor should range from 100 to 900 millivolts (0.1 to 0.9 volt) and switch actively between high and low readings.*
b) *Voltage from a downstream sensor should also read between 100 to 900 millivolts (0.1 to 0.9 volt) but it should not switch actively. The downstream oxygen sensor voltage may stay toward the center of its range (about 400 millivolts) or stay for relatively longer periods of time at the upper or lower limits of the range.*

8 Check the battery voltage supply and ground circuits to the oxygen sensor heater. Disconnect the electrical connector and connect the voltmeter negative (-) lead to the ground terminal and the positive (+) lead to the battery supply terminal of the sensor connector **(see illustration)**. With the ignition ON, the meter should read more than 10 volts. Battery voltage is supplied to the sensors through the ASD relay for only about three seconds when the engine is not running. Have an assistant turn the ignition ON while you read the voltmeter. Refer to the wiring diagrams in Chapter 12 for more information on the circuits and relays.

9 Check the resistance of the oxygen sensor heater. With the connector disconnected. Connect an ohmmeter to the two oxygen sensor terminals of the connector (oxygen sensor side). The oxygen sensor pigtail is generally not color coded, but the heater wires are usually the white wires. The oxygen sensor heater resistance should be 4.0 to 7.0 ohms. If an open circuit or excessive resistance is indicated, replace the oxygen sensor. **Note:** *If the tests indicate that a sensor is good, and not the cause of a driveability problem or diagnostic trouble code, check the wiring harness and connectors between the sensor and the PCM for an open or short circuit. If no problems are found, have the vehicle checked by a dealer service department or other qualified repair shop.*

Replacement

Refer to illustration 11.13

10 The exhaust pipe contracts when cool, and the oxygen sensor may be hard to loosen when the engine is cold. To make sensor removal easier, start and run the engine for a minute or two; then shut it off. Be careful not to burn yourself during the following procedure. Also observe these guidelines when replacing an oxygen sensor.

a) *The sensor has a permanently attached pigtail and electrical connector which should not be removed from the sensor. Damage or removal of the pigtail or electrical connector can harm operation of the sensor.*
b) *Keep grease, dirt and other contaminants away from the electrical connector and the louvered end of the sensor.*
c) *Do not use cleaning solvents of any kind on the oxygen sensor.*
d) *Do not drop or roughly handle the sensor.*

11 Raise the vehicle and place it securely on jackstands.

12 Disconnect the electrical connector

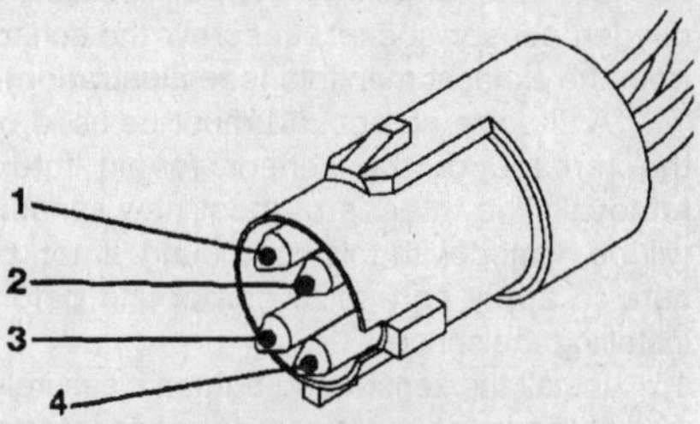

CAV	COLOR	FUNCTION
1	BK	ENGINE GROUND
2	OR/DG	ASD RELAY
3	BK/OR	1/1 02S RETURN
	BK/OR	2/1 02S RETURN
	BK/LB	1/2 SIGNAL RETURN
	BK/LB	2/2 SIGNAL RETURN
4	BK/DG	1/1 02S SIGNAL
	TN/WT	1/2 02S SIGNAL
	LG/RD	2/1 02S SIGNAL
	PK/WT	2/2 02S SIGNAL

11.8 Oxygen sensor terminal identification (looking into the face of the harness connector)

11.13 A special slotted socket, allowing clearance for the wiring harness, may be required for oxygen sensor removal (the tool is available at most auto parts stores)

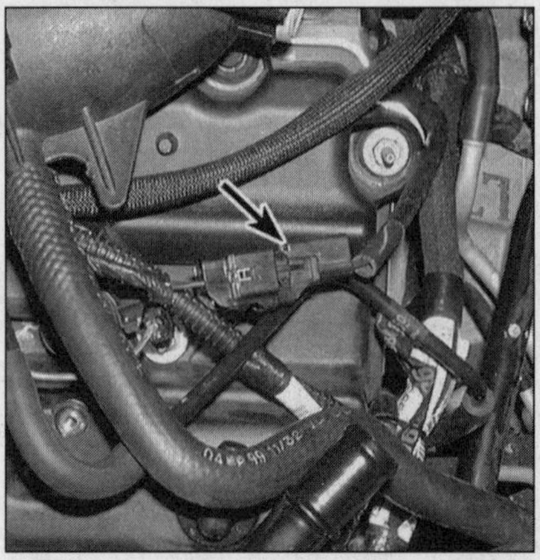

12.2 The knock sensor harness connector location - 2.7L model

12.6 The knock sensor is located under the intake manifold

from the sensor.

13 Using a suitable wrench or specialized oxygen sensor socket, unscrew the sensor from the exhaust manifold **(see illustration)**.

14 Anti-seize compound must be used on the threads of the sensor to aid future removal. The threads of most new sensors will be coated with this compound. If not, be sure to apply anti-seize compound before installing the sensor.

15 Install the sensor and tighten it securely.

16 Reconnect the electrical connector to the sensor and lower the vehicle.

12 Knock sensor - check and replacement

1 The knock sensor detects abnormal vibration (spark knock or pinging) in the engine. The knock control system is designed to reduce spark knock during periods of heavy detonation. This allows the engine to use maximum spark advance to improve driveability. Knock sensors produce AC output voltage which increases with the severity of the knock. The signal is fed into the PCM and the timing is retarded to compensate for the severe detonation. On all models, the knock sensor is located below the intake manifold.

Check

Refer to illustrations 12.2

2 Locate the knock sensor harness connector **(see illustration)**. Backprobe the electrical connector using suitable probes (see Chapter 12 for additional information on how to backprobe a connector). Connect the positive lead of a voltmeter to the knock sensor signal wire and the negative lead to the sensor ground. **Note:** *Refer to the wiring diagrams at the end of Chapter 12 to identify the signal wire and sensor ground by the color code.* Set the voltmeter on the AC volts scale. Start the engine and check for an AC voltage signal from the knock sensor. The AC voltage should increase as the engine speed increases. If a voltage signal is not present, replace the knock sensor.

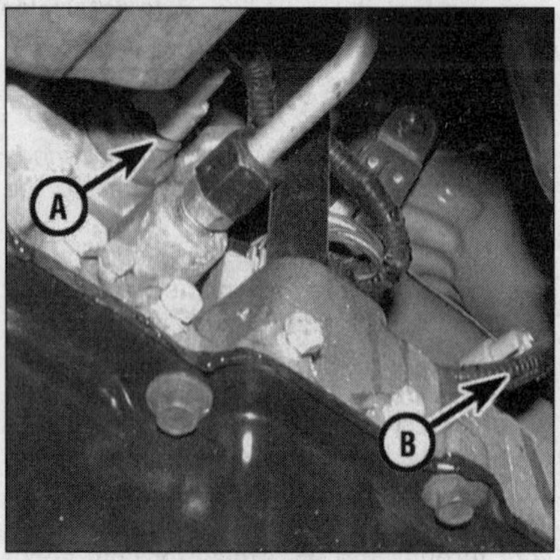

13.2 Vehicle speed sensor location (arrow)

A Input speed sensor
B Output speed sensor

Replacement

Refer to illustration 12.6

3 Remove the upper and lower intake manifolds (see Chapter 2A or 2B).

4 On 2.7L models, remove the right (passengers) side cylinder head (see Chapter 2A).

5 Disconnect the electrical connector from the knock sensor.

6 Remove the sensor from the engine block **(see illustration)**.

7 Installation is the reverse of removal. Tighten the knock sensor or knock sensor bolt to 7 ft-lbs.

13 Vehicle speed sensor - check and replacement

1 The Vehicle Speed Sensor (VSS) is a magnetic pick-up device mounted on the transaxle. The sensor is triggered by the parking pawl lugs as the transaxle output shaft rotates. It produces a pulsating voltage, the frequency of which is proportional to vehicle speed. The transaxle control module and the PCM use the sensor input signal for several different engine and transmission control functions. The VSS signal also drives the speedometer on the instrument panel. A defective VSS can cause various driveability and transaxle problems.

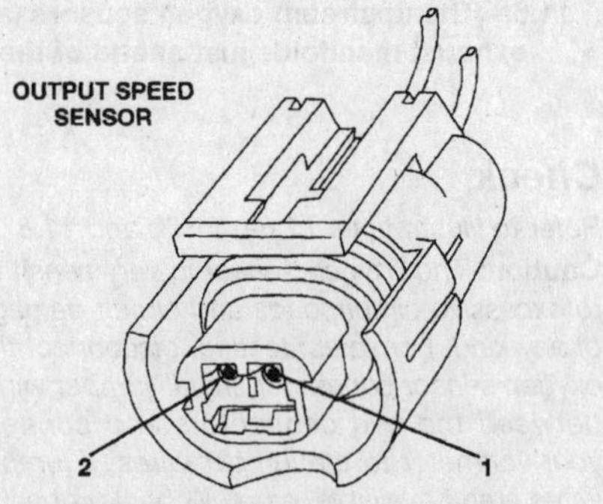

CAV	COLOR	FUNCTION
1	DB/BK	SPEED SENSOR GROUND
2	LG/WT	SPEED SENSOR SIGNAL

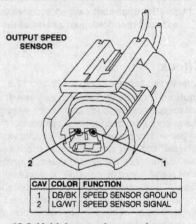

13.3 Vehicle speed sensor harness connector terminal identification

Check

Refer to illustrations 13.2 and 13.3

Note: *Performing the following test will set a diagnostic trouble code and illuminate the Check Engine light. Be prepared to clear the diagnostic trouble code after performing the tests and making the necessary repairs (see Section 2).*

2 Raise the vehicle and support it securely on jackstands. Locate the vehicle speed sensor **(see Illustration)**. Check the terminals in the connector and the wires leading to the sensor for looseness and breaks. Repair as required.

3 Before checking the VSS, check the voltage supply and ground circuits from the transaxle control module. Disconnect the

14.3 The IAC valve is located on the side of the throttle body

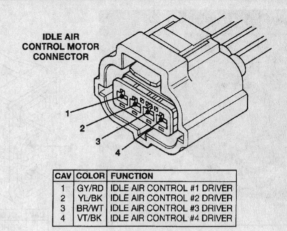

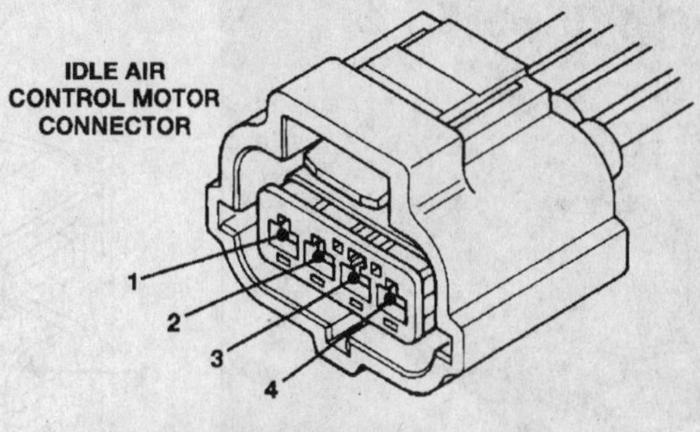

CAV	COLOR	FUNCTION
1	GY/RD	IDLE AIR CONTROL #1 DRIVER
2	YL/BK	IDLE AIR CONTROL #2 DRIVER
3	BR/WT	IDLE AIR CONTROL #3 DRIVER
4	VT/BK	IDLE AIR CONTROL #4 DRIVER

14.4 Idle air control valve harness connector terminal identification

electrical connector from the VSS and connect the positive lead of a voltmeter to the light green/white wire terminal and the negative lead to the dark blue/black wire terminal at the harness connector **(see Illustration)**. Turn the ignition key On - the voltage should read approximately 5.0 volts. If the voltage is incorrect, check the wiring from the VSS to the transaxle control module. If the circuits are good, have the system checked at a dealer service department or other properly equipped repair facility.

4 To check the VSS operation, reconnect the connector to the VSS and using a suitable probe, backprobe the light green/white wire terminal of the VSS connector (see Chapter 12 for additional information on how to backprobe a connector). Connect the positive lead of a voltmeter to the probe and the negative lead to a good chassis ground point. Turn the ignition key On.

5 With the help of an assistant, rotate both front tires by hand and in unison while watching the voltmeter, the voltage should fluctuate between zero and five volts as the transaxle output shaft rotates.

6 If the test results are incorrect, replace the vehicle speed sensor.

Replacement

7 Raise the vehicle and support it securely on jackstands.

8 Disconnect the electrical connector from the VSS.

9 Unscrew the VSS from the transaxle case.

10 Installation is the reverse of removal.

14 Idle air control valve - check and replacement

1 The idle speed is controlled by the Idle Air Control (IAC) valve, located on the throttle body. The IAC valve regulates the air bypassing the throttle plate by moving the pintle in or out of the air passage. The IAC valve is controlled by the PCM, adjusting the idle speed depending upon the running conditions of the engine (air conditioning system, power steering, cold and warm running etc.).

Check

Refer to illustrations 14.3 and 14.4

Note: *Performing the following test will set a diagnostic trouble code and illuminate the Check Engine light. Be prepared to clear the diagnostic trouble code after performing the tests and making the necessary repairs (see Section 2).*

2 A SCAN tool is required for complete testing of the IAC valve and circuits. However, there are several tests the home mechanic can perform on the IAC system to verify operation but they are limited and are useful only in the case of definite IAC valve failure.

3 When the engine is started cold, the IAC valve should vary the idle as the engine begins to warm-up. Allow the engine to warm-up, then disconnect the electrical connector from the IAC valve and listen carefully for a change in the idle **(see illustration)**. Connect the IAC valve electrical connector and place a load on the engine by placing the transmission in gear (automatic), turning the air conditioning on and/or operating the power steering. The idle should remain steady or increase slightly. If the engine stumbles or stalls, or if there are obvious signs that the IAC valve is not working, stop the engine and continue testing.

4 Disconnect the electrical connector from the IAC valve. Using an ohmmeter, measure the resistance across the two outside terminals of the IAC valve, then measure the resistance across the two inside terminals **(see Illustration)** - the resistance should be about the same on both sets. If one or both checks indicate an open circuit, replace the IAC valve.

5 If the IAC valve is good, have the PCM diagnosed by a dealer service department or other qualified repair shop.

14.7 Remove the idle air control valve mounting screws (arrows) and remove it from the throttle body

Replacement

Refer to illustration 14.7

6 Disconnect the electrical connector from the IAC valve.

7 Remove the two mounting screws from the valve and withdraw it from the throttle body **(see illustration)**.

8 Installation is the reverse of removal. Be sure to install a new O-ring.

15 Intake manifold tuning system

1 3.2L/3.5L models and 2000 and later 2.7L models are equipped with an intake manifold tuning system. The intake manifold tuning system consists of a manifold tuning valve, located in the upper intake manifold. 3.2L/3.5L models are also equipped with a short runner valve.

2 The manifold tuning valve opens a crossover passage between the two sides of the upper intake manifold plenum, improving the acoustical tuning qualities of the intake manifold. The PCM energizes the manifold tuning valve solenoid during wide-open throt-

15.5a The manifold tuning valve (arrow) is located at the front of the intake manifold

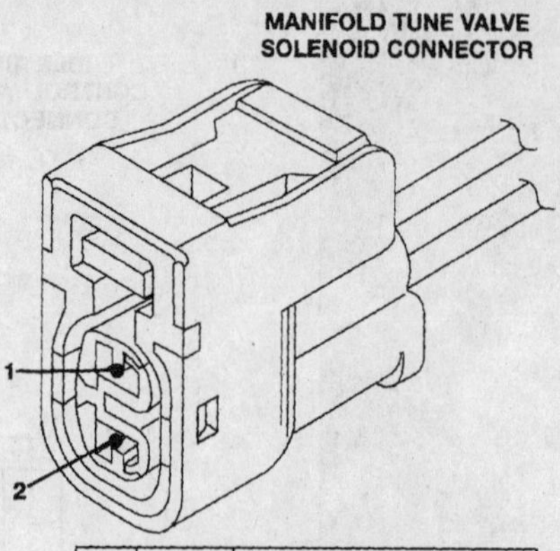

CAV	COLOR	FUNCTION
1	VT/RD	MTV SOLENOID CONTROL
2	DG/LG	ASD RELAY OUTPUT

15.5b Manifold tuning valve harness connector terminal identification

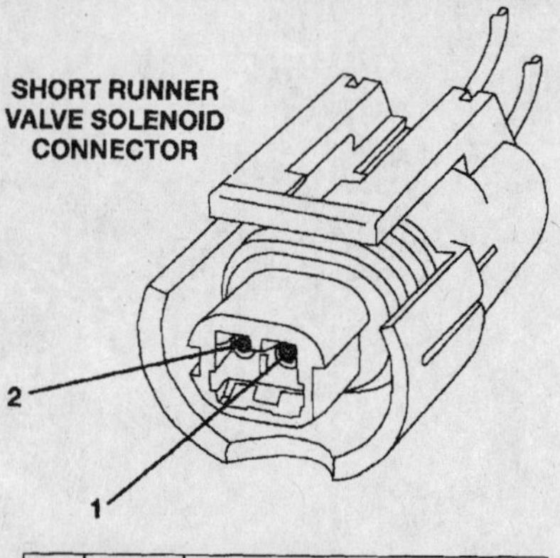

CAV	COLOR	FUNCTION
1	GY/PK	SRV SOLENOID CONTROL
2	OR/DG	FUSED ASD RELAY OUTPUT

15.9 Short runner valve harness connector terminal identification

15.17 Short runner valve vacuum reservoir and control solenoid location

15.20 Short runner valve actuator location

tle operation.

3 The short runner valve diverts the path of the incoming air through the intake manifold, one path being longer than the other. At low engine the short runner valve is closed and air is diverted through the longer path to enhance maximum torque at low speed. At a preset engine speed the PCM energizes the control solenoid, vacuum is applied to the actuator and the short runner valve opens. Air is then drawn through the shorter path enhancing high speed power.

Check

4 A SCAN tool is required for complete testing of the solenoids, valves and circuits. However, there are several tests the home mechanic can perform on the system to verify operation but they are limited and are useful only in the case of definite system failure.

Manifold tuning valve

Refer to illustrations 15.5a and 15.5b

5 Disconnect the electrical connector from the manifold tuning valve. Turn the ignition key On. Using a voltmeter, check for battery voltage at the dark green/light green wire terminal of the harness connector **(see Illustrations)**. If battery voltage is not present, check the ASD relay and the circuit from the ASD relay to the manifold tuning valve (check the fuses first) (see Chapter 12).

6 Using an ohmmeter, measure the resistance across the two terminals of the manifold tuning valve connector. Resistance should be between 10 and 20 ohms. If the resistance is not as specified, replace the manifold tuning valve.

7 If all the above tests are good, have the PCM diagnosed by a dealer service department or other qualified repair shop.

Short runner valve

Refer to illustration 15.9

8 Check the vacuum hoses from the vacuum source to the vacuum reservoir, control solenoid and actuator for leaks or damage. Check the vacuum reservoir to make sure it holds vacuum.

9 Disconnect the electrical connector from the short runner valve control solenoid. Turn the ignition key on and using a voltmeter, check for battery voltage at the orange/dark green terminal of the harness connector **(see Illustration)**. If battery voltage is not present, check the ASD relay and the circuit from the ASD relay to the short runner valve control solenoid (check the fuses first) (see Chapter 12).

10 Using an ohmmeter, measure the resistance across the two terminals of the short runner valve control solenoid connector. Resistance should be between 25 and 35 ohms. If the resistance is not as specified, replace the short runner valve control solenoid.

11 Remove the vacuum hose from the short runner valve actuator. Connect a hand-held vacuum pump to the actuator and apply vacuum. The rod should move and the actuator should hold vacuum. If it doesn't, replace the actuator.

12 If all the above tests are good, have the PCM diagnosed by a dealer service department or other qualified repair shop.

Component replacement

Manifold tuning valve

13 Disconnect the electrical connector from the manual tuning valve.

14 Remove the mounting bolts and withdraw the manual tuning valve from the upper intake manifold.

15 Installation is the reverse of removal.

Short runner valve vacuum reservoir and control solenoid

Refer to illustration 15.17

16 Remove the air filter housing cover and the air intake duct from the throttle body.

17 Disconnect the electrical connector from the solenoid and remove the vacuum hoses from the solenoid valve and vacuum reservoir **(see Illustration)**.

18 Remove the mounting nuts/bolts and remove the vacuum reservoir and solenoid valve assembly.

19 Installation is the reverse of removal.

Short runner valve actuator

Refer to illustration 15.20

20 Disconnect the actuator link from the

short runner valve lever at upper the intake manifold **(see Illustration)**.

21 Disconnect the vacuum hose from the actuator.

22 Remove the mounting bolts and remove the actuator.

23 Installation is the reverse of removal.

16 Positive crankcase ventilation system

Refer to illustrations 16.2a, 16.2b and 16.2c

1 The crankcase ventilation system reduces hydrocarbon emissions by scavenging crankcase vapors. It does this by circulating fresh air from the air cleaner through the crankcase, where it mixes with blow-by gases. The gases are drawn by intake manifold vacuum into the intake manifold, where they mix with the incoming air/fuel mixture and are consumed during normal combustion.

2 The main component of the Positive Crankcase Ventilation (PCV) system is the PCV valve **(see Illustrations)**. Fresh air flows from the air intake duct through a vent tube into the engine. Crankcase vapors are drawn from the crankcase by the PCV valve. To maintain idle quality and good driveability, the PCV valve restricts the flow when the intake manifold vacuum is high **(see Illustration)**. When intake manifold vacuum is lower, maximum vapor flow is allowed through the valve.

3 Checking and replacement of the PCV valve is covered in Chapter 1.

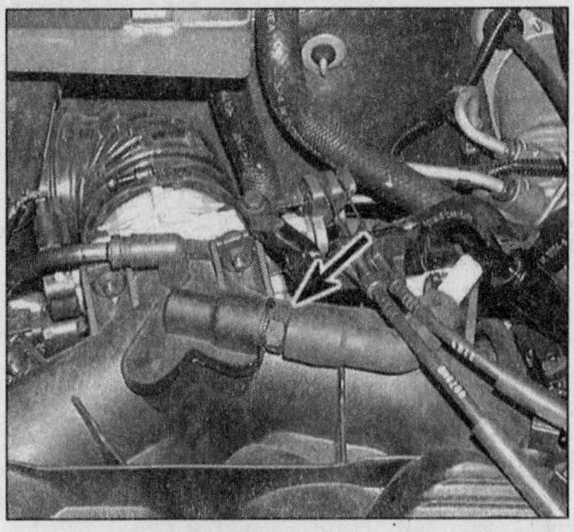

16.2a The PCV valve is located on the upper intake manifold - 2.7L engine

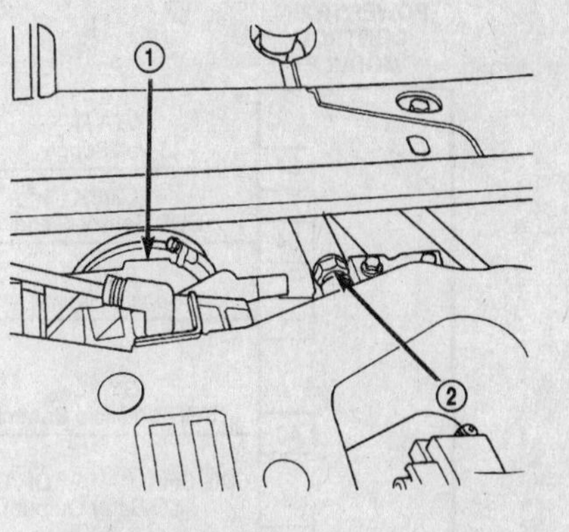

16.2b PCV valve location on 3.2L and 3.5L engines

1 Throttle body
2 PCV valve

17 Exhaust gas recirculation system

1 The Exhaust Gas Recirculation (EGR) system is used to lower NOx (oxides of nitrogen) emission levels caused by high combustion temperatures. The EGR valve recirculates a small amount of exhaust gases into the intake manifold. The additional mixture lowers the temperature of combustion thereby reducing the formation of NOx compounds.

2 The EGR system consists of an electronic EGR valve, an EGR valve position sensor, the EGR tubes and the PCM. The PCM controls the EGR flow rate by energizing the EGR valve solenoid coil, opening or closing the EGR passage in small increments. This system allows for precise control of EGR flow, achieving optimum EGR flow depending on engine operating conditions.

Check

Refer to illustrations 17.4a, 17.4b and 17.6

3 A SCAN tool is required for complete testing of the EGR valve, control system and circuits. However, there are several tests the home mechanic can perform on the system to verify operation but they are limited and are useful only in the case of definite system failure.

4 Check the power supply to the valve. Disconnect the electrical connector from the EGR valve. Connect the negative lead of a voltmeter to a good engine ground point and probe the orange/dark green wire terminal of the EGR valve electrical connector (harness side) with the positive lead **(see Illustrations)**. Turn the ignition key On - battery voltage should be indicated on the meter. If battery voltage is not indicated, check the circuit from the battery to the ASD relay (don't forget to check the fuses), the ASD relay and the circuit from the ASD relay to the EGR valve (see Chapter 12 and the wiring diagrams).

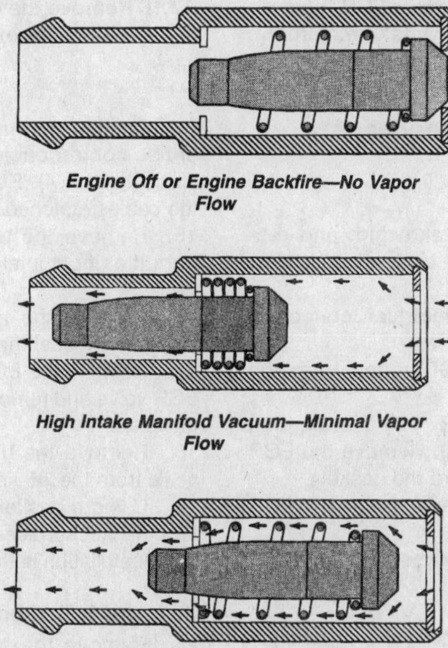

16.2c Typical PCV valve operation

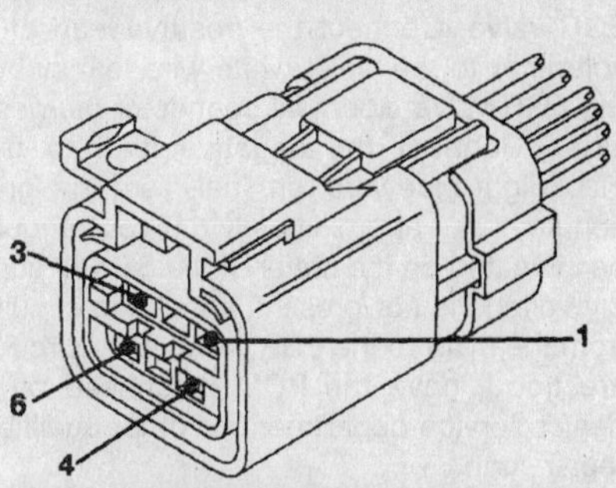

CAV	COLOR	FUNCTION
1	LG/PK	EGR SENSOR SIGNAL
2	VT/WT	5-VOLT SUPPLY
3	BK/LB	SENSOR GROUND
4	GY/YL	EGR SOLENOID CONTROL
6	OR/DG	ASD RELAY OUTPUT

17.4a EGR valve harness connector terminal identification

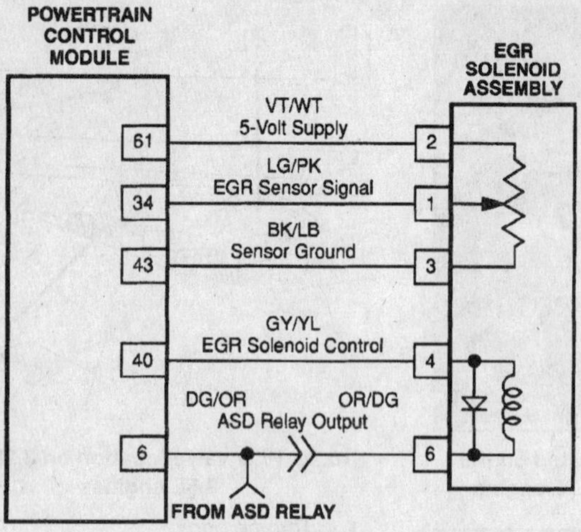

17.4b EGR system schematic

17.6 EGR valve terminal identification

17.10 Remove the EGR valve mounting bolts (arrows)

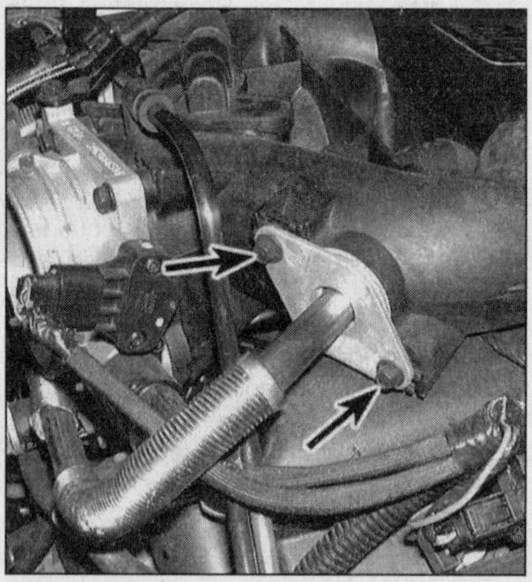

17.15 Remove the upper EGR tube screws from the upper intake manifold

17.16 Remove the lower EGR tube screws from the exhaust manifold

5 Check the voltage supply and ground circuits to the EGR valve position sensor. Disconnect the electrical connector from the EGR valve. Connect the positive lead of a voltmeter to the violet/white wire terminal of the EGR valve electrical connector (harness side). Connect the negative lead to the black/light blue wire terminal. Turn the ignition key On - approximately 5.0 volts should be indicated on the meter. If the 5.0 volt supply voltage is not present, check the circuits from the PCM to the EGR valve. If the circuits are good, have the PCM diagnosed by a dealer service department or other qualified repair shop.

6 To check the EGR valve, use an ohmmeter to measure the resistance of the EGR valve position sensor and the EGR solenoid coil **(see Illustration)**. There should be approximately 4,000 ohms resistance across terminals 2 and 3 (EGR sensor) and approximately 6.0 ohms resistance across terminals 4 and 6 (EGR solenoid coil). If either check reveals an open circuit, replace the EGR valve.

Component replacement

EGR valve

Refer to illustration 17.10

7 Remove the air intake duct and resonator from the throttle body and air filter housing.

8 Disconnect the electrical connector from the EGR valve.

9 Disconnect the EGR tubes from the EGR valve.

10 Remove the EGR valve mounting screws **(see Illustration)**. Remove the EGR valve and gaskets. Discard the gaskets.

11 Using a gasket scraper, clean the EGR valve gasket surfaces.

12 Installation is the reverse of removal.

EGR tubes

Refer to illustrations 17.15, 17.16, 17.22 and 17.23

2.7L models

13 Remove the air intake duct and resonator from the throttle body and air filter housing.

14 Disconnect the accelerator cable and cruise control cable from the throttle body (see Chapter 4). Remove the bracket, with the cables attached, and position it aside.

15 Remove the upper EGR tube screws from the upper intake manifold **(see Illustration)**.

16 Remove the lower EGR tube screws from the exhaust manifold **(see Illustration)**.

17 Remove the EGR tube screws from the EGR valve and remove the tubes. Discard the gaskets.

18 Remove the upper EGR tube silicone seals from the intake manifold.

19 Using a gasket scraper, clean the EGR tube gasket surfaces.

20 Installation is the reverse of removal.

3.2L and 3.5L models

21 Remove the air intake duct and resonator from the throttle body and air filter housing.

22 Remove the throttle body bracket **(see Illustration)**.

23 Remove the EGR tube retaining clips at

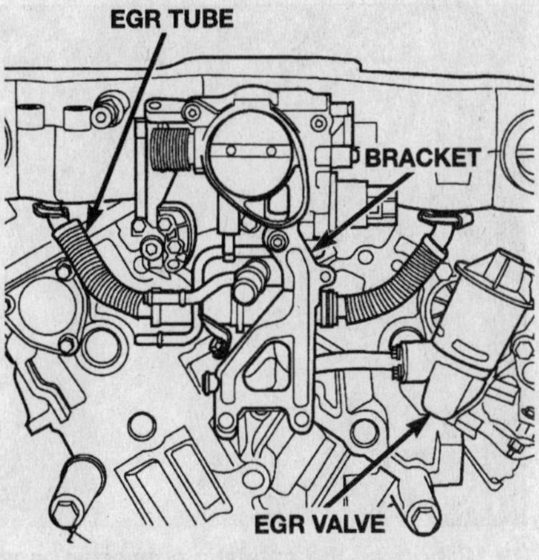

17.22 On 3.2L and 3.5L models, remove the throttle body bracket

the upper intake manifold **(see Illustration)**.

24 Remove the EGR tube screws from the EGR valve and remove the tubes. Discard the gaskets.

25 Remove the upper EGR tube silicone seals from the intake manifold.

26 Using a gasket scraper, clean the EGR tube gasket surfaces.

27 Installation is the reverse of removal.

18 Evaporative emissions control system

1 The fuel evaporative emissions control (EVAP) system absorbs fuel vapors from the fuel tank and, during engine operation, releases them into the engine intake system where they mix with the incoming air/fuel mixture.

2 The evaporative system employs a canister filled with activated charcoal to absorb fuel vapors.

3 The fuel tank filler cap is fitted with a two-way valve as a safety device. The valve vents fuel vapors to the atmosphere if the evaporative control system fails.

4 Another fuel cut-off valve (fuel tank rollover valve), mounted on the fuel tank, regulates fuel vapor flow from the fuel tank to the charcoal canister, based on the pressure or vacuum caused by temperature changes. The fuel tank rollover valve prevents fuel flow to the canister in the event the vehicle rolls over in an accident.

5 After passing through the two-way valve, fuel vapor is carried by vent hoses to the charcoal canister. The activated charcoal in the canister absorbs and stores these vapors.

6 When the engine is running and warmed to a pre-set temperature, a purge control solenoid allows a purge control diaphragm valve in the charcoal canister to be opened by intake manifold vacuum. Fuel vapors from the canister are then drawn through the purge control diaphragm valve by intake manifold vacuum. The duty cycle of the EVAP

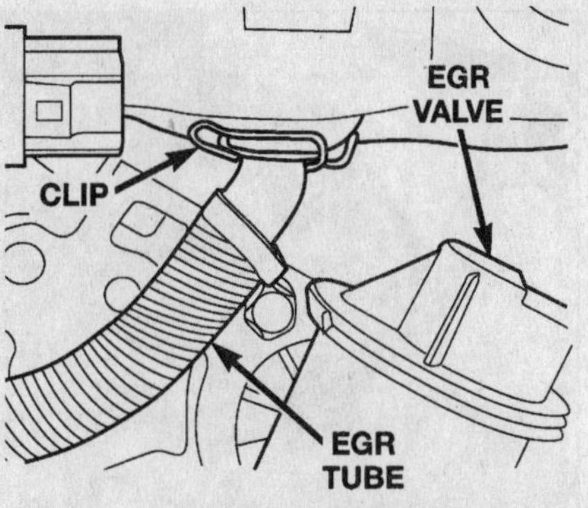

17.23 Carefully remove the EGR tube retaining clips from the upper intake manifold

purge control solenoid regulates the rate of flow of the fuel vapors from the canister to the throttle body. The PCM controls the purge control solenoid. During cold running conditions and hot start time delay, the PCM does not energize the solenoid. After the engine has warmed up to the correct operating temperatures, the PCM purges the vapors into the throttle body according to the running conditions of the engine. The PCM will cycle (ON then OFF) the purge control solenoid about 5 to 10 times per second. The flow rate will be controlled by the pulse width or length of time the solenoid is allowed to be energized.

7 Some models are equipped with a leak detection monitor system. The system is a self-diagnostic system designed to detect a leak in the EVAP system. Each time the engine is started cold, the PCM energizes the leak detection pump. The pump pressurizes the EVAP system then shuts off. The PCM is able to detect a leak if the pump continues to run, unable to pressurize the system. If a leak is detected, the PCM will trigger a diagnostic trouble code (see Section 2).

Check

Refer to illustration 18.8

Note: *The evaporative control system, like all emission control systems, is protected by a Federally-mandated warranty (5 years or 50,000 miles at the time this manual was written). The EVAP system probably won't fail during the service life of the vehicle; however, if it does, the hoses or charcoal canister are usually to blame.*

8 Always check the hoses first. A disconnected, damaged or missing hose is the most likely cause of a malfunctioning EVAP system. Refer to the Vacuum Hose Routing Diagram (attached to the radiator support) to determine whether the hoses are correctly routed and attached. Repair any damaged hoses or replace any missing hoses as necessary **(see Illustration)**.

9 Check the related fuses and wiring to the purge control solenoid. Refer to the wiring diagrams at the end of Chapter 12, if necessary. The purge control solenoid valve is normally closed - no vapors will pass through the ports. When the PCM energizes the solenoid (by completing the circuit to ground), the valve opens and vapors flow through.

10 A SCAN tool is required to thoroughly check the system. If the above checks fail to identify the problem area, have the system diagnosed by a dealer service department or other qualified repair shop.

Component replacement

Refer to illustrations 18.13 and 18.15

EVAP canister and leak detection pump

11 The EVAP canister and leak detection pump are attached to a bracket on top of the fuel tank.

12 Raise the vehicle and support it securely on jackstands. Remove the fuel tank.

13 Label and remove the hoses from the

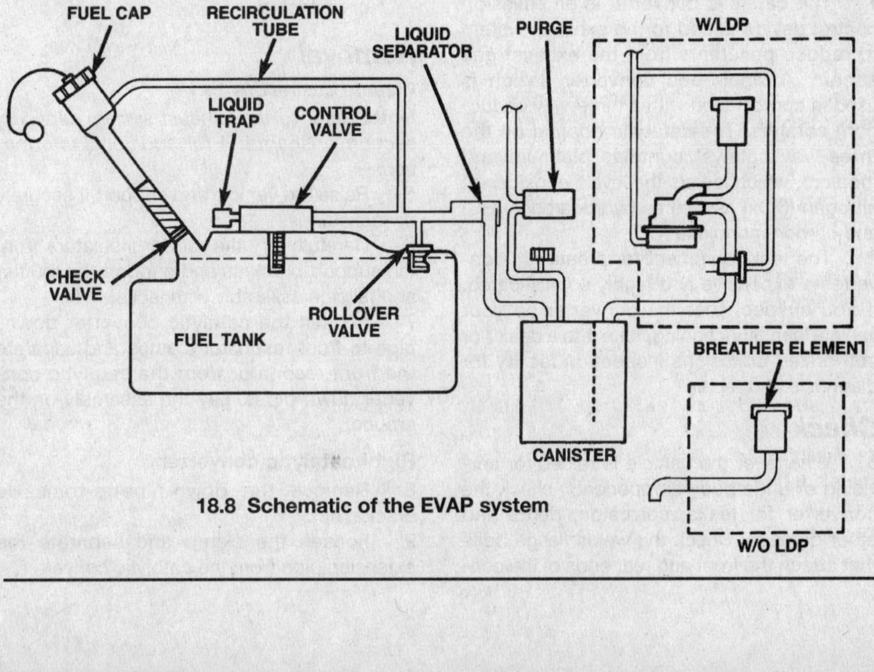

18.8 Schematic of the EVAP system

18.13 The EVAP canister (arrow) is mounted on a bracket attached to the fuel tank

18.15 The purge control solenoid (arrow) is mounted on a bracket near the air filter housing

19.12 Loosen the catalytic converter band clamp (arrow)

canister. Remove the mounting nuts and remove the canister **(see Illustration)**. Remove the leak detection pump from the canister.

14 Installation is the reverse of removal.

Purge control solenoid

15 The purge control solenoid is mounted on a bracket near the air filter housing **(see Illustration)**.

16 Disconnect the electrical connector. Label and remove the hoses from the purge control solenoid.

17 Remove the mounting bolts and remove the purge control solenoid from the bracket.

18 Installation is the reverse of removal.

19 Catalytic converter

Note: *Because of a Federally mandated extended warranty which covers emissions-related components such as the catalytic converter, check with a dealer service department before replacing the converter at your own expense.*

1 The catalytic converter is an emission control device added to the exhaust system to reduce pollutants from the exhaust gas stream. A single-bed converter design is used in combination with a three-way (reduction) catalyst. The catalytic coating on the three-way catalyst contains platinum and rhodium, which lowers the levels of oxides of nitrogen (NOx) as well as hydrocarbons (HC) and carbon monoxide (CO).

2 The test equipment for a catalytic converter is expensive and highly sophisticated. If you suspect that the converter on your vehicle is malfunctioning, take it to a dealer or authorized emissions inspection facility for diagnosis and repair.

Check

3 Whenever the vehicle is raised for servicing of underbody components, check the converter for leaks, corrosion, dents and other damage. Check the welds/flange bolts that attach the front and rear ends of the converter to the exhaust system. If damage is discovered, the converter should be replaced.

4 Although catalytic converters don't break too often, they can become plugged. The easiest way to check for a restricted converter is to use a vacuum gauge to diagnose the effect of a blocked exhaust on intake vacuum.

a) *Connect a vacuum gauge to an intake manifold vacuum source.*
b) *Warm the engine to operating temperature, place the transmission in Park and apply the parking brake.*
c) *Note and record the vacuum reading at idle.*
d) *Open the throttle until the engine speed is about 2000 rpm.*
e) *Release the throttle quickly and record the vacuum reading.*
f) *Perform the test three more times, recording the reading after each test.*
g) *If the reading after the fourth test is more than one in-Hg lower than the reading recorded at idle, the catalytic converter, muffler or exhaust pipes may be plugged or restricted.*

Removal

Refer to illustrations 19.12

Note: *Refer to the exhaust system servicing section in Chapter 4 for additional information.*

5 Raise the vehicle and support it securely on jackstands.

6 Carefully pry the rubber insulators from the support brackets and support the muffler and tailpipe assembly with jackstands.

7 Loosen the catalytic converter down-pipe-to-front resonator clamps and separate the front resonator from the catalytic converter down-pipes. Lay the assembly on the ground.

Right catalytic converter

8 Remove the down-pipe-to-transaxle bracket nut.

9 Loosen the clamp and separate the extension pipe from the catalytic converter.

10 Lower the vehicle and remove the air filter assembly and air intake ducts. On 3.2L/3.5L models, remove the single runner valve and vacuum reservoir.

11 Disconnect the oxygen sensor electrical connector and remove the oxygen sensor from the catalytic converter to prevent damage to the sensor.

12 Loosen the band clamp at the exhaust manifold **(see Illustration)**.

13 Remove the catalytic converter from the engine compartment. Discard the band clamps and obtain new clamps for installation.

Left catalytic converter

14 Disconnect the oxygen sensor electrical connector and remove the oxygen sensor from the catalytic converter to prevent damage to the sensor.

15 Remove the down-pipe-to-transaxle bracket nut.

16 Loosen the band clamp at the exhaust manifold.

17 Remove the catalytic converter from below the vehicle. Be careful not to damage the driveaxle boot. Discard the band clamps and obtain new clamps for installation.

Installation

18 Install the catalytic converter with a new band clamp. Latch the clamp but do not tighten the bolt at this time. Install the extension pipe (right-side only) but do not tighten the clamp at this time.

19 Install the transaxle bracket and tighten the nut securely, then tighten the band clamp to 100 in-lbs and the extension pipe clamp (right-side only) to 45 ft-lbs.

20 Connect the exhaust system to the down-pipes but do not tighten the resonator clamps. Install the exhaust system insulators and make sure the system is aligned and there is sufficient clearance between the exhaust system components and the vehicle body and suspension components. Tighten the resonator clamps to 45 ft-lbs. **Note:** *Apply soapy water to the insulators to make installation easier.*

21 The remainder of installation is the reverse of removal.

Chapter 7 Automatic transaxle

Contents

Specifications

Torque specifications

Torque specifications	**Ft-lbs** (unless otherwise indicated)
Transaxle mounting bolts	75
Torque converter-to-driveplate bolts	60

1 General information

All vehicles covered in this manual are equipped with a 42LE electronic 4-speed automatic transaxle. All information on the automatic transaxle is included in this Chapter.

Due to the complexity of the automatic transaxles covered in this manual and to the specialized equipment necessary to perform most service operations, this Chapter contains only those procedures related to general diagnosis, routine maintenance, adjustment and removal and installation.

If the transaxle requires major repair work, it should be left to a dealer service department or a transmission repair shop. You can, however, remove and install the transaxle yourself and save the expense, even if the repair work is done by a transmission shop.

Some models are equipped with a driver-interactive system known as "Autostick." This system allows the transaxle to be shifted manually. When the shift lever is moved into the Autostick position, the transaxle remains in whatever gear it was in before Autostick was activated. Moving the shift lever to the left (towards the driver) downshifts the transaxle and moving it to the right (towards the passenger seat) upshifts it. The instrument cluster illuminates the gear you have selected. In the Autostick mode, the vehicle can be driven away in first, second or third gear. The cruise control system can be used while in the Autostick mode as long as the shift lever is in third or fourth gear. If the shift lever is moved to second, however, it shuts off the cruise control. Shifting into Overdrive cancels the Autostick mode and the transaxle control module resumes its overdrive shift program.

2 Diagnosis - general

Automatic transaxle malfunctions may be caused by five general conditions:

a) *Poor engine performance*
b) *Improper adjustments*
c) *Hydraulic malfunctions*
d) *Mechanical malfunctions*
e) *Malfunctions in the computer or its signal network*

Diagnosis of these problems should always begin with a check of the easily repaired items: fluid level and condition (see Chapter 1) and shift cable adjustment. Next, perform a road test to determine if the problem has been corrected or if more diagnosis is necessary. If the problem persists after the preliminary tests and corrections are completed, additional diagnosis should be done by a dealer service department or transmission repair shop. Refer to the *Troubleshooting* Section at the front of this manual for information on symptoms of transaxle problems.

Preliminary checks

1 Drive the vehicle to warm the transaxle to normal operating temperature.

2 Check the fluid level as described in Chapter 1.

a) *If the fluid level is unusually low, add enough fluid to bring the level within the designated area of the dipstick, then check for external leaks (see below).*
b) *If the fluid level is abnormally high, drain off the excess, then check the drained fluid for contamination by coolant. The presence of engine coolant in the automatic transmission fluid indicates that a failure has occurred in the internal radiator walls that separate the coolant from the transmission fluid (see Chapter 3).*
c) *If the fluid is foaming, drain it and refill the transaxle, then check for coolant in the fluid, or a high fluid level.*

3 Check the engine idle speed. **Note:** *If*

the engine is malfunctioning, do not proceed with the preliminary checks until it has been repaired and runs normally.

4 Inspect the shift cable (see Section 4). Make sure that it's properly adjusted and that it operates smoothly.

Fluid leak diagnosis

5 Most fluid leaks are easy to locate visually. Repair usually consists of replacing a seal or gasket. If a leak is difficult to find, the following procedure may help.

6 Identify the fluid. Make sure it's transmission fluid and not engine oil or brake fluid (automatic transmission fluid is a deep red color).

7 Try to pinpoint the source of the leak. Drive the vehicle several miles, then park it over a large sheet of cardboard. After a minute or two, you should be able to locate the leak by determining the source of the fluid dripping onto the cardboard.

8 Make a careful visual inspection of the suspected component and the area immediately around it. Pay particular attention to gasket mating surfaces. A mirror is often helpful for finding leaks in areas that are hard to see.

9 If the leak still cannot be found, clean the suspected area thoroughly with a degreaser or solvent, then dry it.

3.2a To remove the handle from the shift lever, loosen the set screw with an Allen wrench . . .

10 Drive the vehicle for several miles at normal operating temperature and varying speeds. After driving the vehicle, visually inspect the suspected component again.

11 Once the leak has been located, the cause must be determined before it can be properly repaired. If a gasket is replaced but the sealing flange is bent, the new gasket will not stop the leak. The bent flange must be straightened.

12 Before attempting to repair a leak, check to make sure that the following conditions are corrected or they may cause another leak. **Note:** *Some of the following conditions cannot be fixed without highly specialized tools and expertise. Such problems must be referred to a transmission shop or a dealer service department.*

Gasket leaks

13 Check the pan periodically. Make sure the bolts are tight, no bolts are missing, the gasket is in good condition and the pan is flat (dents in the pan may indicate damage to the valve body inside).

14 If the pan gasket is leaking, the fluid level or the fluid pressure may be too high, the vent may be plugged, the pan bolts may be too tight, the pan sealing flange may be warped, the sealing surface of the transaxle housing may be damaged, the gasket may be damaged or the transaxle casting may be cracked or porous. If sealant instead of gasket material has been used to form a seal between the pan and the transaxle housing, it may be the wrong sealant.

Seal leaks

15 If a transaxle seal is leaking, the fluid level or pressure may be too high, the vent may be plugged, the seal bore may be damaged, the seal itself may be damaged or improperly installed, the surface of the shaft protruding through the seal may be damaged or a loose bearing may be causing excessive shaft movement.

16 Make sure the dipstick tube seal is in good condition and the tube is properly seated. Periodically check the area around the speedometer gear or sensor for leakage. If transmission fluid is evident, check the O-ring for damage.

Case leaks

17 If the case itself appears to be leaking, the casting is porous and will have to be repaired or replaced.

18 Make sure the oil cooler hose fittings are tight and in good condition.

Fluid comes out vent pipe or fill tube

19 If this condition occurs, the transaxle is overfilled, there is coolant in the fluid, the case is porous, the dipstick is incorrect, the vent is plugged or the drain-back holes are plugged.

3 Shift lever - removal and installation

Refer to illustrations 3.2a, 3.2b and 3.6

Warning: *These models have airbags. Always disable the airbag system before working in the vicinity of any airbag system components to avoid the possibility of accidental deployment of the airbag(s), which could cause personal injury (see Chapter 12).*

Note: *This procedure applies to floor shift levers only.*

Standard shifter

1 Disconnect the negative battery cable from the remote ground terminal (see Chapter 5).

2 Remove the shift lever handle **(see illustrations)**.

3 Remove the console bezel (see Chapter 11).

4 Disconnect the shift cable from the shifter and bracket (see Section 4).

5 Disconnect the shift interlock cable from the lever and the bracket (see Section 5).

6 Remove the shift lever assembly retaining nuts **(see illustration)**. Remove the shift lever assembly.

7 Installation is the reverse of removal. If necessary, adjust the shift cable and the shift interlock cable (see Sections 4 and 5).

3.2b . . . then slide the handle straight up

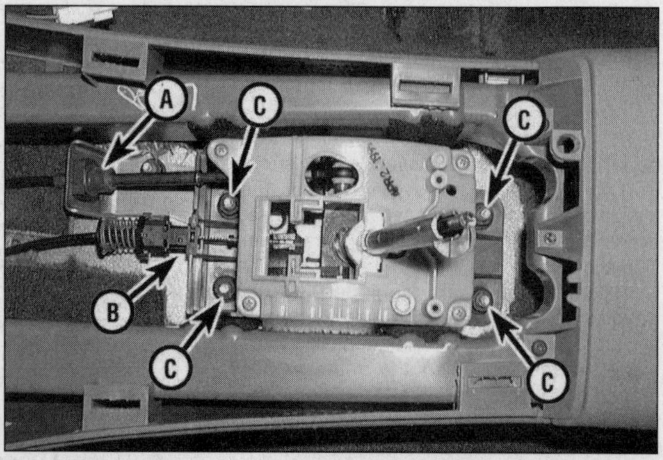

3.6 Detach the shift cable (A) and the shift interlock cable (B), then unscrew the four nuts (C) and remove the shifter assembly

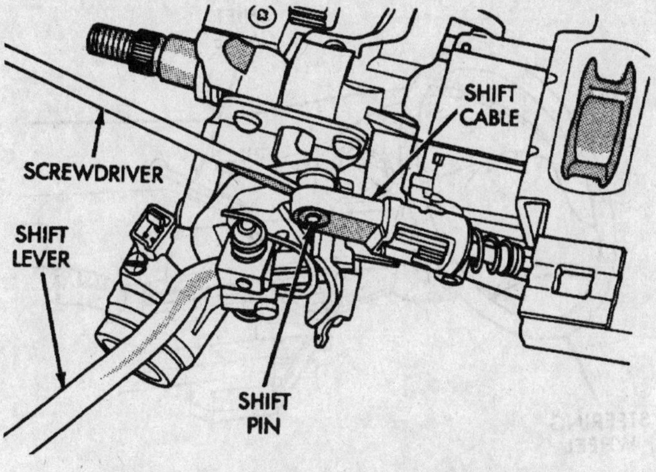

4.6 Disconnect the shift cable from the shift lever pin

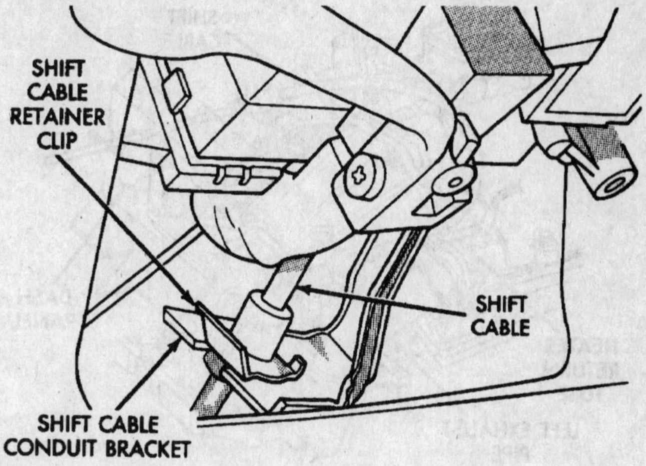

4.7 Remove the cable retainer clip from the shift cable bracket

Autostick shifter

8 The Autostick shifter (see Section 1 for description of operation) is replaced in the same manner as the standard floor shifter. Aside from unplugging the switch in the shift lever base, the replacement procedure is identical to the procedure described above for a conventional shift lever assembly.

4 Shift cable - replacement and adjustment

Warning: *These models have airbags. Always disable the airbag system before working in the vicinity of any airbag system components to avoid the possibility of accidental deployment of the airbag(s), which could cause personal injury (see Chapter 12).*

1 The shift cable must be adjusted when:

- *a) The shift cable is replaced*
- *b) The column shifter is replaced*
- *c) The shift/ignition interlock cable is replaced*
- *d) The transaxle is replaced*
- *e) The valve body is repaired or replaced*
- *f) The engine won't crank over in Park or Neutral*

2 The shift interlock cable (see Section 5) must also be adjusted if:

- *a) The transaxle can be shifted without the key in the ignition*
- *b) The key can be removed with the shifter in Reverse*
- *c) The key cannot be removed with the shift lever in the Park position*

Column-shift cable

Replacement

Refer to illustrations 4.6, 4.7, 4.10, 4.11, 4.12, 4.16 and 4.19

3 Disconnect the negative battery cable from the remote ground terminal (see Chapter 5).

4 Remove the driver's side knee bolster and reinforcement (see Chapter 11). Remove the heater/air conditioning duct from underneath the dash.

5 Remove the steering column covers (see Chapter 11).

6 Disconnect the shift cable from the shift lever pin **(see illustration)**.

7 Remove the cable retainer clip from the shift cable bracket **(see illustration)**.

8 From the engine compartment side of the firewall, pry the grommet out of the firewall and pull out the rear end of the cable from the interior of the vehicle.

9 Raise the front of the vehicle and place it securely on jackstands.

10 Unbolt the fill tube bracket **(see illustration)** and rotate the fill tube out of the way to gain access to the shift cable clamp.

11 Loosen the shift cable clamp and disconnect the shift cable from the shift lever on the transaxle **(see illustration)**. Remove the cable.

12 Route the new cable from underneath the vehicle, between the engine block and the heater return tube **(see illustration)**.

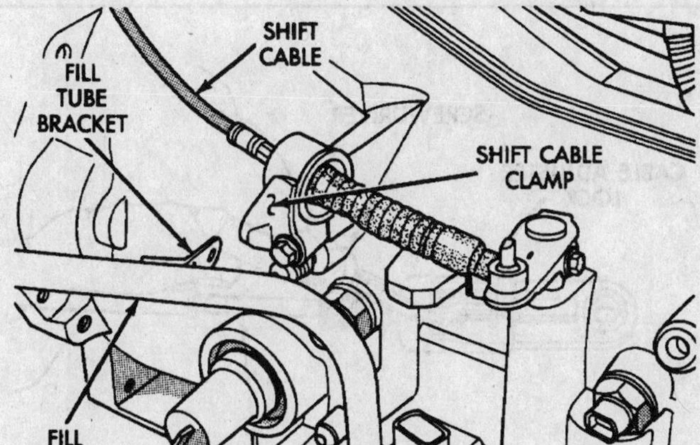

4.10 Unbolt the fill tube bracket and rotate the fill tube out of the way to gain access to the shift cable clamp

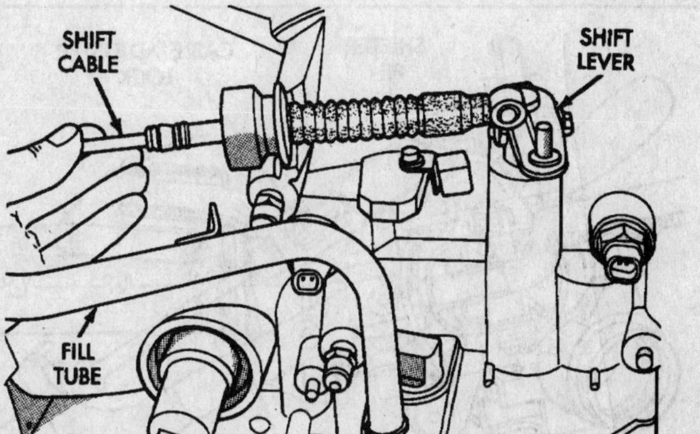

4.11 Loosen the shift cable clamp, disconnect the shift cable from the shift lever on the transaxle and remove the cable

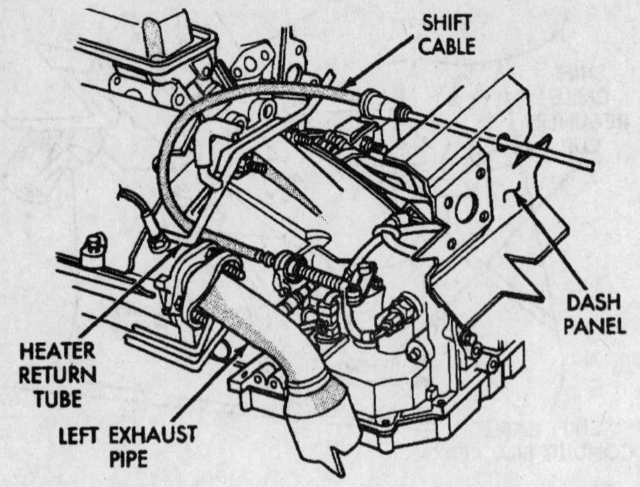

4.12 Route the new cable from underneath the vehicle, between the engine block and the heater return tube

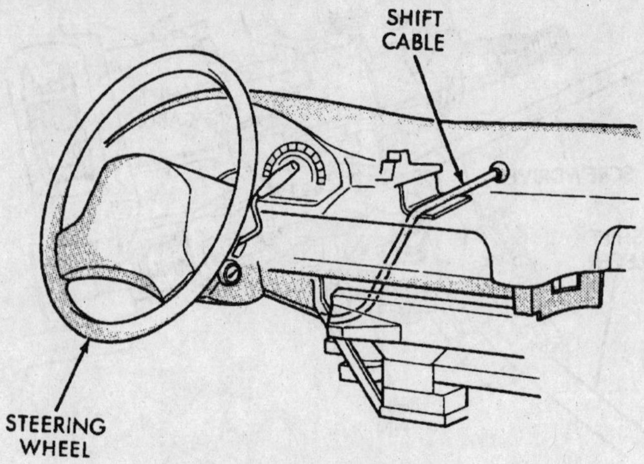

4.16 Route the cable over the under-dash bracket and along the steering column; secure the cable to the bracket with a new retainer clip

13 Connect the new cable to the transaxle shift lever, then set the shift lever to the Park position (the position farthest to the rear).

14 Place the cable in the clamp and tighten the clamp mounting bolt securely. Rotate the fill tube to its proper location and install and tighten the fill tube bracket bolt.

15 Route the cable through the hole in the firewall and install the grommet in the hole.

16 Route the cable over the under-dash bracket and along the steering column **(see illustration)**. Secure the cable to the bracket with a new retainer clip.

17 With the shift lever in the Park position, connect the cable to the shifter pin. Make sure it snaps into place.

18 Tilt the steering column all the way down and put the shift lever at the column into Park with the key removed.

19 Adjust the cable by rotating the adjuster into the Lock position **(see illustration)**. The adjuster will click when the lock is fully adjusted.

20 Install the steering column covers. Install the ducts, reinforcement and knee bolster under the dash.

21 Check the shift lever for proper operation. It should operate smoothly without binding, and the starter should crank only in the Park or Neutral positions.

Adjustment

Refer to illustration 4.23

22 Remove the upper steering column cover (see Chapter 11).

23 Using a small screwdriver, rotate the cable adjuster to its unlocked position **(see illustration)**.

24 Make sure the shift lever at the transaxle is the Park position (the position farthest to the rear) and the parking pawl is fully engaged (the parking pawl must be engaged when adjusting the cable). Rock the vehicle back and forth to ensure that the parking pawl is fully engaged.

25 Tilt the steering column to its full down position and place the shift lever in the Park position with the key removed. Using a small screwdriver, rotate the cable adjuster to its locked position.

26 Install the upper steering column shroud.

27 Check the shift lever for proper operation. It should operate smoothly, without binding. The vehicle should crank only in Park or Neutral.

Floor-shift cable

Replacement

Refer to illustrations 4.31, 4.32 and 4.34

28 Disconnect the negative battery cable from the remote ground terminal (see Chapter 5).

29 Remove the shift lever handle (see Section 3).

30 Remove the console bezel (see Chapter 11).

31 Remove the retaining clip from the shift cable bracket **(see illustration)**.

32 Disconnect the cable from the pin on the shift lever **(see illustration)**.

33 Follow Steps 8 through 15.

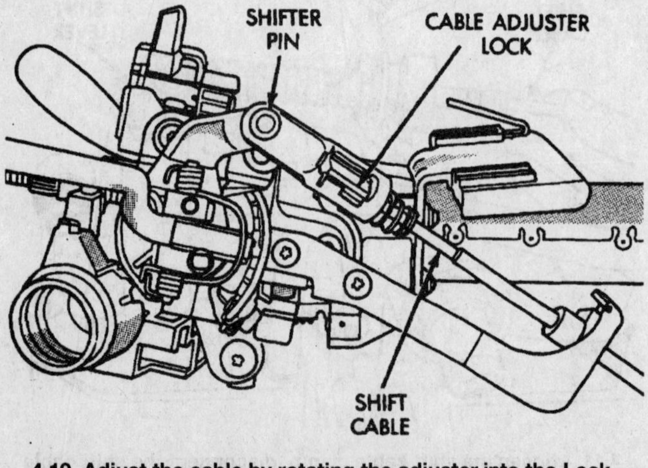

4.19 Adjust the cable by rotating the adjuster into the Lock position; the adjuster will click when the lock is fully adjusted

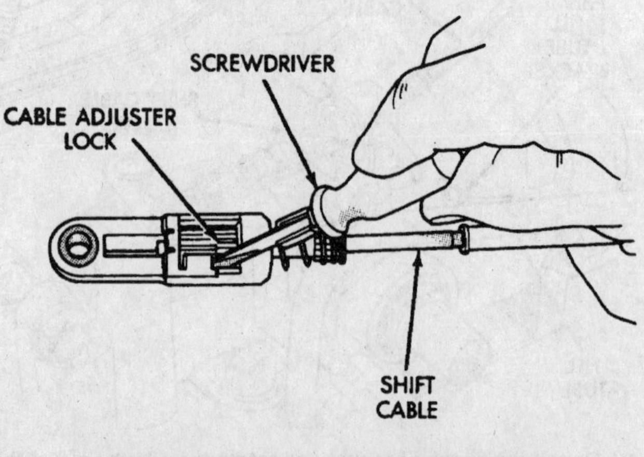

4.23 Using a small screwdriver, rotate the cable adjuster to its unlocked position

4.31 Pry off the clip retaining the shift cable to the bracket

4.32 To disconnect the cable from the pin on the shift lever, pry it off with a screwdriver

34 Route the new cable under the air conditioning duct, over the central distribution duct, through the support strut and airbag mounting bracket. Then route it over the carpeting and down to the shift lever bracket **(see illustration)**.
35 Move the shift lever to Park.
36 Route the cable through the hole in the shift lever bracket and attach the end of the cable to the pin on the shift lever.
37 Install the retainer clip on the cable at the shift lever bracket. If the clip is a loose fit, install a new one.
38 Check the shift lever for proper operation. It should operate smoothly, without binding. The vehicle should crank only in Park or Neutral. If necessary, adjust the cable (see Steps 40 through 47).
39 Install the console bezel and the shift lever handle.

Adjustment

Refer to illustration 4.41

40 Remove the shift lever handle (see Section 3) and the console bezel (see Chapter 11).
41 Loosen the nut on the shift cable adjuster **(see illustration)**.
42 Make sure the shift lever at the transaxle is the Park position (the position farthest to the rear). The parking pawl must be engaged when adjusting the cable. Rock the vehicle back and forth to ensure that the parking pawl is fully engaged.
43 Place the shift lever inside the vehicle in the Park position.
44 Place the ignition key in the Lock position, then remove the key.
45 Tighten the adjuster nut.
46 Check the shift lever for proper operation. It should operate smoothly without binding. The engine should crank only when the lever is in Park or Neutral.
47 Install the console bezel and shift lever handle.

5 Shift interlock system - description, replacement and adjustment

Warning: *These models have airbags. Always disable the airbag system before working in the vicinity of any airbag system components to avoid the possibility of accidental deployment of the airbag(s), which could cause personal injury (see Chapter 12).*

Description

1 The shift interlock system connects the transmission shift lever and the ignition key

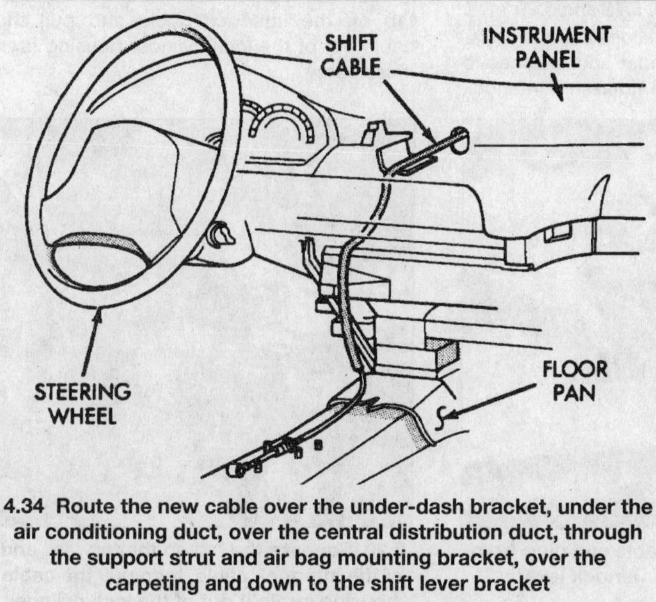

4.34 Route the new cable over the under-dash bracket, under the air conditioning duct, over the central distribution duct, through the support strut and air bag mounting bracket, over the carpeting and down to the shift lever bracket

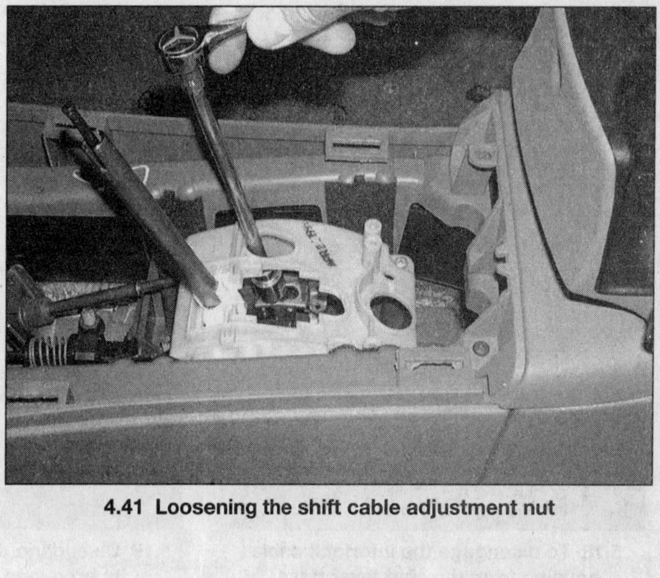

4.41 Loosening the shift cable adjustment nut

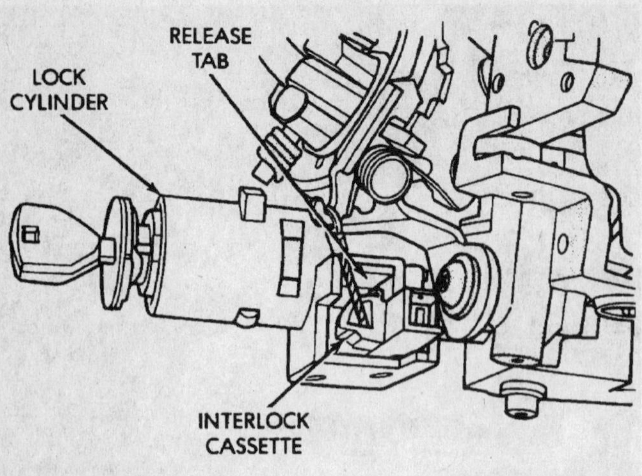

5.2 The interlock cassette on column-shift models slides into its housing behind the key lock cylinder; the interlock cable is attached to a locking arm on the shifter mechanism

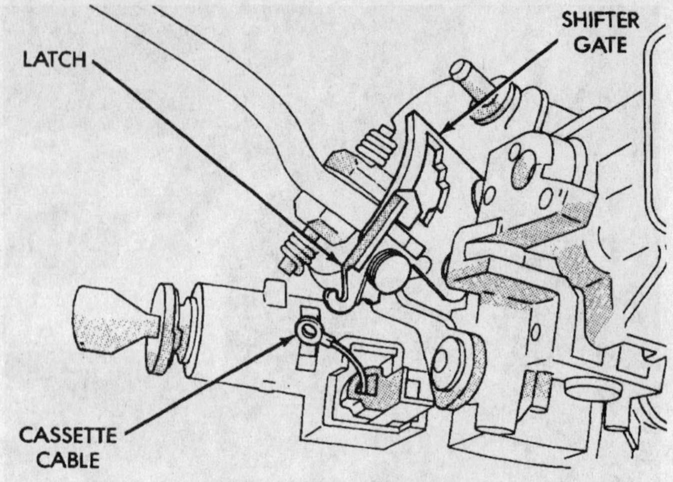

5.6 When installing the new cable, make sure the latch rotates freely on the shifter gate

lock cylinder. With the ignition key in the Off or Accessory position, the interlock system holds the transmission shift lever in Park. When the key is the in the Unlock or Run position, the shift lever is unlocked and can be moved to any position. And if the shift lever is not in Park, the system prevents the operator from turning the ignition switch to the Off or Accessory positions.

Column-shift models

Replacement

Refer to illustrations 5.2 and 5.6

2 The interlock cassette on column-shift models slides into the housing behind the key lock cylinder **(see illustration)**. The cable at the rear of the cassette attaches to a locking arm on the shifter mechanism.

3 Disconnect the negative battery cable from the remote ground terminal (see Chapter 5).

4 Depress the tab on the top of the cassette and slide the interlock cassette out of the housing.

5 Remove the cable from the locking arm on the shift lever mechanism.

6 When installing the new cable, make sure the latch rotates freely on the shifter gate **(see illustration)**.

7 With the shifter in Park and the key removed, install the cable over the hook on the locking arm of the shifter mechanism.

8 Slide the cassette into the housing until it locks in place.

Adjustment

9 The column shift interlock system is adjusted only after installing a new cassette. It cannot be adjusted more than once. If the system operates improperly, install and adjust a new interlock cassette.

10 Push the release tab in until it stops **(see illustration 5.2)**. The adjustment tab will click as it moves into position. Ensure the tab is fully depressed.

Floor-shift models

Replacement

Refer to illustrations 5.18, 5.19 and 5.20

11 The interlock cable slides into the housing behind the lock cylinder and attaches to the shift lever base. The floor-shift interlock system is adjusted by a nut at the shift lever assembly. If the system must be adjusted (but not replaced), adjust it as described below.

12 Disconnect the negative battery cable from the remote ground terminal (see Chapter 5).

13 Remove the shift lever handle (see Section 3).

14 Remove the console bezel (see Chapter 11).

15 Remove the driver's side knee bolster and reinforcement (see Chapter 11).

16 Remove the steering column covers (see Chapter 11).

17 Turn the ignition key to the Run position.

18 Detach the interlock cable from the shift lever base **(see illustration)**.

19 Slide the cable end plug out of its groove in the interlock lever **(see illustration)**.

20 Turn the ignition key to Off. At the ignition key lock cylinder, squeeze the lock tab on the interlock cable and pull the cable out of the lock cylinder housing **(see illustration)**.

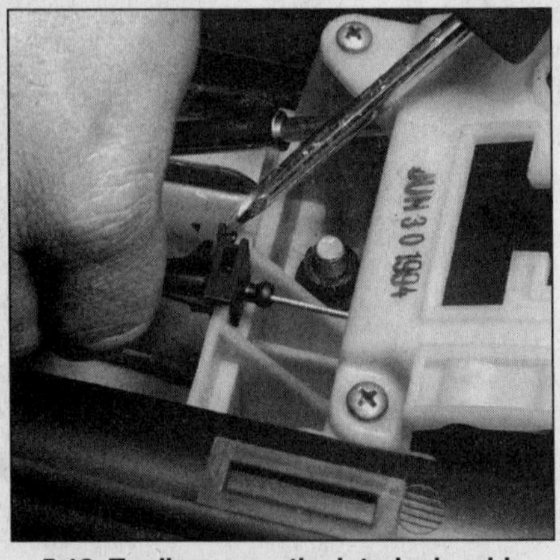

5.18 To disengage the interlock cable housing from the shift lever base, pry up on this small locking tab

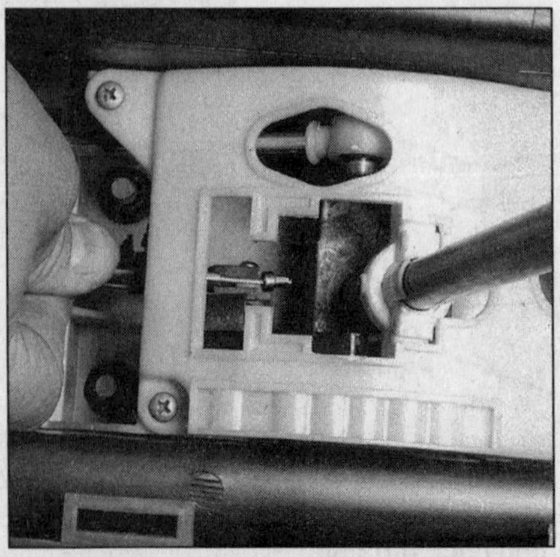

5.19 Disengage the cable end plug from its groove in the interlock lever

5.20 Squeeze the tab on the forward end of the interlock cable, then pull the cable housing straight out of the lock cylinder

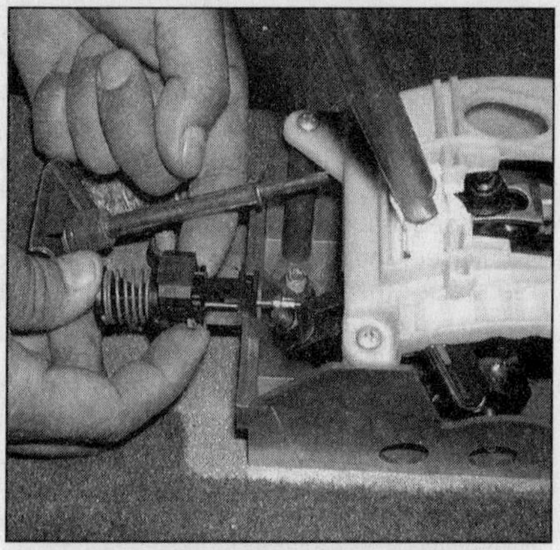

5.30 With the ignition key in the Lock position and the shift lever in the Park position, disengage the locking clip on the interlock cable; the cable will then adjust itself (push the clip back into place after adjustment is complete)

21 Make sure the ignition switch is in the Off position.
22 Route the interlock cable down the steering column and above the air distribution center duct, between the support strut and the airbag module mounting bracket and down to the shift lever assembly.
23 Insert the forward end of the interlock cable into the lock cylinder housing and push it in until it snaps into place.
24 Turn the ignition key to the Off/Lock position and put the shift lever in the Park position.
25 Insert the cable end plug into its groove in the interlock lever. Make sure the plug is properly seated in the groove.
26 Reattach the cable to the shift lever base. The cable housing is fully seated when it snaps into place.
27 Adjust the interlock cable (see Steps 29 through 32).
28 The remainder of installation is the reverse of removal.

Adjustment

Refer to illustration 5.30

29 Remove the ignition key from the lock cylinder with the switch in the Lock position. Make sure the shift lever is still in Park.
30 When the adjustment clip on the interlock cable is disengaged, the cable automatically indexes itself to the correct position. Pull up on the tabs, unlock the clip and allow the cable to do so **(see illustration)**. Snap the clip back into place.
31 With the ignition key in the Off (locked) position, the shift lever should be locked in the Park position. If it isn't, inspect the system for binding and repeat the adjustment procedure.
32 Without starting the engine, place the ignition switch in the Run position. Move the shift lever to the Reverse position. You should be unable to remove the ignition key from the lock cylinder. If you can remove the key at this point, inspect the system for binding and repeat the adjustment procedure.

7.6 Disconnect these two electrical connectors for the transaxle harness

6 Transmission range sensor - general information

The transmission range sensor, which incorporates the Park/Neutral Position (PNP) switch, is fastened to the valve body of the transaxle. Replacement requires removing the transaxle fluid pan and the valve body, since the switch is mounted to the topside of the valve body. If the sensor fails (which may be indicated by failure of the starter motor to crank over, erratic shifting, or a trouble code in the PCM's memory), we recommend having it replaced by a transmission specialist or other qualified repair facility.

7 Transaxle - removal and installation

Refer to illustrations 7.6, 7.7, 7.15, 7.20a, 7.20b and 7.25

Removal

1 Place protective covers on the fenders and cowl and remove the hood (see Chapter 11).
2 Relieve the fuel system pressure (see Chapter 4).
3 Disconnect the negative battery cable from the remote ground terminal (see Chapter 5). Pull out the transaxle fluid dipstick.
4 Remove the cowl cover and strut support brace (see Chapter 11), then remove the windshield wiper module (see Chapter 12).
5 Remove the engine air intake duct (see Chapter 4).
6 Disconnect the transaxle harness electrical connectors near the brake master cylinder **(see illustration)**.
7 Unscrew the nuts from the upper transaxle mounting studs **(see illustration)**.
8 Unbolt the throttle body support bracket.
9 Unscrew the upper transaxle mounting studs **(see illustration 7.7)**.
10 Loosen the front wheel lug nuts, raise the vehicle and support it securely on jackstands. Remove the front wheels. Drain the transaxle fluid and the differential lubricant (see Chapter 1).
11 Remove the exhaust system (see Chapter 4).
12 Disconnect the electrical connectors from the crankshaft position sensor, the transmission range sensor, and the electrical connectors for the input and output speed sensors.
13 Remove the crankshaft position sensor (see Chapter 6).
14 Remove the transaxle fluid dipstick tube, then remove the shift cable from the transaxle (see Section 4).
15 Unscrew the fluid cooler line fittings at the transaxle, using a flare-nut wrench, if available **(see illustration)**. Plug the fittings to prevent fluid leakage and contamination.
16 Detach the lower control arms from the steering knuckles (see Chapter 10).
17 Pry the inner CV joints from the transaxle (see Chapter 8). Pull outward on the steering knuckles, reposition the driveaxles and support them with lengths of wire.

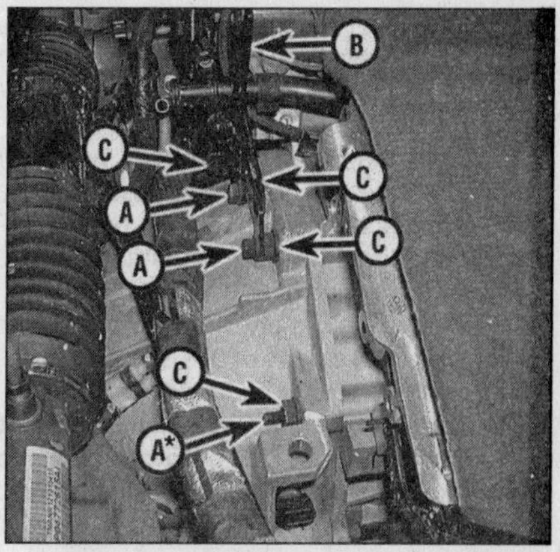

7.7 Remove the nuts (A) from the studs, remove the throttle body support bracket (B), then unscrew the transaxle mounting studs (C). Note: *The nut indicated by (A*) has already been removed to allow the wiring harness to be repositioned for clarity*

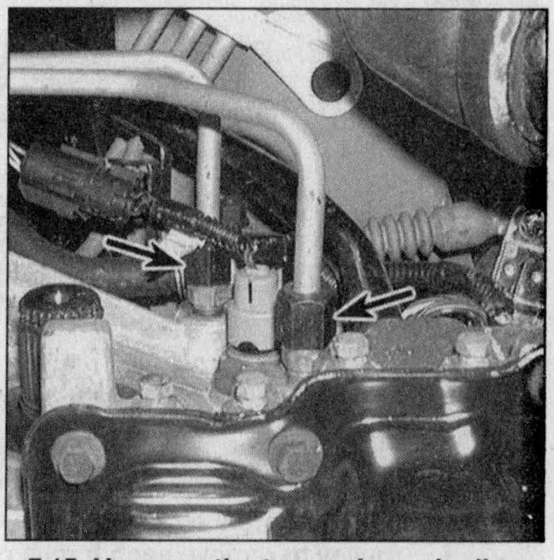

7.15 Unscrew the transaxle cooler line fittings (arrows) from the transaxle (use a flare-nut wrench on the nut and a back-up wrench on the transaxle fitting)

18 Unplug the electrical connectors for the left-side oxygen sensors (one from above, one from below), then remove the left catalytic converter (see Chapter 4).

19 Unbolt the starter motor (see Chapter 5) and set it aside. It's not necessary to actually remove the starter or disconnect the electrical wiring; simply secure the starter aside, between the engine and the frame.

20 Remove the oil pan-to-transaxle support brace (see Chapter 2A or 2B). Mark the relationship of the torque converter to the driveplate **(see illustration)**. Rotate the crankshaft by turning the crankshaft pulley and remove the torque converter bolts **(see illustration)**. **Note:** *Discard these bolts - new ones must be used during reassembly.*

21 Support the transmission with a jack - preferably a jack made for this purpose. Safety chains will help steady the transmission on the jack. **Note:** *Transmission jacks are commonly available from equipment rental yards.*

22 Raise the jack slightly to remove the weight of the transaxle on the rear transaxle mount.

7.20a Mark the relationship of the torque converter to the driveplate . . .

23 Unbolt the rear powertrain mount from the transaxle and crossmember, unbolt the crossmember from each side of the subframe, then remove the crossmember and mount.

24 Slowly lower the transaxle and unplug any electrical connectors still connected to the transaxle.

25 Remove the lower transaxle mounting bolts **(see illustration)**.

26 Recheck to be sure nothing is still connecting the transaxle to the engine or to the vehicle. Label and disconnect anything still attached.

27 Carefully lower the transaxle from the vehicle. Keep the transaxle level and make sure the torque converter at the front does not fall out.

Installation

28 If removed, install the torque converter on the transaxle input shaft. Make sure the converter hub splines are properly engaged with the splines on the transaxle input shaft. Lubricate the torque converter hub with grease (the part that engages the crankshaft).

29 With the transaxle secured to the jack as on removal, and with an assistant holding the torque converter in place, raise the transaxle into position and turn the converter to align the bolt holes in the converter with the bolt holes in the driveplate. Do not use excessive force to install the transaxle - if something binds and the transaxle won't mate with the engine, alter the angle of the transaxle slightly until it does mate. **Caution:** *Do NOT use the transaxle mounting bolts to force the engine and transaxle into alignment. Doing so could crack or damage major components. If you experience difficulties, have an assistant help you line up the dowel pins on the block with the transaxle. Some wiggling of the engine and/or the transaxle will probably be necessary to secure proper alignment of the two.*

30 Install the engine-to-transaxle bolts, tightening them to the torque listed in this Chapter's Specifications.

31 Install the oil pan-to-transaxle support brace. Be sure to tighten the bolts in the proper sequence and to the specified torque values (see Chapter 2A or 2B).

32 Raise the transaxle and install the transaxle mount and crossmember.

33 Install *new* driveplate-to-torque converter bolts; install all of the bolts before tightening any of them. Be sure to tighten them to the torque listed in this Chapter's Specifications.

34 The remainder of installation is the reverse of removal. Before reconnecting the driveaxles, be sure to install new O-ring seals and retainer circlips on the stub shafts (see Chapter 8). After lowering the vehicle, be sure to install the upper transaxle mounting bolts and tighten them to the torque listed in this Chapter's Specifications.

35 Install the wheels and lug nuts. Lower the vehicle and tighten the wheel lug nuts to the torque listed in the Chapter 1 Specifications.

36 Add the specified amounts of automatic transmission fluid and differential lubricant (see Chapter 1).

37 Connect the negative battery cable.

38 Adjust the shift cable (see Section 4).

39 Road test the vehicle to check for proper transaxle operation and check for leakage. If the transaxle operates erratically, it may be necessary to take the vehicle to a dealer service department or other properly equipped repair shop to have the PCM/transmission control module reprogrammed to compensate for the new/different components (this procedure requires a DRB scan tool).

40 Shut off the engine and recheck the fluid levels.

7.20b . . . then rotate the crankshaft by turning the crankshaft pulley to remove each torque converter bolt

7.25 Remove the lower engine-to-transaxle bolts (arrows)

Chapter 8 Driveaxles

Contents

Specifications

Torque specifications

	Ft-lbs (unless otherwise indicated)
Driveaxle/hub nut	
1998 and 1999	120
2000 and 2001	105
Wheel lug nuts	See Chapter 1

1 Driveaxles - general information and inspection

Refer to illustration 1.1

1 Power is transmitted from the transaxle to the wheels through a pair of driveaxles **(see illustration)**. The inner end of each driveaxle is splined to a stub shaft protruding from the differential side gears; the outer end of each driveaxle has a stub shaft that is splined to the front hub and bearing assembly and locked in place with a large nut.

2 The inner ends of the driveaxles are equipped with sliding constant velocity (CV) joints, which are capable of both angular and axial motion. Each inner CV joint assembly consists of a tripod-type bearing and a housing in which the joint is free to slide in-and-out as the driveaxle moves up-and-down with the wheel.

3 The outer ends of the driveaxles are equipped with "ball-and-cage" type CV joints, which are capable of angular but not axial movement. Each outer CV joint consists of six ball bearings running between an inner race and an outer cage.

4 The boots should be inspected periodically for damage and leaking lubricant. Torn CV joint boots must be replaced immediately or the joints will be damaged. If either boot of a driveaxle is damaged, that driveaxle must be removed in order to replace the boot (see Section 2). **Note:** *The inner and outer boots on the vehicles covered in this manual are constructed from different materials: The inner boots are made from a high-temperature application silicone material; the outer boots are made from hytrel plastic. Make sure you obtain a boot made of the correct material for the CV joint boot you're replacing.*

5 Should a boot be damaged, the CV joint can be disassembled and cleaned, but if any parts are damaged, the entire driveaxle assembly must be replaced as a unit (see Section 3).

6 The most common symptom of worn or damaged CV joints, besides lubricant leaks, is a clicking noise in turns, a clunk when accelerating after coasting and vibration at highway speeds. To check for wear in the CV joints and driveaxle shafts, grasp each axle (one at a time) and rotate it in both directions while holding the CV joint housings, feeling for play indicating worn splines or sloppy CV joints. Also check the driveaxle shafts for cracks, dents and distortion.

2 Driveaxle - removal and installation

Note: *The manufacturer states that a new driveaxle/hub nut must be installed whenever it is removed. Be sure to obtain one before beginning this procedure.*

Removal

Refer to illustrations 2.2, 2.6 and 2.8

1 Disconnect the cable from the negative terminal of the battery.

2 If the vehicle has steel wheels, remove the wheel cover. Set the parking brake, place

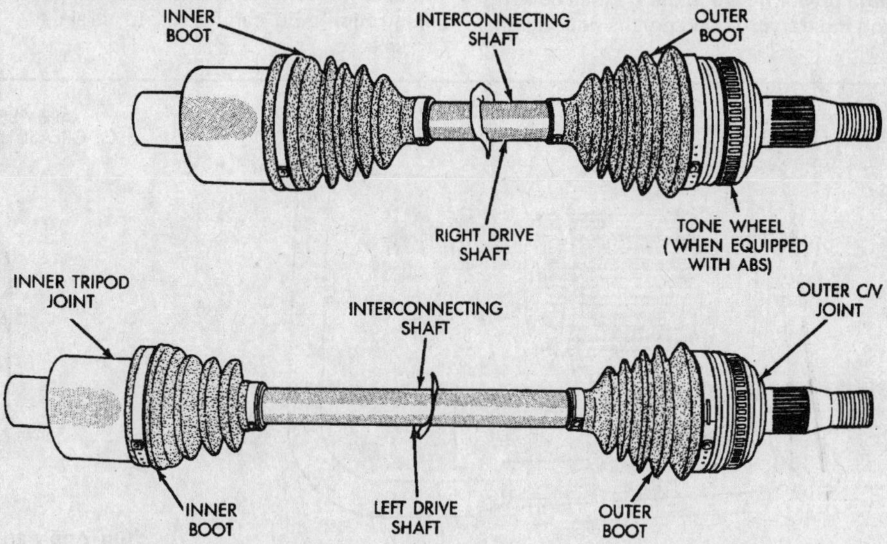

1.1 The right driveaxle (top) and left driveaxle (bottom) assemblies

2.2 To loosen the hub/driveaxle nut on a vehicle with steel wheels, apply the parking brake, place the transaxle in gear and have an assistant apply the brakes firmly, then loosen the nut with a socket and breaker bar

2.6 To separate the outer end of the driveaxle from the steering knuckle, swing the knuckle out until it clears the splined stub shaft of the outer CV joint (be extremely careful - if the splines of the stub shaft nick the lip of the seal on the backside of the knuckle, water could get into the hub bearing assembly

2.8 You might be able to disengage the inner CV joint from the stub shaft by simply pulling it out by the housing; if the joint hangs up on the snap-ring, place a large prybar between the CV joint housing and the transaxle and pry the housing out

the transmission in gear and have an assistant apply the brakes firmly, then loosen the hub/driveaxle nut with a large socket and breaker bar **(see illustration)**. If the vehicle has aluminum wheels, you may not be able to fit a socket through the opening in the center of the wheel; you'll have to wait until the wheel is removed to loosen the nut (see Step 4), or install the spare wheel, lower the vehicle to the ground and loosen the nut.

3 Loosen the front wheel lug nuts, raise the vehicle and support it securely on jackstands. Remove the wheel.

4 Remove the hub/driveaxle nut. If you weren't able to loosen the driveaxle/hub nut in Step 2, insert a large screwdriver or prybar between the wheel studs to immobilize the hub and remove the nut.

5 Separate the lower control arm from the steering knuckle (see Chapter 10).

6 Swing the steering knuckle out and separate it from the driveaxle assembly **(see illustration)**. Be careful not to strain the brake hose.

7 If the driveaxle proves difficult to remove, tap the end of the driveaxle with a soft-faced hammer or a hammer and a brass punch. If the driveaxle is stuck in the hub splines and won't move, it may be necessary to push it from the hub with a puller. If this is the case, the brake caliper and disc will have to be removed (see Chapter 9).

8 Carefully free the inner CV joint from the stub shaft **(see illustration)**. If the joint hangs up on the snap-ring on the stub shaft, pop it loose by levering it out with a large prybar or screwdriver. Do not use the axleshaft to pull on the inner CV joint. Doing so will separate the spider assembly from the tripod joint housing.

9 Remove the driveaxle assembly, being careful not to overextend the inner CV joint or damage the driveaxle boots.

Installation

Refer to illustrations 2.10a and 2.10b

10 Installation is the reverse of the removal procedure, but note the following additional

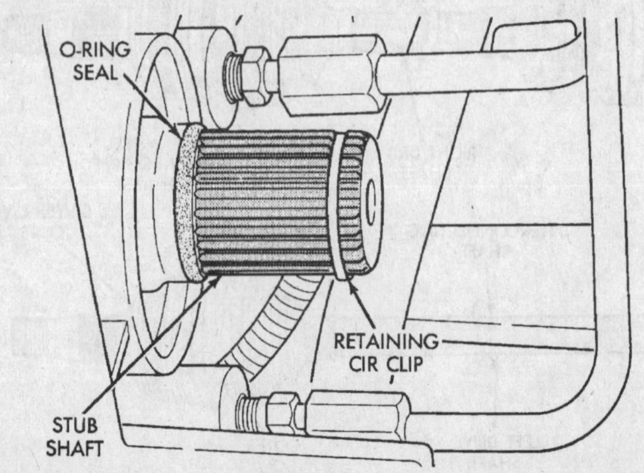

2.10a Be sure to replace the O-ring seal and the retaining circlip on the stub shaft

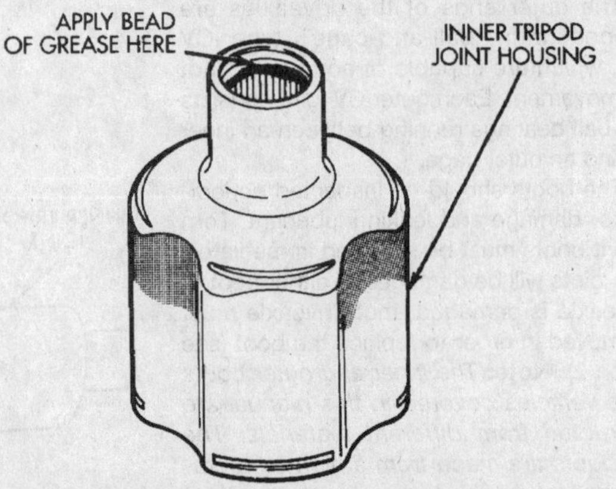

2.10b Apply an even coat of multi-purpose grease to the indicated area, where the inner CV joint seats against the O-ring on the stub shaft

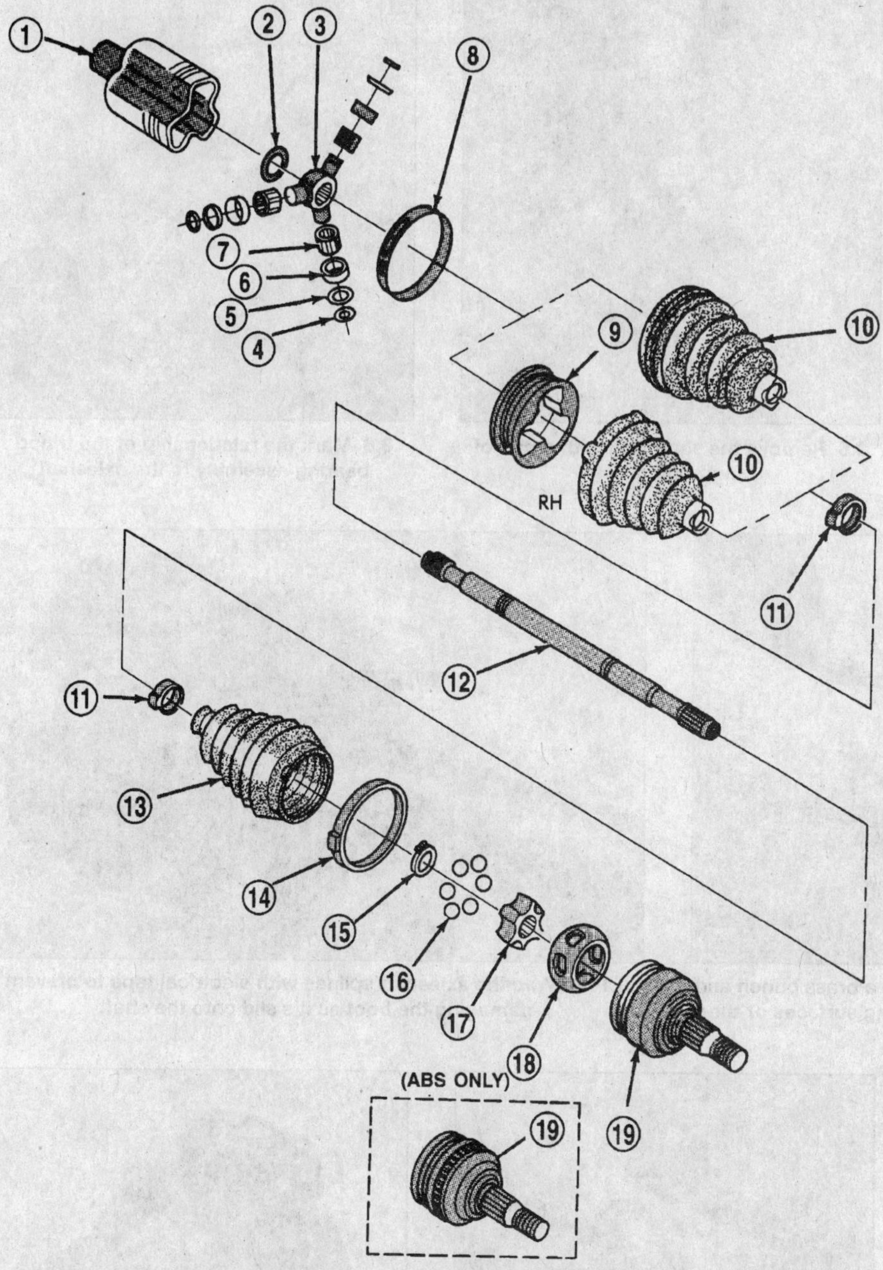

3.3a An exploded view of the driveaxle assembly

1	*Inner CV joint housing*	7	*Needle roller bearing*	14	*Boot retaining clamp*
2	*Spacer ring*	8	*Boot retaining clamp*	15	*Race retaining ring*
3	*Tripod joint spider*	9	*Tripod bushing*	16	*Ball bearings*
4	*Retaining ring*	10	*Driveaxle inner boot*	17	*CV joint inner race*
5	*Ball and roller retainer*	11	*Boot retaining clamp*	18	*CV joint cage*
6	*Tripod joint ball*	12	*Axleshaft*	19	*CV joint outer race*
		13	*Driveaxle outer boot*		

points:

a) *Be sure to install a new O-ring seal and retainer circlip on the stub shaft* **(see illustration).**

b) *Apply an even bead of multi-purpose grease around the spline of the inner CV joint, where the joint seats against the O-ring on the stub shaft* **(see illustration).**

c) *When installing the driveaxle, push it sharply in to seat the snap-ring on the stub shaft into its groove inside the splined female end of the inner CV joint housing.*

d) *Install a NEW driveaxle/hub nut and tighten it to the torque listed in this Chapter's Specifications.*

e) *Install the wheel and lug nuts, lower the vehicle and tighten the lug nuts to the torque listed in the Chapter 1 Specifications.*

3.3b Cut the old boot clamps off and discard them

3 Driveaxle boot replacement

Note 1: *The inner and outer boots on the vehicles covered in this manual are constructed from different materials: The inner boots are made from a high-temperature application silicone material; the outer boots are made from hytrel plastic. Make sure you obtain a boot made of the correct material for the CV joint boot you're replacing.*

Note 2: *If the CV joint boot(s) must be replaced, explore all options before beginning the job. Complete, rebuilt driveaxles may be available on an exchange basis, eliminating much time and work. Whichever route you choose to take, check on the cost and availability of parts before disassembling the vehicle.*

1 Remove the driveaxle (see Section 2).

2 Mount the driveaxle in a vise with wood lined jaws (to prevent damage to the axleshaft). Check the CV joint for excessive play in the radial direction, which indicates worn parts. Check for smooth operation throughout the full range of motion for each CV joint. If a boot is torn, the recommended procedure is to disassemble the joint, clean the components and inspect for damage due to loss of lubrication and possible contamination by foreign matter. If the CV joint is in good condition, lubricate it with CV joint grease and install a new boot.

Inner CV joint

Disassembly

Refer to illustrations 3.3a, 3.3b, 3.4, 3.5, 3.6 and 3.7

3 Using diagonal cutters, cut the boot clamps **(see illustrations)**, remove the clamps and discard them.

4 Using a screwdriver, carefully pry up on the edge of the CV boot, pull it off the CV

3.4 Remove the boot from the inner CV joint and slide the tripod from the joint housing

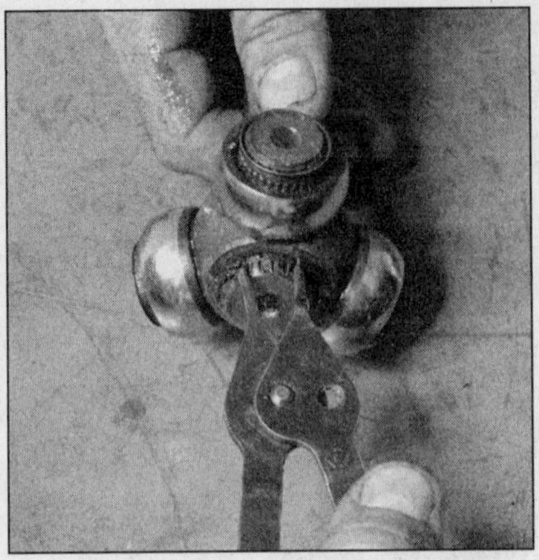

3.5 Remove the snap-ring with a pair of snap-ring pliers

3.6 Mark the relationship of the tripod bearing assembly to the axleshaft

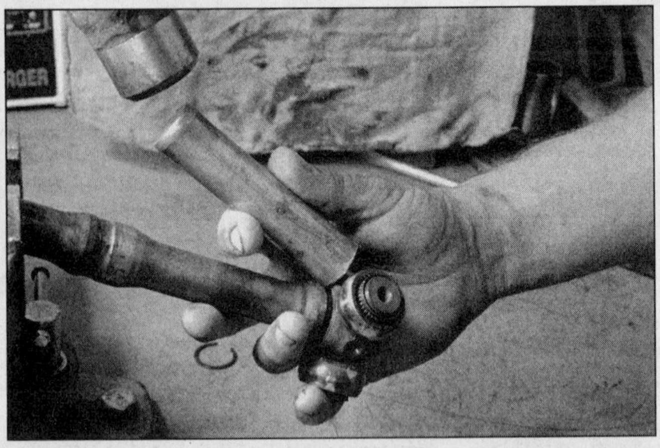

3.7 Drive the tripod joint off the axleshaft with a brass punch and hammer; be careful not to damage the bearing surfaces or the splines on the shaft

3.10a Wrap the axleshaft splines with electrical tape to prevent damaging the boot as it's slid onto the shaft

joint housing and slide it down the axleshaft, exposing the tripod spider assembly **(see illustration)**. To separate the axleshaft and spider assembly from the inner CV joint housing, simply pull them straight out.

5 Remove the tripod joint snap-ring with a pair of snap-ring pliers **(see illustration)**.

6 Mark the tripod to the axleshaft **(see illustration)** to ensure that they are reassembled properly.

7 Use a hammer and a brass punch to drive the tripod joint from the driveaxle **(see illustration)**.

8 Cut the boot clamps for the outer CV joint boot and slide off or cut off both boots.

Check

9 Thoroughly clean all components with solvent until the old CV joint grease is completely removed. Inspect the bearing surfaces of the inner tripods and housings for cracks, pitting, scoring and other signs of wear. If any part of the inner CV joint is worn, you must replace the entire driveaxle assembly (inner CV joint, axleshaft and outer CV joint). The only components which can be purchased separately are the boots themselves and the boot clamps.

3.10b Install the tripod spider on the axleshaft (make sure your match mark is facing out)

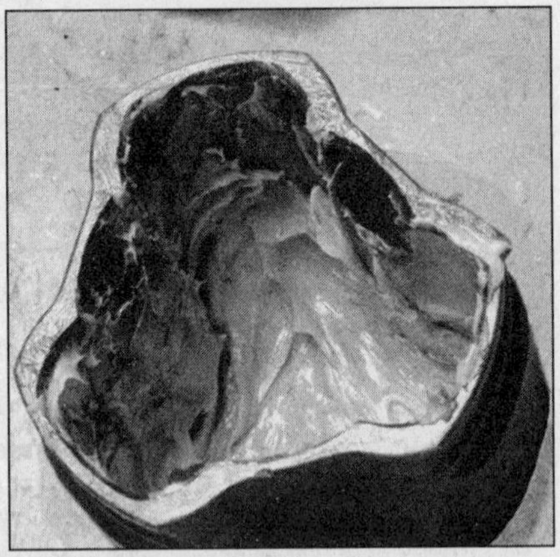

3.10c Place grease at the bottom of the CV joint housing

Reassembly

Refer to illustrations 3.10a, 3.10b, 3.10c, 3.10d, 3.11a, 3.11b and 3.13

10 Wrap the splines on the inner end the axleshaft with electrical tape to protect the boots from the sharp edges of the splines **(see illustration)**. Slide the clamps and boot onto the axleshaft, then remove the tape and place the tripod on the shaft. Apply grease to the tripod assembly and inside the housing. Insert the tripod into the housing and pack the remainder of the grease around the tripod **(see illustrations)**. If you're repacking the

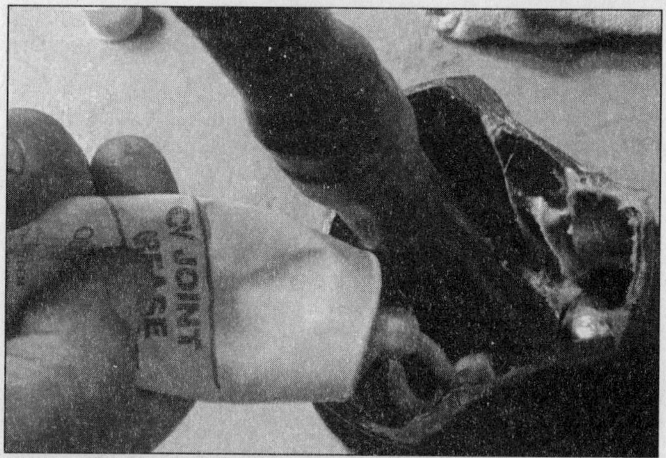

3.10d Install the boot and clamps onto the axleshaft, then insert the tripod into the housing, followed by the rest of the grease

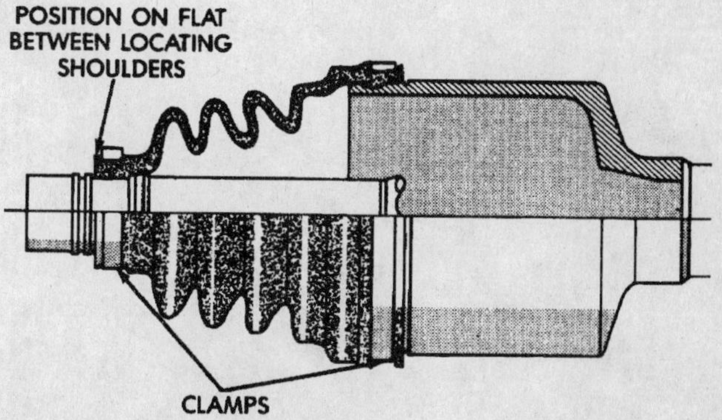

3.11a Slide the boot into place, making sure the small end seats in the flat spot on the axleshaft between the locating shoulders

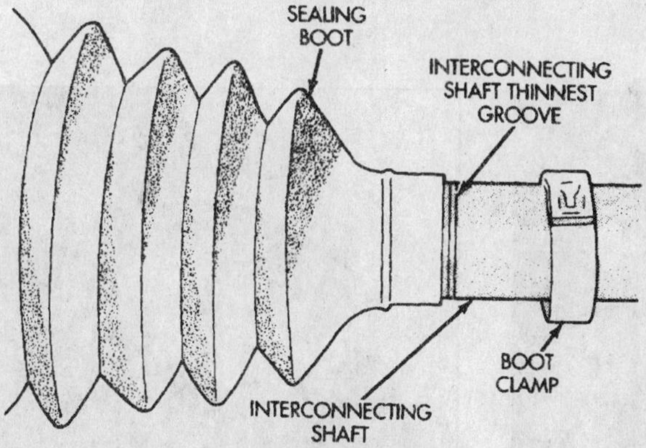

3.11b Make sure that the thinnest groove on the axleshaft is the only one showing

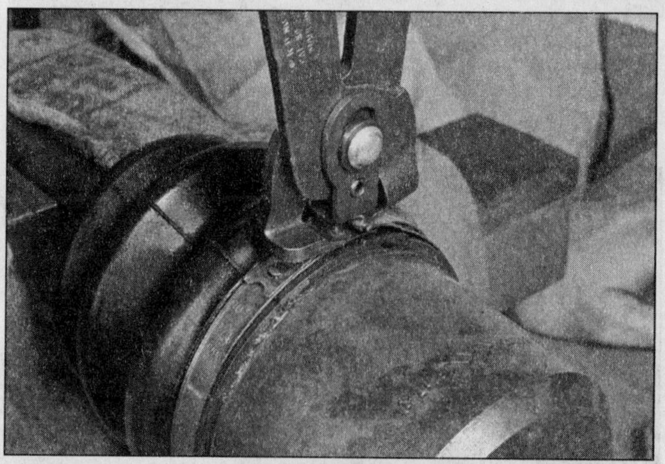

3.13 This type of clamp crimping tool, available at most auto parts stores, will work for tightening the clamps on the inner boots (the outer boot clamps require a tool that generates much more clamping force)

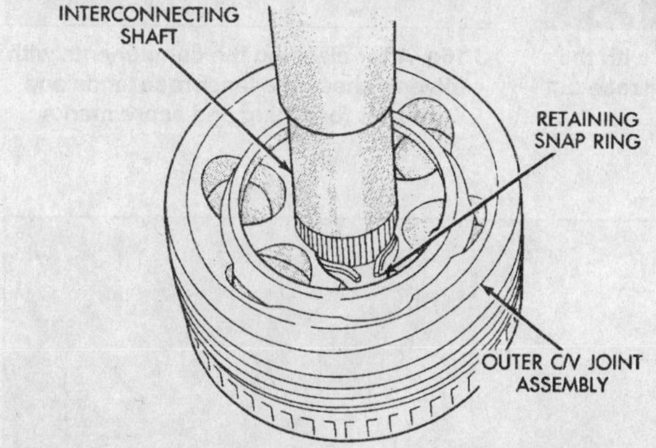

3.16a Once the boot for the outer CV joint has been slid back out of the way and some of the old grease is wiped off, you'll see a retaining ring buried in there

3.16b Use a pair of snap-ring pliers to release the snap-ring, then slide the outer CV joint assembly off the axleshaft and discard the old boot

outer joint, be sure to work the entire tube of CV joint grease (included with the boot kit) into the bearing assembly.

11 Slide the boot into place, making sure the small end seats in the flat spot on the axleshaft between the locating shoulders **(see illustration)**. Also make sure that the thinnest groove on the axleshaft is the only one showing **(see illustration)**.

12 Make sure each end of the boot is seated properly, and that the boot is not distorted. Equalize the pressure inside of the boot by inserting a small, dull screwdriver between the boot and the CV joint housing.

13 Clamp the new boot clamps onto the boot with a crimping tool, available at most auto parts stores **(see illustration)**.

14 The driveaxle is now ready for installation (see Section 2).

Outer CV joint

Refer to illustrations 3.16a through 3.16u

15 Cut off the old boot clamps.

16 To disassemble an outer CV joint for inspection, reassemble it, and install a new boot, referring to the accompanying photo sequence **(see illustrations)**. Be sure to stay in order and read the caption under each illustration.

17 The driveaxle is now ready for installation (see Section 2).

3.16c Place the outer CV joint assembly in a vise, then press down on the inner race far enough to allow a ball bearing to be removed; if it's difficult to tilt, gently tap the cage and inner race with a brass punch and hammer

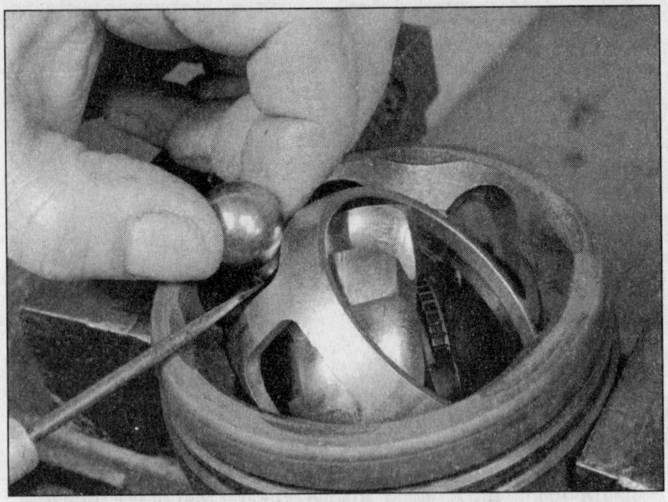

3.16d Pry the balls out of the cage, one at a time, with a dull screwdriver or wooden tool

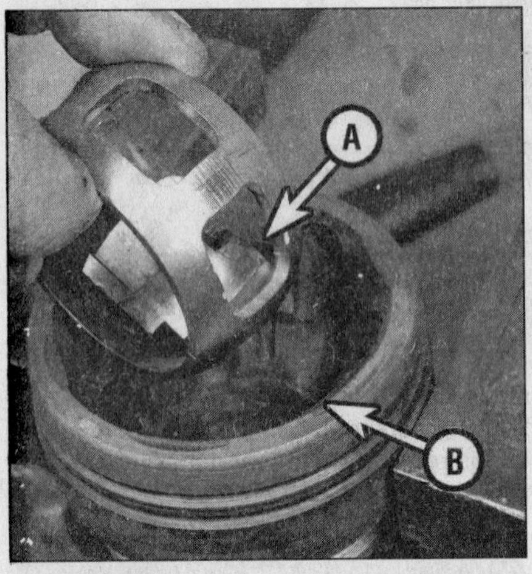

3.16e Tilt the inner race and cage 90-degrees, then align the windows (A) in the cage with the lands (B) of the housing and rotate the inner race up and out of the outer race

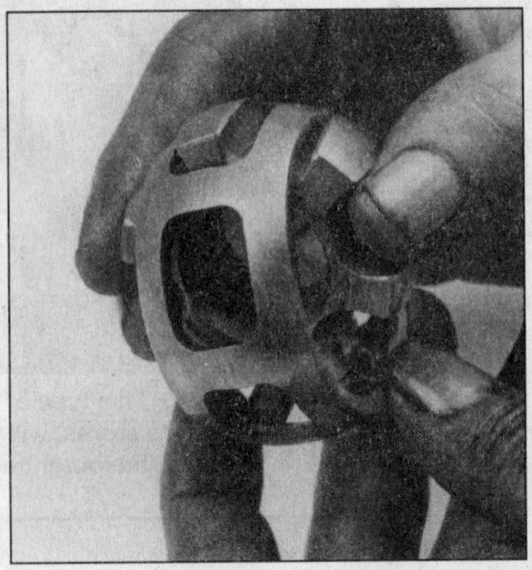

3.16f Align the inner race lands with the cage window and rotate the inner race out of the cage

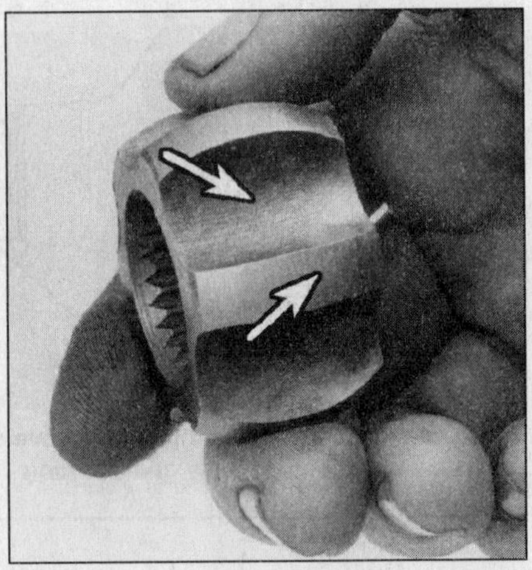

3.16g After cleaning the components with solvent, check the inner race lands and grooves for pitting and score marks

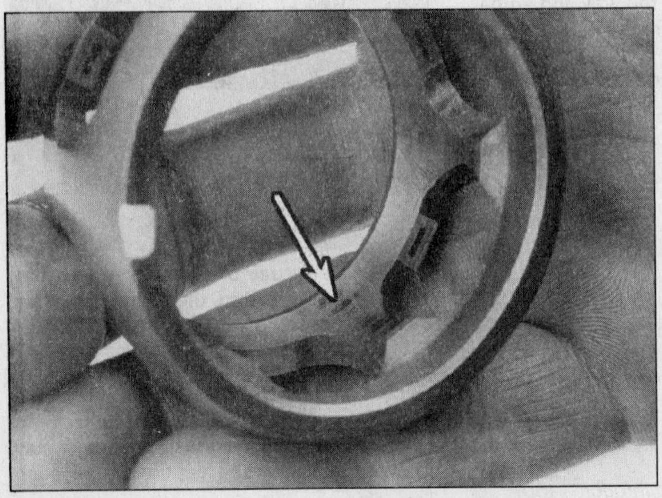

3.16h Check the cage for cracks, pitting and score marks - shiny spots are normal and don't affect operation

3.16i With the race and cage tilted at 90-degrees, lower the assembly into the housing

3.16j Rotate the assembly by gently tapping with a hammer and brass punch . . .

3.16k . . . then press the balls into the cage windows, repeating until all of the balls are installed

3.16l Use needle-nose pliers to lower the retaining ring into the groove . . .

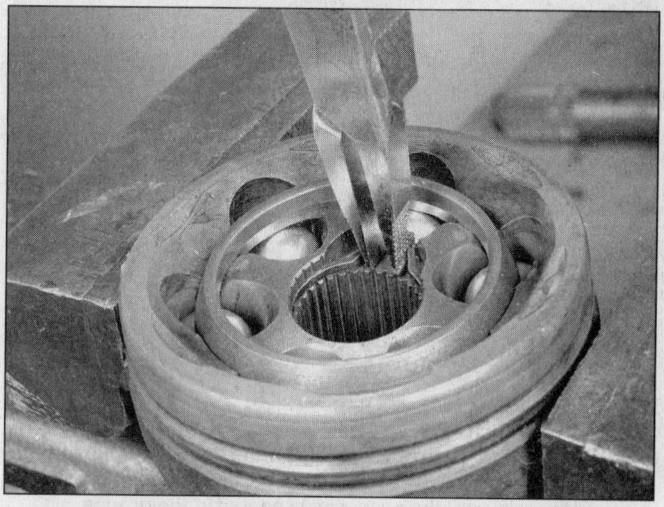

3.16m . . . then seat it into the groove with snap-ring pliers

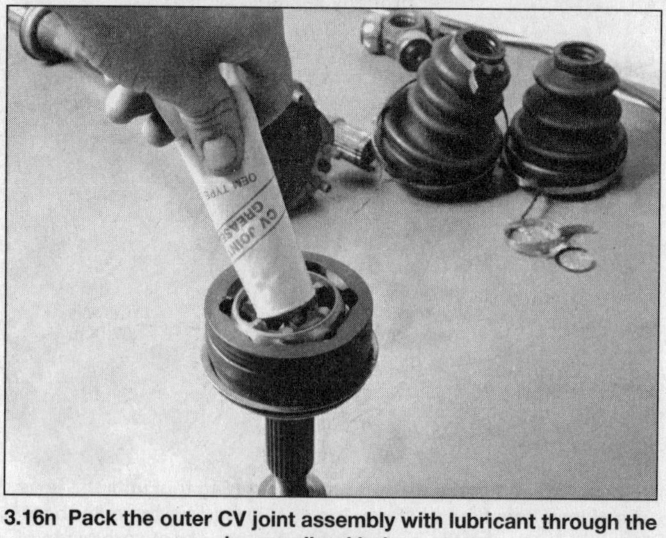

3.16n Pack the outer CV joint assembly with lubricant through the inner splined hole . . .

3.16o . . . then insert a wooden dowel (with a diameter slightly less than that of the axle) through the splined hole and push down - the dowel will force the grease into the joint - repeat until the bearing is completely packed

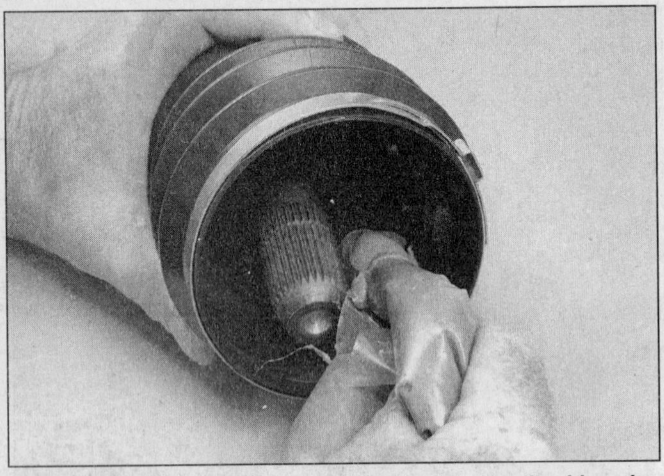

3.16p Install the small clamp and the new boot on the driveaxle (see illustration 3.10a), then apply grease to the inside of the boot until . . .

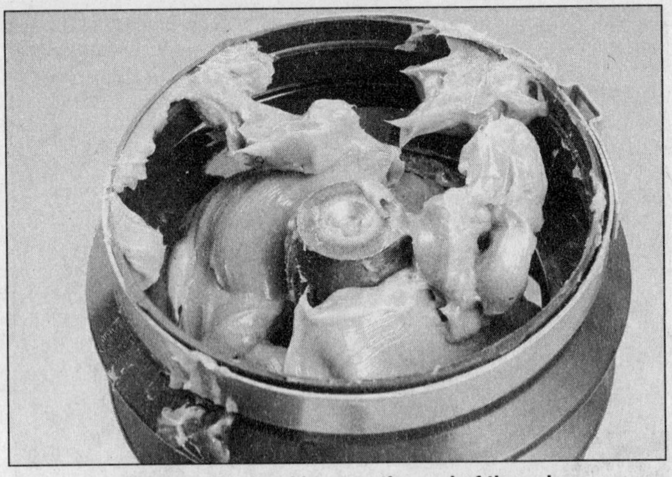

3.16q . . . the level is up to the end of the axle

3.16r Position the CV joint assembly on the driveaxle, aligning the splines, then use a soft-face hammer to drive the joint onto the driveaxle until the snap-ring is seated in the groove

3.16s Seat the small end of the boot in the flat area on the axleshaft between the locating shoulders, with only one groove (the thinnest) showing (see illustrations 3.11a and 3.11b) and install the new retaining clamp. Then install the other clamp on the larger end of the boot, again making sure the boot is properly seated

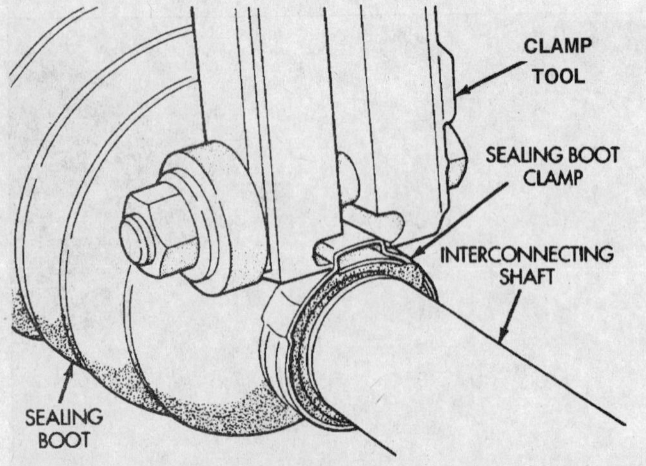

3.16t Equalize the pressure in the boot by inserting a small screwdriver between the boot and the housing, then clamp the new boot clamps onto the boot with a crimping tool such as this one (available at most auto parts stores). Place the crimping tool over the bridge of each new boot clamp . . .

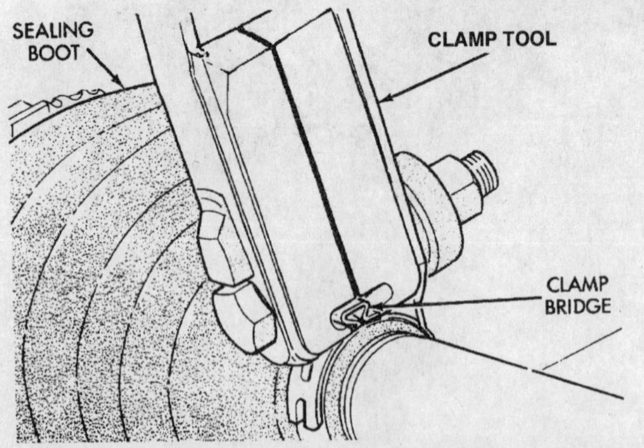

3.16u . . . then tighten the nut on the crimping tool until the jaws are closed (this type of clamp tool is required for the outer boot clamps; because of the material that the outer boots are made of, much greater crimping force is required than the tool used on the inner clamps is capable of generating

Chapter 9 Brakes

Contents

Specifications

General

Brake fluid type	See Chapter 1
Wheel speed sensor resistance	
Between terminals	800 to 1400 ohms
Between each terminal and ground	15,000 ohms minimum

Disc brakes

Brake pad minimum thickness	See Chapter 1
Disc lateral runout limit	0.005 inch
Disc minimum thickness	Cast into disc
Thickness variation	0.0005 inch

Torque specifications

	Ft-lbs (unless otherwise indicated)
Brake booster mounting nuts	21
Brake hose banjo bolt-to-caliper	35
Caliper guide pin bolts	16
Master cylinder-to-brake booster mounting nuts	21
Parking brake pedal assembly mounting bolts/nuts	21

1 General information

General

All models covered by this manual are equipped with a hydraulically operated brake system. All models are equipped with front and rear disc brakes. All brakes are self-adjusting.

The hydraulic system is split diagonally - the left front and right rear brakes are on one circuit, the right front and left rear on the other. If one circuit fails, the other circuit will remain functional and a warning indicator will light up on the dashboard when a substantial amount of brake fluid is lost, showing that a failure has occurred.

Calipers

All disc brakes used by the vehicles covered in this manual are equipped with a double-pin floating caliper, a single-piston design that "floats" on two steel guide pins. When the brake pedal is depressed, hydraulic pressure pushing on the piston is transmitted to the inner brake pad and against the inner surface of the brake disc. As the force against the disc from the inner pad is increased, the caliper assembly moves in, sliding on the guide pins and pulling the outer pad against the disc, providing a pinching force on the disc.

Master cylinder

The master cylinder is located under the hood on the driver's side, and can be identified by the large fluid reservoir on top. The master cylinder has two separate circuits to accommodate the diagonally split system.

Power brake booster

The power brake booster uses engine manifold vacuum to provide assistance to the brakes. It is mounted on the firewall in the engine compartment, directly behind the master cylinder.

Parking brake system

The parking brake pedal actuates the rear brakes via a series of cables. The parking brake cables pull on a lever attached to the parking brake shoe assembly, causing the shoes to expand against the drum surfaces inside the rear discs.

Precautions

There are some general precautions and warnings related to the brake system:

a) *Use only brake fluid conforming to DOT 3 specifications.*
b) *The brake pads and linings may contain asbestos fibers which are hazardous to your health if inhaled. Whenever you work on brake system components, clean all parts with brake system cleaner. Do not allow the fine dust to become airborne.*
c) *Safety should be paramount whenever any servicing of the brake components is performed. Do not use parts or fasteners which are not in perfect condition, and be sure all clearances and torque specifications are adhered to. If you are at all unsure about a certain procedure, seek professional advice. Upon completion of any brake system work, test the brakes carefully in a controlled area before driving the vehicle in traffic.*
d) *If a problem is suspected in the brake system, don't drive the vehicle until it's fixed.*

2 Anti-lock Brake System (ABS) - general information

Description

The Anti-lock Brake System (ABS) prevents wheel lock-up under heavy braking conditions on virtually any road surface. Preventing the wheels from locking up maintains vehicle maneuverability, preserves directional stability, and allows optimal deceleration. How does ABS work? Basically, by monitoring the rotational speed of the wheels and controlling the brake line pressure to the calipers/wheel cylinders at each wheel during braking.

Components

Integrated Control Unit (ICU)

The Integrated Control Unit consists of the Hydraulic Control Unit (HCU) and the Controller Anti-lock Brake (CAB). It is located in front of the left front wheel, behind the splash shield.

Controller Anti-lock Brake (CAB)

The CAB is mounted to the bottom of the HCU and consists of a pair of microprocessors which monitor wheel speeds and control the anti-lock and traction control functions. The CAB constantly monitors the system. If a malfunction is detected, the CAB turns off the ABS and traction control functions, and turns on the warning lights.

Hydraulic Control Unit (HCU)

The HCU contains the valve block assembly, the pump/motor assembly and the fluid accumulator.

Valve block assembly

The valve block assembly contains eight valve/solenoids: four inlet valves and four outlet valves. The inlet valves are spring-loaded in the open position and the outlet valves are spring-loaded in the closed position. During ABS operation, these valves are cycled to maintain the proper slip ratio for each channel. If a wheel locks, the inlet valve is closed to prevent a further increase in pressure. Simultaneously, the outlet valve is opened to release the pressure back to the accumulators until the wheel is no longer slipping. Once the wheel no longer slips, the outlet valve closes and the inlet valve opens to allow pressure to the wheel caliper or wheel cylinder.

Pump/motor assembly

The pump/motor assembly consists of an electric motor and a dual-piston pump. The pump provides high-pressure brake fluid to the hydraulic control unit when the ABS system is activated.

Fluid accumulators

The two fluid accumulators in the HCU are for the primary and secondary hydraulic circuits, respectively. The accumulators temporarily store brake fluid that is blocked during ABS operation. This fluid is re-routed to the pump.

Proportioning valves

See Section 7.

Wheel speed sensors

A speed sensor is mounted at each wheel. The speed sensors send variable voltage signals to the HCU. These analog voltage outputs are proportional to the speed of rotation of each wheel.

Diagnosis and repair

The ABS system has self-diagnostic capabilities. Each time the ignition key is turned to On, the system runs a self-test. If it finds a problem, the ABS and traction control warning lights come on and remain on. If there's no problem with the system, the lights go out after approximately five seconds.

If the ABS and traction control warning lights come on and stay on during vehicle operation, there is a problem in the ABS system. Two things now happen: The controller stores a diagnostic trouble code (which can be displayed with a DRB III scanner at the dealer) and the ABS system is shut down. Once the ABS system is disabled, it will remain disabled until the problem is fixed and the trouble code is erased. However, the regular brake system will continue to function normally.

Although a DRB III (a special electronic tester) is necessary to properly diagnose the system (and access the trouble codes), you can make a few preliminary checks before taking the vehicle to a dealer:

a) *Make sure the brake calipers are in good condition.*
b) *Check the electrical connector at the controller.*
c) *Check the fuses.*
d) *Follow the wiring harness to the speed sensors and brake light switch and make sure all connections are secure and the wiring isn't damaged.*
e) *Follow the wiring harness from each wheel speed sensor up to its electrical connector. Unplug the connector and measure the resistance across the two terminals (on the sensor side of the harness). Also check the resistance between each terminal and a good ground. Compare your resistance readings with the values listed in this Chapter's Specifications. If any sensor is out of range, replace it.*

If the above preliminary checks don't rectify the problem, the vehicle should be diagnosed by a dealer service department or other properly equipped repair shop.

3 Disc brake pads - replacement

Refer to illustrations 3.3 and 3.4a through 3.4o

Warning: *Disc brake pads must be replaced on both front or rear wheels at the same time - never replace the pads on only one wheel. Also, the dust created by the brake system may contain asbestos, which is harmful to your health. Never blow it out with compressed air and don't inhale any of it. An approved filtering mask should be worn when working on the brakes. Do not, under any circumstances, use petroleum-based solvents to clean brake parts. Use brake system cleaner only!*

Note 1: *This procedure applies to both the front and the rear disc brakes.*

Note 2: *Always replace the retractor clips when the brake pads are replaced.*

1 Loosen the wheel lug nuts, raise the vehicle and support it securely on jackstands. Apply the parking brake. Remove the wheels.

3.3 Use a C-clamp to depress the piston into its bore

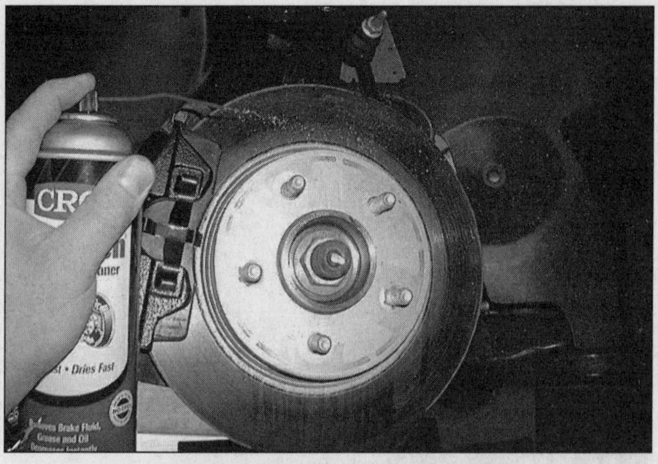

3.4a Wash the disc and brake pads with brake system cleaner to remove brake dust; DO NOT blow brake dust off with compressed air

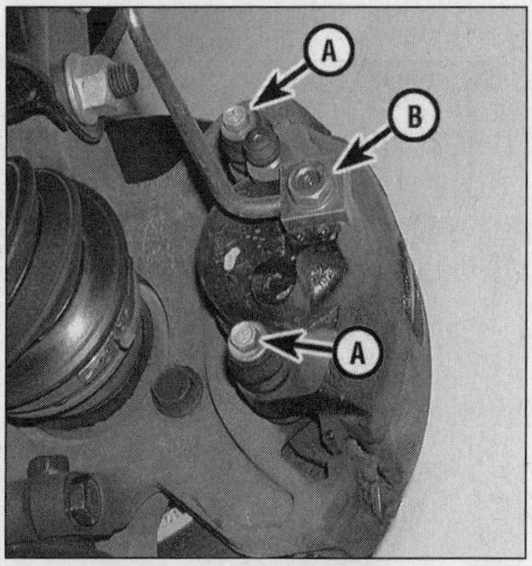

3.4b To remove the front caliper, remove the guide pin bolts (A); the brake hose banjo fitting bolt (B) doesn't have to be removed unless the caliper or brake hose is being replaced

2 Remove about two-thirds of the fluid from the master cylinder reservoir and discard it. Position a drain pan under the brake assembly.

3.4c To remove the rear caliper, remove these guide pin bolts (arrows)

3 Push the piston back into its bore to provide room for the new brake pads with a C-clamp **(see illustration)**. As the piston is depressed to the bottom of the caliper bore, the fluid in the master cylinder will rise. Make sure it doesn't overflow. If necessary, siphon off some of the fluid.

3.4d Hang the caliper from the strut coil spring with a piece of wire - don't let it hang by the brake hose

4 To replace the brake pads, follow the accompanying photos, beginning with **illustration 3.4a**. Be sure to stay in order and read the caption under each illustration.

3.4e Pry the outer brake pad retaining spring from the caliper . . .

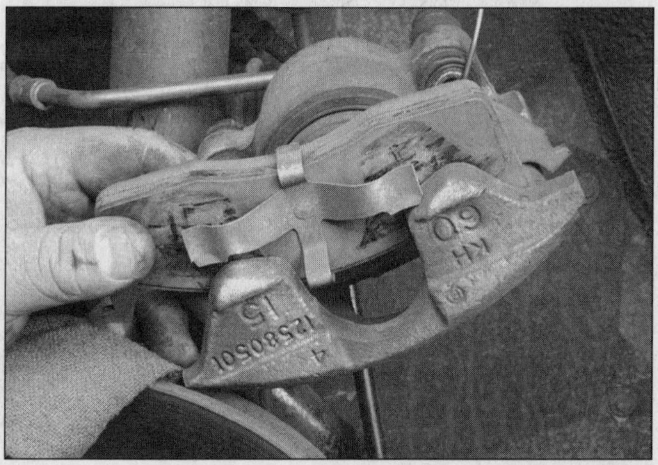

3.4f . . . and remove the outer brake pad

3.4g Pull the inner brake pad retaining spring loose from the piston and remove the pad

3.4h Remove the guide pin bushings

3.4i Remove the bushing boots, inspect them for tears and replace as necessary

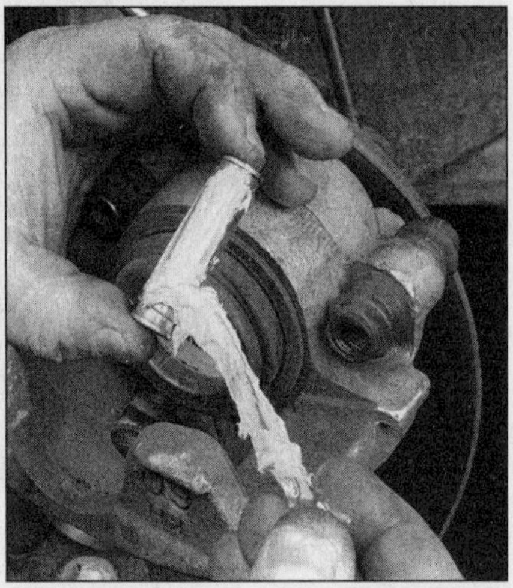

3.4j Lubricate the guide pin bushings with multi-purpose grease before installing them

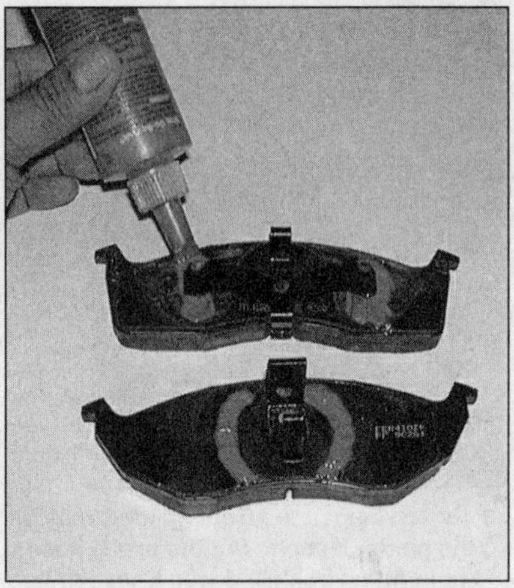

3.4k Apply a film of disc brake anti-squeal compound to the backs of the new pads (follow the directions on the product)

3.4l Install the inner brake pad - make sure the retaining spring is fully seated into its bore in the piston

3.4m Install the outer brake pad - make sure the retaining spring is properly engaged with the caliper body

3.4n Slip the caliper and pads over the brake disc, then install the upper retractor clip (arrow) . . .

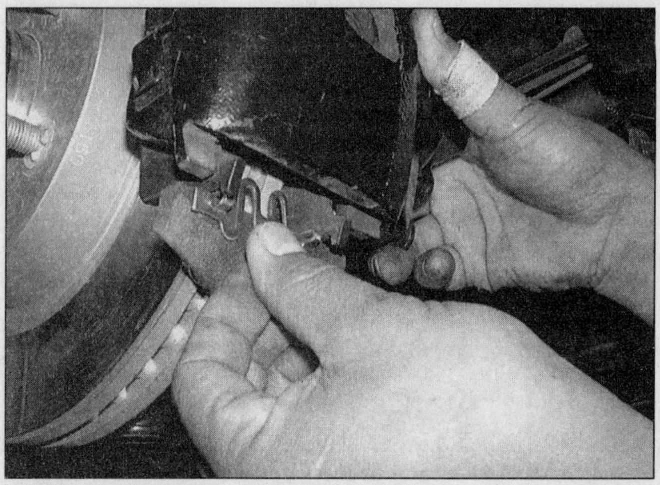

3.4o . . . and the lower retractor clip. Install the guide pin bolts, tightening them to the torque listed in this Chapter's Specifications

5 While the pads are removed, inspect the caliper for brake fluid leaks and ruptures of the piston boot. Replace the caliper if necessary (see Section 4). Also inspect the brake disc carefully (see Section 5). If machining is necessary, follow the information in that Section to remove the disc.

6 Before installing the caliper guide pin bolts, clean them and check them for corrosion and damage. If they're significantly corroded or damaged, replace them. Be sure to tighten the caliper guide pin bolts to the torque listed in this Chapter's Specifications.

7 Install the brake pads on the opposite wheel, then install the wheels and lower the vehicle. Tighten the lug nuts to the torque listed in the Chapter 1 Specifications. Add brake fluid to the reservoir until it's full (see Chapter 1).

8 Pump the brakes several times to seat the pads against the disc, then check the fluid level again.

9 Check the operation of the brakes before driving the vehicle in traffic. Try to avoid heavy brake applications until the brakes have been applied lightly several times to seat the pads.

4 Brake caliper - removal and installation

Warning: *Dust created by the brake system may contain asbestos, which is harmful to your health. Never blow it out with compressed air and don't inhale any of it. An approved filtering mask should be worn when working on the brakes. Do not, under any circumstances, use petroleum-based solvents to clean brake parts. Use brake system cleaner only.*

Note: *Always replace the calipers in pairs on the same axle (front or rear) - never replace just one of them.*

Removal

1 Loosen the wheel lug nuts, raise the vehicle and support it securely on jackstands. Remove the wheels.

2 Unscrew the banjo bolt from the caliper and detach the hose. **Note:** *If you're just removing the caliper for access to other components, don't disconnect the hose.* Discard the sealing washers on each side of the fitting and use new ones during installation. Wrap a plastic bag around the end of the hose to prevent fluid loss and contamination.

3 Remove the caliper guide pin bolts and remove the caliper **(see illustration 3.4b or 3.4c)**. Clean the caliper assembly with brake system cleaner. DO NOT use kerosene, gasoline or petroleum-based solvents. Be sure to check the pads as well and replace them if necessary (see Section 3).

Installation

4 Install the caliper assembly, tightening the caliper guide pin bolts to the torque listed in this Chapter's Specifications.

5 Connect the brake hose to the caliper using new sealing washers. Tighten the banjo bolt to the torque listed in this Chapter's Specifications.

6 Bleed the brakes (see Section 9).

7 Install the wheels and lug nuts. Lower the vehicle and tighten the lug nuts to the torque listed in the Chapter 1 Specifications.

8 After the job has been completed, firmly depress the brake pedal a few times to bring the pads into contact with the disc.

9 Check the operation of the brakes before driving the vehicle in traffic.

5.2 The brake pads on this vehicle were obviously neglected, as they wore down completely and cut deep grooves into the disc - wear this severe means the disc must be replaced

5 Brake disc - inspection, removal and installation

Inspection

Refer to illustrations 5.2, 5.3, 5.4a and 5.4b

1 Loosen the wheel lug nuts, raise the front of the vehicle and support it securely on jackstands. Apply the parking brake. Remove the front wheels. Reinstall the lug nuts, flat side toward the disc, to hold the disc firmly against the hub. **Note:** *It may be necessary to install washers under the lug nuts if they don't tighten down on the disc.*

2 Remove the brake caliper as described in Section 4. Visually inspect the disc surface for score marks and other damage **(see illus-**

5.3 Use a dial indicator to check disc runout - if the reading exceeds the specified runout limit, the disc will have to be machined or replaced

5.4a The minimum thickness is cast into the disc

tration). Light scratches and shallow grooves are normal after use and won't affect brake operation. Deep grooves - over 0.015-inch deep - require disc removal and refinishing by an automotive machine shop. Be sure to check both sides of the disc.

3 To check disc runout, place a dial indicator at a point about 1/2-inch from the outer edge of the disc **(see illustration)**. Set the indicator to zero and turn the disc. The indicator reading should not exceed the runout limit listed in this Chapter's Specifications. If it does, the disc should be refinished by an automotive machine shop. **Note:** *Professionals recommend resurfacing the brake discs regardless of the dial indicator reading (to produce a smooth, flat surface that will eliminate brake pedal pulsations and other undesirable symptoms related to questionable discs). At the very least, if you elect not to have the discs resurfaced, deglaze them with sandpaper or emery cloth.*

4 The disc must not be machined to a thickness less than the specified minimum thickness. The minimum (or discard) thickness is cast into the disc **(see illustration)**. The disc thickness can be checked with a micrometer **(see illustration)**.

Removal and installation

Refer to illustration 5.8

5 Loosen the wheel lug nuts, raise the vehicle and place it securely on jackstands.

6 Remove the wheel. If you're removing a rear disc, block the front wheels and release the parking brake.

7 Remove the caliper (see Section 4).

8 Remove the retaining clips, if present, from the wheel studs **(see illustration)**.

9 Pull the disc off the hub.

10 If you're removing a rear disc and the disc won't come off, remove the plug from the parking brake adjusting access hole. Turn the adjusting star wheel with a suitable tool (such as a screwdriver or brake adjusting tool) and retract the parking brake shoes.

11 Installation is the reverse of removal. Make sure you tighten the caliper guide pin bolts to the torque listed in this Chapter's Specifications.

6 Master cylinder - removal, reservoir replacement and installation

Removal

Refer to illustrations 6.2 and 6.4

Note: *Although not absolutely necessary, removing the cowl cover and strut brace will improve access to the master cylinder (see Chapter 11).*

1 Place rags under the brake line fittings and prepare caps or plastic bags to cover the ends of the lines once they're disconnected. **Caution:** *Brake fluid will damage paint. Cover all painted surfaces and avoid spilling fluid during this procedure.*

2 Unplug the electrical connector from the brake fluid level sensor **(see illustration)**.

3 Loosen the tube nuts at the ends of the brake lines where they enter the master cylinder. To prevent rounding off the flats on these nuts, a flare-nut wrench, which wraps around the nut, should be used **(see illustration 6.2)**.

5.4b Use a micrometer to measure the thickness of the disc at several points

5.8 Cut off and discard the disc retaining washers, if present (it isn't necessary to reinstall them)

6.2 Unplug the electrical connector from the fluid level warning switch (arrow), then disconnect the brake line fittings with a flare-nut wrench

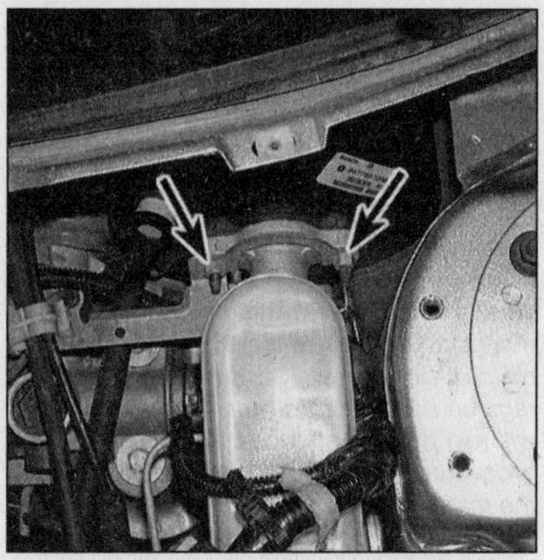

6.4 To detach the master cylinder from the power brake booster, remove these nuts (arrows), then pull the master cylinder assembly straight off the mounting studs

Pull the brake lines away from the master cylinder slightly and plug the ends to prevent contamination. Also plug the openings in the master cylinder to prevent fluid spillage.

4 Remove the two master cylinder mounting nuts **(see illustration)** and unbolt the bracket. Move the bracket aside slightly, taking care not to kink the hydraulic lines. Remove the master cylinder from the vehicle.

5 Remove the reservoir cap, then discard any fluid remaining in the reservoir.

Reservoir replacement

Refer to illustrations 6.8, 6.9 and 6.10

Note: *The master cylinders used on the vehicles covered by this manual are not rebuildable. However, you can replace the reservoir and/or the sealing grommets between the reservoir and the master cylinder.*

6 Remove the master cylinder, if you haven't already done so (see Steps 1 through 5).

7 Remove the cap and drain the brake fluid into a container. Clean the exterior of the master cylinder with brake system cleaner.

8 Knock out the reservoir retaining pins **(see illustration)**.

9 Remove the reservoir by rocking it back-and-forth and pulling up on it **(see illustration)**.

10 Remove the reservoir-to-master cylinder grommets **(see illustration)**.

11 Lubricate a pair of new grommets with clean brake fluid and install them into the bores in the master cylinder.

12 Install the reservoir into the grommets; make sure the reservoir is completely seated and the reservoir cap is at the front.

13 Install the reservoir retaining pins.

Installation

Refer to illustrations 6.15 and 6.23

14 Bench bleed the new master cylinder before installing it. Mount the master cylinder in a vise, with the jaws of the vise clamping on the mounting flange.

15 Attach a pair of master cylinder bleeder tubes to the outlet ports of the master cylinder **(see illustration)**.

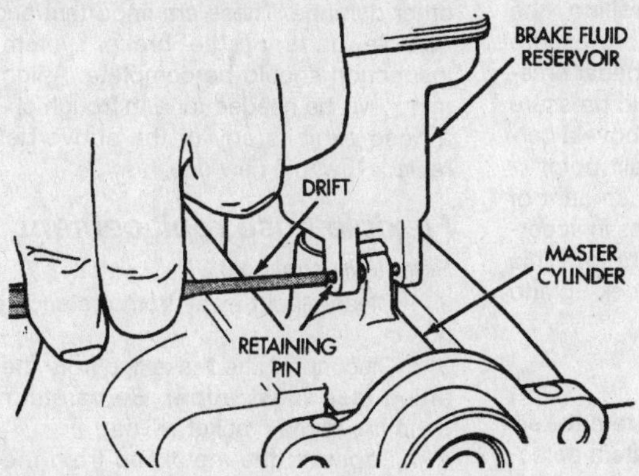

6.8 Remove the reservoir retaining pins with a small punch

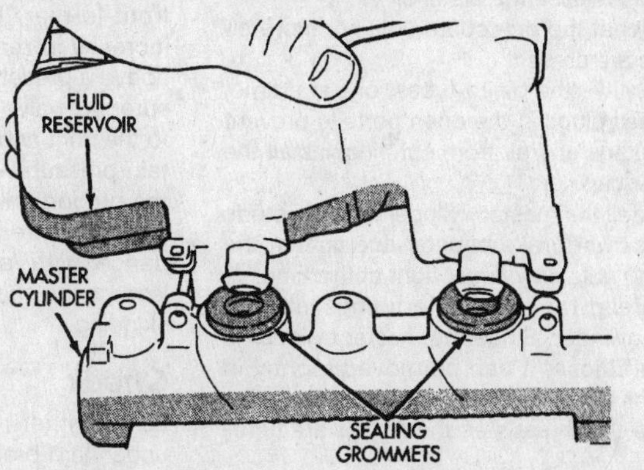

6.9 To separate the reservoir from the master cylinder, rock the reservoir back and forth and pull up at the same time

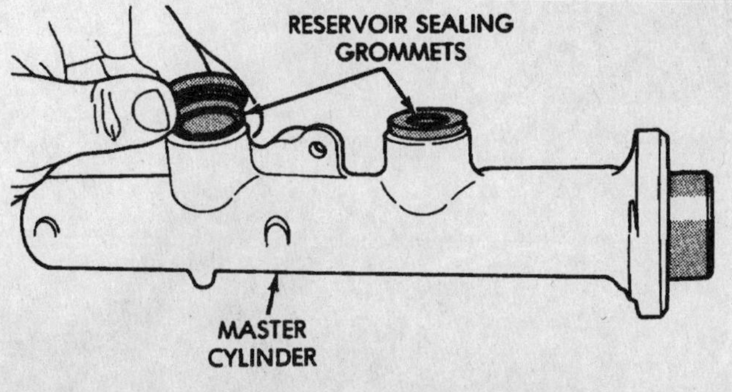

6.10 Remove the old grommets; if a grommet is difficult to remove, pry it out carefully with a small screwdriver but make sure you don't gouge the aluminum master cylinder housing

6.15 The best way to bleed air from the master cylinder before installing it on the vehicle is with a pair of bleeder tubes that direct brake fluid into the reservoir during bleeding

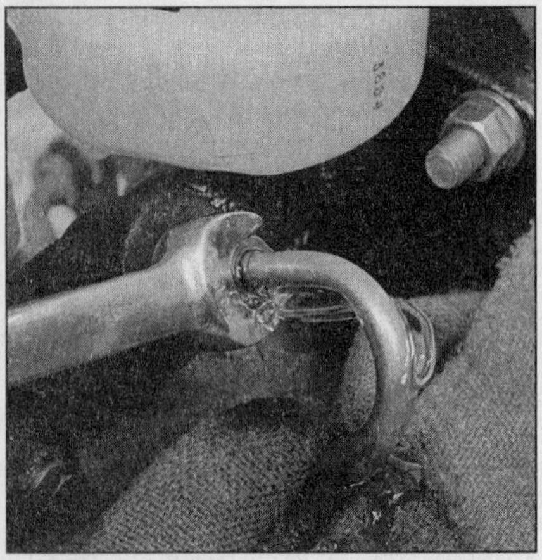

6.23 Have an assistant depress the brake pedal and hold it down, then loosen the fitting nut, allowing air and fluid to escape; repeat this procedure on both fittings until the fluid is clear of air bubbles

16 Fill the reservoir with brake fluid of the recommended type (see Chapter 1).

17 Slowly push the pistons into the master cylinder (a large Phillips screwdriver can be used for this) - air will be expelled from the pressure chambers and into the reservoir. Because the tubes are submerged in fluid, air can't be drawn back into the master cylinder when you release the pistons.

18 Repeat the procedure until nor more air bubbles are present.

19 Remove the bleed tubes, one at a time, and install plugs in the open ports to prevent fluid leakage and air from entering. Install the reservoir cap.

20 Install the master cylinder over the studs on the power brake booster and tighten the attaching nuts only finger tight at this time.

21 Thread the brake line fittings into the master cylinder. Since the master cylinder is still a bit loose, it can be moved slightly in order for the fittings to thread in easily. Do not strip the threads as the fittings are tightened.

22 Tighten the mounting nuts to the torque listed in this Chapter's Specifications, then the brake line fittings.

23 Fill the master cylinder reservoir with fluid, then bleed the master cylinder and the rest of the brake system as described in Section 9. To bleed the cylinder on the vehicle, have an assistant depress the brake pedal and hold the pedal to the floor. Loosen the fitting nut to allow air and fluid to escape **(see illustration)**. Repeat this procedure on both fittings at the master cylinder until the fluid is clear of air bubbles. **Caution:** *Have plenty of rags on hand to catch the fluid - brake fluid will ruin painted surfaces. After the bleeding procedure is completed, rinse the area under the master cylinder with clean water.*

24 Test the operation of the brake system carefully before placing the vehicle into normal service. **Warning:** *Do not operate the vehicle if you are in doubt about the effectiveness of the brake system.*

7 Proportioning valve(s) - description, check and replacement

Description

Refer to illustration 7.1

1 All models have two in-line proportioning valves **(see illustration)** that balance front-to-rear braking by controlling the increase in rear system hydraulic pressure above a preset level. Under light pedal pressure, the valve allows full hydraulic pressure to the front and rear brakes. But above a certain pressure - known as the "split point" - the proportioning valve limits the amount of pressure increase to the rear brakes in accordance with a predetermined ratio. This lessens the chance of rear wheel lock-up and skidding.

Check

2 If either rear wheel skids prematurely under hard braking, it could indicate a defective proportioning valve. If this occurs, have the system checked out by a dealer service department or other qualified repair shop. A pair of special pressure gauges are required for diagnosing the proportioning valve.

Replacement

Caution: *Brake fluid will damage paint. Cover all painted surfaces and avoid spilling fluid during this procedure.*

3 Raise the rear of the vehicle and place it securely on jackstands.

4 Unscrew the proportioning valve(s) from the brake line(s) **(see illustration 7.1)**. Use a flare-nut wrench to prevent rounding off the corners of the fittings. Back off the fittings and detach the lines. Plug the ends of the lines to prevent loss of brake fluid and the entry of dirt.

5 Installation is the reverse of removal.

6 Bleed the system after the replacement valve has been installed.

8 Brake hoses and lines - check and replacement

1 About every six months, with the vehicle raised and placed securely on jackstands, the flexible hoses which connect the steel brake lines with the front and rear brake assemblies should be inspected for cracks, chafing of the outer cover, leaks, blisters and other damage. These are important and vulnerable parts of the brake system and inspection should be complete. A light and mirror will be needed for a thorough check. If a hose exhibits any of the above defects, replace it with a new one.

Flexible hose replacement

Refer to illustration 8.3

2 Clean all dirt away from the ends of the hose.

3 Disconnect the brake line from the hose fitting **(see illustration)**. Be careful not to bend the frame bracket or line.

4 Separate the metal line from the connection and unbolt the hose bracket from the

7.1 The proportioning valves are located in each rear brake line, near the rear suspension crossmember

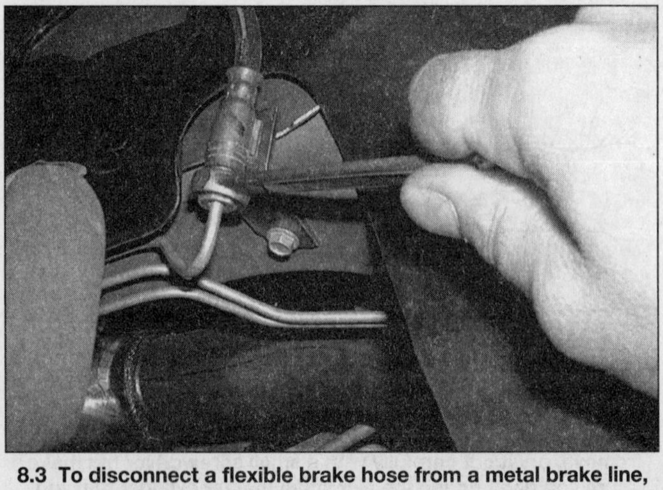

8.3 To disconnect a flexible brake hose from a metal brake line, unscrew the fitting nut with a flare nut wrench

vehicle. Immediately plug the metal line to prevent excessive fluid loss or contamination.
5 Unscrew the banjo bolt at the caliper and disconnect the hose from the caliper, discarding the sealing washers on either side of the fitting.
6 Using new sealing washers, attach the new brake hose to the caliper. Tighten the banjo bolt to the torque listed this Chapter's Specifications.
7 Make sure the hose isn't kinked or twisted, then attach metal line to the hose. Position the hose bracket on the frame and install the bolt, tightening it securely.
8 Carefully check to make sure the suspension or steering components don't make contact with the hose. Have an assistant push down on the vehicle while you check to see if the hose interferes with suspension operation. If you're replacing a front hose, have your assistant turn the steering wheel lock-to-lock while you make sure the hose doesn't interfere with the steering linkage or the steering knuckle.
9 Bleed the brake system (see Section 9).

Metal brake lines

10 When replacing brake lines, be sure to use the correct parts. Don't use copper tubing for any brake system components. Purchase steel brake lines from a dealer parts department or an auto parts store.
11 Prefabricated brake line, with the tube ends already flared and fittings installed, is available at auto parts stores and dealer parts departments. These lines can be bent to the proper shapes using a tubing bender.
12 When installing the new line make sure it's well supported in the brackets and has plenty of clearance between moving or hot components. Make sure you tighten the fittings securely.
13 After installation, check the master cylinder fluid level and add fluid as necessary. Bleed the brake system as outlined in Section 9 and test the brakes carefully before placing the vehicle into normal operation.

9 Brake system bleeding

Refer to illustration 9.8

Warning: *Wear eye protection when bleeding the brake system. If the fluid comes in contact with your eyes, immediately rinse them with water and seek medical attention.*

Note: *Bleeding the brake system is necessary to remove any air that's trapped in the system when it's opened during removal and installation of a hose, line, caliper, wheel cylinder or master cylinder.*

1 If a brake line was disconnected only at a wheel, then only that caliper or wheel cylinder must be bled.
2 On conventional (non-ABS) brake systems, if air has entered the system due to low fluid level, all four brakes must be bled. **Warning:** *If this has occurred on a model with an Anti-lock Brake System (ABS), or if the lines to the Hydraulic Control Unit (HCU) have been disconnected, the vehicle must be towed to a dealer service department or other repair shop equipped with a DRB II scan tool to have the system properly bled.*
3 If a brake line is disconnected at a fitting located between the master cylinder and any of the brakes, that part of the system served by the disconnected line must be bled.
4 Remove any residual vacuum from the brake power booster (if equipped) by applying the brake several times with the engine off.
5 Remove the master cylinder reservoir cover and fill the reservoir with brake fluid. Reinstall the cover. **Note:** *Check the fluid level often during the bleeding operation and add fluid as necessary to prevent the fluid level from falling low enough to allow air bubbles into the master cylinder.*
6 Have an assistant on hand, as well as a supply of new brake fluid, an empty clear container, a length of clear tubing to fit over the bleeder valve and a wrench to open and close the bleeder valve.
7 Beginning at the right rear wheel, loosen the bleeder screw slightly, then tighten it to a point where it's snug but can still be loosened quickly and easily.
8 Place one end of the tubing over the bleeder screw fitting and submerge the other end in brake fluid in the container **(see illustration)**.
9 Have the assistant slowly depress the brake pedal and hold the pedal firmly to the floor.
10 While the pedal is held depressed, open the bleeder screw just enough to allow a flow of fluid to leave the valve. Watch for air bubbles to exit the submerged end of the tube. When the fluid flow slows after a couple of seconds, tighten the screw and have your assistant release the pedal.
11 Repeat Steps 9 and 10 until no more air is seen leaving the tube, then tighten the bleeder screw and proceed to the left front wheel, the left rear wheel and the right front wheel, in that order, and perform the same procedure. Be sure to check the fluid in the master cylinder reservoir frequently.
12 Never use old brake fluid. It contains moisture which can boil if the temperature of the brake fluid rises high enough, which will render the brakes useless.
13 Refill the master cylinder with fluid at the end of the operation.
14 Check the operation of the brakes. The pedal should feel solid when depressed, with no sponginess. If necessary, repeat the entire process. **Warning:** *Do not operate the vehicle if the pedal feels low or spongy, if the ABS light on the dash won't go off or if you have any doubts as to the effectiveness of the brake system.*

10 Power brake booster - check, removal and installation

Operating check

1 Depress the brake pedal several times with the engine off and make sure that there is no change in the pedal reserve distance.
2 Depress the pedal and start the engine. If the pedal goes down slightly, operation is normal.

Airtightness check

3 Start the engine and turn it off after one or two minutes. Depress the brake pedal several times slowly. If the pedal goes down farther the first time but gradually rises after the second or third depression, the booster is airtight.
4 Depress the brake pedal while the engine is running, then stop the engine with the pedal depressed. If there is no change in the pedal reserve travel after holding the pedal for 30 seconds, the booster is airtight.

Removal

Refer to illustration 10.9

5 The power brake booster unit requires no special maintenance apart from periodic inspection of the vacuum hose and the case. The power brake booster cannot be repaired. If a problem develops, a new unit must be installed.

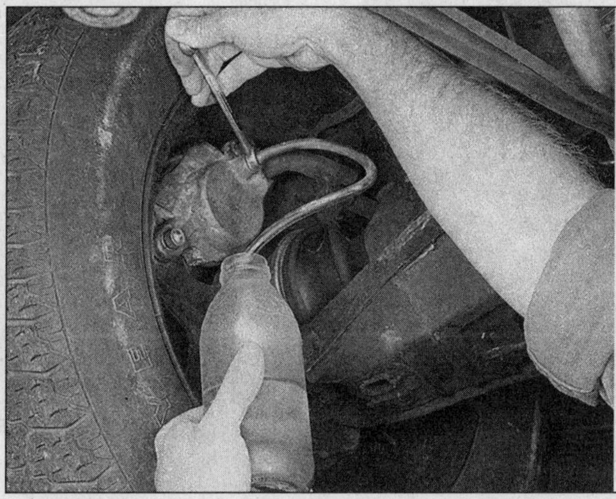

9.8 When bleeding the brakes, a hose is connected to the bleed screw at the caliper or wheel cylinder and then submerged in brake fluid - air will be seen as bubbles in the tube and container (all air must be expelled before moving to the next wheel)

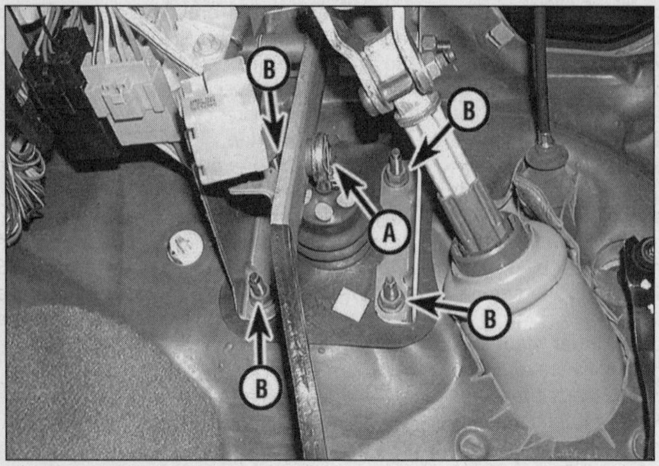

10.9 Pry off the retaining clip (A) and detach the pushrod from the brake pedal, then remove the booster mounting nuts (B)

11.5 Wash the parking brake assembly with brake system cleaner so you don't inhale any brake dust

6 Remove the cowl cover and strut brace (see Chapter 11) and the windshield wiper module (see Chapter 12).

7 Remove the master cylinder (see Section 6). It isn't necessary to actually disconnect the brake lines from the master cylinder; simply slide the master cylinder off the mounting studs and push it aside (just make sure you don't kink the metal brake lines).

8 Disconnect the vacuum hose from the check valve on the power brake booster. **Caution:** *Don't remove the check valve from the booster.*

9 Working under the dash, disconnect the power brake pushrod from the top of the brake pedal by prying off the retainer clip **(see illustration)**. Discard the old retainer clip and buy a new clip for reassembly.

10 Remove the nuts attaching the booster to the firewall.

11 Carefully lift the booster unit away from the firewall and out of the engine compartment.

Installation

12 To install the booster, place it into position and tighten the retaining nuts to the torque listed in this Chapter's Specifications. Connect the brake pedal. **Warning:** *Use a new retainer clip. Do not re-use the old clip.*

13 Install the master cylinder and vacuum hose.

14 Carefully test the operation of the brakes before placing the vehicle in normal operation.

11 Parking brake shoes - removal, inspection and installation

Warning: *Dust created by the brake system may contain asbestos, which is harmful to your health. Never blow it out with compressed air and don't inhale any of it. An approved filtering mask should be worn when working on the brakes. Do not, under any circumstances, use petroleum-based solvents to clean brake parts. Use brake system cleaner only.*

Note: *Parking brake shoes should be replaced on both wheels at the same time - never replace the shoes on only one wheel.*

Removal

Refer to illustrations 11.5 and 11.6a through 11.6h

1 The parking brake system should be checked as a normal part of driving. With the vehicle parked on a hill, apply the brake, place the transmission in Neutral and verify that the parking brake alone with hold the vehicle (be sure to stay in the vehicle during this check). Additionally, every 24 months - and any time a fault is suspected - the assembly itself should be visually inspected.

2 Loosen the rear wheel lug nuts, raise the rear of the vehicle and support it securely on jackstands. Block the front wheels and remove the rear wheels. Release the parking brake.

3 Remove the rear calipers (see Section 4). Support the caliper assemblies with a coat hanger or heavy wire and don't disconnect the brake line from the caliper.

4 Remove the rear discs (see Section 5). Remove the rear hub and bearing assemblies (see Chapter 10).

5 Clean the parking brake assembly with brake system cleaner **(see illustration)**.

6 Follow the accompanying sequence of

11.6a Remove the forward parking brake shoe hold-down clip by pushing in on the clip and turning the retaining pin 90-degrees

11.6b Remove the rear shoe hold-down clip

11.6c Pull the upper end of the rear shoe away from the parking brake actuator lever . . .

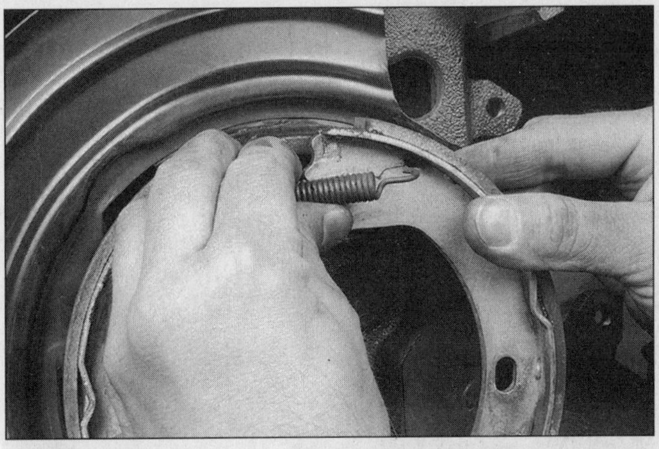

11.6d . . . then unhook the upper spring from the rear shoe

11.6e Disengage the lower end of the rear shoe from the adjuster . . .

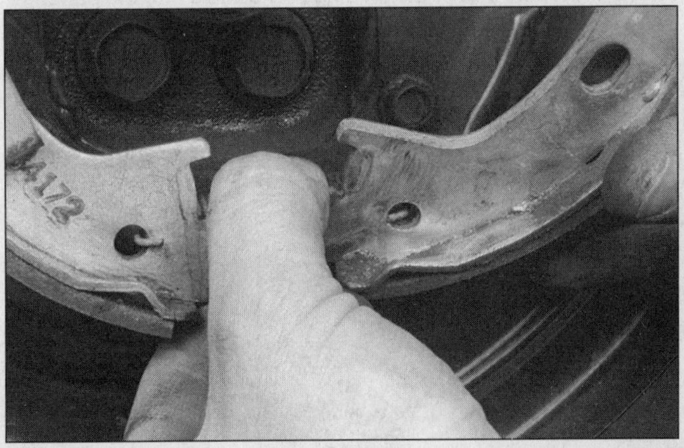

11.6f . . . then unhook the lower spring from the rear shoe and remove the rear shoe

photos to remove the parking brake shoes **(see illustrations)**. Be sure to stay in order and read the caption under each illustration.

Inspection

7 Inspect the lining contact pattern to determine whether the shoes are bent or have been improperly adjusted. The lining should show contact across the entire width, extending from head to toe. Shoes showing contact only on one side should be replaced.

8 Clean the backing plate with brake system cleaner.

9 Inspect the drum surface inside the disc for score marks, deep grooves, hard spots (which will appear as small, discolored areas) and cracks. If the disc/drum is worn, scored or out of round, it can be resurfaced by an automotive machine shop.

Installation

Refer to illustrations 11.10a through 11.10l

10 Follow the accompanying sequence of photos to install the new shoes **(see illustra-**

11.6g Unhook the lower spring from the front shoe

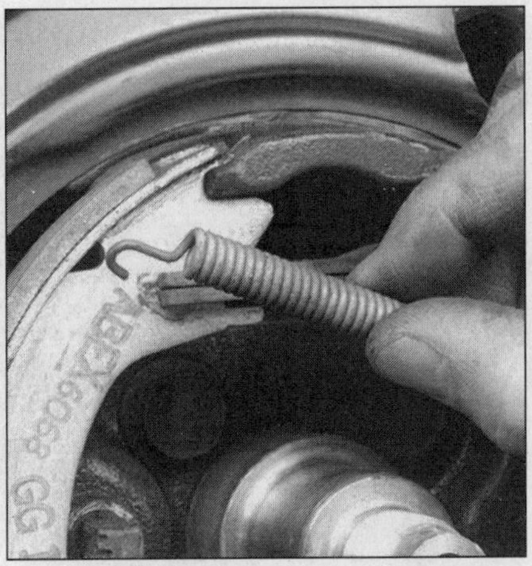

11.6h Unhook the upper spring from the front shoe

11.10a Lubricate the friction points on the brake backing plate with high-temperature grease

11.10b Insert the end of the parking brake cable into the parking brake actuator lever, if removed

11.10c Insert the pin for the hold-down clip through the brake backing plate

11.10d Install the front shoe

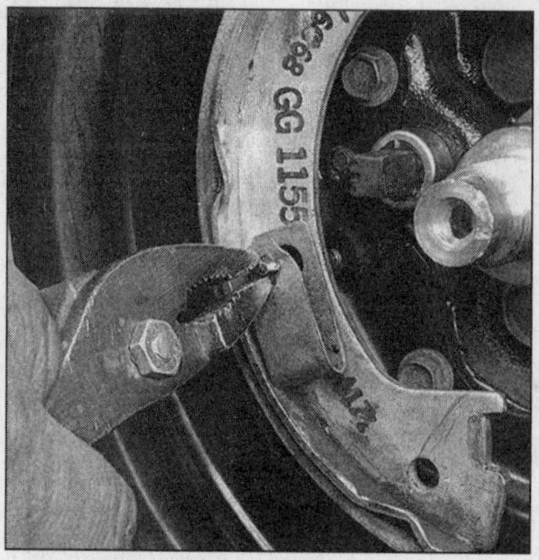

11.10e Install the front shoe hold-down clip

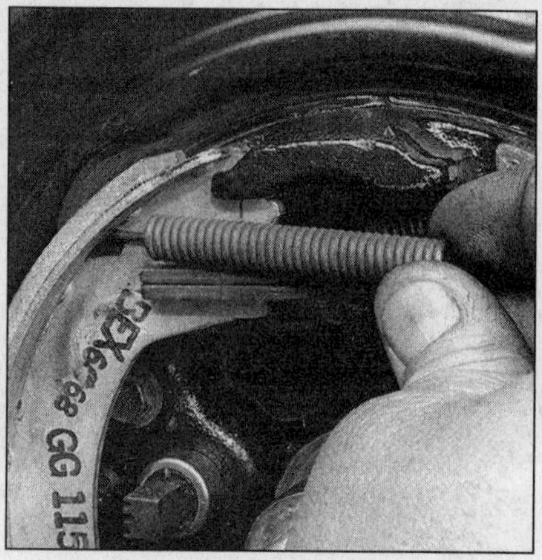

11.10f Hook the upper return spring to the front shoe

tions), then install the hub and bearing assemblies (see Chapter 10).

11 Before installing the disc, rotate the star wheel on the adjuster until the distance across the friction surfaces of the parking brake shoes is 6-3/4 inches.

12 Install the disc (see Section 5). Using a screwdriver or brake adjusting tool, turn the star wheel on the parking brake shoe adjuster until the shoes slightly drag as the disc is turned, then back-off the adjuster until the shoes don't drag.

13 Install the caliper (see Section 4).

14 Repeat this sequence for the other parking brake shoes at the other rear wheel.

11.10g Hook the lower return spring to the front shoe

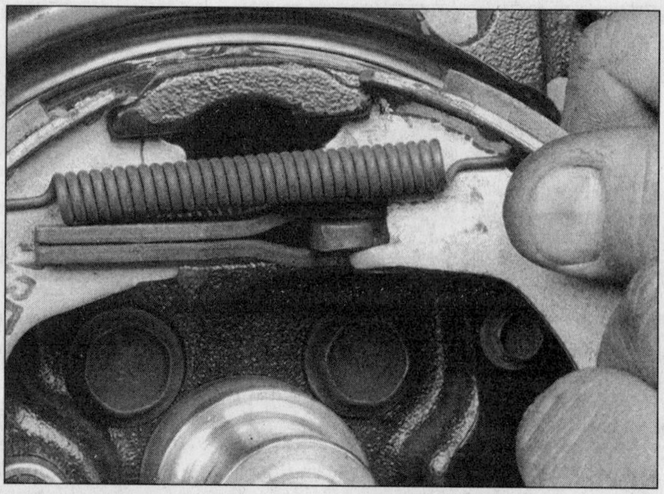

11.10h Hook the upper return spring to the rear shoe

11.10i Hook the lower return spring to the rear shoe

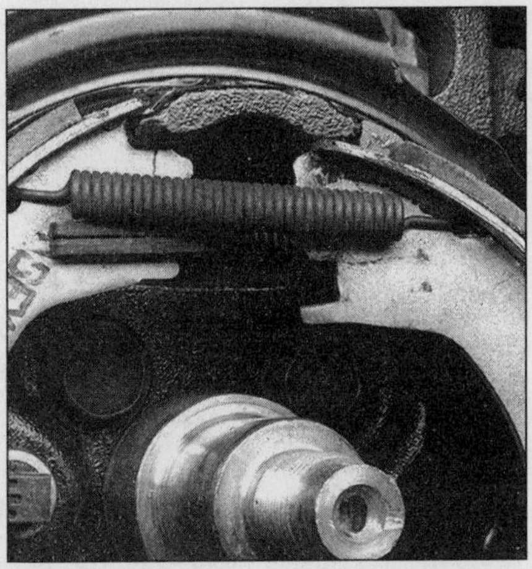

11.10j Pull the rear shoe back and engage it with the actuator lever

11.10k Insert the pin for the rear hold-down clip through the backing plate and install the clip

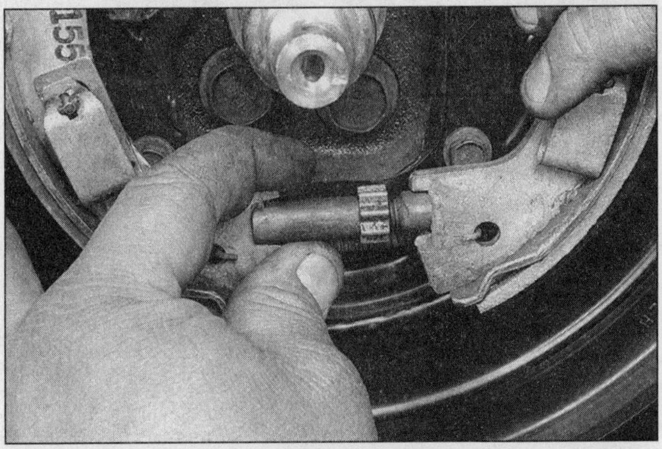

11.10l Install the adjuster between the parking brake shoes, then turn the adjuster star wheel until the distance across the friction surfaces of the shoes is 6-3/4 inches. Note: *The long portion of the adjuster should be pointing to the front of the vehicle*

12.2 Loosen the adjusting nut at the tensioner (arrow)

12 Parking brake - adjustment

Refer to illustrations 12.2 and 12.5

Note: *This is not a routine adjustment; if the parking brake shoes are adjusted properly, cable adjustment is only required when a cable or the tensioner is disconnected or replaced.*

1 Raise the rear of the vehicle and support it securely on jackstands. Block the front wheels to prevent the vehicle from rolling.

2 Loosen the adjusting nut at the tensioner enough to create slack in the cables **(see illustration)**.

3 Adjust the parking brake shoes as described in Section 11, Step 12.

4 Verify that the discs rotate freely without drag, then fully apply the parking brake.

5 Mark the tensioner rod about 1/4-inch from the tensioner bracket **(see illustration)**.

6 Tighten the adjusting nut at the tensioner until the mark on the tensioner rod moves into alignment with the tensioner bracket. **Caution:** *Do NOT loosen or tighten the tensioner adjusting nut for any reason after completing this adjustment.*

7 Release the parking brake pedal and verify that the rear wheels rotate freely without any drag.

8 Remove the jackstands and lower the vehicle.

9 Test the operation of the parking brake on an incline (be sure to remain in the vehicle for this check!).

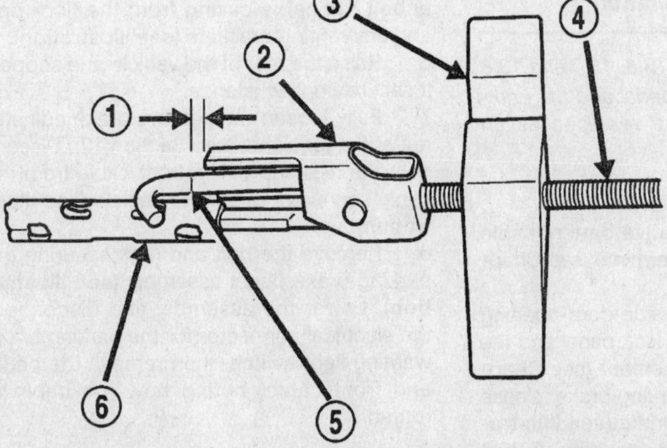

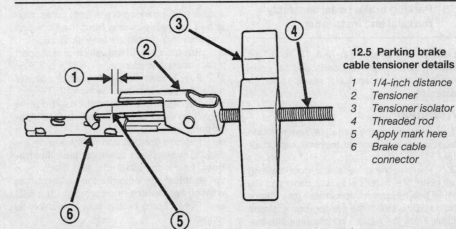

12.5 Parking brake cable tensioner details

1 *1/4-inch distance*
2 *Tensioner*
3 *Tensioner isolator*
4 *Threaded rod*
5 *Apply mark here*
6 *Brake cable connector*

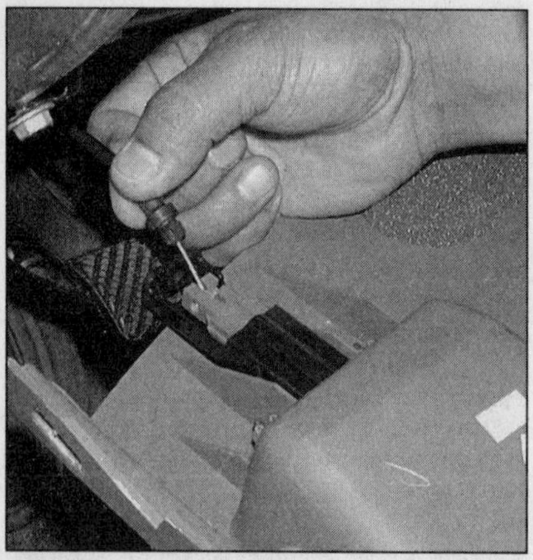

13.2 Disconnecting the parking brake release cable from the release handle

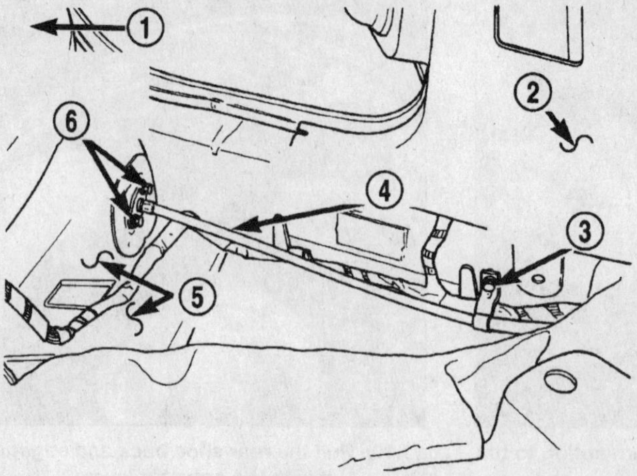

13.5 The rear end of the front parking brake cable casing is bolted to the floor pan

1 *Rear seat*
2 *Pillar between the front and rear doors*
3 *Cable bracket*
4 *Parking brake cable*
5 *Floor pan*
6 *Cable casing bolts*

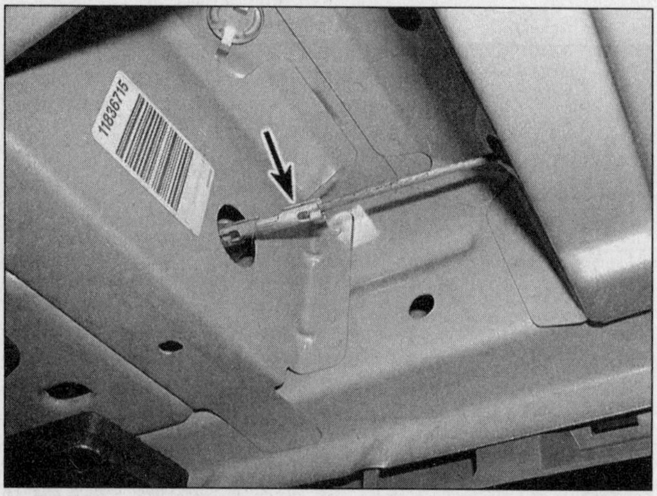

13.7 Disconnect the front parking brake cable from the cable connector, right behind where the front cable comes through the floor pan

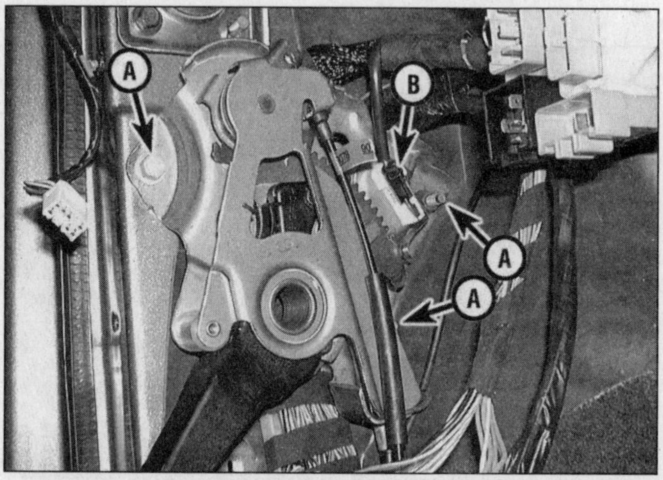

13.8 Unscrew the fasteners (A), lower the parking brake pedal assembly and disconnect the switch wire (B), then remove the pedal and cable from the vehicle (instrument panel removed for clarity)

13 Parking brake pedal assembly - removal and installation

Refer to illustrations 13.2, 13.5, 13.7 and 13.8

Note: *The parking brake pedal and the parking brake front cable are replaced as an assembly.*

Removal

1 Disconnect the negative battery cable from the remote ground terminal (see Chapter 5).

2 Remove the driver's side door-opening sill plate, the driver's side kick panel and the knee bolster and reinforcement (see Chapter 11). Disconnect the parking brake release cable from the release handle **(see illustration)**. Also, remove the air conditioning duct from under the steering column.

3 Unbolt the fuse block and move it aside.

4 Open the left rear door and remove the sill plate.

5 Remove the driver's seat belt anchor bolt at the bottom of the pillar between the front and rear doors. Peel up the carpet for access to the parking brake front cable, then unbolt the cable casing from the floor pan and any routing brackets **(see illustration)**.

6 Raise the rear of the vehicle and support it securely on jackstands.

7 Fully loosen the parking brake adjuster nut at the tensioner (see Section 12). Disconnect the rear end of the front cable from the cable connector under the vehicle **(see illustration)**.

8 Remove the bolt and nuts securing the parking brake pedal assembly **(see illustration)**. Lower the assembly and disconnect the electrical connector for the parking brake warning light switch, then remove the pedal and front cable, noting how the cable is routed.

Installation

9 Insert the rear end of the front parking brake cable through its hole in the floor pan. Route the parking brake cable along the left side of the floor and install the cable casing-to-floor pan bolts, tightening them securely.

10 From under the vehicle, engage the end of the front cable to the cable connector.

11 Move the pedal assembly into place under the dash, connect the electrical connector for the warning light switch, then raise the pedal assembly up and onto the mounting studs. Install the mounting bolt and nuts, tightening them to the torque listed in this Chapter's Specifications.

12 The remainder of installation is the reverse of removal. Before lowering the vehicle, adjust the parking brake cable as described in Section 12.

14 Parking brake cables - replacement

Front cable

1 The front parking brake cable is an integral part of the parking brake pedal assembly and can't be replaced separately. If the front cable requires replacement, replace the parking brake pedal assembly (see Section 13).

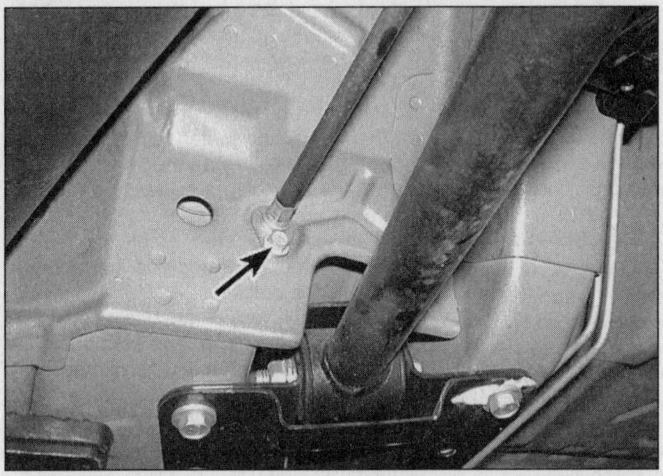

14.5 Unbolt the intermediate cable casing from the floor pan

14.14 Remove the clip retaining the rear cable to the crossmember

14.18 Use a screwdriver to depress the tangs on the rear cable casing retainer at the caliper mounting bracket (two of the three tangs shown)

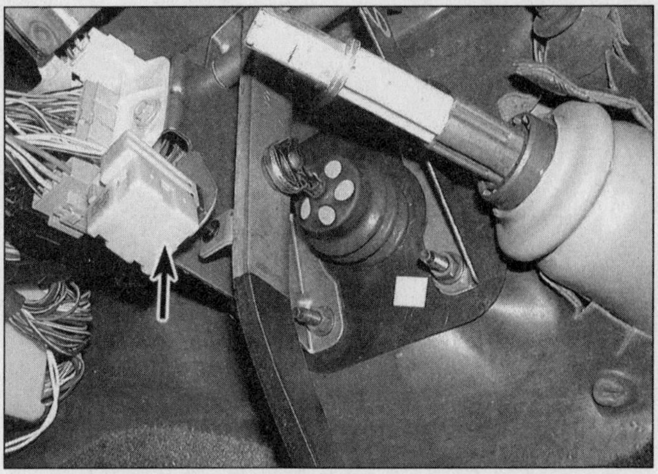

15.1 The brake light switch is located on a bracket near the top of the brake pedal (arrow)

Intermediate cable

Refer to illustration 14.5

2 Raise the rear of the vehicle and support it securely on jackstands.

3 Loosen the adjusting nut at the parking brake cable tensioner **(see illustration 12.2)**.

4 Detach the front end of the intermediate cable from the connector that joins it to the front cable **(see illustration 13.7)**.

5 Unbolt the cable casing from the floor pan **(see illustration)**.

6 Detach the rear end of the intermediate cable from the connector at the right rear parking brake cable.

7 Squeeze the retainer tangs and disconnect the intermediate cable from the cable tensioner. **Note:** *A 1/2-inch box-end wrench, slipped over the retainer, will depress all three tangs simultaneously.*

8 Note how the cable is routed, then detach it from any remaining clips or brackets.

9 Installation is the reverse of removal. Be sure to adjust the parking brake as described in Section 12.

Rear cable(s)

Refer to illustrations 14.14 and 14.18

10 Loosen the rear wheel lug nuts, raise the rear of the vehicle and support it securely on jackstands. Remove the wheel(s).

11 Loosen the adjusting nut at the parking brake cable tensioner **(see illustration 12.2)**.

12 If you're removing the left rear cable, detach it from the connector at the cable tensioner.

13 If you're removing the right rear cable, detach it from the connector that joins it to the intermediate cable.

14 Remove the clip that retains the cable to the crossmember **(see illustration)**.

15 Remove the caliper and brake disc (see Sections 4 and 5). Support the caliper with a piece of wire - don't let it hang by the brake hose.

16 Remove the parking brake shoes (see Section 11).

17 Detach the parking brake actuator from the cable end.

18 Depress the retainer tangs and pass the cable and casing through the caliper mounting bracket **(see illustration)**.

19 Installation is the reverse of removal. Be sure to tighten the caliper guide pin bolts to the torque listed in this Chapter's Specifications. Adjust the parking brake shoes as described in Section 11, Step 12, then adjust the parking brake cables as described in Section 12.

15 Brake light switch - check, replacement and adjustment

Refer to illustration 15.1

1 The brake light switch is a normally open switch that controls the operation of the brake lights. The switch is located near the top of the brake pedal **(see illustration)**. When the brake pedal is applied, a spring-loaded plunger closes the circuit to the brake lights.

2 On models with cruise control, the brake light switch also deactivates the cruise control system when the brake pedal is depressed. When the brake pedal is applied

on these models, the switch opens the ground circuit for the switch sensor inside the and the powertrain control module deactivates the cruise control system.

Check

3 If the brake lights don't come on when the brake pedal is applied, check the fuses (see Chapter 12). If the fuse is bad, look for a short in the brake light circuit.

4 If the fuse is okay, use a test light or voltmeter to verify that there's voltage to the switch on terminal no. 6 (the pink/dark blue wire). If there's no voltage to the switch, look for an open or short in the power wire to the switch.

5 If there's voltage to the switch, depress the pedal and check for power at terminal no. 5 (the white/tan wire). If no voltage is present, replace the switch.

6 If there is voltage present at terminal no. 5 when the brake is applied, but the brake lights don't come on when the brake pedal is applied, check the wiring between the switch and the brake lights for an open circuit. Also check the brake light bulbs.

Replacement and adjustment

7 Depress and hold the brake pedal, then rotate the brake light switch about 30-degrees in a counterclockwise direction.

8 Pull the switch to the rear and remove it from its mounting bracket.

9 Unplug the electrical connector from the switch.

10 Hold the brake light switch firmly and pull out on the plunger until it ratchets out to its fully extended position.

11 Plug the electrical connector into the switch.

12 Depress the brake pedal as far as it will go, then install the switch in the bracket by aligning the index key on the switch with the slot at the top of the square hole in the mounting bracket. When the switch is fully installed in the bracket, rotate the switch clockwise about 30-degrees to lock the switch into the bracket.

13 Gently pull back on the brake pedal until the pedal stops moving. The switch plunger will ratchet backward to the correct position. **Caution:** *Don't use excessive force when pulling back on the brake pedal to adjust the switch. If you use too much force, you will damage the switch or the striker.*

Chapter 10
Suspension and steering systems

Contents

Specifications

Torque specifications

	Ft-lbs (unless otherwise indicated)
Front suspension	
Control arm pivot bushing-to-cradle bracket bolt	105
Hub and bearing-to-steering knuckle bolts	80
Stabilizer bar link-to-strut nut	70
Stabilizer bar link-to-stabilizer bar nut	65
Stabilizer bushing/retainer bolts	45
Steering knuckle-to-balljoint stud pinch bolt	40
Strut upper mounting nuts	28
Strut shaft nut	70
Strut-to-steering knuckle nuts	150
Tension strut-to-cradle bracket nut	95
Tension strut-to-control arm nut	105
Hub and bearing stub axle nut	
1998 through 2000	135
2001 and later	105

Rear suspension

Hub and bearing assembly-to-spindle nut	124
Lateral link-to-spindle bolt	100
Lateral link-to-rear crossmember bolt	70
Stabilizer-to-link nuts	70
Stabilizer bushing retainer bolts	
Front	30
Rear	75
Strut upper mounting nuts	19
Strut shaft nut	55
Spindle-to-strut pinch bolt	40
Trailing arm-to-bracket bolt	75
Trailing arm-to-spindle bracket bolt	75
Trailing arm bracket-to-spindle bolts	80
Trailing arm bracket-to-chassis bolts	45

Steering system

Airbag module retaining screws	75 in-lbs
Power steering pump mounting bolts	21
Power steering fluid discharge fitting	62
Steering gear mounting bolts	43
Steering gear mount-to-gear (right side)	27
Power steering fluid line tube fittings	35
Steering wheel nut	45
Steering column	
Mounting nuts	105 in-lbs
Mounting bolts	105 in-lbs
Intermediate shaft coupler bolt	20
Tie-rod	
Tie-rod end-to-steering arm nut	27
Tie-rod end adjuster pinch bolt	28
Tie-rod-to-steering gear bolt	
1998 through 2000	60
2001 and later	74
Wheel lug nuts	See Chapter 1

1.1a Front suspension and steering components

1 *Stabilizer bar*
2 *Strut/coil spring assembly*
3 *Tie-rod end*
4 *Tension strut*
5 *Steering knuckle*
6 *Balljoint*
7 *Stabilizer bar link*
8 *Control arm*

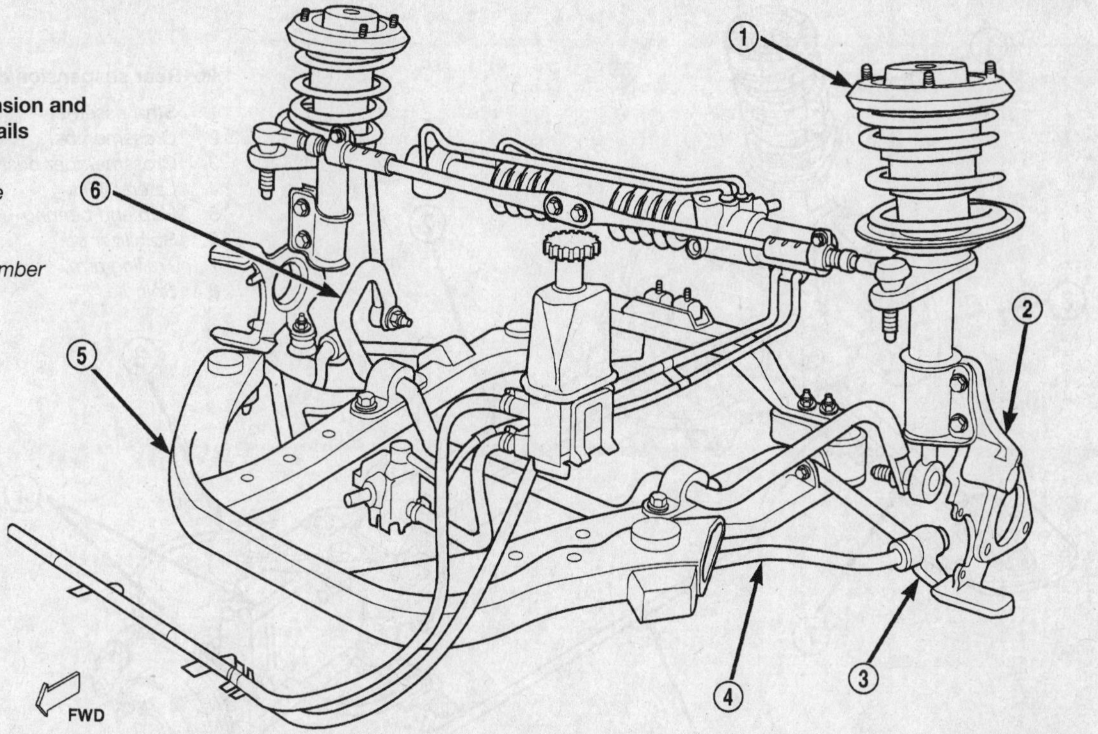

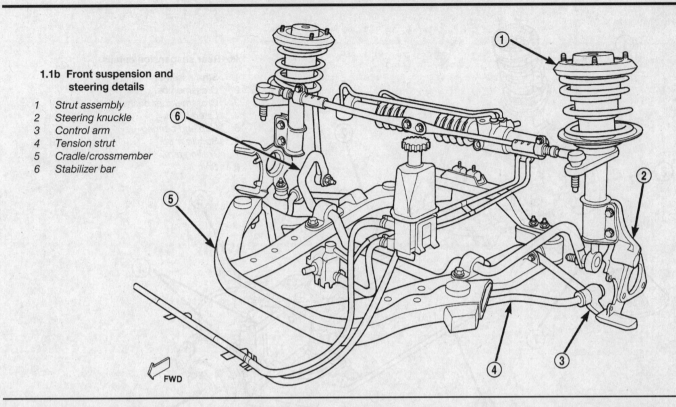

1.1b Front suspension and steering details

1. *Strut assembly*
2. *Steering knuckle*
3. *Control arm*
4. *Tension strut*
5. *Cradle/crossmember*
6. *Stabilizer bar*

1 General information

Refer to illustrations 1.1a, 1.1b, 1.2a and 1.2b

The front suspension **(see illustrations)** is a Macpherson strut design. The upper end of each strut/coil spring assembly is attached to the vehicle body. The lower end of each strut is bolted to the upper end of the steering knuckle. The lower end of the steering knuckle is attached to a balljoint mounted in the outer end of the control arm. The control arm is positioned longitudinally by a tension strut. A stabilizer bar bolted to the frame and connected to the strut/coil assemblies reduces body roll during cornering.

The rear suspension **(see illustrations)** also uses strut/coil spring assemblies. The upper end of each strut is attached to the vehicle body. The lower end of the strut is attached to a spindle. The spindle is located by a pair of lateral links on each side, and a longitudinally mounted trailing arm between the body and each spindle.

1.2a Rear suspension components

1. *Stabilizer bar*
2. *Stabilizer bar bracket*
3. *Stabilizer bar link*
4. *Lateral link (front)*
5. *Trailing arm*
6. *Spindle*
7. *Lateral link (rear)*
8. *Strut/coil spring assembly*

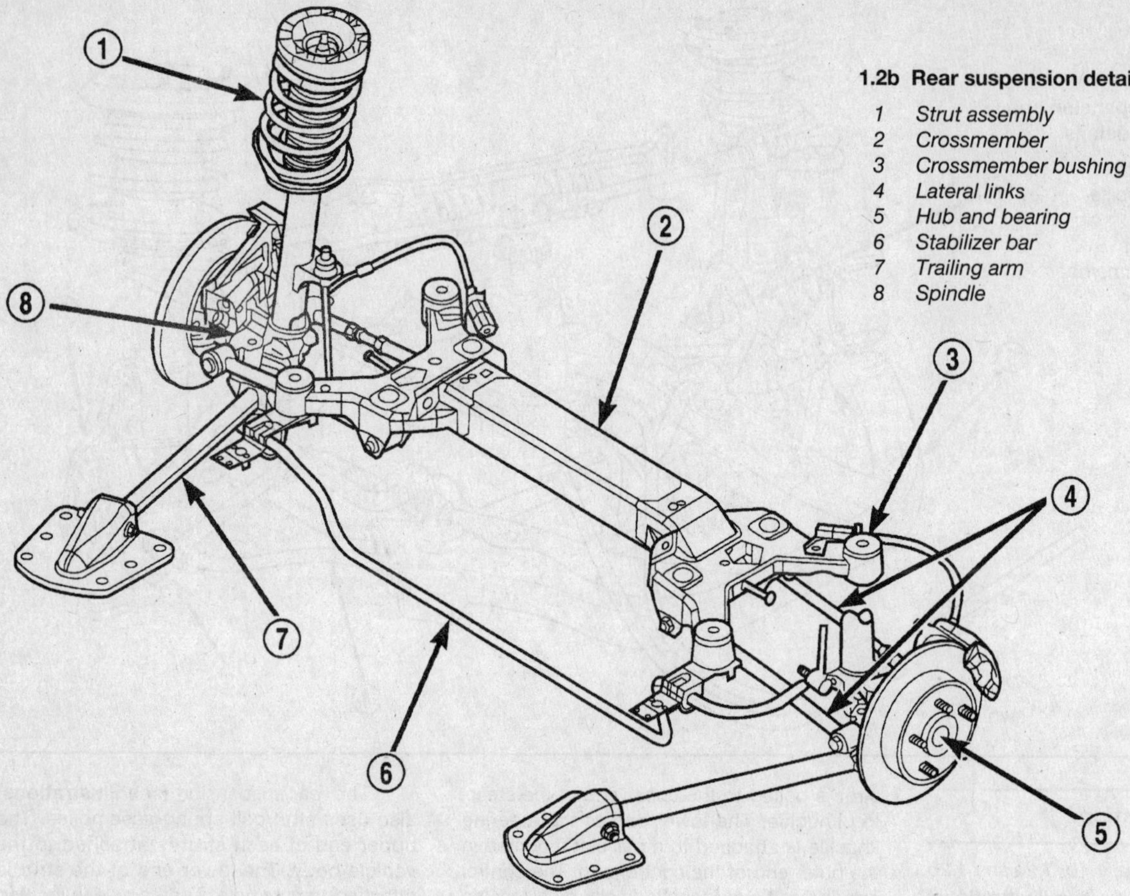

1.2b Rear suspension details

1. *Strut assembly*
2. *Crossmember*
3. *Crossmember bushing*
4. *Lateral links*
5. *Hub and bearing*
6. *Stabilizer bar*
7. *Trailing arm*
8. *Spindle*

All models are equipped with rack-and-pinion steering. The steering gear - which is located behind the engine, above the transaxle, in front of the firewall - operates the steering knuckles via tie rods connected to steering arms on the strut assemblies. The tie-rod ends can be replaced by unscrewing them from the inner tie rods. Adjustment sleeves between the inner tie rods and the tie-rod ends are used to adjust front wheel toe.

The power assist system consists of a belt-driven pump and associated lines and hoses. The fluid level in the power steering pump reservoir should be checked periodically (see Chapter 1).

The steering wheel operates the steering shaft, which actuates the steering gear through a short steering column and a couple of universal joints. Looseness in the steering can be caused by wear in these universal joints, the steering gear, the tie-rod ends and loose retaining bolts.

Frequently, when working on the suspension or steering system components, you may come across fasteners which seem impossible to loosen. These fasteners on the underside of the vehicle are continually subjected to water, road grime, mud, etc., and can become rusted or "frozen," making them extremely difficult to remove. In order to unscrew these stubborn fasteners without damaging them (or other components), be sure to use lots of penetrating oil and allow it to soak in for a while. Using a wire brush to clean exposed threads will also ease removal of the nut or bolt and prevent damage to the threads. Sometimes a sharp blow with a hammer and punch will break the bond between a nut and bolt threads, but care must be taken to prevent the punch from slipping off the fastener and ruining the threads. Heating the stuck fastener and surrounding area with a torch sometimes helps too, but isn't recommended because of the obvious dangers associated with fire. Long breaker bars and extension, or "cheater," pipes will increase leverage, but never use an extension pipe on a ratchet - the ratcheting mechanism could be damaged. Sometimes tightening the nut or bolt first will help to break it loose. Fasteners that require drastic measures to remove should always be replaced with new ones.

Since most of the procedures dealt with in this Chapter involve jacking up the vehicle and working underneath it, a good pair of jackstands will be needed. A hydraulic floor jack is the preferred type of jack to lift the vehicle, and it can also be used to support certain components during various operations. **Warning:** *Never, under any circumstances, rely on a jack to support the vehicle while working on it. Whenever any of the suspension or steering fasteners are loosened or removed they must be inspected and, if necessary, replaced with new ones of the same part number or of original equipment quality and design. Torque specifications must be followed for proper reassembly and component retention. Never attempt to heat or straighten any suspension or steering components. Instead, replace any bent or damaged part with a new one.*

2 Strut/coil spring assembly (front) - removal, inspection and installation

Removal

Refer to illustrations 2.4, 2.6 and 2.8

1 Loosen the wheel lug nuts, raise the vehicle and support it securely on jackstands. Remove the wheel.

2 Disconnect the stabilizer bar link from the strut assembly **(see illustration 6.3a)**.

3 Disconnect the tie-rod end from the steering arm (see Section 16).

4 If the vehicle is equipped with ABS, remove the speed sensor wire harness grommets from the wire harness bracket **(see illustration)** and remove the bracket.

5 Support the control arm with a floor jack.

6 Remove the strut-to-knuckle nuts **(see illustration)** and knock the bolts out with a hammer and punch. **Caution:** *Don't turn the bolts; they are serrated to prevent them from turning, and to do so would ruin the bolts and*

2.4 If the vehicle is equipped with ABS, remove the ABS wire harness grommets from the small bracket on the strut, then remove the bracket retaining bolt (arrow) and detach the bracket

2.6 To detach the lower end of the strut from the steering knuckle, remove these two large nuts and knock out the bolts with a punch and hammer

strip out the serrations in the steering knuckle.

7 Separate the strut from the steering knuckle. Be careful not to overextend the inner CV joint. Also, don't let the steering knuckle fall out, as the brake hose could be damaged - wire it in place if necessary.

8 Support the strut and spring assembly and remove the strut upper mounting nuts **(see illustration)**. It would be a good idea to have an assistant help you do this. Remove the assembly out from the fenderwell.

Inspection

9 Check the strut body for leaking fluid, dents, cracks and other obvious damage which would warrant repair or replacement.

10 Check the coil spring for chips or cracks in the spring coating (this can cause premature spring failure due to corrosion). Inspect the spring seat for cuts, hardness and general deterioration.

11 If any undesirable conditions exist, proceed to the strut disassembly procedure (see Section 3).

Installation

12 Guide the strut assembly up into the fenderwell and insert the upper mounting studs through the holes in the shock tower. Once the studs protrude from the shock tower, install the nuts so the strut won't fall back through. This is most easily accomplished with the help of an assistant, as the strut is quite heavy and awkward.

13 Slide the steering knuckle into the strut flange and insert the two bolts. Install the nuts and tighten them to the torque listed in this Chapter's Specifications. Do not turn the bolts; hold them while you tighten the nuts.

14 Connect the stabilizer bar link to the strut and tighten the nut to the torque listed in this Chapter's Specifications.

15 If the vehicle is equipped with ABS, install the speed sensor wiring harness bracket, tighten the bolt securely and push the wire harness grommets back into the bracket.

16 Install the wheel and lug nuts, then lower the vehicle and tighten the lug nuts to the torque listed in the Chapter 1 Specifications.

17 Tighten the upper mounting nuts to the torque listed in this Chapter's Specifications.

3 Strut/coil spring - replacement

1 If the struts or coil springs exhibit the telltale signs of wear (leaking fluid, loss of damping capability, chipped, sagging or cracked coil springs) explore all options before beginning any work. The strut/shock absorber assemblies are not serviceable and must be replaced if a problem develops. However, strut assemblies complete with springs may be available on an exchange basis, which eliminates much time and work. Whichever route you choose to take, check on the cost and availability of parts before disassembling your vehicle. **Warning:** *Disassembling a strut is potentially dangerous and utmost attention must be directed to the job, or serious injury may result. Use only a high-quality spring compressor and carefully follow the manufacturer's instructions furnished with the tool. After removing the coil spring from the strut assembly, set it aside in a safe, isolated area.*

Disassembly

Refer to illustrations 3.2, 3.4, 3.5, 3.6, 3.7 and 3.8

2 Remove the strut and spring assembly following the procedure described in Section 2 (front) or Section 9 (rear). Mount the strut assembly in a vise. Line the vise jaws with wood or rags to prevent damage to the unit and don't tighten the vise excessively. To ensure proper reassembly, use paint to mark the relationship of the upper end of the coil spring to the seat/bearing assembly and upper strut mount, and the lower end of the spring to the strut as shown **(see illustration)**.

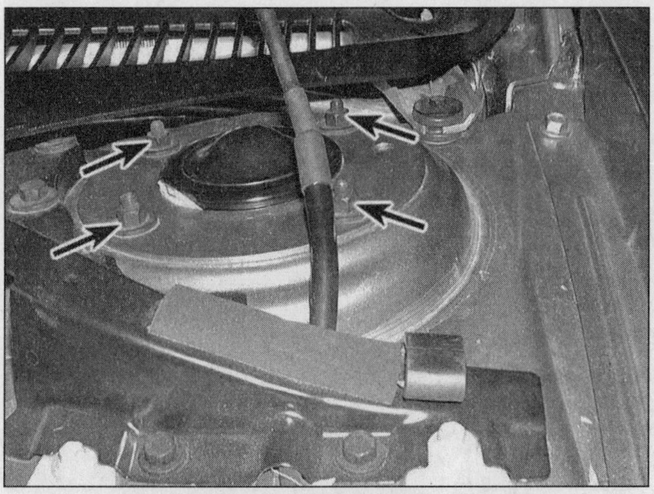

2.8 To detach the upper end of the strut from the body, remove these four nuts

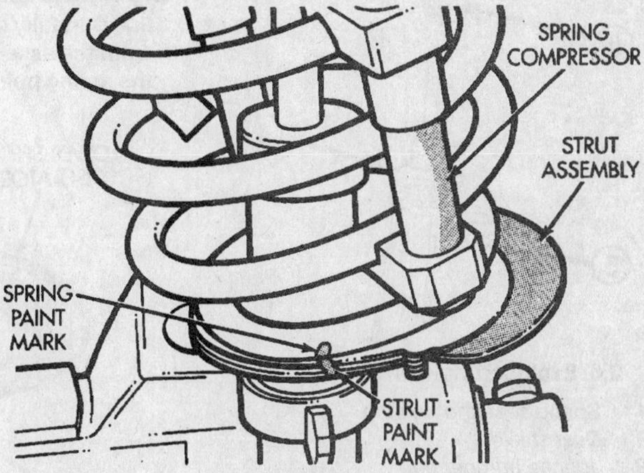

3.2 To ensure proper reassembly, use paint to mark the relationship of the upper end of the coil spring to the seat/bearing assembly and upper strut mount (not shown), and the lower end of the spring to the strut

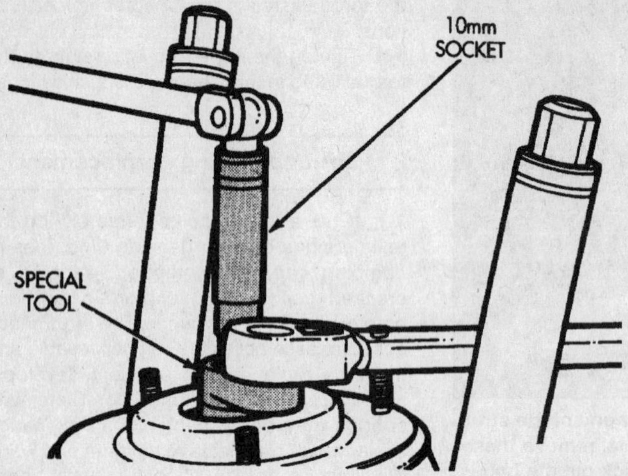

3.4 Loosen and remove the strut shaft nut with a special tool like this one while holding the shaft with a 10mm wrench or socket

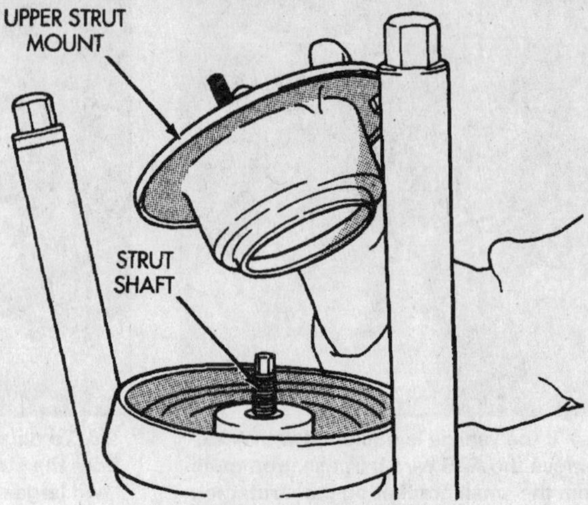

3.5 Remove the upper strut mount

3 Following the tool manufacturer's instructions, install the spring compressor (which can be obtained at most auto parts stores or equipment yards on a daily rental basis) on the spring and compress it sufficiently to relieve all pressure from the upper spring seat **(see illustration 3.2)**. This can be verified by wiggling the spring. **Caution:** *The coil spring on 1998 models is equipped with a sleeve. Don't allow the spring compressor to contact the spring in an area covered by the sleeve.*

4 Loosen and remove the strut shaft nut **(see illustration)** while holding the shaft with a 10mm wrench or socket. **Note:** *Because the nut is so recessed in the upper mount, a special socket, available at most auto parts stores or specialty tool suppliers, is required.*

5 Remove the upper strut mount **(see illustration)**.

6 Remove the seat/bearing, dust shield and jounce bumper **(see illustration)**.

7 Carefully lift the compressed spring from the assembly **(see illustration)** and set it in a safe place. **Warning:** *Never place your head near the end of the spring!*

8 Remove the lower spring isolator from the strut assembly **(see illustration)**.

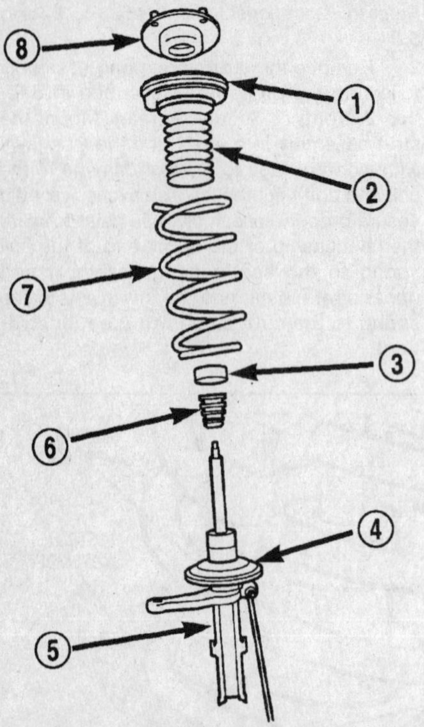

3.6 Exploded view of a front strut

1 *Spring seat and bearing*
2 *Dust shield*
3 *Jounce bumper cup*
4 *Lower spring isolator*
5 *Strut*
6 *Jounce bumper*
7 *Coil spring*
8 *Upper mount*

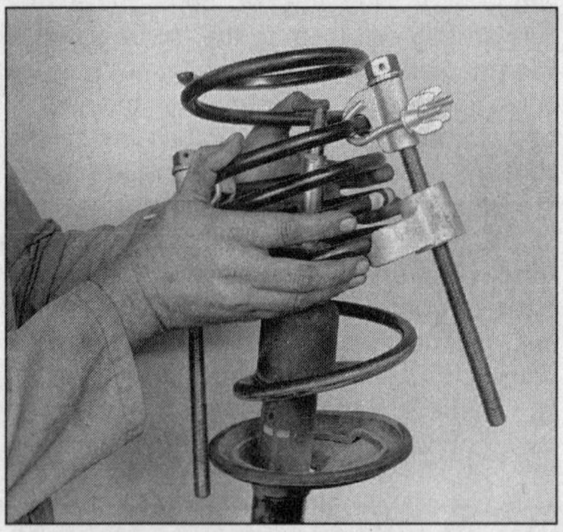

3.7 Carefully lift the compressed spring from the assembly, keeping the ends of the spring pointed away from your body

Inspection

9 Inspect all disassembled parts for signs of excessive wear or failure. Replace all broken, damaged or worn parts. Inspect the strut unit for excessive oil leakage. If the strut is leaking, replace it. Also check the strut for loss of gas charge by pushing the strut shaft into the body of the strut and releasing it. The strut shaft should return to its fully extended position. If it doesn't, replace the strut.

Reassembly

Refer to illustrations 3.13, 3.14a and 3.14b

10 Install the lower spring isolator, making sure it rests properly on the strut **(see illustration 3.8)**.

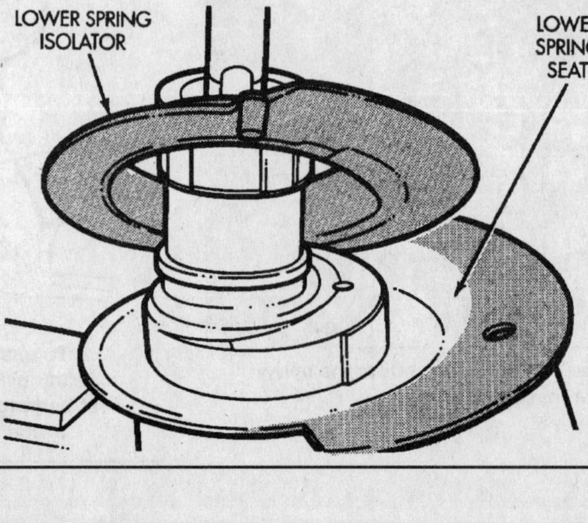

3.8 Remove the lower spring isolator from the strut assembly

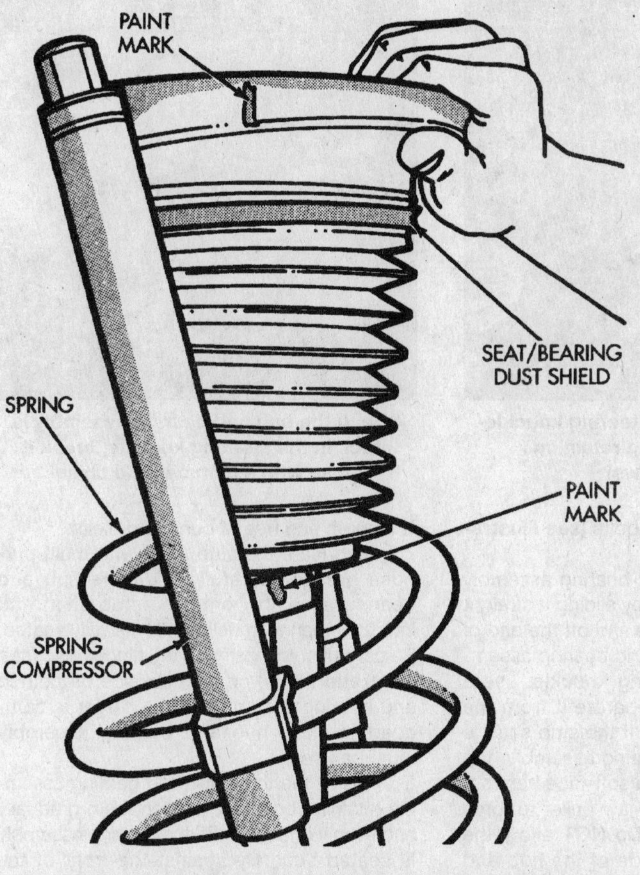

3.13 Lower the seat/bearing assembly and dust shield onto the strut/coil spring assembly; be sure to align the paint mark you made on the seat/bearing assembly with the mark on the upper end of the coil spring

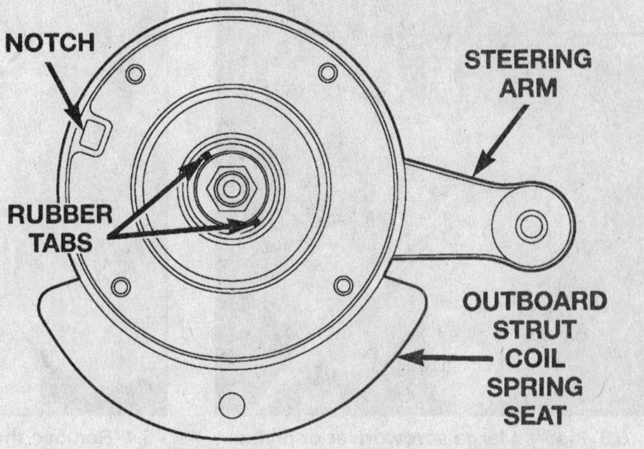

3.14a Proper positioning of the right front strut mount

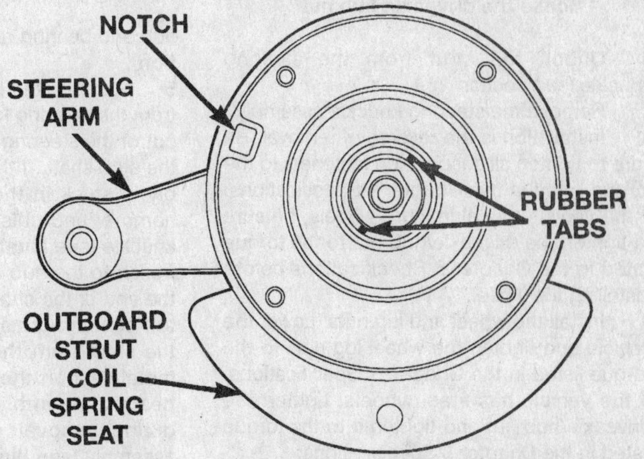

3.14b Proper positioning of the left front strut mount

11 Extend the damper rod to its full length and install the jounce bumper (with the smaller diameter end of the bumper pointing down). Install the cup on top of the jounce bumper.

12 Carefully place the coil spring onto the lower isolator, with the marked end of the spring aligned with the mark on the strut **(see illustration 3.2)**.

13 Lower the seat/bearing assembly and dust shield onto the strut/coil spring assembly. Align the paint mark you made on the seat/bearing assembly with the mark on the upper end of the coil spring **(see illustration)**.

14 Install the upper strut mount. Again, make sure the paint mark on the upper strut mount is aligned with the mark on the spring. **Note:** *Make sure you install the correct upper mount on the strut (they are directional). When looking down at the top of the strut, the square hole should be in the notch in the 10 o'clock position, and the rubber tabs visible in the center of the strut mount should be positioned as shown* **(see illustrations)**.

15 Using the same technique as in Step 4, tighten the damper shaft nut to the torque listed in this Chapter's Specifications.

16 Slowly loosen the spring compressor until all tension is removed from the coil spring.

17 Install the strut in the vehicle (see Section 2 [front] or Section 9 [rear]).

18 Repeat this procedure for the other strut.

4 Steering knuckle - removal and installation

Refer to illustration 4.3

Warning: *Dust created by the brake system may contain asbestos, which is harmful to your health. Never blow it out with compressed air and don't inhale any of it. Do not, under any circumstances, use petroleum-based solvents to clean brake parts. Use brake system cleaner only.*

1 If the vehicle has steel wheels, remove the wheel cover or hubcap and loosen the driveaxle/hub nut now (see Chapter 8); if the vehicle has aluminum wheels, the nut can't be loosened until the wheel is removed **(see illustration 8.3)** because the hole in the center of the wheel is too small for a regular socket (you need a special thin-walled socket to fit through the hole for the nut). Loosen the wheel lug nuts, raise the vehicle and support it securely on jackstands. Remove the wheel.

2 Remove the brake caliper, support it with a piece of wire, and remove the brake disc from the hub and bearing assembly (see Chapter 9).

4.3 To remove the speed sensor from the steering knuckle, remove the sensor retaining bolt (arrow), then pull out the sensor

3 If the vehicle is equipped with ABS, remove the speed sensor from the steering knuckle **(see illustration)**.

4 Remove the hub and bearing assembly (see Section 5).

5 Remove the balljoint stud pinch bolt and separate the control arm from the steering knuckle (see Section 7).

5.3 Insert a large screwdriver or prybar between the studs to hold the hub and use a large breaker bar to break loose the driveaxle hub nut

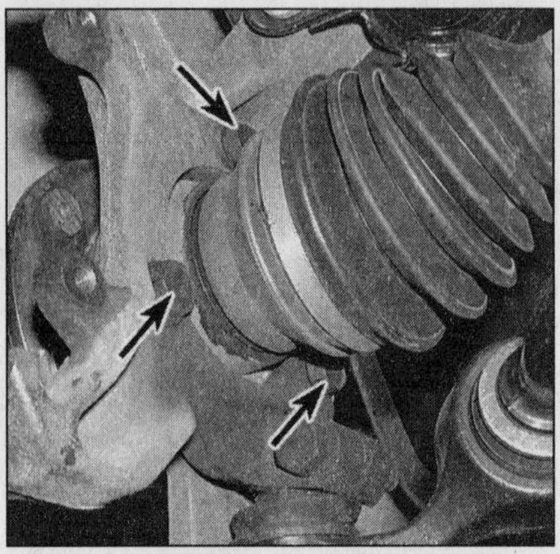

5.4 Remove the three steering knuckle-to-hub and bearing retaining bolts (arrows)

5.5a If the hub and bearing assembly is stuck in the steering knuckle, break it loose with a hammer and chisel

6 Unbolt the strut from the steering knuckle (see Section 2).

7 Remove the steering knuckle assembly.

8 Installation is the reverse of removal. Be sure to tighten all suspension fasteners to the torque listed in this Chapter's Specifications. If the vehicle has aluminum wheels, be sure to tighten the driveaxle/hub nut to the torque listed in the Chapter 8 Specifications before installing the wheel.

9 Install the wheel and lug nuts. Lower the vehicle and tighten the wheel lug nuts to the torque listed in the Chapter 1 Specifications. If the vehicle has steel wheels, tighten the driveaxle/hub nut and tighten it to the torque listed in the Chapter 8 Specifications.

5 Hub and bearing assembly (front) - removal and installation

Refer to illustrations 5.3, 5.4, 5.5a, 5.5b and 5.6

Warning: *Dust created by the brake system may contain asbestos, which is harmful to your health. Never blow it out with compressed air and don't inhale any of it. Do not, under any circumstances, use petroleum-based solvents to clean brake parts. Use brake system cleaner only.*

1 If the vehicle has steel wheels, loosen the driveaxle/hub nut (see Chapter 8); if the vehicle has aluminum wheels, the nut can't be loosened until the wheel is removed because the hole in the center of the wheel is too small for a regular socket (you need a special thin-walled socket to fit through the hole for the nut). Loosen the wheel lug nuts, raise the front of the vehicle, support it securely on jackstands and remove the wheel.

2 Remove the brake caliper, support it with a piece of wire and remove the brake disc from the hub and bearing assembly (see Chapter 9).

3 Remove the driveaxle/hub nut **(see illustration)**.

4 Remove the three steering knuckle-to-hub and bearing retaining bolts **(see illustration)**.

5 Remove the hub and bearing assembly from the steering knuckle by sliding it straight out of the steering knuckle and off the end of the stub shaft. If the hub and bearing assembly is stuck in the steering knuckle, use a hammer and chisel to separate it from the knuckle **(see illustration)**. If the stub shaft is frozen to the hub and bearing assembly, tap the end of the shaft with a soft-face hammer to free it up, or use a two-jaw puller to force the shaft from the hub. Do NOT allow the metal seal on the backside of the hub and bearing assembly to be bent or damaged during removal of the hub and bearing assembly **(see illustration)**. If the metal seal is frozen to the steering knuckle and becomes bent, damaged or dislodged removal of the hub and bearing assembly, DO NOT reuse the old hub and bearing assembly.

6 Make sure that the mounting surface inside the steering knuckle **(see illustration)** is smooth and free of burrs and nicks.

7 Lubricate the stub shaft with multi-purpose grease. Carefully slide the hub and bearing assembly onto the stub shaft and into the steering knuckle until it's fully seated. Be careful not to damage the flinger disc **(see illustration 5.5b)** on the backside of the hub and bearing assembly. If the flinger is damaged, a NEW hub and bearing assembly must be used.

8 Install the three hub and bearing assembly retaining bolts and tighten them gradually and evenly until the hub and bearing assembly is seated squarely against the front of the steering knuckle. Then tighten the bolts to the torque listed in this Chapter's Specifications.

9 Install a NEW driveaxle/hub nut and tighten it securely. If the vehicle has factory aluminum wheels, you'll have to tighten the nut to the torque listed in this Chapter's Specifications now; if it has steel wheels, you can torque the nut after the vehicle is on the ground. If the vehicle has aluminum wheels, place a large screwdriver or prybar between

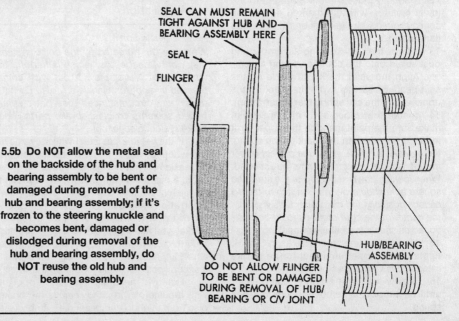

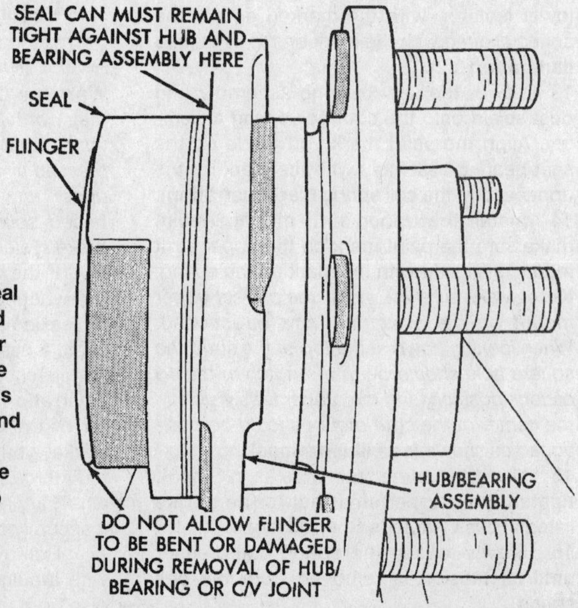
SEAL CAN MUST REMAIN
TIGHT AGAINST HUB AND
BEARING ASSEMBLY HERE
SEAL
FLINGER
HUB/BEARING
ASSEMBLY
DO NOT ALLOW FLINGER
TO BE BENT OR DAMAGED
DURING REMOVAL OF HUB/
BEARING OR C/V JOINT

5.5b Do NOT allow the metal seal on the backside of the hub and bearing assembly to be bent or damaged during removal of the hub and bearing assembly; if it's frozen to the steering knuckle and becomes bent, damaged or dislodged during removal of the hub and bearing assembly, do NOT reuse the old hub and bearing assembly

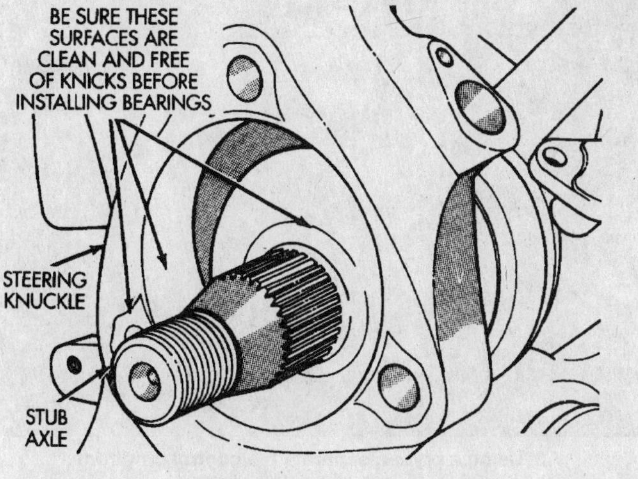

5.6 Make sure that the mounting surface inside the steering knuckle is smooth and free of burrs and nicks

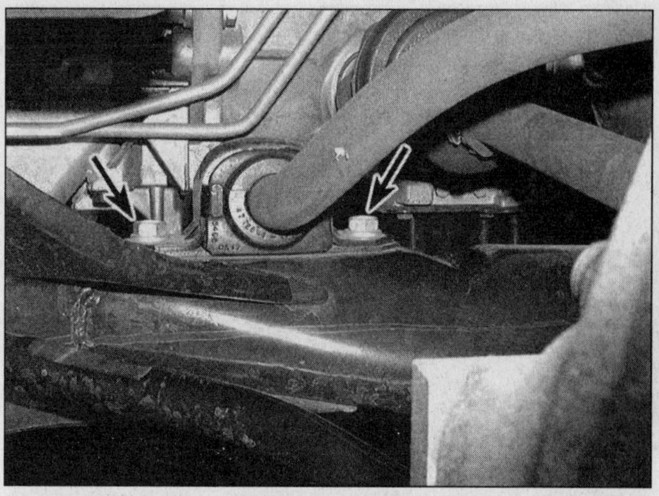

6.2 To detach the stabilizer bar bushing retainers from the engine cradle, remove the two bolts

the studs and tighten the nut to the torque listed in the Chapter 8 Specifications.

10 Install the brake disc and the caliper (see Chapter 9).

11 Install the wheel and lug nuts. Lower the vehicle and tighten the lug nuts to the torque listed in the Chapter 1 Specifications.

12 If the vehicle has steel wheels, tighten the driveaxle nut to the torque listed in the Chapter 8 Specifications.

6 Stabilizer bar and bushings (front) - removal and installation

6.3a To disconnect the upper end of the stabilizer bar link from the strut/coil spring assembly, remove this nut (arrow)

6.3b To disconnect the lower end of the stabilizer bar link from the stabilizer bar itself, remove this nut (arrow)

Bushings and links

Refer to illustrations 6.2, 6.3a, 6.3b and 6.6

1 Loosen the front wheel lug nuts. Raise the front of the vehicle and support it securely on jackstands. Apply the parking brake and block the rear wheels to keep the vehicle from rolling off the stands. Remove the front wheels.

2 Remove the bolts from the stabilizer bar bushing retainers **(see illustration)**. Remove the retainers from the bushings, prying them off, if necessary.

3 Remove the nuts that attach the upper and lower ends of the stabilizer links to the strut/coil spring assembly and to the stabilizer bar **(see illustrations)**. Detach the links.

4 Inspect the retainer bushings for cracks and tears. If either bushing is broken, damaged, distorted or worn, replace both of them. If the ballstuds on the links are loose or otherwise worn, replace the links.

5 Install the links, tightening the link nuts to the torque listed in this Chapter's Specifications.

6 Install the retainer bushings. Clean the areas on the stabilizer bar where the bushings are located. Lubricate the inside and outside of the new bushings with vegetable oil (used in cooking) to simplify reassembly. **Caution:** *Don't use petroleum or mineral-based lubricants or brake fluid - they will lead to deterioration of the bushings.* These bushings are split so that you can install them without having to slide them onto the ends of the stabilizer bar. Install the bushings with the slit in each bushing facing forward **(see illustration)**.

7 Install the retainers and bolts, tightening the bolts to the torque listed in this Chapter's Specifications. **Caution:** *Make sure the lower part of the stabilizer bar is centered in the middle of the cradle assembly.*

8 Install the wheels and lug nuts. Lower the vehicle and tighten the lug nuts to the torque listed in the Chapter 1 Specifications.

Stabilizer bar

Stabilizer bar removal involves raising the engine and transaxle assembly off the cradle, removing the right front strut and maneuvering the bar out the right side of the vehicle. Stabilizer bars rarely wear out, and if one becomes damaged it is most likely the result of an accident that was severe enough to damage other major components (such as the cradle itself). Damage this severe will require the services of an auto body shop. For this reason, front stabilizer bar removal and installation is not covered in this manual.

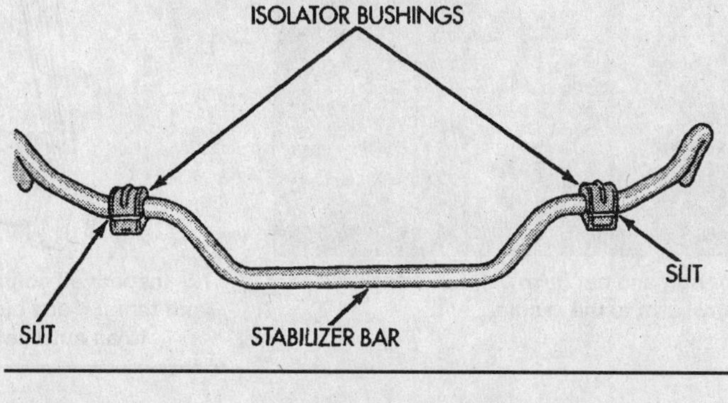

6.6 When installing the stabilizer bar bushings, make sure that the slit on each bushing faces forward

7.2 Remove the pinch bolt (arrow) which secures the balljoint stud to the steering knuckle (do NOT remove the big nut that attaches the rear end of the tension strut to the control arm unless the control arm and tension strut have already been removed from the vehicle)

7.3 Using a prybar, separate the control arm from the steering knuckle

7 Control arm and tension strut - removal, inspection and installation

Removal

Refer to illustrations 7.2, 7.3, 7.4 and 7.5

1 Loosen the wheel lug nuts, raise the front of the vehicle, support it securely on jackstands and remove the wheel.

2 Remove the pinch bolt that secures the balljoint stud to the steering knuckle **(see illustration)**.

3 Using a prybar, separate the control arm from the steering knuckle **(see illustration)**.

4 Remove the nut that attaches the tension strut to the cradle **(see illustration)**.

5 Remove the pivot bolt that attaches the control arm to the engine cradle **(see illustration)**.

6 Detach the control arm from the cradle, then slide the tension strut out of the isolator bushing.

Inspection

Refer to illustration 7.8

7 Make sure the control arm and tension strut are straight. If either component is bent, replace it. Do not attempt to straighten a bent control arm or tension strut.

8 Inspect all bushings **(see illustration)** for cracks and tears. If any bushing is torn or worn out, take the assembly to an automotive machine shop to have the bushing(s) replaced.

Installation

9 Insert the tension strut through the cradle, slip the isolator bushing over the threaded end of the strut, then install the lower control arm pivot bushing into the cradle.

10 Install the control arm-to-cradle bolt and nut, but don't tighten the nut yet.

11 Install the washer on the tension strut isolator bushing, then install a NEW nut on the tension strut and tighten it to the torque listed in this Chapter's Specifications. While tightening the new nut, prevent the tension strut from turning by holding it at the machined flat with a wrench **(see illustration 7.4)**.

12 Install the control arm balljoint stud into the steering knuckle, install the pinch bolt and tighten it to the torque listed in this Chapter's Specifications.

7.4 To loosen the nut that attaches the tension strut to the cradle, hold the tension strut with a wrench on its machined flat

7.5 Remove the pivot bolt and nut (arrows) that attach the control arm to the cradle

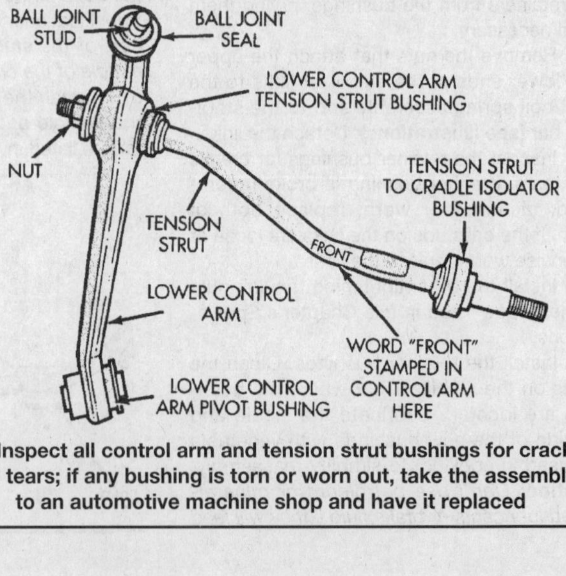

7.8 Inspect all control arm and tension strut bushings for cracks and tears; if any bushing is torn or worn out, take the assembly to an automotive machine shop and have it replaced

9.6 To separate the spindle from the lower end of the strut, remove this pinch bolt (arrow)

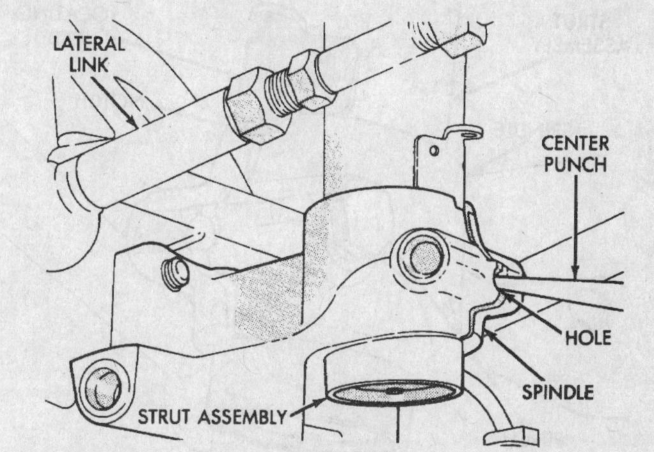

9.7 To spread the spindle so it can be knocked off the end of the strut, tap a center punch into the hole in the split in the spindle

13 Using a floor jack placed under the lower balljoint, raise the control arm to simulate normal ride height. Now tighten the control arm-to-cradle bolt/but to the torque listed in this Chapter's Specifications.

14 Install the wheel and lug nuts, lower the vehicle and tighten the lug nuts to the torque listed in the Chapter 1 Specifications.

8 Balljoints - check and replacement

1 Raise the vehicle and support it securely on jackstands. Make sure the tires are not contacting the ground.

2 Grasp the tire at top and bottom and try to rock it in and out. The balljoints on these vehicles are not supposed to have any freeplay, so if any movement is evident, the balljoint must be replaced.

3 The balljoints on these vehicles are not serviceable, nor can they be removed from the control arms. If a balljoint is bad, replace the control arm (see Section 7).

4 The balljoint seal, however, is replaceable. If the seal is damaged, remove the control arm and take it to an automotive machine shop to have the old seal pressed off and the new seal pressed on.

5 Remove the jackstands and lower the vehicle.

9 Strut/coil spring assembly (rear) - removal, inspection and installation

Removal

Refer to illustrations 9.6, 9.7, 9.8 and 9.10

1 Loosen the rear wheel lug nuts, raise the rear of the vehicle and support it securely on jackstands. Block the front wheels and remove the rear wheels.

2 Remove the rear brake caliper and support it with a piece of wire, then remove the brake disc (see Chapter 9).

3 If the vehicle is equipped with ABS, detach the ABS sensor from the caliper mounting bracket. **Caution:** *If the spindle and trailing arm assembly is lowered from the strut with the ABS sensor wire attached to the strut bracket and the trailing arm, the sensor wire will be damaged.*

4 Remove the through-bolt that attaches the lateral links to the spindle (see Section 13).

5 Disconnect the stabilizer bar link from the stabilizer bar (see Section 12).

6 Loosen and remove the spindle-to-strut pinch bolt **(see illustration)**.

7 Insert a center punch into the hole on the inside of the spindle **(see illustration)** and tap the punch until it's jammed into the hole. This spreads the spindle casting enough to disengage it from the lower end of the strut. **Warning:** *Make sure the tip of the punch does not contact the strut body.*

8 Using a hammer and brass drift, tap on the top of the spindle casting **(see illustration)** until it drops down far enough to fall off the lower end of the strut.

9 Remove the rear seat back, the quarter panel trim, and the parcel shelf (see Chapter 11). Also remove the rear speaker and its mounting plate (see Chapter 12).

10 Have an assistant support the strut. Locate the three upper strut-to-body mounting nuts and remove them **(see illustration)**. Remove the strut assembly.

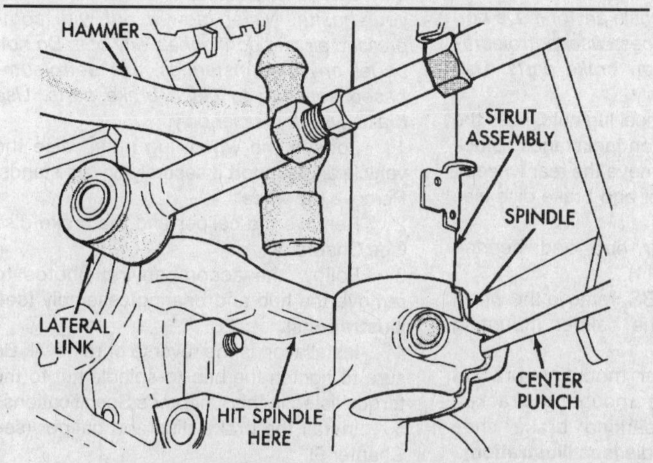

9.8 To separate the spindle from the lower end of the strut, knock it off with a hammer

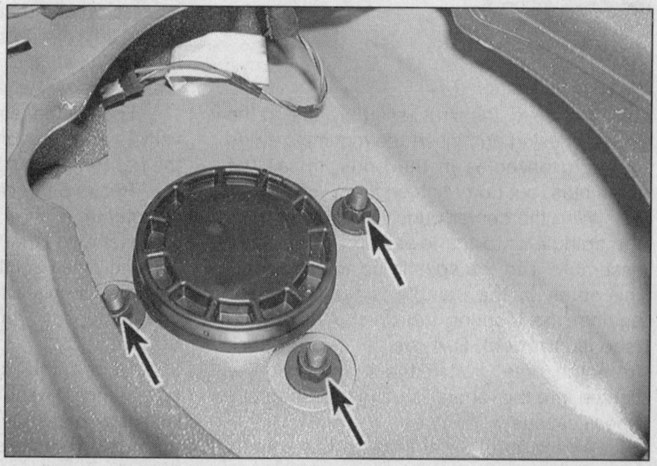

9.10 The three upper strut-to-body nuts are accessible from inside the vehicle, after the rear seat back, quarter panel trim, parcel shelf and speaker/mounting plate have been removed

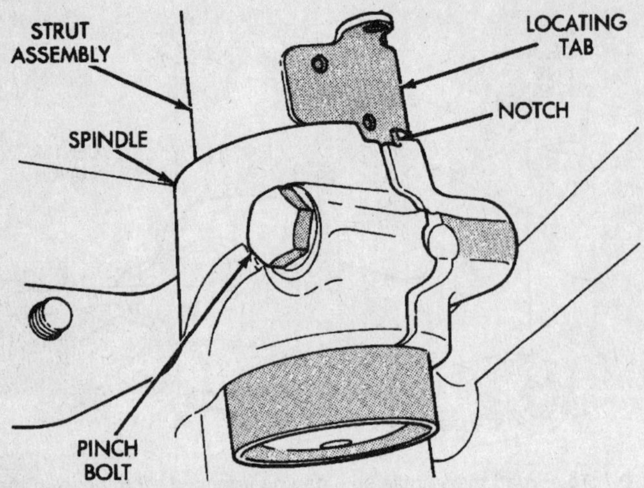

9.13 When installing the spindle onto the lower end of the strut, tap the spindle on until it's fully seated against the locating tab on the strut body

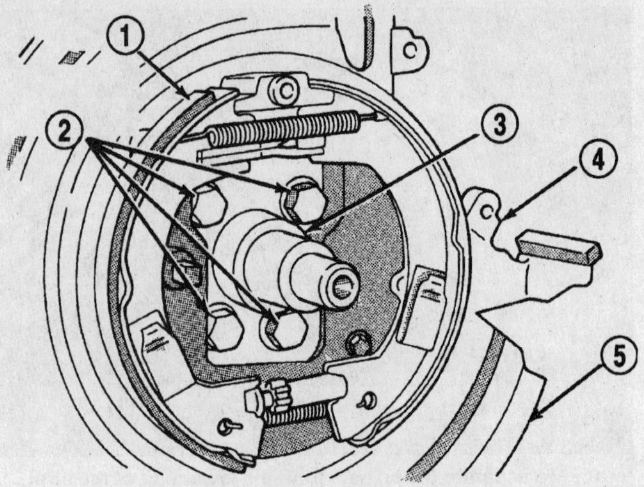

10.5 Remove the caliper mounting bracket bolts and separate the bracket/backing plate/parking brake assembly from the spindle

1 *Parking brake shoes*
2 *Caliper mounting bracket bolts*
3 *Spindle*
4 *Caliper mounting bracket*
5 *Backing plate*

11.3a Remove the dust cap

Inspection

11 Follow the inspection procedures described in Section 2. If you determine that the strut assembly must be disassembled for replacement of the strut or the coil spring, refer to Section 3.

Installation

Refer to illustration 9.13

12 Maneuver the strut assembly up into the wheel housing and insert the mounting studs through the holes in the body. Install the three nuts, but don't tighten them yet.

13 With the center punch in its hole, push the spindle onto the lower end of the strut assembly. Tap the spindle up the strut until the notch in the spindle is tightly seated against the locating tab on the strut body **(see illustration)**. Remove the center punch from the hole. Install the pinch bolt and tighten it to the torque listed in this Chapter's Specifications.

14 Attach the lateral links to the spindle with the through-bolt. Using a floor jack placed under the trailing arm bracket/spindle, raise the suspension to simulate normal ride height and tighten the bolt to the torque listed in this Chapter's Specifications.

15 Connect the stabilizer bar to the link and tighten the nut to the torque listed in this Chapter's Specifications.

16 Install the ABS wheel speed sensor, if equipped.

17 Install the brake disc and brake caliper (see Chapter 9).

18 Repeat this procedure for the other strut.

19 Install the wheel and lug nuts, lower the vehicle and tighten the lug nuts to the torque listed in the Chapter 1 Specifications.

10 Spindle - removal and installation

Refer to illustration 10.5

Warning: *Dust created by the brake system may contain asbestos, which is harmful to your health. Never blow it out with compressed air and don't inhale any of it. Do not, under any circumstances, use petroleum-based solvents to clean brake parts. Use brake system cleaner only.*

1 Loosen the rear wheel lug nuts, raise the vehicle and support it on jackstands. Block the front wheels and remove the rear wheel.

2 Remove the caliper and brake disc (see Chapter 9).

3 Remove the rear hub and bearing assembly (see Section 11).

4 On models with ABS, remove the wheel speed sensor from the caliper mounting bracket.

5 Unbolt the caliper mounting bracket bolts and detach the mounting bracket, backing plate and parking brake shoe assembly from the spindle **(see illustration)**.

6 Remove the nut and bolt that attach the trailing arm to the bracket on the spindle (see Section 13).

7 Remove the nut and bolt that attach the lateral links to the spindle (see Section 13).

8 Disconnect the spindle from the strut (see Section 9).

9 Installation is the reverse of removal. Be sure to tighten all suspension fasteners to the torque listed in this Chapter's Specifications. **Note:** *Don't tighten the trailing arm or lateral link fasteners until the rear suspension has been raised with a floor jack to simulate normal ride height.*

10 Install the wheel and lug nuts. Lower the vehicle and tighten the lug nuts to the torque listed in the Chapter 1 Specifications.

11 Hub and bearing assembly (rear) - removal and installation

Refer to illustrations 11.3a through 11.3g

Warning: *Dust created by the brake system may contain asbestos, which is harmful to your health. Never blow it out with compressed air and don't inhale any of it. Do not, under any circumstances, use petroleum-based solvents to clean brake parts. Use brake system cleaner only.*

1 Loosen the wheel lug nuts, raise the vehicle and support it securely on jackstands. Remove the wheel.

2 Remove the caliper and the brake disc (see Chapter 9).

3 Follow the accompanying photos to remove the hub and bearing assembly **(see illustrations)**.

4 Installation is the reverse of removal. Be sure to tighten the hub-to-spindle nut to the torque listed in this Chapter's Specifications.

5 Install the brake disc and caliper (see Chapter 9).

6 Install the wheel and lug nuts. Lower the vehicle and tighten the lug nuts to the torque listed in the Chapter 1 Specifications.

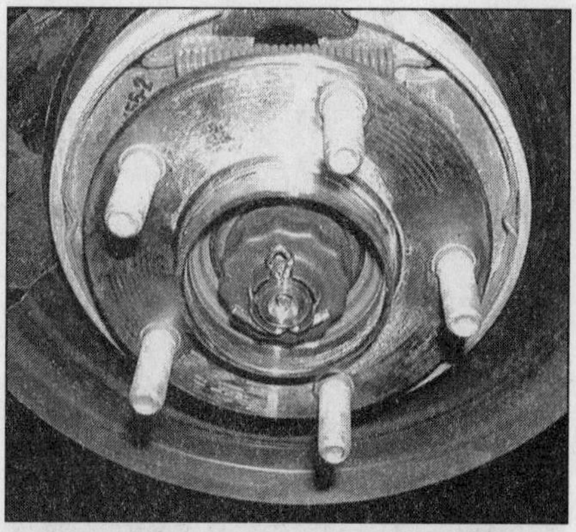

11.3b Remove the cotter pin

11.3c Remove the nut retainer

11.3d Remove the wave washer

11.3e Remove the hub retaining nut

11.3f Remove the large washer

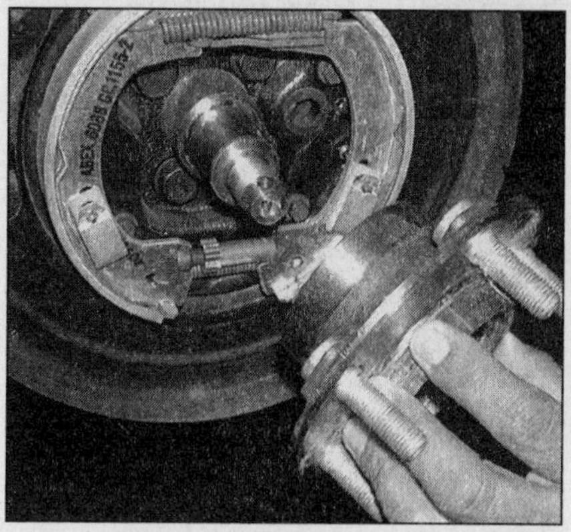

11.3g Remove the hub and bearing assembly

12.3 To disconnect a rear stabilizer bar link from the bar, remove this nut (arrow); if the link stud turns with the nut, hold the stud with a wrench or socket

12.4 Each stabilizer bar bracket is retained by two bolts; the left side also has a bracket line bracket bolt that must be removed

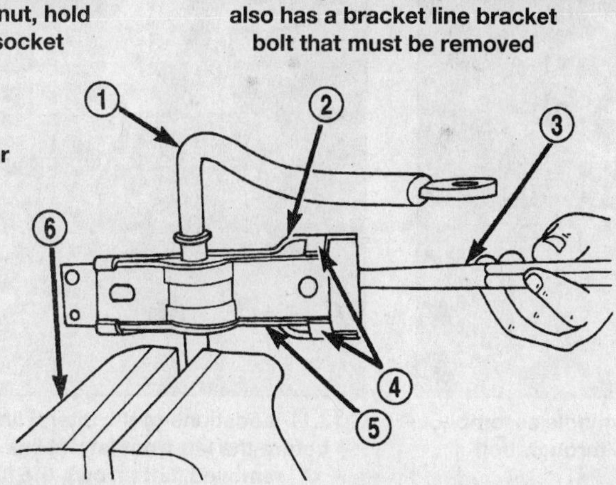

12.6 Removal details of the rear stabilizer bar bushing

1 *Stabilizer bar*
2 *Upper half of retainer*
3 *Punch*
4 *Retainer tabs (pried open)*
5 *Lower half of retainer*
6 *Vise*

12 Stabilizer bar (rear) - removal and installation

Refer to illustrations 12.3, 12.4 and 12.6

1 Loosen the rear wheel lug nuts. Raise the rear of the vehicle and place it securely on jackstands. Block the front wheels and remove the rear wheels.

2 Unbolt the brake line bracket from the left side bushing retainer.

3 Remove the stabilizer bar-to-link nuts **(see illustration)**.

4 Unbolt the stabilizer bar bushing retainers **(see illustration)** and remove the stabilizer bar from the vehicle.

5 Inspect the stabilizer bushings for cracks and tears. If the bushings are damaged, distorted or excessively worn, replace them.

6 To replace the bushings, the retainer halves must be separated. To do this, mount the stabilizer bar in a vise and pry back the tabs on the wider end of the upper retainer, then drive the upper portion of the retainer off the lower part **(see illustration)**.

7 When installing the bushings, make sure the slits face the front of the vehicle, and the elongated hole in the lower half of the retainer also faces the front of the vehicle. Reassemble the halves of the retainer brackets by driving the upper half onto the lower half until the bolt holes are aligned, then bend the tabs on the upper half of the retainer over the lower half.

8 The remainder of installation is the reverse of removal. Tighten the stabilizer bar-to-link nuts and the stabilizer bushing retainer bolts to the torque listed in this Chapter's Specifications.

9 Install the wheels and lug nuts, lower the vehicle and tighten the lug nuts to the torque listed in the Chapter 1 Specifications.

13 Suspension arms (rear) - removal and installation

Trailing arm

Refer to illustrations 13.2, 13.3 and 13.5

1 Loosen the rear wheel lug nuts, raise the rear of vehicle and support it securely on jackstands. Block the front wheels and remove the rear wheel.

2 Unscrew the nut and remove the trailing arm-to-spindle bracket bolt **(see illustration)**.

3 Remove the four bolts from the trailing arm-to-body bracket **(see illustration)** and detach the trailing arm from the vehicle.

4 If you're replacing the trailing arm, remove the nut and bolt and detach the arm from the bracket.

5 The trailing arm must be properly positioned in the mounting bracket before the nut and bolt are tightened. Place the bracket, open side down, on a level surface. Using a protractor or bubble-type angle gauge, adjust the angle of the arm to five degrees **(see illustration)**, then tighten the nut and bolt to the torque listed in this Chapter's Specifications. **Note:** *Once the arm is installed on the vehicle, this bolt can't be tightened.*

6 Install the arm on the vehicle, tightening the mounting bracket bolts to the torque listed in this Chapter's Specifications.

7 Using a floor jack and block of wood placed under the trailing arm/spindle area, raise the suspension to simulate normal ride height, then tighten the trailing arm-to-spindle bolt/nut to the torque listed in this Chapter's Specifications. Tighten the wheel lug nuts to the torque listed in the Chapter 1 Specifications.

13.2 To remove the rear end of the trailing arm from the bracket bolted to the spindle, remove this nut and bolt (arrows)

13.3 To remove the forward end of the trailing arm, unscrew these bracket bolts (arrows)

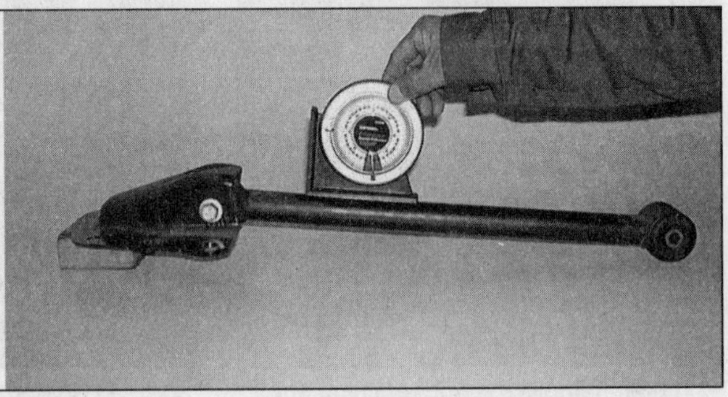

13.5 Before tightening the front mounting bracket bolt/nut, the arm must be set at a 5-degree angle to the mounting surface of the bracket

Lateral links

Refer to illustrations 13.9 and 13.11

8 Loosen the rear wheel lug nuts, raise the rear of the vehicle and support it securely on jackstands. Remove the rear wheel.

9 Unscrew the nut and remove bolt that attaches the lateral links to the spindle **(see illustration)**.

Left front lateral link

10 Remove the bolt that attaches the brake line bracket to the left stabilizer bar retainer. Unbolt the stabilizer bar bushing retainers and allow the stabilizer bar to hang down (see Section 12).

11 Remove the nut from the pivot bolt at the inner end of the left front lateral link **(see illustration)**. Don't try to remove the bolt yet.

12 Unbolt the fuel filler tube from the left side frame rail.

13 Refer to Chapter 4, *Fuel tank - removal and installation*, and lower the fuel tank

13.9 To disconnect the lateral links from the spindle assembly, remove this nut (arrow) and knock out the through-bolt with a long punch

13.11 Locations of the lateral link-to-crossmember bolts/nuts; before the left front lateral link-to-crossmember bolt can be removed (left arrow), the fuel tank must be lowered

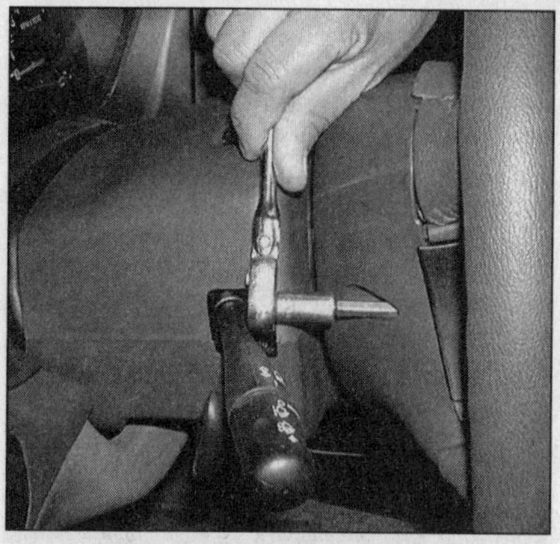

14.3a On models with cruise control, remove the cruise control switch screw . . .

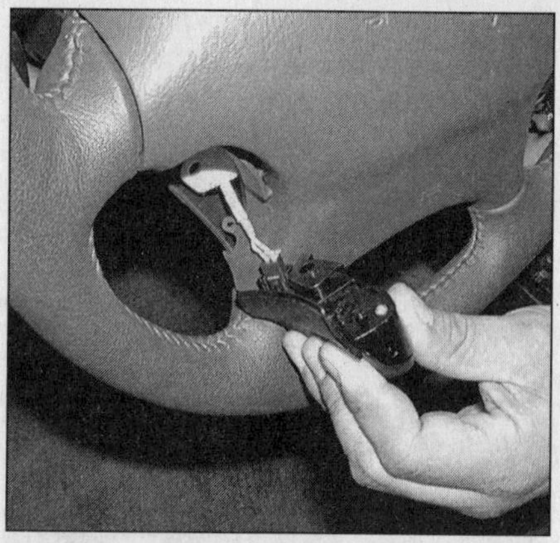

14.3b . . . and remove the switches (left switch shown, right switch identical)

14.4 To detach the airbag module from the steering wheel, remove the two module retaining bolts (arrows)

enough to allow the inner pivot bolt for the lateral link to be removed.

14 Remove the lateral link from the vehicle.

15 Installation is the reverse of removal. Be sure to install the inner pivot bolt the same way it was removed - with the bolt head facing forward. Place a floor jack under the trailing arm/spindle area and raise the rear suspension to simulate normal ride height, then tighten the lateral link inner pivot bolt and the lateral link-to-spindle bolt to the torque listed in this Chapter's Specifications. Proceed too Step 18.

Left rear lateral link and both right lateral links

16 Remove the lateral link-to-crossmember nut and bolt **(see illustration 13.11)**.

17 Installation is the reverse of removal. If you removed the left rear lateral link, make sure the bolt head is facing the rear of the vehicle. On both right lateral links, the bolt heads should be facing the front of the vehicle. Place a floor jack under the trailing arm/spindle area and raise the rear suspension to simulate normal ride height, then tighten the lateral link inner pivot bolt and the lateral link-to-spindle bolt to the torque listed in this Chapter's Specifications. Proceed to the next Step.

All lateral links

18 Install the wheel and lug nuts, then lower the vehicle to the ground. Tighten the wheel lug nuts to the torque listed in the Chapter 1 Specifications.

19 Have the rear wheel toe checked by an alignment shop.

14 Steering wheel - removal and installation

Warning: *These models have airbags. Always disable the airbag system before working in the vicinity of any airbag system components to avoid the possibility of accidental deployment of the airbag(s), which could cause personal injury (see Chapter 12).*

Removal

Refer to illustrations 14.3a, 14.3b, 14.4, 14.5a, 14.5b, 14.8, 14.9a and 14.9b

1 Park the vehicle with the front wheels pointing straight ahead.

2 Disconnect the negative battery cable from the remote ground terminal (see Chapter 5). Wait at least two minutes before proceeding.

3 Remove the two cruise control switches **(see illustrations)** from the steering wheel to gain access to the airbag module retaining bolts. **Note:** *The screws can be removed with either a 5.5 mm socket or a T-15 Torx bit.* If the vehicle isn't equipped with cruise control, pry off the covers on the sides of the steering wheel for access.

4 Remove the two airbag module retaining bolts **(see illustration)**.

5 Lift the airbag module off the steering wheel and unplug the airbag electrical connector **(see illustrations)**. Also unplug the electrical connector for the horn. **Warning:** *Set the airbag module aside in a safe, isolated location. Carry the airbag module with the trim side facing away from you and set it down with the trim side facing up.*

6 Turn the steering wheel 180-degrees (1/2-turn) clockwise from the straight ahead position. Place the ignition key in the LOCK position, then remove the key. **Warning:** *Don't allow the steering shaft to turn after the steering wheel has been removed, as the airbag system clockspring could be damaged.*

7 Remove the steering wheel retaining nut. **Note:** *It isn't necessary to mark the relationship of the steering wheel to the shaft,*

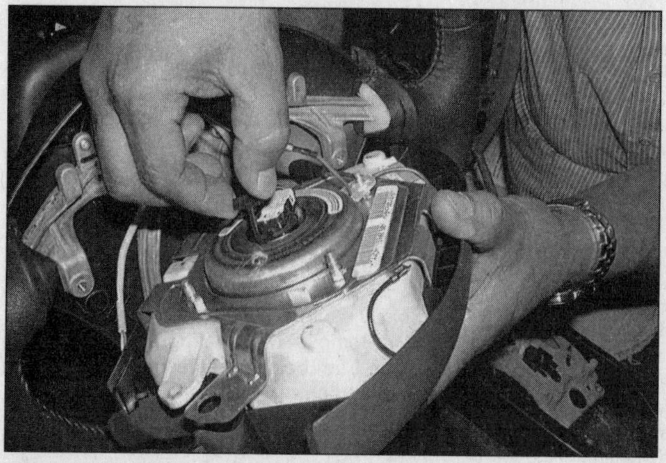

14.5a Pull up on the connector lock . . .

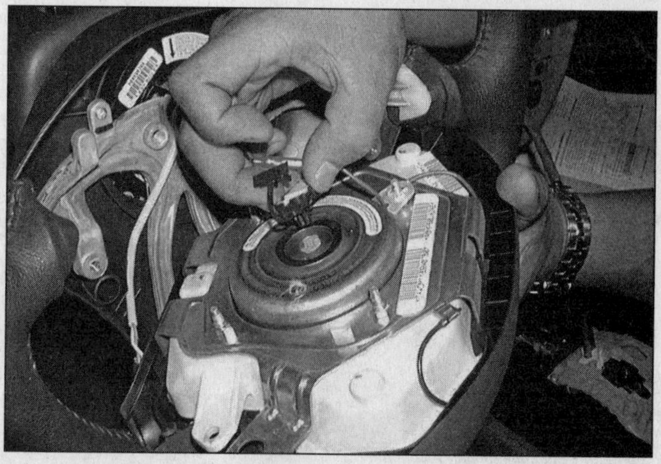

14.5b . . . then unplug the electrical connector from the airbag module

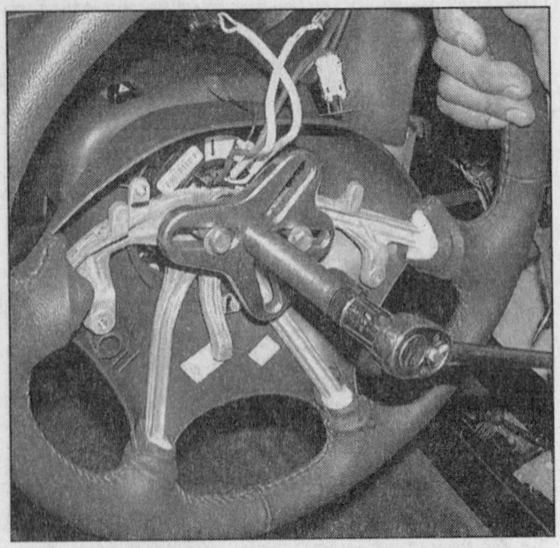

14.8 Use a steering wheel puller to remove the wheel from the shaft

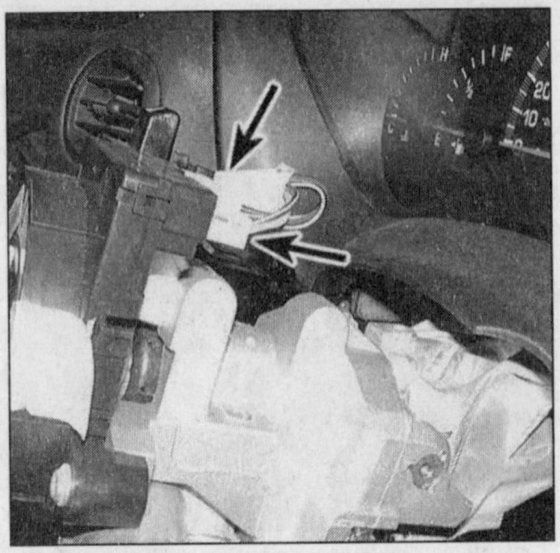

14.9a Unplug the electrical connectors (arrows) from the back of the airbag clockspring

14.9b The clockspring is secured to the steering column with two screws

since the hole in the steering wheel hub has one larger spline, allowing the wheel to fit in only one position.

8 Use a puller to disconnect the steering wheel from the shaft **(see illustration)**. Don't try to remove the steering wheel using any other method.

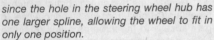

14.12 When the clockspring is in the centered position, the window on the left side of the clockspring body will be yellow (arrow) and the drive pin will be aligned with the arrow at the top of the clockspring body

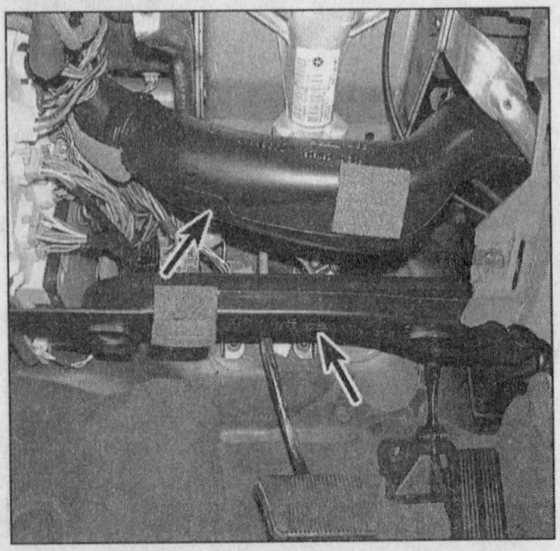

15.5 Remove these two ducts from below the steering column (arrows)

9 If it's necessary to remove the airbag system clockspring (for steering column removal, for example), remove the steering column covers (see Chapter 11), unplug the electrical connectors, remove the clockspring mounting screws and lift the clockspring off the steering column **(see illustrations)**. **Note:** *The clockspring has a locking device to prevent the hub from turning when the steering wheel is off, but it is a good idea to place a piece of tape across the body of the clockspring and the hub, in case the lock pin is inadvertently depressed.*

Installation

Refer to illustration 14.12

10 Verify that the steering column is still in the correct position; the blank spline on the steering column shaft will be pointing straight down.

11 If the clockspring was removed, position it on the steering column, install the mounting screws and tighten them securely. Reconnect the clockspring electrical connectors.

12 Whether or not the clockspring was removed, verify that it is centered. If it is in the centered position, the window in the clockspring body will be yellow and the arrow on the clockspring body will be pointing at the drive pin **(see illustration)**.

13 If it isn't in the centered position, push in on the plastic locking pin to free the locking mechanism and, while holding the pin depressed, turn the clockspring hub *clockwise* until it stops (don't apply too much force; you could damage the clockspring). Now, turn the clockspring hub counterclockwise until the window in the clockspring turns yellow and the arrow on the clockspring points to the drive pin on the clockspring hub. Release the locking pin.

14 Align the large spline on the steering wheel hub with the area with the missing splines on the steering shaft and slip the wheel onto the shaft; at the same time, guide the wiring for the airbag module, horn and combination switch through the opening in the steering wheel. Install the nut and tighten it to the torque listed in this Chapter's Specifications.

15 Rotate the steering wheel 180-degrees (1/2-turn) counterclockwise so the steering wheel is in the straight ahead position.

16 Guide the airbag module into position and plug in the horn and airbag module electrical connectors.

17 Install the airbag module and tighten the module retaining bolts to the torque listed in this Chapter's Specifications.

18 Plug in and install the cruise control switches and tighten the screws securely. On vehicles without cruise control, install the covers.

19 Connect the negative battery cable.

15 Steering column - removal and installation

Refer to illustrations 15.5, 15.9 and 15.11

Warning: *These models have airbags. Always disable the airbag system before working in the vicinity of any airbag system components to avoid the possibility of accidental deployment of the airbag(s), which could cause personal injury (see Chapter 12).*

Removal

1 Park the vehicle with the front wheels pointing straight ahead.

2 Disconnect the negative battery cable from the remote ground terminal (see Chapter 5). Wait at least two minutes before proceeding.

3 Remove the steering wheel and clockspring (see Section 14). **Caution:** *Be sure to turn the steering wheel 180-degrees clockwise before removing it, as described in Section 14.*

4 Remove the knee bolster and the knee bolster reinforcement (see Chapter 11).

5 Remove the heating/air conditioning ducts from below the steering column **(see illustration)**.

6 Remove the tilt lever and steering column covers (see Chapter 11), then unplug the electrical connectors from the combination switch and ignition switch (see Chapter 12).

15.9 On this model, the pinch bolt on the steering column coupler has a round head and the bolt is indexed to the shaft, so the nut has to be unscrewed, not the bolt; remove the clip (arrow) then unscrew the nut

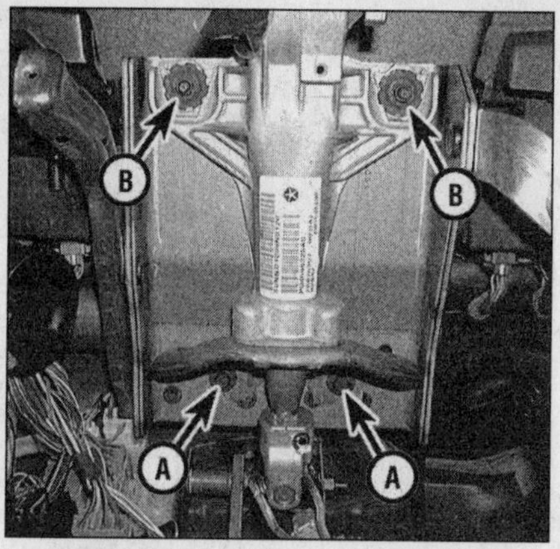

15.11 Loosen - but don't remove - the bolts (A), remove the nuts (B), then slide the column back and remove it

7 On floor shift models, detach the park lock cable from the ignition lock cylinder housing (see Chapter 7).

8 On column shift models, unplug the electrical connector from the brake transmission shift interlock (BTSI) solenoid. Also, detach the shift cable from its mounting pin, then remove the screws and detach the cable mounting bracket from the steering column (see Chapter 7).

9 Remove the clip from the steering column coupler pinch bolt **(see illustration)**. On some models the pinch bolt head is round and can't be unscrewed; if your vehicle is like this, unscrew the nut and drive the bolt out of the coupler. If the bolt has a hex head, unscrew the bolt - not the nut.

10 Separate the steering column coupler from the intermediate shaft.

11 Loosen (but don't remove) the two bolts securing the lower end of the steering column to the support bracket, then remove the two nuts that secure the upper end of the steering column to the support bracket **(see illustration)**. Lower the upper end of the steering column and pull it to the rear to remove it from the support bracket.

16.2 Loosen the adjustment sleeve pinch bolt nut (arrow)

Installation

12 Engage the slotted openings at the lower end of the column with the lower mounting bolts, then push the holes in the upper end of the column over the upper mounting studs and install the nuts. Tighten the nuts and bolts finger-tight only at this time.

13 Center the steering column on its support bracket, then tighten the upper mounting nuts to the torque listed in this Chapter's Specifications. Now tighten the lower mounting bolts to the torque listed in this Chapter's Specifications.

14 The remainder of installation is the reverse of the removal procedure. Be sure to tighten all fasteners to the proper torque values, and carefully follow the steering wheel and clockspring installation procedure described in Section 14.

16 Tie-rod ends - removal and installation

Removal

Refer to illustrations 16.2, 16.3, 16.4 and 16.5

1 Loosen the wheel lug nuts. Raise the front of the vehicle, support it securely on jackstands and set the parking brake. Remove the front wheels.

2 Loosen the pinch bolt on the adjustment sleeve **(see illustration)**.

3 Loosen the nut on the tie-rod end stud a few turns, but don't remove it yet **(see illustration)**.

4 Disconnect the tie-rod from the steering arm with a puller **(see illustration)**. Remove the nut and separate the tie-rod.

5 Measure the distance from the center of the tie-rod end to the outer edge of the adjuster sleeve and write down this measurement **(see illustration)**.

6 Unscrew the tie-rod end from the adjustment sleeve.

Installation

Refer to illustration 16.7

7 Screw the tie-rod end into the adjustment sleeve until the distance from the center of the new tie-rod end to the outer edge of the adjustment sleeve matches the measurement you made before removing the old tie-

16.3 Prevent the tie-rod end stud from turning by holding it with a wrench, then loosen the stud nut with another wrench, but don't remove it yet

16.4 Install a puller and push the tie-rod end stud out of the steering arm

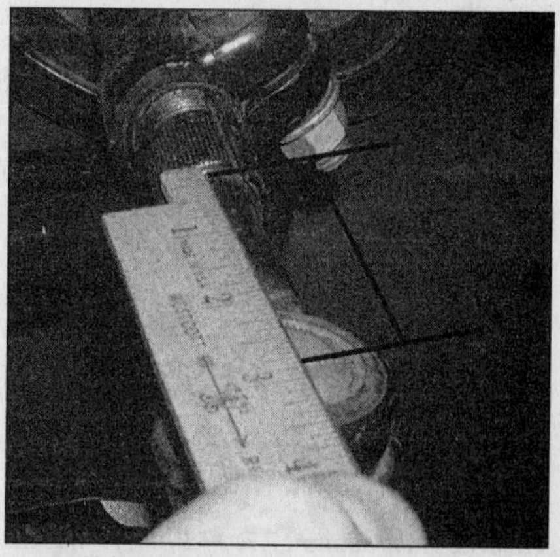

16.5 Measuring the distance from the adjuster sleeve to the center of the tie-rod end

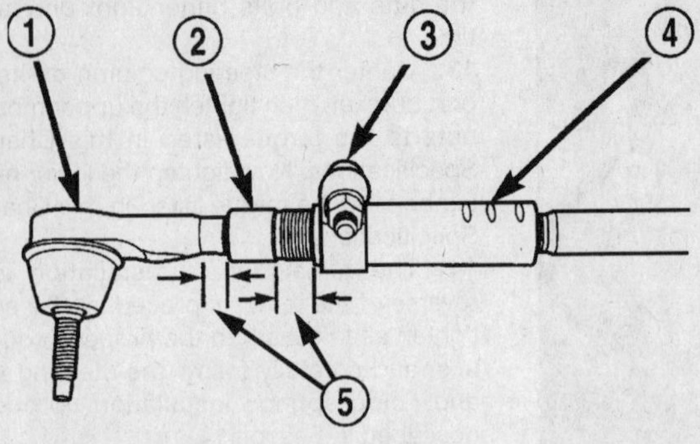

16.7 There must not be more than 25/32-inch of combined thread exposure on the tie-rod end and adjuster sleeve

1 *Tie-rod end*
2 *Adjuster sleeve*
3 *Pinch bolt*
4 *Inner tie-rod*
5 *Measure the amount of thread exposure in these areas*

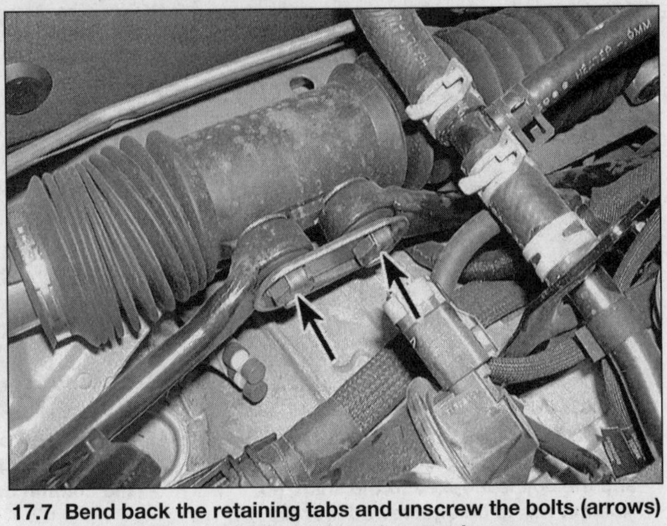

17.7 Bend back the retaining tabs and unscrew the bolts (arrows) retaining the tie-rods to the steering gear

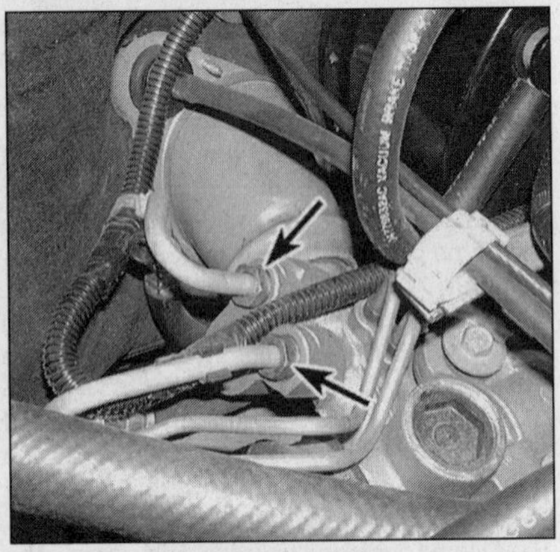

17.9 Unscrew the power steering fluid line fittings (arrows)

17.11 The left-side steering gear mounting bolts (arrows) can be removed with a long extension and a socket with a U-joint attachment; if you don't have a U-joint attachment, you'll probably have to remove the brake master cylinder for access to the bolts

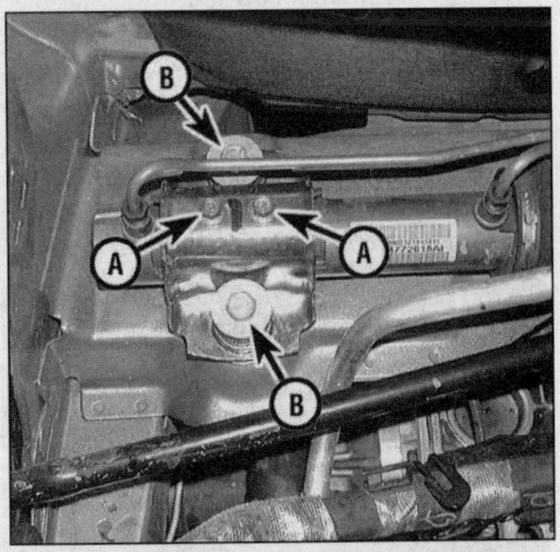

17.12 Remove the bolts that attach the mounting bracket to the right side of the steering gear (A), then remove the bracket-to-chassis bolts (B)

rod end. **Warning:** *There must not be more than 25/32-inch (20 mm) of combined thread exposure on the adjuster and tie-rod end* **(see illustration)**.

8 Install the tie-rod end stud into the steering arm, install the stud nut and tighten it to the torque listed in this Chapter's Specifications.

9 Tighten the pinch bolt on the adjuster sleeve to the torque listed in this Chapter's Specifications.

10 Install the wheel and lug nuts. Lower the vehicle and tighten the lug nuts to the torque listed in the Chapter 1 Specifications.

11 Have the front end alignment checked and, if necessary, adjusted.

17 Steering gear - removal and installation

Removal

Refer to illustrations 17.7, 17.9, 17.11, 17.12 and 17.14

Warning: *These models are equipped with airbags. Make sure the steering column shaft is not turned while the steering gear is removed or you could damage the airbag system. To prevent the shaft from turning, turn the ignition key to the lock position before beginning work or run the seat belt through the steering wheel and clip the seat belt into place. Due to the possible damage to the airbag system, we recommend only experienced mechanics attempt this procedure.*

1 Park the vehicle with the wheels pointing straight ahead.

2 Disconnect the negative battery cable from the remote ground terminal (see Chapter 5).

3 Remove the windshield wiper arms, wiper module cover, cowl cover and strut tower reinforcement (see Chapters 11 and 12).

4 Remove the windshield wiper module (see Chapter 12).

5 Remove the air intake duct and resonator (see Chapter 4).

6 Separate the steering column coupler from the intermediate shaft (see Section 15).

7 Bend back the retaining tabs for the bolts that attach the inner ends of the tie rods to the steering gear **(see illustration)**. Remove these bolts and detach the tie-rods from the steering gear.

8 Siphon as much fluid as possible from the power steering fluid reservoir.

9 Detach the power steering pressure and return lines from the steering gear **(see illustration)**. Cap or plug the fittings to prevent excessive fluid loss and contamination.

10 If the vehicle is equipped with speed proportional steering, disconnect the electrical connector for the solenoid valve, located under the brake master cylinder.

11 Remove the mounting bolts from the left side of the steering gear **(see illustration)**. **Note:** *Removal of the rear bolt will require the use of a long extension and a U-joint socket or adapter. If you don't have a U-joint socket or adapter, you'll have to remove the brake master cylinder mounting nuts and reposition the bracket that supports the wiring harness.*

12 Unbolt the right side steering gear bracket from the steering gear, then unbolt the bracket from the chassis **(see illustration)**. Remove the bracket.

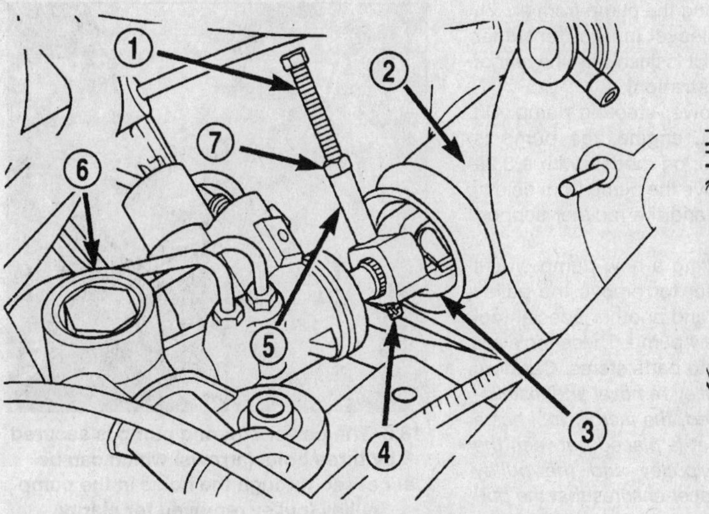

17.14 Steering coupler roll pin removal details (using a roll pin remover)

1 *Roll pin removal tool*
2 *Boot*
3 *Coupler*
4 *Knurled nut (part of tool)*
5 *Sleeve*
6 *Steering gear*
7 *Nut*

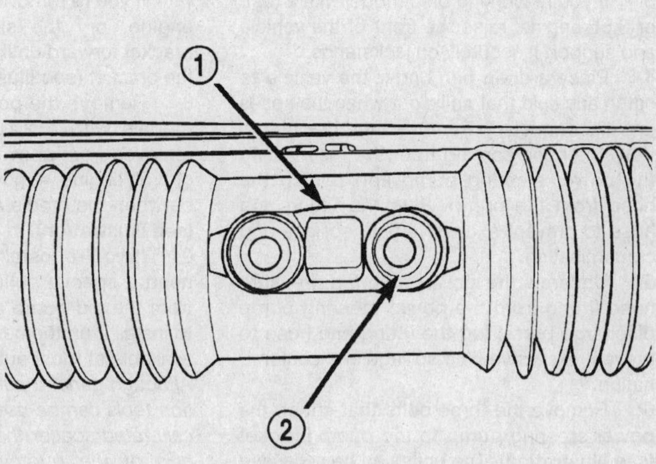

17.32 Before connecting the tie-rods to the steering gear, make sure the spacer block holes are aligned with the holes in the rack

1 *Steering gear boot*
2 *Spacer block*

13 Move the steering gear forward for access to the roll pin that secures the intermediate shaft to the steering gear input shaft. Mark the relationship of the steering coupler to the steering gear shaft to ensure proper reassembly.

14 Using a roll pin remover (available at specialty tool suppliers), remove the roll pin from the joint **(see illustration)**. If a roll pin remover is not available, you may be able to remove it using a small pin punch and hammer. Detach the intermediate shaft from the steering gear.

15 Loosen the right front wheel lug nuts, raise the front of the vehicle and support it securely on jackstands. Remove the wheel.

16 Detach the right tie-rod end from the steering arm **(see illustration 16.4)**. Remove the tie-rod.

17 If the vehicle is equipped with a 2.7 liter engine, turn the front of the left front wheel outward. This will position the left tie-rod to give the maximum amount of clearance for steering gear removal.

18 Maneuver the steering gear to the right side of the vehicle, passing it into the opening for the right tie-rod about half way.

19 Raise the left end of the steering gear, move the steering gear back toward the center of the vehicle, then guide it up between the cowl and the engine to remove it. **Caution:** *Be careful not to let power steering fluid drip on the vehicle's paint.*

Installation

Refer to illustration 17.32

20 Before installing the steering gear, make sure the center take-off for the tie rods is centered. To ensure that it is, turn the steering gear input shaft all the way in one direction, then turn it the other way, counting the number of turns until it reaches the end of its travel. Divide that number by two, then turn the input shaft in the opposite direction that many turns.

21 Guide the steering gear back into position the same way it was removed. It may be necessary to reposition the left front wheel to move the left tie-rod into a position that gives the most clearance.

22 Guide the right side tie-rod through its hole in the inner fender panel and connect the tie-rod end to the steering arm (see Section 16). Tighten the nut to the torque listed in this Chapter's Specifications.

23 Install the right front wheel and lug nuts. Lower the vehicle and tighten the lug nuts to the torque listed in this Chapter's Specifications.

24 If you're installing the old steering gear, align the mark on the steering coupler with the mark on the steering gear shaft and insert the shaft into the coupler. If you're installing a new steering gear, align the master spline on the steering gear shaft with the master spline on the coupler, then insert the shaft into the coupler.

25 Install the steering coupler-to-steering shaft roll pin, pushing it in with the roll pin tool or carefully tapping it in until it's flush with the top of the coupler.

26 Push the steering gear into position, making sure the boot on the firewall slides over the steering gear without folding.

27 Install the steering gear left-side mounting bolts, but don't tighten them yet.

28 Install the right-side steering gear mount, installing the mount-to-crossmember bolts and the mount-to-steering gear bolts finger tight only. Now, tighten the mount-to-crossmember bolt to the torque listed in this Chapter's Specifications.

29 Tighten the left-side mounting bolts to the torque listed in this Chapter's Specifications.

30 Tighten the right-side mount-to-steering gear bolts to the torque listed in this Chapter's Specifications.

31 Connect the power steering fluid pressure and return lines to the steering gear, tightening the fittings securely.

32 Check to see that the holes in the spacer block inside the steering gear boot are lined-up with the holes in the steering rack **(see illustration)**, then attach the inner ends of the tie-rods to the steering gear, making sure the washers are positioned between the steering gear and the tie-rods. **Note:** *It may be necessary to raise the front wheels off the ground slightly to turn the wheels in or out to position the tie-rods properly.* Also, make sure the plate and lock tabs are properly positioned. After tightening the tie-rod-to-steering gear bolts to the torque listed in this Chapter's Specifications, bend the lock tabs over the bolt heads.

33 The remainder of installation is the reverse of removal. Be sure to bleed the power steering system (see Section 19).

18 Power steering pump - removal and installation

Refer to illustrations 18. 6, 18.7, 18.8, 18.9a, 18.9b and 18.9c

1 Disconnect the negative battery cable from the remote ground terminal (see Chapter 5). Remove the drivebelt (see Chapter 1).

2 Unplug the electrical connector from the pressure sensor on the side of the power steering pump. Using a large syringe or suction gun, suck as much fluid out of the power steering fluid reservoir as possible.

3 If you're working on a model with a 3.2L or 3.5L engine, raise the front of the vehicle and support it securely on jackstands.

4 Place a drain pan under the vehicle to catch any fluid that spills out when the hoses are disconnected. Remove the hose clamp from the hose coming from the reservoir to the power steering pump and detach the hose from the pump. Plug the fitting and hose to prevent excessive fluid spillage and contamination.

5 Unscrew the power steering pressure hose fitting from the power steering pump discharge port. Plug the fitting and hose to prevent excessive fluid spillage and contamination.

6 Remove the three bolts that attach the power steering pump to the pump bracket **(see illustration)**. The bolts can be accessed through the holes in the power steering pump pulley.

7 If you're removing the pump from a 2.7L engine, pry the sleeve in the tensioner bracket forward until it is flush with the rear of the bracket **(see illustration)**.

8 Remove the power steering pump. On models with a 2.7L engine, the pump is removed from above; on models with a 3.2L or 3.5L engine, remove the pump from below, between the cradle and the radiator support **(see illustration)**.

9 If you're installing a new pump, you'll need a special puller to remove the pulley from the old pump and another special tool to install it on the new pump. These tools are available at most auto parts stores. **Caution:** *Although generic pulley removal and installation tools can be used, the factory tool has a calibrated spacer that is placed between the hub of the pump pulley and the pulley installer tool; this spacer ensures that the pulley is installed to the correct position on the*

18.6 The power steering pump is secured by three bolts (arrows) which can be accessed through the holes in the pump pulley (pulley removed for clarity)

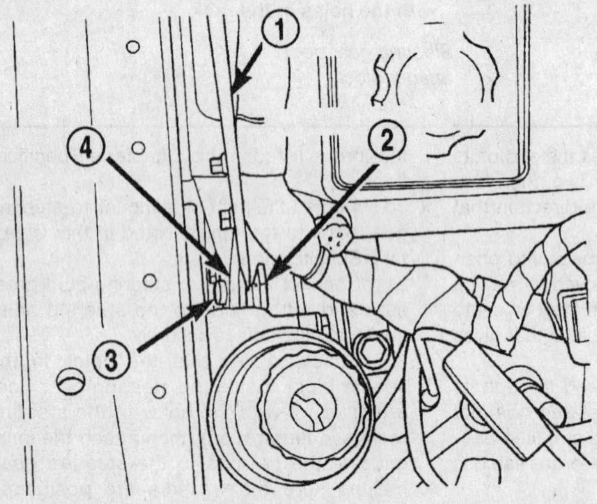

18.7 Power steering pump removal details (2.7L engine)

1 *Screwdriver (pry the sleeve forward)*
2 *Power steering pump*
3 *Sleeve*
4 *Tensioner bracket*

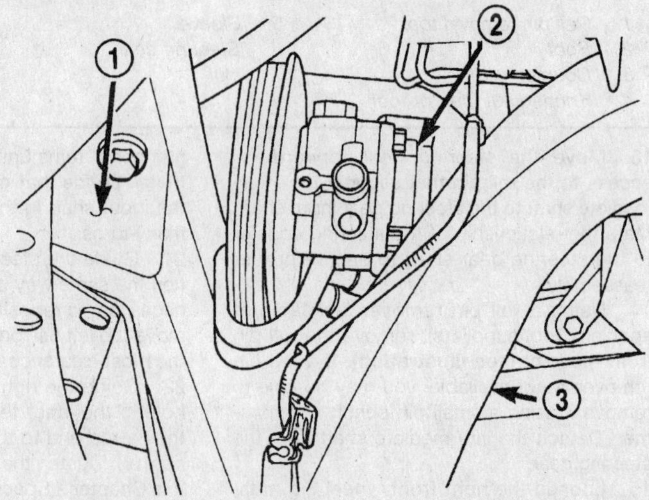

18.8 Power steering pump removal details (3.2L and 3.5L engines)

1 *Radiator support (lower)*
2 *Power steering pump*
3 *Engine cradle*

18.9a Before removing the pulley from the power steering pump, measure the depth of the shaft in the pulley hub; the pulley must be pressed onto the new pump to the exact same position

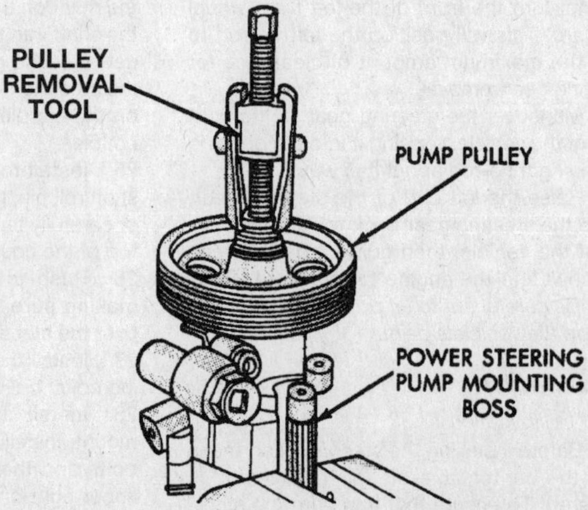

18.9b You'll need a special puller to remove the pulley from the power steering pump . . .

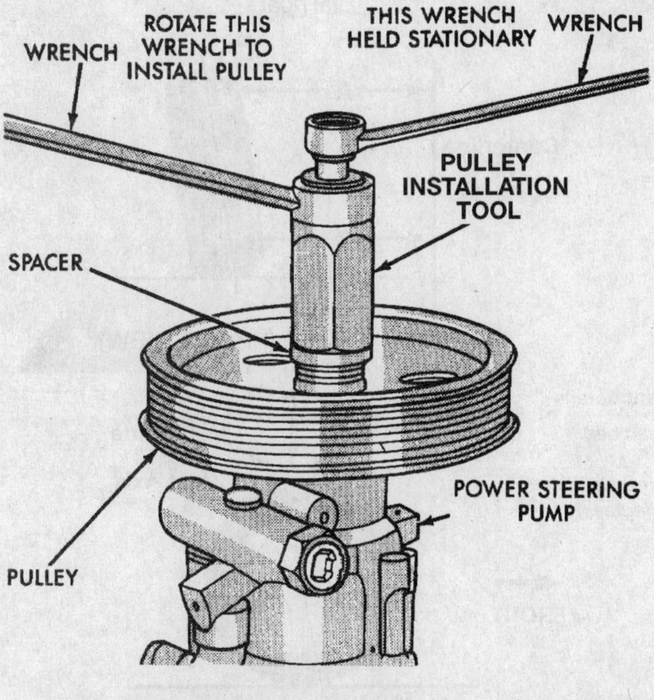

18.9c ... and another special tool to install it on the new pump (these tools are available at most auto parts stores) - make sure the pulley is pressed onto the shaft until the previously measured depth is the same as on the old pump

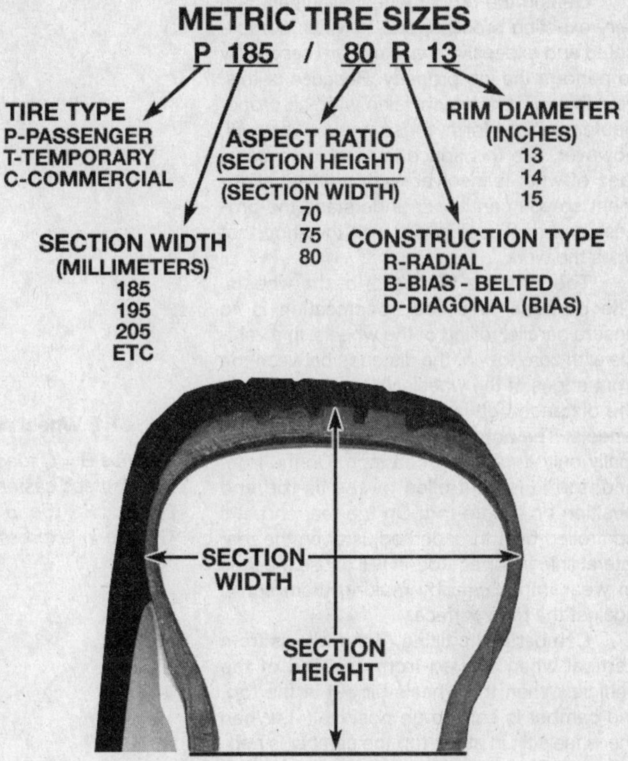

20.1 Metric tire size code

shaft, which is critical for drivebelt alignment. If you are using a generic installer tool, measure the distance from the pulley hub to the end of the shaft using a vernier or dial caliper (or some other type of depth gauge) before you remove the pulley from the old pump **(see illustrations)**. *Press the pulley onto the new pump to the exact same position.*

10 Installation is the reverse of removal. Be sure to tighten the power steering pump bolts to the torque listed in this Chapter's Specifications. Tighten the pressure hose fitting securely.

11 Refill the fluid in the reservoir (see Chapter 1) and bleed the system (see Section 19).

19 Power steering system - bleeding

1 Following any operation in which the power steering fluid lines have been disconnected, the power steering system must be bled to remove all air and obtain proper steering performance.

2 With the front wheels in the straight ahead position, check the power steering fluid level and, if low, add fluid until it reaches the Cold mark on the reservoir.

3 Start the engine and allow it to run at fast idle. Recheck the fluid level and add more if necessary to reach the Cold mark on the reservoir.

4 Bleed the system by turning the wheels from side to side, without hitting the stops. This will work the air out of the system. Keep the reservoir full of fluid as this is done.

5 When the air is worked out of the system, return the wheels to the straight ahead position and leave the vehicle running for several more minutes before shutting it off.

6 Road test the vehicle to be sure the steering system is functioning normally and noise free.

7 Recheck the fluid level to be sure it is up to the Hot mark on the reservoir while the engine is at normal operating temperature. Add fluid if necessary (see Chapter 1).

20 Wheels and tires - general information

Refer to illustration 20.1

1 All vehicles covered by this manual are equipped with metric-sized fiberglass or steel belted radial tires **(see illustration)**. Use of other size or type of tires may affect the ride and handling of the vehicle. Don't mix different types of tires, such as radials and bias belted, on the same vehicle as handling may be seriously affected. It's recommended that tires be replaced in pairs on the same axle, but if only one tire is being replaced, be sure it's the same size, structure and tread design as the other.

2 Because tire pressure has a substantial effect on handling and wear, the pressure on all tires should be checked at least once a month or before any extended trips (see Chapter 1).

3 Wheels must be replaced if they are bent, dented, leak air, have elongated bolt holes, are heavily rusted, out of vertical symmetry or if the lug nuts won't stay tight. Wheel repairs that use welding or peening are not recommended.

4 Tire and wheel balance is important in the overall handling, braking and performance of the vehicle. Unbalanced wheels can adversely affect handling and ride characteristics as well as tire life. Whenever a tire is installed on a wheel, the tire and wheel should be balanced by a shop with the proper equipment.

21 Wheel alignment - general information

Refer to illustration 21.1

A wheel alignment refers to the adjustments made to the wheels so they are in proper angular relationship to the suspension and the ground. Wheels that are out of proper alignment not only affect vehicle control, but also increase tire wear. The alignment angles normally measured are camber, caster and toe-in **(see illustration)**. Toe-in is the only adjustable angle on the front or the rear. The other angles should be measured to check for bent or worn suspension parts.

Getting the proper wheel alignment is a very exacting process, one in which complicated and expensive machines are necessary to perform the job properly. Because of this, you should have a technician with the proper equipment perform these tasks. We will, however, use this space to give you a basic idea of what is involved with a wheel alignment so you can better understand the process and deal intelligently with the shop that does the work.

Toe-in is the turning in of the wheels. The purpose of a toe specification is to ensure parallel rolling of the wheels. In a vehicle with zero toe-in, the distance between the front edges of the wheels will be the same as the distance between the rear edges of the wheels. The actual amount of toe-in is normally only a fraction of an inch. On the front end, toe-in is controlled by the tie-rod end position on the tie-rod. On the rear end, it's controlled by a threaded adjuster on the rear lateral link. Incorrect toe-in will cause the tires to wear improperly by making them scrub against the road surface.

Camber is the tilting of the wheels from vertical when viewed from one end of the vehicle. When the wheels tilt out at the top, the camber is said to be positive (+). When the wheels tilt in at the top the camber is negative (-). The amount of tilt is measured in degrees from vertical and this measurement is called the camber angle. This angle affects the amount of tire tread which contacts the road and compensates for changes in the suspension geometry when the vehicle is cornering or traveling over an undulating surface.

Caster is the tilting of the front steering axis from the vertical. A tilt toward the rear is positive caster and a tilt toward the front is negative caster.

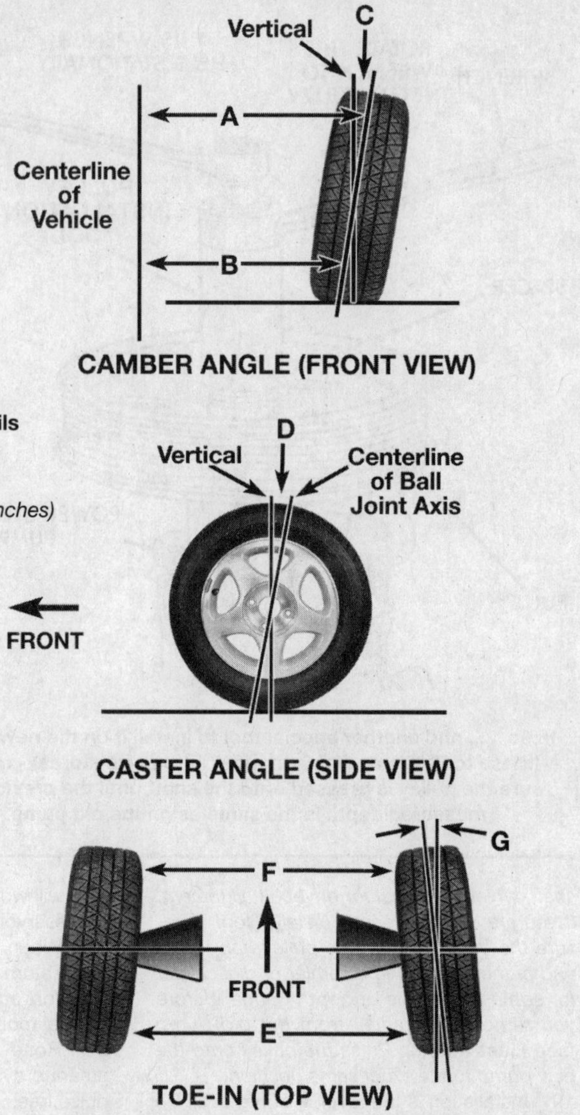

21.1 Wheel alignment details

A minus B = C (degrees camber)
D = degrees caster
E minus F = toe-in (measured in inches)
G = toe-in (expressed in degrees)

Chapter 11 Body

Contents

1 General information

The Chrysler LH models feature a "unibody" layout, using a floor pan with front and rear frame side rails which support the body components, front and rear suspension systems and other mechanical components. Certain components are particularly vulnerable to accident damage and can be unbolted and repaired or replaced. Among these parts are the body moldings, bumpers, front fenders, doors, the hood and trunk lid. Only general body maintenance practices and body panel repair procedures within the scope of the do-it-yourselfer are included in this chapter.

Although all covered models are very similar, some procedures may differ somewhat from one body to another.

2 Body - maintenance

1 The condition of your vehicle's body is very important, because the resale value depends a great deal on it. It's much more difficult to repair a neglected or damaged body than it is to repair mechanical components. The hidden areas of the body, such as the wheel wells, the frame and the engine compartment, are equally important, although they don't require as frequent attention as the rest of the body.

2 Once a year, or every 12,000 miles, it's a good idea to have the underside of the body steam cleaned. All traces of dirt and oil will be removed and the area can then be inspected carefully for rust, damaged brake lines, frayed electrical wires, damaged cables and other problems. The front suspension components should be greased after completion of this job.

3 At the same time, clean the engine and the engine compartment with a steam cleaner or water-soluble degreaser.

4 The wheel wells should be given close attention, since undercoating can peel away and stones and dirt thrown up by the tires can cause the paint to chip and flake, allowing rust to set in. If rust is found, clean down to the bare metal and apply an anti-rust paint.

5 The body should be washed about once a week. Wet the vehicle thoroughly to soften the dirt, then wash it down with a soft sponge and plenty of clean soapy water. If the surplus dirt is not washed off very carefully, it can wear down the paint.

6 Spots of tar or asphalt thrown up from the road should be removed with a cloth soaked in solvent.

7 Once every six months, wax the body and chrome trim. If a chrome cleaner is used to remove rust from any of the vehicle's plated parts, remember that the cleaner also removes part of the chrome, so use it sparingly. After cleaning chrome trim, apply paste wax to preserve it.

3 Vinyl trim - maintenance

Don't clean vinyl trim with detergents, caustic soap or petroleum-based cleaners. Plain soap and water works just fine, with a soft brush to clean dirt that may be ingrained. Wash the vinyl as frequently as the rest of the vehicle. After cleaning, application of a high-quality rubber and vinyl protectant will help prevent oxidation and cracks. The protectant can also be applied to weatherstripping, vacuum lines and rubber hoses, which often fail as a result of chemical degradation, and to the tires.

4 Upholstery and carpets - maintenance

1 Every three months remove the floormats and clean the interior of the vehicle (more frequently if necessary). Use a stiff whiskbroom to brush the carpeting and loosen dirt and dust, then vacuum the upholstery and carpets thoroughly, especially along seams and crevices.
2 Dirt and stains can be removed from carpeting with basic household or automotive carpet shampoos available in spray cans. Follow the directions and vacuum again, then use a stiff brush to bring back the "nap" of the carpet.
3 Most interiors have cloth or vinyl upholstery, either of which can be cleaned and maintained with a number of material-specific cleaners or shampoos available in auto supply stores. Follow the directions on the product for usage, and always spot-test any upholstery cleaner on an inconspicuous area (bottom edge of a backseat cushion) to ensure that it doesn't cause a color shift in the material.
4 After cleaning, vinyl upholstery should be treated with a protectant. **Note:** *Make sure the protectant container indicates the product can be used on seats - some products may make a seat too slippery.* **Caution:** *Do not use protectant on vinyl-covered steering wheels.*
5 Leather upholstery requires special care. It should be cleaned regularly with saddlesoap or leather cleaner. Never use alcohol, gasoline, water, nail polish remover or thinner to clean leather upholstery.
6 After cleaning, regularly treat leather upholstery with a leather conditioner, rubbed in with a soft cotton cloth. Never use car wax on leather upholstery.
7 In areas where the interior of the vehicle is subject to bright sunlight, cover leather seating areas of the seats with a sheet if the vehicle is to be left out for any length of time.

5 Body repair - minor damage

Plastic body panels (front and rear bumper fascia)

The following repair procedures are for minor scratches and gouges. Repair of more serious damage should be left to a dealer service department or qualified auto body shop. Below is a list of the equipment and materials necessary to perform the following repair procedures on plastic body panels. Although a specific brand of material may be mentioned, it should be noted that equivalent products from other manufacturers may be used instead.

Wax, grease and silicone removing solvent
Cloth-backed body tape
Sanding discs
Drill motor with three-inch disc holder
Hand sanding block
Rubber squeegees
Sandpaper
Non-porous mixing palette
Wood paddle or putty knife
Curved-tooth body file
Flexible parts repair material

1 Remove the damaged panel, if necessary or desirable. In most cases, repairs can be carried out with the panel installed.
2 Clean the area(s) to be repaired with a wax, grease and silicone removing solvent applied with a water-dampened cloth.
3 If the damage is structural, that is, if it extends through the panel, clean the backside of the panel area to be repaired as well. Wipe dry.
4 Sand the rear surface about 1-1/2 inches beyond the break.
5 Cut two pieces of fiberglass cloth large enough to overlap the break by about 1-1/2 inches. Cut only to the required length.
6 Mix the adhesive from the repair kit according to the instructions included with the kit, and apply a layer of the mixture approximately 1/8-inch thick on the backside of the panel. Overlap the break by at least 1-1/2 inches.
7 Apply one piece of fiberglass cloth to the adhesive and cover the cloth with additional adhesive. Apply a second piece of fiberglass cloth to the adhesive and immediately cover the cloth with additional adhesive in sufficient quantity to fill the weave.
8 Allow the repair to cure for 20 to 30 minutes at 60-degrees to 80-degrees F.
9 If necessary, trim the excess repair material at the edge.
10 Remove all of the paint film over and around the area(s) to be repaired. The repair material should not overlap the painted surface.
11 With a drill motor and a sanding disc (or a rotary file), cut a "V" along the break line approximately 1/2-inch wide. Remove all dust and loose particles from the repair area.
12 Mix and apply the repair material. Apply a light coat first over the damaged area; then continue applying material until it reaches a level slightly higher than the surrounding finish.
13 Cure the mixture for 20 to 30 minutes at 60-degrees to 80-degrees F.
14 Roughly establish the contour of the area being repaired with a body file. If low areas or pits remain, mix and apply additional adhesive.
15 Block sand the damaged area with sandpaper to establish the actual contour of the surrounding surface.
16 If desired, the repaired area can be temporarily protected with several light coats of primer. Because of the special paints and techniques required for flexible body panels, it is recommended that the vehicle be taken to a paint shop for completion of the body repair.

Steel body panels

See photo sequence

Repair of minor scratches

17 If the scratch is superficial and does not penetrate to the metal of the body, repair is very simple. Lightly rub the scratched area with a fine rubbing compound to remove loose paint and built up wax. Rinse the area with clean water.
18 Apply touch-up paint to the scratch, using a small brush. Continue to apply thin layers of paint until the surface of the paint in the scratch is level with the surrounding paint. Allow the new paint at least two weeks to harden, then blend it into the surrounding paint by rubbing with a very fine rubbing compound. Finally, apply a coat of wax to the scratch area.
19 If the scratch has penetrated the paint and exposed the metal of the body, causing the metal to rust, a different repair technique is required. Remove all loose rust from the bottom of the scratch with a pocketknife, then apply rust inhibiting paint to prevent the formation of rust in the future. Using a rubber or nylon applicator, coat the scratched area with glaze-type filler. If required, the filler can be mixed with thinner to provide a very thin paste, which is ideal for filling narrow scratches. Before the glaze filler in the scratch hardens, wrap a piece of smooth cotton cloth around the tip of a finger. Dip the cloth in thinner and then quickly wipe it along the surface of the scratch. This will ensure that the surface of the filler is slightly hollow. The scratch can now be painted over as described earlier in this Section.

Repair of dents

20 When repairing dents, the first job is to pull the dent out until the affected area is as close as possible to its original shape. There is no point in trying to restore the original

shape completely as the metal in the damaged area will have stretched on impact and cannot be restored to its original contours. It is better to bring the level of the dent up to a point that is about 1/8-inch below the level of the surrounding metal. In cases where the dent is very shallow, it is not worth trying to pull it out at all.

21 If the backside of the dent is accessible, it can be hammered out gently from behind using a soft-face hammer. While doing this, hold a block of wood firmly against the opposite side of the metal to absorb the hammer blows and prevent the metal from being stretched.

22 If the dent is in a section of the body which has double layers, or some other factor makes it inaccessible from behind, a different technique is required. Drill several small holes through the metal inside the damaged area, particularly in the deeper sections. Screw long, self-tapping screws into the holes just enough for them to get a good grip in the metal. Now pulling on the protruding heads of the screws with locking pliers can pull out the dent.

23 The next stage of repair is the removal of paint from the damaged area and from an inch or so of the surrounding metal. This is easily done with a wire brush or sanding disk in a drill motor, although it can be done just as effectively by hand with sandpaper. To complete the preparation for filling, score the surface of the bare metal with a screwdriver or the tang of a file or drill small holes in the affected area. This will provide a good grip for the filler material. To complete the repair, see the Section on filling and painting.

Repair of rust holes or gashes

24 Remove all paint from the affected area and from an inch or so of the surrounding metal using a sanding disk or wire brush mounted in a drill motor. If these are not available, a few sheets of sandpaper will do the job just as effectively.

25 With the paint removed, you will be able to determine the severity of the corrosion and decide whether to replace the whole panel, if possible, or repair the affected area. New body panels are not as expensive as most people think and it is often quicker to install a new panel than to repair large areas of rust.

26 Remove all trim pieces from the affected area except those which will act as a guide to the original shape of the damaged body, such as headlight shells, etc. Using metal snips or a hacksaw blade, remove all loose metal and any other metal that is badly affected by rust. Hammer the edges of the hole in to create a slight depression for the filler material.

27 Wire-brush the affected area to remove the powdery rust from the surface of the metal. If the back of the rusted area is accessible, treat it with rust inhibiting paint.

28 Before filling is done, block the hole in some way. This can be done with sheet metal riveted or screwed into place, or by stuffing the hole with wire mesh.

29 Once the hole is blocked off, the affected area can be filled and painted. See the following subsection on filling and painting.

Filling and painting

30 Many types of body fillers are available, but generally speaking, body repair kits which contain filler paste and a tube of resin hardener are best for this type of repair work. A wide, flexible plastic or nylon applicator will be necessary for imparting a smooth and contoured finish to the surface of the filler material. Mix up a small amount of filler on a clean piece of wood or cardboard (use the hardener sparingly). Follow the manufacturer's instructions on the package, otherwise the filler will set incorrectly.

31 Using the applicator, apply the filler paste to the prepared area. Draw the applicator across the surface of the filler to achieve the desired contour and to level the filler surface. As soon as a contour that approximates the original one is achieved, stop working the paste. If you continue, the paste will begin to stick to the applicator. Continue to add thin layers of paste at 20-minute intervals until the level of the filler is just above the surrounding metal.

32 Once the filler has hardened, the excess can be removed with a body file. From then on, progressively finer grades of sandpaper should be used, starting with a 180-grit paper and finishing with 600-grit wet-or-dry paper. Always wrap the sandpaper around a flat rubber or wooden block, otherwise the surface of the filler will not be completely flat. During the sanding of the filler surface, the wet-or-dry paper should be periodically rinsed in water. This will ensure that a very smooth finish is produced in the final stage.

33 At this point, the repair area should be surrounded by a ring of bare metal, which in turn should be encircled by the finely feathered edge of good paint. Rinse the repair area with clean water until all of the dust produced by the sanding operation is gone.

34 Spray the entire area with a light coat of primer. This will reveal any imperfections in the surface of the filler. Repair the imperfections with fresh filler paste or glaze filler and once more smooth the surface with sandpaper. Repeat this spray-and-repair procedure until you are satisfied that the surface of the filler and the feathered edge of the paint are perfect. Rinse the area with clean water and allow it to dry completely.

35 The repair area is now ready for painting. Spray painting must be carried out in a warm, dry, windless and dust free atmosphere. These conditions can be created if you have access to a large indoor work area, but if you are forced to work in the open, you will have to pick the day very carefully. If you are working indoors, dousing the floor in the work area with water will help settle the dust that would otherwise be in the air. If the repair area is confined to one body panel, mask off the surrounding panels. This will help minimize the effects of a slight mismatch in paint color. Trim pieces such as chrome strips, door handles, etc., will also need to be masked off or removed. Use masking tape and several thickness of newspaper for the masking operations.

36 Before spraying, shake the paint can thoroughly, then spray a test area until the spray painting technique is mastered. Cover the repair area with a thick coat of primer. The thickness should be built up using several thin layers of primer rather than one thick one. Using 600-grit wet-or-dry sandpaper, rub down the surface of the primer until it is very smooth. While doing this, the work area should be thoroughly rinsed with water and the wet-or-dry sandpaper periodically rinsed as well. Allow the primer to dry before spraying additional coats.

37 Spray on the top coat, again building up the thickness by using several thin layers of paint. Begin spraying in the center of the repair area and then, using a circular motion, work out until the whole repair area and about two inches of the surrounding original paint is covered. Remove all masking material 10 to 15 minutes after spraying on the final coat of paint. Allow the new paint at least two weeks to harden, then use a very fine rubbing compound to blend the edges of the new paint into the existing paint. Finally, apply a coat of wax.

6 Body repair - major damage

1 Major damage must be repaired by an auto body shop specifically equipped to perform unibody repairs. These shops have the specialized equipment required to do the job properly.

2 If the damage is extensive, the body must be checked for proper alignment or the vehicle's handling characteristics may be adversely affected and other components may wear at an accelerated rate.

3 Due to the fact that all of the major body components (hood, fenders, etc.) are separate and replaceable units, any seriously damaged components should be replaced rather than repaired. Sometimes the components can be found in a wrecking yard that specializes in used vehicle components, often at considerable savings over the cost of new parts.

7 Hinges and locks - maintenance

Once every 3000 miles, or every three months, the hinges and latch assemblies on the doors, hood and trunk should be given a few drops of light oil or lock lubricant. The door latch strikers should also be lubricated with a thin coat of grease to reduce wear and ensure free movement. Lubricate the door and trunk locks with spray-on graphite lubricant.

These photos illustrate a method of repairing simple dents. They are intended to supplement *Body repair - minor damage* in this Chapter and should not be used as the sole instructions for body repair on these vehicles.

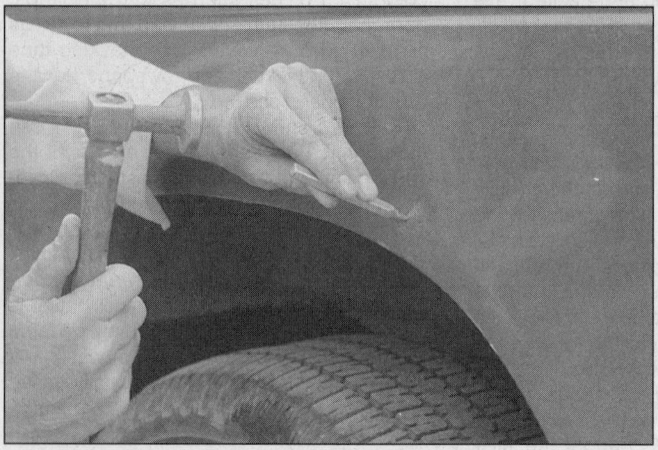

1 If you can't access the backside of the body panel to hammer out the dent, pull it out with a slide-hammer-type dent puller. In the deepest portion of the dent or along the crease line, drill or punch hole(s) at least one inch apart . . .

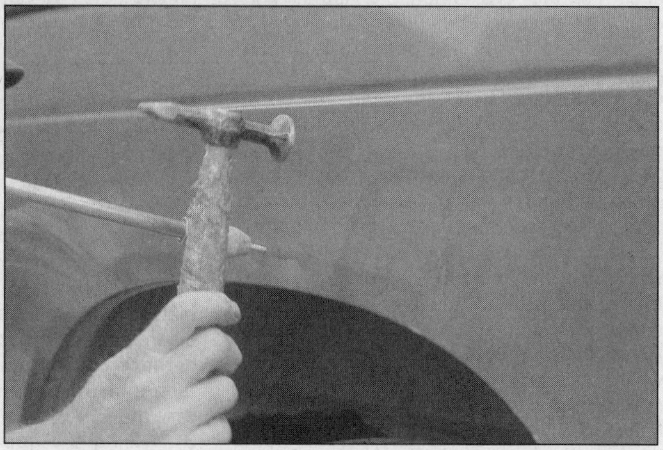

2 . . . then screw the slide-hammer into the hole and operate it. Tap with a hammer near the edge of the dent to help 'pop' the metal back to its original shape. When you're finished, the dent area should be close to its original contour and about 1/8-inch below the surface of the surrounding metal

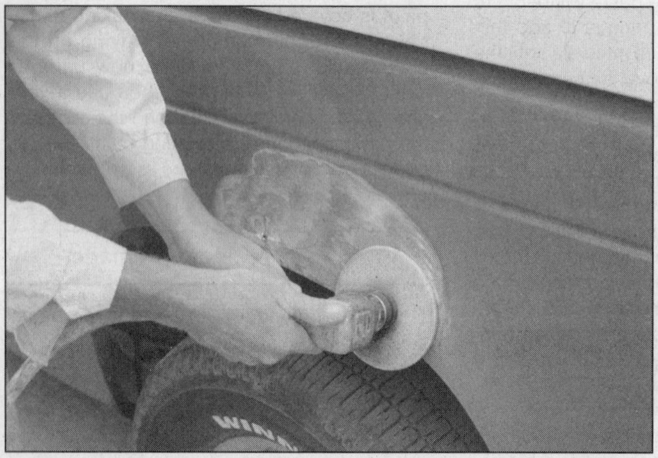

3 Using coarse-grit sandpaper, remove the paint down to the bare metal. Hand sanding works fine, but the disc sander shown here makes the job faster. Use finer (about 320-grit) sandpaper to feather-edge the paint at least one inch around the dent area

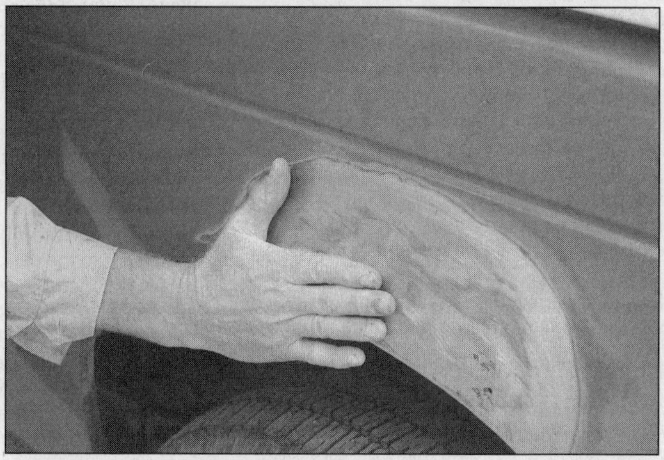

4 When the paint is removed, touch will probably be more helpful than sight for telling if the metal is straight. Hammer down the high spots or raise the low spots as necessary. Clean the repair area with wax/silicone remover

5 Following label instructions, mix up a batch of plastic filler and hardener. The ratio of filler to hardener is critical, and, if you mix it incorrectly, it will either not cure properly or cure too quickly (you won't have time to file and sand it into shape)

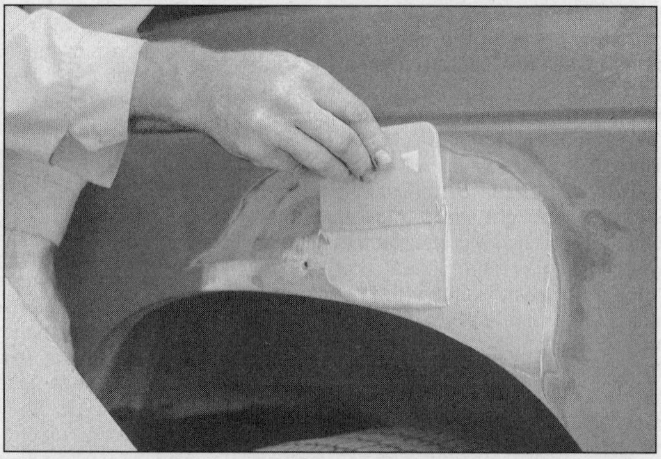

6 Working quickly so the filler doesn't harden, use a plastic applicator to press the body filler firmly into the metal, assuring it bonds completely. Work the filler until it matches the original contour and is slightly above the surrounding metal

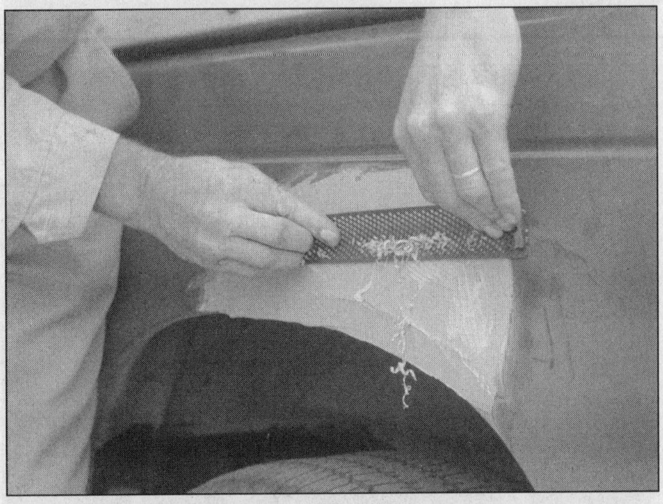

7 Let the filler harden until you can just dent it with your fingernail. Use a body file or Surform tool (shown here) to rough-shape the filler

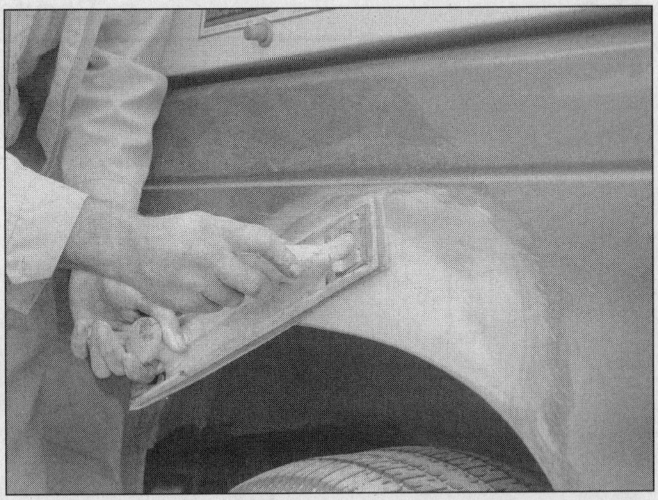

8 Use coarse-grit sandpaper and a sanding board or block to work the filler down until it's smooth and even. Work down to finer grits of sandpaper - always using a board or block - ending up with 360 or 400 grit

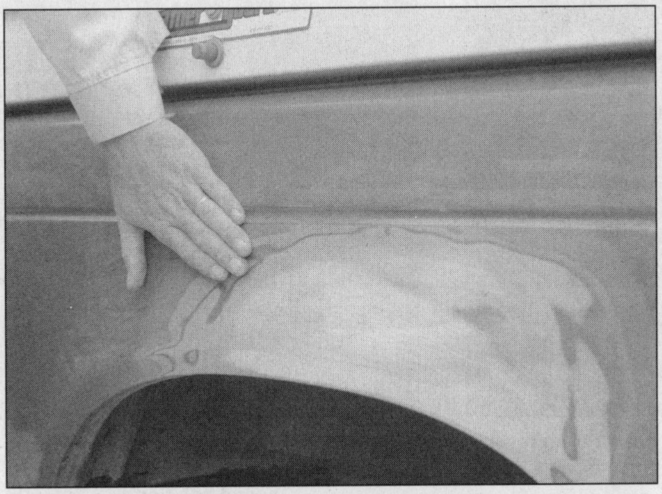

9 You shouldn't be able to feel any ridge at the transition from the filler to the bare metal or from the bare metal to the old paint. As soon as the repair is flat and uniform, remove the dust and mask off the adjacent panels or trim pieces

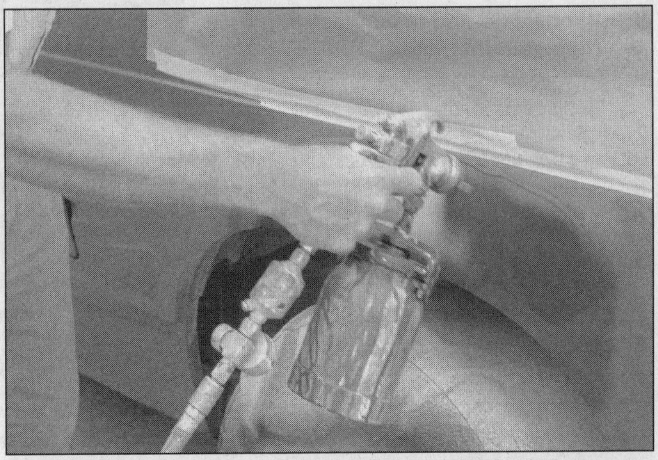

10 Apply several layers of primer to the area. Don't spray the primer on too heavy, so it sags or runs, and make sure each coat is dry before you spray on the next one. A professional-type spray gun is being used here, but aerosol spray primer is available inexpensively from auto parts stores

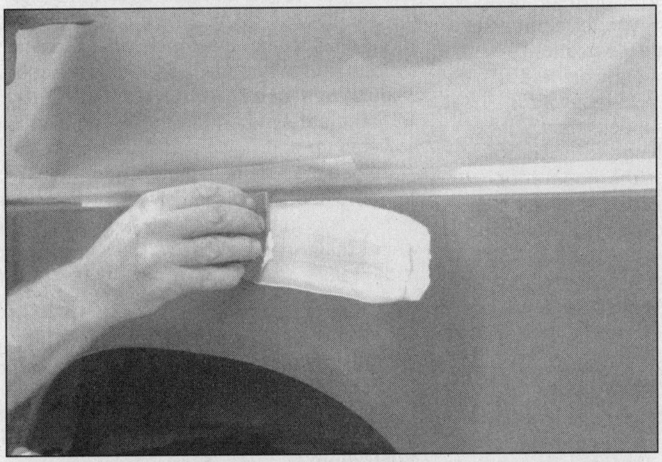

11 The primer will help reveal imperfections or scratches. Fill these with glazing compound. Follow the label instructions and sand it with 360 or 400-grit sandpaper until it's smooth. Repeat the glazing, sanding and respraying until the primer reveals a perfectly smooth surface

12 Finish sand the primer with very fine sandpaper (400 or 600-grit) to remove the primer overspray. Clean the area with water and allow it to dry. Use a tack rag to remove any dust, then apply the finish coat. Don't attempt to rub out or wax the repair area until the paint has dried completely (at least two weeks)

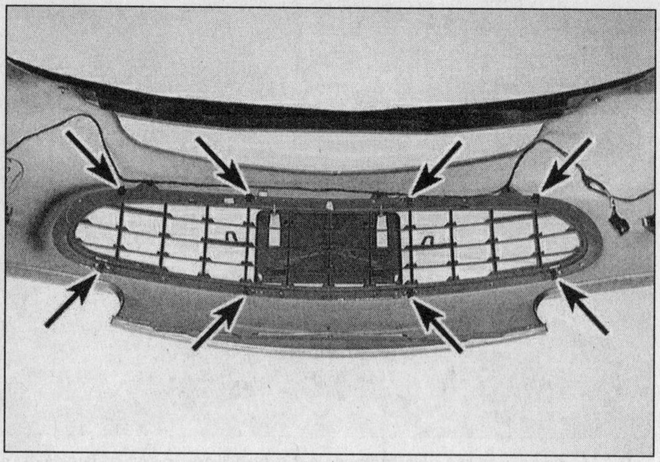

9.3 Release the tabs (arrows) from behind the front bumper fascia to release the grille

10.2 Use a marking pen to outline the hinge plate and bolt heads

8 Windshield and fixed glass - replacement

Replacement of the windshield and fixed glass requires the use of special fast-setting adhesive/caulk materials and some specialized tools and techniques. These operations should be left to a dealer service department or a shop specializing in glass work.

9 Radiator grille - removal and installation

Refer to illustration 9.3

1 The size and shape of the grille varies with the model (Intrepid models do not have a grille), but the removal procedure is basically the same for all models that have a grille.

2 Refer to Section 12 and remove the front bumper fascia. The grille will come with it.

3 From behind the fascia, remove the plastic clips and detach the grille **(see illustration)**.

4 To install, place the grille in position and seat the tabs into the holes in the fascia.

5 The remainder of the installation is the reverse of removal.

10 Hood and hood support struts - removal, installation and adjustment

Note: *The hood is heavy and somewhat awkward to remove and install - at least two people should perform this procedure.*

Removal and installation

Refer to illustration 10.2

1 Use blankets or pads to cover the cowl area of the body and the fenders. This will protect the body and paint as the hood is lifted off.

10.10 Adjust the hood height by screwing the hood bumpers in or out

2 Scribe alignment marks around the bolt heads to insure proper alignment during installation (a permanent-type felt-tip marker also will work for this) **(see illustration)**.

3 Disconnect any cables or wire harnesses that will interfere with removal.

4 Have an assistant support the weight of the hood. Remove the hinge-to-hood bolts. **Note:** *The upper end of the hood support struts are attached to the hood hinges and do not need to be disconnected for hood removal.*

5 Lift off the hood.

6 Installation is the reverse of removal.

Adjustment

Refer to illustrations 10.10 and 10.11

7 Fore-and-aft and side-to-side adjustment of the hood is done by moving the hood in relation to the hinge plate after loosening the bolts.

8 Scribe or trace a line around the entire hinge plate so you can judge the amount of movement.

9 Loosen the bolts and move the hood into correct alignment. Move it only a little at a time. Tighten the hinge bolts or nuts and carefully lower the hood to check the alignment.

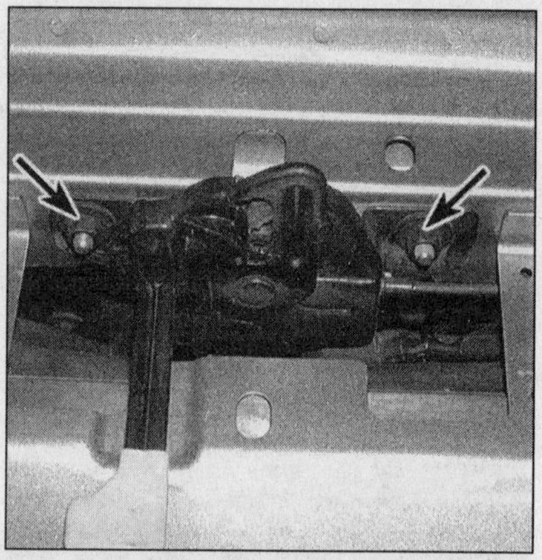

10.11 Loosen the nuts (arrows) and move the latch to adjust the hood in closed position

10 Adjust the hood bumpers on the radiator support so the hood is flush with the fenders when closed **(see illustration)**.

11 The safety latch assembly can also be adjusted up-and-down and side-to-side after loosening the nuts **(see illustration)**.

12 The hood latch assembly, as well as the hinges, should be periodically lubricated with white lithium-base grease to prevent sticking and wear.

Hood support struts

Refer to illustrations 10.14 and 10.15

13 Open the hood and support it.

14 Use a screwdriver to pry out the plastic retainer from the top end of the strut **(see illustration)**.

15 At the bottom end of the strut, slide the plastic clip back and remove the forked end of the strut from the mounting post **(see illustration)**.

16 Installation is the reverse of removal.

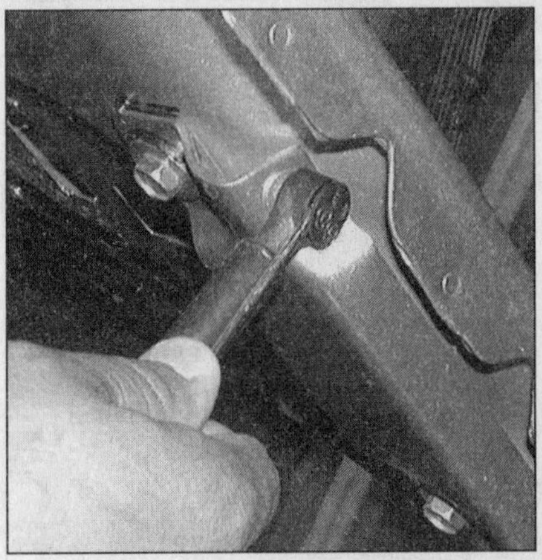

10.14 Use a screwdriver to push out the plastic retainer from the top end of the strut

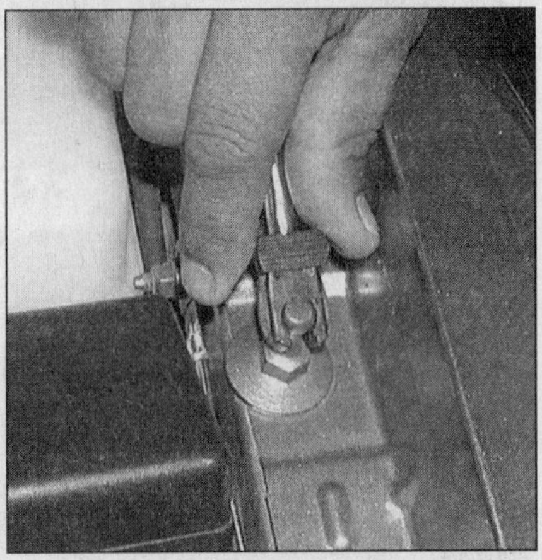

10.15 Detach the strut lower end by pushing back the plastic clip until the forked end of the strut can be removed from the mounting post

11.3 Detach the cable end (A) from the latch and the cable body from the bracket (B)

11 Hood latch and release cable - removal and installation

Refer to illustrations 11.3, 11.6 and 11.7

Latch

1 Open the hood.

2 Remove the nuts and detach the latch assembly **(see illustration 10.11)**.

3 Detach the cable end from the back of the latch assembly, the remove the latch **(see illustration)**.

4 Installation is the reverse of removal.

Cable

5 Use a screwdriver to release the cable end, then detach the cable case from the bracket on the back of the latch **(see illustration 11.3)**.

6 In the passenger compartment, remove the two screws and detach the kick panel for access to the hood release handle **(see illustration)**.

7 Remove the hood release handle mounting bolts **(see illustration)**.

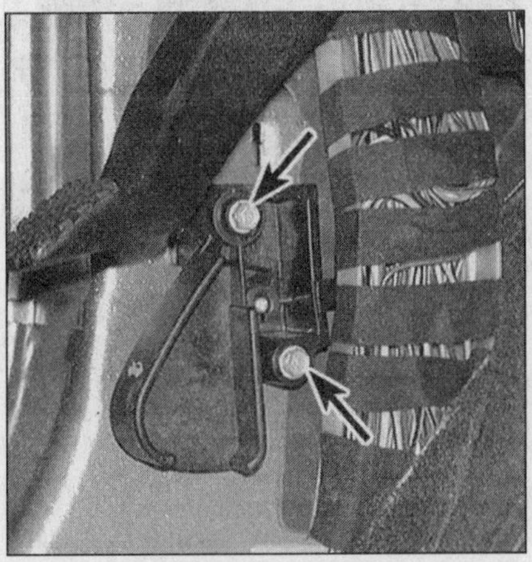

11.7 Hood release handle mounting bolts (arrows)

8 Under the dash, remove the cable grommet from the firewall.

9 Remove the fasteners at the outer edge of the left front fenderwell splash shield and, working behind the splash shield, feel along the hood release cable until you have pulled out the clips securing the cable.

10 Attach a wire or string to the hood end of the old cable and pull the cable through into the vehicle's interior.

11 Connect the string or wire to the new cable and pull it through the firewall into the engine compartment.

12 The remainder of installation is the reverse of removal.

12 Bumpers - removal and installation

1 Front and rear bumpers on all models are composed of a plastic fascia, or exterior cover, and a foam-covered structural beam.

Front bumper

Refer to illustrations 12.3, 12.4, 12.5, 12.6, 12.8, 12.9a and 12.9b

2 Apply the parking brake, raise the vehicle and support it securely on jackstands.

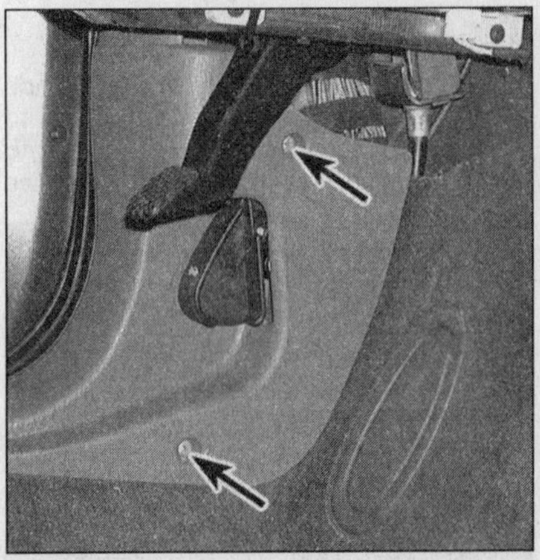

11.6 Remove the two screws (arrows) and angle the kick panel out

3 Working under the vehicle, detach the fasteners securing the lower edges of the bumper cover **(see illustration)**. **Note:** *Use a small screwdriver to pop the center button up on the plastic fasteners, but do not try to remove the center buttons. They stay in the ferrules.*

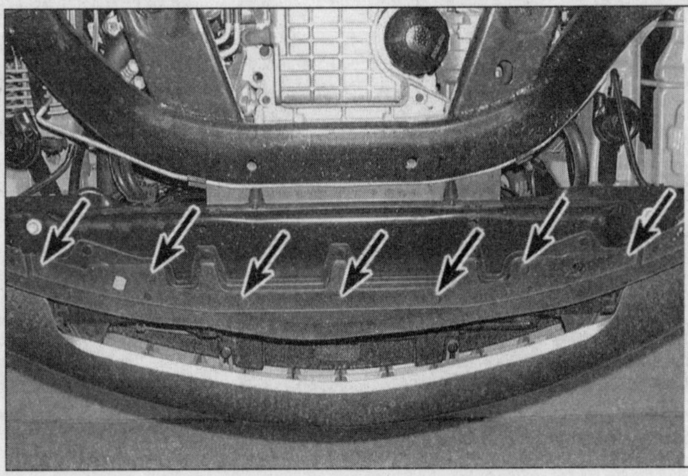

12.3 Remove the fasteners (arrows) securing the lower edge of the front bumper cover

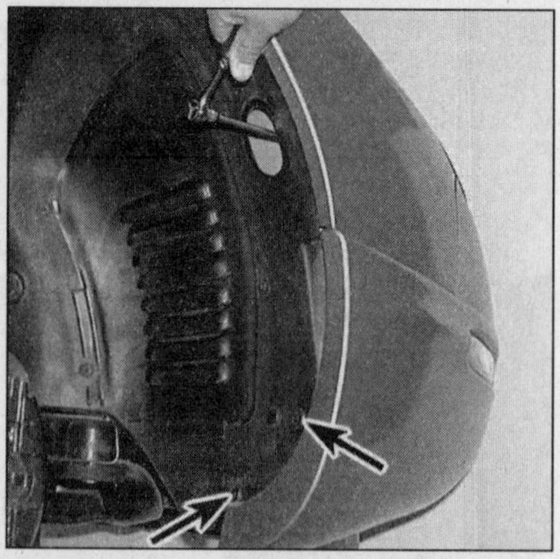

12.4 With the rubber access plug removed, the nut securing the bumper cover to the fender can be removed with a socket and long extension - arrows indicate two plastic rivets that must be cut off from behind

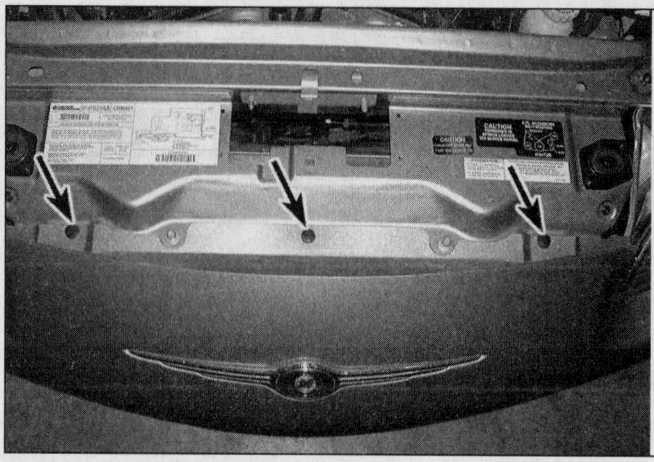

12.5 At the front of the engine compartment, remove the fasteners (arrows) securing the bumper cover to the radiator support panel

4 Remove the large rubber plug in each front fenderwell splash shield for access to the fasteners securing the bumper cover to the front fenders **(see illustration)**. **Note:** *The plastic rivets in the fenderwell must be cut off with side-cutter pliers. The rivets can be replaced with small bolts, washers and nuts on reassembly.*

5 Working at the top, detach the plastic pushpin fasteners securing the bumper cover to the hood latch support panel **(see illustration)**. Remove the cover.

6 On models with turn signal or fog lamps mounted in the fascia, disconnect the electrical connectors at the lamps **(see illustration)**.

7 Installation is the reverse of removal. Make sure the tabs on the bumper cover fit into the corresponding clips on the body before attaching the bolts and screws. An assistant is helpful.

8 If the foam inserts need to be replaced, remove the two screws in the grille area **(see illustration)**. **Note:** *The foam inserts stay with the fascia when it is removed from the vehicle.*

9 The bumper reinforcement beam can now be unbolted from the chassis **(see illustrations)**.

10 Installation is the reverse of the removal procedure.

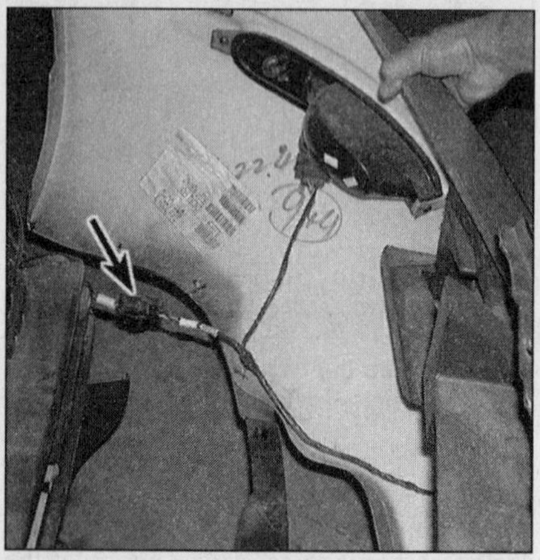

12.6 Pull the fascia forward until the electrical connectors (arrow) can be disconnected

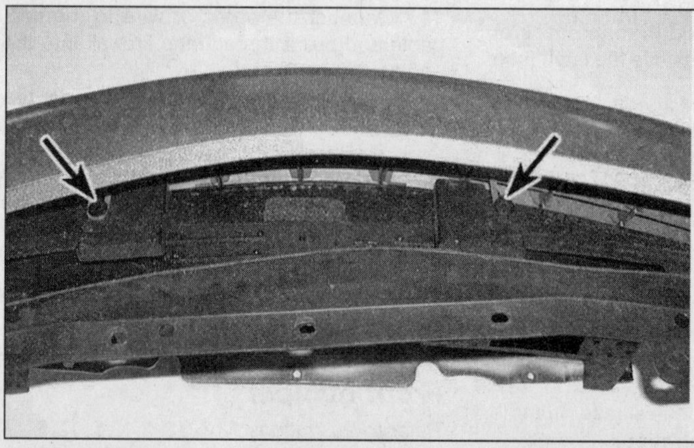

12.8 Remove the screws (arrows) to separate the foam inserts from the fascia

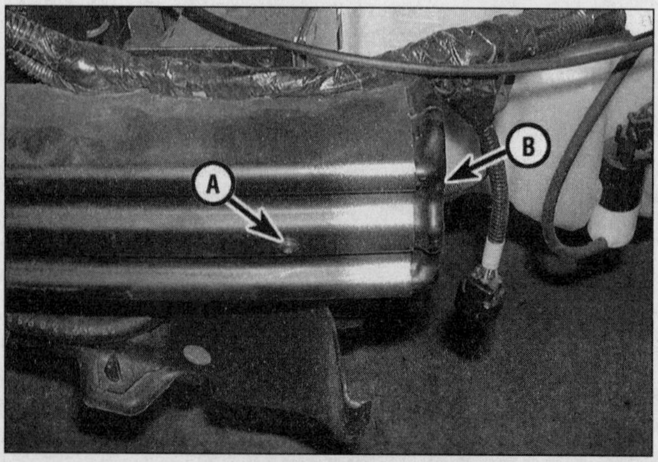

12.9a Remove the screw (A) at each end of the bumper beam, then remove the rubber end cap (B) . . .

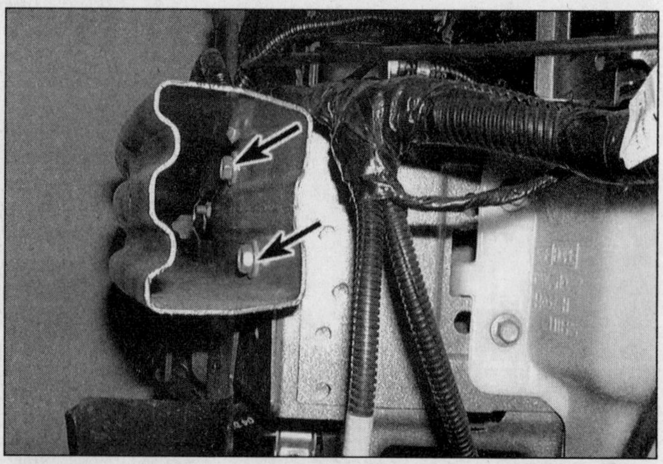

12.9b . . . to access the front bumper reinforcement beam mounting bolts (arrows)

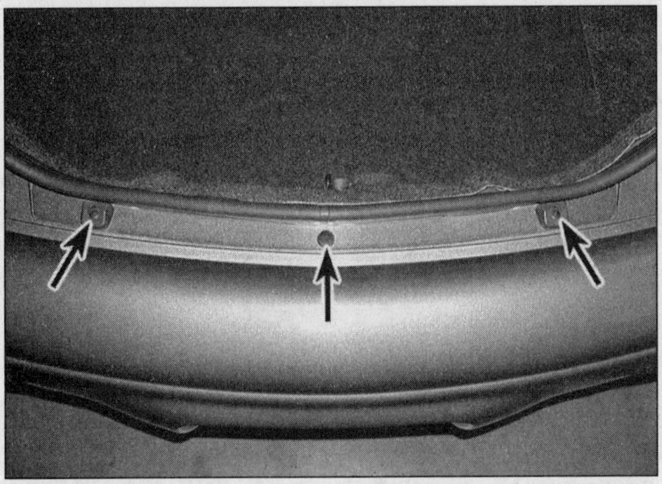

12.11 Remove the three pull-up plastic fasteners (arrows) along the trunk opening

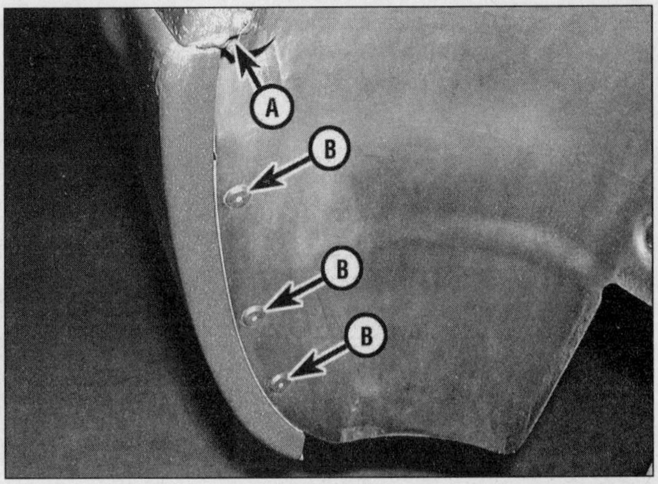

12.12 In each rear fenderwell, remove the one screw (A), then cut off the three rivets (B)

Rear bumper

Refer to illustrations 12.11, 12.12, 12.13 and 12.14

11 Open the trunk and remove the bumper cover pushpin fasteners **(see illustration)**. **Note:** *Use a small screwdriver to pop the center button up on the plastic fasteners, but do not try to remove the center buttons. They stay in the ferrules.*

12 Remove the fasteners securing the bumper cover in each rear wheel opening **(see illustration)**.

13 Pull the bumper cover assembly sharply out and away from the vehicle to disengage the clips at the quarter panels, then disconnect the electrical connectors **(see illustration)**. **Note:** *One some models, the fascia must be flexed to extract it from around the taillight housing, on other models, the taillight housing must be removed* (see Chapter 12).

14 If the rear bumper reinforcement beam is to be removed, remove the bolt and nuts **(see illustration)**.

15 Installation is the reverse of removal.

13 Front fender - removal and installation

Refer to illustrations 13.3, 13.4a, 13.4b, 13.4c and 13.5

1 Loosen the front wheel lug nuts, raise the vehicle, support it securely on jackstands and remove the front wheel.

2 Apply wide masking tape along the front edge of the door to prevent scratching the paint during fender removal. Refer to Section 10, open the hood and support it, then remove the hood support strut from the stud on top of the fender.

3 There are two bolts securing the lower front edge of the fender to the body **(see illustration)**. These are easiest to get at with the bumper fascia removed, but can be accessed from below with the cover in place.

4 Remove the fender-to-cowl mounting bolts **(see illustrations)**. **Note:** *On 2000 and later models, you may have to drill a 1-1/16 inch hole in the plastic splash shield to access the upper fender bolt at the cowl. On other models, remove the splash shield screws and pull it back for access.*

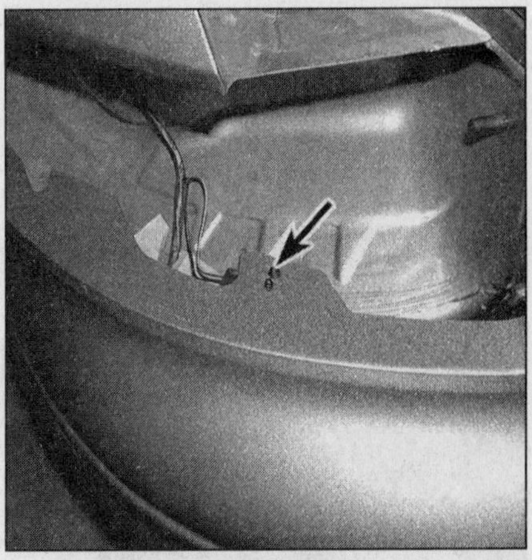

12.13 With the fascia pulled away, push out the plastic pins (arrow) holding the electrical connector to the lip of the fascia

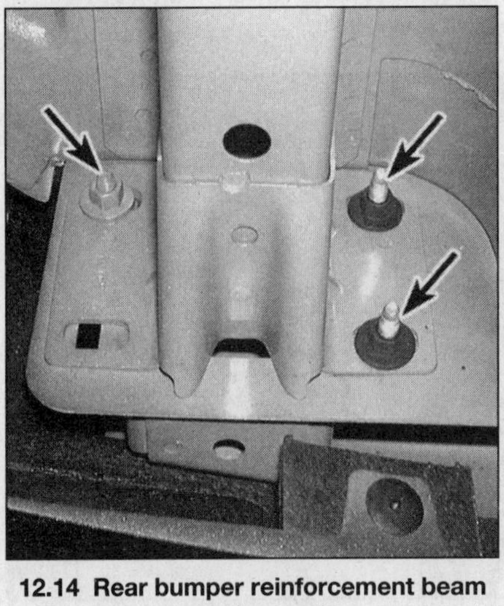

12.14 Rear bumper reinforcement beam nuts (arrows)

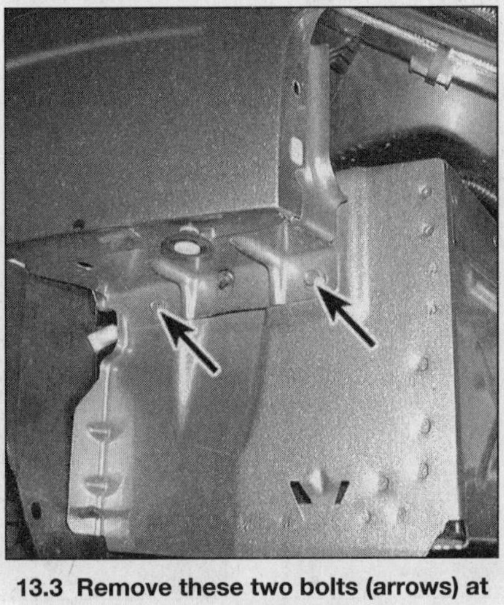

13.3 Remove these two bolts (arrows) at the lower front of the fender (bumper fascia removed for clarity)

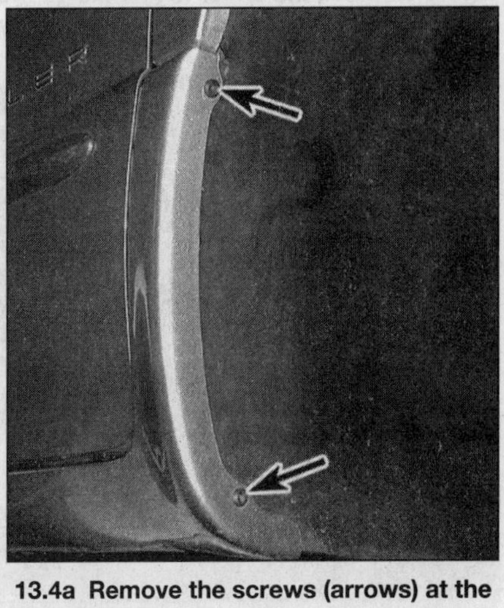

13.4a Remove the screws (arrows) at the front edge of the plastic rocker panel . . .

5 Working in the engine compartment, remove the bolts securing the fender to the body and detach the fender **(see illustration)**. The fender may have to be angled to clear the front bumper cover and headlight.

6 Installation is the reverse of removal.

7 Tighten all nuts, bolts and screws securely.

14 Cowl cover and strut support - removal and installation

Cowl cover

Refer to illustrations 14.2a and 14.2b

1 Open the hood, then refer to Chapter 12 and remove the wiper arms.

2 Remove the Torx screws securing the two halves of the cowl cover to the cowl **(see illustrations)**.

3 Remove the cowl cover.

4 Installation is the reverse of removal.

Strut support

Refer to illustrations 14.7a and 14.7b

5 For access to repair procedures such as windshield wiper motor replacement, power brake booster removal or work on the rack-and-pinion steering gear, the strut support must be removed.

6 Refer to Steps 1 through 3 and remove the cowl cover.

7 Remove the one bolt that secures the wiper motor to the strut support, then the

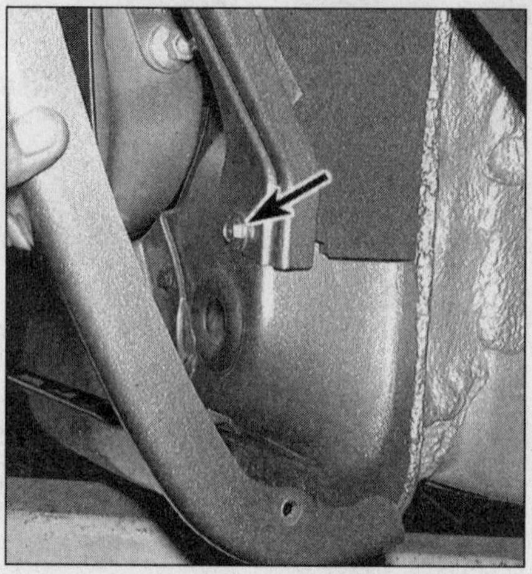

13.4b ... then bend it out enough to access the lower fender-to-cowl bolt (arrow)

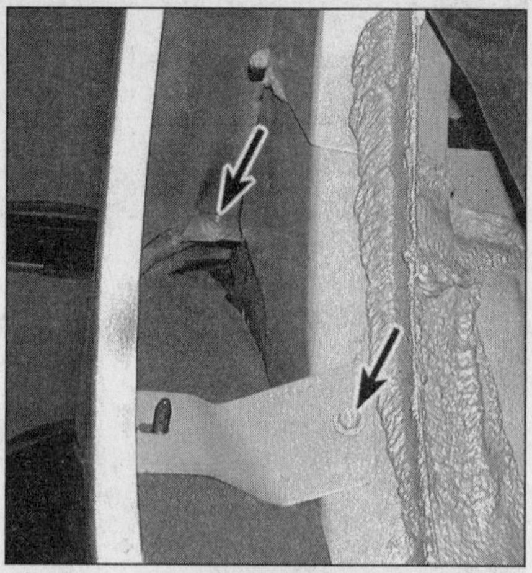

13.4c Remove the plastic fasteners at the rear edge of the fenderwell liner to access the middle and upper fender-to-cowl mounting bolts (arrows)

13.5 Remove the upper fender flange mounting bolts (arrows) and remove the fender

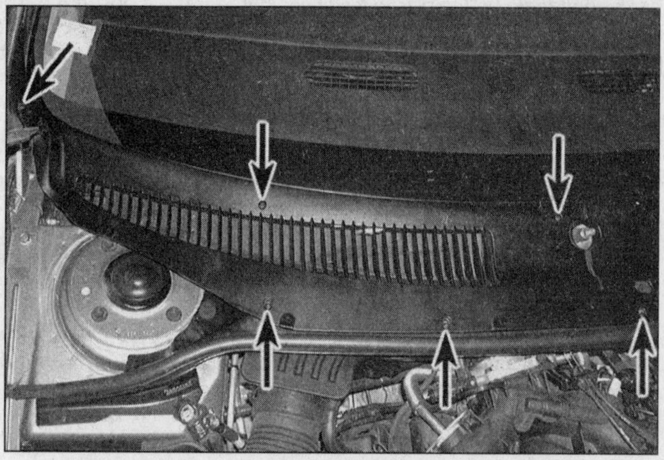

14.2a Remove the Torx screws (arrows) on the right cowl cover half . . .

14.2b . . . and the left cowl cover half

14.7a To remove the strut tower support, remove the wiper motor bolt (A), then the bolts (arrows) at the left strut tower . . .

14.7b . . . and the bolts (arrows) at the right strut tower

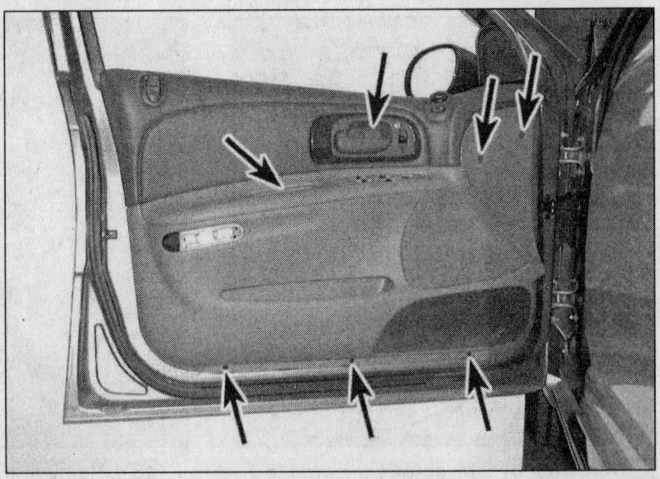

15.3 Remove the screws (arrows) securing the door panel - there are also three screws in the speaker area (speaker grille not yet removed in this photo)

eight bolts at the left and right strut towers and remove the support **(see illustrations)**.

8 Installation is the reverse of the removal procedure.

15 Door trim panels - removal and installation

Refer to illustrations 15.3, 15.5a, 15.5b and 15.6

1 Disconnect the negative battery cable from the remote ground terminal (see Chapter 5).

2 Remove the main speaker grille by prying it out with a plastic or wooden trim tool, then remove the small upper speaker, if equipped (see Chapter 12).

3 Remove the screws retaining the door panel to the door **(see illustration)**. **Note:** *Remove the plastic screw covers in the door pull pocket and the inside door handle pocket to expose the screws there.*

4 Using a trim tool, pry along the rear edge of the door panel to disengage the clips.

5 Grasp the trim panel and pull up sharply to detach it from the door. Disconnect the inner door handle lock rod from the handle **(see illustration)**. Unplug any electrical connectors and remove the door panel **(see illustration)**.

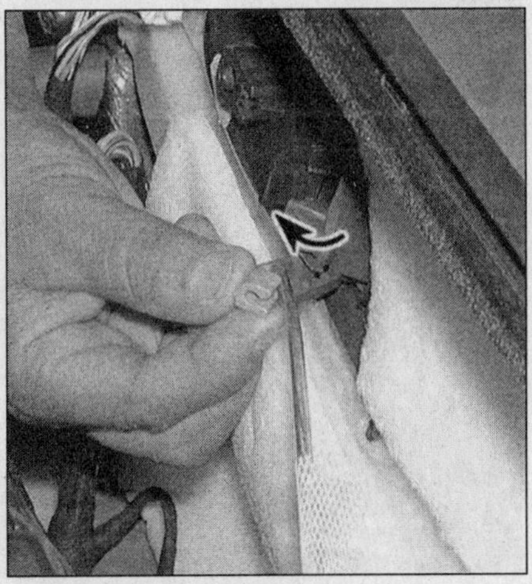

15.5a Rotate the clip in the direction shown to disconnect the door handle rod

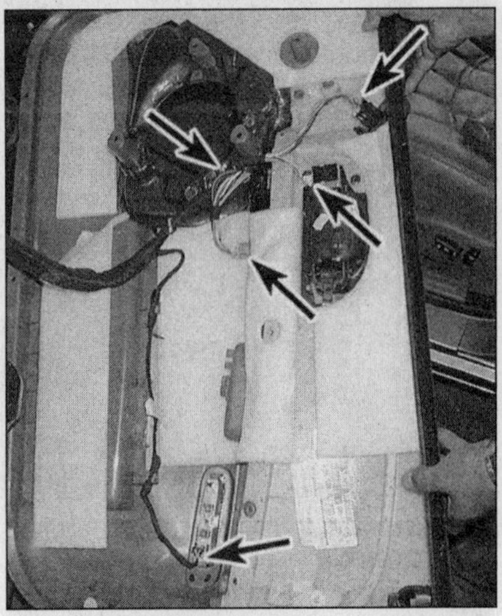

15.5b Disconnect the electrical connectors (arrows) at the door panel

6 If other procedures are to be done inside the door, such as glass or regulator replacement, carefully peel back the plastic watershield on the door for access **(see illustration)**. The watershield is reusable if not torn.

7 To install the panel, connect the wire harness connectors and door handle rod, then place the panel in position in the door. Press the trim panel down into place until the clips are seated.

8 Install the screws and screw covers, where used. Reconnect the negative battery cable.

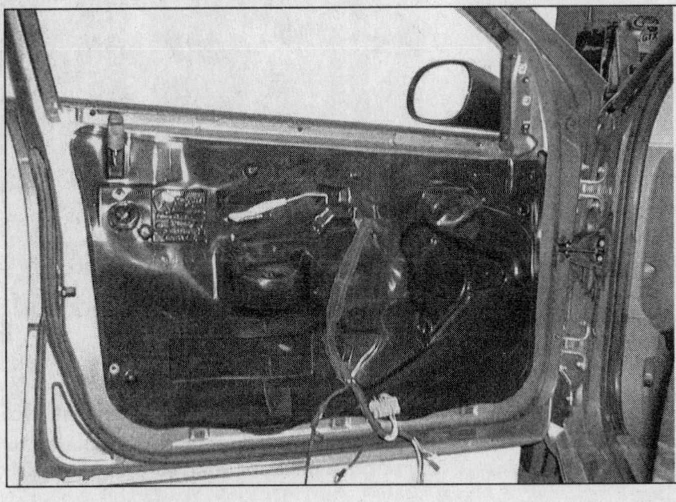

15.6 The plastic watershield can be peeled off the door for access to interior parts

16 Door - removal, installation and adjustment

Refer to illustrations 16.2, 16.4 and 16.6

1 Remove the door trim panel (see Section 15).

2 Remove the screws securing the door

16.2 Remove the screws (arrows) to detach the door stay from the body - pull the rubber boot out (lower arrow) and feed the door wiring harness out

16.4 Remove the hinge nut and bolt (arrows) and lift the door off (upper hinge shown, lower hinge similar)

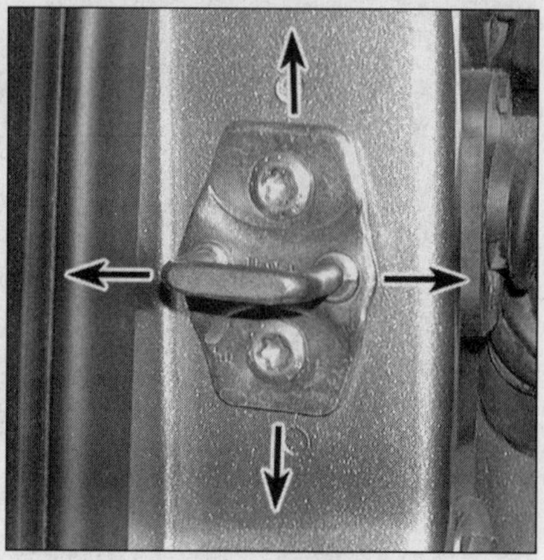

16.6 The striker can be loosened and moved slightly to achieve secure latch engagement

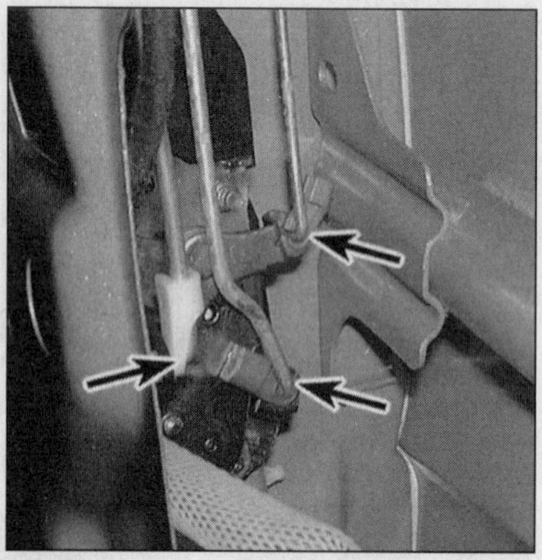

17.2 Working through the door opening, disconnect the link rods (arrows) from the latch

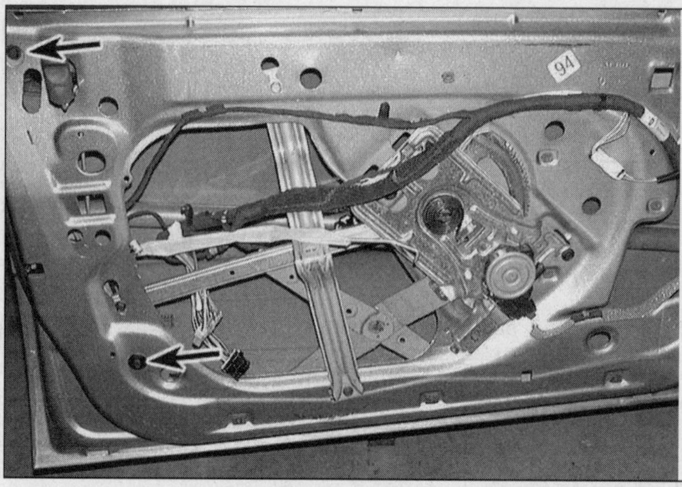

17.3 Remove the rear glass run channel bolts (arrows), allowing the channel to be moved for latch removal clearance

check strap to the door jamb **(see illustration)**. Pull the rubber wiring harness boot away from the door, and feed the wiring harness out from the door through the large hole.

3 Place a jack under the door or have an assistant on hand to support it when the hinge bolts are removed. **Note:** *If a jack is used, place a rag between it and the door to protect the door's painted surfaces.*

4 Scribe around the mounting bolts/nuts with a marking pen, remove the bolts/nuts and carefully lift off the door **(see illustration)**.

5 Installation is the reverse of removal, making sure to align the hinge with the marks made during removal before tightening the bolts.

6 Following installation of the door, check the alignment and adjust it if necessary as follows:

a) Up-and-down and in-and-out adjustments are made by loosening the hinge-to-door bolts/nuts and moving the door as necessary.

b) Forward-and-backward adjustments are made by loosening the hinge-to-body bolts and moving the door as necessary.

c) The door lock striker can also be adjusted both up-and-down and sideways to provide positive engagement with the lock mechanism. This is done by loosening the mounting screws and moving the striker as necessary **(see illustration)**.

17 Door latch, lock cylinder and outside handle - removal and installation

1 Close the window completely and remove the door trim panel (see Section 15).

Latch

Refer to illustrations 17.2, 17.3 and 17.4

2 Disconnect the link rods from the latch **(see illustration)**.

3 Remove the two bolts and move the rear glass run channel out of the way of the latch **(see illustration)**.

4 Remove the three Torx-head mounting screws from the end of the door (it may be necessary to use an impact-type screwdriver to loosen them) and detach the latch from the door **(see illustration)**.

5 Place the latch in position, install the screws and tighten them securely.

6 Connect the link rods to the latch and bolt the glass run channel in place.

17.4 A Torx-head tool may be required to remove the door latch screws (arrows)

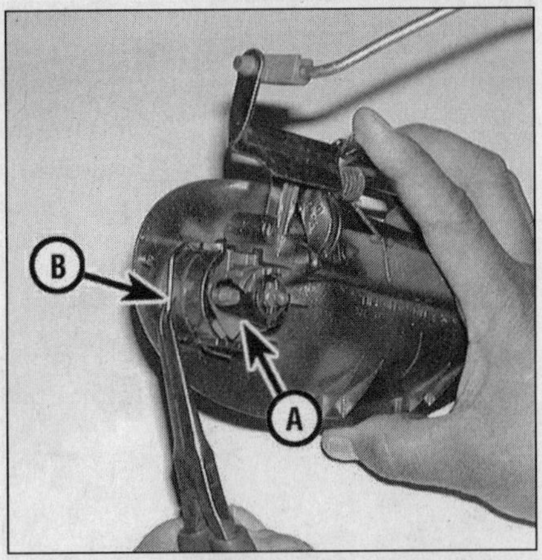

17.7 Lock cylinder removal details - disengage the clip (A) and the rod, then pull the retainer clip (B) and remove the lock cylinder from the door handle

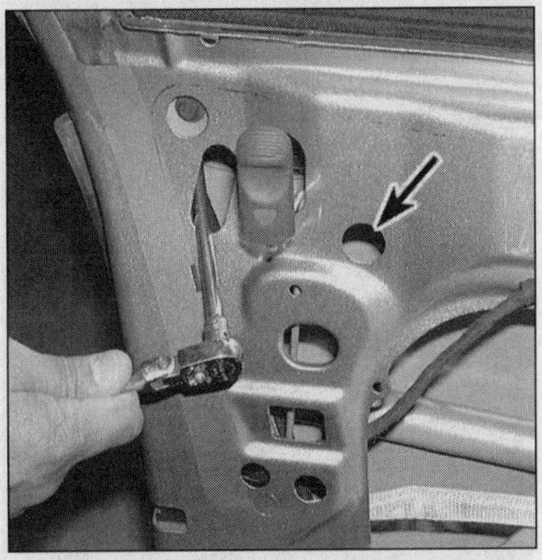

17.9 Through holes in the door, remove the two bolts holding the outside door handle to the door

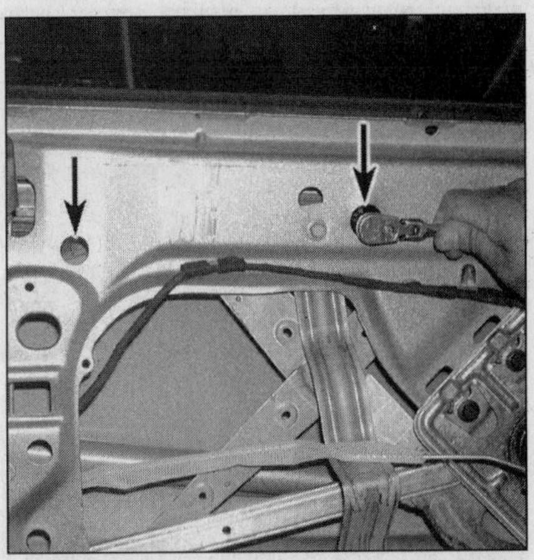

18.2 Loosen the nuts (arrows) and slide the roller channel rearward so the nuts line up with the keyhole slots (front door shown, rear door similar)

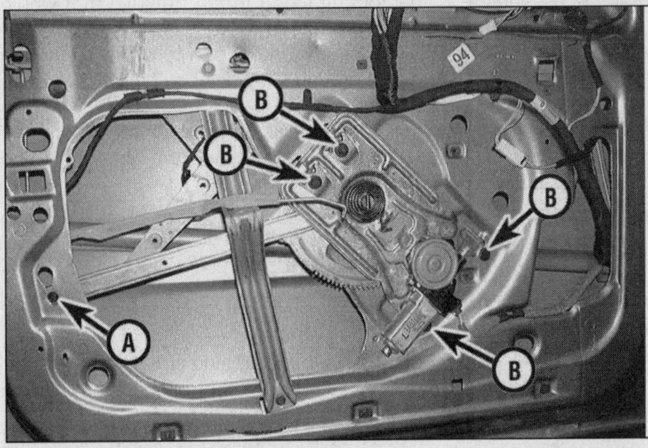

19.4 Loosen the regulator support brace bolts (A), then remove the remaining regulator mounting bolts (B) - front door shown, rear regulator mounting similar

Lock cylinder

Refer to illustration 17.7

7 Disconnect the link, use a screwdriver to push the key lock cylinder retainer off and withdraw the lock cylinder from the door handle assembly **(see illustration)**.

8 Installation is the reverse of removal.

Outside handle

Refer to illustration 17.9

9 Disconnect the links, remove the mounting bolts and detach the handle from the door **(see illustration)**.

10 Place the handle in position, attach the links and install the bolts. Tighten the bolts securely. **Note:** *Make sure to reinstall the rear glass run channel after the latch is in place.*

18 Door window glass - removal and installation

Removal

Refer to illustration 18.2

1 Lower the window glass to six inches below full Up, then remove the door trim panel (see Section 15).

2 Through the two holes in the door, use a socket and extension to loosen the nuts retaining the regulator roller channel to the glass, slide the channel toward the rear so the nuts pass through the keyhole slots, then detach the glass and lift it up and out of the door **(see illustration)**.

Installation

3 Lower the glass into the door, insert the nuts through the keyhole slots in the channel, then slide the channel forward to lock the glass in place. Tighten the nuts.

4 If adjustment is necessary, loosen the adjustment nuts, adjust the glass position, and tighten the nuts.

19 Door window glass regulator - removal and installation

Refer to illustration 19.4

Warning: *Do not remove the motor from the regulator assembly without first clamping the sector gear to the mounting plate or serious injury may result.*

1 Remove the door trim panel (see Section 15).

2 Remove the door window glass (see Section 18).

3 Disconnect the electrical connector for the window regulator.

4 Loosen the bolt retaining the regulator support brace, remove the regulator mounting bolts and remove the regulator assembly through the opening in the door **(see illustration)**.

5 Installation is the reverse of removal.

20 Mirrors - removal and installation

Refer to illustrations 20.1 and 20.5

Interior

1 Use a Phillips head screwdriver to remove the set screw, then slide the mirror up off the button on the windshield **(see illustration)**.

2 Installation is the reverse of removal.

Exterior

3 Remove the two screws and detach the small speaker at the top front of the door (see Chapter 12).

20.1 The interior mirror fits over a button on the glass and is held in position by a screw

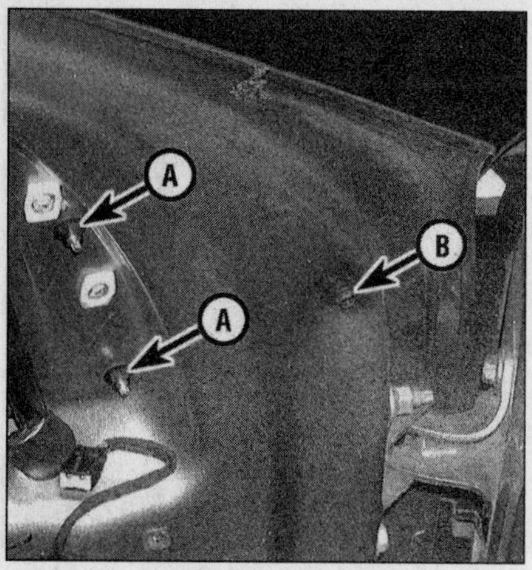

20.5 Exterior mirror mounting nuts (A) and screw (B)

4 Remove the screws and detach the mirror knob and bezel. On power mirrors, unplug the electrical connector.

5 Remove the two nuts and one screw and detach the mirror from the door **(see illustration)**.

6 Installation is the reverse of removal.

21 Trunk lid and trunk lid support struts - removal, installation and adjustment

Note: *The trunk lid is heavy and somewhat awkward to remove and install - at least two people should perform this procedure.*

Trunk lid

Refer to illustrations 21.3 and 21.7

1 Open the trunk lid and cover the edges of the trunk compartment with pads or cloths to protect the painted surfaces when the lid is removed.

2 Disconnect any cables or electrical connectors attached to the trunk lid that would interfere with removal..

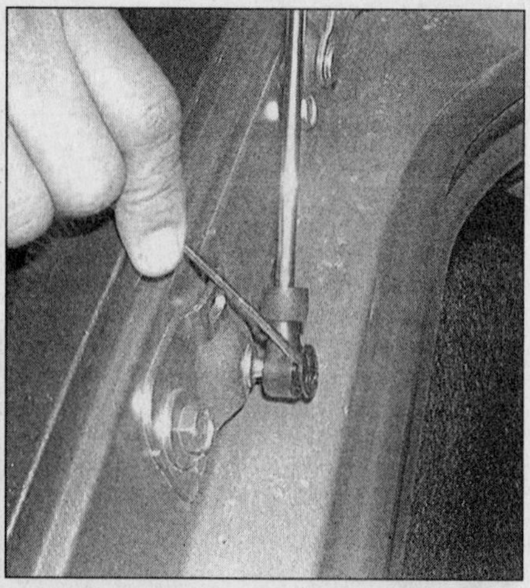

21.10 Pry the trunk lid support strut locking caps out, then pry the ends from their mounting studs (lower end shown, upper end similar)

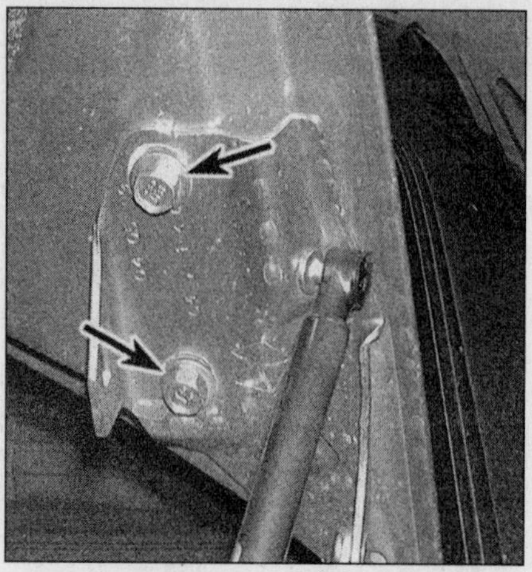

21.3 Draw around the bolt heads with a marking pen so the trunk lid can be installed in the same position

3 Use a marking pen to make alignment marks around the hinge bolt heads **(see illustration)**.

4 While an assistant supports its weight, remove the hinge bolts from both sides and lift the trunk lid off.

5 Installation is the reverse of removal. **Note:** *When reinstalling the trunk lid, align the hinge bolt heads with the marks made during removal.*

6 After installation, close the lid and see if it's in proper alignment with the surrounding panels. Fore-and-aft and side-to-side adjustments of the lid are controlled by the position of the hinge bolts in the holes. To adjust it, loosen the hinge bolts, reposition the lid and retighten the bolts.

7 The height of the lid in relation to the surrounding body panels when closed can be adjusted by loosening the lock striker bolts, repositioning the striker and retightening the bolts **(see illustration)**.

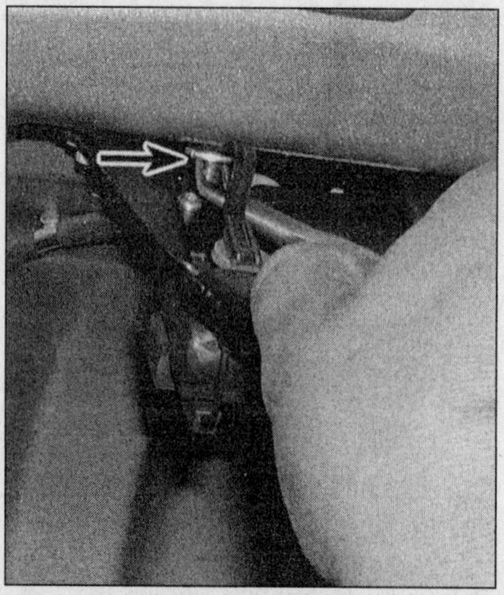

22.3 Use needle-nose pliers to disconnect the lock cylinder rod (arrow) from the latch

21.7 To adjust the striker, mark around the edges with a pen, then loosen the bolts and move the striker slightly and retighten

Trunk lid support struts

Refer to illustration 21.10

8 The trunk lid supports are attached to the upper and lower brackets of the trunk lid hinges. They do not need to be removed to remove the trunk lid.

9 To replace trunk lid supports, open the trunk lid and support it with a prop.

10 Pry out the locking caps at the top and bottom of the support struts and pull the struts from their mounting studs **(see illustration)**. **Note:** *Always replace support struts as a pair, but install the new one on one side of the vehicle before removing the old one from the other side. Always have one strut in place.*

11 Installation is the reverse of the removal procedure.

22 Trunk lid latch and lock cylinder - removal and installation

Trunk lid latch

Refer to illustrations 22.3 and 22.4

1 Open the trunk and use a trim tool to pry up the plastic buttons securing the lower portion of the trunk lid inner panel to expose the latch assembly.

2 Scribe a line around the trunk lid latch assembly for a reference point to aid the installation procedure.

3 Disconnect the electrical connector and pop the link from the rod connecting the latch and the lock cylinder **(see illustration)**.

4 Detach the two retaining bolts and remove the latch **(see illustration)**.

5 Installation is the reverse of removal.

Trunk lock cylinder

Refer to illustration 22.7

6 On Concorde models, remove the trunk lid latch (see above). The lock cylinder mount

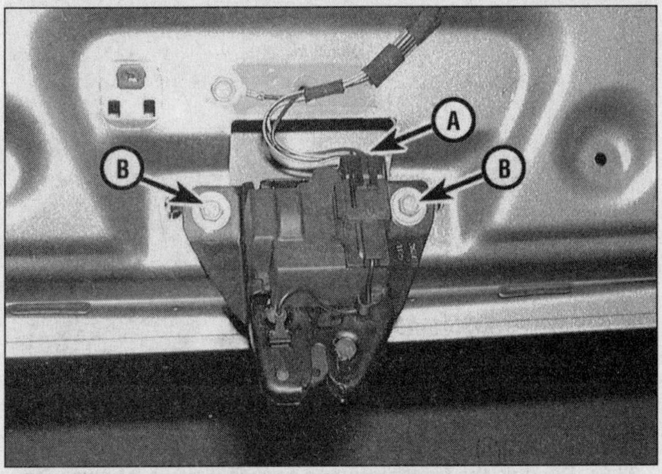

22.4 Disconnect the electrical connector (A), then remove the two latch mounting bolts (B)

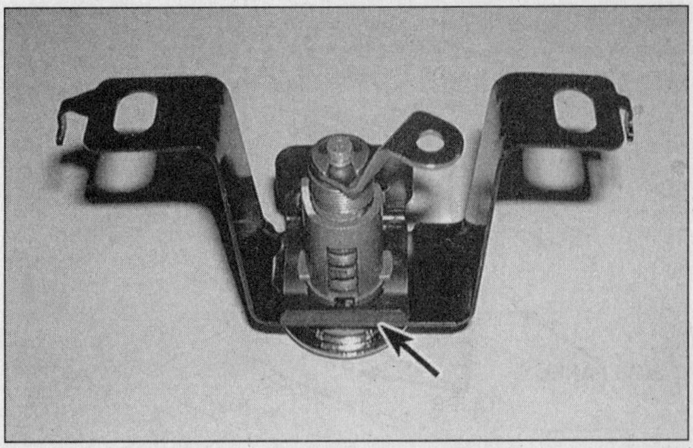

22.7 Remove the latch to access the lock cylinder's retaining clip (arrow) - remove the clip and push the cylinder out to the outside of the trunk lid (shown with lock assembly removed from the vehicle for clarity)

23.3 Pry up the center console shift bezel

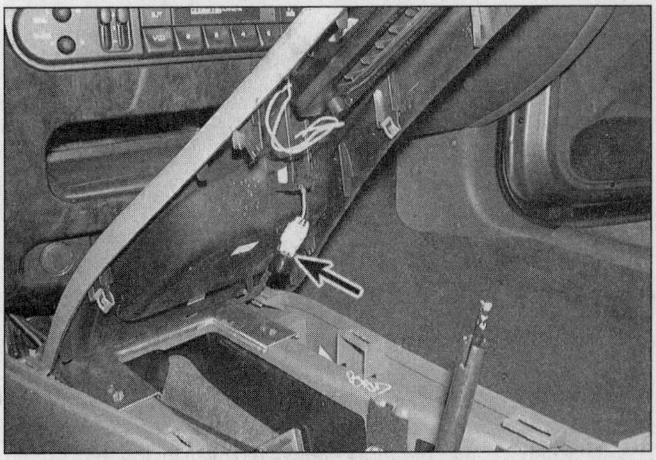

23.4 Disconnect any electrical connectors (arrow) under the shift bezel

is retained by the latch on these models.

7 Remove the lock cylinder's retaining clip and remove the cylinder from the outside of the trunk lid **(see illustration)**.

8 Installation is the reverse of removal.

23 Center console and overhead console - removal and installation

Warning: *The models covered by this manual are equipped with Supplemental Restraint Systems (SRS), more commonly known as airbags. Always disable the airbag system before working in the vicinity of any airbag system components to avoid the possibility of accidental deployment of the airbags, which could cause personal injury* (see Chapter 12).

Console shift bezel

Refer to illustrations 23.3 and 23.4

1 Disconnect the negative battery cable from the remote ground terminal (see Chapter 5).

2 With the parking brake applied, place the shift lever in Neutral, loosen the shift knob screw and remove the knob.

3 Lift out the ashtray for access and carefully pry up the console shift bezel with a plastic trim tool **(see illustration)**. **Note:** *On some LHS and 300M models, the center instrument panel bezel will have to be removed first* (see Section 24).

4 Mark and disconnect the electrical connectors at the front end of the console shift bezel and remove the bezel **(see illustration)**.

Center console

Refer to illustrations 23.6, 23.7, 23.8a and 23.8b

5 Remove the shift bezel (see Steps 1 through 4).

6 On Concorde models, use a trim tool to release the left and right side panels from the console **(see illustration)**.

7 On all other models, refer to Section 24

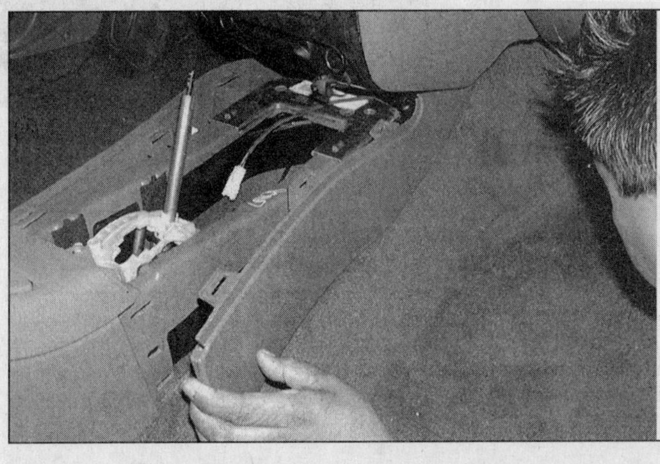

23.6 Pry out the side panels on Concorde models

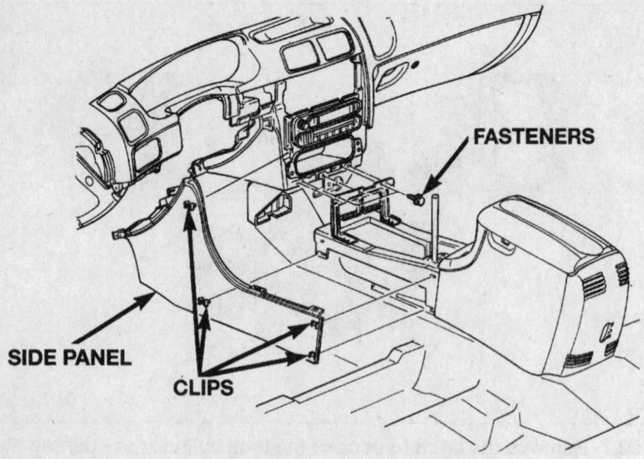

23.7 On Intrepid, LHS and 300M models, remove the screws at the front of each side panel, then pry the panels out to release the clips

23.8a Remove the front mounting screws (arrows, shown with ashtray removed) and . . .

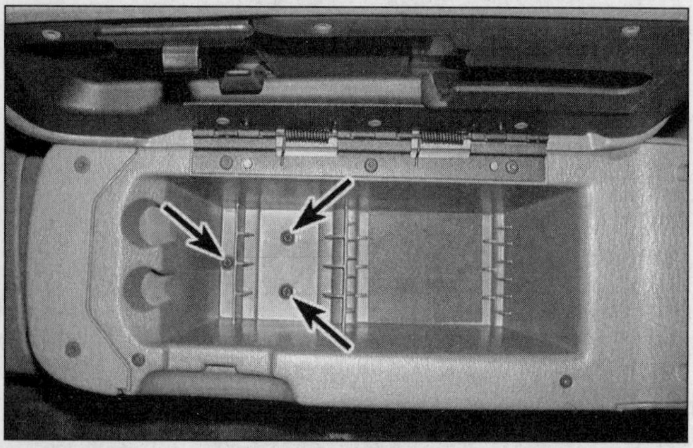

23.8b . . . and the three screws (arrows) inside the armrest/storage area

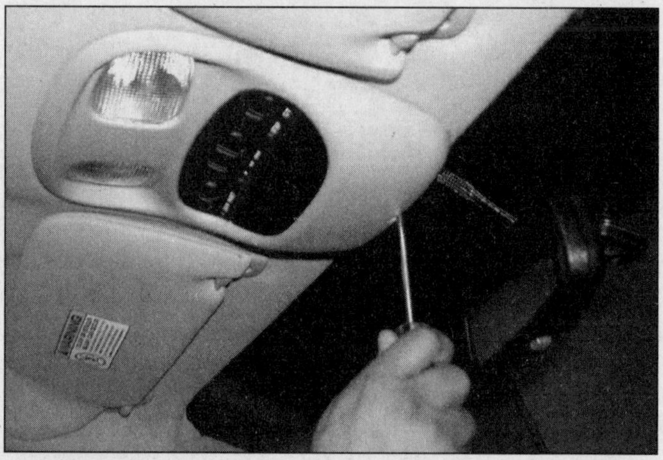

23.12 Remove the screw at the front of the overhead console

and remove the driver's knee bolster to access the screws for removal of the left console side panel, then open the glove box for access to the screws for the right-side console panel **(see illustration).**

8 At the front of the console, remove the mounting bolt(s) at the bottom of the instrument panel, then open the armrest and remove the bolts at the bottom of the storage compartment **(see illustrations)**.

9 Lift up the console enough to disconnect any electrical connectors, then remove the console. **Note:** *You may have to tilt the rear of the console up until it is higher than the instrument panel to work the front mounting bracket out from under the dash.*

10 Installation is the reverse of removal.

Overhead console

Refer to illustrations 23.12 and 23.13

11 Disconnect the negative battery cable from the remote ground terminal (see Chapter 5).

12 Remove the screw at the front of the overhead console **(see illustration)**.

13 Use a trim tool to pry down the rear of the overhead console **(see illustration)**. Disconnect the electrical connectors.

23.13 Pry down the overhead console with a trim tool

14 Installation is the reverse of the removal procedure.

24 Dashboard trim panels - removal and installation

Warning: *The models covered by this manual are equipped with Supplemental Restraint Systems (SRS), more commonly known as airbags. Always disable the airbag system before working in the vicinity of any airbag system components to avoid the possibility of accidental deployment of the airbags, which could cause personal injury* (see Chapter 12).

Dashboard end caps

1 The end caps are held in place by clips.

2 Grasp the cover securely and pull sharply to remove it. If necessary, gently pry with a trim tool.

3 Installation is the reverse of removal.

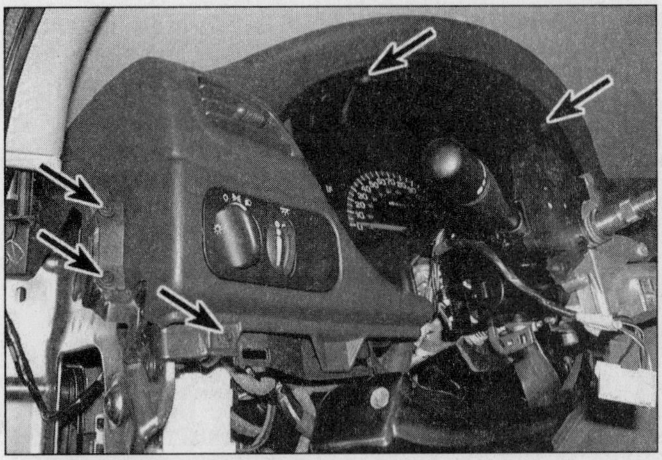

24.4 Remove the screws (arrows) and detach the cluster bezel (shown with steering wheel removed for clarity)

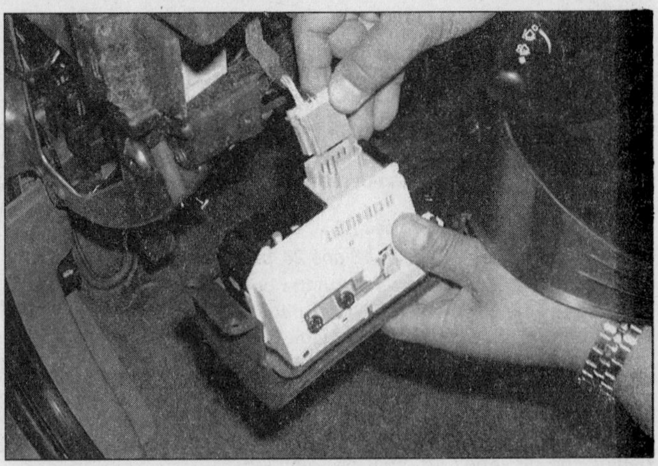

24.9 Disconnect the electrical connector on the back of the headlight switch

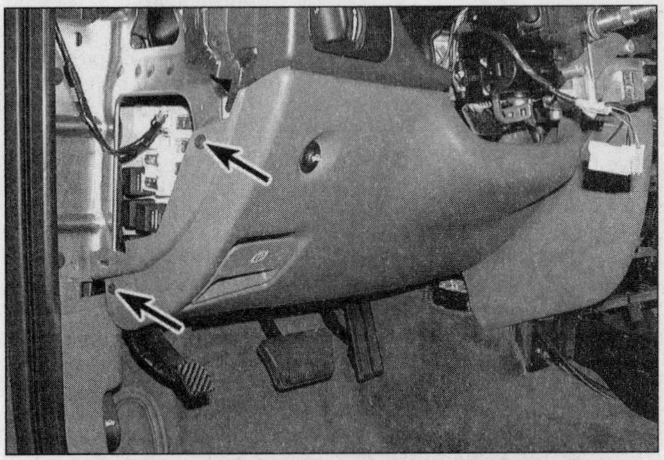

24.11 Remove the driver's knee bolster screws (arrows)

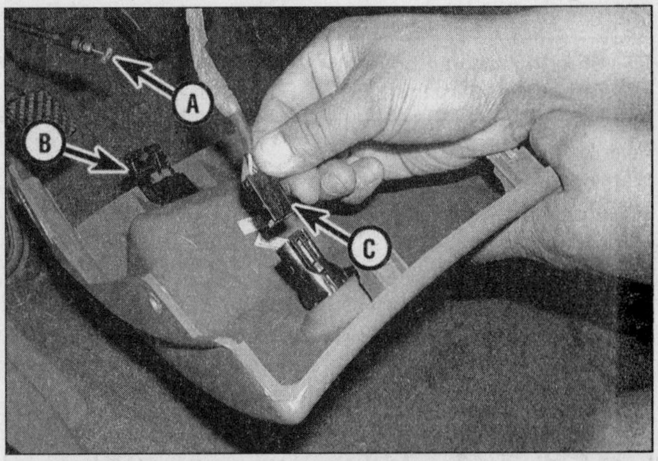

24.12 Remove the brake release cable end (A) from the handle's notch (B), then disconnect the connector (C) at the trunk release

Instrument cluster bezel

Refer to illustrations 24.4 and 24.9

4 Remove the left dashboard end cap and remove the two screws securing the lower-left edge of the cluster bezel **(see illustration)**.

5 Remove the driver's knee bolster (see below) and the one cluster bezel screw behind it **(see illustration 24.4)**.

6 Lower the tilt steering wheel to its lowest position.

7 Remove the steering column covers (see Section 25).

8 Remove the screws and detach the bezel. **Note:** *On some models, there are only clips, no screws, and careful use of a plastic trim tool is required.*

9 Disconnect the electrical connector on the back of the headlight switch **(see illustration)**.

10 Installation is the reverse of removal.

Driver's knee bolster

Refer to illustrations 24.11, 24.12 and 24.13

11 Remove the dashboard end cap on the left side, then remove the screws retaining the bolster to the instrument panel **(see illustration)**.

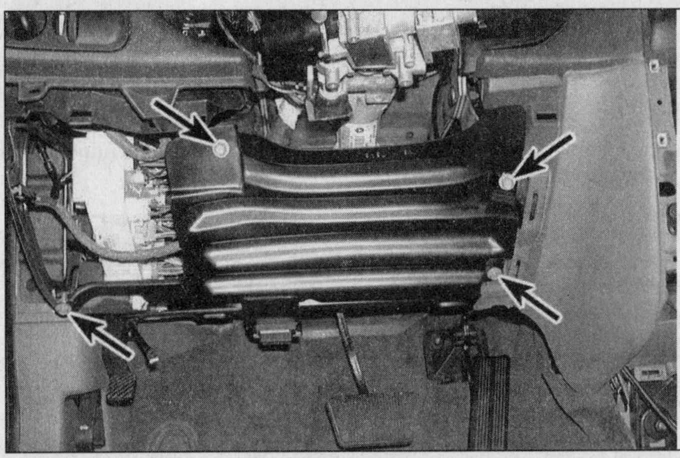

24.13 Remove the bolts (arrows) and the reinforcement panel

12 Pull backward on the bolster to release the clips, then disconnect the cable end from the brake release handle and disconnect the electrical connector at the trunk release **(see illustration)**.

13 If the reinforcement panel needs to be removed to perform a repair procedure, remove the reinforcement panel bolts **(see illustration)**.

14 Installation is the reverse of removal.

Center trim panel

Refer to illustrations 24.15a and 24.15b

15 Using a plastic trim tool, detach the panel and unplug the electrical connectors from the back of the heating/air conditioning

controls **(see illustrations)**. **Note:** *The heating/air conditioning control unit is attached to the back of the panel with screws. On some models, the traction control switch and power outlet are also on this panel and must be disconnected to remove the panel.*

16 Installation is the reverse of removal.

Glove box

Refer to illustrations 24.17, 24.18 and 24.19

17 Remove the four screws along the bottom edge of the glove box **(see illustration)**.

18 Turn the glove box at an angle and remove the glove box from the dashboard **(see illustration)**.

19 For some repair procedures, such as disabling the passenger airbag, the panel behind the glovebox lid must be removed. Remove the screws and the panel **(see illustration)**.

20 Installation is the reverse of removal.

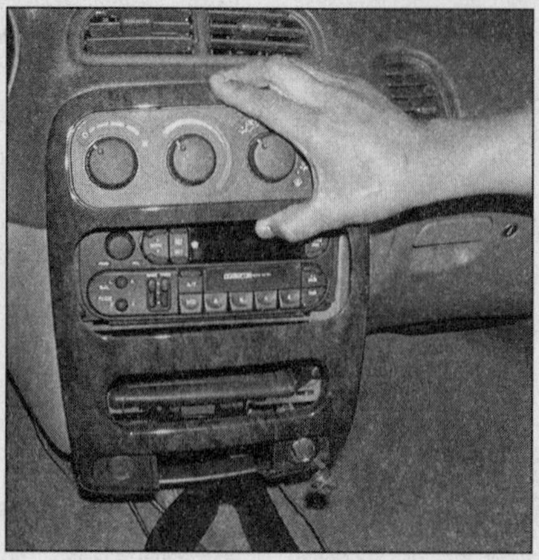

24.15a Pry the center trim panel out and . . .

24.15b . . . disconnect the electrical connectors at the heating/air conditioning controls (and the traction control switch if applicable)

25 Steering column covers - removal and installation

Refer to illustrations 25.2 and 25.3

Warning: *The models covered by this manual are equipped with Supplemental Restraint Systems (SRS), more commonly known as airbags. Always disable the airbag system before working in the vicinity of any airbag system components to avoid the possibility of accidental deployment of the airbags, which could cause personal injury* (see Chapter 12).

1 Disconnect the negative battery cable from the remote ground terminal (see Chapter 5).

2 Remove the upper cover by pressing in on the right seam nearest the instrument cluster until it snaps loose from the lower cover, then release it from the clips on the left side **(see illustration)**.

3 Remove the screw and detach the steering column tilt lever, then remove the

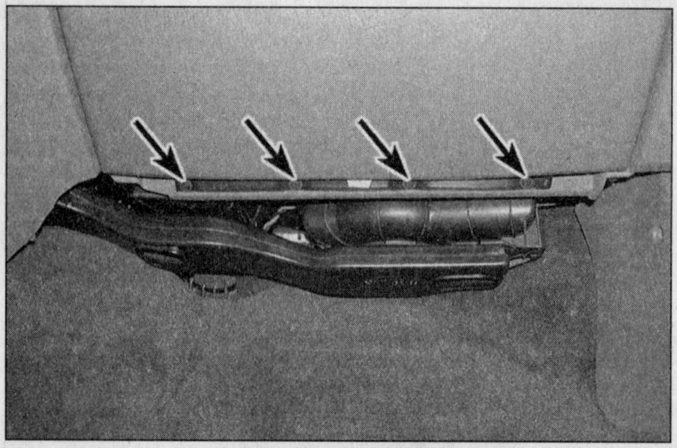

24.17 Remove the screws (arrows) at the bottom of the glovebox hinge

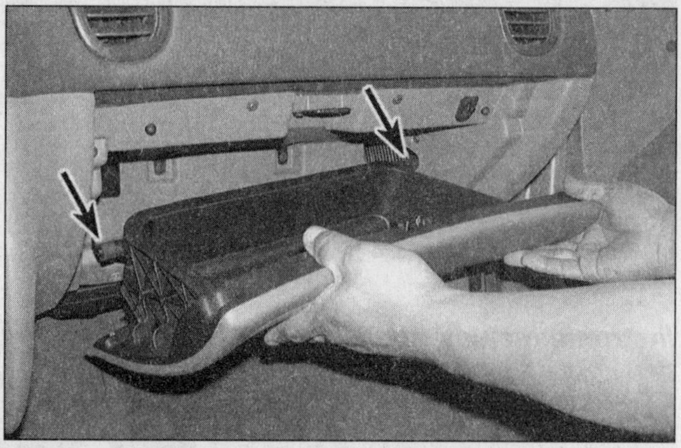

24.18 Angle the glovebox until the projecting pins (arrows) clear the notches and remove the glovebox

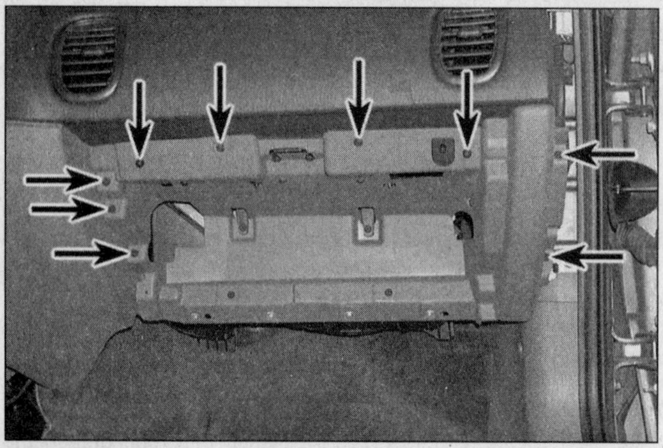

24.19 Remove the screws (arrows) and the panel behind the glovebox lid

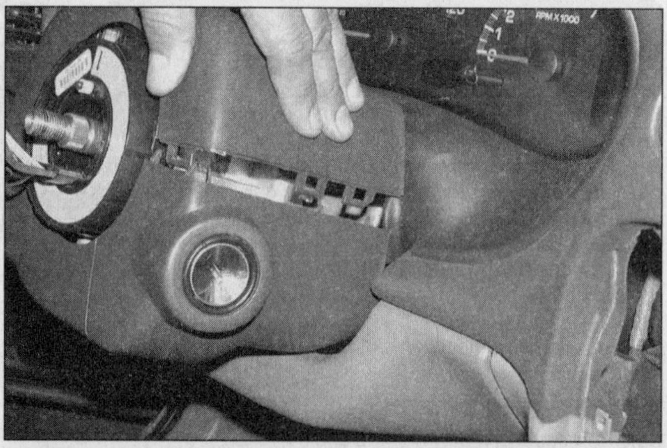

25.2 Push in on the upper cover's right seam to release the clips, then release the left seam

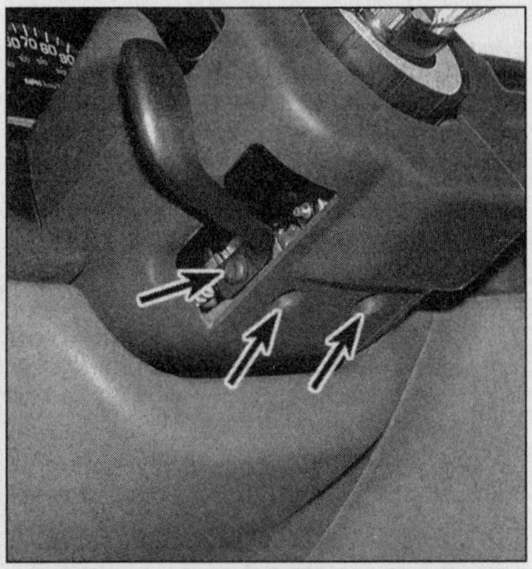

25.3 Remove the tilt lever screw and tilt lever, then the two screws in the lower cover (arrows)

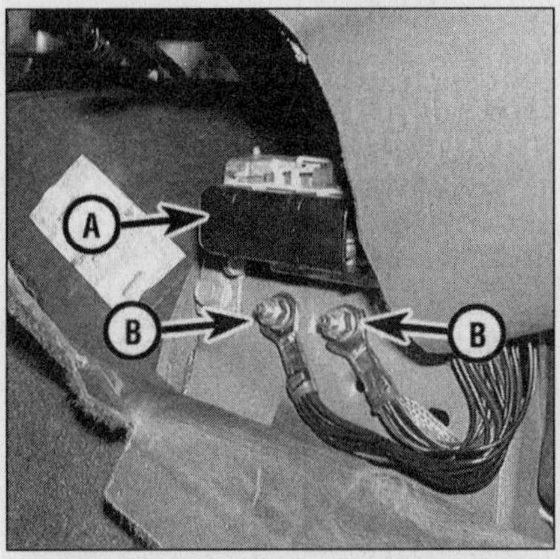

26.9a At the center and below the dash, disconnect the airbag control module connector (A) and the instrument panel grounds (B)

26.9b Disconnect the main heating/air conditioning control connector (arrow)

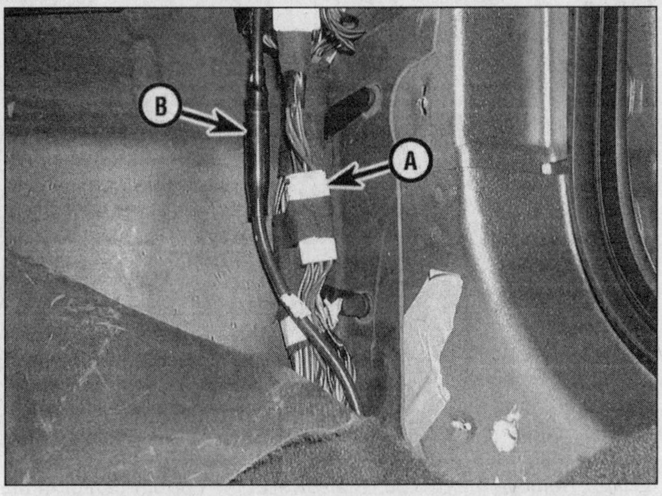

26.9c At the right kick panel area, disconnect the electrical connector (A) and the antenna connector (B)

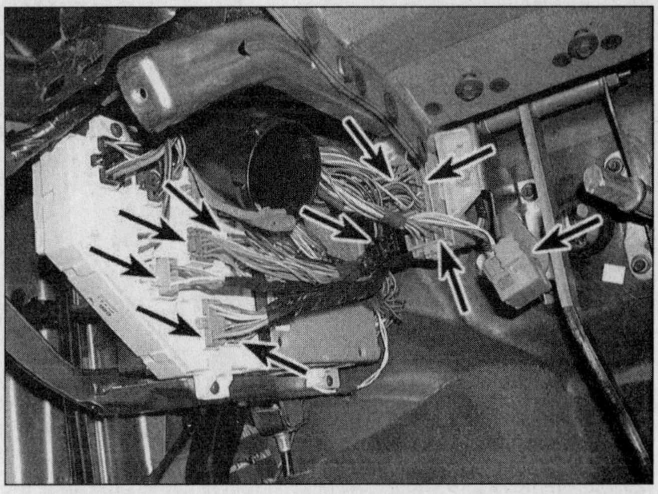

26.9d At the left end of the instrument panel, disconnect all the connectors (arrows)

cover screws and the lower cover **(see illustration)**.

4 Installation is the reverse of removal.

26 Instrument panel - removal and installation

Refer to illustrations 26.9a, 26.9b, 26.9c, 26.9d, 26.10, 26.11, 26.12a, 26.12b, 26.12c, 26.12d and 26.12e

Warning: *The models covered by this manual are equipped with Supplemental Restraint Systems (SRS), more commonly known as airbags. Always disable the airbag system before working in the vicinity of any airbag system components to avoid the possibility of accidental deployment of the airbags, which could cause personal injury* (see Chapter 12).

Note: *This is a difficult procedure for the home mechanic, involving tedious disassembly and the disconnection/reconnection of numerous electrical connectors. If you do attempt this procedure, make sure you take good notes and mark all matching connectors (and their mounting points) to aid reassembly.*

1 Disconnect the negative battery cable from the remote ground terminal (see Chapter 5).

2 Remove the center console (see Section 23).

3 Remove the steering column covers (see Section 25).

4 Remove the dashboard trim panels (see Section 24).

5 Remove the audio components (see Chapter 12).

6 Refer to Chapter 10 and remove the steering column.

8 Remove the kick panels at each side (see Section 11).

9 Mark and disconnect all of the electrical connectors at the center and left and right sides of the instrument panel **(see illustrations)**. **Note:** *Refer to Chapter 12 for disconnecting the connector at the passenger airbag.*

10 Remove the left and right trim strips along the interior of each windshield post **(see illustration)**.

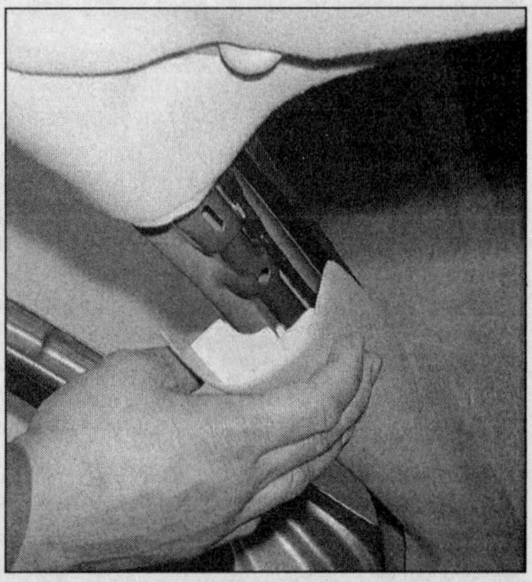

26.10 Use a trim tool to pry up the windshield post trim panels

11 At the top of the instrument panel where

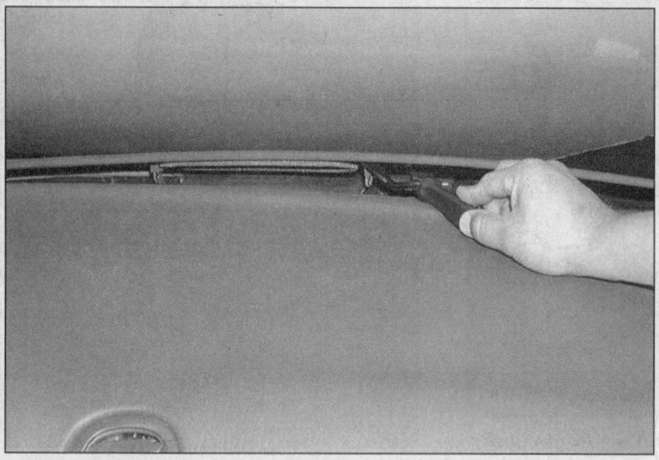

26.11 Pry up the defroster grilles with a trim tool to access the screws on the top edge of the instrument panel

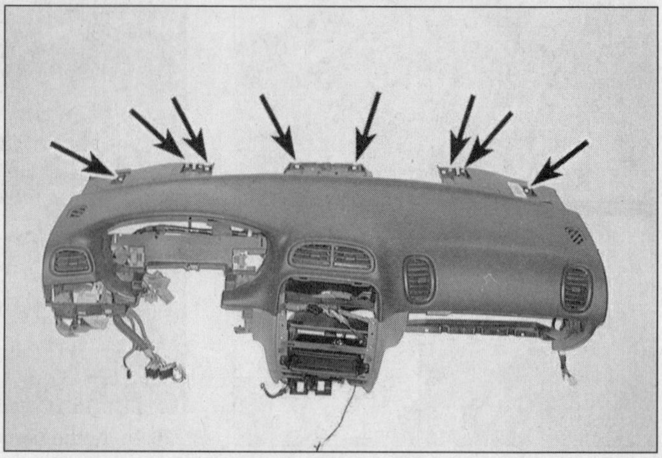

26.12a Upper instrument panel fasteners (arrows)

26.12b Remove this one screw (arrow) that is accessible after the steering column has been removed

26.12c Remove the two bolts (arrows) at the bottom-center of the instrument panel

it meets the windshield, pry up the defroster grilles to access the upper bolts of the instrument panel **(see illustration)**.

12 Remove all of the fasteners securing the instrument panel, and any electrical connectors still attached to the panel **(see illustrations)**. Pull the panel back and out of the vehicle.

13 Installation is the reverse of removal.

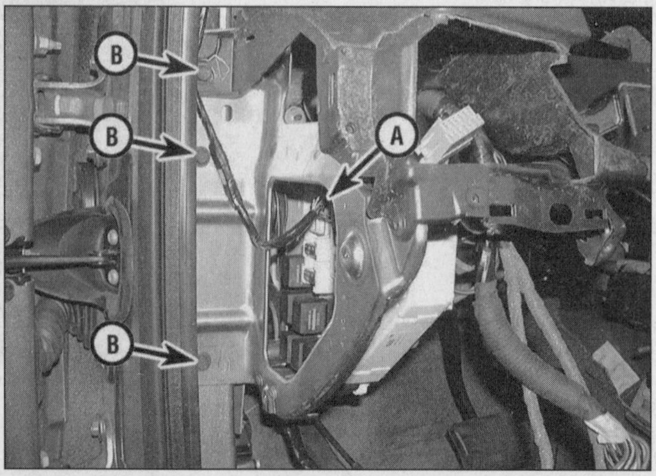

26.12d Disconnect the electrical connector (A) at the fuse panel, then remove the three bolts (B) from the left end of the instrument panel

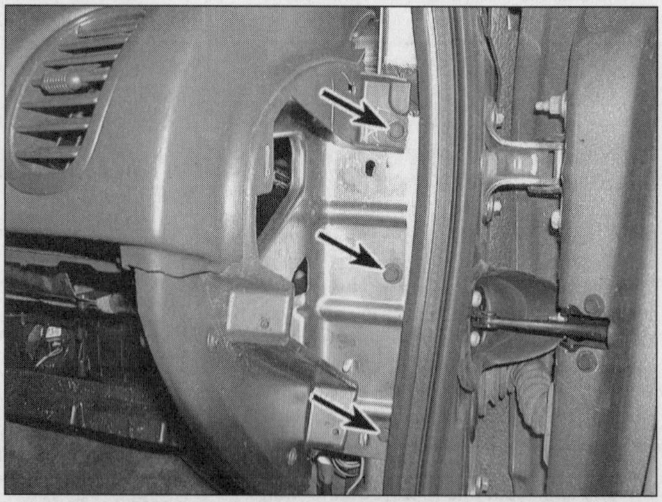

26.12e Remove the three instrument panel mounting bolts (arrows) at the right end

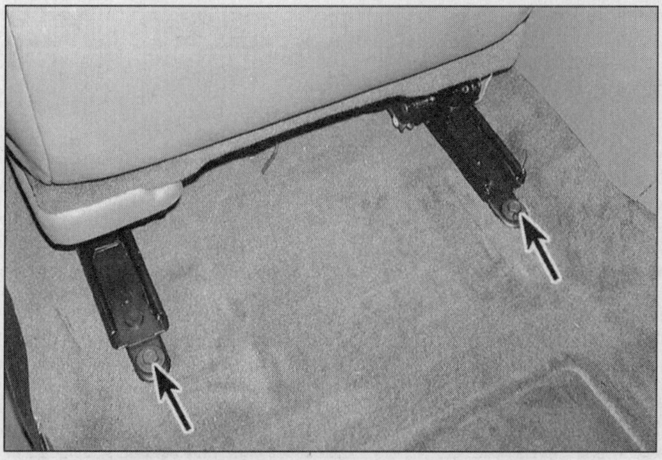

27.2a Front seat rear mounting bolts (arrows)

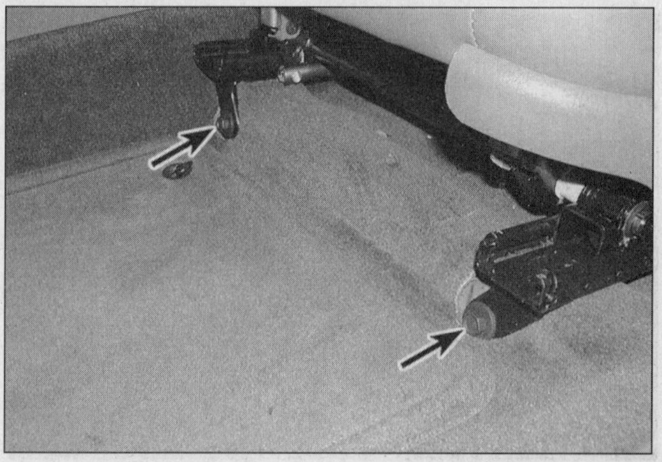

27.2b Front seat front mounting bolts (arrows)

27.5 Pull up the rear seat bottom cushion until the clips (arrow indicates one of two) release from slots in the floorpan

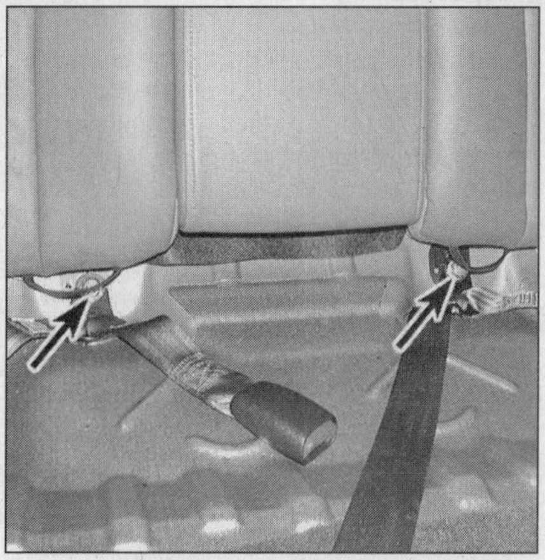

27.6 Remove the two nuts (arrows) at the bottom of the seat back

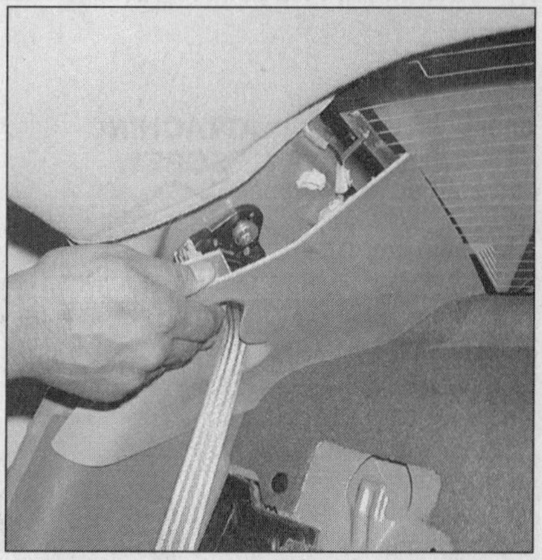

28.2 Removing the upper trim panels - the rubber door seal must be pulled away from the body where it covers the forward edge of the trim panel

27 Seats - removal and installation

Refer to illustrations 27.2a, 27.2b, 27.5 and 27.6

Front

1 Move the seat forward.

2 Remove the rear seat track bolts, move the seat rearward and remove the front seat track bolts and unplug any electrical connectors attached to the seat **(see illustrations)**.

3 Lift the seat from the vehicle.

4 Installation is the reverse of removal.

Rear

5 Remove the seat bottom cushion by grasping the front edge securely, then pulling up sharply to detach the cushion **(see illustration)**. Remove the seat bottom from the vehicle.

6 Remove the seat back and seat belt retaining nuts and lift the seat back out of the vehicle **(see illustration)**.

7 Installation is the reverse of removal. Torque the two seat back/seat belt nuts to 32 ft-lbs.

28 Rear package shelf - removal and installation

Refer to illustrations 28.2, 28.3, 28.4 and 28.5

1 Remove the back seat (see Section 27).

2 Use a trim tool or a taped screwdriver to pry the rear roof pillar trim panels out **(see illustration)**. The rear shoulder belts are routed through the panels. If you are just removing the package shelf to replace the rear speakers, just slide the panels along the belts, out of the way.

3 Pull back the rubber weatherstripping around the rear door opening, away from the body, and pry out the lower side trim panels **(see illustration)**.

4 Remove the push-in plastic fasteners at

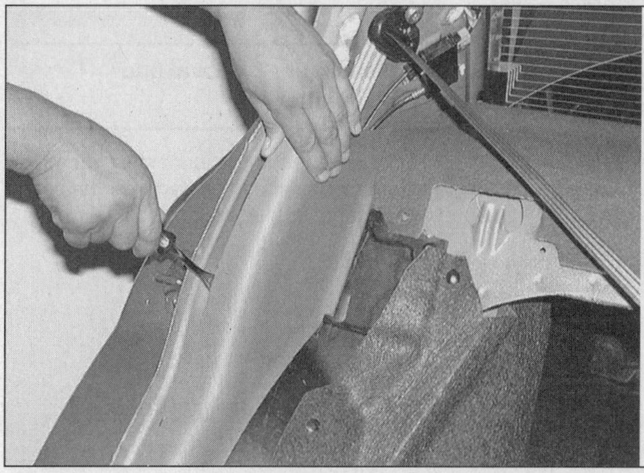

28.3 After pulling the rubber door seal away from the body lip, use a trim tool to remove the lower trim panels

28.4 Remove the plastic push-in fasteners (arrows indicate two of the three), then pull the package shelf forward, not up

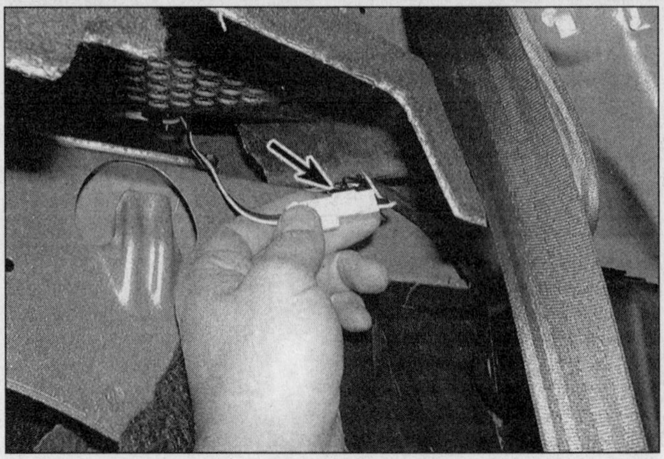

28.5 Disconnect the electrical connector (arrow) from the high-mounted brake light

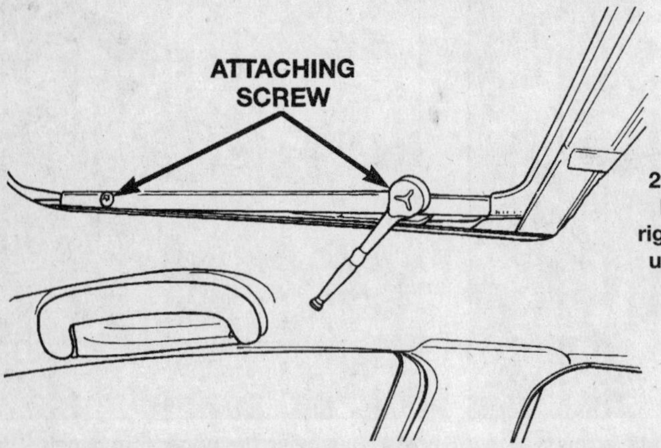

29.4 The sunroof glass has four screws (two right-side screws shown) used to adjust the fit of the glass to the roof

the front edge of the package shelf, then pull the shelf forward to disengage it from the clips at the rear **(see illustration)**.

5 Disconnect the electrical connector at the high-mounted brake light and remove the package shelf **(see illustration)**.

6 Installation is the reverse of the removal.

29 Sunroof - adjustment

Refer to illustration 29.4

1 The electric drive system for the power sunroof is not adjustable. See Chapter 12 for troubleshooting the sunroof system. **Warning:** *Do not remove the sunroof motor unless the sunroof is completely closed. Otherwise a new motor will have to be installed and timed with a tool that comes with the new motor.*

2 The position of the glass panel can be adjusted in the following manner.

3 Open the interior sunshade all the way back and operate the sunroof until it is fully closed.

4 There are two glass mounting screws on each side of the sunroof opening, inside the vehicle. Loosen the two front screws **(see illustration)**. Set the front edge of the glass to be just (1/32-inch) below the surface of the roof. Tighten the front screws.

5 Loosen the rear glass adjustment screws and adjust the glass to be just above (1/32-inch) the roof at the rear. Tighten the rear screws.

30 Headliner - removal and installation

1 To access the components of the sunroof or other overhead procedures, the headliner must be removed.

2 Removing the front seats (see Section 27) makes the job easier, but the headliner can be removed with the seats reclined to their full back position.

3 Remove the interior side trim at the windshield posts (see Section 26). Disconnect the electrical connector at the pillar connecting the overhead electrical items to the vehicle harness.

4 Remove the screws and remove the overhead console and sunvisors, disconnecting the electrical connectors if the visors are equipped with lighted vanity mirrors.

5 At the post just behind the front doors, remove the cover over the upper seat belt swivel, then remove the bolt securing the seat belt swivel to the sliding adjuster.

6 Remove the knob on the seat belt adjuster, then use a plastic trim tool to pry behind the upper post trim cover to release the clips.

7 Remove the screws and remove the assist handles, disconnecting the electrical connectors at the rear handles, if equipped with courtesy lights.

8 Remove the upper interior trim panels at each side of the rear window (see Section 28).

9 Pull the headliner down and angle it out through one of the back doors. This is a an awkward procedure and requires two people.

10 There is a large plastic clip that secures the headliner just above the rear window. The clip will probably come out with the headliner. If so, remove the clip from the body and snap it into the base plate that is glued to the back of the headliner.

11 The remainder of the installation is the reverse of the removal procedure.

Chapter 12
Chassis electrical system

Contents

1 General information

The electrical system is a 12-volt, negative ground type. Power for the lights and all electrical accessories is supplied by a lead/acid-type battery that is charged by the alternator.

This Chapter covers the various electrical components not associated with the engine. Information on the battery, alternator, distributor and starter motor can be found in Chapter 5.

It should be noted that when portions of the electrical system are serviced, the cable should be disconnected from the negative battery terminal to prevent electrical shorts and/or fires.

Warning: *The models covered by this manual are equipped with Supplemental Restraint Systems (SRS), more commonly known as airbags. Always disable the airbag system before working in the vicinity of any airbag system components to avoid the possibility of accidental deployment of the airbags, which could cause personal injury* (see Section 29).

2 Electrical troubleshooting - general information

Refer to illustrations 2.5a, 2.5b, 2.6, 2.9 and 2.15

A typical electrical circuit consists of an electrical component, any switches, relays, motors, fuses, fusible links or circuit breakers related to that component and the wiring and connectors that link the component to both the battery and the chassis. To help you pinpoint an electrical circuit problem, wiring dia-

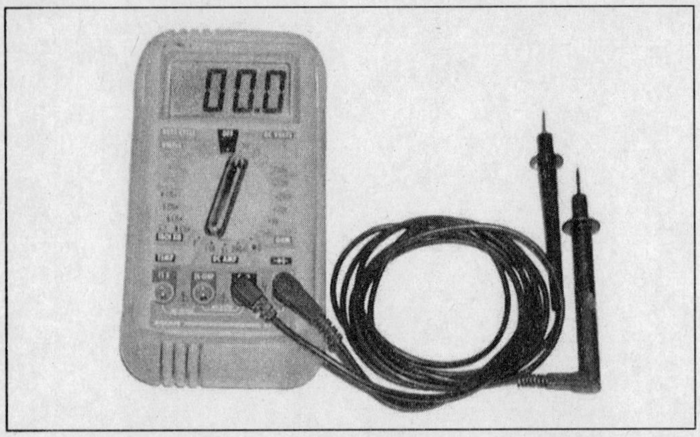

2.5a The most useful tool for electrical troubleshooting is a digital multimeter that can measure volts, amps and resistance

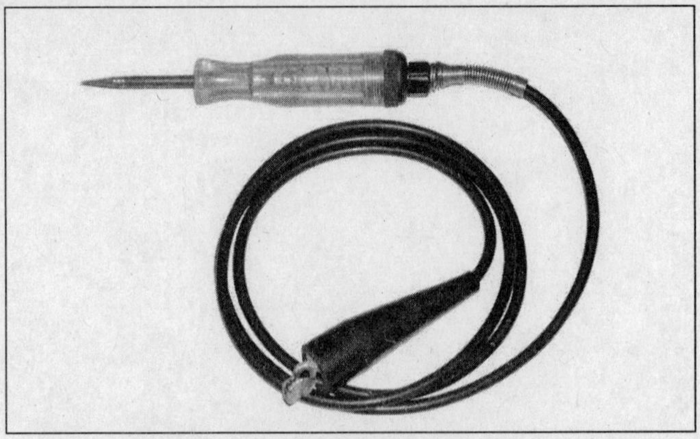

2.5b A simple test light is very handy, especially when testing for voltage

grams are included at the end of this Chapter.

Before tackling any troublesome electrical circuit, first study the appropriate wiring diagrams to get a complete understanding of what makes up that individual circuit. Trouble spots, for instance, can often be narrowed down by noting if other components related to the circuit are operating properly. If several components or circuits fail at one time, chances are the problem is in a fuse or ground connection, because several circuits are often routed through the same fuse and ground connections.

Electrical problems usually stem from simple causes, such as loose or corroded connections, a blown fuse, a melted fusible link or a failed relay. Visually inspect the condition of all fuses, wires and connections in a problem circuit before troubleshooting the circuit.

If test equipment and instruments are going to be utilized, use the diagrams to plan ahead of time where you will make the necessary connections in order to accurately pinpoint the trouble spot.

The basic tools needed for electrical troubleshooting include a circuit tester or voltmeter (a 12-volt bulb with a set of test leads can also be used), a continuity tester, which includes a bulb, battery and set of test leads, and a jumper wire, preferably with a circuit breaker incorporated, which can be used to bypass electrical components **(see illustrations)**. Before attempting to locate a problem with test instruments, use the wiring diagram(s) to decide where to make the connections.

Voltage checks

Voltage checks should be performed if a circuit is not functioning properly. Connect one lead of a circuit tester to either the negative battery terminal or a known good ground. Connect the other lead to a connector in the circuit being tested, preferably nearest to the battery or fuse **(see illustration)**. If the bulb of the tester lights, voltage is present, which means that the part of the circuit between the connector and the battery is problem free.

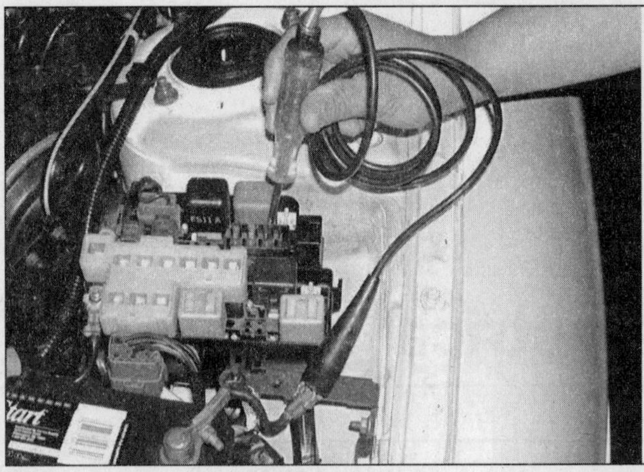

2.6 In use, the test light lead is clipped to a known good ground, then the pointed probe can test connectors, wires or electrical sockets - if the bulb lights, the circuit being tested has battery voltage

Continue checking the rest of the circuit in the same fashion. When you reach a point at which no voltage is present, the problem lies between that point and the last test point with voltage. Most of the time the problem can be traced to a loose connection. **Note:** *Keep in mind that some circuits receive voltage only when the ignition key is in the Accessory or Run position.*

Finding a short

One method of finding shorts in a circuit is to remove the fuse and connect a test light or voltmeter in place of the fuse terminals. There should be no voltage present in the circuit. Move the wiring harness from side-to-side while watching the test light. If the bulb goes on, there is a short to ground somewhere in that area, probably where the insulation has rubbed through. The same test can be performed on each component in the circuit, even a switch.

Ground check

Perform a ground test to check whether a component is properly grounded. Disconnect the battery and connect one lead of a continuity tester or multimeter (set to the ohms scale), to a known good ground. Connect the other lead to the wire or ground connection being tested. If the resistance is low (less than 5 ohms), the ground is good. If the bulb on a self-powered test light does not go on, the ground is not good.

Continuity check

A continuity check is done to determine if there are any breaks in a circuit - if it is passing electricity properly. With the circuit off (no power in the circuit), a self-powered continuity tester or multimeter can be used to check the circuit. Connect the test leads to both ends of the circuit (or to the "power" end and a good ground), and if the test light comes on the circuit is passing current properly **(see illustration)**. If the resistance is low (less than 5 ohms), there is continuity; if the reading is 10,000 ohms or higher, there is a break somewhere in the circuit. The same procedure can be used to test a switch, by connecting the continuity tester to the switch terminals. With the switch turned On, the test light should come on (or low resistance should be indicated on a meter).

Finding an open circuit

When diagnosing for possible open circuits, it is often difficult to locate them by sight because the connectors hide oxidation or terminal misalignment. Merely wiggling a connector on a sensor or in the wiring harness may correct the open circuit condition. Remember this when an open circuit is indicated when troubleshooting a circuit. Inter-

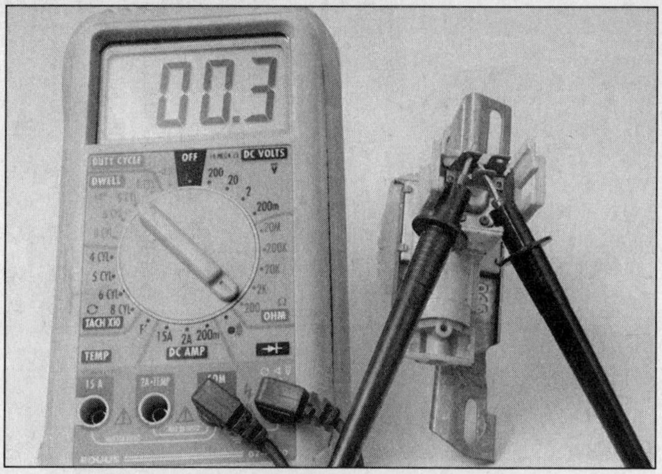

2.9 With a multimeter set to the ohms scale, resistance can be checked across two terminals - when checking for continuity, a low reading indicates continuity, a high reading indicates lack of continuity

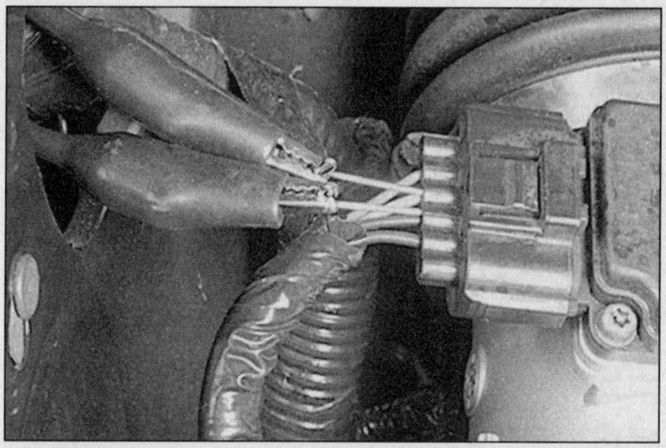

2.15 To backprobe a connector, insert a small, sharp probe (such as a straight-pin) into the back of the connector alongside the desired wire until it contacts the metal terminal inside; connect your meter leads to the probes - this allows you to test a functioning circuit

mittent problems may also be caused by oxidized or loose connections.

Electrical troubleshooting is simple if you keep in mind that all electrical circuits are basically electricity running from the battery, through the wires, switches, relays, fuses and fusible links to each electrical component (light bulb, motor, etc.) and to ground, from which it is passed back to the battery. Any electrical problem is an interruption in the flow of electricity to and from the battery.

Connectors

Most electrical connections on these vehicles are made with multiwire plastic connectors. The mating halves of many connectors are secured with locking clips molded into the plastic connector shells. The mating halves of large connectors, such as some of those under the instrument panel, are held together by a bolt through the center of the connector.

To separate a connector with locking clips, use a small screwdriver to pry the clips apart carefully, then separate the connector halves. Pull only on the shell, never pull on the wiring harness as you may damage the individual wires and terminals inside the connectors. Look at the connector closely before trying to separate the halves. Often the locking clips are engaged in a way that is not immediately clear. Additionally, many connectors have more than one set of clips.

Each pair of connector terminals has a male half and a female half. When you look at the end view of a connector in a diagram, be sure to understand whether the view shows the harness side or the component side of the connector. Connector halves are mirror images of each other, and a terminal shown on the right side end-view of one half will be on the left side end view of the other half.

Backprobing a connector

It is often necessary to take circuit voltage measurements with a connector connected. Whenever possible, carefully insert a small straight pin (not your meter probe) into the rear of the connector shell to contact the terminal inside, then clip your meter lead to the pin. This kind of connection is called "backprobing" **(see illustration)**. When inserting a test probe into a male terminal, be careful not to distort the terminal opening. Doing so can lead to a poor connection and corrosion at that terminal later. Using the small straight pin instead of a meter probe results in less chance of deforming the terminal connector.

3 Fuses and fusible links - general information

Fuses

Refer to illustrations 3.1a, 3.1b and 3.3

The electrical circuits of the vehicle are protected by a combination of fuses, circuit breakers and fusible links. The fuse blocks are located under the instrument panel on the

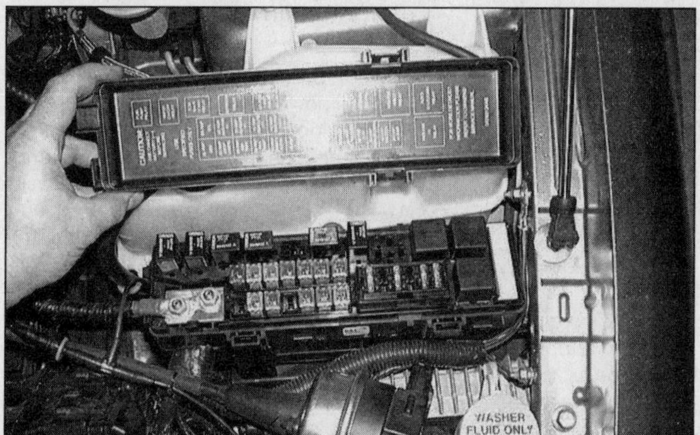

3.1a The power distribution center is located on the left side of the engine compartment and contains fuses and relays - the inside of the cover has a legend to identify the fuses and relays

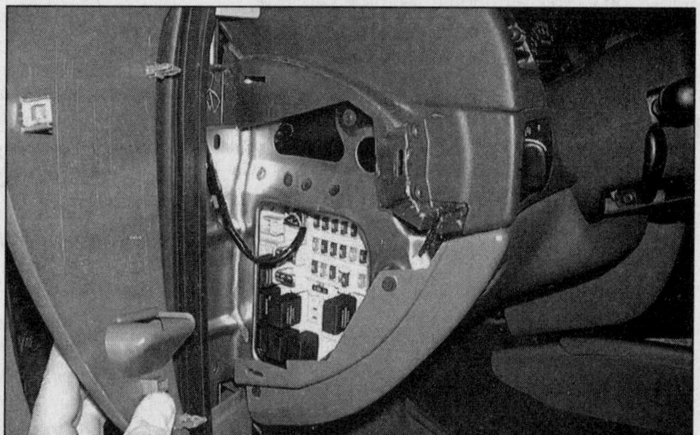

3.1b Under the left dashboard endcap is the junction block or interior fuse center, which contains, fuses and several relays - the inside of the instrument panel end cap has the identification legends cast into the plastic (not visible in this photo)

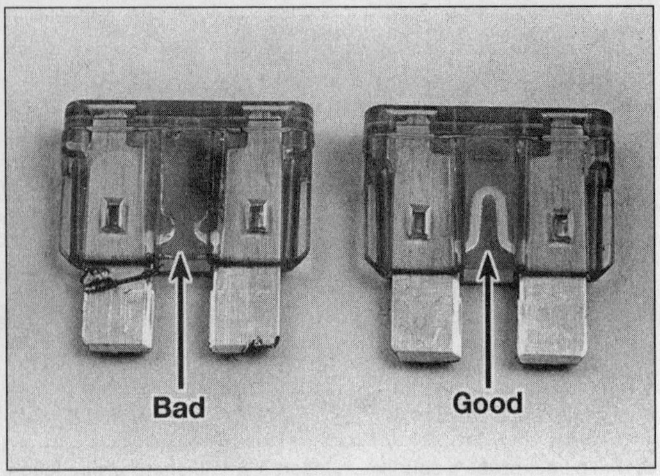

3.3 The fuses on these models can be easily checked visually to see if they are blown

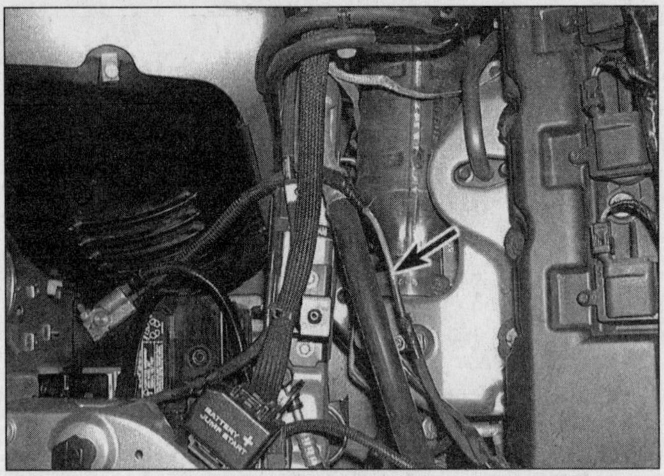

3.7 The fusible link (arrow) is in the circuit from the alternator to the battery

left side of the dashboard and in the engine compartment **(see illustrations)**.

Each of the fuses is designed to protect a specific circuit, and the various circuits are identified on the fuse panel itself.

Miniaturized fuses are employed in the fuse blocks. These compact fuses, with blade terminal design, allow fingertip removal and replacement. If an electrical component fails, always check the fuse first. The best way to check the fuses is with a test light. Check for power at the exposed terminal tips of each fuse. If power is present at one side of the fuse but not the other, the fuse is blown. A blown fuse can also be identified by visually inspecting it **(see illustration)**.

Be sure to replace blown fuses with the correct type. Fuses of different ratings are physically interchangeable, but only fuses of the proper rating should be used. Replacing a fuse with one of a higher or lower value than specified is not recommended. Each electrical circuit needs a specific amount of protection. The amperage value of each fuse is molded into the fuse body.

If the replacement fuse immediately fails, don't replace it again until the cause of the problem is isolated and corrected. In most cases, this will be a short circuit in the wiring caused by a broken or deteriorated wire.

Fusible links

Refer to illustrations 3.7 and 3.9

Some circuits are protected by fusible links. The links are used in circuits that are not ordinarily fused, such as the alternator circuit.

The fusible link for the alternator circuit is located on the right side of the engine compartment, and is easily identified **(see illustration)**. The link is a short length of green heavy wire spliced into the alternator cable to the battery, and the ends are wrapped with tape.

To replace a fusible link, first disconnect the negative battery cable from the remote

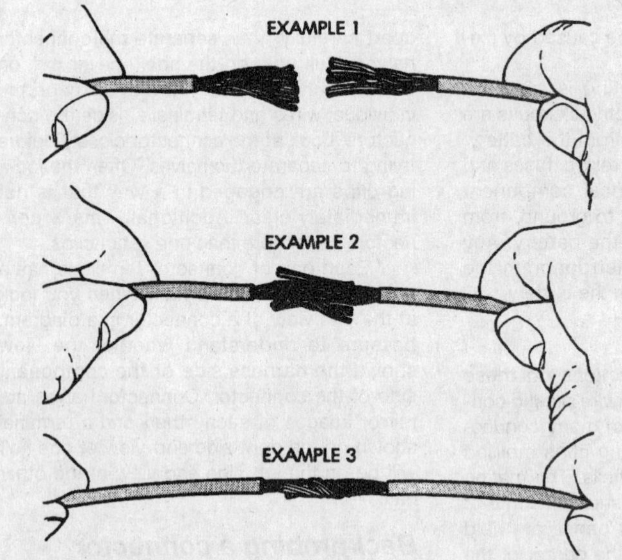

3.9 To repair a fusible link, cut out the damaged section, then join a new section by stripping the wire and twisting it together, as shown here. When securely joined, solder the connections and wrap them with electrical tape

ground terminal (see Chapter 5).

Although the fusible links appear to be a heavier gauge than the wires they're protecting, the appearance is due to the thick insulation. All fusible links are four wire gauges smaller than the wire they're designed to protect. Fusible links can't be repaired, but a new link of the same size wire can be installed. The procedure is as follows:

a) *Cut the damaged fusible link out of the wire just behind the connector.*
b) *Strip the insulation back approximately 1-inch.*
c) *Spread the strands of the exposed wire apart, push them together and twist them in place* **(see illustration)**.
d) *Use rosin core and solder the wires together to obtain a good connection.*
e) *Use plenty of electrical tape around the soldered joint. No wires should be exposed.*
f) *Connect the negative battery cable. Test the circuit for proper operation.*

4 Circuit breakers - general information and check

Circuit breakers protect certain circuit, such as the power windows, power seats and power door locks. There are two 20-amp circuit breakers, each located in the interior fuse/relay box at the left end of the dashboard.

Because the circuit breakers reset automatically, an electrical overload in a circuit-breaker-protected system will cause the circuit to fail momentarily, then come back on. If the circuit does not come back on, check it immediately.

For a basic check, pull the circuit breaker up out of its socket on the fuse panel, but just far enough to probe with a voltmeter. The breaker should still contact the sockets.

With the voltmeter negative lead on a good chassis ground, tough each end prong

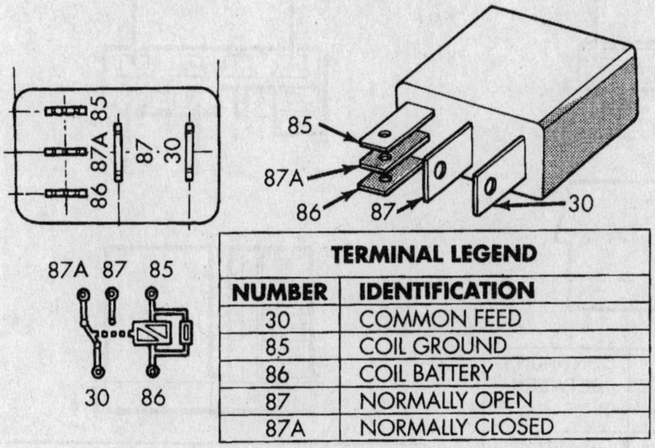

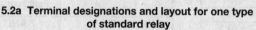

TERMINAL LEGEND	
NUMBER	IDENTIFICATION
30	COMMON FEED
85	COIL GROUND
86	COIL BATTERY
87	NORMALLY OPEN
87A	NORMALLY CLOSED

5.2a Terminal designations and layout for one type of standard relay

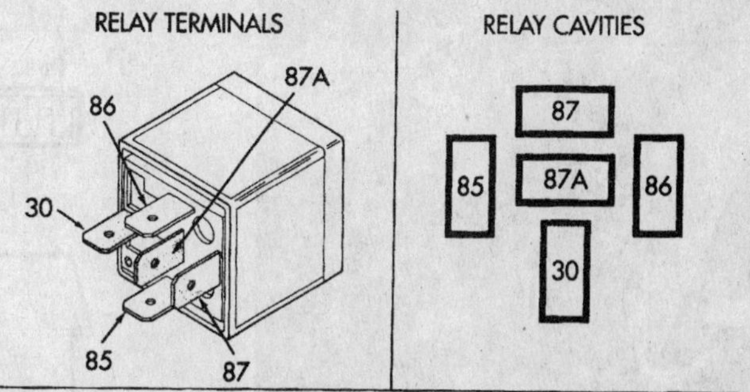

TERMINAL LEGEND	
NUMBER	IDENTIFICATION
30	COMMON FEED
85	COIL GROUND
86	COIL BATTERY
87	NORMALLY OPEN
87A	NORMALLY CLOSED

5.2b Terminal designations and layout for a second type of standard relay

of the circuit breaker with the positive meter probe. There should be battery voltage at each end. If there is battery voltage only at one end, the circuit breaker must be replaced.

5 Relays - general information and testing

General information

1 Several electrical accessories in the vehicle, such as the fuel injection system, horns, starter, and fog lamps use relays to transmit the electrical signal to the component. Relays use a low-current circuit (the control circuit) to open and close a high-current circuit (the power circuit). If the relay is defective, that component will not operate properly. Most relays are mounted in the engine compartment and interior fuse/relay boxes. If a faulty relay is suspected, it can be removed and tested using the procedure below or by a dealer service department or a repair shop. Defective relays must be replaced as a unit.

Testing

Refer to illustrations 5.2a and 5.2b

2 Most of the relays used in these vehicles are often called "ISO" relays, which refers to the International Standards Organization. The terminals of ISO relays are numbered to indicate their usual circuit connections and functions. There are two basic layouts of terminals on the relays used in the covered vehicles **(see illustrations)**.

3 Refer to the wiring diagram for the circuit to determine the proper connections for the relay you're testing. If you can't determine the correct connection from the wiring diagrams, however, you may be able to determine the test connections from the information that follows.

4 Two of the terminals are the relay control circuit and connect to the relay coil. The other relay terminals are the power circuit. When the relay is energized, the coil creates a magnetic field that closes the larger contacts of the power circuit to provide power to the circuit loads.

5 Terminals 85 and 86 are normally the control circuit. If the relay contains a diode, terminal 86 must be connected to battery positive (B+) voltage and terminal 85 to ground. If the relay contains a resistor, terminals 85 and 86 can be connected in either direction with respect to B+ and ground.

6 Terminal 30 is normally connected to the battery voltage (B+) source for the circuit loads. Terminal 87 is connected to the ground side of the circuit, either directly or through a load. If the relay has several alternate terminals for load or ground connections, they usually are numbered 87A, 87B, 87C, and so on.

7 Use an ohmmeter to check continuity through the relay control coil.

a) *Connect the meter according to the polarity shown in* **illustrations 5.2a or 5.2b** *for one check; then reverse the ohmmeter leads and check continuity in the other direction.*
b) *If the relay contains a resistor, resistance should be the specified value with the ohmmeter in either direction.*
c) *If the relay contains a diode, resistance should be the specified coil resistance value with the ohmmeter in the forward polarity direction. With the meter leads reversed, resistance should be lower.*
d) *If the ohmmeter shows infinite resistance in both directions, replace the relay.*

8 Remove the relay from the vehicle and use the ohmmeter to check for continuity between the relay power circuit terminals. There should be no continuity between terminal 30 and 87 with the relay de-energized.

9 Connect a fused jumper wire to terminal 86 and the positive battery terminal. Connect another jumper wire between terminal 85 and ground. When the connections are made, the relay should click.

10 With the jumper wires connected, check for continuity between the power circuit terminals. Now, there should be continuity between terminals 30 and 87.

11 If the relay fails any of the above tests, replace it.

6 Turn signal/hazard flashers - check and replacement

Refer to illustration 6.4

Warning: *The models covered by this manual are equipped with Supplemental Restraint Systems (SRS), more commonly known as airbags. Always disable the airbag system before working in the vicinity of any airbag system components to avoid the possibility of accidental deployment of the airbags, which could cause personal injury* (see Section 29).

1 The turn signal and hazard flasher is a single combination unit.

2 When the flasher unit is functioning properly, an audible click can be heard during its operation. If the turn signals fail on one side or the other and the flasher unit does not make its characteristic clicking sound, a faulty turn signal bulb is indicated.

3 If both turn signals fail to blink, the problem may be due to a blown fuse, a faulty flasher unit, a broken switch or a loose or open connection. If a quick check of the fuse box indicates that the turn signal fuse has blown, check the wiring for a short before installing a new fuse.

4 To replace the flasher, disconnect the electrical connector and remove the flasher unit from its mounting bracket located under the instrument panel to the left of the steering

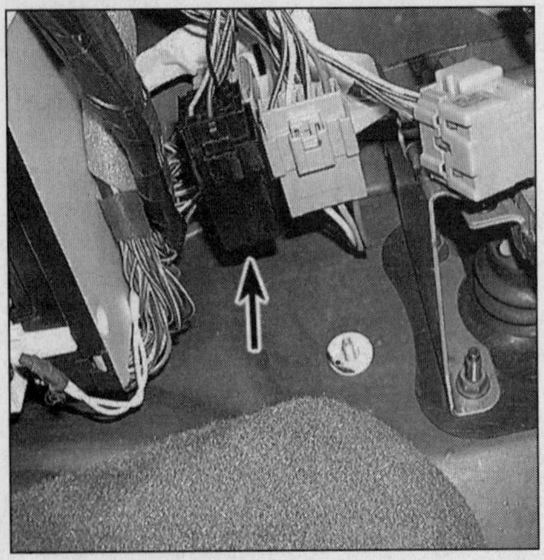

6.4 Turn signals and hazard flasher unit location (arrow), under the left end of the instrument panel (heating duct removed for clarity)

column **(see illustration)**. Refer to Chapter 11 for removal of the driver's knee bolster for access to the flasher, which is black and mounted on a bracket.

5 Make sure that the replacement unit is identical to the original. Compare the old one to the new one before installing it.

6 Installation is the reverse of removal.

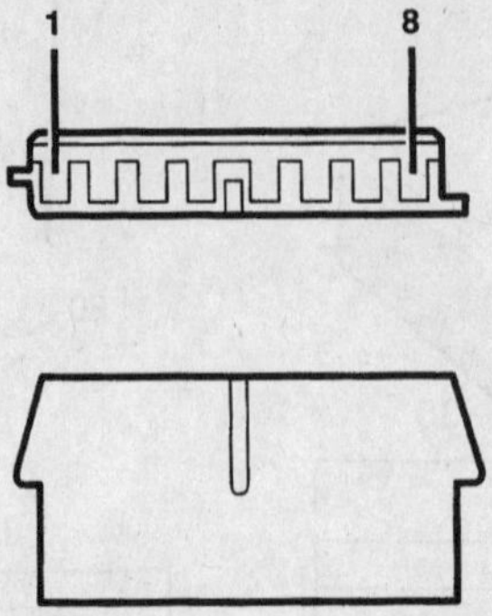

SWITCH POSITION		CONTINUITY BETWEEN
TURN SIGNAL	HAZARD WARNING	
NEUTRAL	OFF	1 AND 2
LEFT	OFF	7 AND 6
RIGHT	OFF	7 AND 8
NEUTRAL	ON	2 AND 3 7 AND 8 7 AND 6 4 AND 5

7.3a Terminal identification and continuity chart for the turn signal/hazard switch portion of the combination switch

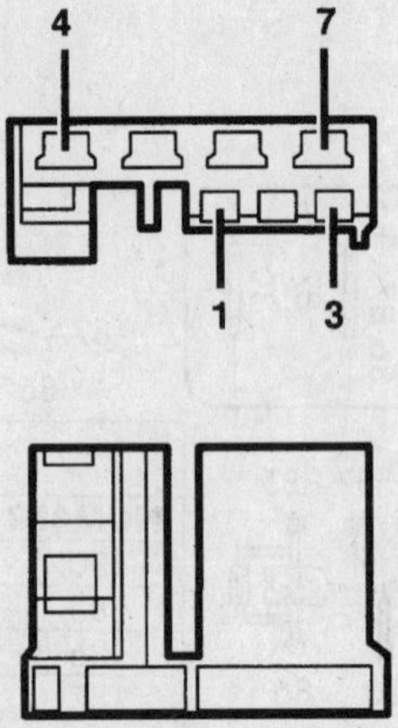

SWITCH POSITION	CONTINUITY BETWEEN
LOW BEAM	7 AND 5
HIGH BEAM	7 AND 4
OPTICAL HORN	6 AND 4

7.3b Terminal identification and continuity chart for the headlight beam selection switch portion of the combination switch

7 Steering column switches - check and replacement

Warning: *The models covered by this manual are equipped with Supplemental Restraint Systems (SRS), more commonly known as airbags. Always disable the airbag system before working in the vicinity of any airbag system components to avoid the possibility of accidental deployment of the airbags, which could cause personal injury* (see Section 29).

Multi-function switch

Check

Refer to illustrations 7.3a, 7.3b and 7.3c

1 Disconnect the negative battery cable from the remote ground terminal (see Chapter 5).

2 Refer to the replacement procedure below to remove the multi-function switch for testing.

3 Using an ohmmeter, check for continuity between the indicated terminals with the various switches in each of the indicated positions **(see illustrations)**.

4 If the continuity is not as specified, replace the multi-function switch.

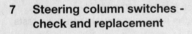

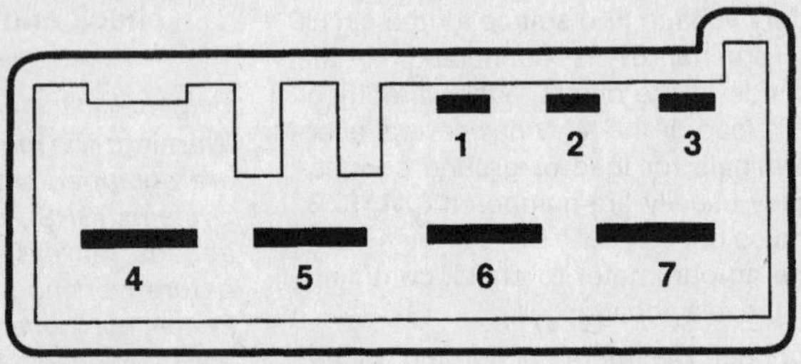

SWITCH POSITION		TERMINALS	RESISTANCE VALUE
OFF		PINS 1 T0 3	OPEN 300 K OHMS
DELAY LEVEL	1	PINS 1 TO 3	9.72 K OHMS
	2	PINS 1 TO 3	8.22 K OHMS
	3	PINS 1 TO 3	6.61 K OHMS
	4	PINS 1 TO 3	5.12 K OHMS
	5	PINS 1 TO 3	3.67 K OHMS
	6	PINS 1 TO 3	2.22 K OHMS
LOW		PINS 1 TO 3	1.02 K OHMS
HIGH		PINS 1 TO 3	0.51 K OHMS
WASH		PINS 1 TO 2	0 OHMS

7.3c Terminal identification and continuity chart for the wiper/washer switch portion of the combination switch

7.7 The multi-function switch is held in place by two screws (arrows, steering wheel removed for clarity)

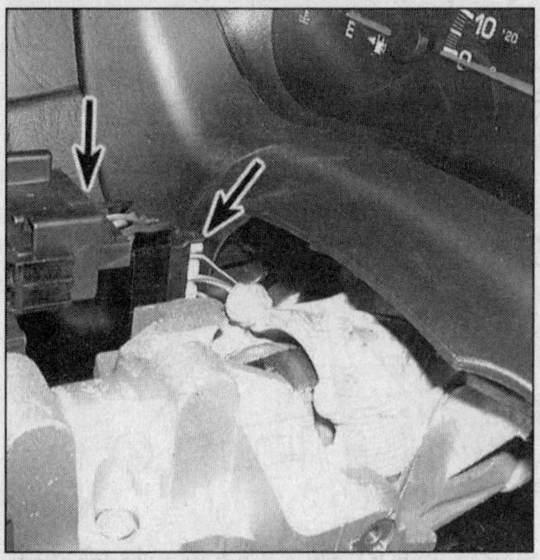

7.8 Unplug the electrical connectors (arrows) from the multi-function switch

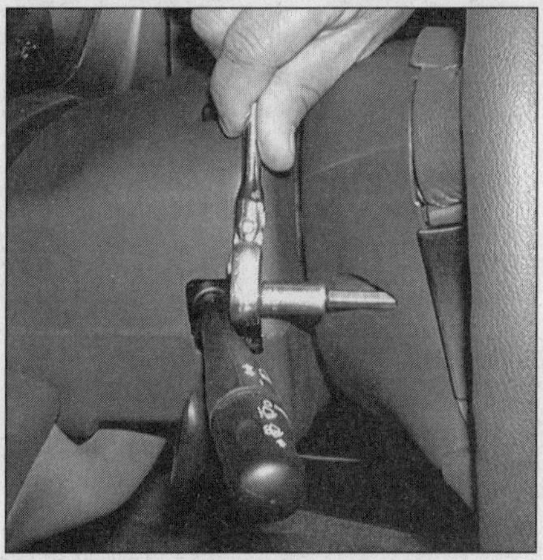

7.14a From the back of the steering wheel, remove the cruise switch mounting screws (one screw for each pod)

7.14b Pull the cruise switch pod (left pod shown) out and disconnect the electrical connector

Replacement

Refer to illustrations 7.7 and 7.8

5 Disconnect the negative battery cable from the remote ground terminal (see Chapter 5).

6 Remove the steering column covers (see Chapter 11).

7 Remove the multi-function switch retaining screws **(see illustration)**. **Note:** *The screws are male Torx type*.

8 Remove the multi-function switch. Slide the switch up off the column and unplug the connectors **(see illustration)**.

9 Insert the connectors into the new multi-function switch, pushing in until they are securely locked in place.

10 The remainder of installation is the reverse of removal.

Cruise control switches

Check

11 The cruise control switch pods are located on the steering wheel. Refer to the replacement procedure below to remove the cruise control switches for testing.

12 The cruise control switches are part of the vehicle's multiplexing communication system with the PCM, and send/receive information through the steering wheel's airbag clockspring connector. Standard troubleshooting will not give a true picture of the switch operation. If you suspect a problem with either cruise control switch pod, have the system checked with a factory scan tool at a dealership.

Replacement

Refer to illustrations 7.14a and 7.14b

13 Disconnect the negative battery cable from the remote ground terminal (see Chapter 5).

14 From the back of the steering wheel, remove the switch mounting screws, remove the switches and disconnect the electrical connectors **(see illustrations)**.

15 Installation is the reverse of removal.

8 Ignition switch and key lock cylinder - check and replacement

Warning: *The models covered by this manual are equipped with Supplemental Restraint Systems (SRS), more commonly known as airbags. Always disable the airbag system before working in the vicinity of any airbag system components to avoid the possibility of accidental deployment of the airbags, which could cause personal injury* (see Section 29).

Ignition switch

Check

Refer to illustrations 8.4, 8.5 and 8.6

1 Disable the airbag system (see Section 29).

2 Remove the steering column covers (see Chapter 11).

3 Remove the multi-function switch (see Section 7).

4 On models with Sentry Key alarm systems, remove the Sentry Key Immobilizer module from the ignition switch and lock cylinder **(see illustration)**.

5 Disconnect the ignition switch electrical connector on the left end of the ignition switch **(see illustration)**.

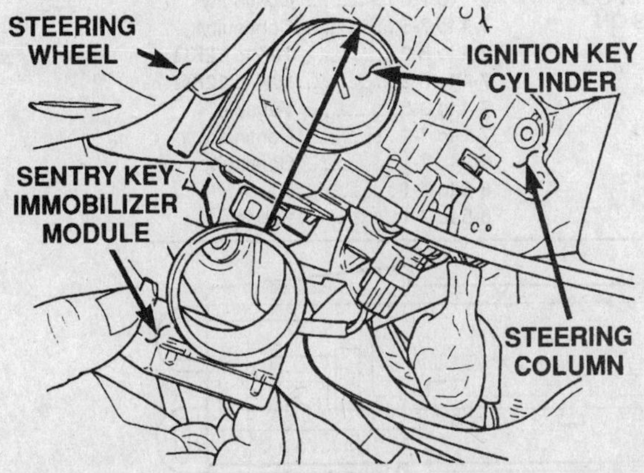

8.4 Where equipped, remove the Sentry Key Immobilizer module prior to removing the ignition switch from the steering column

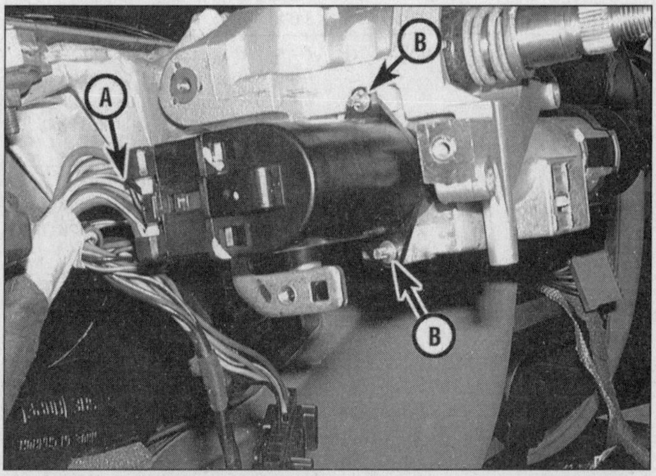

8.5 Disconnect the electrical connector (A) at the ignition switch - remove the two screws (B) to remove the switch

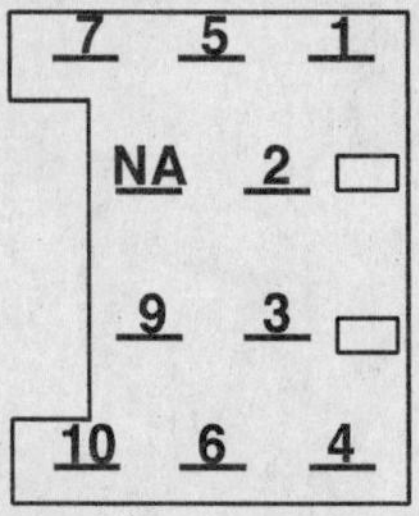

SWITCH POSITION	CONTINUITY BETWEEN
Start	1 and 5, 4 and 5 5 and 9,
Run	1 and 5, 4 and 5 5 and 6, 7 and 10
Off	1 and 5
Acc	5 and 6

8.6 Ignition switch terminal identification and continuity chart

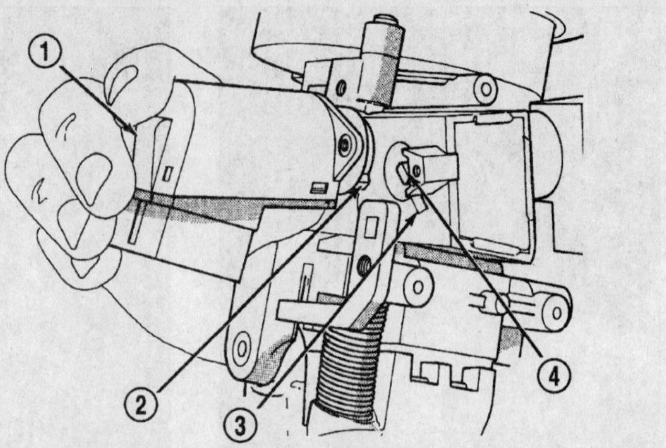

8.11 To install the ignition switch (1), align the key cylinder shaft (4) with the notch (3), then align the tab (2) on the switch and install with the two screws (switch viewed from below)

8.15 In the Run position, depress the lock tab (arrow) and remove the lock cylinder

6 Check the switch for continuity between the indicated terminals with the key in each position **(see illustration). Note:** *There is continuity between 2 and 3 in all positions, since this is the key-in-lock switch that indicates to the BCM that the key is in place. There is no continuity at any terminals in the Lock position, except for 2 and 3 when the key is in.*

7 If the continuity is not as specified, replace the switch.

8 Check the lock cylinder in each position to make sure it isn't worn or loose and that the key position corresponds to the markings on the housing.

Replacement

Refer to illustration 8.11

9 Follow Steps 1 through 4 above to access the ignition switch.

10 Disconnect the electrical connector and remove the switch mounting screws to remove the switch **(see illustration 8.5)**.

11 Install the new switch, making sure the tab on the switch fits against the notch on the key cylinder, and that the slot on the shaft of the switch aligns with the projecting tang on the key cylinder **(see illustration). Note:** *Use the key in the cylinder to align the cylinder with the switch.*

12 The remainder of the installation is the reverse of the removal procedure.

Lock cylinder

Refer to illustration 8.15

13 Follow Steps 1 through 4 above to

POSITION	TERMINALS	RESISTANCE VALUE
ALL SWITCHES OFF	7-5 to 8-2	10K to 12KΩ
	7-5 to 8-6	10K to 12KΩ
	8-2 to 8-6	6 to 7
	7-5 to 8-5	Variable
	8-2 to 8-5	Variable
	8-6 to 8-5	Variable
HEADLAMPS ON	7-7 to 7-6	Continuity
	7-4 to 7-5	Continuity
	7-4 to 8-2	10K to 12KΩ
	7-4 to 8-6	10K to 12KΩ
	7-4 to 8-5	Variable
PARKING LAMPS ON	7-4 to 7-5	Continuity
	7-4 to 8-2	10K to 12KΩ
	7-4 to 8-6	10K to 12KΩ
	7-4 to 8-5	Variable
THUMBWHEEL-DIM POSITION	7-5 to 8-5	900 to 1.2KΩ
	8-2 to 8-5	10K to 12KΩ
	8-6 to 8-5	10K to 12KΩ
THUMBWHEEL-BRIGHT POSITION	7-5 to 8-5	10K to 12KΩ
	8-2 to 8-5	Continuity
	8-6 to 8-5	Continuity
THUMBWHEEL-DOME LAMPS POSITION	7-5 to 8-5	10K to 12KΩ
	8-2 to 8-5	Continuity
	8-6 to 8-5	Continuity
	8-2 to 8-3	Continuity
FRONT FOG LAMPS ON	7-7 to 7-6	Continuity
	7-4 to 7-5	Continuity
	7-4 to 8-2	10K to 12KΩ
	7-4 to 8-6	10K to 12KΩ
	7-4 to 8-5	Variable
	7-1 to 7-2	Continuity
	8-2 to 7-1	Continuity
	8-6 to 7-1	6 to 7
	8-5 to 7-1	Variable

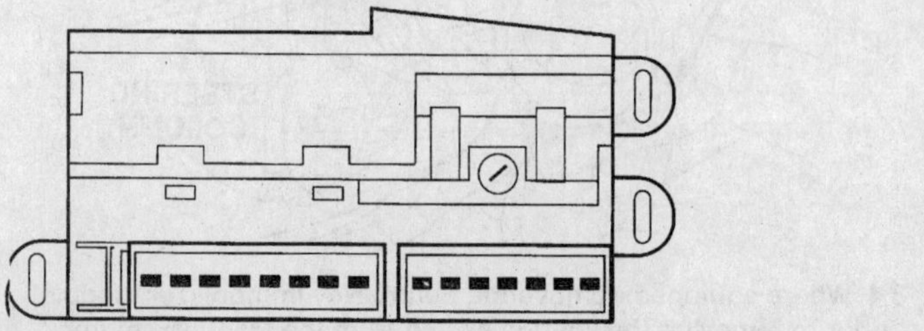

9.2a Headlight switch terminal identification and tests - 1998 models

POSITION	TERMINALS	RESISTANCE VALUES
OFF	6 & 12	3600 Ω - 5400 Ω
PARK LAMP ON	6 & 12	44.65 Ω - 49.35 Ω
PARK LAMP W/FRONT FOG	6 & 12	64.6 Ω - 71.4 Ω
HEADLAMP ON	6 & 12	209.2 Ω - 231 Ω
HEADLAMP W/FRONT FOG	6 & 12	446.5 Ω - 493.5 Ω
AUTO	6 & 12	370.5 Ω - 409.5 Ω
AUTO WFRONT FOG	6 & 12	400 Ω - 1100 Ω
RHEOSTAT (THUMBWHEEL) DIM POSITION	6 & 3	180 Ω - 1870 Ω (POT)
RHEOSTAT (THUMBWHEEL) BRIGHT POSITION (FUNERAL MODE)	6 & 3	2280 Ω - 2520 Ω
DOME LAMP	6 & 3	3230 Ω - 3570 Ω

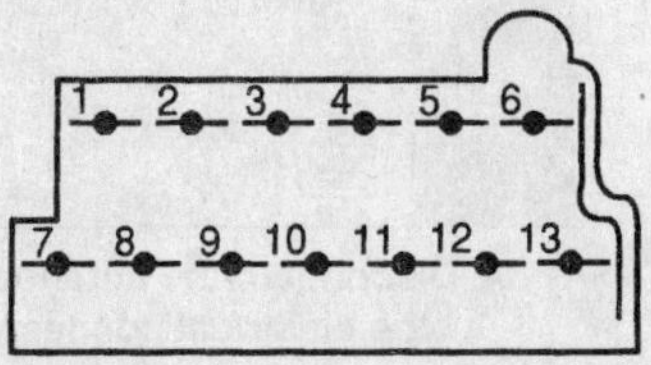

9.2b Headlight switch terminal identification and tests - 1999 and later models

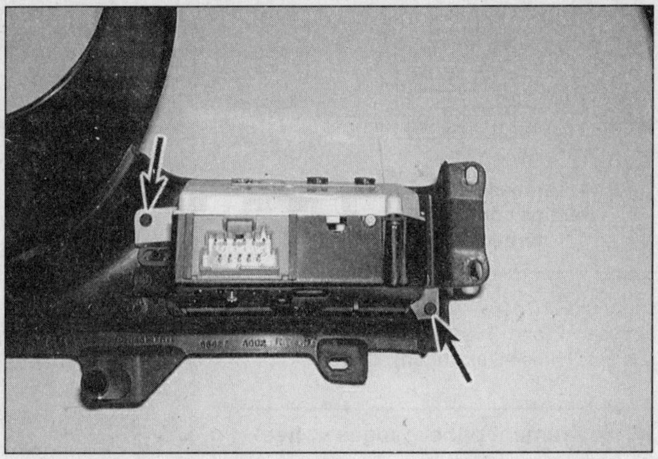

9.4 Remove the headlight switch mounting screws (arrows)

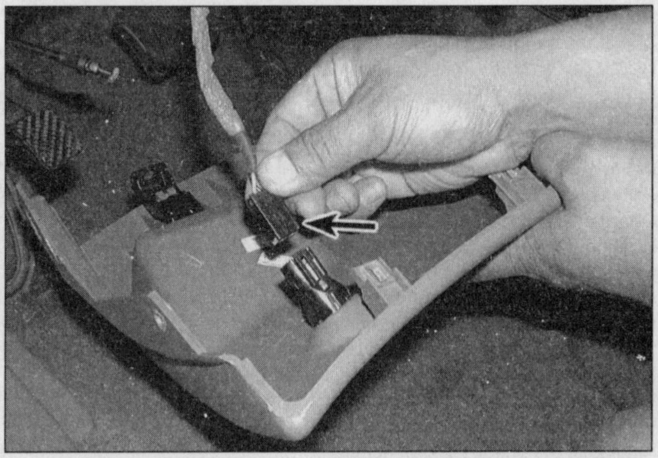

9.8 Depress the tab (arrow) to release the connector from the back of the trunk release switch

access the ignition switch.

14 Insert the key and turn the ignition switch to the Run position.

15 Using a small screwdriver, depress the tab on the lock cylinder and use the key to withdraw the cylinder from the housing **(see illustration)**.

16 To install a new cylinder, insert the key and turn to the Run position. You can feel the correct position by pushing on the lock tab; if it can be pushed, the cylinder is in the correct position.

17 Insert the cylinder to the housing until the locking tab comes out in the housing slot.

18 Refer to Chapter 7 for adjustment of the interlock cassette or cable end at the lock cylinder. The remainder of installation is the reverse of the removal procedure.

9 Instrument panel switches - check and replacement

Warning: *The models covered by this manual are equipped with Supplemental Restraint Systems (SRS), more commonly known as airbags. Always disable the airbag system before working in the vicinity of any airbag system components to avoid the possibility of accidental deployment of the airbags, which could cause personal injury* (see Section 29).

Headlight switch

Refer to illustrations 9.2a, 9.2b and 9.4

Check

1 Refer to Steps below to remove the headlight switch for testing.

2 Test the switch terminals with an ohmmeter **(see illustrations)**. If the switch fails the tests, replace it.

Replacement

3 Refer to Chapter 11 for removal of the instrument cluster trim bezel (which includes the headlight switch).

4 Remove the hex-head screws from the back of the bezel to remove the headlight switch **(see illustration)**.

5 Installation is the reverse of the removal procedure.

Trunk release switch

Refer to illustration 9.8

6 Disconnect the negative battery cable from the remote ground terminal (see Chapter 5).

7 On 1998 models, remove the center trim bezel from the instrument panel (see Chapter 11). On 1999 and later models, remove the driver's knee bolster (see Chapter 11).

8 Disconnect the electrical connector on the back of the switch **(see illustration)**.

9 Using an ohmmeter, check that there is continuity between the two switch terminals only when the switch is depressed.

10 To replace the switch, squeeze all four of the "wing" tabs on the back of the switch and pull it out of the panel. The new switch must be pushed into the panel with a tab on the side aligned with a notch in the panel.

Traction control switch

Refer to illustration 9.14

11 Disable the airbag system (see Section 29).

12 Refer to Chapter 11 for removal of the center instrument panel bezel.

13 With the bezel pulled away from the instrument panel, disconnect the electrical connector at the traction control switch.

14 Using an ohmmeter, test the switch for

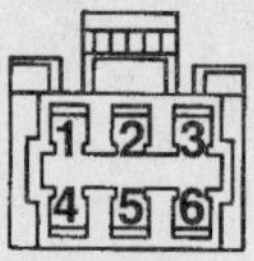

9.14 Terminal identification for the traction control switch (not all terminals are used)

continuity. There should be continuity between 2 and 3 only when the switch is pushed On **(see illustration)**.

10 Instrument panel gauges - check

1 All tests below require the ignition switch to be turned to Off position before testing.

2 If the gauge pointer does not move from the empty or cold positions when the key is turned On, check the fuses, referring to the wiring diagrams at the end of this chapter for the fuses controlling the circuit in question. If the fuse is OK, locate the particular sending unit for the circuit you're working on (see Chapter 2 for the oil pressure sending unit location, Chapter 3 for the temperature gauge sending unit location, and Chapter 4 for fuel sending unit location). Each of these Chapters has a basic test for the sending unit.

3 If the fuses are OK, check that the cooling system is in good condition (see Chapter 3), the fuel tank does have fuel, and that there is proper oil pressure with the engine running. If the gauges do not accurately reflect actual conditions and the fuses and sending units are OK, have the instrument panel diagnosed with a factory scan tool at a dealership.

11 Instrument cluster - removal and installation

Refer to illustration 11.3

Warning: *The models covered by this manual are equipped with Supplemental Restraint Systems (SRS), more commonly known as airbags. Always disable the airbag system before working in the vicinity of any airbag system components to avoid the possibility of accidental deployment of the airbags, which could cause personal injury* (see Section 29).

1 Disable the airbag system (see Section 29).

2 Remove the instrument cluster bezel (see Chapter 11).

3 Remove the retaining screws and pull the cluster forward sharply to disengage it from the body **(see illustration)**. **Note:** *The bottom corners of the instrument cluster have recesses where a hook tool can be used if necessary to provide a sharper pull on the cluster*. The electrical connectors will stay with the body when the cluster is removed.

4 Installation is the reverse of the removal procedure.

11.3 Remove the mounting screws (arrows) and pull the instrument cluster away from the dash

12.3 Remove the audio unit mounting screws (arrows)

12.4 Disconnect the antenna lead (A) and the electrical connectors (B)

12 Radio and speakers - removal and installation

Warning: *The models covered by this manual are equipped with Supplemental Restraint Systems (SRS), more commonly known as airbags. Always disable the airbag system before working in the vicinity of any airbag system components to avoid the possibility of accidental deployment of the airbags, which could cause personal injury* (see Section 29).

Radio/CD player

Refer to illustrations 12.3 and 12.4

1 Disable the airbag system (see Section 29).

2 Remove the center bezel panel from the dash (see Chapter 11).

3 Remove the screws and pull the radio/CD player assembly away from the dash **(see illustration)**.

4 Disconnect the antenna lead and the electrical connectors, then remove the audio unit **(see illustration)**.

5 Installation is the reverse of removal.

Speakers

Front

Refer to illustrations 12.7a, 12.7b and 12.7c

6 Using a trim tool, pry off the speaker covers in the front door. **Note:** *Higher-level audio systems have similar speakers in the rear doors, and they are accessed and removed in the same way.*

7 Remove the speaker retaining screws. Unplug the electrical connector and remove the speaker **(see illustrations)**.

8 Installation is the reverse of removal.

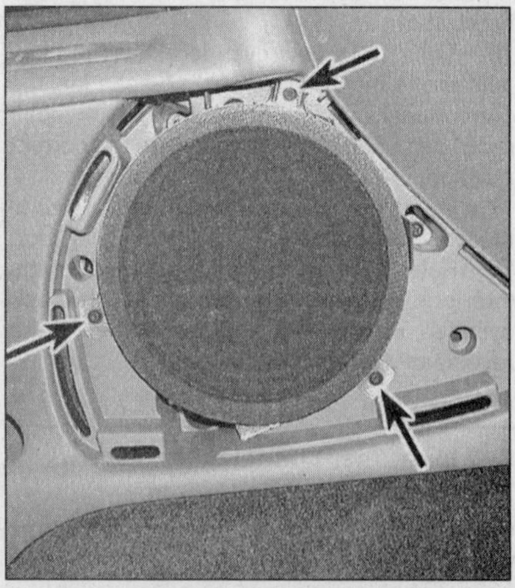

12.7a With the grille removed, remove the front speaker mounting screws (arrows)

12.7b On optional audio systems, small speakers are used at the front of the window opening on the front doors - remove the two screws (arrows) to remove the speaker, then disconnect the electrical connector

Rear

Refer to illustration 12.10

9 Remove the rear package shelf (see Chapter 11).

10 Lift the package shelf up for access and remove the rear speaker mounting screws **(see illustration)**.

11 Installation is the reverse of removal.

13 Antenna - check and replacement

Intrepid models

1 On Intrepid models, remove the antenna mast-retaining nut. Apply masking tape around the antenna mount to avoid scratching the paint.

2 Working in the trunk, pry out the plastic clips securing the passenger side trunk finishing panels to allow access to the antenna connections.

12.7c If the mirrors are to be replaced or a door panel removed, remove the two screws (arrows) and the upper speaker's mounting plate

3 Detach the antenna lead and remove the antenna from the vehicle.

4 Installation is the reverse of removal.

LHS, Concorde and 300M models

Refer to illustration 13.7

5 Most models have a wire-grid antenna in the rear window. The antenna grid for the AM reception occupies the upper portion of the rear window only, while the FM antenna shares the main grid with the rear window defogger.

6 The antenna grid can be tested for continuity in the same manner as outlined in Section 21, and if there is a break in the grid, it can be repaired in the same manner as the rear defogger grid (see Section 21).

7 Models with a grid antenna also have a rear window antenna module, mounted behind the upper right interior panel, above the package shelf **(see illustration)**.

8 Remove the trim panel to access the module, which connects the antenna grid,

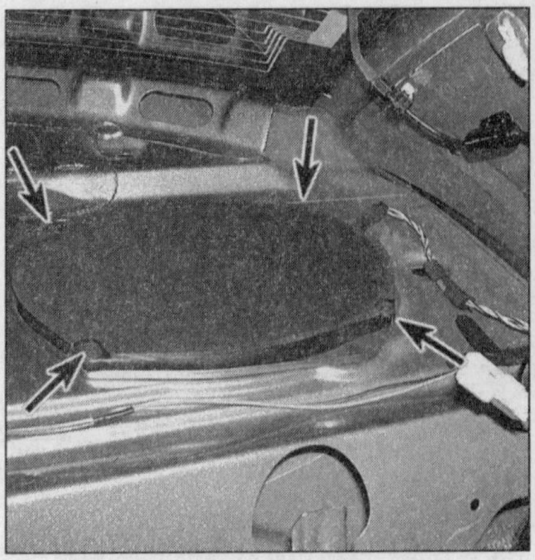

12.10 Rear speaker mounting screws (arrows)

the defogger grid, and the coax cable from the audio unit (see Chapter 11).

14 Headlight bulb - replacement

Refer to illustrations 14.2, 14.3, 14.7 and 14.8

All models except 300M Special

Warning: *These models are equipped with halogen gas-filled bulbs, which are under pressure and may shatter if the surface is scratched or the bulb is dropped. Wear eye protection and handle the bulbs carefully, grasping only the base whenever possible. Do not touch the surface of the bulb with your fingers because the oil from your skin could cause it to overheat and fail prematurely. If you do touch the bulb surface, clean it with rubbing alcohol.*

1 The headlight housing must be removed to access the bulbs on the back of the housing (see Section 16).

2 Remove the retaining ring **(see illustration)**.

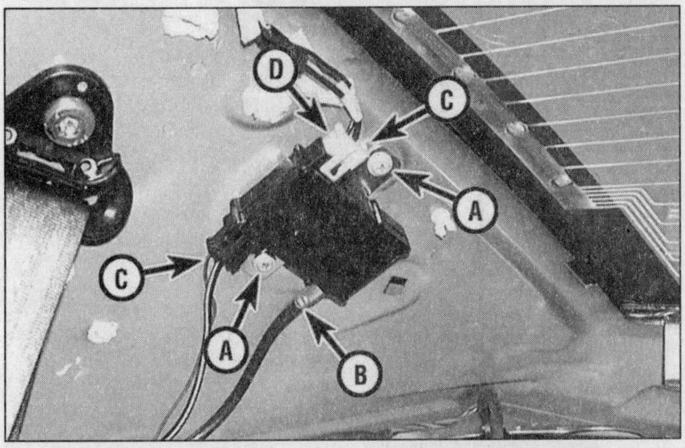

13.7 Rear window antenna/defogger module details

A Module mounting screws
B Coax cable connector
C Battery voltage feed connector
D Connector to grid lines

14.2 Twist the retaining rings (arrows) and slide them back over the harness

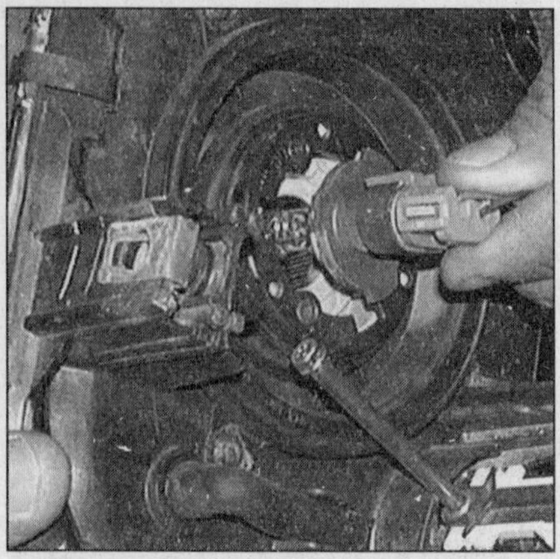

14.3 Twist, then pull out the bulb holder and replace the bulb

3 Withdraw the bulb assembly from the headlight housing **(see illustration)**.

4 Without touching the glass with your bare fingers, insert the new bulb assembly into the headlight housing and secure it with the retaining ring.

5 Plug in the electrical connector. Reinstall the headlight housing (see Section 16), then test headlight operation.

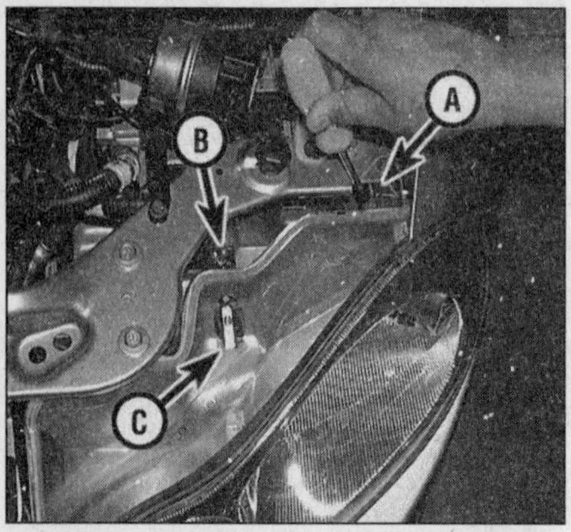

15.1a Use a Torx screwdriver or small wrench to adjust the headlights - the adjuster closest to the fender (A) controls the horizontal movement and the one closest to the radiator (B), vertical movement, C is the bubble level - Concorde, LHS and 300M models

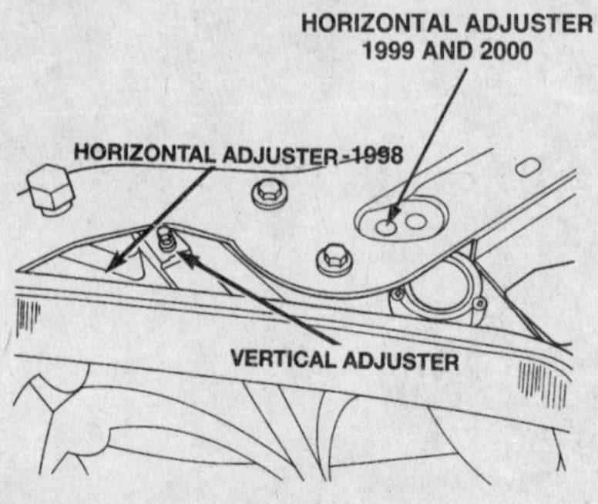

15.1b Headlight adjusters, Intrepid models

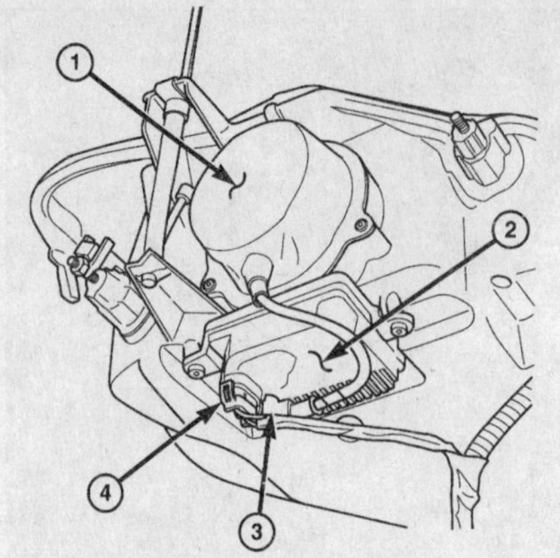

14.7 HID system components

1 *Water shield*
2 *Ballast module*
3 *Igniter/lamp assembly*
4 *Electrical connector*

300M Special Models

Warning: *These models are equipped with the High Intensity Discharge (HID) xenon gas filled headlight bulbs which are under pressure and may shatter if the surface is scratched or the bulb is dropped. Wear eye protection and handle the bulbs carefully, grasping only the base whenever possible. Do not touch the surface of the bulb with your fingers because the oil from your skin could cause the bulb to overheat and fail prematurely. If you do touch the bulb surface, clean it with rubbing alcohol.*

6 Remove the headlight housing (see Section 16).

7 Disconnect the headlight igniter assembly electrical connector from the ballast module **(see illustration)**.

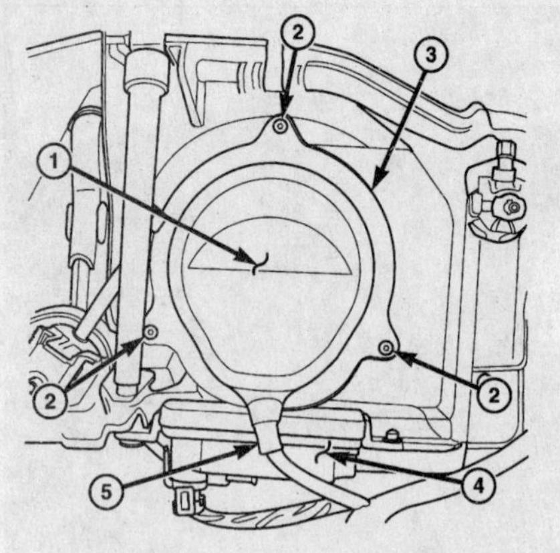

14.8 HID igniter/lamp components

1 *Igniter/lamp assembly and water shield*
2 *Retaining screw*
3 *Water shield retaining ring*
4 *Ballast module*
5 *Electrical wire and connector*

8 Remove the water shield retaining ring screws **(see illustration)**.

9 Carefully pull up on the water shield and pull it back over the igniter wire.

10 Release the igniter/lamp assembly retaining spring and pull the assembly straight out of the headlight housing. The lamp and igniter are an integral unit and are replaced as an assembly.

11 Install the igniter/lamp assembly into the headlight housing and install the spring retainer onto the igniter/lamp assembly.

12 Install the water shield into the groove, making sure it is positioned correctly, then push down on the edge to completely seat the shield in the retaining groove.

13 Install the retaining ring over the water shield and install the retaining screws.

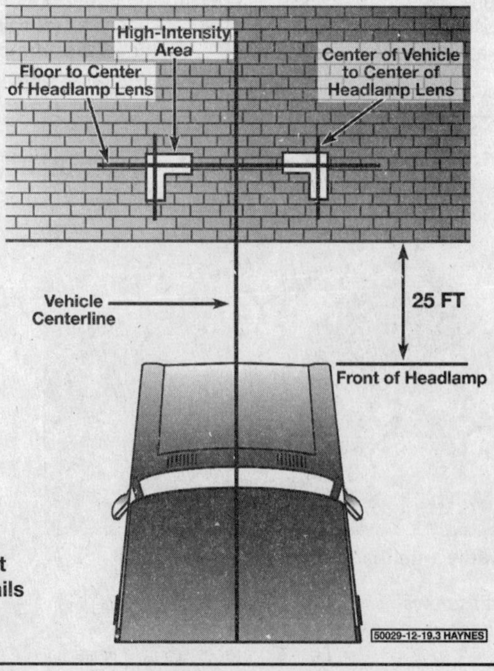

15.2 Headlight adjustment details

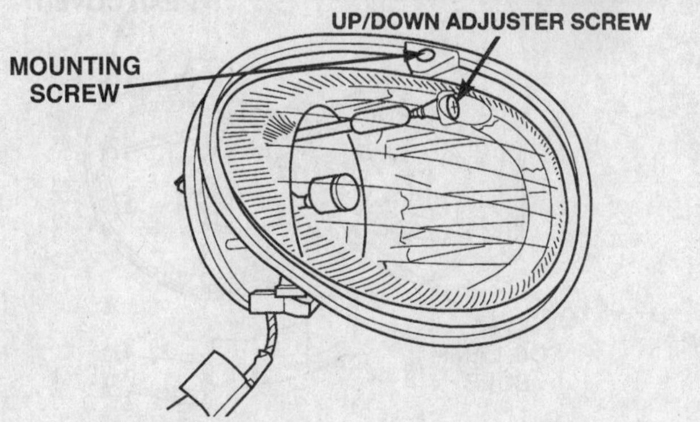

15.11 Fog lamp adjusting and mounting screws - Intrepid models

16.1 Remove the two long bolts (arrows) on the headlight housing

14 Connect the headlight igniter assembly electrical connector onto the ballast module (see illustration 14.7).

15 Install the headlight housing (see Section 16), then test headlight operation.

15 Headlights and fog lights - adjustment

Headlights

Refer to illustrations 15.1a, 15.1b and 15.2

Note: *It is important that the headlights are aimed correctly. If adjusted incorrectly they could blind the driver of an oncoming vehicle and cause a serious accident or seriously reduce your ability to see the road. The headlights should be checked for proper aim every 12 months and any time a new headlight is installed or front end body work is performed. It should be emphasized that the following procedure is only an interim step that will provide temporary adjustment until the headlights can be adjusted by a properly equipped shop.*

1 These models are equipped with composite headlights with two adjustment screws, one controlling left-and-right movement and one for up-and-down movement **(see illustrations)**. Concorde, LHS and 300M models also have a bubble-level built into the top of the headlight housings for quick alignment.

2 There are several methods of adjusting the headlights. The simplest method requires a blank wall 25 feet in front of the vehicle and a level floor **(see illustration)**.

3 Position masking tape vertically on the wall in reference to the vehicle centerline and the centerlines of both headlights.

4 Position a horizontal tape line in reference to the centerline of all the headlights. **Note:** *It may be easier to position the tape on the wall with the vehicle parked only a few inches away.*

5 Adjustment should be made with the vehicle sitting level, the gas tank half-full and no unusually heavy load in the vehicle.

6 Starting with the low beam adjustment, position the high intensity zone so it is two inches below the horizontal line and two inches to the side of the vertical headlight line away from oncoming traffic. Twist the adjustment screws until the desired level has been achieved.

7 With the high beams on, the high intensity zone should be vertically centered with the exact center just below the horizontal line. **Note:** *It may not be possible to position the headlight aim exactly for both high and low beams. If a compromise must be made, keep in mind that the low beams are the most used and have the greatest effect on driver safety.*

8 Have the headlights adjusted by a dealer service department at the earliest opportunity.

Fog lights

Refer to illustration 15.11

9 On Intrepid models, the fog lights can be aimed just like headlights.

10 Position tape on a wall 25 feet in front of the vehicle **(see illustration 15.2)**. Tape a horizontal line on the wall that represents the height of the fog lamps, and another four inches below that line.

11 Using the adjusting screws on the fog lamps, adjust the pattern on the wall so that the top of the fog lamp beam meets the lower line on the wall **(see illustration)**.

16 Headlight housing - replacement

Refer to illustrations 16.1 and 16.3

1 Open the hood and remove the two long bolts at the top of the headlight housing **(see illustration)**. On Intrepid models, remove the headlight housing and refer to Section 14 to disconnect the electrical connectors and remove the bulbs.

2 To remove the headlight housings on Concorde, LHS and 300M models, remove all of the fasteners from the front bumper fascia (see Chapter 11) except for the bottom fasteners, then pull the plastic fascia ahead enough to angle the headlight housing out.

3 Disconnect the electrical connectors **(see illustration)**.

4 Installation is the reverse of removal.

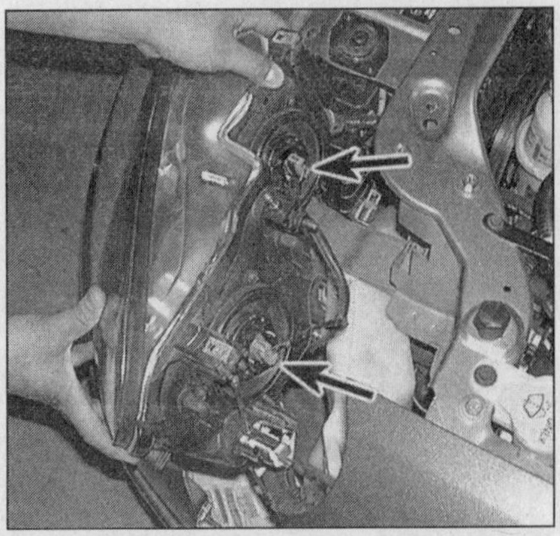

16.3 Disconnect the electrical connectors (arrows) at the back of the headlight housing

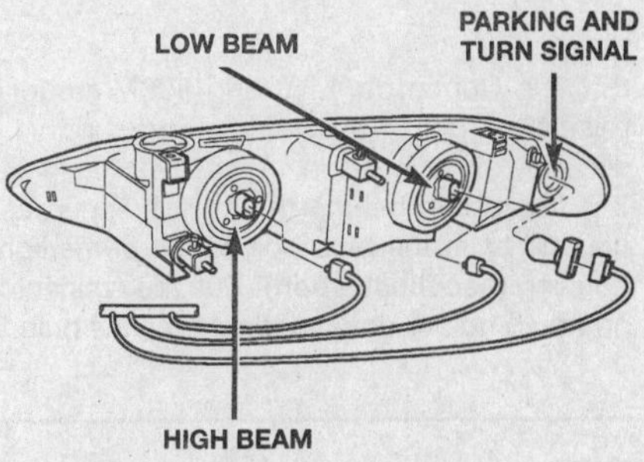

17.1 On Intrepid models, the front park turn and side marker bulbs are access from the back of the headlight housing

17 Bulb replacement

Front side marker/park/turn signal lights

Refer to illustrations 17.1 and 17.3

1 On Intrepid models, the park, turn and side marker light is part of the headlight housing. See Section 16 for removal of the headlight housing to access this bulb **(see illustration)**.

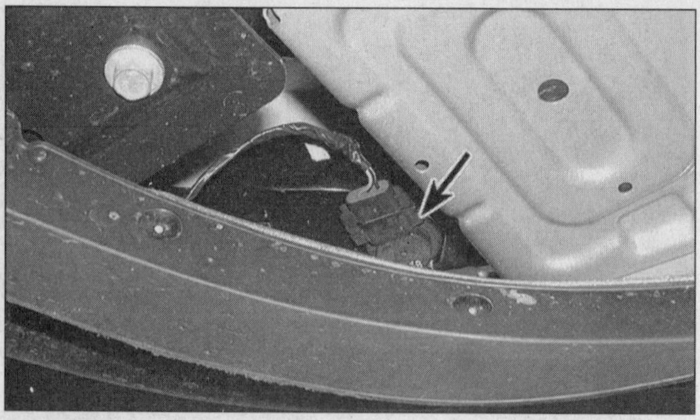

17.3 On Concorde, LHS and 300M models, the marker/park/turn bulb (arrow) is accessed from below and behind the front bumper fascia

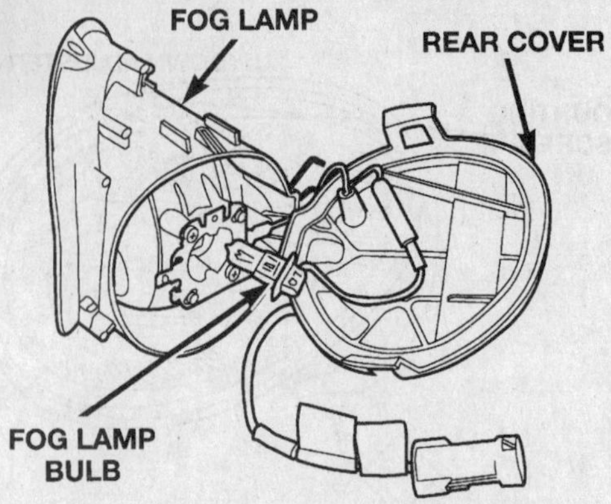

17.6 Fog light bulb replacement - Intrepid models

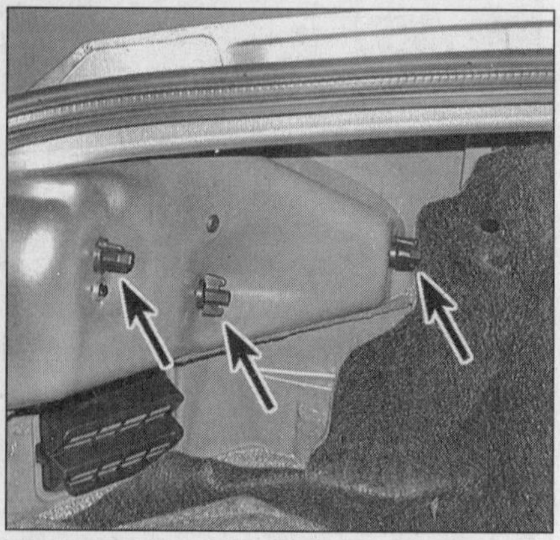

17.7 Remove the plastic pushpins and pull back the trunk liner to access the taillight housing wingnuts (arrows) - Concorde shown, Intrepid similar

17.9 Bulb holders (arrows) on the taillight housing

17.10 The license light bulb can be accessed by removing the lens screws (arrows), or by reaching up behind the bumper fascia and withdrawing the bulb holder from behind

2 On Concorde, LHS and 300M models, raise the front of the vehicle and support it securely on jackstands.

3 Reach up behind the front bumper fascia and twist the bulb holder out of the light housing **(see illustration)**. Pull the connector and bulb holder down and replace the bulb.

Fog lights (Intrepid models only)

Refer to illustration 17.6

4 Front the front of the vehicle, remove the mounting screw for the fog lamp **(see illustration 15.11)**.

5 Pull out the fog lamp assembly and pull off the rear cover, which snaps over two projections on the housing.

6 Squeeze the wire clip securing the bulb holder, pull the holder out and exchange the bulb **(see illustration)**.

Tail/stop/turn and back-up lights

Refer to illustrations 17.7 and 17.9

7 Open the trunk and pull back the trim

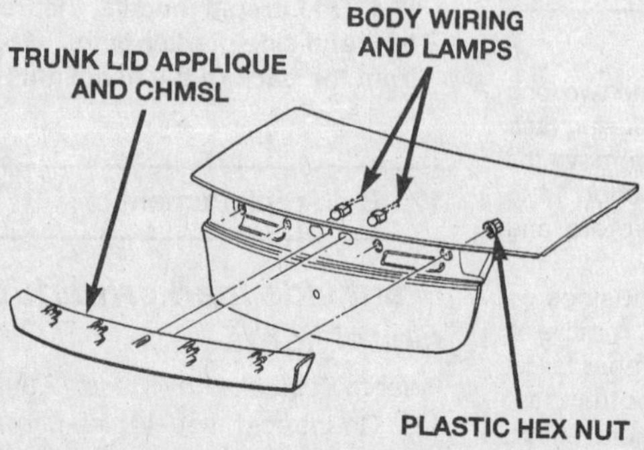

17.12 The high-mount brake light bulb holders on Intrepid models, are accessed from the interior of the trunk lid

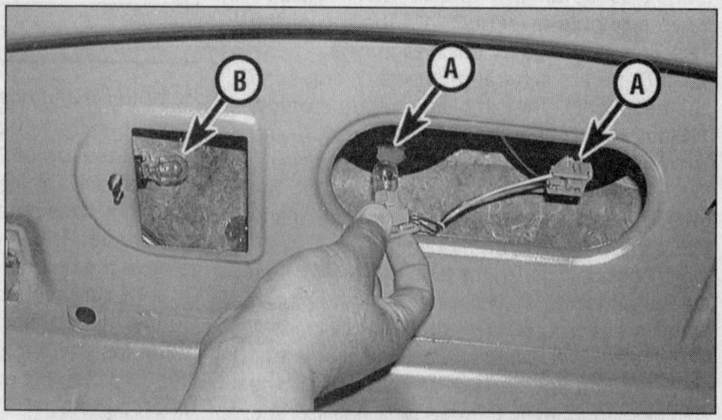

17.14 The bulb holders for the high-mount brake light (A) on Concorde, LHS and 300M models are under the rear package shelf, and accessed through the trunk - (B) is the bulb for the trunk light

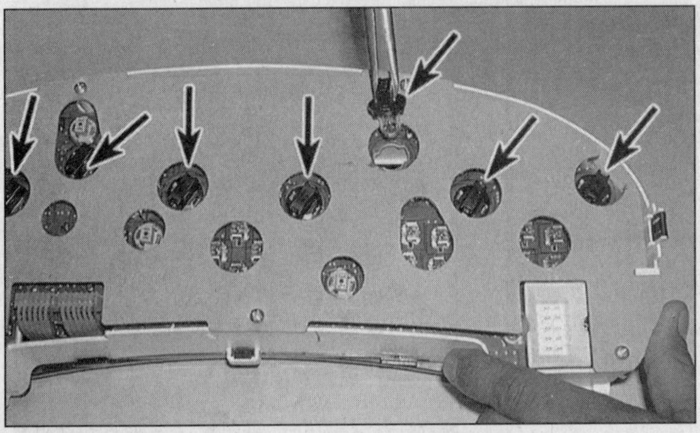

17.15 To remove an instrument cluster light bulb (arrows), depress it and turn it counterclockwise to release it

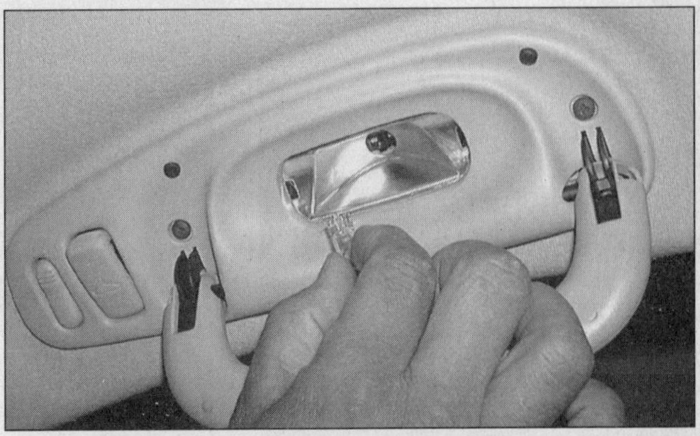

17.16 Pry off the plastic lenses for the courtesy lights (shown) or vanity mirror lights, then remove the bulbs

17.17 With the overhead console pulled down, pull out the map light bulbholders (arrow indicates one) and replace the bulbs

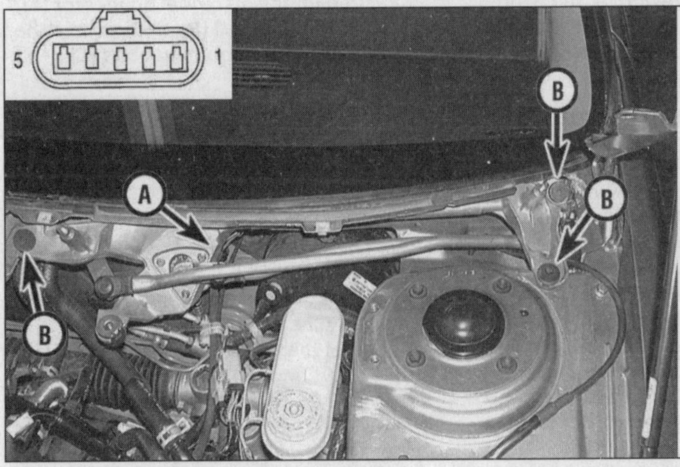

18.2 Backprobe the connector (A) at the wiper motor to check for power at terminal 2 (low) or 1 (high), then check for a good continuity to ground at terminal 5 - (B) indicates wiper assembly mounting bolts

cover for access to the fasteners on the back of the taillight housing **(see illustration)**.

8 Pull the taillight housing out enough to access the bulb holders.

9 Twist the bulbholders out, then push in on the bulbs and rotate them counterclockwise to remove them from the holder **(see illustration)**.

License plate light

Refer to illustration 17.10

10 Reach up behind the rear bumper fascia until you feel the license light bulb holder. Twist the bulb holder out and pull it down for access to the bulb **(see illustration)**.

11 Pull the bulb straight out to replace it.

High-mounted brake light

Refer to illustrations 17.12 and 17.14

12 On Intrepid models, the high-mounted brake light is part of a trim panel across the back of the trunk lid, Pull back the lower portion of the trunk lid liner and remove the two bulb holders **(see illustration)**. Install new bulbs in the holders.

13 On Concorde, LHS and 300M models, open the trunk and use a trim tool to pull down the rear of the trunk liner just behind the rear seat.

14 Twist out the two bulb holders from beneath the high-mounted brake light housing and replace the bulbs **(see illustration)**.

Instrument cluster illumination

Refer to illustration 17.15

15 To gain access to the instrument cluster illumination lights, the instrument cluster will have to be removed (see Section 11). The bulbs can then be removed and replaced from the rear of the cluster **(see illustration)**.

Interior lights

Refer to illustrations 17.16 and 17.17

16 Remove the lenses for the courtesy or vanity mirror lights by prying the cover off with a small screwdriver **(see illustration)**.

17 To replace the map light bulbs, remove the overhead console (see Chapter 11) and remove the bulbs from behind **(see illustration)**.

18 Wiper motor - check and replacement

Check

Refer to illustration 18.2

Note: *Refer to the wiring diagrams for wire colors and locations in the following checks. When checking for voltage, probe a grounded 12-volt test light to each terminal at a connector until it lights; this verifies voltage (power) at the terminal. If the following checks fail to locate the problem, have the system diagnosed by a dealer service department or other properly equipped repair facility.*

1 If the wipers work slowly, make sure the battery is in good condition and has a strong charge (see Chapter 1). If the battery is in good condition, remove the wiper motor (see below) and operate the wiper arms by hand. Check for binding linkage and pivots. Lubricate or repair the linkage or pivots as necessary. Reinstall the wiper motor. If the wipers still operate slowly, check for loose or corroded connections, especially the ground connection. If all connections look OK, replace the motor.

2 If the wipers fail to operate when activated, check the fuse. If the fuse is OK, connect a jumper wire between the wiper motor and ground, then retest. If the motor works now, repair the ground connection. If the motor still doesn't work, turn the wiper switch to the HI position and check for voltage at the motor **(see illustration)**. **Note:** *The cowl cover will have to be removed (see Chapter 11).* If there's voltage at the connector, remove the motor and check it off the vehicle with fused jumper wires from the battery. If

18.6 Use a small screwdriver to pry off the wiper arm nut cover, then remove the nut and pull the arm straight off its splined shaft

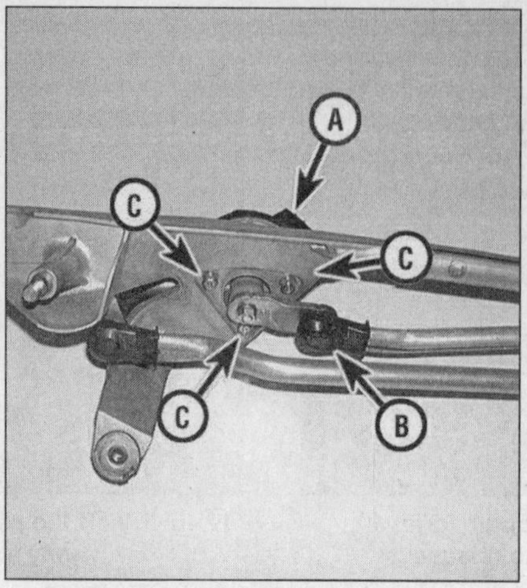

18.10 Unplug the electrical connector (A), pry off the linkage rod (B), and remove the wiper motor mounting bolts (C)

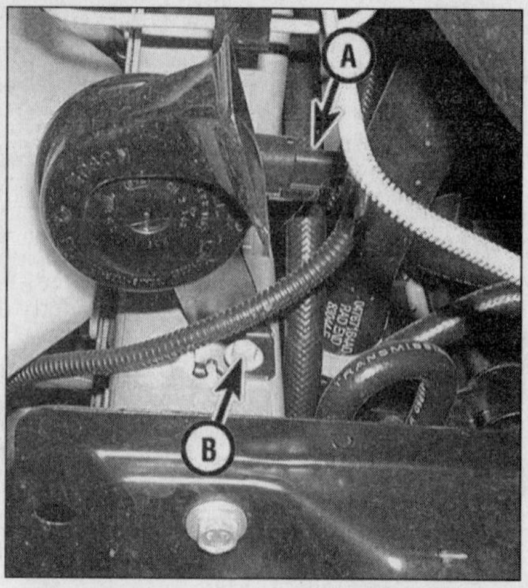

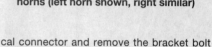

19.1 Unplug the electrical connector (A) and remove the bolt (B), then detach the horns (left horn shown, right similar)

the motor now works, check for binding linkage (see Step 1 above). If the motor still doesn't work, replace it. If there's no voltage to the motor, check for voltage at the wiper control relays in the power distribution center (see Section 5 for relay testing). If there's voltage at the wiper control relays and no voltage at the wiper motor, check the multi-function switch for continuity (see Section 7).

3 If the wipers stop at the position they're in when the switch is turned off (fail to park), check for a good ground on the connector side at the motor. With an ohmmeter connected between any of the black wire terminals and a known ground, resistance should be less than 5 ohms.

4 If the wipers won't shut off unless the ignition is OFF, disconnect the wiring from the wiper control switch. If the wipers stop, replace the switch. If the wipers keep running, there's a defective limit switch in the motor; replace the motor.

5 If the wipers won't retract below the hood line, check for mechanical obstructions in the wiper linkage or on the vehicle's body that would prevent the wipers from parking. If there are no obstructions, check the wiring between the switch and motor for continuity. If the wiring is OK, replace the wiper motor.

Replacement

Refer to illustrations 18.6 and 18.10

6 Remove the windshield wiper arms **(see illustration)**.

7 Remove the cowl cover and the strut tower reinforcement (see Chapter 11).

8 Disconnect the electrical connector from the wiper motor **(see illustration 18.2)**.

9 Detach the wiper motor/linkage assembly from the cowl **(see illustration 18.2)**.

10 Remove the wiper motor retaining bolts and remove the motor **(see illustration)**.

11 Installation is the reverse of removal.

19 Horn - check and replacement

Refer to illustration 19.1

Note: *Check the fuse before beginning electrical diagnosis.*

1 Unplug the electrical connector from the horns **(see illustration)**.

2 To test the horns, refer to the wiring diagrams and connect battery voltage to the dark green/red-wire terminals, and temporarily ground the two black-wire terminals with a pair of jumper wires. If the horns don't sound, replace them. If they do sound, the problem lies in the switch, relay or the wiring between the components.

3 Refer to Section 5 for testing of the relay, which is located in the interior fuse/relay box.

4 To replace the horn, unplug the electrical connector and remove the bracket bolt **(see illustration 19.1)**.

5 Installation is the reverse of removal.

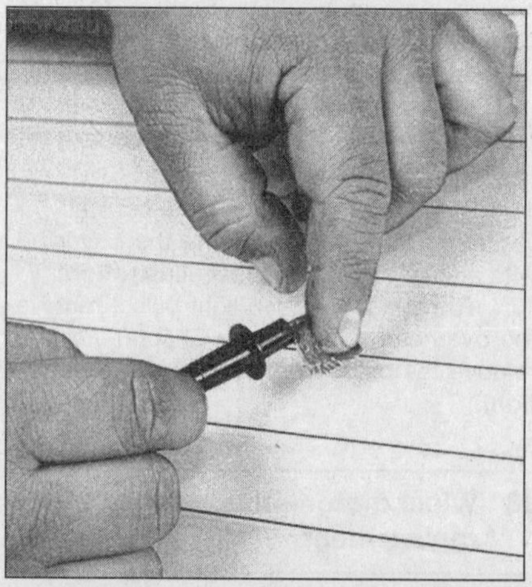

21.5 When measuring the voltage at the rear window defogger grid, wrap a piece of aluminum foil around the negative probe of the voltmeter and press the foil against the wire with your finger

20 Daytime Running Lights (DRL) - general information

The Daytime Running Lights (DRL) system used on Canadian models turns the headlights on whenever the engine is started. The only exception is when the engine is turned on when the parking brake is engaged. Once the parking brake is released, the lights will remain on as long as the ignition switch is on, even if the parking brake is later applied.

The DRL system supplies reduced power to the headlights so they won't be too bright for daytime use while prolonging headlight life.

21 Rear window defogger - check and repair

1 The rear window defogger consists of a number of horizontal heating elements baked onto the inside surface of the glass. Power is supplied through a large fuse from the power distribution box in the engine compartment. The heater is controlled by the instrument panel switch, which is part of the heating/air-conditioning controls. Test the switch for continuity (see Chapter 3). **Note:** *On Intrepid models, the rear window grid is used as a defogger only, while on Concorde, LHS and 300M models, the defogger grid also serves as the antenna for the FM portion of the radio. On those models, a separate, two-line grid (above the defogger grid) is unheated and used for the AM antenna.*

2 Small breaks in the element can be repaired without removing the rear window.

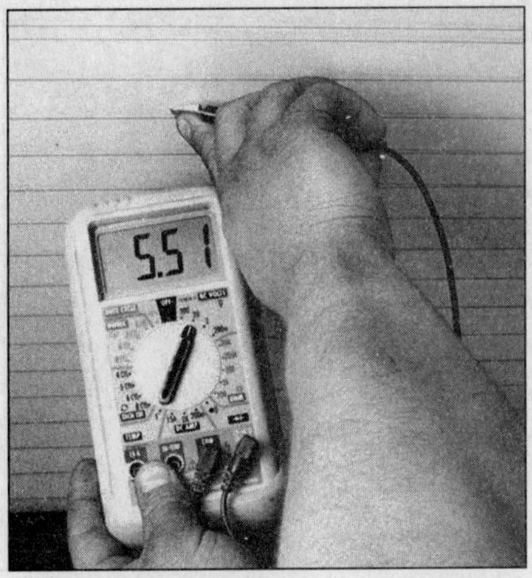

21.6 To determine if a heating element has broken, check the voltage at the center of each element - if the voltage is 6-volts, the element is unbroken

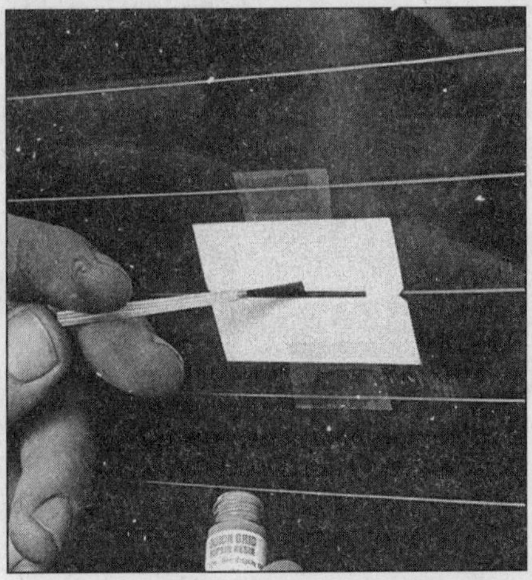

21.14 To use a defogger repair kit, apply masking tape to the inside of the window at the damaged area, then brush on the special conductive coating

Check

Refer to illustrations 21.5 and 21.6

3 Turn the ignition switch and defogger switches to the ON position.

4 Using a voltmeter, place the positive probe against the defogger grid positive terminal and the negative probe against the ground terminal. If battery voltage is not indicated, check the fuse, defogger switch, defogger relay and related wiring. If voltage is indicated, but all or part of the defogger doesn't heat, proceed with the following tests.

5 When measuring voltage during the next two tests, wrap a piece of aluminum foil around the tip of the voltmeter positive probe and press the foil against the heating element with your finger **(see illustration)**. Place the negative probe on the defogger grid ground terminal.

6 Check the voltage at the center of each heating element **(see illustration)**. If the voltage is 5 to 6 volts, the element is okay (there is no break). If the voltage is 0 volts, the element is broken between the center of the element and the positive end. If the voltage is 10 to 12 volts the element is broken between the center of the element and the ground side. Check each heating element.

7 If none of the elements are broken, connect the negative probe to a good chassis ground. The voltage reading should stay the same, if it doesn't the ground connection is bad.

8 To find the break, place the voltmeter negative probe against the defogger ground terminal. Place the voltmeter positive probe with the foil strip against the heating element at the positive side and slide it toward the negative side. The point at which the voltmeter deflects from several volts to zero is the point where the heating element is broken.

Repair

Refer to illustration 21.14

9 Repair the break in the element using a repair kit specifically for this purpose, such as Dupont paste No. 4817 (or equivalent). The kit includes conductive plastic epoxy.

10 Before repairing a break, turn off the system and allow it to cool for a few minutes.

11 Lightly buff the element area with fine steel wool; then clean it thoroughly with rubbing alcohol.

12 Use masking tape to mask off the area being repaired.

13 Thoroughly mix the epoxy, following the kit instructions.

14 Apply the epoxy material to the slit in the masking tape, overlapping the undamaged area about 3/4-inch on either end **(see illustration)**.

15 Allow the repair to cure for 24 hours before removing the tape and using the system.

22 Cruise control system - description and check

Refer to illustrations 22.5 and 22.8

1 The cruise control system maintains vehicle speed with a vacuum-actuated servo motor located on the left fenderwell near the battery, which is connected to the throttle linkage by a cable. The system consists of the servo motor, brake switch, vacuum pump, control switches, a relay and associated vacuum hoses. Some features of the system require special testers and diagnostic procedures that are beyond the scope of the home mechanic. Listed below are some general procedures that may be used to locate common problems.

2 Check the fuse (see Section 3).

3 The brake pedal position (BPP) switch (or stop lamp switch) deactivates the cruise control system. Have an assistant press the brake pedal while you check the stop lamp operation.

4 If the brake lights do not operate properly, correct the problem and retest the cruise control.

5 Check the control cable between the cruise control servo/amplifier and the throttle linkage and replace as necessary **(see illustration)**. There is no separate adjustment of cable length for the cruise control system, but refer to Chapter 4 for adjustment of the throttle linkage, which is on the same bracket as the cruise control cable.

6 The cruise control system uses information from the PCM, including the Vehicle Speed Sensor, which is located in the transmission. To test the speed sensor, see Chapter 6.

7 The testing of the steering-wheel-mounted cruise control switches is covered in Section 7. **Note:** *Make sure the horn works before testing the cruise control system, as the cruise control switch gets power from the horn relay.*

8 Some tests of the servo can be made by the home mechanic. Turn the cruise control and ignition key to On (engine not running). Disconnect the electrical connector at the

22.5 The cruise control servo (A) is located near the underhood fuse/relay box, - make sure the cruise control cable (B) mounted on the throttle body is not damaged and that it operates smoothly when the throttle is opened, C indicates the servo mounting bolts

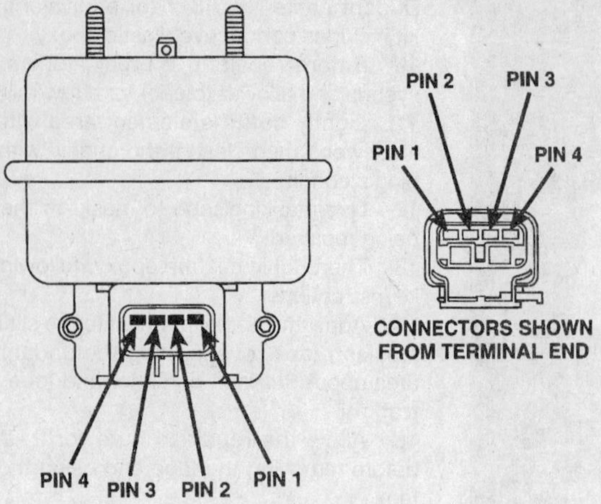

22.8 Pin identification for the cruise control servo and its connector

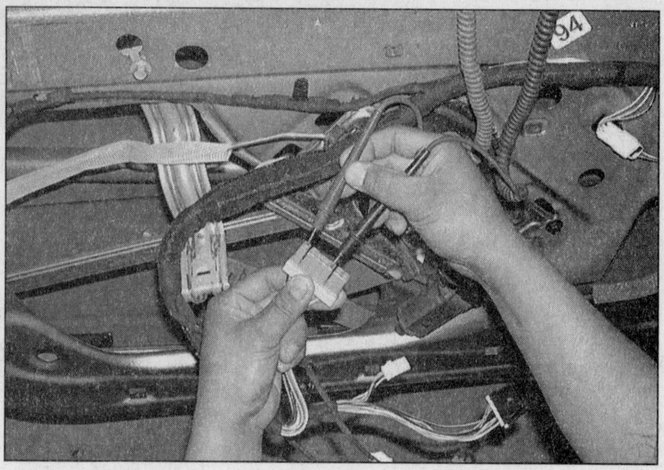

23.12a With the door panel removed, check for power at Pin 1 on the master power window switch connector (attach voltmeter ground to pin 10)

servo and hook pin 3 on each side (at the servo and at the connector) with a jumper wire **(see illustration)**. Attach jumpers to pins 2 and 4 on the servo and ground them in the engine compartment.

9 Using a hand-held vacuum pump, apply 10-15 inches of vacuum to the vacuum port on the servo. If the cable moves, the servo must be replaced. If it didn't move, now ground pin 1 at the servo with a jumper wire and the cable should move the throttle.

10 Also check that proper vacuum is available to the servo. Attach a vacuum gauge to the hose leading to the cruise control servo, and make sure that it shows at least 10 inches of vacuum with the engine running. If not, look for a vacuum leak somewhere.

11 Test-drive the vehicle to determine if the cruise control is now working. If it isn't, take it to a dealer service department or an automotive electrical specialist for further diagnosis.

23 Power window system - description and check

Refer to illustrations 23.12a, 23.12b and 23.15

1 The power window system operates the electric motors mounted in the doors which lower and raise the windows. The system consists of the control switches, the motors (regulators), glass mechanisms and associated wiring.

2 Power windows are wired so they can be lowered and raised from the master control switch by the driver or by remote switches located at the individual windows. Each window has a separate motor that is reversible. The position of the control switch determines the polarity and therefore the direction of operation. Some systems are equipped with relays that control current flow to the motors.

3 Some vehicles are equipped with a separate circuit breaker for each motor in addition to the fuse or circuit breaker protecting the whole circuit. This prevents one stuck window from disabling the whole system.

4 The power window system will only operate when the ignition switch is ON. In addition, many models have a window lock-out switch at the master control switch which, when activated, disables the switches at the rear windows and, sometimes, the switch at the passenger's window also.

SWITCH POSITION		CONTINUITY BETWEEN TERMINALS
OFF		PIN 8 to 10 PIN 8 to 11 PIN 8 to 7 PIN 8 to 6 PIN 8 to 3 PIN 8 to 4 PIN 8 to 9 PIN 8 to 2
UP	DRIVER'S	PIN 8 to 10 PIN 5 to 11
UP	RIGHT FRONT	PIN 8 to 7 PIN 5 to 6
UP	LEFT REAR	PIN 8 to 3 PIN 5 to 4
UP	RIGHT REAR	PIN 8 to 9 PIN 5 to 2
DOWN	DRIVER'S	PIN 8 to 11 PIN 5 to 10
DOWN	RIGHT FRONT	PIN 8 to 6 PIN 5 to 7
DOWN	LEFT REAR	PIN 8 to 4 PIN 5 to 3
DOWN	RIGHT REAR	PIN 8 to 2 PIN 5 to 9
WINDOW LOCK		PIN 5 to 1

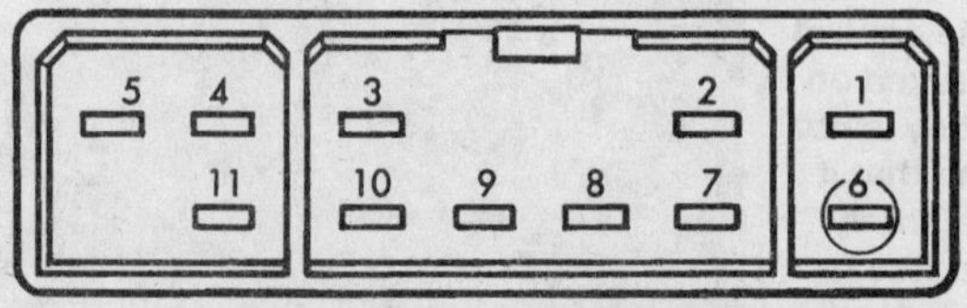

23.12b Pin identification and continuity test for master power window switch

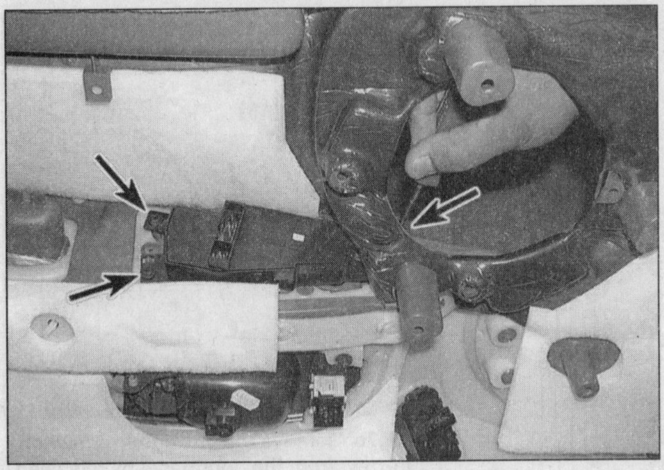

23.15 Remove the three mounting screws (arrows) from the door panel to replace the power window master switch

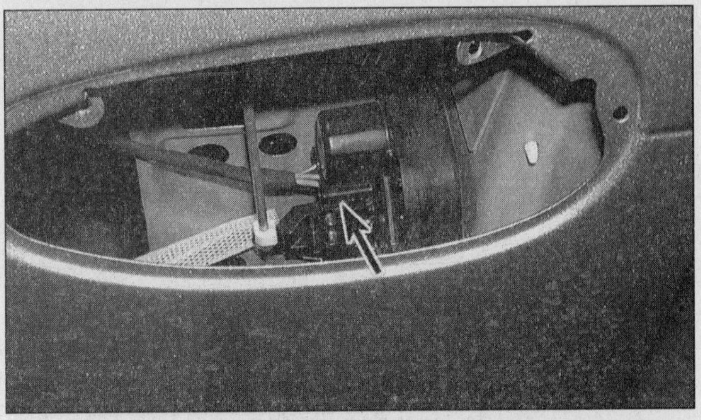

24.10 Check for power at the door lock actuator connector (arrow) with the switch depressed - check the door lock actuator itself by disconnecting the connector and using jumper wires to temporarily apply battery voltage and ground directly (shown through door handle opening)

Always check these items before troubleshooting a window problem.

5 These procedures are general in nature, so if you can't find the problem using them, take the vehicle to a dealer service department.

6 If the power windows don't work at all, check the fuse or circuit breaker.

7 If only the rear windows are inoperative, or if the windows only operate from the master control switch, check the rear window lockout switch for continuity in the unlocked position. Replace it if it doesn't have continuity.

8 Check the wiring between the switches and fuse panel for continuity. Repair the wiring, if necessary.

9 If only one window is inoperative from the master control switch, try the other control switch at the window. **Note:** *This doesn't apply to the drivers door window*.

10 If the same window works from one switch, but not the other, check the switch for continuity.

11 If the switch tests OK, check for a short or open in the wiring between the affected switch and the window motor.

12 If one window is inoperative from both switches, remove the trim panel from the affected door and check for voltage at the switch and at the motor while the switch is operated. First check for voltage at the connector side **(see illustration)**. If voltage is there, use an ohmmeter to check the continuity of the switch in each position **(see illustration)**.

13 If voltage is reaching the motor and the switch is OK, disconnect the glass from the regulator (see Chapter 11). Move the window up and down by hand while checking for binding and damage. Also check for binding and damage to the regulator. If the regulator is not damaged and the window moves up and down smoothly, replace the motor. If there's binding or damage, lubricate, repair or replace parts, as necessary.

14 If voltage isn't reaching the motor, check the wiring in the circuit for continuity between the switches and motors. You'll need to consult the wiring diagram for the vehicle. Some power window circuits are equipped with relays. If equipped, check that the relays are grounded properly and receiving voltage from the switches. Also check that each relay sends voltage to the motor when the switch is turned on. If it doesn't, replace the relay.

15 Test the windows after you are done to confirm proper repairs. If the main power window switch is to be replaced, remove the mounting screws from the back of the door panel **(see illustration)**.

24 Power door lock system and keyless entry - description and check

Refer to illustration 24.10

1 The power door lock system operates the door lock actuators mounted in each door. The system consists of the switches, actuators and associated wiring. Diagnosis can usually be limited to simple checks of the wiring connections and actuators for minor faults that can be easily repaired.

2 Power door lock systems are operated by bi-directional solenoids located in the doors. The lock switches have two operating positions: Lock and Unlock. These switches activate a relay, which in turn connects voltage to the door lock solenoids. Depending on which way the relay is activated, it reverses polarity, allowing the two sides of the circuit to be used alternately as the feed (positive) and ground side.

3 Some vehicles may have keyless entry, electronic control modules and anti-theft systems incorporated into the power locks. If you are unable to locate the trouble using the following general steps, consult your dealer service department. **Note:** *Some vehicles also have control switches connected to the key locks in the doors, which unlock all the doors when one is unlocked.*

4 Always check the circuit protection first. Some vehicles use a combination of circuit breakers and fuses. Refer to the wiring diagrams at the end of this Chapter.

5 Operate the door lock switches in both directions (Lock and Unlock) with the engine off. Listen for the faint click of the relay operating.

6 If there's no click, check for voltage at the switches. If no voltage is present, check the wiring between the fuse panel and the switches for shorts and opens.

7 If voltage is present but no click is heard, test the switch for continuity. Replace it if there's not continuity in both switch positions.

8 If the switch has continuity but the relay doesn't click, check the wiring between the switch and relay for continuity. Repair the wiring if there's no continuity.

9 If the relay is receiving voltage from the switch but is not sending voltage to the solenoids, check for a bad ground at the relay case. If the relay case is grounding properly, replace the relay.

10 If all but one lock solenoids operate, remove the trim panel from the affected door (see Chapter 11) and check for voltage at the solenoid while the lock switch is operated **(see illustration)**. One of the wires should have voltage in the Lock position; the other should have voltage in the Unlock position.

11 If the inoperative solenoid is receiving voltage, replace the solenoid.

12 If the inoperative solenoid isn't receiving voltage, check for an open or short in the wire between the lock solenoid and the relay. **Note:** *It's common for wires to break in the portion of the harness between the body and door (opening and closing the door fatigues and eventually breaks the wires).*

13 On the models covered by this manual, power door lock system communication goes through the Body Control Module. If the above tests do not pinpoint a problem, take the vehicle to a dealer or qualified shop with the proper scan tool to retrieve trouble codes from the BCM.

SWITCH POSITION MOVE BUTTON	CONTINUITY BETWEEN TERMINALS
MIRROR IN "L" POSITION	
UP	PIN 11 TO 12 PIN 12 TO 13 PIN 9 TO 1
RIGHT	PIN 11 TO 1 PIN 9 TO 7 PIN 9 TO 8
DOWN	PIN 11 TO 1 PIN 9 TO 12 PIN 9 TO 13
LEFT	PIN 11 TO 7 PIN 11 TO 8 PIN 9 TO 1
MIRROR IN "R" POSITION	
UP	PIN 11 TO 12 PIN 11 TO 13 PIN 9 TO 2
RIGHT	PIN 11 TO 6 PIN 9 TO 7 PIN 9 TO 8
DOWN	PIN 11 TO 6 PIN 9 TO 12 PIN 9 TO 13
LEFT	PIN 11 TO 7 PIN 11 TO 8 PIN 9 TO 6

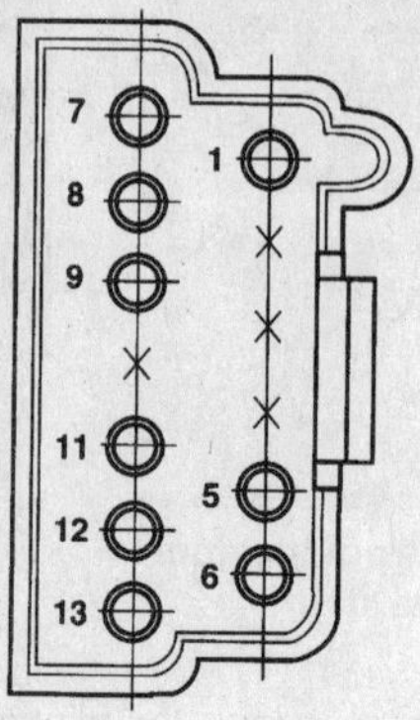

25.7a Power mirror switch terminal identification and continuity tests

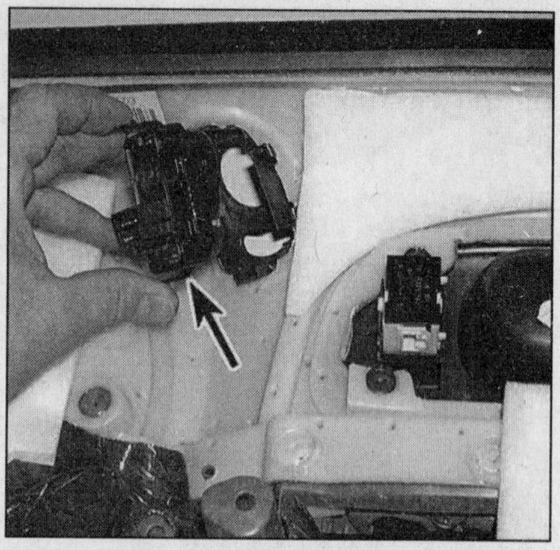

25.7b Remove the power mirror switch (arrow) from the door panel by releasing the clips

Keyless entry system

14 The keyless entry system consists of a remote control transmitter that sends a coded infrared signal to a receiver, which then operates the door, lock system.

15 Replace the batteries when the transmitter doesn't operate the locks at a distance of 10 feet. Normal range should be about 30 feet.

16 Use a small screwdriver to carefully separate the case halves.

17 Replace the two CR2016 lithium batteries.

18 Snap the case halves together.

25 Electric side view mirrors - description and check

Refer to illustration 25.7a and 25.7b

1 Most electric side view mirrors use two motors to move the glass; one for up and down adjustments and one for left-right adjustments.

2 The control switch has a selector portion that sends voltage to the left or right side mirror. With the ignition ON but the engine OFF, roll down the windows and operate the mirror control switch through all functions (left-right and up-down) for both the left and right side mirrors.

3 Listen carefully for the sound of the electric motors running in the mirrors.

4 If the motors can be heard but the mirror glass doesn't move, there's probably a problem with the drive mechanism inside the mirror. Remove and disassemble the mirror to locate the problem.

5 If the mirrors don't operate and no sound comes from the mirrors, check the fuse (see Chapter 1).

6 If the fuse is OK, remove the mirror control switch from its mounting without disconnecting the wires attached to it (see Chapter 11 for door panel removal). Turn the ignition ON and check for voltage at the switch. There should be voltage at terminal 1. If there's no voltage at the switch, check for an open or short in the wiring between the fuse panel and the switch.

7 If there's voltage at the switch, disconnect it. Check the switch for continuity in all its operating positions **(see illustration)**. If the switch does not have continuity, replace it **(see illustration)**.

8 Re-connect the switch. Locate the wire going from the switch to ground. Leaving the switch connected, connect a jumper wire between this wire and ground. If the mirror works normally with this wire in place, repair the faulty ground connection.

9 If the mirror still doesn't work, remove the mirror and check the wires at the mirror for voltage. Check with ignition ON and the mirror selector switch on the appropriate side. Operate the mirror switch in all its positions. There should be voltage at one of the switch-to-mirror wires in each switch position (except the neutral "off" position).

10 If voltage isn't present in each switch position, check the wiring between the mirror and control switch for opens and shorts.

11 If there's voltage, remove the mirror and test it off the vehicle with jumper wires. Replace the mirror if it fails this test.

26 Electric sunroof motor/module - check and replacement

Check

1 The electric sunroof is powered by a single motor located in the roof behind the headliner, near the overhead console. When sunlight isn't desired, an interior sliding panel can be closed.

2 The control switch (tilt and slide) sends a ground signal to the sunroof motor when the switch is pressed. With the ignition On but the engine Off, operate the sunroof control switch through the tilt and slide functions.

3 Listen carefully for the sound of the sunroof motor running in the roof.

4 If the motors can be heard but the sunroof glass doesn't move, there's probably a problem with the drive mechanism or drive cables.

5 If the sunroof does not operate and no sound comes from the motor, check the fuse (10-amp fuse number 14 in the interior fuse panel, and 20-amp fuse F in the PDC.

6 If the fuses are OK, further testing or repairs require the interior headliner be removed (see Chapter 11). Turn the ignition On and check for voltage at the red wire (battery power) and the dark blue/white wire (voltage with ignition On) at the motor. If there's voltage at the motor, check for power and ground at the switch. If power and ground exist at the motor and there's still no voltage at the switch replace the switch.

7 If there's voltage at the switch, disconnect it. Check the switch for continuity in all its operating positions. If the switch does not have continuity, replace it.

8 If the switch has continuity re-connect the switch. Locate the wire going from the switch to ground. Leaving the switch connected, connect a jumper wire between this wire and ground. If the motor works normally with this wire in place, repair the faulty ground connection.

Replacement

9 Refer to Chapter 11 for headliner removal.

SWITCH POSITION	CONTINUITY BETWEEN PINS	
	DRIVER	PASSENGER
OFF	PIN 5 TO 4 PIN 5 TO 3 PIN 5 TO 2 PIN 5 TO 10 PIN 5 TO 9 PIN 5 TO 8 PIN 5 TO 7 PIN 5 TO 6	PIN 5 TO 4 PIN 5 TO 3 PIN 5 TO 2 PIN 5 TO 10 PIN 5 TO 9 PIN 5 TO 8 PIN 5 TO 7 PIN 5 TO 6
FRONT RISER UP	PIN 5 TO 6 PIN 1 TO 9	PIN 5 TO 9 PIN 1 TO 6
FRONT RISER DOWN	PIN 5 TO 9 PIN 1 TO 6	PIN 5 TO 6 PIN 1 TO 9
CENTER SWITCH FORWARD	PIN 5 TO 3 PIN 1 TO 10	PIN 5 TO 3 PIN 1 TO 10
CENTER SWITCH REARWARD	PIN 5 TO 10 PIN 3 TO 1	PIN 5 TO 10 PIN 3 TO 1
REAR RISER UP	PIN 5 TO 7 PIN 1 TO 8	PIN 5 TO 8 PIN 1 TO 7
REAR RISER DOWN	PIN 5 TO 8 PIN 1 TO 7	PIN 5 TO 7 PIN 1 TO 8
RECLINER UP	PIN 5 TO 2 PIN 4 TO 1	PIN 5 TO 2 PIN 4 TO 1
RECLINER DOWN	PIN 5 TO 4 PIN 2 TO 1	PIN 5 TO 4 PIN 2 TO 1

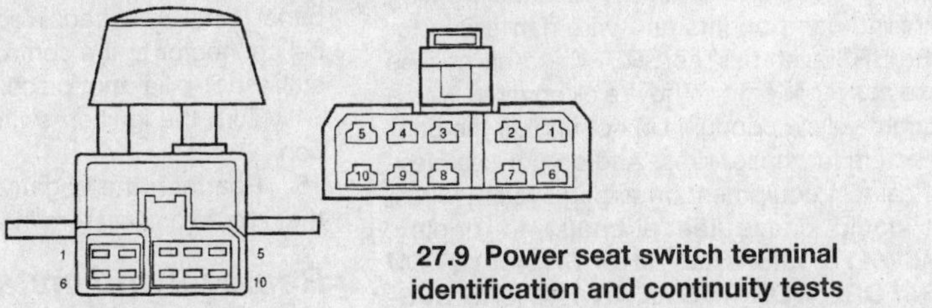

27.9 Power seat switch terminal identification and continuity tests

10 The sunroof must be fully closed if the motor is to be removed. **Warning:** *Do not remove the sunroof motor unless the sunroof is completely closed. Otherwise a new motor will have to be installed and timed with a tool that comes with the new motor.*

11 The motor and the sunroof express module are both accessible once the headliner is removed.

12 Disconnect the electrical connector at the motor/module.

13 Remove the motor mounting bolts and remove the motor from the housing.

14 Installation is the reverse of removal procedure. **Note:** *A gauge for timing the cables to the motor comes with a new motor.*

27 Power seats - description and check

Refer to illustration 27.9

1 Power seats allow you to adjust the position of the seat with little effort. The optional power seats on these models adjust forward and backward, up and down and tilt forward and backward.

2 The power seat system consists of a motor, a switch on the seat, and the #2 circuit breaker (under the left end of the instrument panel).

3 Look under the seat for any objects which may be preventing the seat from moving.

4 If the seat won't work at all, check the circuit breaker (see Section 4).

5 With the engine off to reduce the noise level, operate the seat controls in all directions and listen for sound coming from the seat motors.

6 If the motors run or click but the seat doesn't move, the seat drive mechanism is damaged and the motor assembly must be replaced.

7 If the motor doesn't work or make noise, check for voltage at the motor while an assistant operates the switch.

8 If the motor is getting voltage but doesn't run, test it off the vehicle with jumper wires. If it still doesn't work, replace it (see Chapter 11 for seat removal).

9 If the motor isn't getting voltage, check for voltage at the switch. If there's no voltage at the switch, check the wiring between the fuse panel and the switch. If there's voltage at the switch, check the switch for continuity in all its operating positions **(see illustration)**. Replace the switch if there's no continuity.

10 If the switch is OK, check for a short or open in the wiring between the switch and motor.

11 Test the completed repairs.

28 Programmable Communications Interface (PCI) - description

1 The vehicles covered by this manual have a complex electrical system, encompassing many power accessories, and a number of separate electronic modules.

2 The Powertrain Control Module (PCM) is mainly responsible for engine and transaxle control, but also communicates with other modules around the vehicle through a PCI Bus terminal. Many of the computer functions involved in the operation of body systems are routed through the Body Control Module (BCM), which communicates with the PCM through the PCI port.

3 Among the systems connected to the BCM and PCI are the instrument cluster, windshield wiper/washer, power door locks, security system and heating/air-conditioning system.

4 All of the modules in the vehicle have associated trouble codes. When other troubleshooting procedures fail to pinpoint the problem, check the wiring diagrams at the end of this Chapter to see if the BCM or PCI are involved in the circuit. If so, bring your vehicle to a dealer with the factory diagnostic tools to extract the trouble codes.

29 Airbag system - general information

Refer to illustrations 29.1, 29.11 and 29.18

1 These models are equipped with Supplemental Restraint System (SRS), more commonly known as airbags, designed to protect the driver and front seat passenger from serious injury in the event of a head-on, or frontal collision, and on 2001 and later models, in the event of a side impact collision. All models have a diagnostic/control unit located under the dashboard, just ahead of the floor console **(see illustration)**.

Airbag modules

2 The airbag modules consist of a housing

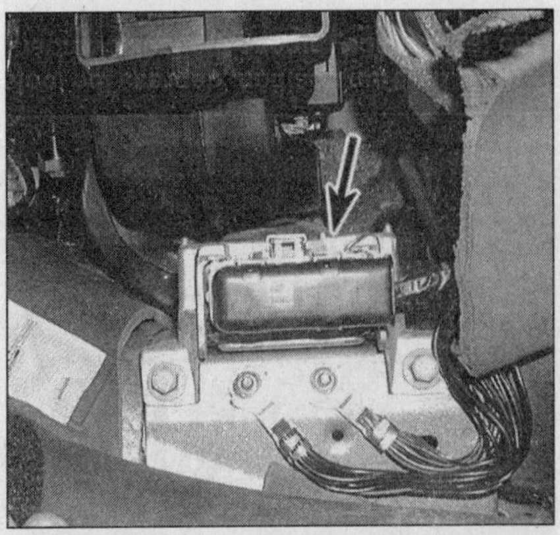

29.1 The airbag Control Module (arrow) is located on the floor ahead of the floor console, just under the dashboard

29.11 Disconnect the passenger airbag module connector (arrow)

incorporating the cushion (airbag) and inflator unit. The inflator assembly is mounted on the back of the housing over a hole through which gas is expelled, inflating the bag almost instantaneously when an electrical signal is sent from the system. The specially-wound wire on the driver's side that carries this signal to the module is called a spiral cable. The spiral cable is a flat, ribbon-like electrically conductive tape that is wound many times so that it can transmit an electrical signal regardless of steering wheel position.

Diagnostic/control unit and sensors

3 The diagnostic/control unit contains an on-board microprocessor which monitors the operation of the system, and also contains a crash sensor. It checks this system every time the vehicle is started, causing the "AIRBAG" light to go on then off after six or seven seconds, if the system is operating properly. If there is a fault in the system, the light will go on and continue, either illuminated steadily or blinking, and the unit will store fault codes indicating the nature of the fault.

Operation

4 For the airbag(s) to deploy, one or both impact sensors and the safing sensor must be activated. When this condition occurs, the circuit to the airbag inflator is closed and the airbag inflates. If the battery is destroyed by the impact, or is too low to power the inflator, a back-up power unit inside the SRS unit provides power.

Self-diagnosis system

5 A self-diagnosis circuit in the SRS unit displays a light on the instrument panel when the ignition switch is turned to the On position. If the system is operating normally, the light should go out after about seven seconds. If the light doesn't come on, or doesn't go out after seven seconds, or if it comes on while you're driving the vehicle, or if it blinks at any time, there's a malfunction in the SRS system. Have it inspected and repaired as soon as possible. Do not attempt to troubleshoot or service the SRS system yourself. Even a small mistake could cause the SRS system to malfunction when you need it.

Servicing components near the SRS system

6 Nevertheless, there are times when you need to remove the steering wheel, radio or service other components on or near the dashboard. At these times, you'll be working around components and wire harnesses for the SRS system. The SRS wiring harnesses are easy to identify: They're all covered with a bright yellow conduit. Do not unplug the connectors for these wires. And do not use electrical test equipment on airbag system wires; it could cause the airbag(s) to deploy. ***ALWAYS DISABLE THE SRS SYSTEM BEFORE WORKING NEAR THE SRS SYSTEM COMPONENTS OR RELATED WIRING.***

Disabling the SRS system

Warning: *Any time you are working in the vicinity of airbag wiring or components, DISABLE THE SRS SYSTEM.*

7 Disconnect the negative battery cable from the remote ground terminal (see Chapter 5). Wait at least two minutes for the backup power supply to be depleted before beginning work.

Driver's side airbag

8 Remove the steering column covers and unplug the two-pin connector between the airbag and the spiral cable reel (see Chapter 10).

Passenger's side airbag

9 Open the glove box. Refer to Chapter 11 to remove the glove box.

10 Remove the screws and the glove box liner.

11 At the right of the glove box opening, disconnect the two-pin electrical connector (yellow harness) between the passenger side airbag and the SRS main wiring harness **(see illustration)**.

Side air bag

12 Remove the lower B-pillar trim piece. Disconnect the electrical connector from the side airbag control module.

Enabling the system

13 After you've disabled the airbag and performed the necessary service, reconnect the two-pin airbag connector into the two-pin spiral cable reel connector (driver's side), the SRS main harness (passenger's side) Reinstall the lid to the underside of the steering wheel or reinstall the glove box or seat back panel. On side airbags, reconnect the electrical connector to the control module and reinstall the B-pillar trim piece.

14 Turn the ignition switch to the Off position.

15 Reattach the negative battery cable to the remote ground terminal (see Chapter 5).

Removal and installation

Driver's side airbag

16 Refer to Chapter 10 for removal and installation of the driver's side airbag.

Passenger side airbag

17 Disable the airbag system, see the **Warning** above.

18 On 1998 models, the passenger airbag can't be removed unless the instrument panel is removed (see Chapter 11). On 1999 and later models, the instrument panel needs to be "almost" removed, i.e. only the right end of the instrument panel needs to be raised, and the main electrical connectors on the left end do not need to be disconnected.

19 Disconnect the two-pin connector **(see illustration 29.11)**. Remove the screws and gently pry the airbag unit from the back of the dashboard with a screwdriver **(see illustration)**. **Caution:** *The airbag assembly is heavier than it looks, use both hands when removing it from the dash.*

20 Installation is the reverse of the removal procedure.

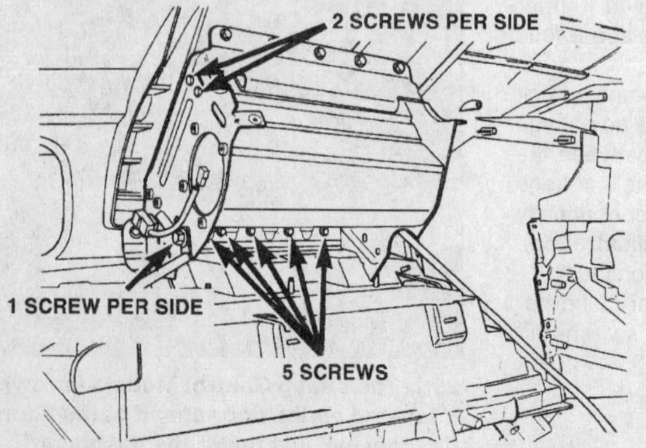

29.18 The passenger airbag is hard to access (this view is of the back of the instrument panel, removed from the vehicle) - remove the screws to the pencil braces first, then the side screws, and the lower screws

Side air bag

21 Disassemble the airbag system, see the **Warning** above.

22 Remove the lower B-pillar trim piece. Disconnect the electrical connector from the side airbag control module.

23 Remove the front seat (see Chapter 11, section 27).

COLOR CODE	COLOR	STANDARD TRACER COLOR
BL	BLUE	WT
BK	BLACK	WT
BR	BROWN	WT
DB	DARK BLUE	WT
DG	DARK GREEN	WT
GY	GRAY	BK
LB	LIGHT BLUE	BK
LG	LIGHT GREEN	BK
OR	ORANGE	BK
PK	PINK	BK or WT
RD	RED	WT
TN	TAN	WT
VT	VIOLET	WT
WT	WHITE	BK
YL	YELLOW	BK
*	WITH TRACER	

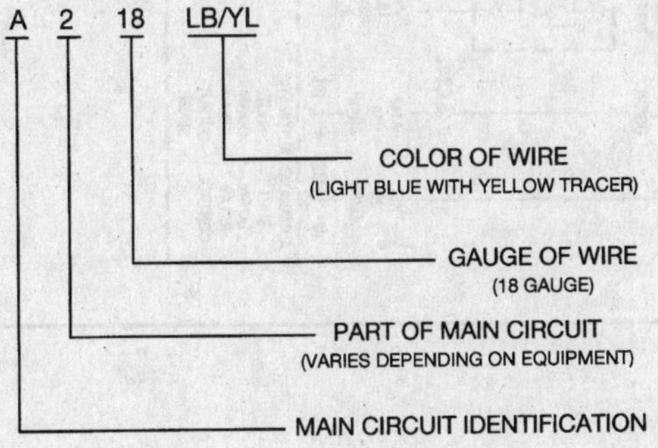

CIRCUIT	FUNCTION
A	BATTERY FEED
B	BRAKE CONTROLS
C	CLIMATE CONTROLS
D	DIAGNOSTIC CIRCUITS
E	DIMMING ILLUMINATION CIRCUITS
F	FUSED CIRCUITS
G	MONITORING CIRCUITS (GAUGES)
H	OPEN
I	NOT USED
J	OPEN
K	POWERTRAIN CONTROL MODULE
L	EXTERIOR LIGHTING
M	INTERIOR LIGHTING
N	NOT USED
O	NOT USED
P	POWER OPTION (BATTERY FEED)
Q	POWER OPTIONS (IGNITION FEED)
R	PASSIVE RESTRAINT
S	SUSPENSION/STEERING
T	TRANSMISSION/TRANSAXLE/ TRANSFER CASE
U	OPEN
V	SPEED CONTROL, WIPER/WASHER
W	OPEN
X	AUDIO SYSTEMS
Y	OPEN
Z	GROUNDS

30.4 Wire color code chart

24 Remove the plastic back panel from the seat back.

25 Disengage the seat back trim cover J-strap from the upper, lower and airbag side of the seat back.

26 Disconnect the airbag electrical connector and slide the yellow locking tab down to unlock. The push the two side retaining tabs in, then pull the connector straight from the airbag module.

27 Remove the nuts securing the side air bag module to the seat back frame.

28 Grasp the upper airbag side of the seat back trim cover, then pull the trim cover and cushion over the top of the seat back frame.

29 Carefully unhook the airbag studs from the nylon sleeve and slide the airbag module out of the sleeve. Do not tear the nylon sleeve, if damaged it will affect the deployment of the airbag.

30 Carefully slide the airbag module into the nylon sleeve and align the mounting studs with the holes in the nylon sleeve. ***Warning:*** *The airbag module must be correctly located within the nylon sleeve prior to installing the mounting nuts. Failure to do so will adversely affect the deployment of the airbag.*

31 Correctly locate the airbag and nylon sleeve into position on the seat back frame. Install the nuts and tighten securely.

32 Install the upper seat back trim cover and cushion over the seat back frame.

33 Connect the airbag electrical connector and slide the yellow locking tab up to LOCKED position. Pull on the connector to ensure it is secured in place.

34 Install the seat back trim cover and install the seat back trim cover J-straps on the upper, lower and airbag side of the seat.

35 Use new push pins and secure the plastic back panel onto the seat back.

36 Install the front seat (see Chapter 11, section 27).

30 Wiring diagrams - general information

Refer to illustration 30.4

Since it isn't possible to include all wiring diagrams for every year covered by this manual, the following diagrams are those that are typical and most commonly needed.

Prior to troubleshooting any circuits, check the fuse and circuit breakers (if equipped) to make sure they are in good condition. Make sure the battery is properly charged and has clean, tight cable connections (see Chapter 1).

When checking the wiring system, make sure that all electrical connectors are clean, with no broken or loose pins. When unplugging an electrical connector, do not pull on the wires, only on the connector housings themselves.

Refer to the accompanying chart for an explanation of the wire color codes applicable to your vehicle **(see illustration)**.

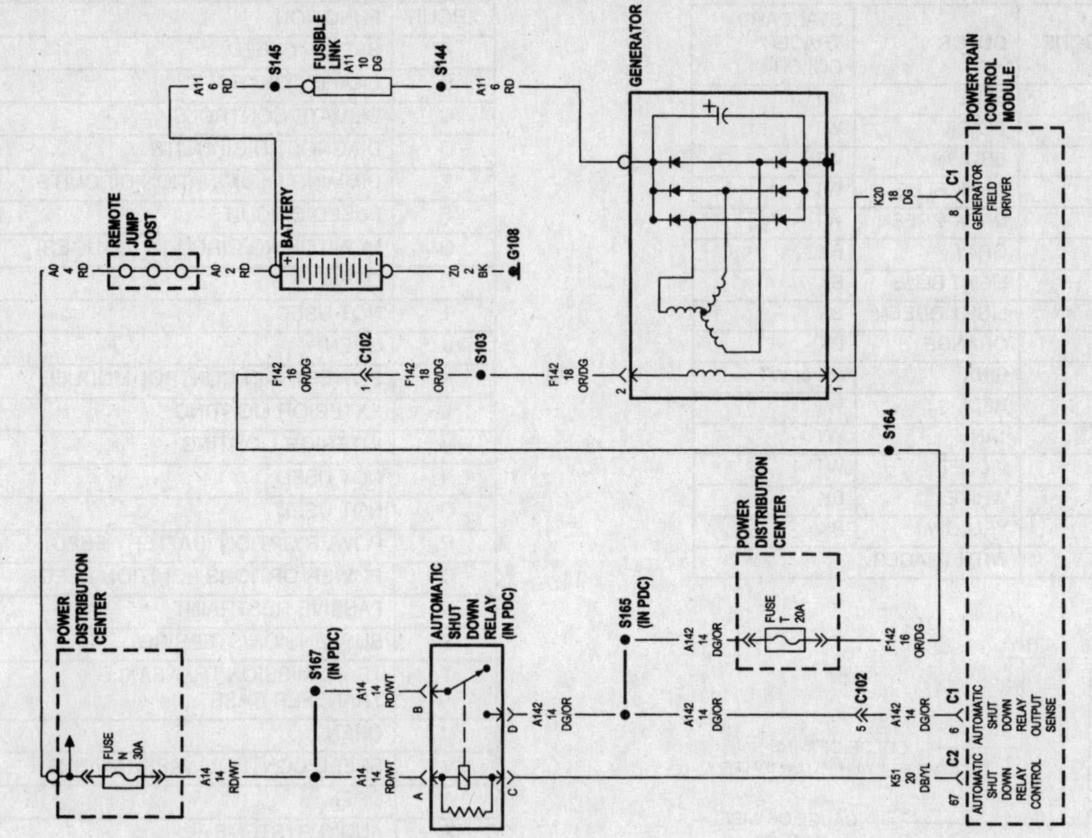

Charging system

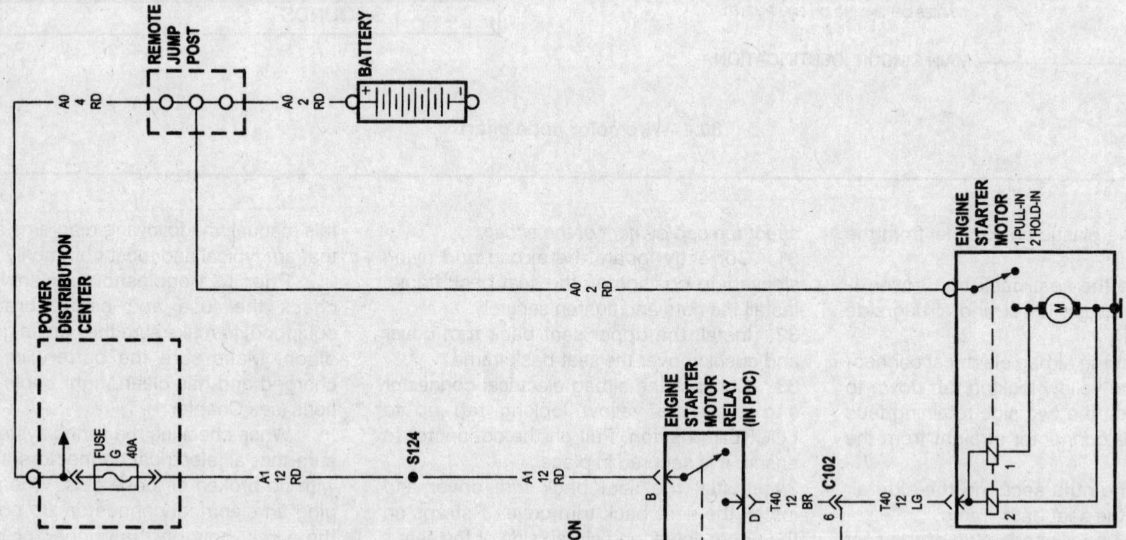

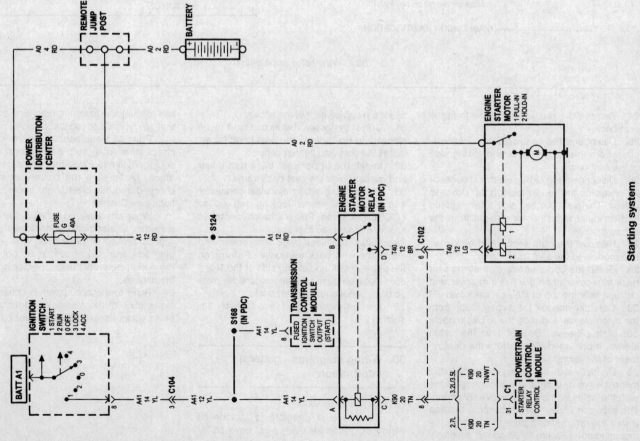

Starting system

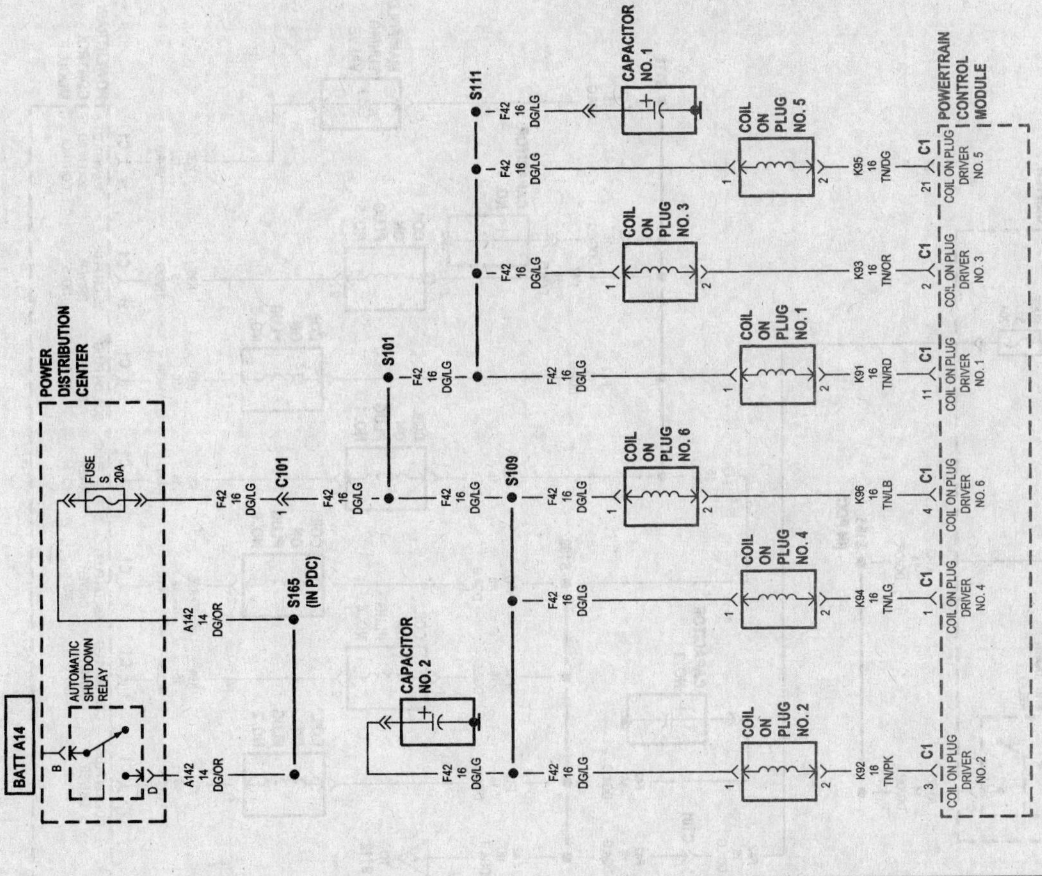

Engine control system (2.7L ignition coils)

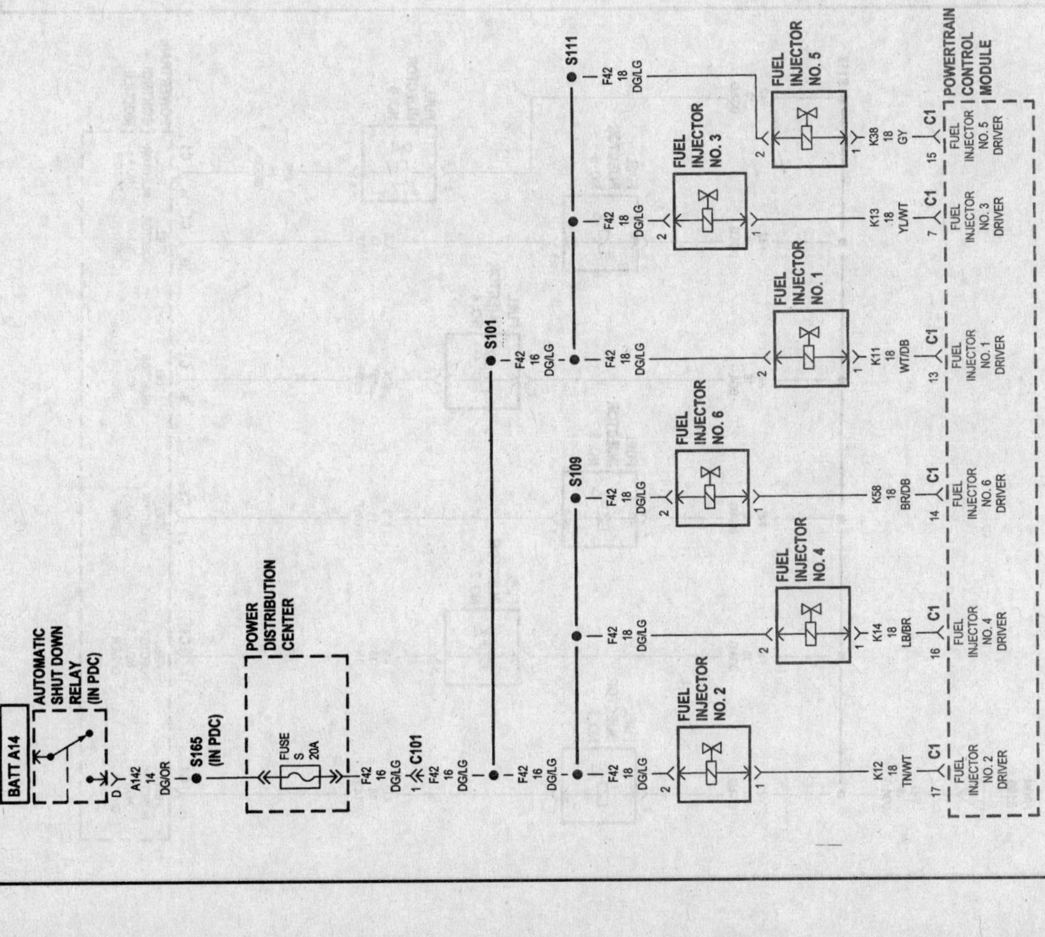

Engine control system (2.7L fuel injectors)

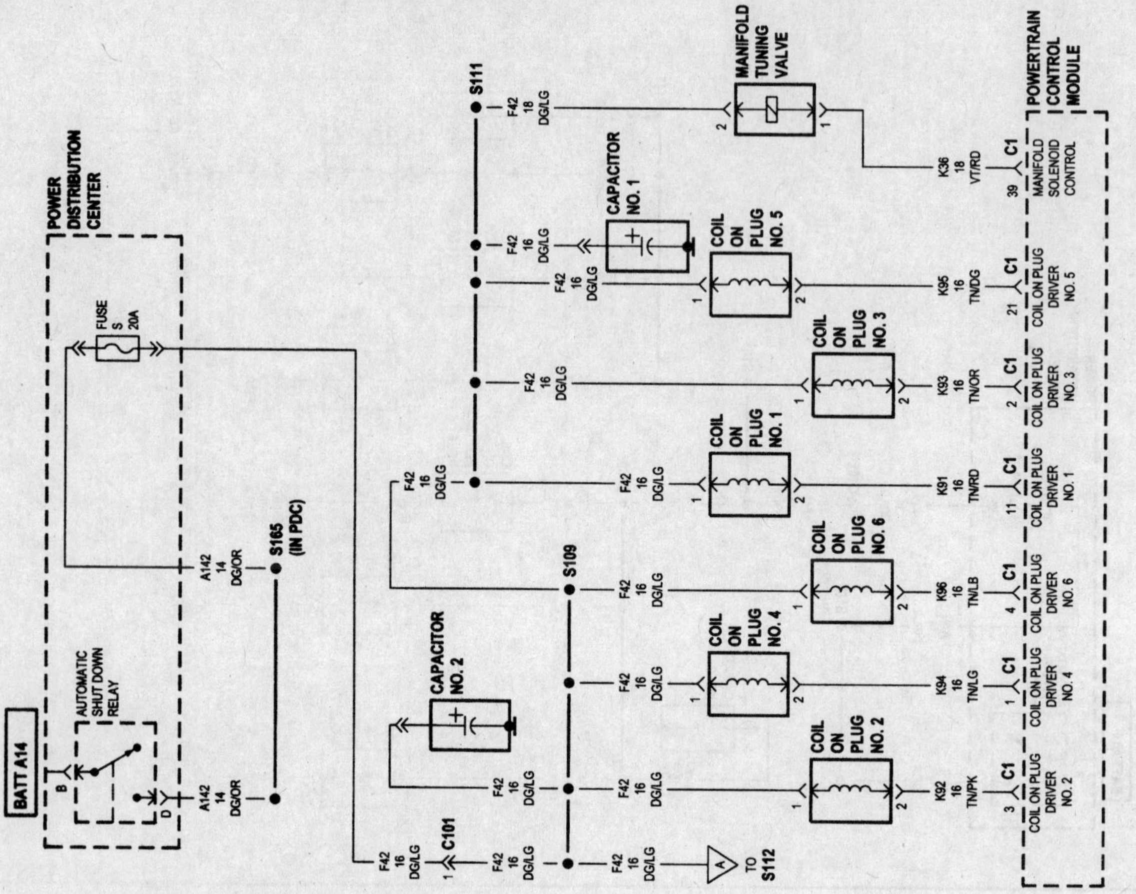

Engine control system (3.2L/3.5L ignition coils)

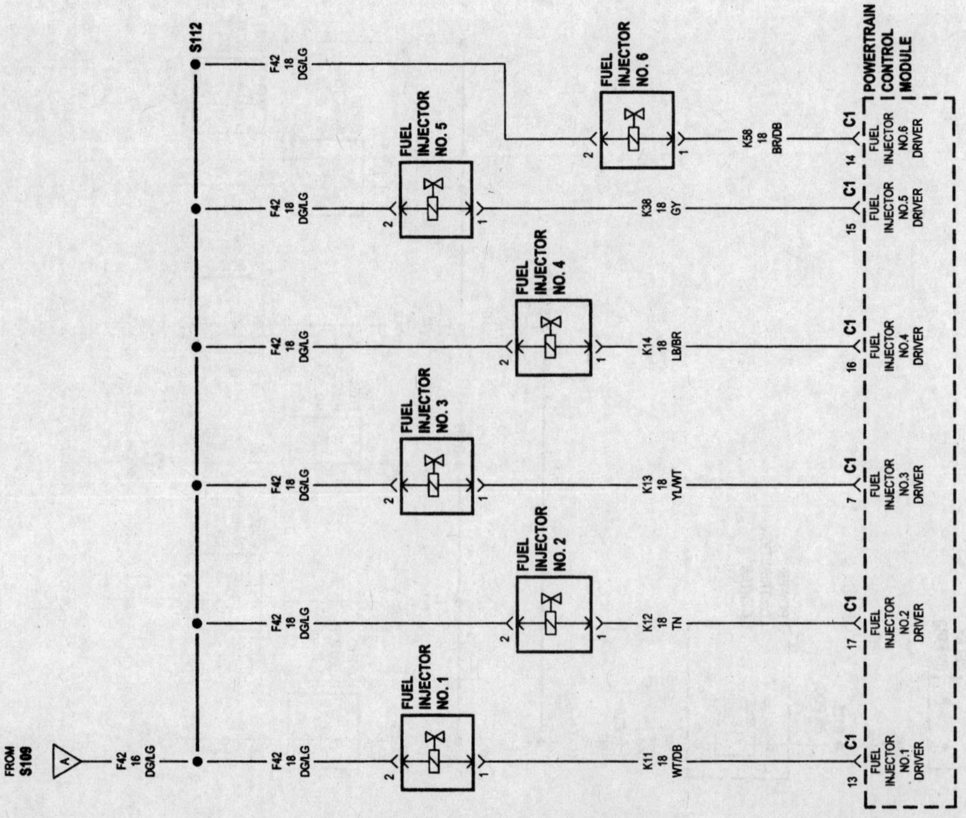

Engine control system (3.2L/3.5L fuel injectors)

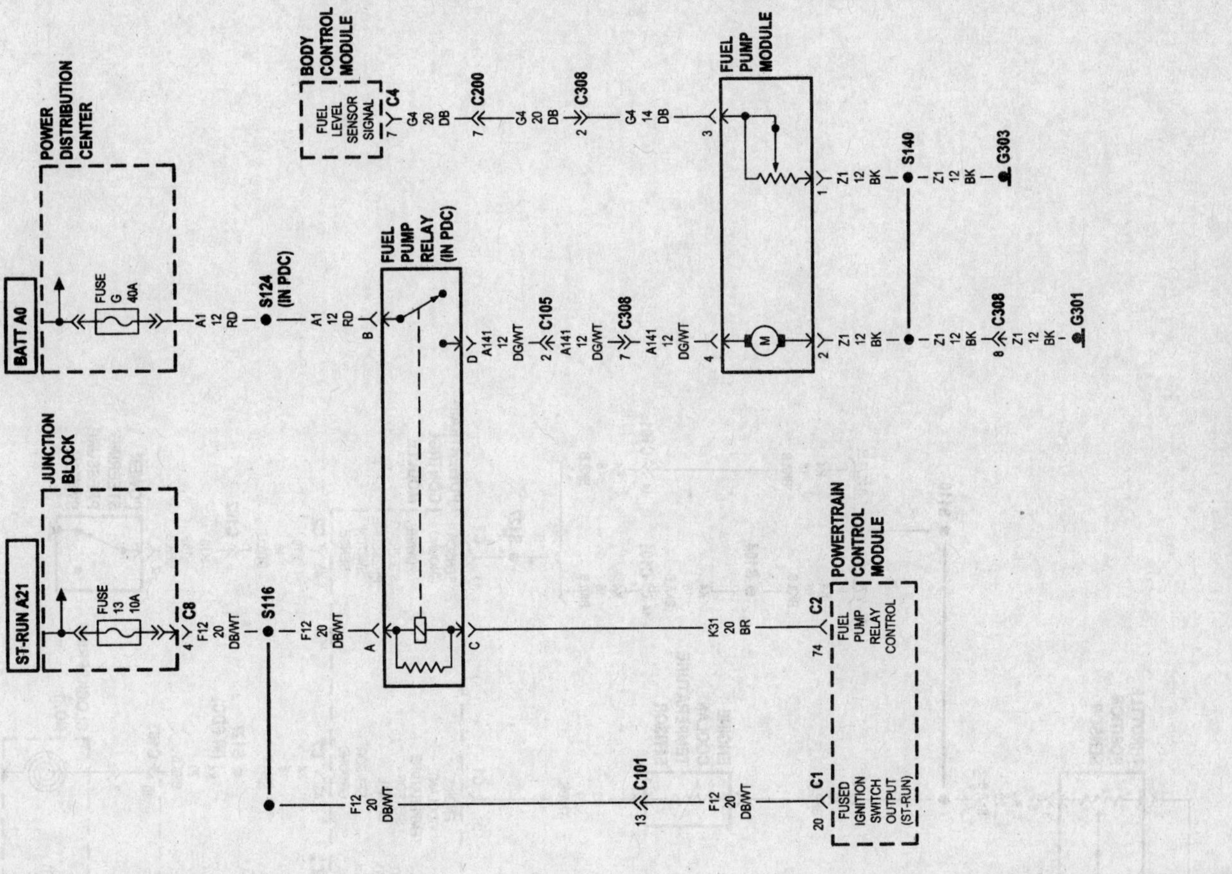

Engine control system (fuel pump circuit)

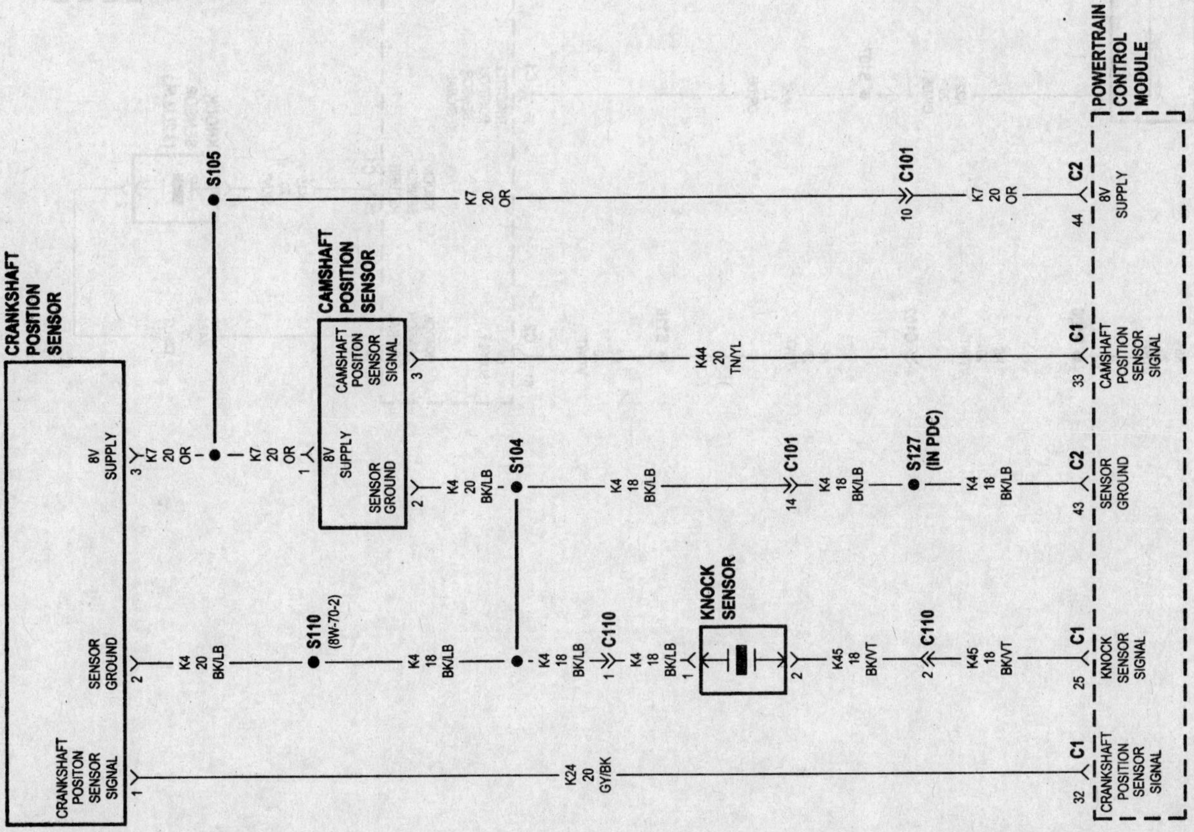

Engine control system (2.7L sensors)

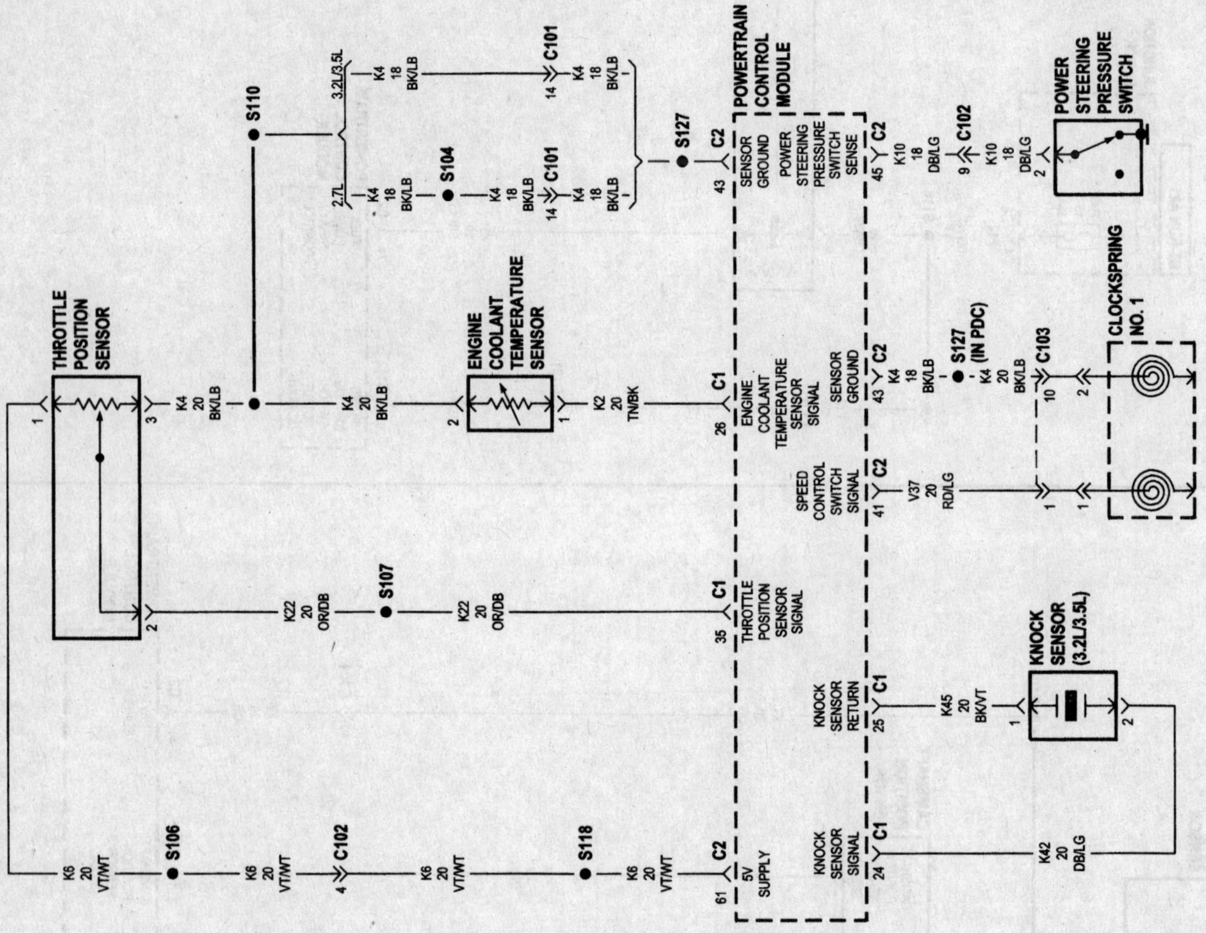

Engine control system (sensors)

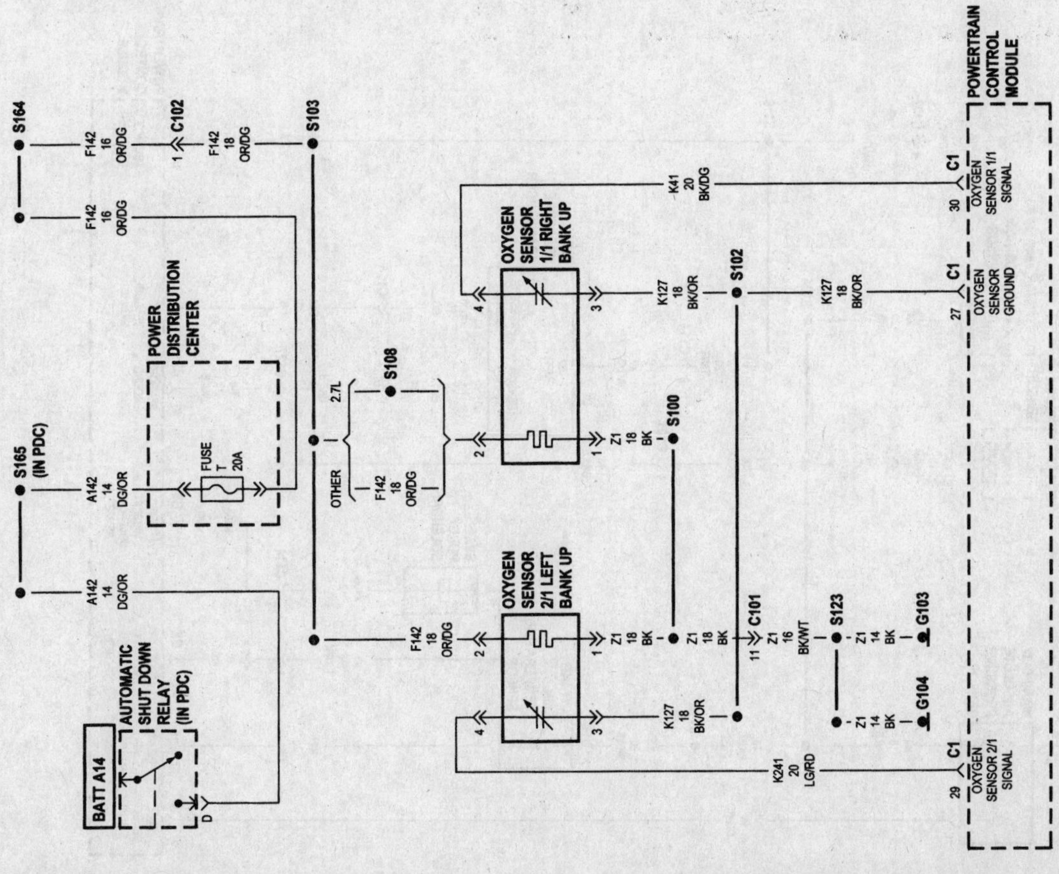

Engine control system - oxygen sensors (Part 1 of 2)

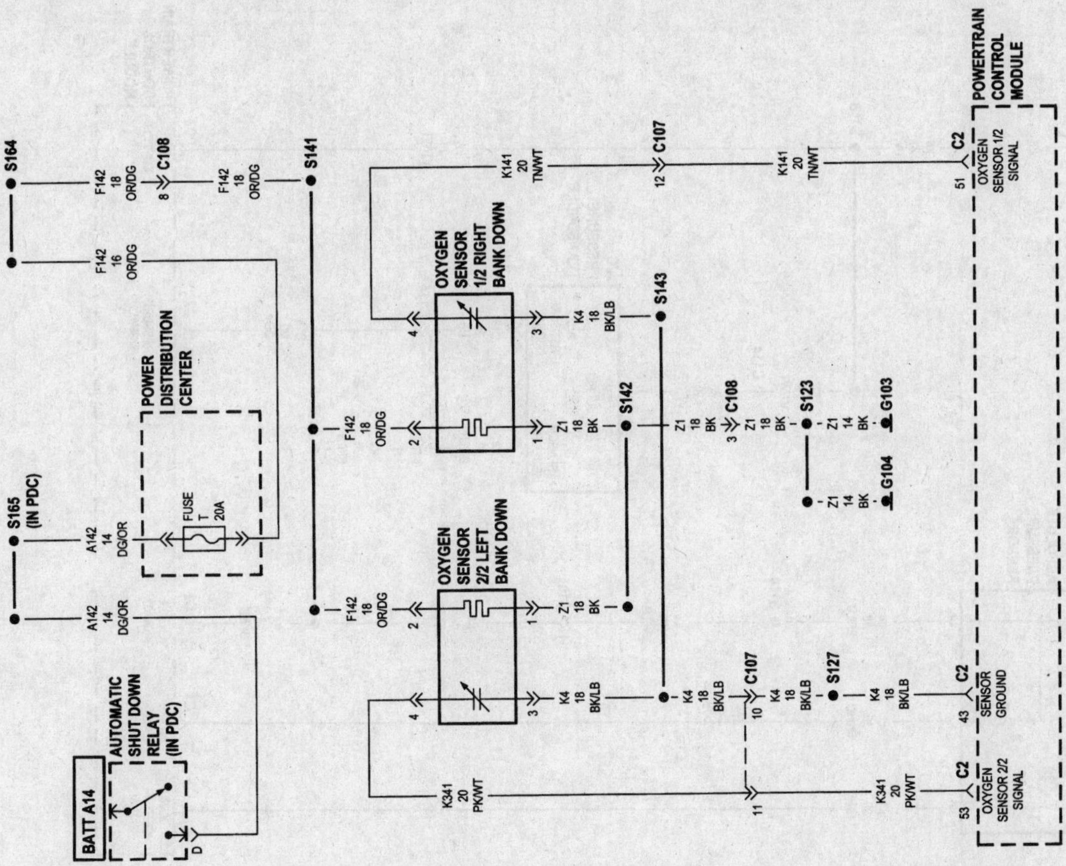

Engine control system - oxygen sensors (Part 2 of 2)

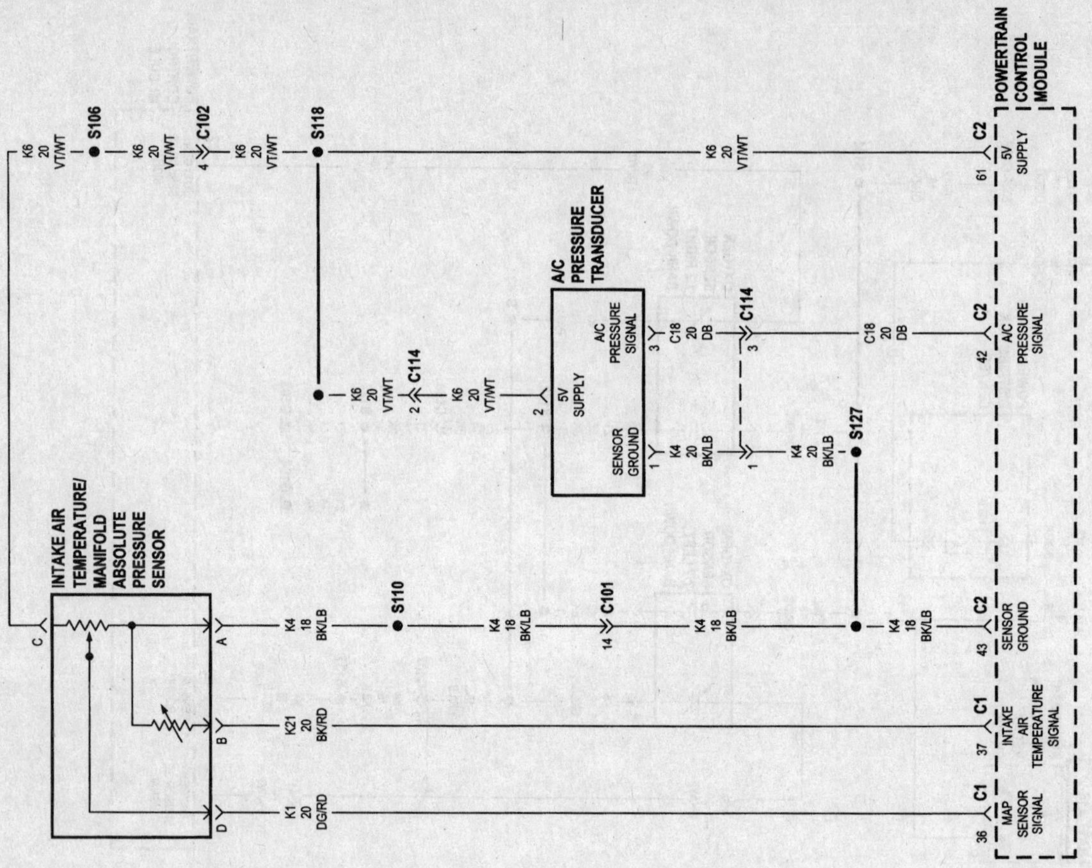

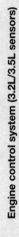

Engine control system (3.2L/3.5L sensors)

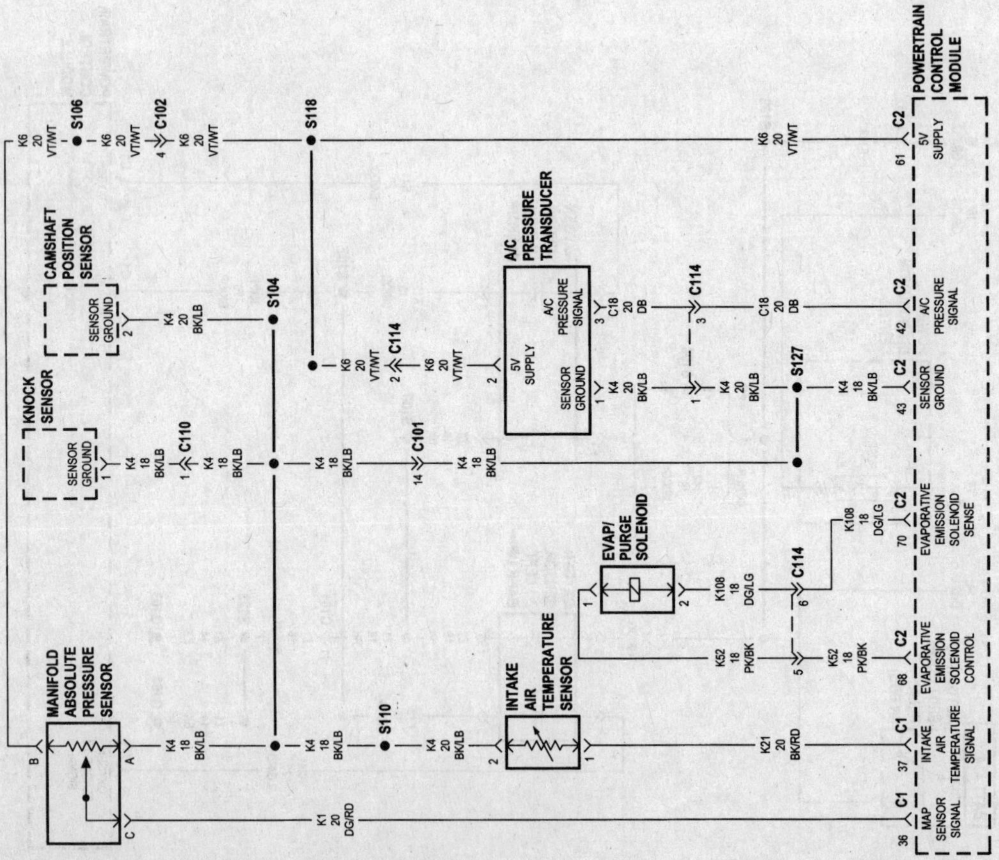

Engine control system (2.7L sensors)

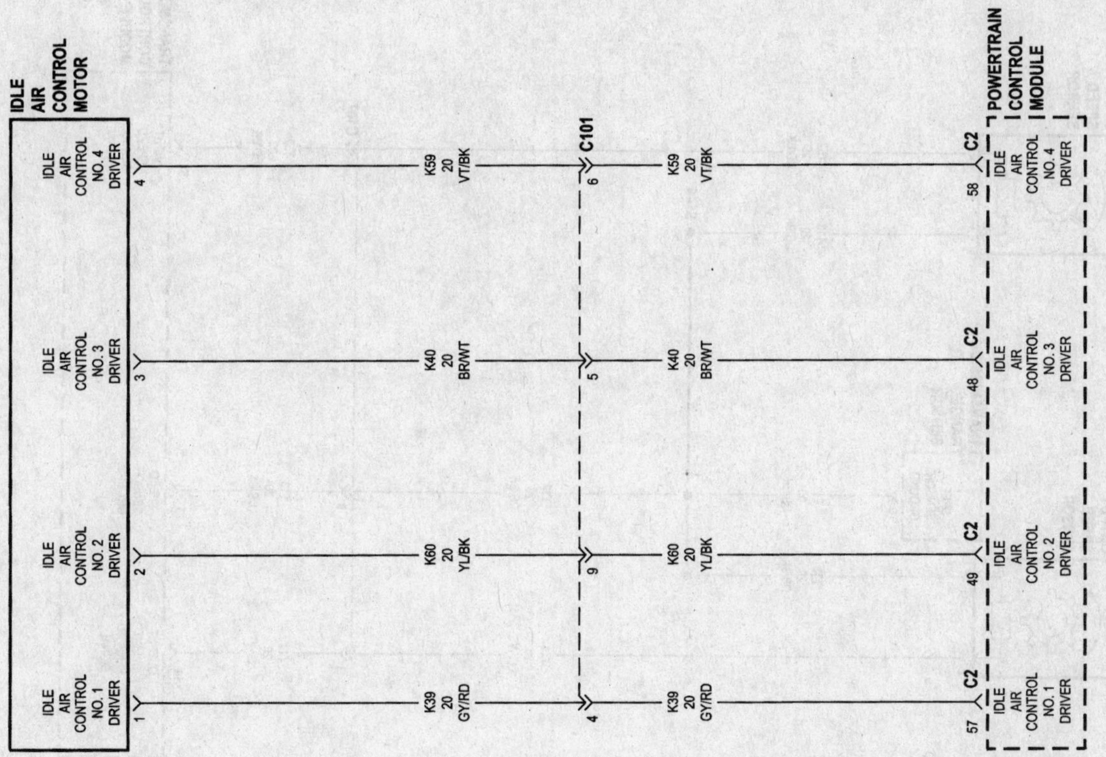

Engine control system (idle air control motor)

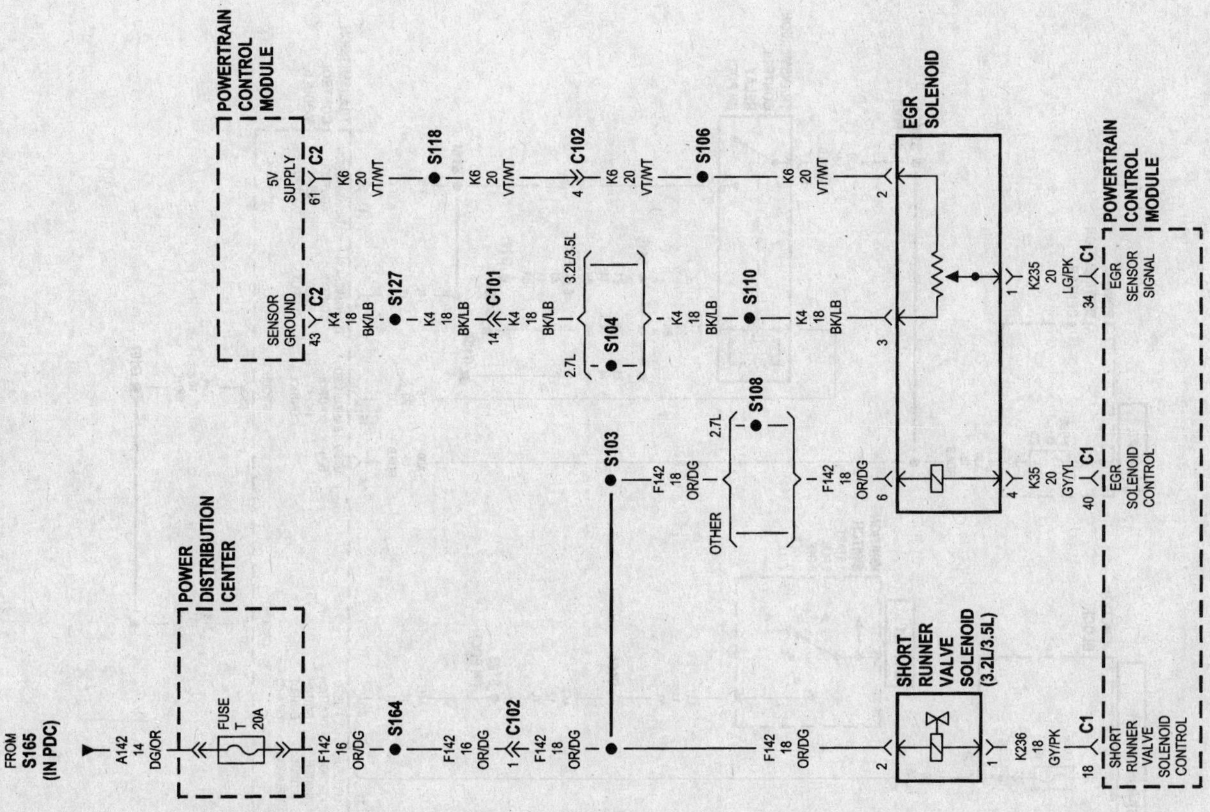

Engine control system (solenoids)

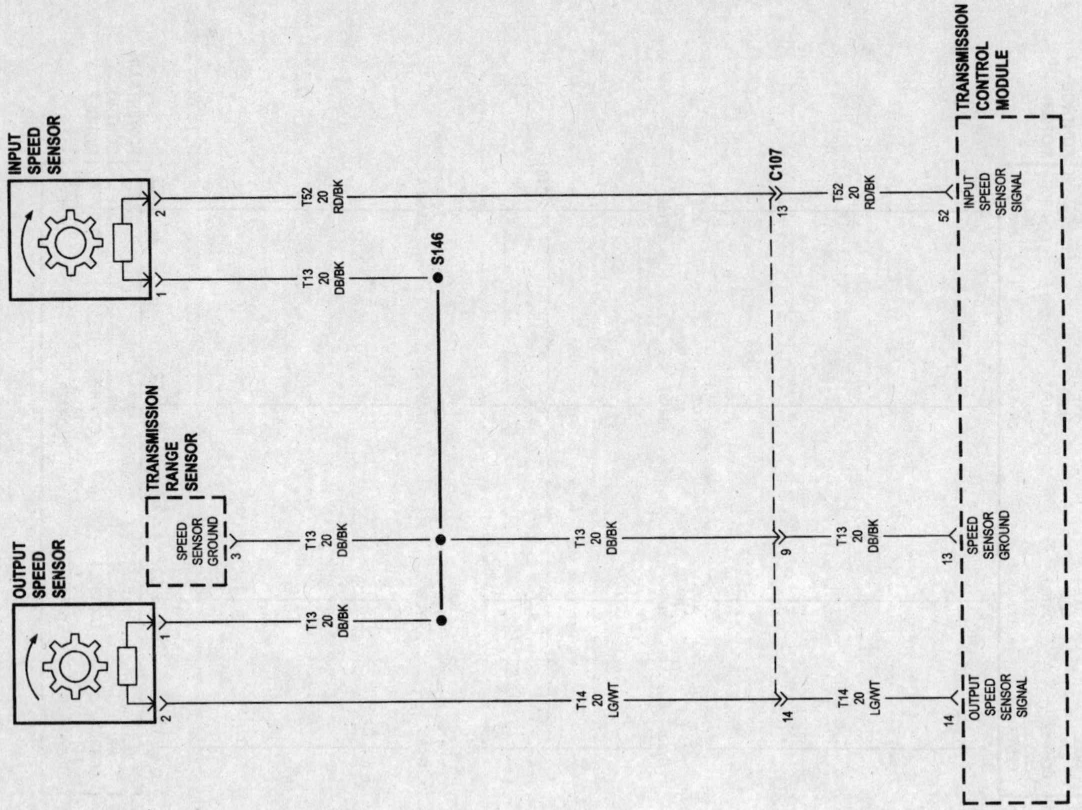

Transaxle control system (Part 2 of 7)

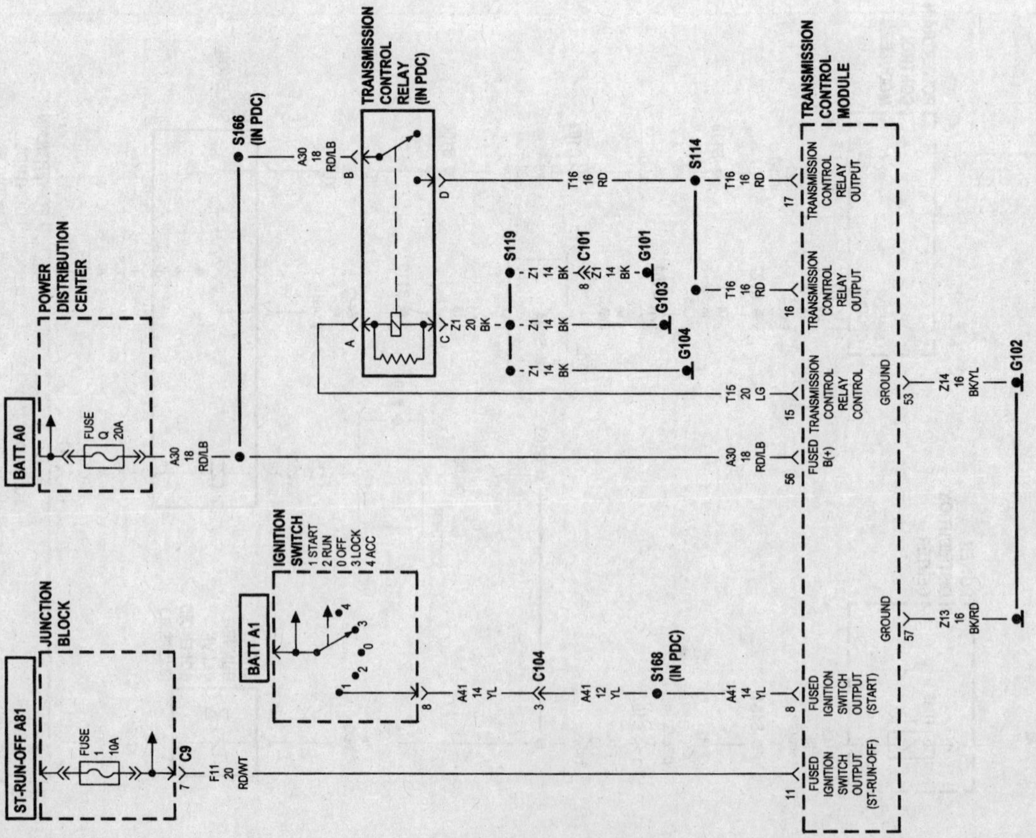

Transaxle control system (Part 1 of 7)

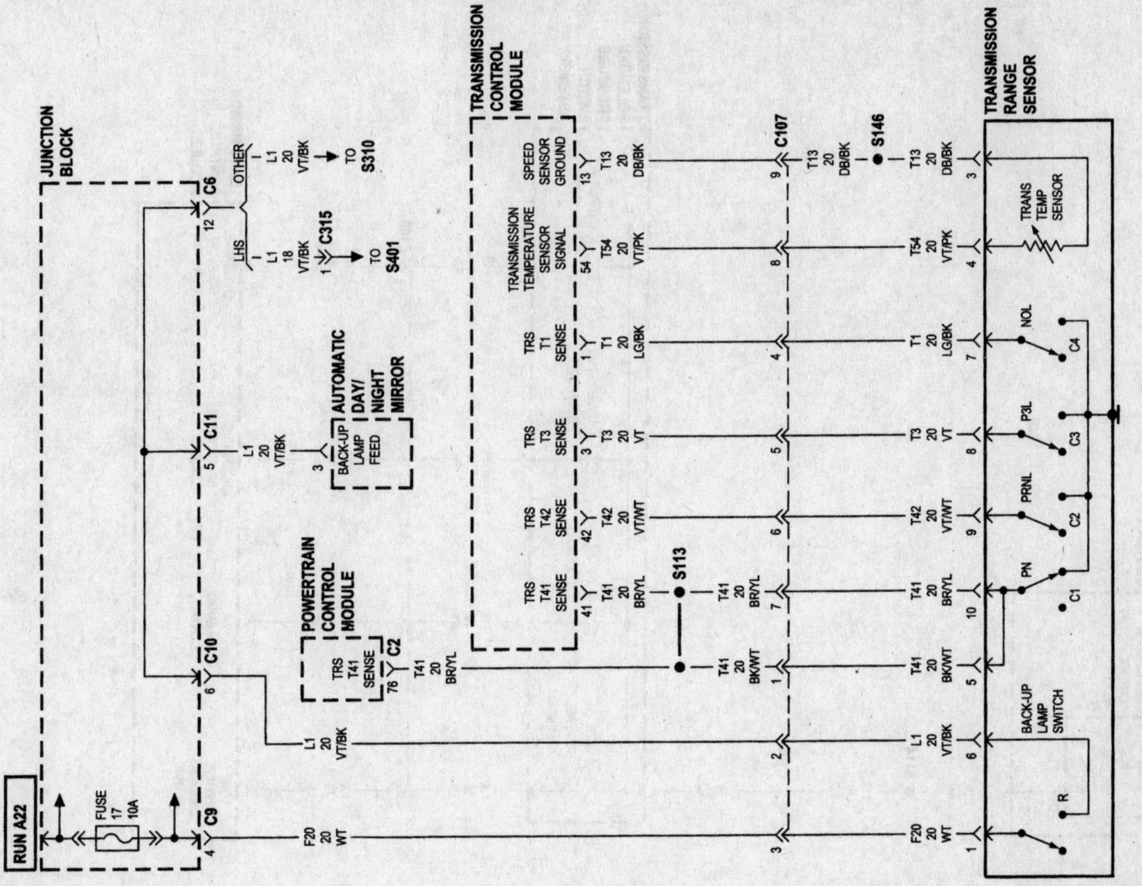

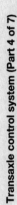

Transaxle control system (Part 4 of 7)

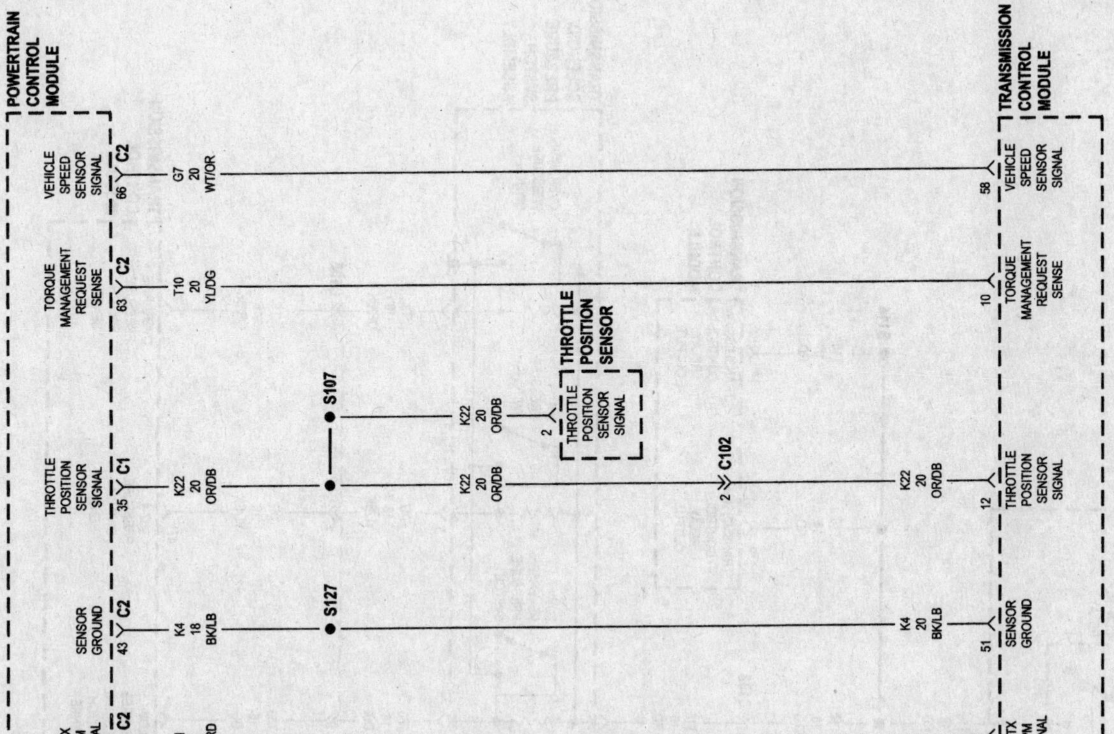

Transaxle control system (Part 3 of 7)

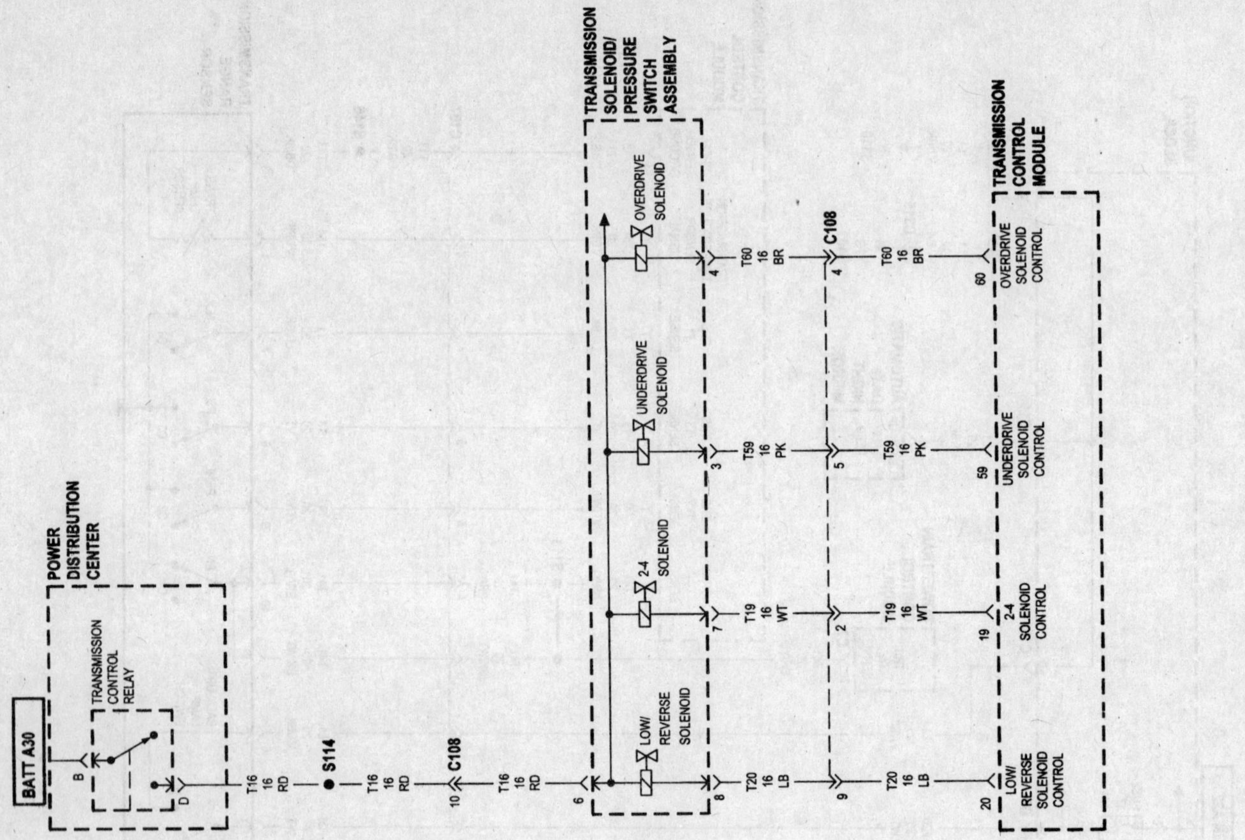

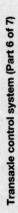

Transaxle control system (Part 6 of 7)

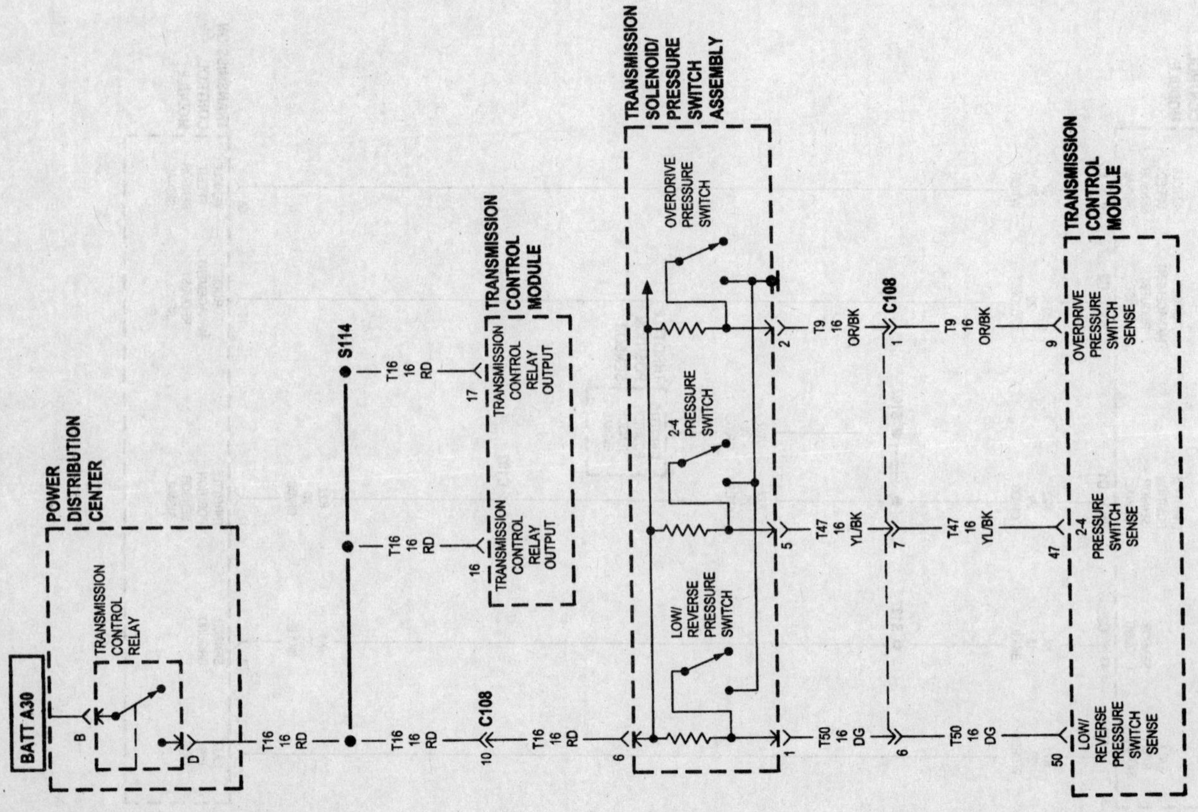

Transaxle control system (Part 5 of 7)

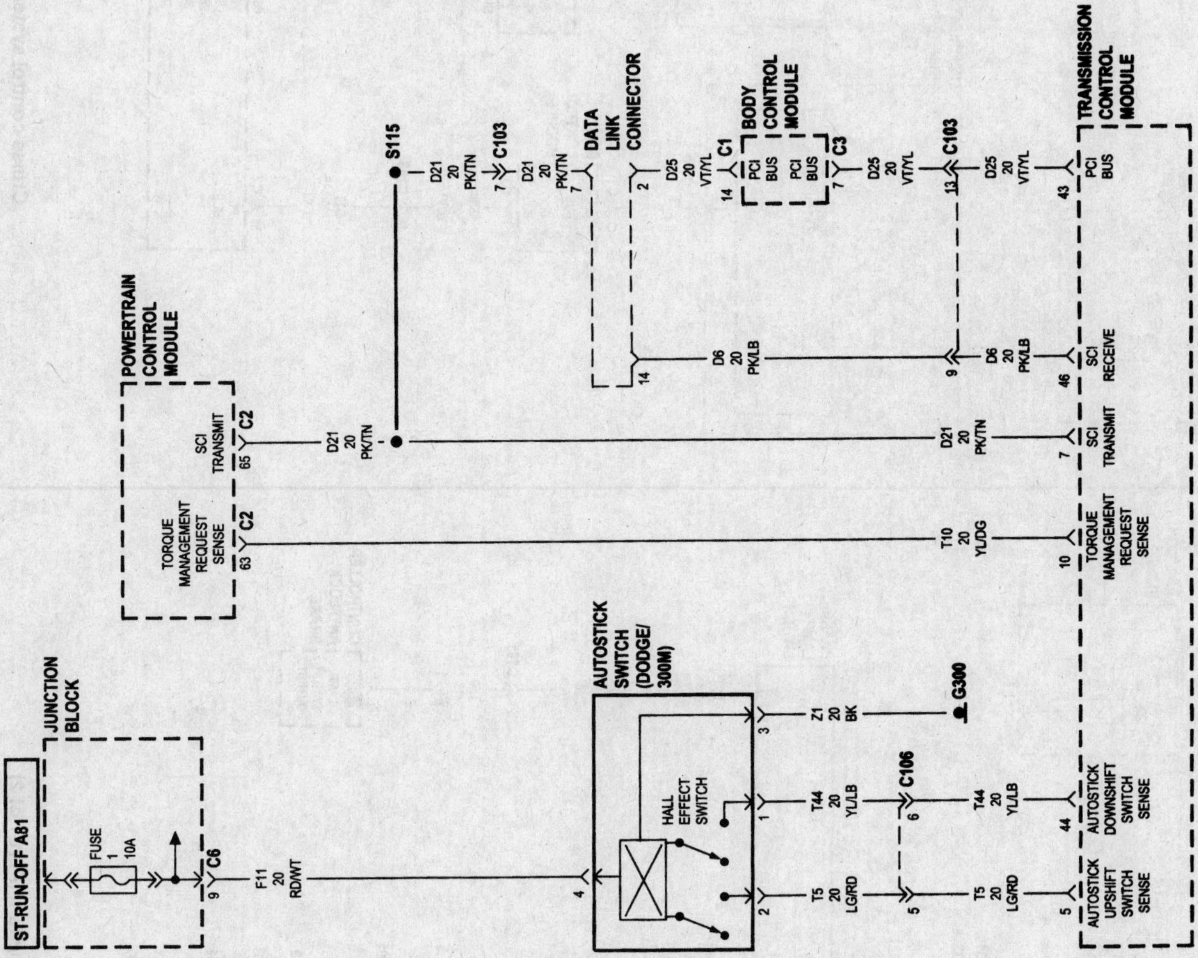

Transaxle control system (Part 7 of 7)

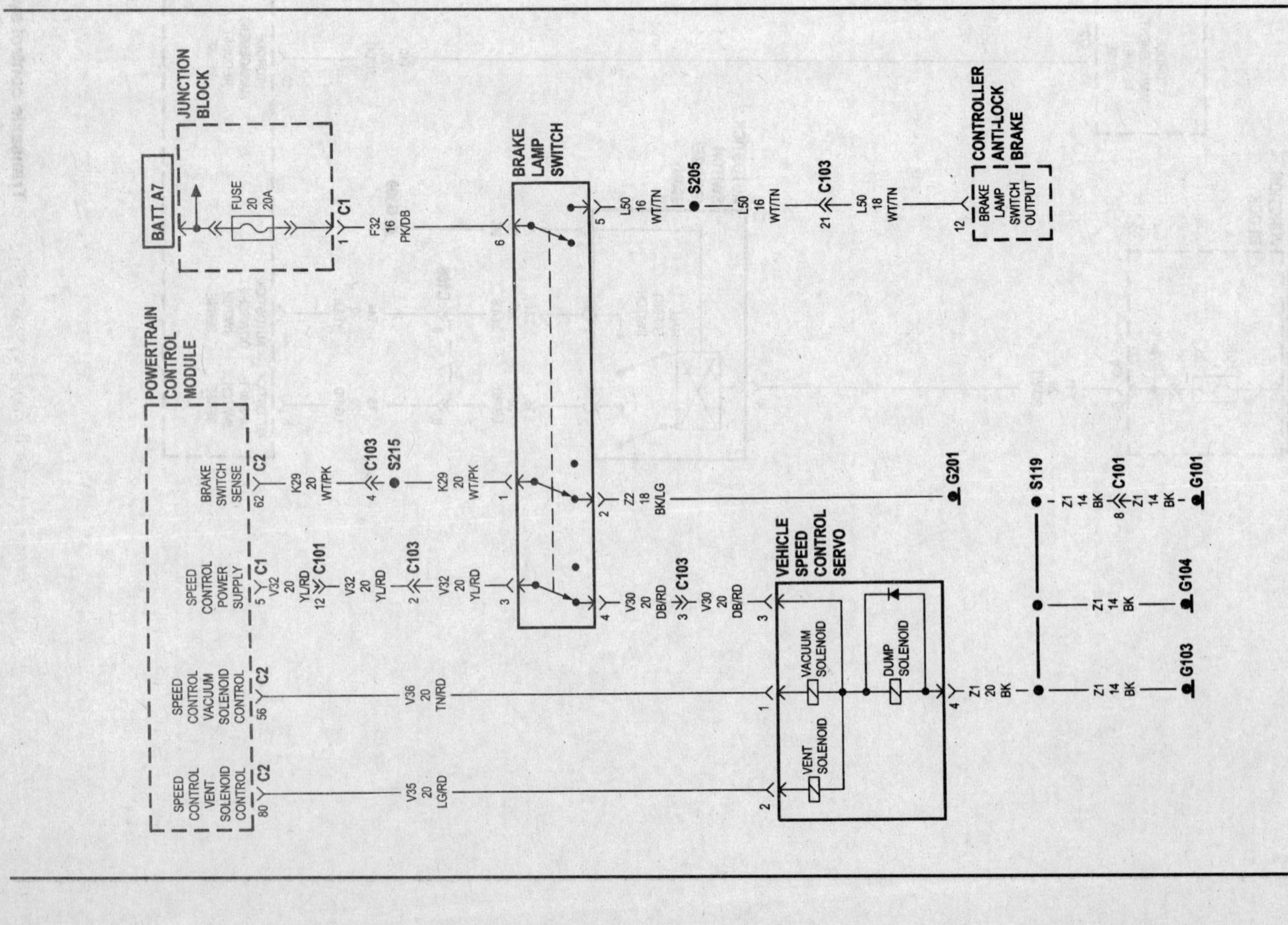

Cruise control system (Part 1 of 2)

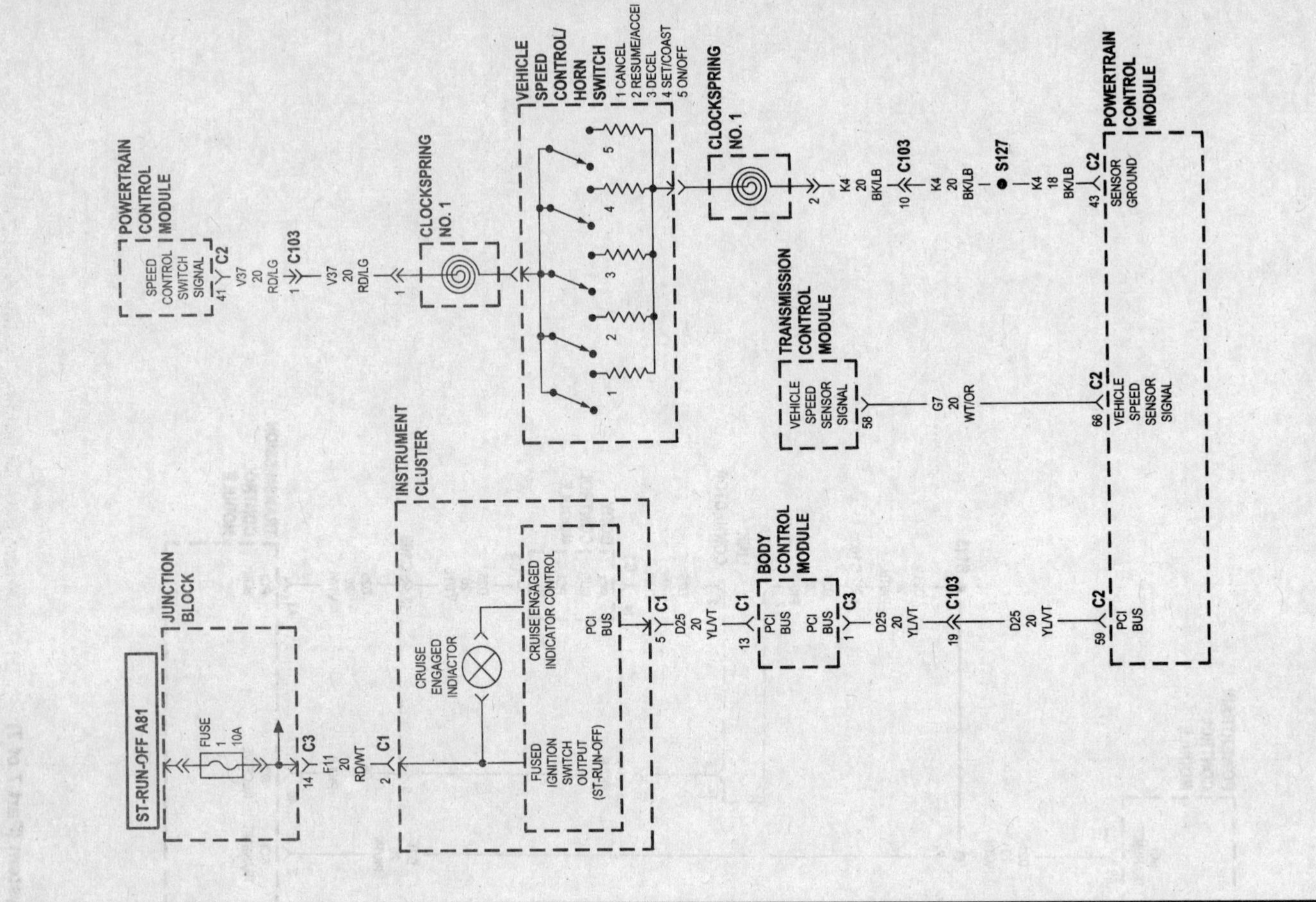

Cruise control system (Part 2 of 2)

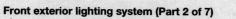

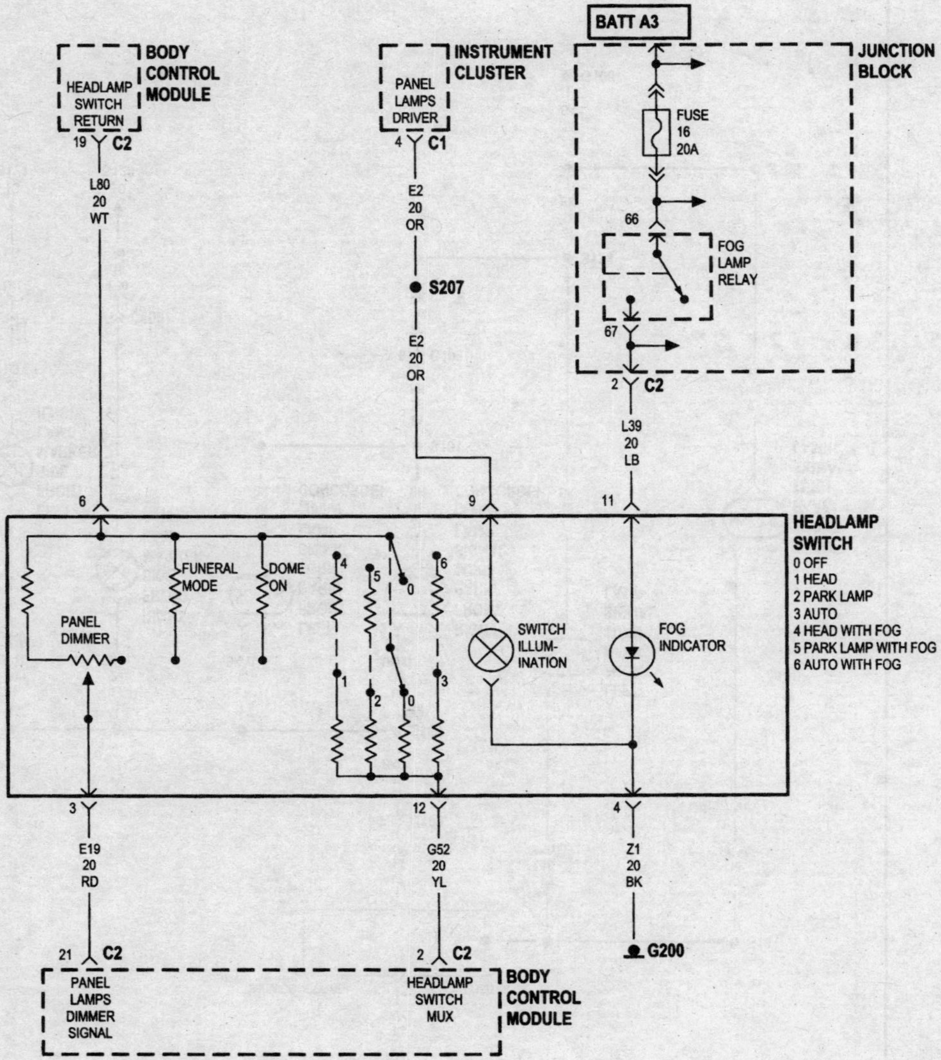

Front exterior lighting system (Part 1 of 7)

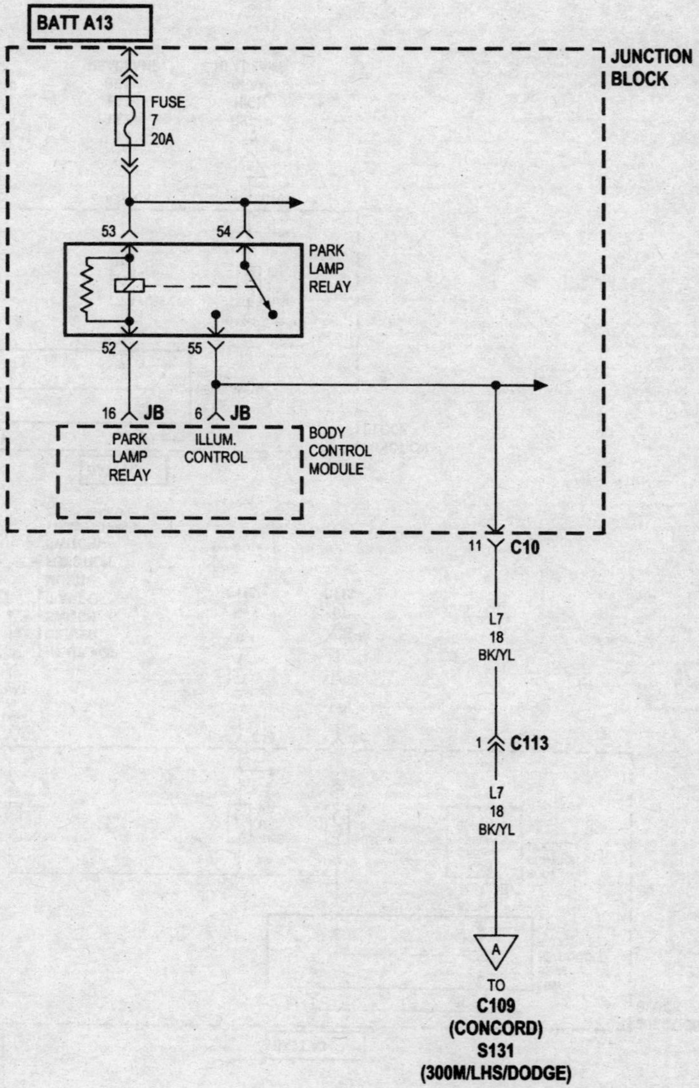

Front exterior lighting system (Part 2 of 7)

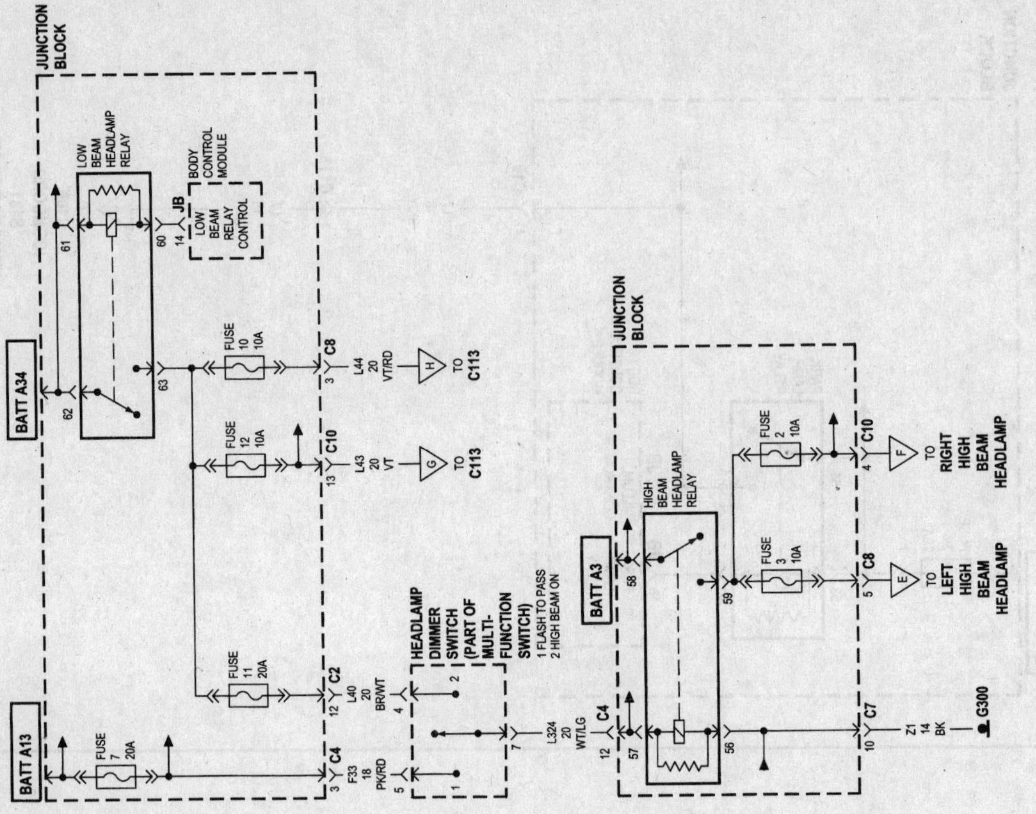

Front exterior lighting system (Part 4 of 7)

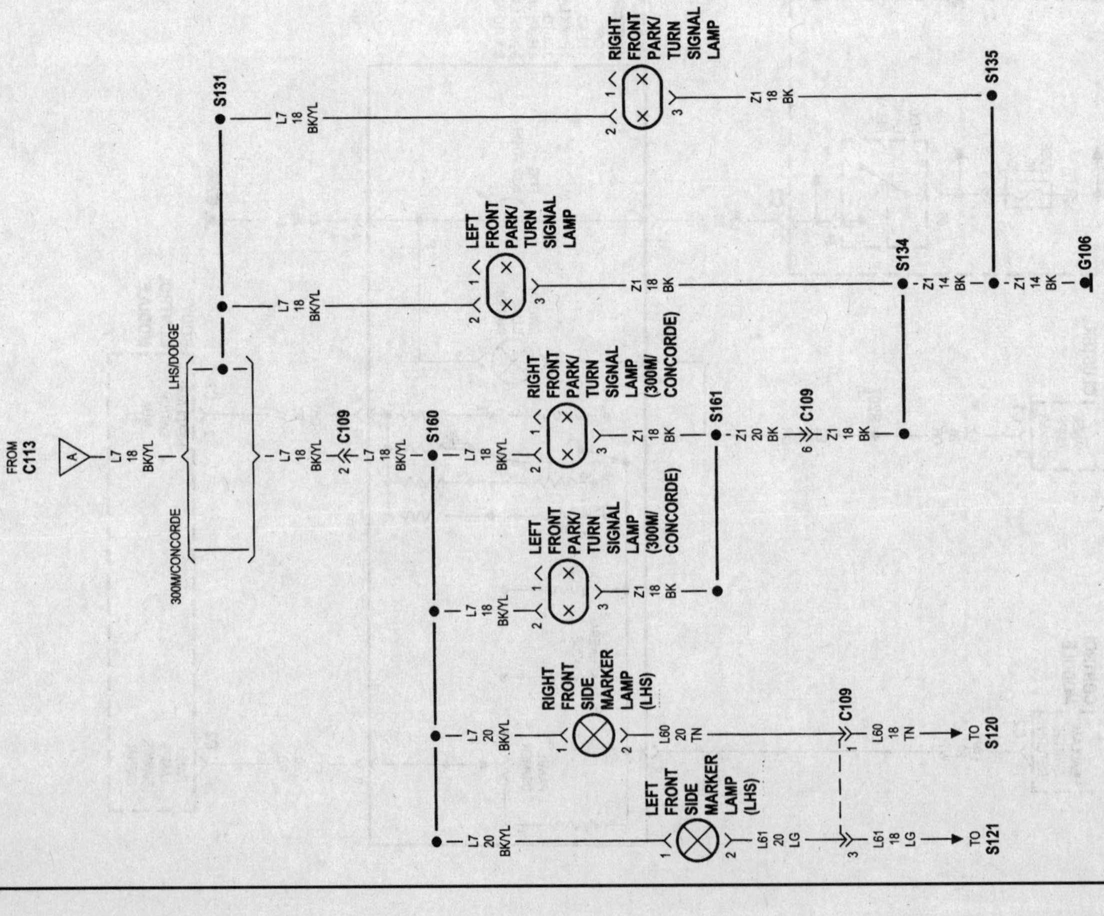

Front exterior lighting system (Part 3 of 7)

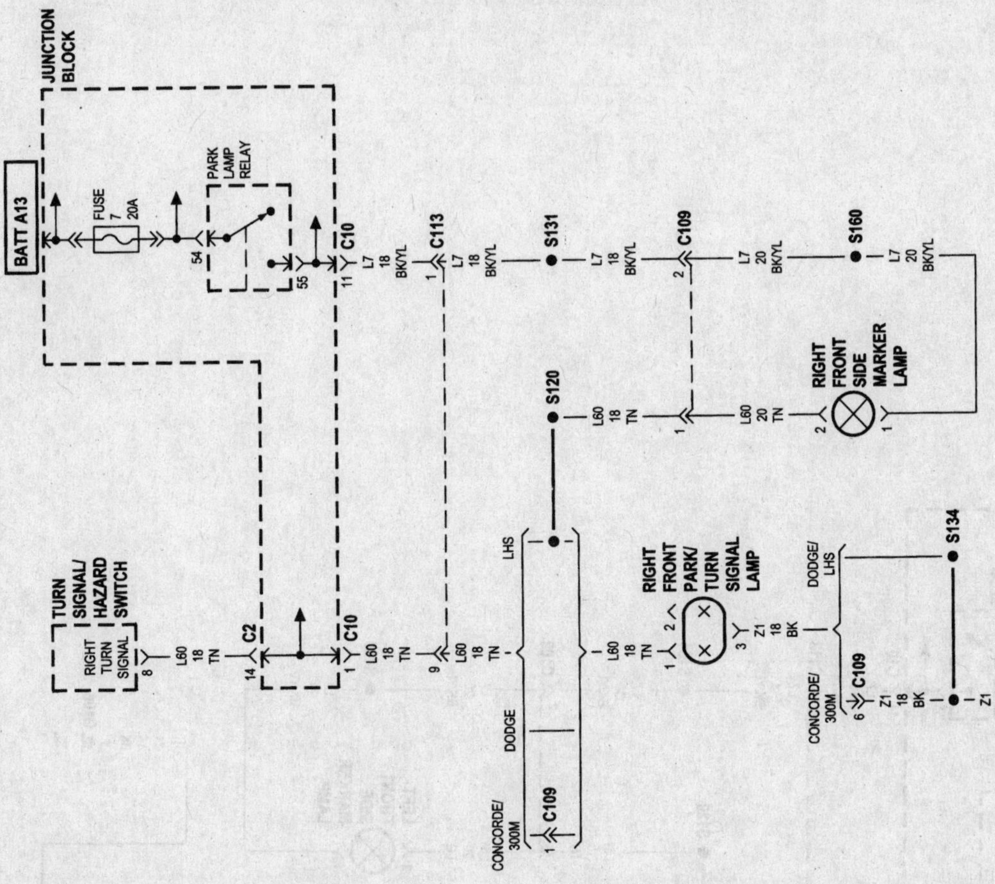

Front exterior lighting system (Part 6 of 7)

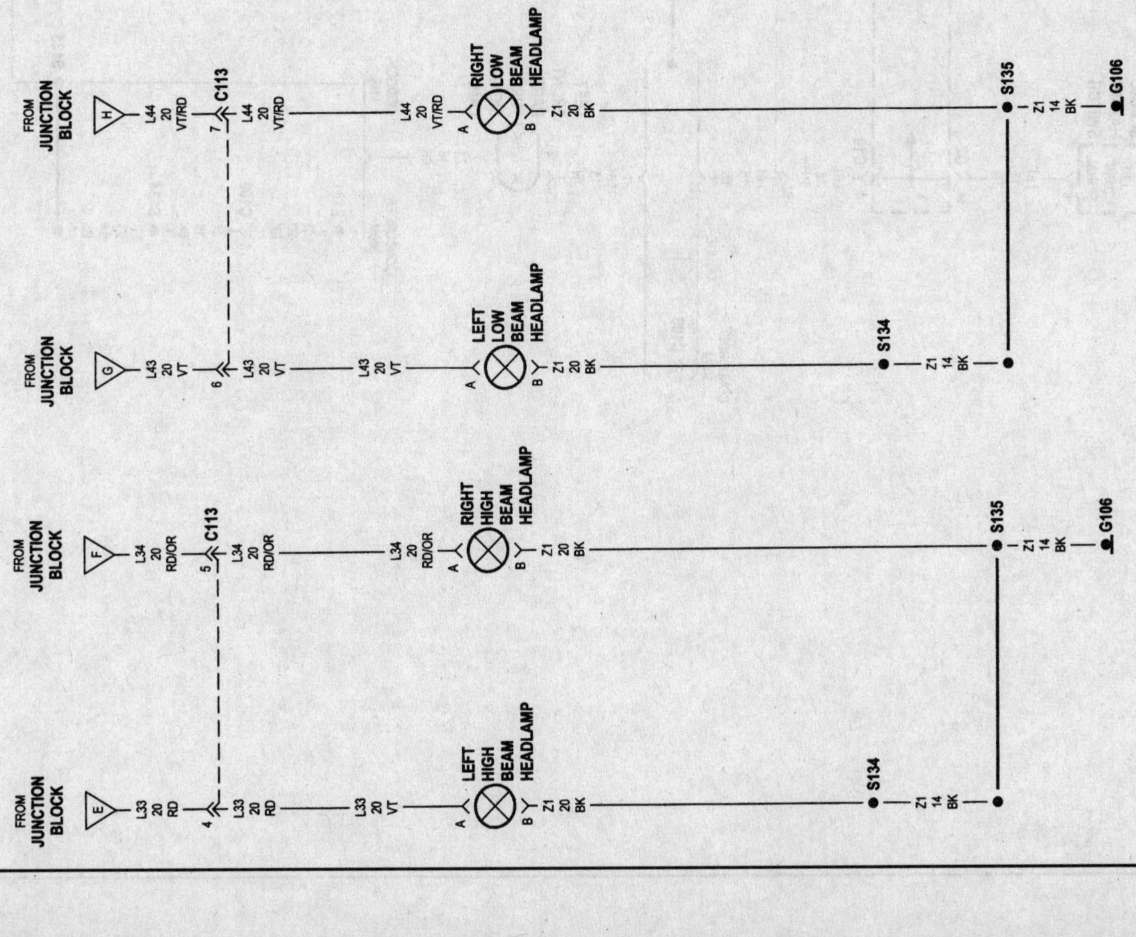

Front exterior lighting system (Part 5 of 7)

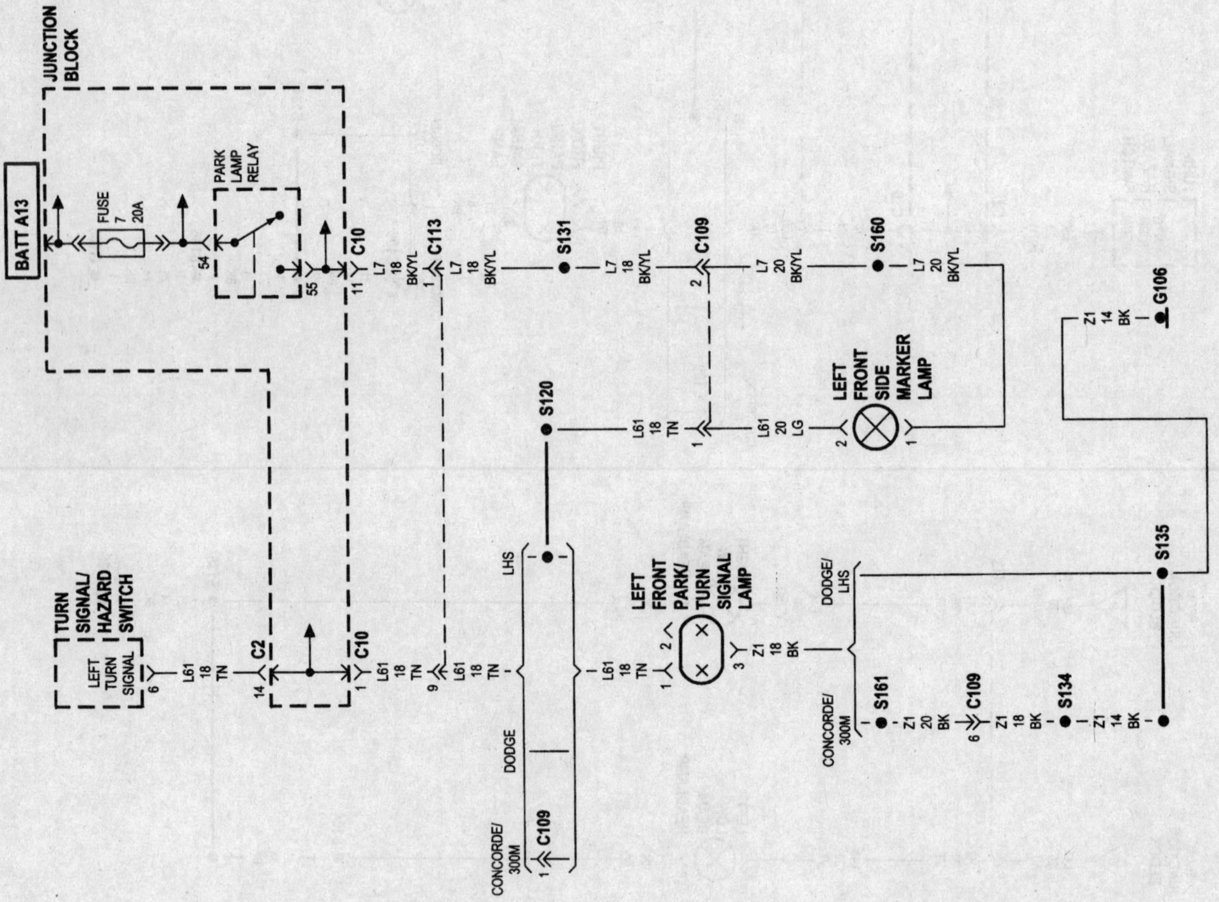

Front exterior lighting system (Part 7 of 7)

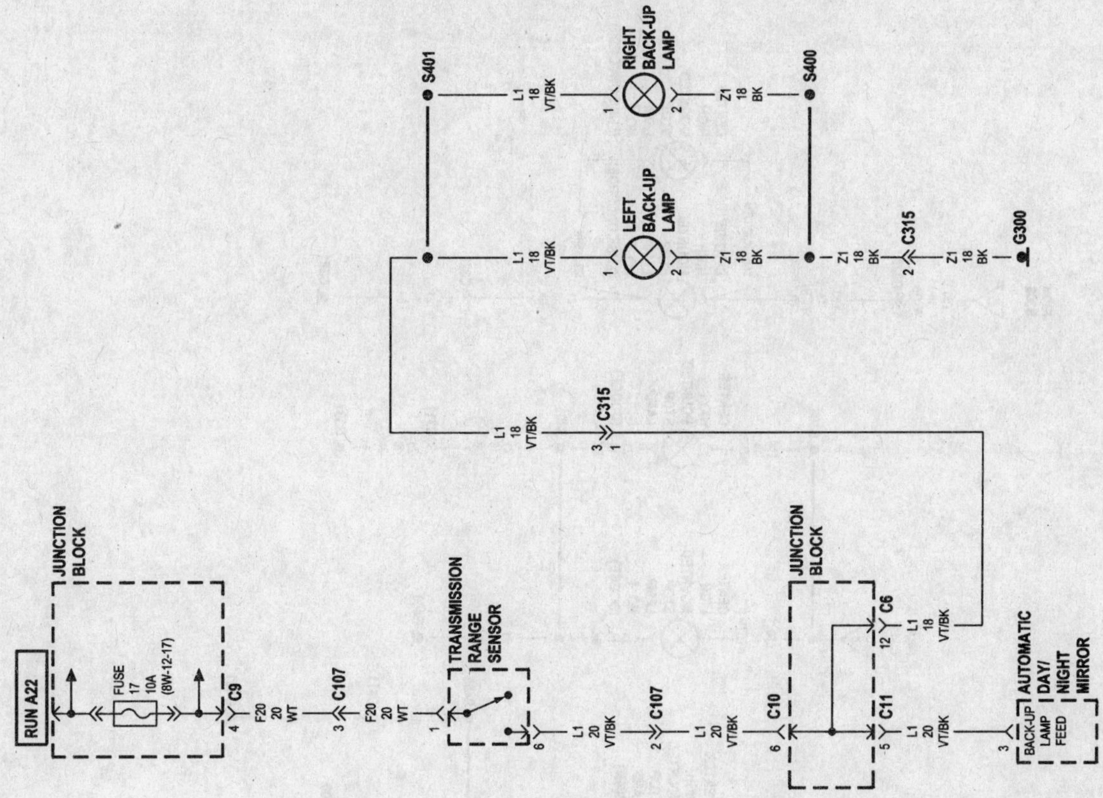

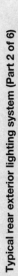

Typical rear exterior lighting system (Part 2 of 6)

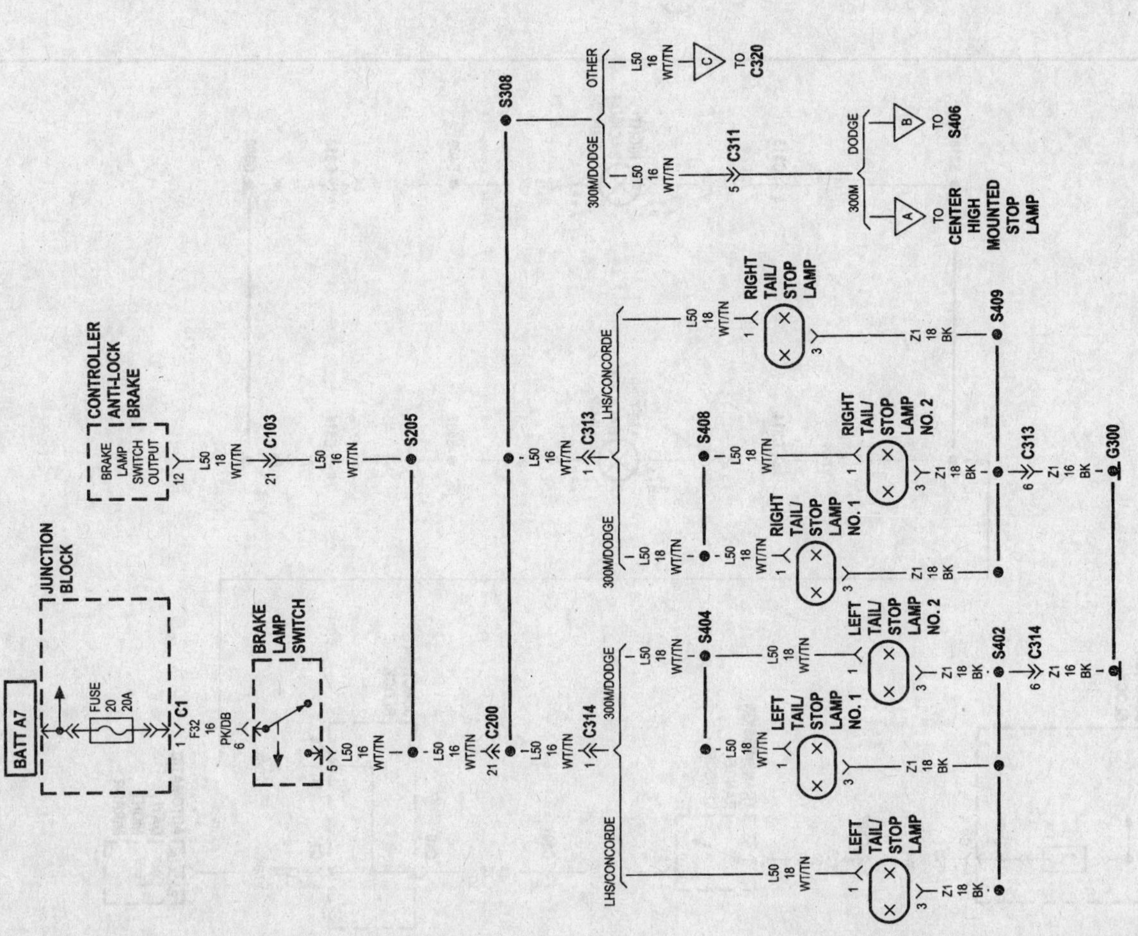

Typical rear exterior lighting system (Part 1 of 6)

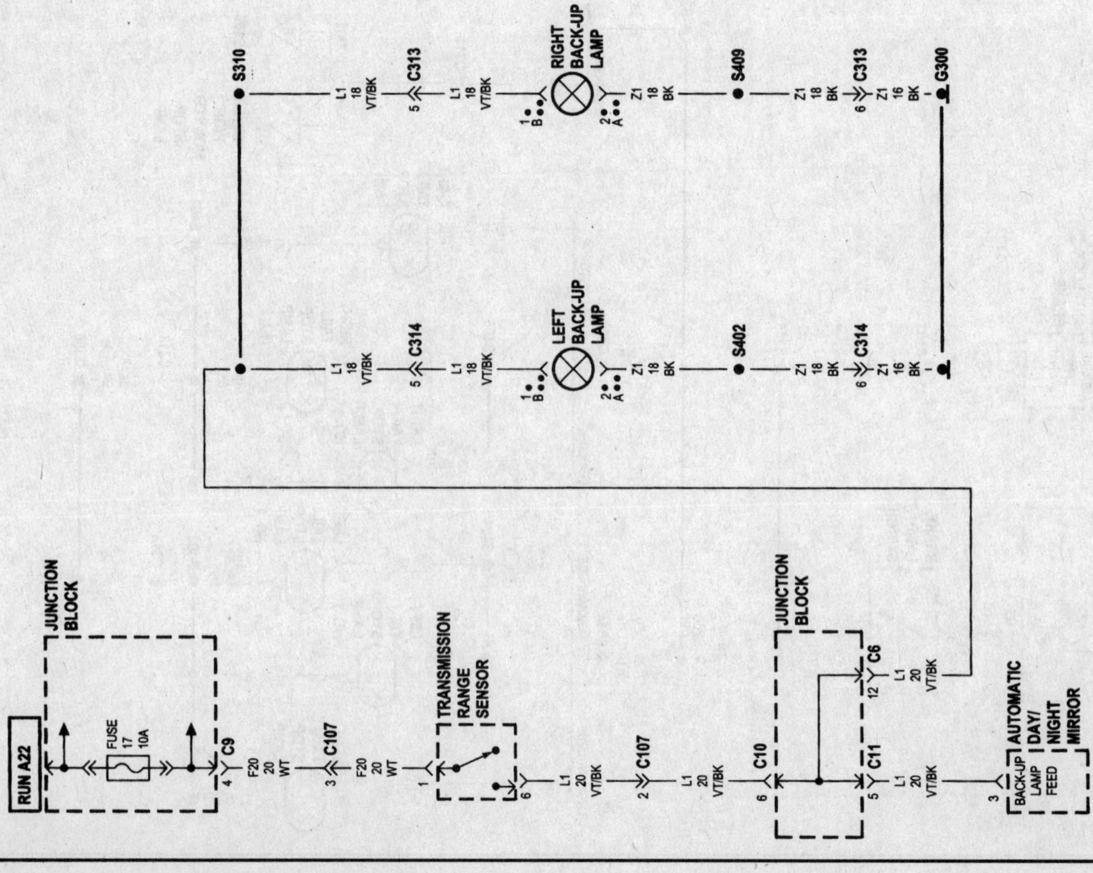

Typical rear exterior lighting system (Part 3 of 6)

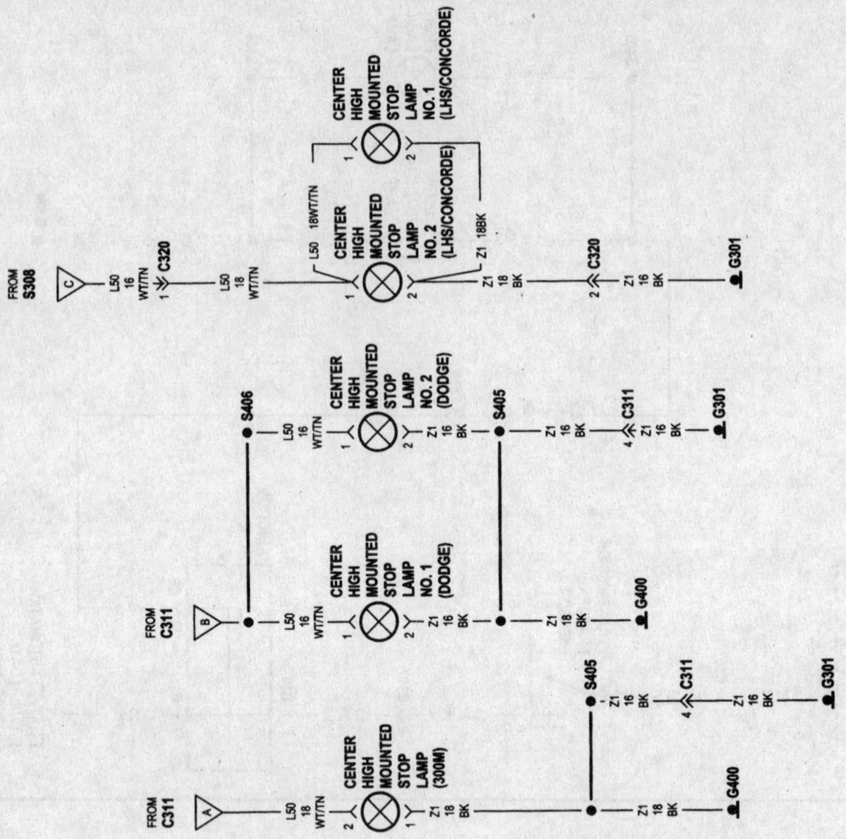

Typical rear exterior lighting system (Part 4 of 6)

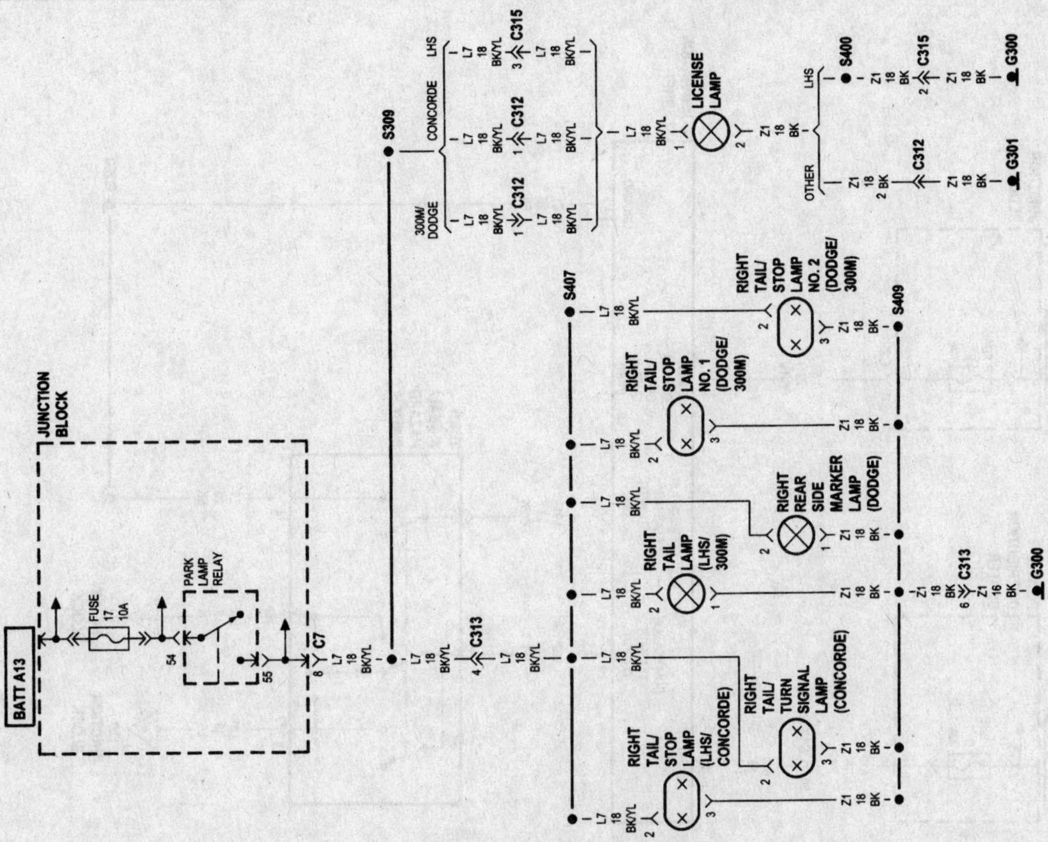

Typical rear exterior lighting system (Part 5 of 6)

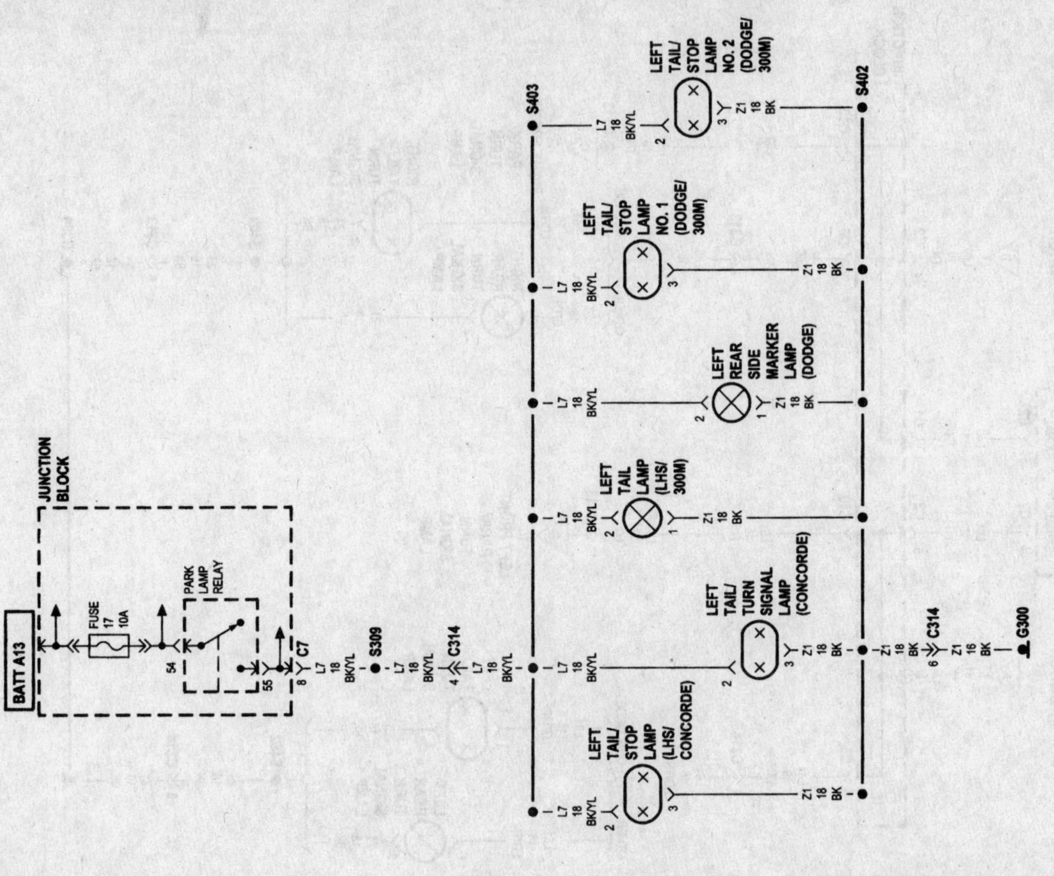

Typical rear exterior lighting system (Part 6 of 6)

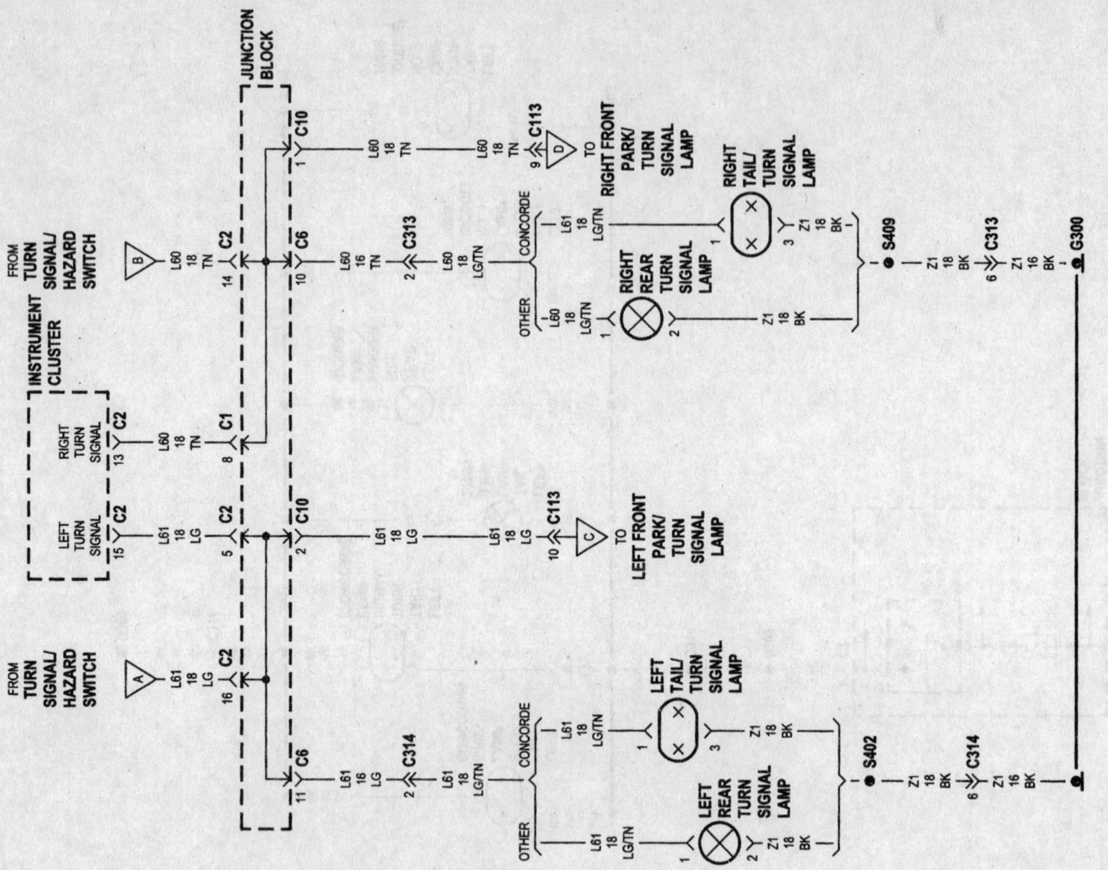

Turn signal/hazard flasher system (Part 2 of 3)

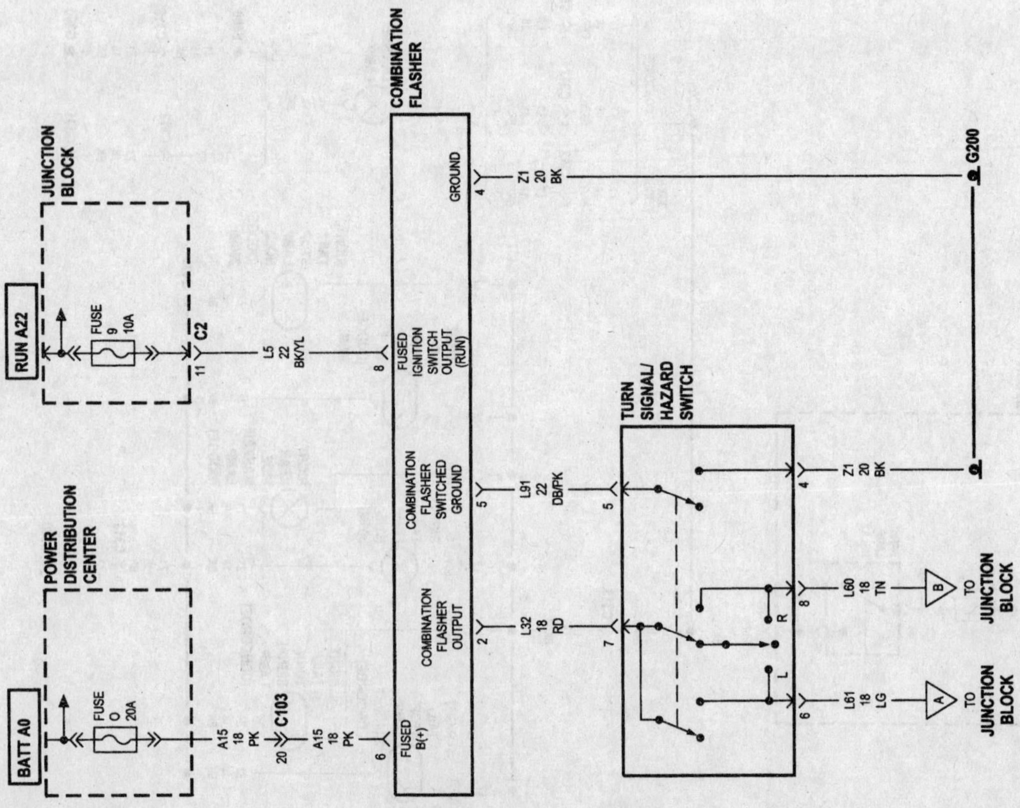

Turn signal/hazard flasher system (Part 1 of 3)

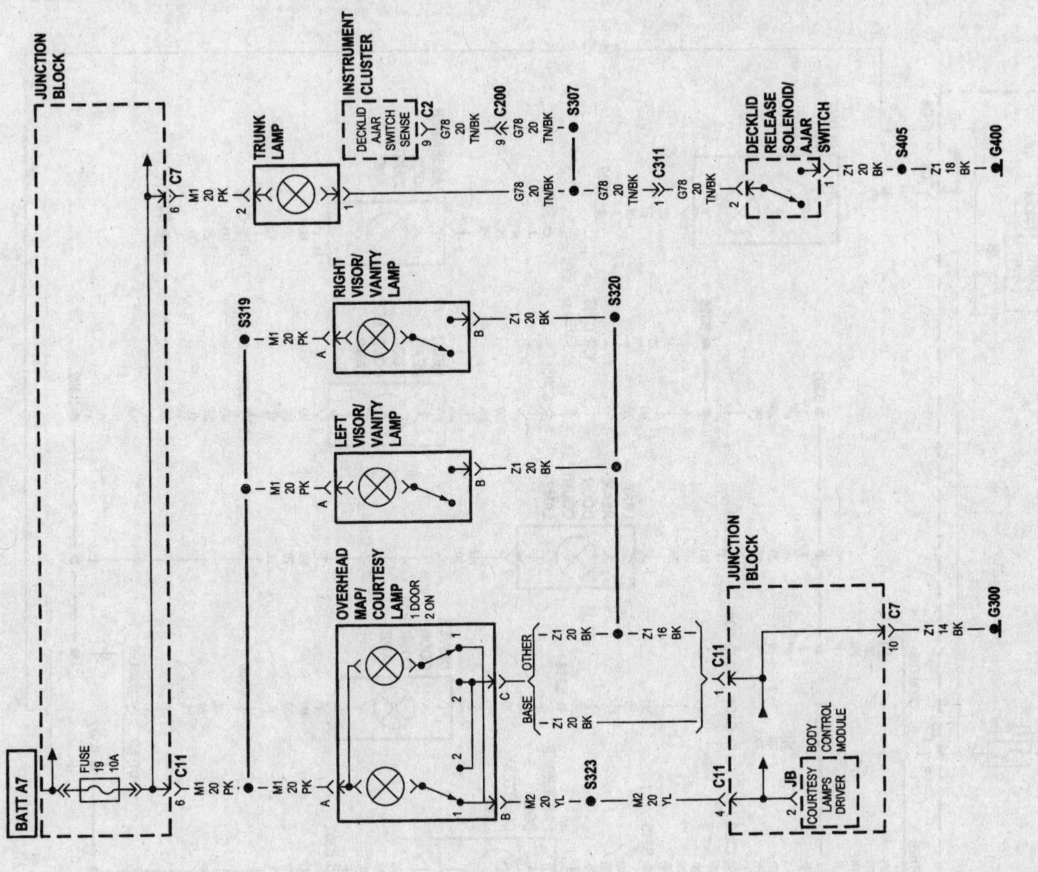

Interior lighting system (Part 1 of 5)

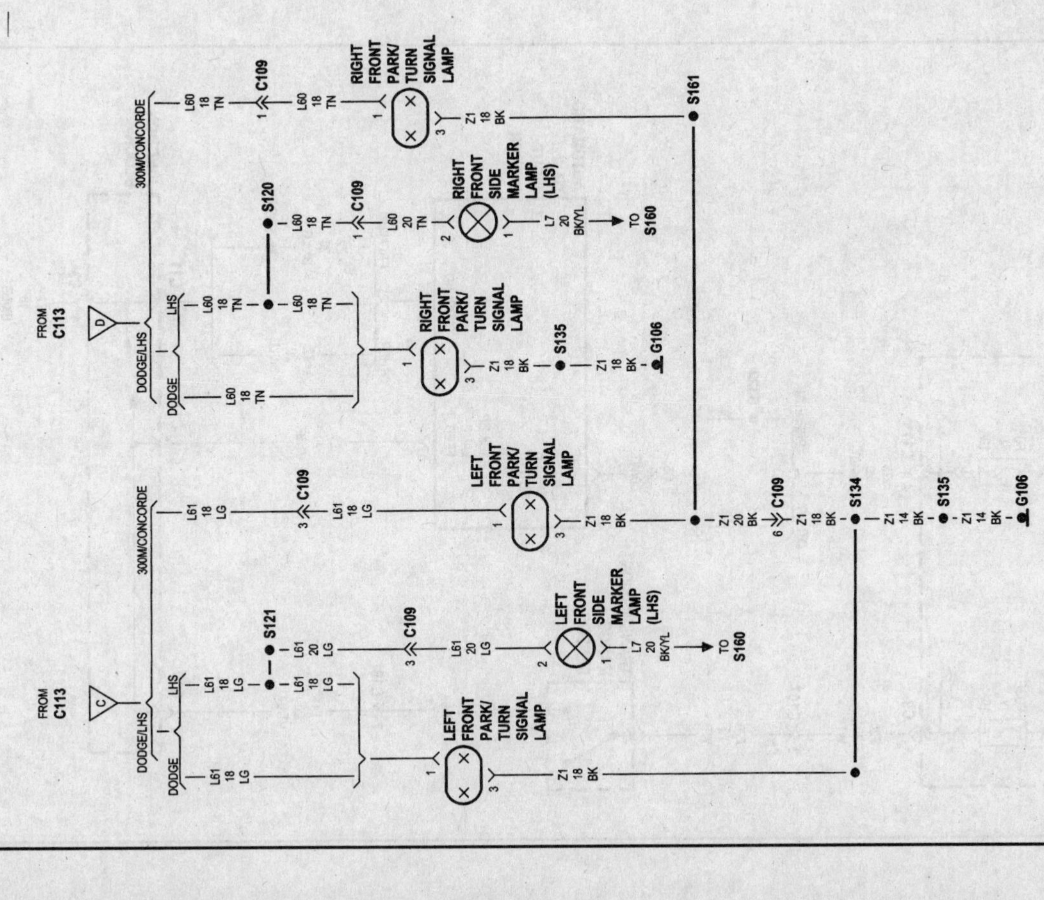

Turn signal/hazard flasher system (Part 3 of 3)

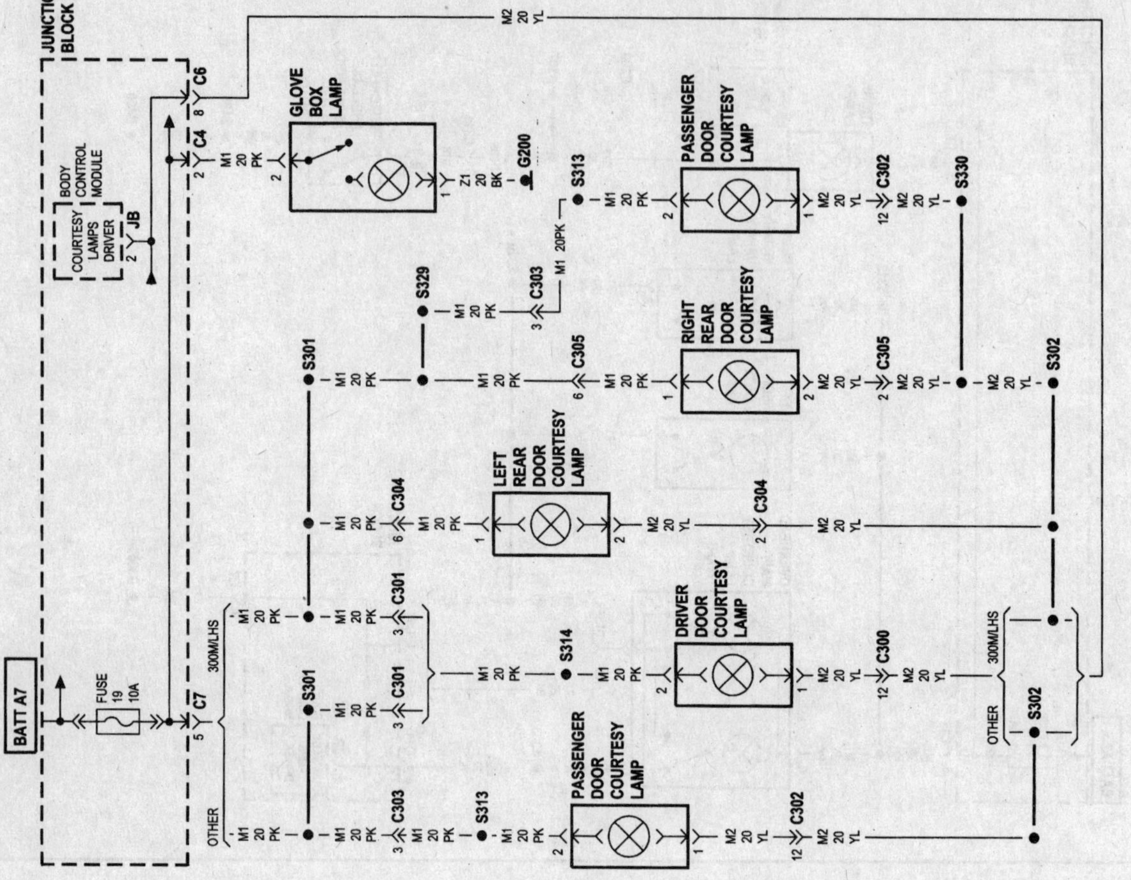

Typical interior lighting system (Part 3 of 5)

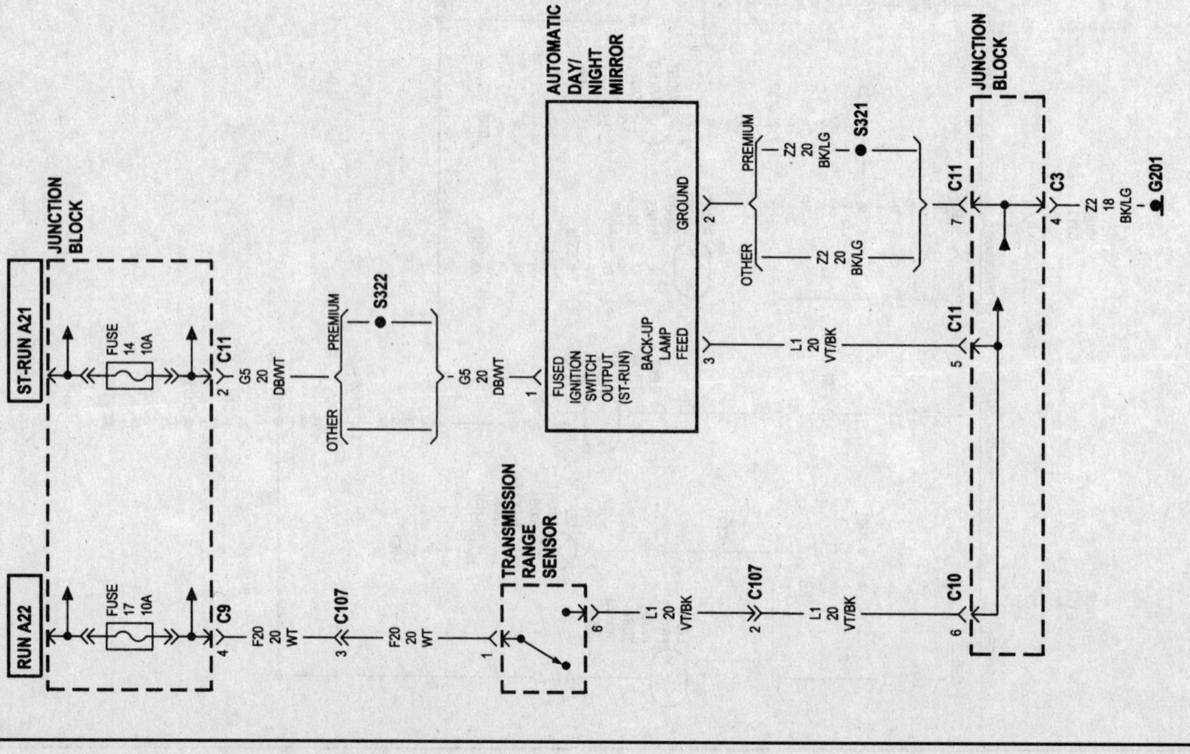

Typical interior lighting system (Part 2 of 5)

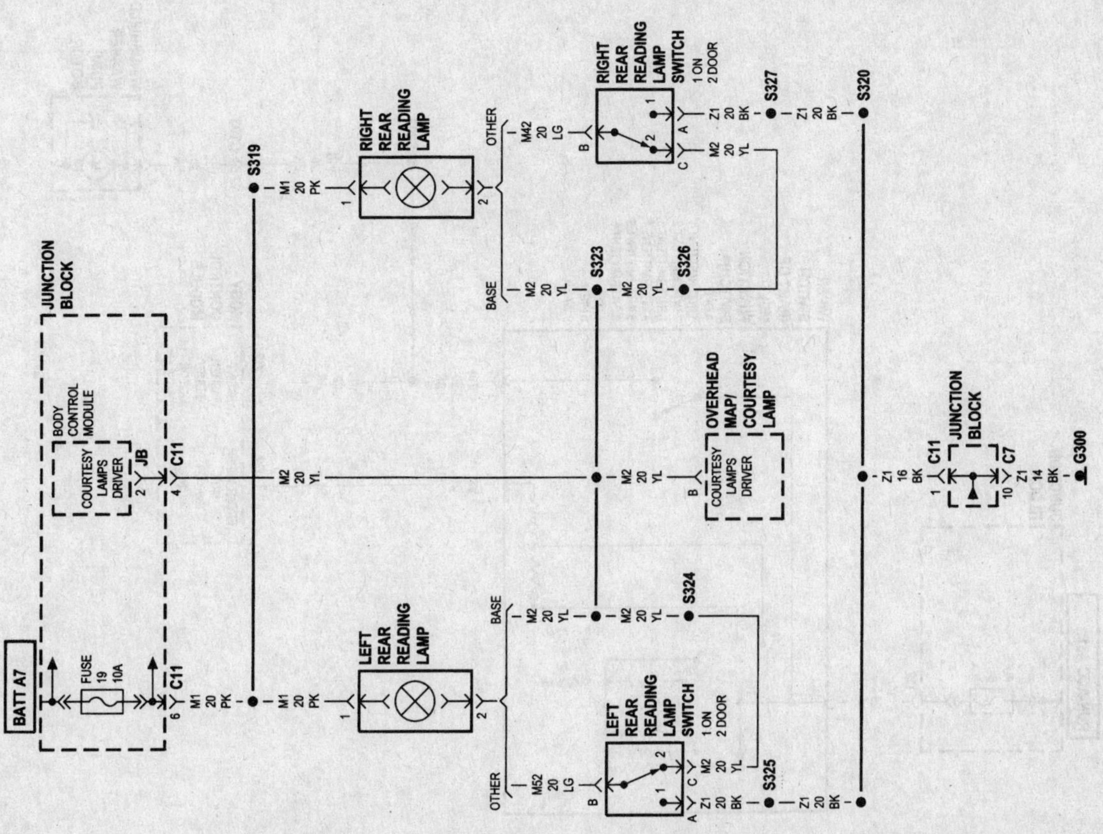

Typical interior lighting system (Part 4 of 5)

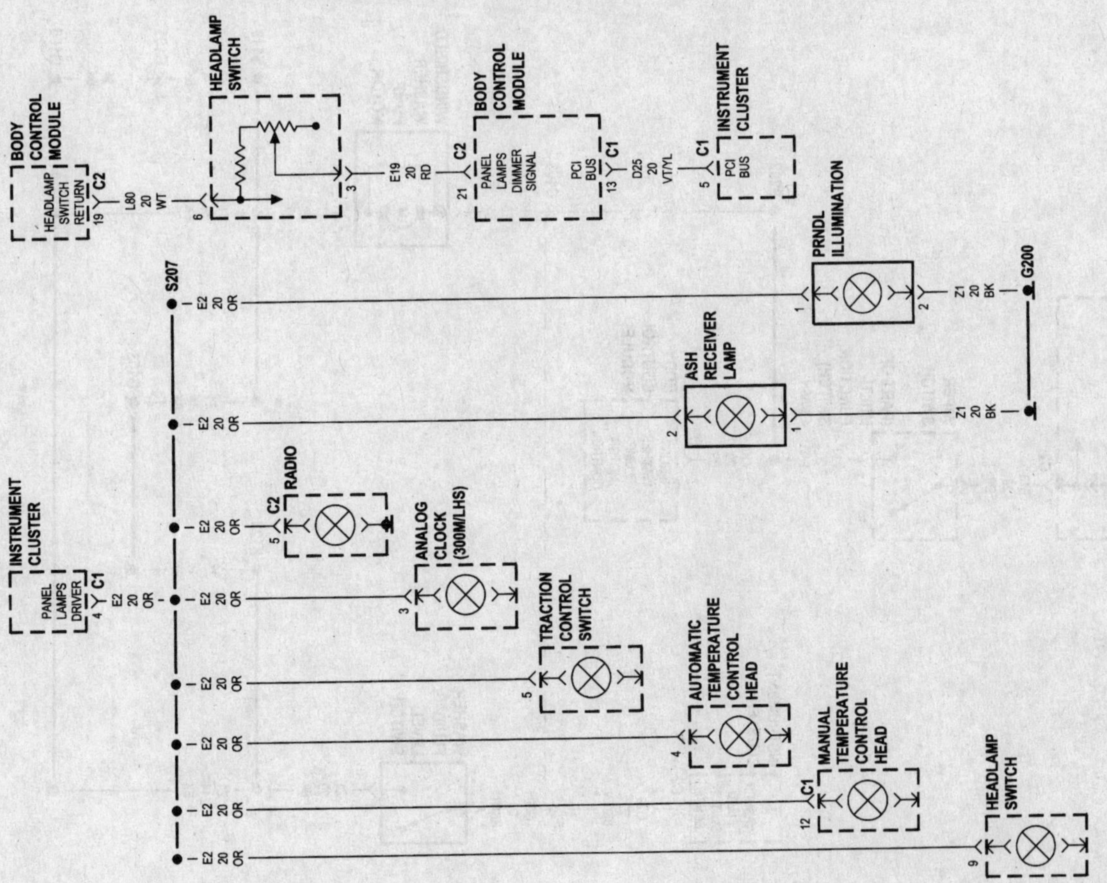

Typical interior lighting system (Part 5 of 5)

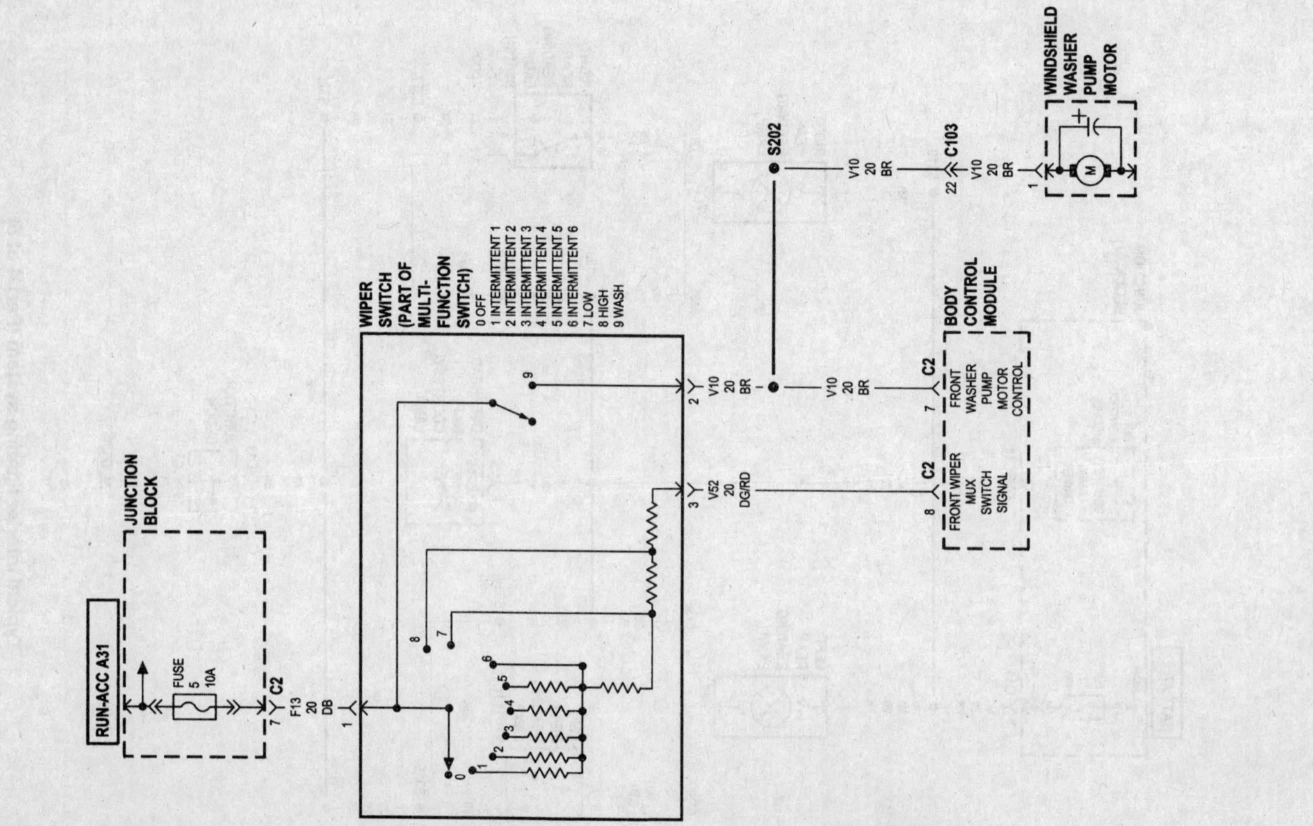

Windshield wiper/washer system (Part 1 of 3)

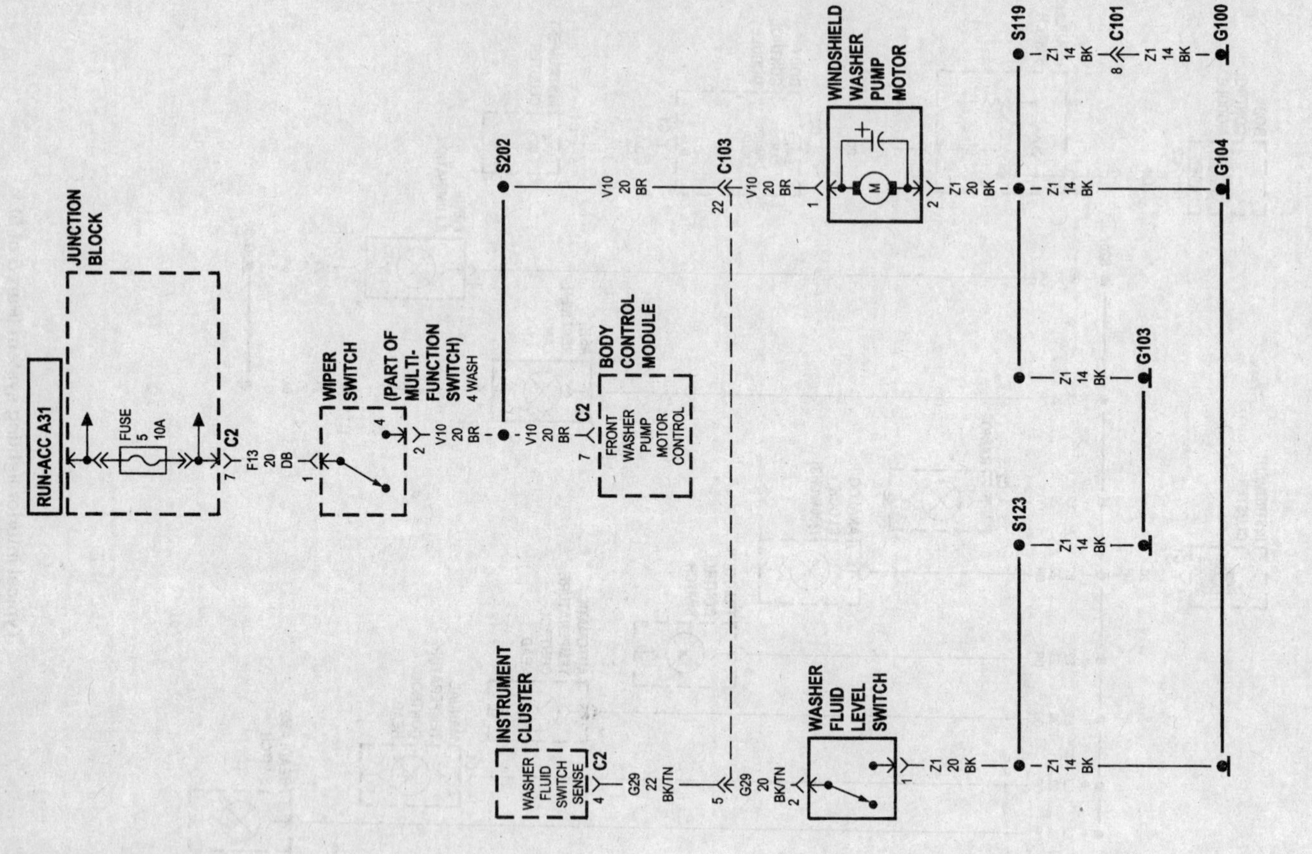

Windshield wiper/washer system (Part 2 of 3)

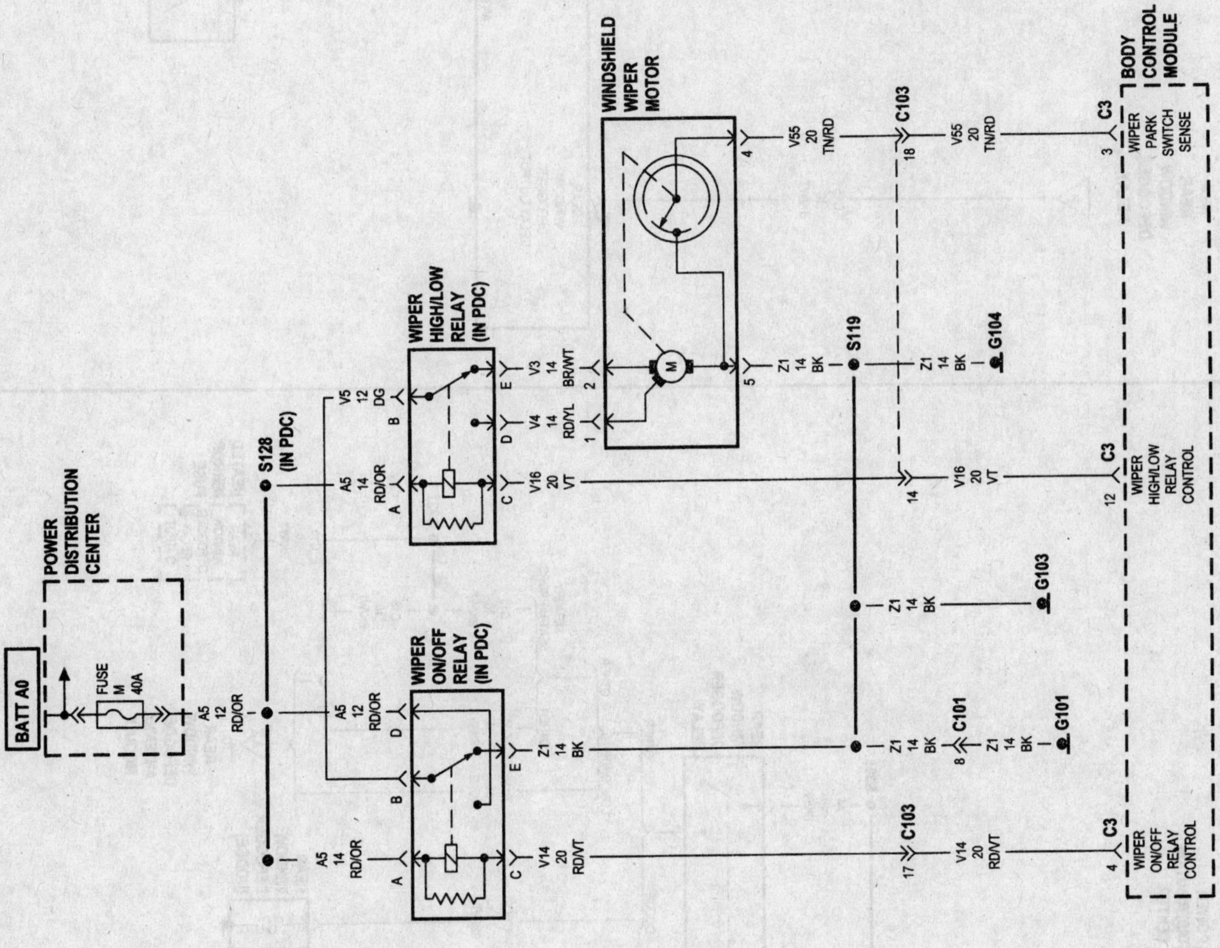

Windshield wiper/washer system (Part 3 of 3)

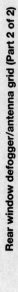

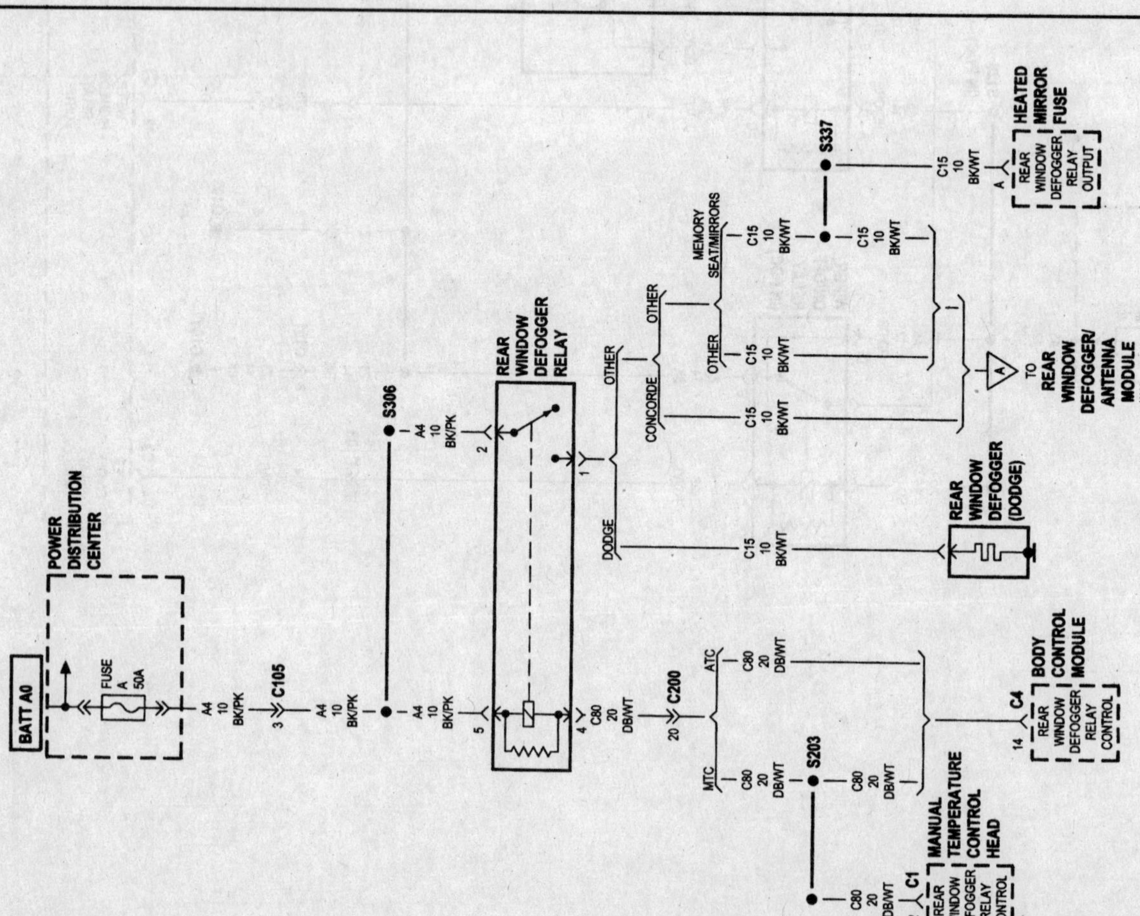

Rear window defogger/antenna grid (Part 1 of 2)

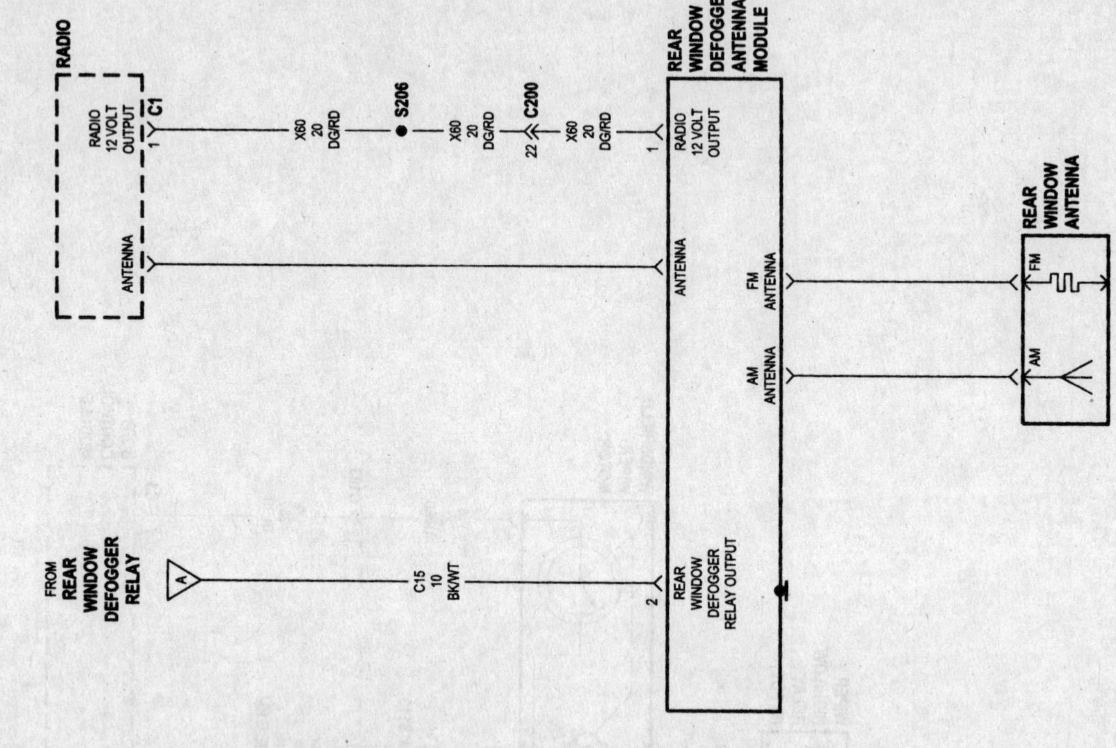

Rear window defogger/antenna grid (Part 2 of 2)

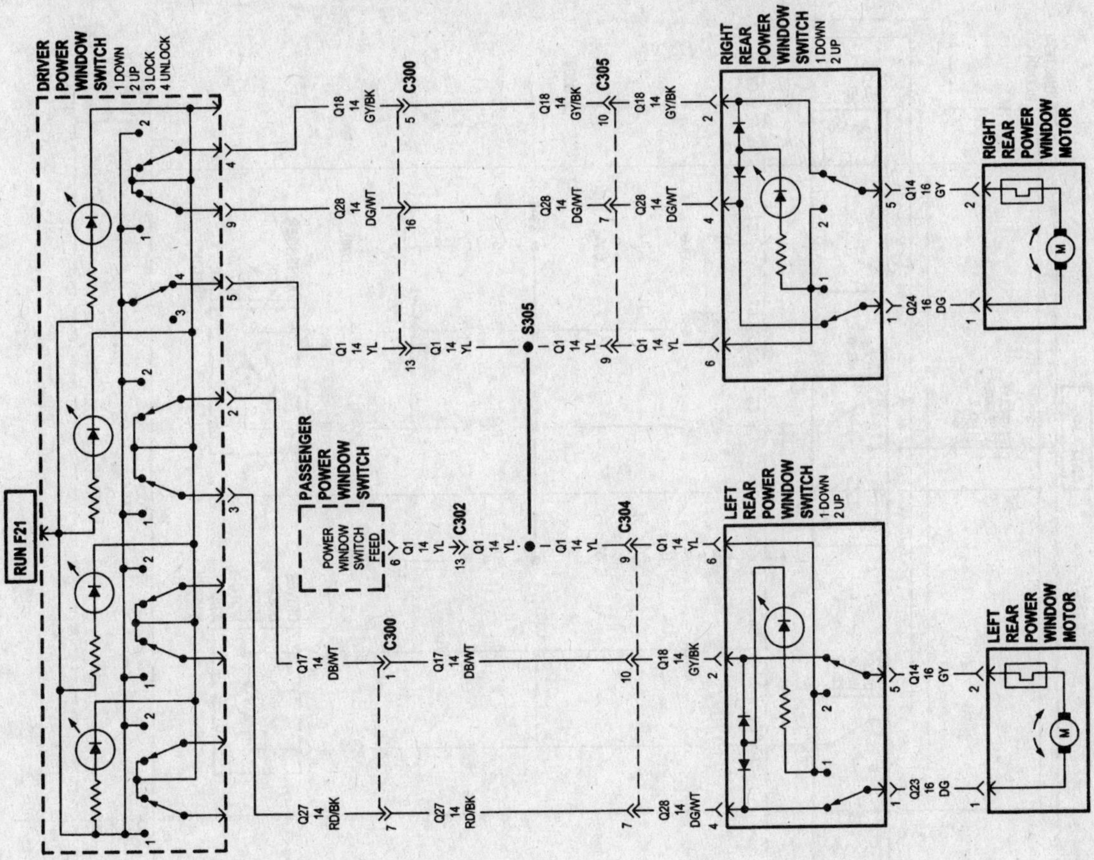

Power window system (Part 2 of 2)

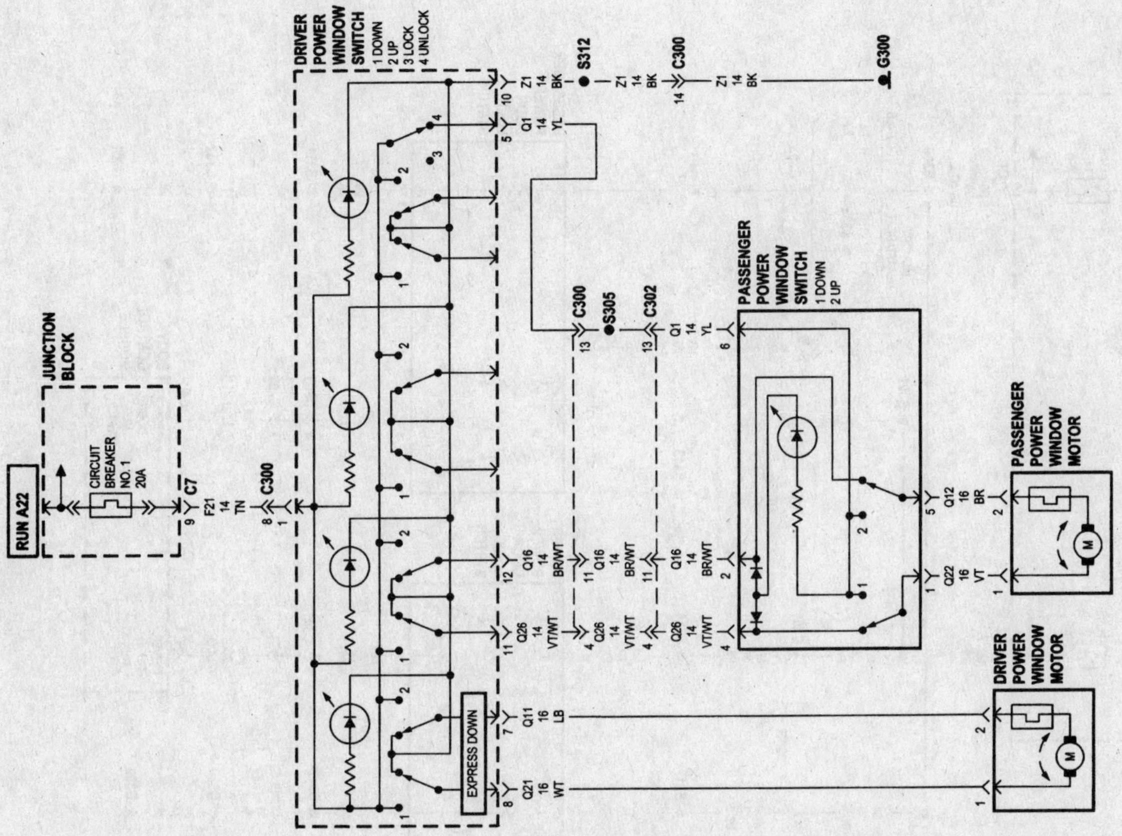

Power window system (Part 1 of 2)

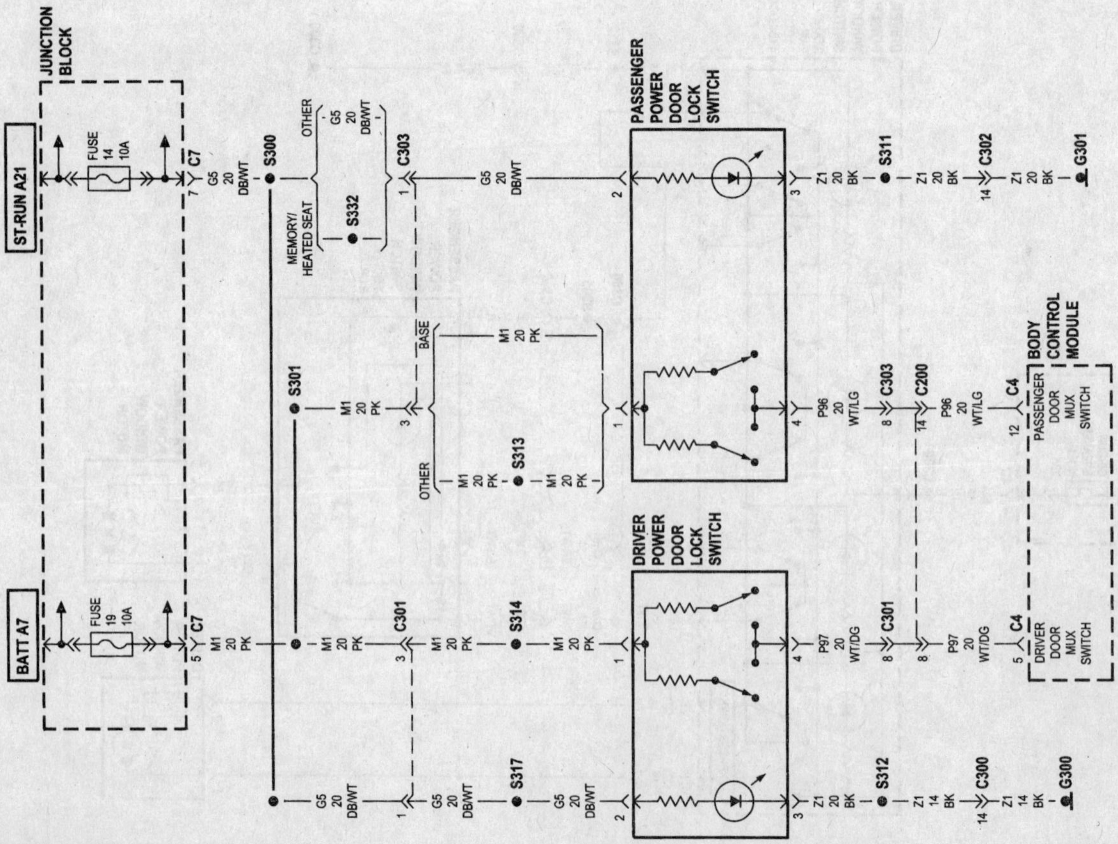

Power door lock system (Part 1 of 4)

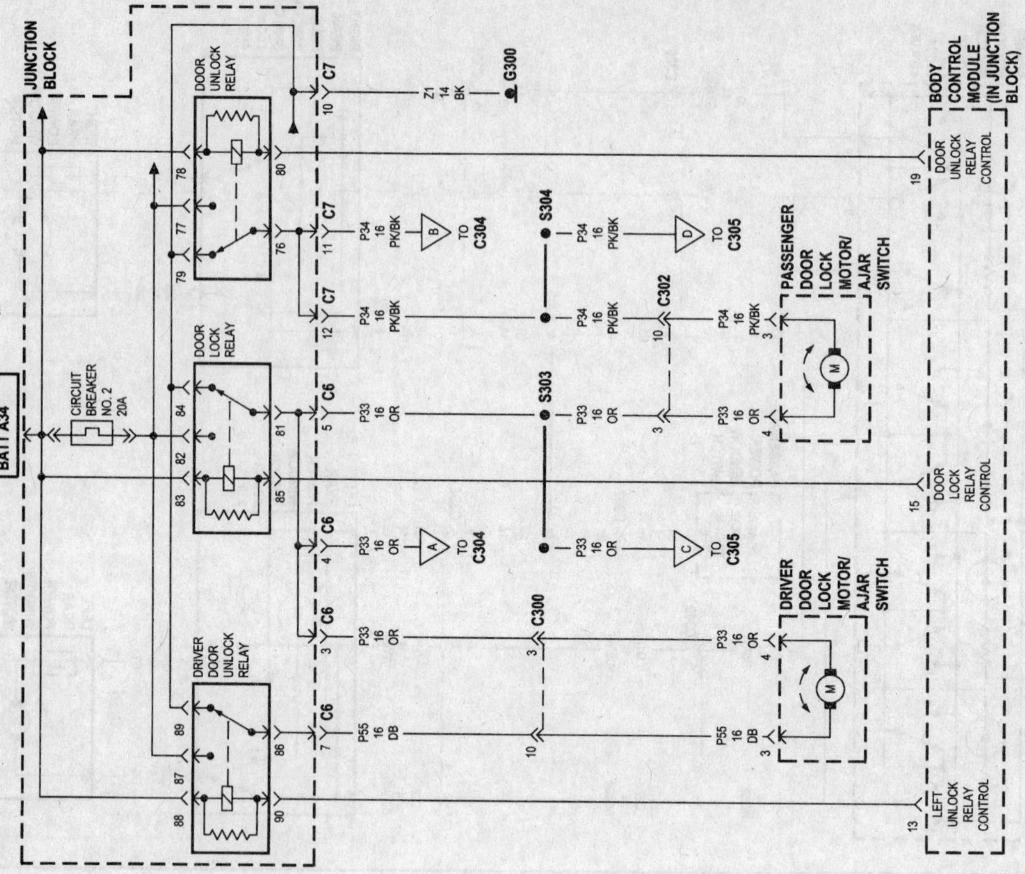

Power door lock system (Part 2 of 4)

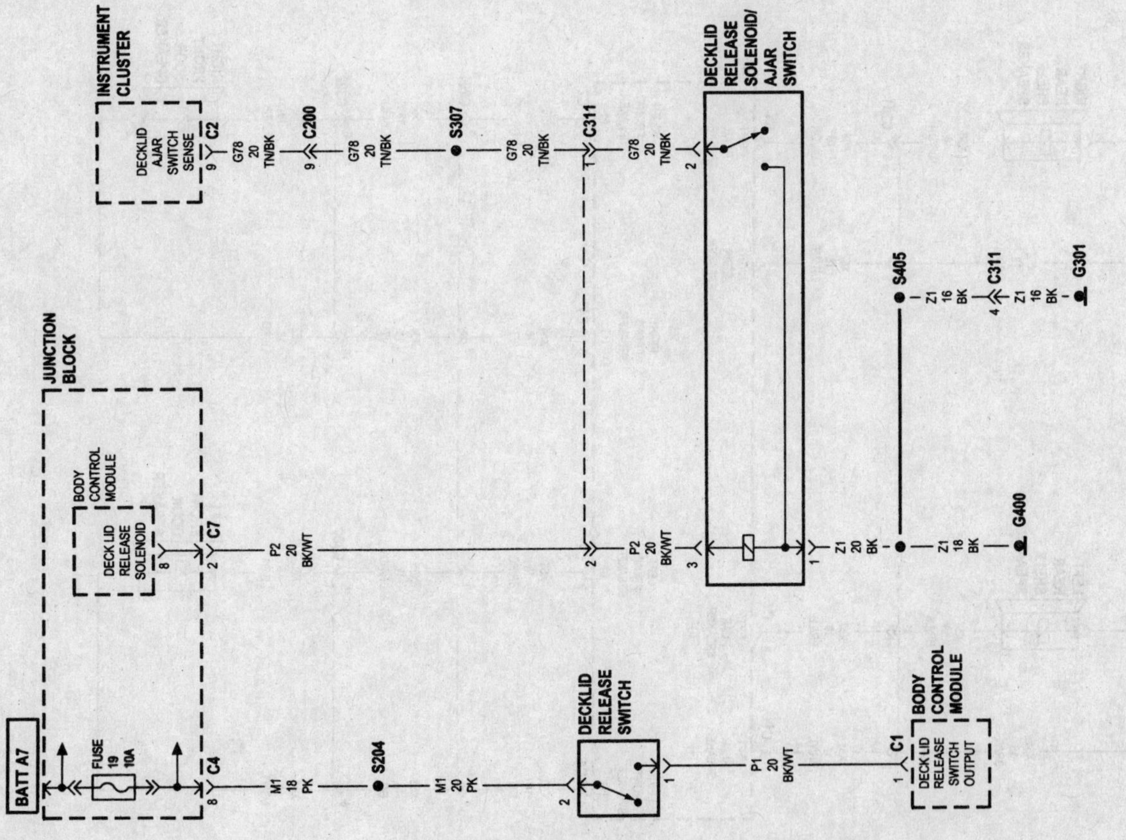

Power door lock system (Part 4 of 4)

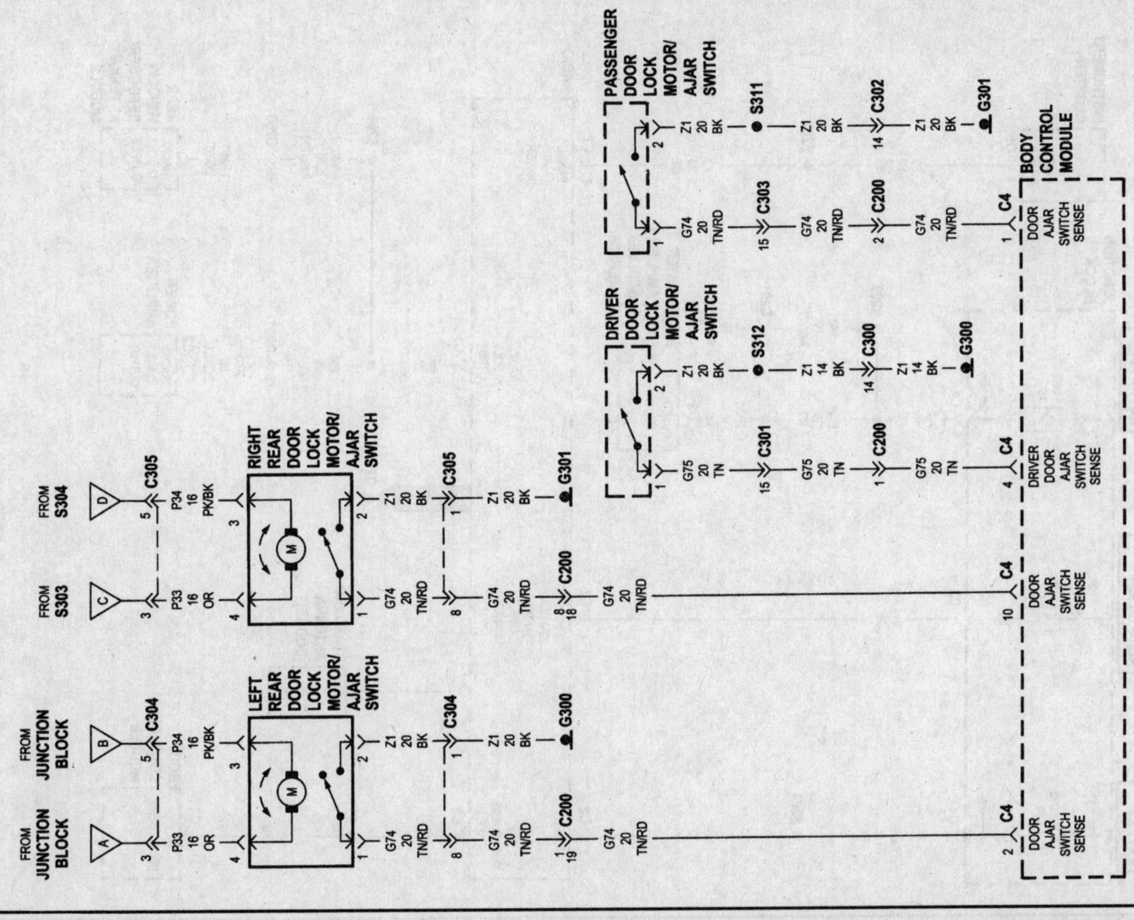

Power door lock system (Part 3 of 4)

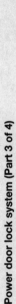

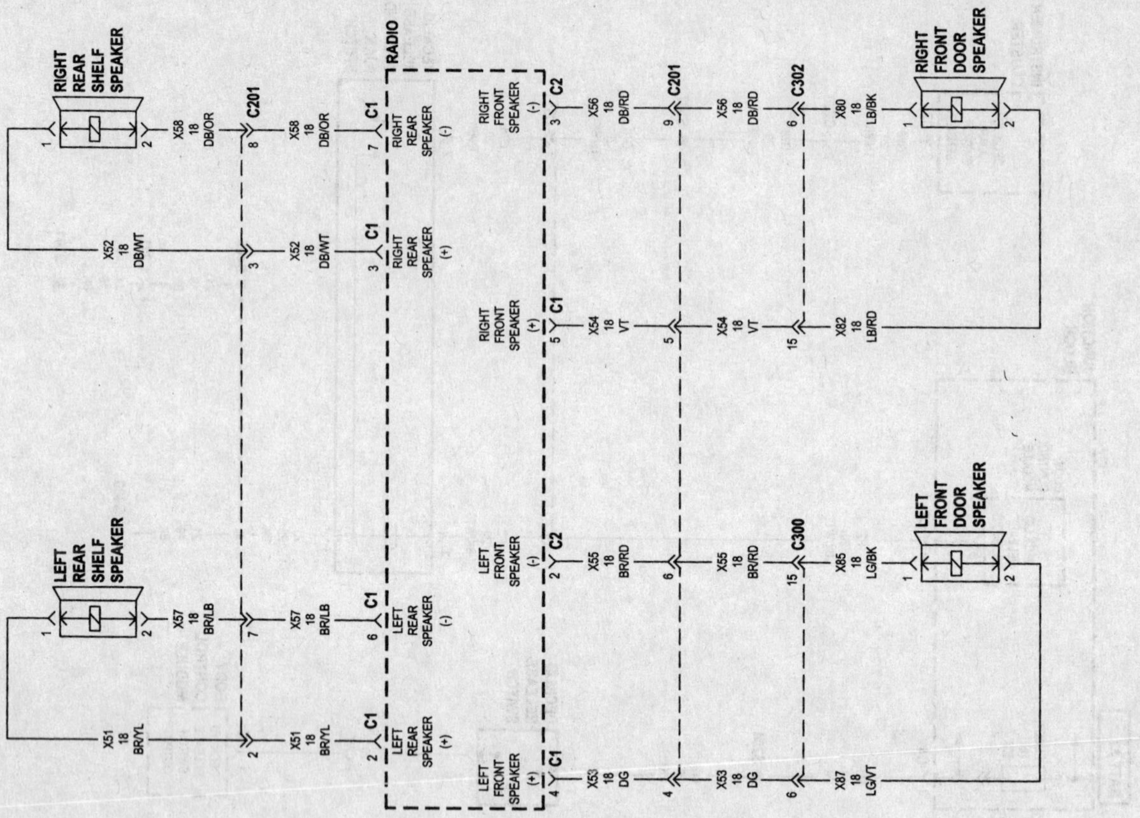

Base audio system (Part 2 of 2)

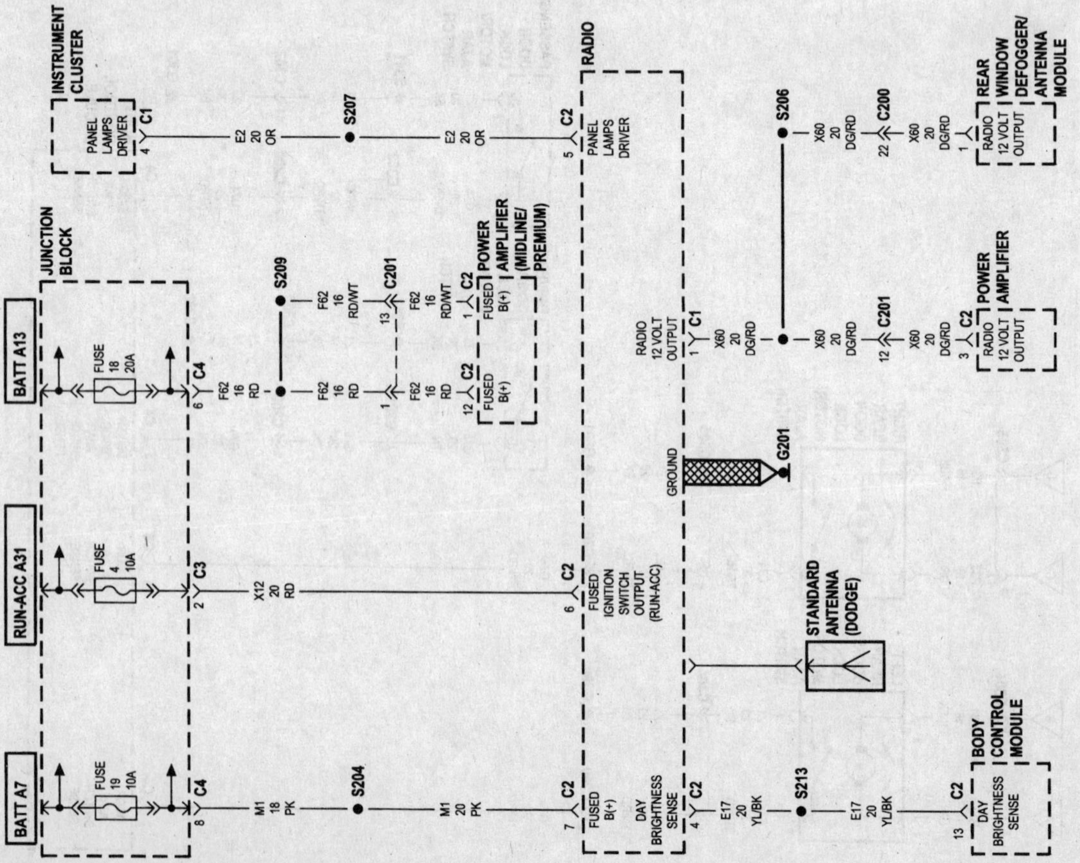

Base audio system (Part 1 of 2)

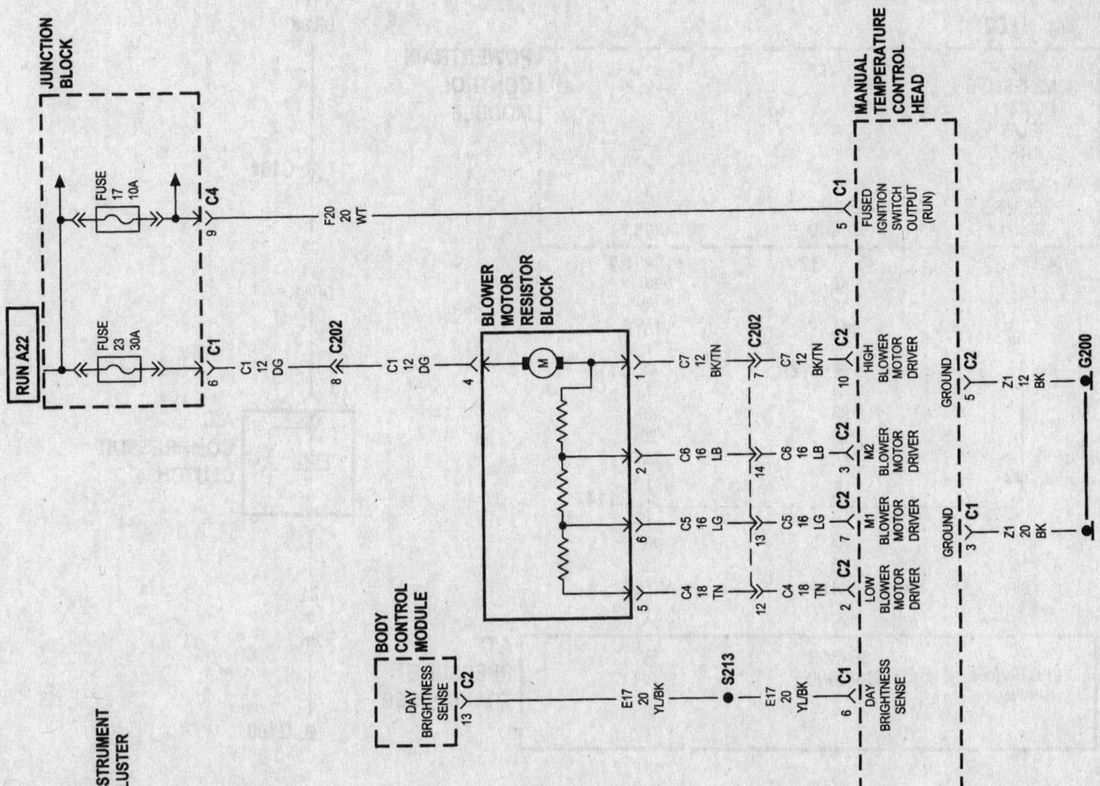

Heating/air conditioning - manual system (Part 1 of 2)

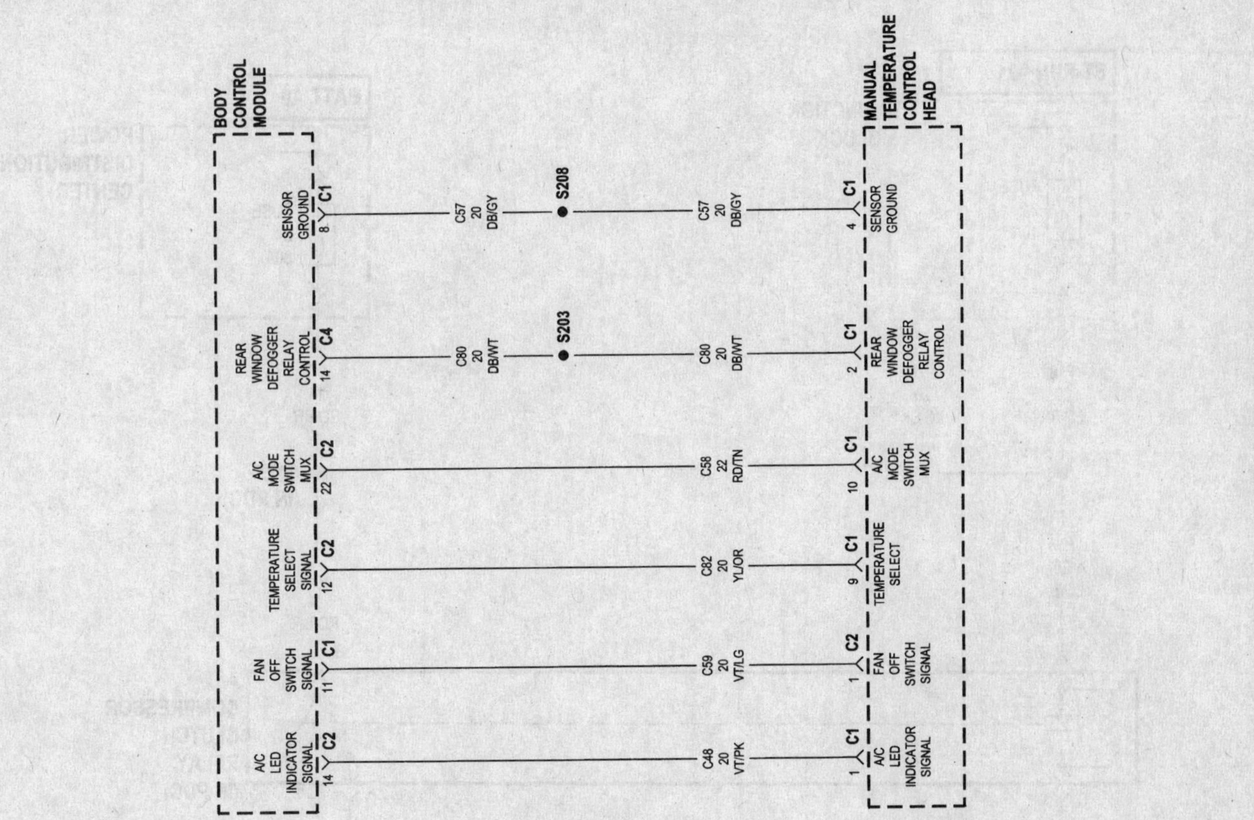

Heating/air conditioning - manual system (Part 2 of 2)

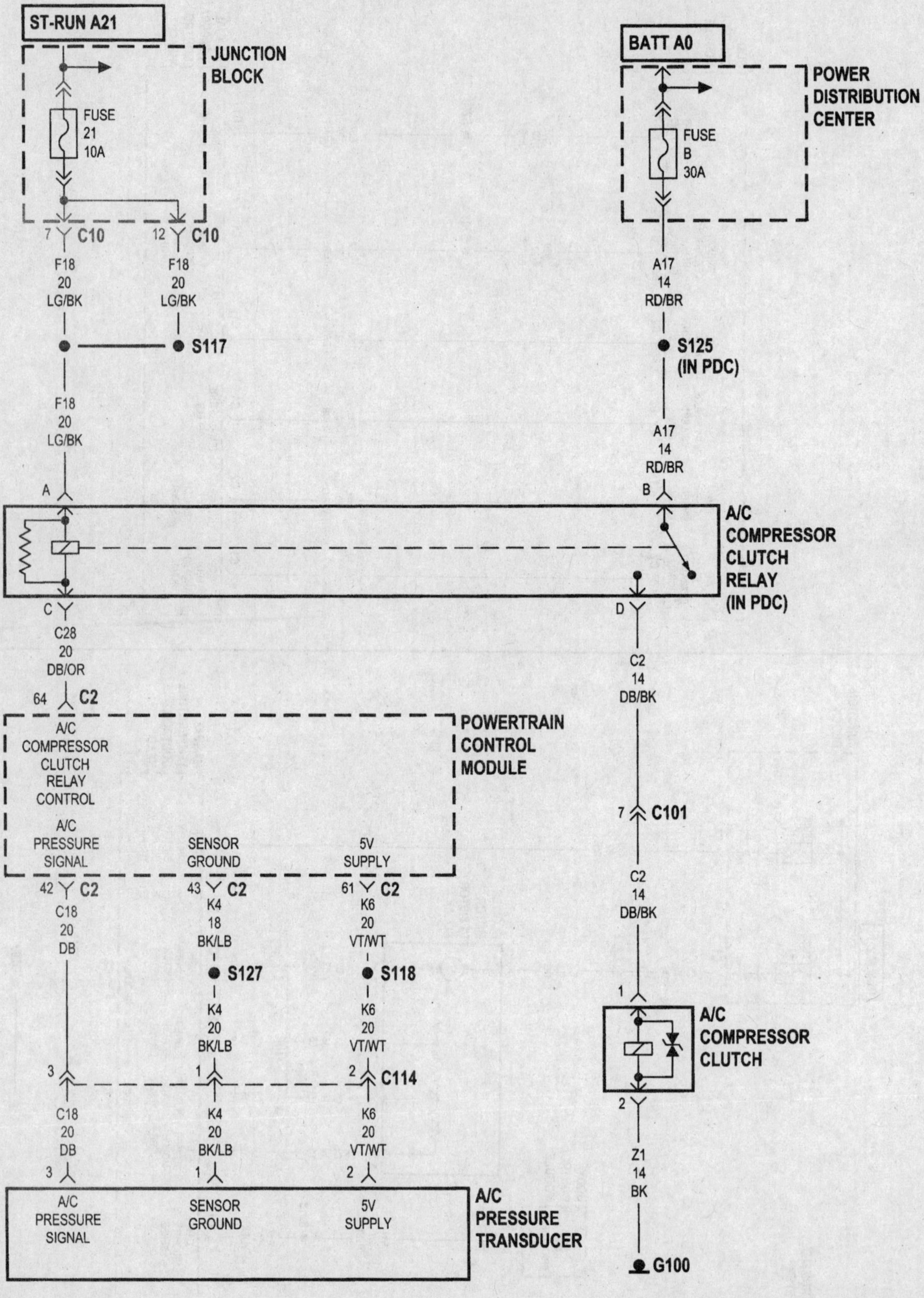

Heating/air conditioning system - compressor circuit

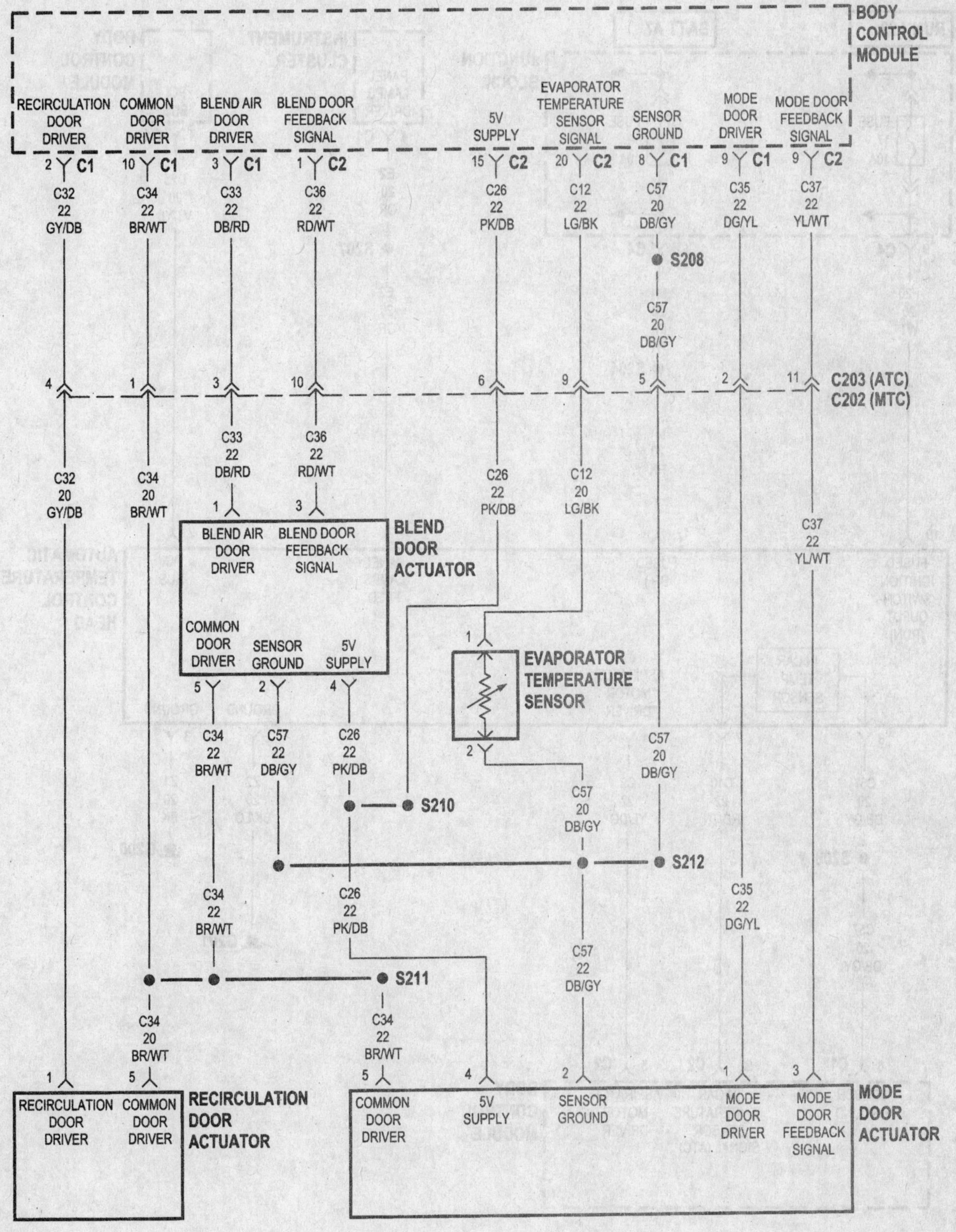

Heating/air conditioning - ATC system (Part 1 of 3)

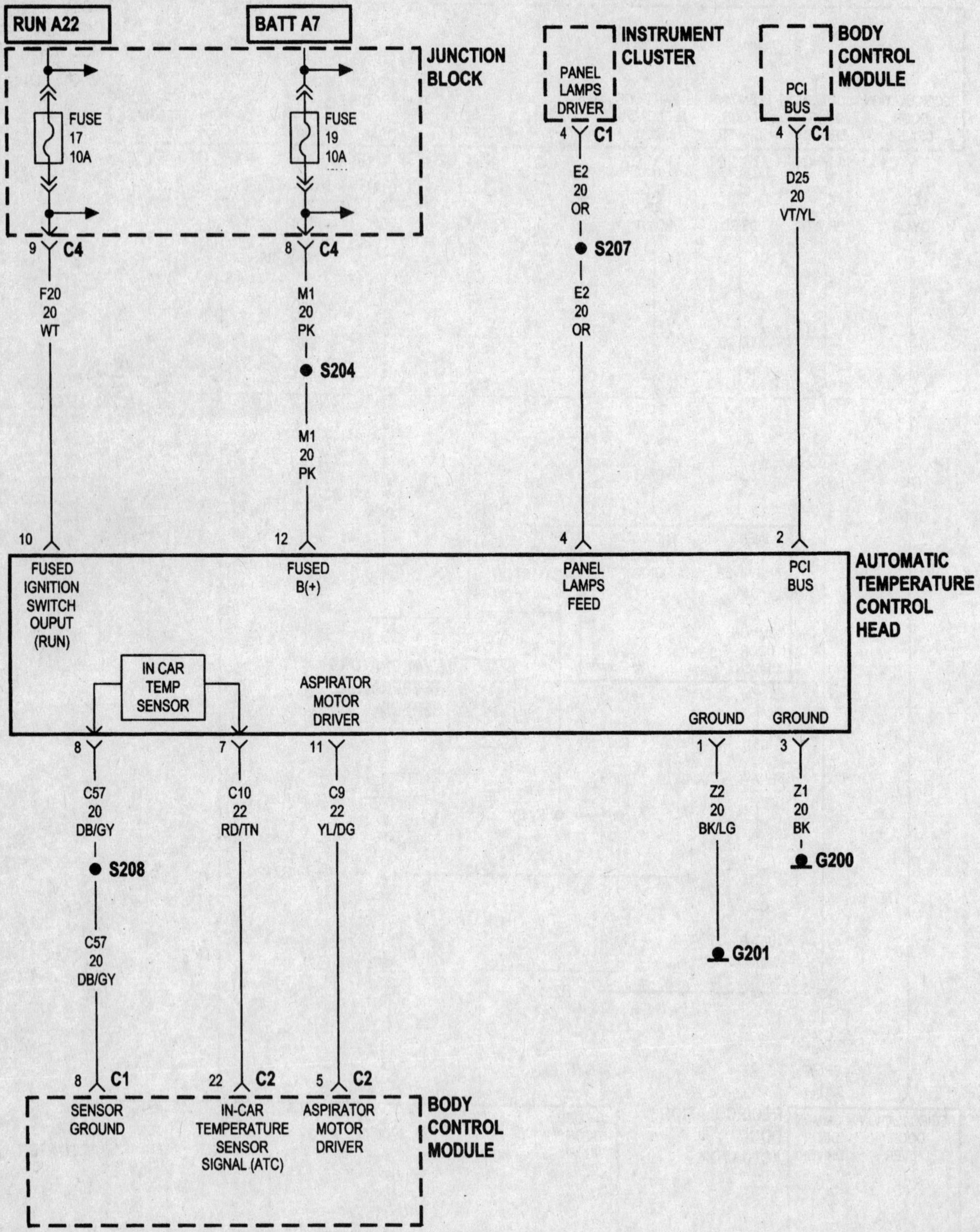

Heating/air conditioning - ATC system (Part 2 of 3)

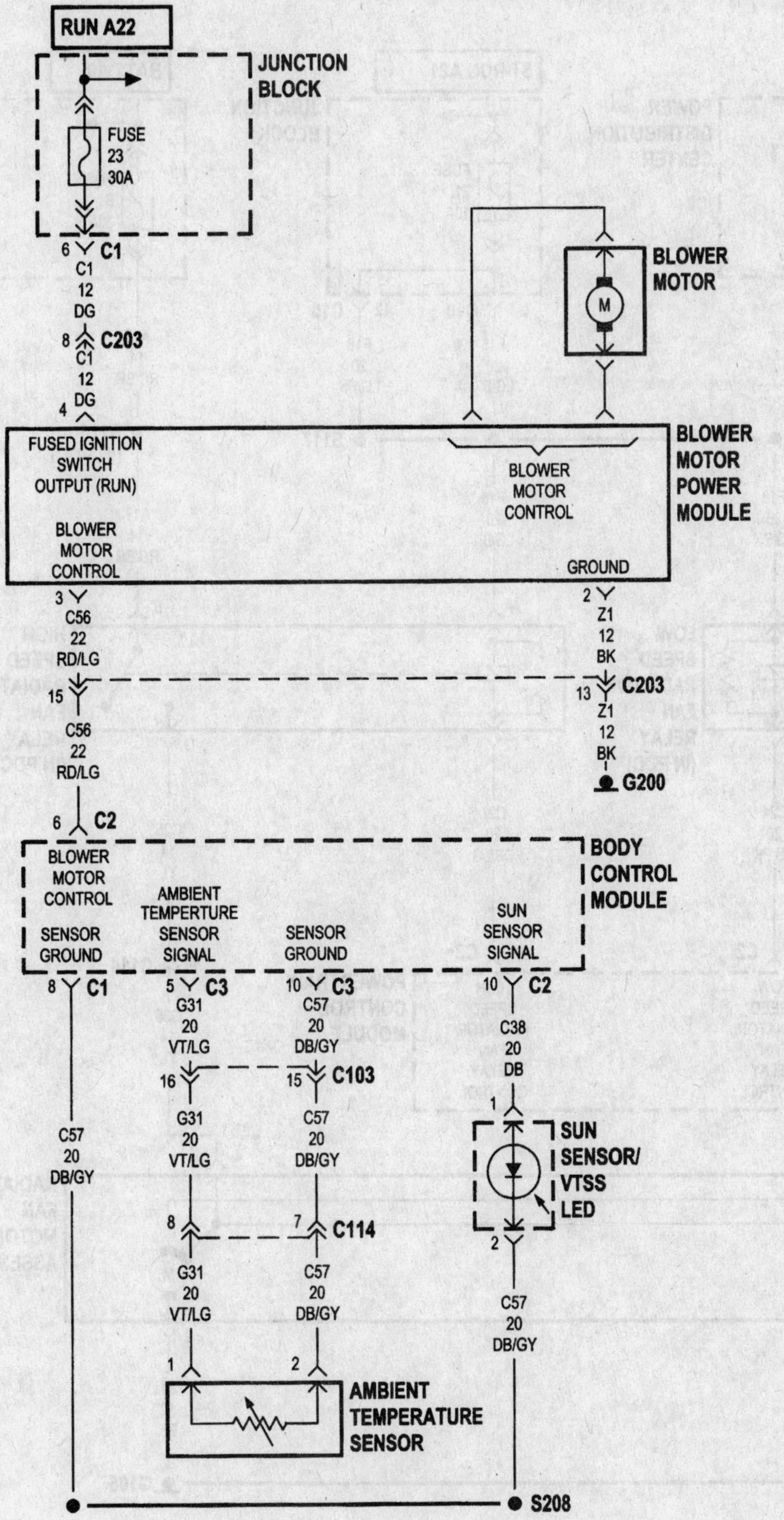

Heating/air conditioning - ATC system (Part 3 of 3)

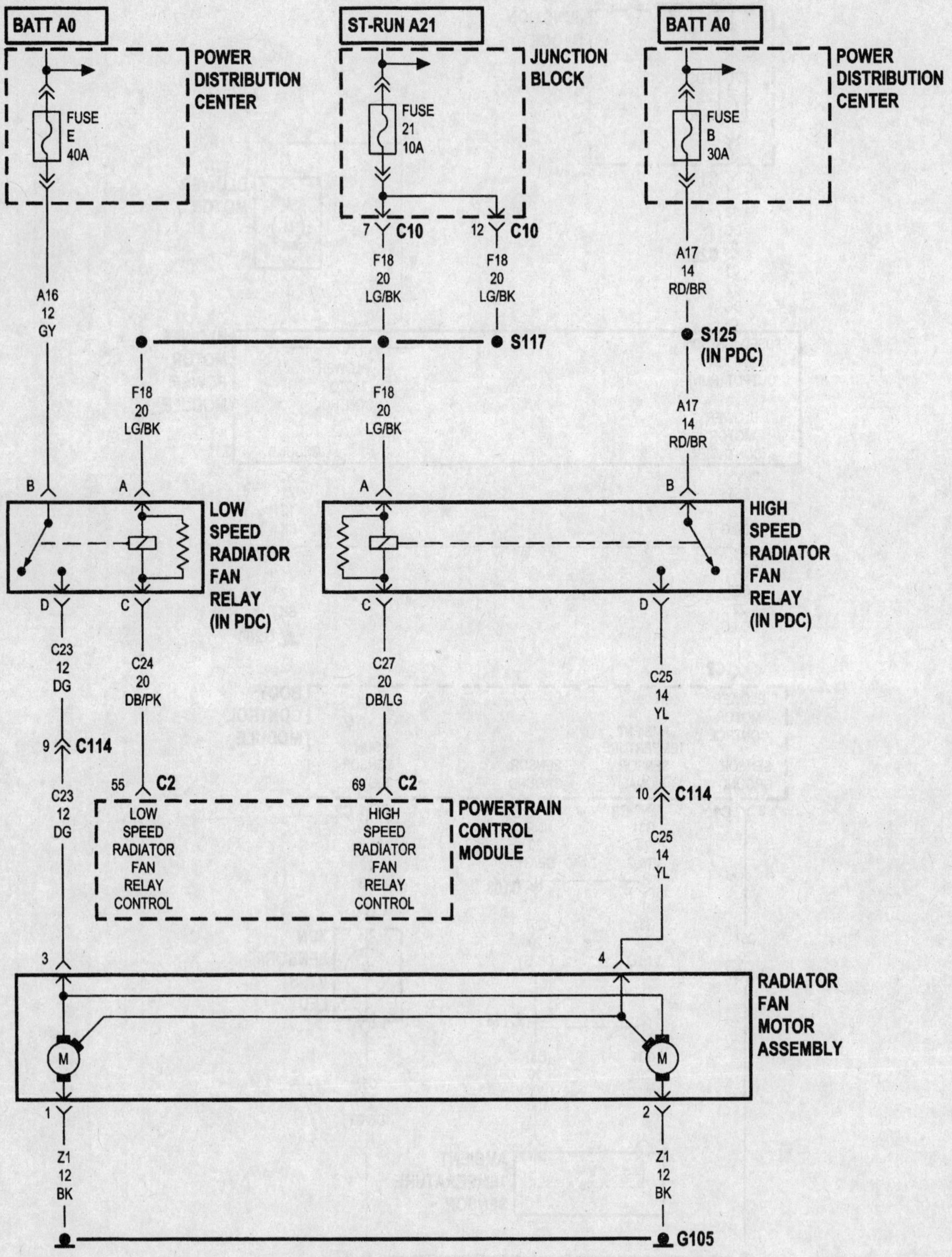

Engine cooling fan system

Index

A

B

F

O

P

R

S

T

U

V

W

Notes

Haynes Automotive Manuals

NOTE: If you do not see a listing for your vehicle, consult your local Haynes dealer for the latest product information.

HAYNES XTREME CUSTOMIZING
11101 Sport Compact Customizing
11102 Sport Compact Performance
11110 In-car Entertainment
11150 Sport Utility Vehicle Customizing
11213 Acura
11255 GM Full-size Pick-ups
11314 Ford Focus
11315 Full-size Ford Pick-ups
11373 Honda Civic

ACURA
12020 Integra '86 thru '89 & Legend '86 thru '90
12021 Integra '90 thru '93 & Legend '91 thru '95

AMC
Jeep CJ - *see JEEP (50020)*
14020 Mid-size models '70 thru '83
14025 (Renault) Alliance & Encore '83 thru '87

AUDI
15020 4000 all models '80 thru '87
15025 5000 all models '77 thru '83
15026 5000 all models '84 thru '88

AUSTIN-HEALEY
Sprite - *see MG Midget (66015)*

BMW
18020 3/5 Series not including diesel or all-wheel drive models '82 thru '92
18021 3-Series incl. Z3 models '92 thru '98
18022 3-Series, E46 chassis '99 thru '05, Z4 models '03 thru '05
18025 320i all 4 cyl models '75 thru '83
18050 1500 thru 2002 except Turbo '59 thru '77

BUICK
19010 Buick Century '97 thru '05
Century (front-wheel drive) - *see GM (38005)*
19020 Buick, Oldsmobile & Pontiac Full-size (Front-wheel drive) '85 thru '05
Buick Electra, LeSabre and Park Avenue; Oldsmobile Delta 88 Royale, Ninety Eight and Regency; Pontiac Bonneville
19025 Buick Oldsmobile & Pontiac Full-size (Rear wheel drive)
Buick Estate '70 thru '90, Electra'70 thru '84, LeSabre '70 thru '85, Limited '74 thru '79
Oldsmobile Custom Cruiser '70 thru '90, Delta 88 '70 thru '85,Ninety-eight '70 thru '84
Pontiac Bonneville '70 thru '81, Catalina '70 thru '81, Grandville '70 thru '75, Parisienne '83 thru '86
19030 Mid-size Regal & Century all rear-drive models with V6, V8 and Turbo '74 thru '87
Regal - *see GENERAL MOTORS (38010)*
Riviera - *see GENERAL MOTORS (38030)*
Roadmaster - *see CHEVROLET (24046)*
Skyhawk - *see GENERAL MOTORS (38015)*
Skylark - *see GM (38020, 38025)*
Somerset - *see GENERAL MOTORS (38025)*

CADILLAC
21030 Cadillac Rear Wheel Drive all gasoline models '70 thru '93
Cimarron - *see GENERAL MOTORS (38015)*
DeVille - *see GM (38031 & 38032)*
Eldorado - *see GM (38030 & 38031)*
Fleetwood - *see GM (38031)*
Seville - *see GM (38030, 38031 & 38032)*

CHEVROLET
24010 Astro & GMC Safari Mini-vans '85 thru '03
24015 Camaro V8 all models '70 thru '81
24016 Camaro all models '82 thru '92
24017 Camaro & Firebird '93 thru '02
Cavalier - *see GENERAL MOTORS (38016)*
Celebrity - *see GENERAL MOTORS (38005)*
24020 Chevelle, Malibu & El Camino '69 thru '87
24024 Chevette & Pontiac T1000 '76 thru '87
Citation - *see GENERAL MOTORS (38020)*
24027 Colorado & GMC Canyon '04 thru '06
24032 Corsica/Beretta all models '87 thru '96
24040 Corvette all V8 models '68 thru '82
24041 Corvette all models '84 thru '96
10305 Chevrolet Engine Overhaul Manual
24045 Full-size Sedans Caprice, Impala, Biscayne, Bel Air & Wagons '69 thru '90
24046 Impala SS & Caprice and Buick Roadmaster '91 thru '96
Impala - *see LUMINA (24048)*
Lumina '90 thru '94 - *see GM (38010)*
24048 Lumina & Monte Carlo '95 thru '05
Lumina APV - *see GM (38035)*
24050 Luv Pick-up all 2WD & 4WD '72 thru '82
Malibu '97 thru '00 - *see GM (38026)*
24055 Monte Carlo all models '70 thru '88
Monte Carlo '95 thru '01 - *see LUMINA (24048)*
24059 Nova all V8 models '69 thru '79
24060 Nova and Geo Prizm '85 thru '92
24064 Pick-ups '67 thru '87 - Chevrolet & GMC, all V8 & in-line 6 cyl, 2WD & 4WD '67 thru '87; Suburbans, Blazers & Jimmys '67 thru '91
24065 Pick-ups '88 thru '98 - Chevrolet & GMC, full-size pick-ups '88 thru '98, C/K Classic '99 & '00, Blazer & Jimmy '92 thru '94; Suburban '92 thru '99; Tahoe & Yukon '95 thru '99
24066 Pick-ups '99 thru '06 - Chevrolet Silverado & GMC Sierra '99 thru '06, Suburban/Tahoe/ Yukon/Yukon XL/Avalanche '00 thru '06
24070 S-10 & S-15 Pick-ups '82 thru '93, Blazer & Jimmy '83 thru '94,
24071 S-10 & Sonoma Pick-ups '94 thru '04, Blazer & Jimmy '95 thru '04, Hombre '96 thru '01
24072 Chevrolet TrailBlazer & TrailBlazer EXT, GMC Envoy & Envoy XL, Oldsmobile Bravada '02 thru '06
24075 Sprint '85 thru '88 & Geo Metro '89 thru '01
24080 Vans - Chevrolet & GMC '68 thru '96
24081 Chevrolet Express & GMC Savana Full-size Vans '96 thru '05

CHRYSLER
25015 Chrysler Cirrus, Dodge Stratus, Plymouth Breeze '95 thru '00
10310 Chrysler Engine Overhaul Manual
25020 Full-size Front-Wheel Drive '88 thru '93
K-Cars - *see DODGE Aries (30008)*
Laser - *see DODGE Daytona (30030)*
25025 Chrysler LHS, Concorde, New Yorker, Dodge Intrepid, Eagle Vision, '93 thru '97
25026 Chrysler LHS, Concorde, 300M, Dodge Intrepid, '98 thru '03
25027 Chrysler 300, Dodge Charger & Magnum '05 thru '07
25030 Chrysler & Plymouth Mid-size front wheel drive '82 thru '95
Rear-wheel Drive - *see Dodge (30050)*
25035 PT Cruiser all models '01 thru '03
25040 Chrysler Sebring, Dodge Avenger '95 thru '05
Dodge Stratus '01 thru 05

DATSUN
28005 200SX all models '80 thru '83
28007 B-210 all models '73 thru '78
28009 210 all models '79 thru '82
28012 240Z, 260Z & 280Z Coupe '70 thru '78
28014 280ZX Coupe & 2+2 '79 thru '83
300ZX - *see NISSAN (72010)*
28018 510 & PL521 Pick-up '68 thru '73
28020 510 all models '78 thru '81
28022 620 Series Pick-up all models '73 thru '79
720 Series Pick-up - *see NISSAN (72030)*
28025 810/Maxima all gasoline models, '77 thru '84

DODGE
400 & 600 - *see CHRYSLER (25030)*
30008 Aries & Plymouth Reliant '81 thru '89
30010 Caravan & Plymouth Voyager '84 thru '95
30011 Caravan & Plymouth Voyager '96 thru '02
30012 Challenger/Plymouth Saporro '78 thru '83
30013 Caravan, Chrysler Voyager, Town & Country '03 thru '06
30016 Colt & Plymouth Champ '78 thru '87
30020 Dakota Pick-ups all models '87 thru '96
30021 Durango '98 & '99, Dakota '97 thru '99
30022 Dodge Durango models '00 thru '03
Dodge Dakota models '00 thru '04
30023 Dodge Durango '04 thru '06, Dakota '05 and '06
30025 Dart, Demon, Plymouth Barracuda, Duster & Valiant 6 cyl models '67 thru '76
30030 Daytona & Chrysler Laser '84 thru '89
Intrepid - *see CHRYSLER (25025, 25026)*
30034 Neon all models '95 thru '99
30035 Omni & Plymouth Horizon '78 thru '90
30036 Dodge and Plymouth Neon '00 thru'05
30040 Pick-ups all full-size models '74 thru '93
30041 Pick-ups all full-size models '94 thru '01
30042 Dodge Full-size Pick-ups '02 thru '05
30045 Ram 50/D50 Pick-ups & Raider and Plymouth Arrow Pick-ups '79 thru '93
30050 Dodge/Plymouth/Chrysler RWD '71 thru '89
30055 Shadow & Plymouth Sundance '87 thru '94
30060 Spirit & Plymouth Acclaim '89 thru '95
30065 Vans - Dodge & Plymouth '71 thru '03

EAGLE
Talon - *see MITSUBISHI (68030, 68031)*
Vision - *see CHRYSLER (25025)*

FIAT
34010 124 Sport Coupe & Spider '68 thru '78
34025 X1/9 all models '74 thru '80

FORD
10355 Ford Automatic Transmission Overhaul
36004 Aerostar Mini-vans all models '86 thru '97
36006 Contour & Mercury Mystique '95 thru '00
36008 Courier Pick-up all models '72 thru '82
36012 Crown Victoria & Mercury Grand Marquis '88 thru '06
10320 Ford Engine Overhaul Manual
36016 Escort/Mercury Lynx all models '81 thru '90
36020 Escort/Mercury Tracer '91 thru '00
36022 Ford Escape & Mazda Tribute '01 thru '03
36024 Explorer & Mazda Navajo '91 thru '01
36025 Ford Explorer & Mercury Mountaineer '02 thru '06
36028 Fairmont & Mercury Zephyr '78 thru '83
36030 Festiva & Aspire '88 thru '97
36032 Fiesta all models '77 thru '80
36034 Focus all models '00 thru '05
36036 Ford & Mercury Full-size '75 thru '87
36044 Ford & Mercury Mid-size '75 thru '86
36048 Mustang V8 all models '64-1/2 thru '73
36049 Mustang II 4 cyl, V6 & V8 models '74 thru '78
36050 Mustang & Mercury Capri all models Mustang, '79 thru '93; Capri, '79 thru '86
36051 Mustang all models '94 thru '04
36052 Mustang '05 thru '07
36054 Pick-ups & Bronco '73 thru '79
36058 Pick-ups & Bronco '80 thru '96
36059 F-150 & Expedition '97 thru '03, F-250 '97 thru '99 & Lincoln Navigator '98 thru '02
36060 Super Duty Pick-ups, Excursion '99 thru '06
36061 F-150 full-size '04 thru '06
36062 Pinto & Mercury Bobcat '75 thru '80
36066 Probe all models '89 thru '92
36070 Ranger/Bronco II gasoline models '83 thru '92
36071 Ranger '93 thru '05 & Mazda Pick-ups '94 thru '05
36074 Taurus & Mercury Sable '86 thru '95
36075 Taurus & Mercury Sable '96 thru '05
36078 Tempo & Mercury Topaz '84 thru '94
36082 Thunderbird/Mercury Cougar '83 thru '88
36086 Thunderbird/Mercury Cougar '89 and '97
36090 Vans all V8 Econoline models '69 thru '91
36094 Vans full size '92 thru '05
36097 Windstar Mini-van '95 thru '03

GENERAL MOTORS
10360 GM Automatic Transmission Overhaul
38005 Buick Century, Chevrolet Celebrity, Oldsmobile Cutlass Ciera & Pontiac 6000 all models '82 thru '96
38010 Buick Regal, Chevrolet Lumina, Oldsmobile Cutlass Supreme & Pontiac Grand Prix (FWD) '88 thru '05
38015 Buick Skyhawk, Cadillac Cimarron, Chevrolet Cavalier, Oldsmobile Firenza & Pontiac J-2000 & Sunbird '82 thru '94
38016 Chevrolet Cavalier & Pontiac Sunfire '95 thru '04
38017 Chevrolet Cobalt & Pontiac G5 '05 thru '07
38020 Buick Skylark, Chevrolet Citation, Olds Omega, Pontiac Phoenix '80 thru '85
38025 Buick Skylark & Somerset, Oldsmobile Achieva & Calais and Pontiac Grand Am all models '85 thru '98
38026 Chevrolet Malibu, Olds Alero & Cutlass, Pontiac Grand Am '97 thru '03
38027 Chevrolet Malibu '04 thru '07
38030 Cadillac Eldorado '71 thru '85, Seville '80 thru '85, Oldsmobile Toronado '71 thru '85, Buick Riviera '79 thru '85
38031 Cadillac Eldorado & Seville '86 thru '91, DeVille '86 thru '93, Fleetwood & Olds Toronado '86 thru '92, Buick Riviera '86 thru '93
38032 Cadillac DeVille '94 thru '05 & Seville '92 thru '04
38035 Chevrolet Lumina APV, Olds Silhouette & Pontiac Trans Sport all models '90 thru '96
38036 Chevrolet Venture, Olds Silhouette, Pontiac Trans Sport & Montana '97 thru '05
General Motors Full-size Rear-wheel Drive - see BUICK (19025)

GEO
Metro - *see CHEVROLET Sprint (24075)*
Prizm - *'85 thru '92 see CHEVY (24060), '93 thru '02 see TOYOTA Corolla (92036)*

(Continued on other side)

Haynes Automotive Manuals (continued)

NOTE: If you do not see a listing for your vehicle, consult your local Haynes dealer for the latest product information.

40030 **Storm** all models '90 thru '93
Tracker - *see SUZUKI Samurai (90010)*

GMC

Vans & Pick-ups - *see CHEVROLET*

HONDA

42010 **Accord CVCC** all models '76 thru '83
42011 **Accord** all models '84 thru '89
42012 **Accord** all models '90 thru '93
42013 **Accord** all models '94 thru '97
42014 **Accord** all models '98 thru '02
42015 **Honda Accord** models '03 thru '05
42020 **Civic 1200** all models '73 thru '79
42021 **Civic 1300 & 1500 CVCC** '80 thru '83
42022 **Civic 1500 CVCC** all models '75 thru '79
42023 **Civic** all models '84 thru '91
42024 **Civic & del Sol** '92 thru '95
42025 **Civic** '96 thru '00, **CR-V** '97 thru '01, **Acura Integra** '94 thru '00
42026 **Civic** '01 thru '04, **CR-V** '02 thru '04
42035 **Honda Odyssey** all models '99 thru '04
42037 **Honda Pilot** '03 thru '07, **Acura MDX** '01 thru '07
42040 **Prelude CVCC** all models '79 thru '89

HYUNDAI

43010 **Elantra** all models '96 thru '01
43015 **Excel & Accent** all models '86 thru '98

ISUZU

Hombre - *see CHEVROLET S-10 (24071)*
47017 **Rodeo** '91 thru '02; **Amigo** '89 thru '94 and '98 thru '02; **Honda Passport** '95 thru '02
47020 **Trooper & Pick-up** '81 thru '93

JAGUAR

49010 **XJ6** all 6 cyl models '68 thru '86
49011 **XJ6** all models '88 thru '94
49015 **XJ12 & XJS** all 12 cyl models '72 thru '85

JEEP

50010 **Cherokee, Comanche & Wagoneer Limited** all models '84 thru '01
50020 **CJ** all models '49 thru '86
50025 **Grand Cherokee** all models '93 thru '04
50029 **Grand Wagoneer & Pick-up** '72 thru '91 Grand Wagoneer '84 thru '91, Cherokee & Wagoneer '72 thru '83, Pick-up '72 thru '88
50030 **Wrangler** all models '87 thru '03
50035 **Liberty** '02 thru '04

KIA

54070 **Sephia** '94 thru '01, **Spectra** '00 thru '04

LEXUS

ES 300 - *see TOYOTA Camry (92007)*

LINCOLN

Navigator - *see FORD Pick-up (36059)*
59010 **Rear-Wheel Drive** all models '70 thru '05

MAZDA

61010 **GLC Hatchback (rear-wheel drive)** '77 thru '83
61011 **GLC (front-wheel drive)** '81 thru '85
61015 **323 & Protogé** '90 thru '00
61016 **MX-5 Miata** '90 thru '97
61020 **MPV** all models '89 thru '94
Navajo - *see Ford Explorer (36024)*
61030 **Pick-ups** '72 thru '93
Pick-ups '94 thru '00 - *see Ford Ranger (36071)*
61035 **RX-7** all models '79 thru '85
61036 **RX-7** all models '86 thru '91
61040 **626** (rear-wheel drive) all models '79 thru '82
61041 **626/MX-6 (front-wheel drive)** '83 thru '92
61042 **626** '93 thru '01, **MX-6/Ford Probe** '93 thru '01

MERCEDES-BENZ

63012 **123 Series Diesel** '76 thru '85
63015 **190 Series** four-cyl gas models, '84 thru '88
63020 **230/250/280** 6 cyl sohc models '68 thru '72
63025 **280 123 Series** gasoline models '77 thru '81
63030 **350 & 450** all models '71 thru '80

MERCURY

64200 **Villager & Nissan Quest** '93 thru '01
All other titles, see FORD Listing.

MG

66010 **MGB** Roadster & GT Coupe '62 thru '80
66015 **MG Midget, Austin Healey Sprite** '58 thru '80

MITSUBISHI

68020 **Cordia, Tredia, Galant, Precis & Mirage** '83 thru '93
68030 **Eclipse, Eagle Talon & Ply. Laser** '90 thru '94
68031 **Eclipse** '95 thru '01, **Eagle Talon** '95 thru '98
68035 **Mitsubishi Galant** '94 thru '03
68040 **Pick-up** '83 thru '96 **& Montero** '83 thru '93

NISSAN

72010 **300ZX** all models including Turbo '84 thru '89
72015 **Altima** all models '93 thru '04
72020 **Maxima** all models '85 thru '92
72021 **Maxima** all models '93 thru '04
72030 **Pick-ups** '80 thru '97 **Pathfinder** '87 thru '95
72031 **Frontier Pick-up** '98 thru '04, **Xterra** '00 thru '04, **Pathfinder** '96 thru '04
72040 **Pulsar** all models '83 thru '86
Quest - *see MERCURY Villager (64200)*
72050 **Sentra** all models '82 thru '94
72051 **Sentra & 200SX** all models '95 thru '04
72060 **Stanza** all models '82 thru '90

OLDSMOBILE

73015 **Cutlass** V6 & V8 gas models '74 thru '88
For other OLDSMOBILE titles, see BUICK, CHEVROLET or GENERAL MOTORS listing.

PLYMOUTH

For PLYMOUTH titles, see DODGE listing.

PONTIAC

79008 **Fiero** all models '84 thru '88
79018 **Firebird** V8 models except Turbo '70 thru '81
79019 **Firebird** all models '82 thru '92
79040 **Mid-size Rear-wheel Drive** '70 thru '87
For other PONTIAC titles, see BUICK, CHEVROLET or GENERAL MOTORS listing.

PORSCHE

80020 **911** except Turbo & Carrera 4 '65 thru '89
80025 **914** all 4 cyl models '69 thru '76
80030 **924** all models including Turbo '76 thru '82
80035 **944** all models including Turbo '83 thru '89

RENAULT

Alliance & Encore - *see AMC (14020)*

SAAB

84010 **900** all models including Turbo '79 thru '88

SATURN

87010 **Saturn** all models '91 thru '02
87011 **Saturn Ion** '03 thru '07
87020 **Saturn** all L-series models '00 thru '04

SUBARU

89002 **1100, 1300, 1400 & 1600** '71 thru '79
89003 **1600 & 1800** 2WD & 4WD '80 thru '94
89100 **Legacy** all models '90 thru '99
89101 **Legacy & Forester** '00 thru '06

SUZUKI

90010 **Samurai/Sidekick & Geo Tracker** '86 thru '01

TOYOTA

92005 **Camry** all models '83 thru '91
92006 **Camry** all models '92 thru '96
92007 **Camry, Avalon, Solara, Lexus ES 300** '97 thru '01
92008 **Toyota Camry, Avalon and Solara and Lexus ES 300/330** all models '02 thru '05
92015 **Celica Rear Wheel Drive** '71 thru '85
92020 **Celica Front Wheel Drive** '86 thru '99
92025 **Celica Supra** all models '79 thru '92
92030 **Corolla** all models '75 thru '79
92032 **Corolla** all rear wheel drive models '80 thru '87
92035 **Corolla** all front wheel drive models '84 thru '92
92036 **Corolla & Geo Prizm** '93 thru '02
92037 **Corolla** models '03 thru '05
92040 **Corolla Tercel** all models '80 thru '82
92045 **Corona** all models '74 thru '82
92050 **Cressida** all models '78 thru '82
92055 **Land Cruiser** FJ40, 43, 45, 55 '68 thru '82
92056 **Land Cruiser** FJ60, 62, 80, FZJ80 '80 thru '96
92065 **MR2** all models '85 thru '87
92070 **Pick-up** all models '69 thru '78
92075 **Pick-up** all models '79 thru '95
92076 **Tacoma** '95 thru '04, **4Runner** '96 thru '02, **& T100** '93 thru '98
92078 **Tundra** '00 thru '05 **& Sequoia** '01 thru '05
92080 **Previa** all models '91 thru '95
92081 **Prius** all models '01 thru '08
92082 **RAV4** all models '96 thru '05
92085 **Tercel** all models '87 thru '94
92090 **Toyota Sienna** all models '98 thru '02
92095 **Highlander & Lexus RX-330** '99 thru '06

TRIUMPH

94007 **Spitfire** all models '62 thru '81
94010 **TR7** all models '75 thru '81

VW

96008 **Beetle & Karmann Ghia** '54 thru '79
96009 **New Beetle** '98 thru '05
96016 **Rabbit, Jetta, Scirocco & Pick-up** gas models '75 thru '92 & Convertible '80 thru '92
96017 **Golf, GTI & Jetta** '93 thru '98 **& Cabrio** '95 thru '98
96018 **Golf, GTI, Jetta & Cabrio** '99 thru '02
96020 **Rabbit, Jetta & Pick-up** diesel '77 thru '84
96023 **Passat** '98 thru '01, **Audi A4** '96 thru '01
96030 **Transporter 1600** all models '68 thru '79
96035 **Transporter 1700, 1800 & 2000** '72 thru '79
96040 **Type 3 1500 & 1600** all models '63 thru '73
96045 **Vanagon** all air-cooled models '80 thru '83

VOLVO

97010 **120, 130 Series & 1800 Sports** '61 thru '73
97015 **140 Series** all models '66 thru '74
97020 **240 Series** all models '76 thru '93
97040 **740 & 760 Series** all models '82 thru '88
97050 **850 Series** all models '93 thru '97

TECHBOOK MANUALS

10205 **Automotive Computer Codes**
10206 **OBD-II & Electronic Engine Management Systems**
10210 **Automotive Emissions Control Manual**
10215 **Fuel Injection Manual, 1978 thru 1985**
10220 **Fuel Injection Manual, 1986 thru 1999**
10225 **Holley Carburetor Manual**
10230 **Rochester Carburetor Manual**
10240 **Weber/Zenith/Stromberg/SU Carburetors**
10305 **Chevrolet Engine Overhaul Manual**
10310 **Chrysler Engine Overhaul Manual**
10320 **Ford Engine Overhaul Manual**
10330 **GM and Ford Diesel Engine Repair Manual**
10333 **Building Engine Power Manual**
10340 **Small Engine Repair Manual,** 5 HP & Less
10341 **Small Engine Repair Manual,** 5.5 - 20 HP
10345 **Suspension, Steering & Driveline Manual**
10355 **Ford Automatic Transmission Overhaul**
10360 **GM Automatic Transmission Overhaul**
10405 **Automotive Body Repair & Painting**
10410 **Automotive Brake Manual**
10411 **Automotive Anti-lock Brake (ABS) Systems**
10415 **Automotive Detailing Manual**
10420 **Automotive Electrical Manual**
10425 **Automotive Heating & Air Conditioning**
10430 **Automotive Reference Manual & Dictionary**
10435 **Automotive Tools Manual**
10440 **Used Car Buying Guide**
10445 **Welding Manual**
10450 **ATV Basics**
10452 **Scooters, Automatic Transmission 50cc to 250cc**

SPANISH MANUALS

98903 **Reparación de Carrocería & Pintura**
98904 **Carburadores para los modelos Holley & Rochester**
98905 **Códigos Automotrices de la Computadora**
98910 **Frenos Automotriz**
98913 **Electricidad Automotriz**
98915 **Inyección de Combustible 1986 al 1999**
99040 **Chevrolet & GMC Camionetas** '67 al '87 Incluye Suburban, Blazer & Jimmy '67 al '91
99041 **Chevrolet & GMC Camionetas** '88 al '98 Incluye Suburban '92 al '98, Blazer & Jimmy '92 al '94, Tahoe y Yukon '95 al '98
99042 **Chevrolet & GMC Camionetas Cerradas** '68 al '95
99055 **Dodge Caravan & Plymouth Voyager** '84 al '95
99075 **Ford Camionetas y Bronco** '80 al '94
99077 **Ford Camionetas Cerradas** '69 al '91
99088 **Ford Modelos de Tamaño Mediano** '75 al '86
99091 **Ford Taurus & Mercury Sable** '86 al '95
99095 **GM Modelos de Tamaño Grande** '70 al '90
99100 **GM Modelos de Tamaño Mediano** '70 al '88
99106 **Jeep Cherokee, Wagoneer & Comanche** '84 al '00
99110 **Nissan Camioneta** '80 al '96, **Pathfinder** '87 al '95
99118 **Nissan Sentra** '82 al '94
99125 **Toyota Camionetas y 4Runner** '79 al '95

Over 100 Haynes motorcycle manuals also available

10-07

Haynes North America, Inc., 861 Lawrence Drive, Newbury Park, CA 91320-1514 • (805) 498-6703